Soldier in the Sinai

FOREIGN MILITARY STUDIES

History is replete with examples of notable military campaigns and
exceptional military leaders and theorists. Military professionals and
students of the art and science of war cannot afford to ignore these
sources of knowledge or limit their studies to the history of the U.S.
armed forces. This series features original works, translations, and
reprints of classics outside the American canon that promote a deeper
understanding of international military theory and practice.

The Institute for Advanced Military Thinking (IAMT) was formed by
retired senior officers of the Israel Defense Forces to serve as a bridge
between the theories and policies of the academic world and the doctrine, training, and other preparations required for field operations.
The IAMT applies this approach across the full spectrum of future land
warfare by:

- initiating and supporting joint discussions regarding the
  historical lessons offered by land warfare in the Middle East;
- encouraging innovative thinking and open debate about current
  critical defense issues;
- supporting decision makers as they prepare for future
  challenges.

SERIES EDITORS: Roger Cirillo and Gideon Avidor

An AUSA Book

SOLDIER
IN THE SINAI

A General's Account
OF THE
Yom Kippur War

Major General Emanuel Sakal, IDF (Ret.)

TRANSLATED BY MOSHE TLAMIM

UNIVERSITY PRESS OF KENTUCKY

Published by the University Press of Kentucky
Scholarly publisher for the Commonwealth,
serving Bellarmine University, Berea College, Centre College of Kentucky,
Eastern Kentucky University, The Filson Historical Society, Georgetown
College, Kentucky Historical Society, Kentucky State University, Morehead
State University, Murray State University, Northern Kentucky University,
Transylvania University, University of Kentucky, University of Louisville, and
Western Kentucky University.
All rights reserved.

Editorial and Sales Offices: The University Press of Kentucky
663 South Limestone Street, Lexington, Kentucky 40508-4008
www.kentuckypress.com

All photographs are courtesy of Lieutenant Colonel Avi Gur (Ret.), IDF
Spokesperson's Unit, Government Press Office.

Library of Congress Cataloging-in-Publication Data

Sakal, Emanuel.
  [Ha-sadir yivlom? English]
  Soldier in the Sinai : a general's account of the Yom Kippur war / Major
General Emanuel Sakal, IDF (Ret.) ; translated by Moshe Tlamim.
      p. cm. — (Foreign military studies)
  Includes bibliographical references and index.
  ISBN 978-0-8131-5080-2 (hardcover : alk. paper) — ISBN 978-0-8131-5081-9 (pdf)
  — ISBN 978-0-8131-5082-6 (epub)
  1. Israel-Arab War, 1973. 2. Israel. Tseva haganah le-Yisra'el—Campaigns.
I. Tlamim, Moshe, translator. II. Title.
  DS128.1.S2613 2014
  956.04'8—dc23   2014017667

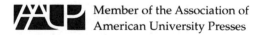

In memory of my son,
Sergeant Yoav Sakal
(Golani Reconnaissance Unit),
who fell in battle in Lebanon
on September 5, 1986

Contents

Foreword

When the Yom Kippur War broke out, Israel found itself fighting a strategic defensive campaign on two fronts: on the Golan Heights against the Syrian invasion, and on the Suez Canal against the Egyptian onslaught. In the north, Israel succeeded in blocking the Syrian advance. In Sinai, the first stage of the defensive battle ended without Israel achieving an operational decision. The author, Major General Emanuel Sakal (Ret.), has analyzed the defensive battle in the south and posits eight reasons for its failure:

1. The disproportionate number of Egyptian troops and Israeli regulars.
2. The delay in mobilizing Israel Defense Forces (IDF) reservists due to dilatory decision making before the war's outbreak.
3. Failure to implement the IDF's deployment plan, code-named Dovecote (in Hebrew, *Shovach Yonim*).
4. Failure to carry out a preventive counterstrike against Egyptian bridging and crossing equipment situated on the western bank of the Suez Canal.
5. Failure of the first IDF counterattack.
6. Ineffective air support for IDF ground forces owing to the nonimplementation of Operation Scratch (*Sreeta*).
7. The IDF's ineffective use of armor in the first twenty-four hours of fighting.
8. Failure to evacuate the Israeli strongholds during the first night of the war (October 6–7).

Sakal is a war hero. He began his regular army service in the Golani Infantry Brigade. As a reservist, he commanded a platoon of recoilless guns during the Six-Day War. Thereafter, he joined the standing army. In my role as commander of Israel's Armored Corps, I interviewed Sakal when he applied for a commission in the corps. He spoke ardently about the lessons of the Six-Day War and argued that future wars would be decided by mobile armored forces. Even then, at the very start of his career, I recognized that he had the makings of a fine senior officer.

In the Yom Kippur War, Sakal commanded a regular army tank battalion that fought in the most desperate battles in Sinai. He switched tanks three times after his own were hit. His defensive maneuvering and fighting capability proved him to be an exemplary armored officer. For his bravery and excellence under murderous fire, he received the Medal of Courage. After the war he rose through the ranks in a series of command roles, reaching the rank of major general and serving as corps commander and later commander of the Israeli Ground Corps Command.

During his military service, Sakal acquired vast experience in the art of war. Today he is recognized as an expert in mobile and armored warfare. He attended the U.S. Army Command and General Staff College and excels in deep and original military thinking. His background is perfectly suited for research on a classic armored campaign such as the Yom Kippur War. His personal experience, combined with his academic qualifications and in-depth knowledge of the IDF, makes his description and analysis of the fighting an authoritative account of the highest order.

Major General Israel Tal (Ret.)
Deputy Chief of Staff in the Yom Kippur War

Abbreviations

AGCR	*Agranat Commission Report*
APC	armored personnel carrier
ASC	air support center
CBU	cluster bomb unit
CCP	central command post (IAF)
EW	electronic warfare
FCG	forward command group
GHQ	General Staff Headquarters
GSO	General Staff Operations
IAF	Israeli Air Force
IDF	Israel Defense Forces
MI	military intelligence
RPG	rocket-propelled grenade
TOC	tactical operations center
TOW	tube-launched, optically tracked, wire-guided antitank missile

Introduction

Between the 1967 Six-Day War and the 1973 Yom Kippur War, Israel's political and military leadership believed its military strength would deter the Arab states—especially Egypt and Syria—from launching a war to recoup their losses in the Six-Day War. Belief in deterrence notwithstanding, no one dismissed the possibility that the Arabs might try to break the political deadlock by undertaking a military move that would force the superpowers to pressure Israel to make concessions and give up territory. The Arabs were aware that, if they did so, the Israel Defense Forces (IDF) would probably annihilate their armies again, but it was conceivable that they might choose the path of war anyway, even at the cost of a million lives, as Egypt's president Anwar Sadat declared.

Israel assumed that, whether they were forewarned or surprised, and even if they were attacked on two fronts simultaneously, the IDF regulars on the front lines—supported by members of the Israeli Air Force (IAF), most of whom were also regulars—would be able to block any Arab military attack. This belief was encapsulated in the expression "The regulars will hold [the line]!" The IDF estimated that during the brief defensive battle—expected to last from a few hours to a few days—the reservists would mobilize and, once they were at the front, would expand the regulars' attack across the Suez Canal, transfer the fighting to the enemy's rear, and attain an operational decision on enemy soil.

The operational concept of "the regulars will hold" evolved during the War of Attrition (which officially began in March 1969 but actually erupted on July 1, 1967) and was strongly supported by Lieutenant General Haim Bar-Lev, who served as chief of the IDF General Staff from 1968 to 1971. It remained standard IDF dogma throughout the cease-fire (August 8, 1970, to October 6, 1973). Bar-Lev's successor, Lieutenant General David "Dado" Elazar, fully subscribed to this belief and adopted it as the basis for IDF operational plans.

As artillery duels intensified on the canal, General Headquarters (GHQ) held long and intensive discussions on the defense of Western Sinai and the canal line. In November–December 1968 a plan was devised that revealed sharp disagreements over defense of the territory and the government's unwritten directive: Egypt must be allowed no territorial gain. During these discussions, commanders presented various concepts based on static versus mobile defense. The media oversimplified this difference of opinion, reporting that Generals Israel Tal and Ariel "Arik" Sharon supported mobile defense on the canal, while Chief of Staff Bar-Lev and Major General Avraham "Bren" Adan favored static defense. In reality, the differences revolved around how to apply the armored force in the area east of the canal up to the line of hills (which would later be paved and become known as Artillery Road) or even up to the Gidi and Mitla mountain passes thirty to forty kilometers east of the canal. During the GHQ discussions, some of which were attended by defense minister Moshe Dayan, there was consensus on implementing the political directive to deny the enemy any territorial gain, which demanded a physical military presence on the canal. This aim could be achieved by erecting a chain of fortresses, later called strongholds (in Hebrew, *ma'ozim*), along an extended defensive line that came to be known as the Bar-Lev Line.

GHQ was divided over tactical deployment on the waterline. Often, this was a matter of minor details, such as the emplacement of the strongholds' periscopes, flanking and frontal fire capability, the exact location of communications trenches on the rear slope, and so forth. Although these issues were important in their own right, they were secondary to the general concept.

The military leadership, followed by the political leadership, adopted the IDF's recommendations for defense of the canal but noted two basic conditions that had to be met in the event of a surprise attack, despite Israel's deterrence capability: (1) a four- to five-day (but no less than forty-eight-hour) warning of an impending Arab offensive (based on intelligence), and (2) flexible and readily available air support to guarantee that the regulars could carry out a holding defensive operation. The unqualified superiority of Israeli armor over Egyptian and Syrian armor ensured that the regular army would be able to hold the canal line, provided it had enough time to scramble into position, and provided the IAF destroyed enemy concentrations on both sides of the canal while the reserve complement was mobilizing. This book questions the concept of "the regulars will hold" and examines how it was implemented and whether it stood the test of fire. Thus, the main subject here is the defensive battle on the Sinai front.

States and armies take many complex factors into consideration when choosing a security concept (doctrine) and striking the correct balance among defense, attack, and deterrence.[1] Balance is the major issue discussed in political and military echelons, and it is the secret of the art of war. Since the dawn of history, armies, generals, states, and national leaders have deliberated over the optimal combination of defense and attack, with deterrence as an additional factor in the equation. Many considerations, not all of which are military, influence the selection of a particular security doctrine:

- Domestic political considerations: the balance of power among the party in control, the opposition, and nonpartisan groups representing radically different views (in Israel, the dovish Peace Now Movement, the Greater Israel Settlers Movement, and so forth).
- Societal considerations: size, composition, and resilience of the population in wartime, as well as the cultural and economic status of the population.
- Force composition: Should the force be based on conscript troops? What is the optimal size of the regular army? In the overall balance of forces, what percentage should reservists constitute? Which military arm (air, sea, or land) should receive priority in budgeting and replenishment? What is the correct balance of forces within each branch?
- Past experience: experience accumulated in past wars and the political, military, technological, economic, and social lessons learned.
- Economic considerations: the state's ability to weather an extended period during which it must supply its military with modern weapons. Further, should the emphasis be placed on defensive or offensive weapons?
- Geographic considerations: How big is the state? Is it landlocked or open to the sea? Can it endure a surprise attack, or does it have to launch a preventive war or preemptive strike?

Once a security doctrine has been chosen, it must not lead to chronic tunnel vision. Doctrines can change on short notice. Just before World War II, the British Royal Air Force shifted from an offensive doctrine—deep-penetration strategic bombing—to a defensive one. At the onset of the Germans' attack in the west in

May 1940, the French army entered neutral Belgium—an offensive act—even though France had declared its commitment to a defensive doctrine.[2] IDF doctrine, too, underwent a change: a primarily offensive perspective dominated military planning until the Six-Day War, followed by a defensive doctrine on the Suez Canal and the Golan Heights based on the dictum of no ground gained by the enemy. This shift to the defensive, which was not based solely on doctrinal and operational analyses, is also examined herein.

Soldier in the Sinai describes the impact of the security concept on Israel's defensive doctrine in Western Sinai after the Six-Day War, especially during the War of Attrition and the subsequent cease-fire. There were deficiencies on all levels—tactical, operational, and strategic—but the cult of the offense dominated the security doctrine and IDF thinking, to the detriment of defensive strategy. This lopsided view was expressed in doctrine, operational planning, battle procedure, officer training, unit exercises, organization, weapons procurement, and deployment on the contact line, as well as during the Yom Kippur War itself. Because of the continuous disregard for defense, neither the IDF nor Southern Command possessed contingency plans to defend Sinai. This deficiency had fatal implications in the initial days of the war and contributed to the high number of casualties.

This book examines the modus operandi and performance of the ground troops on October 6–15 (especially October 6–9) and their total dependence on airpower and IAF versatility, especially in the event of a surprise attack (as indeed occurred). It also tackles the question of the "preemptive strike" in Israel's security doctrine before and after the Six-Day War and in the critical days before October 6, 1973. It analyzes the decision not to attack on the morning of Yom Kippur, addresses the sources and ramifications of that decision, and examines whether it aided or impeded the war effort and the regulars' ability to hold the line. The American position, as Israeli leaders understood it, is also clarified.

Despite a difficult beginning, the IDF squandered the opportunity to achieve a quick operational decision in the defensive battle that could have resulted in fewer Israeli casualties, less equipment lost, a shorter war, a significant reduction in the Egyptian advance, more impressive Israeli military and political achievements, and less dependence on American assistance and therefore no dictates from Washington regarding a cease-fire and the release of Egyptian Third Army from the IDF's choking encirclement. To prove this assumption, this book describes the errors that could have been prevented and assesses the results of a defensive battle if they had been avoided. Wherever possible, the author presents a quantitative estimate of the potential improvement in outcome. The major blunders were as follows: failure to deploy the regulars according to the Dovecote plan, failure to evacuate the strongholds on the night of October 6–7, and misuse of tanks on the canal line, especially on the morning of October 7 (leaving them in a static position to the rear of the strongholds rather than engaging the enemy in a maneuver). This book also treats one of the major shortcomings of the war— ineffectual air support in the defensive phase of the ground battle— and analyzes the main flaws in the counterattack (on October 8 and the morning of October 9) that could have been avoided with earlier staff work on battle procedure and ground operations.

In addition to these blunders and their operational consequences, this book points out the opportunity lost by not attacking the Egyptians' bridging and fording equipment—an action that could have been carried out in a preemptive or parallel air strike on October 6. If such an attack had been executed, it would have changed the course of the war by seriously impairing the ability of Egyptian armor formations to cross the canal and reinforce the infantry divisions already on the eastern bank.

The author has employed operations research, simulation, and computerized war games to assess the virtual results of (1) an alternative application of IDF tanks in the first two days of fighting, (2) a preemptive or parallel attack by the IAF against Egyptian bridging and crossing equipment on the first day of the war, and (3) the influence of concentrated Israeli artillery fire on enemy infantry dug in on the eastern bank between October 9 (October 8 in the southern sector) and October 11. A qualitative and quantitative analysis of the major blunders in the IDF's use of force in the Yom Kippur War, whether by commission or omission, confirms the assumption that an operational decision in the defensive battle on the eastern bank could have been achieved within a few days.

The critical prewar mistakes—Israel's military "concept,"[3] the estimate of a low likelihood of war, and the nonmobilization of reservists—are mentioned only in passing. This book focuses on a tactical and operational analysis of the defensive battle on the southern front from 04:30 on October 6, 1973 (when the chief of staff was notified by his aide that war would break out that evening), to the evening of October 15 (the date 14th Armored Brigade commenced the breakthrough battle for the canal crossing). Within this range of events, the book surveys the operational and strategic decisions made by the chief of staff and the defense minister, mainly regarding the defensive campaign, the preemptive or parallel air strike, and the counterattack. The author discusses the fighting in the sector north of Kantara only in general terms; this is a complex and difficult sector that deserves a separate study. The research concentrates on the fighting south of Kantara down to Ras Masala on the shore of the Gulf of Suez.

Owing to his long-term familiarity with Sinai and the Suez Canal as a company commander in the War of Attrition and a battalion commander in the Yom Kippur War, the author has a deep understanding of the events described. However, his personal involvement does not detract from the objectivity of the research. This book is based on primary sources in the IDF and Defense Ministry archives; secondary sources, such as literature on the war, Ma'arachot (Israel Defense Ministry) publications, and books produced by combat units; and oral documentation and interviews with commanders who fought in the War of Attrition and the Yom Kippur War and statesmen in Israel and abroad. Regarding "new discoveries" in the study of the Yom Kippur War—a subject tackled by many erudite and talented writers—the author finds it fitting to quote from Max Hastings's monumental work *Armageddon: The Battle for Germany 1944–45*: "After almost sixty years, it is unreasonable to think that great secrets about how the Second World War was managed still remain hidden. The challenge lies in improving our concept of the war and finding a new interpretation of the existing evidence. Most of the current books that claim to reveal sensational discoveries have turned out to be pure poppycock. I have no truck with innovation for the sake of innovation."[4]

Criticism of IDF commanders (some of whom occupied senior posts during the war) by historians, the Agranat Commission, and the author abounds in the following pages. This criticism, especially in this book, is not intended to detract one iota from the admiration and respect the author feels for these people who gave their best years—and sometimes their very lives—for the defense of their country. The author cites the following passage written by Colonel Yehoshua Nevo (Ret.) after the Yom Kippur War: "Some say that it's easier to write and criticize than to make war. But it is not easy to criticize decisions and assessments that your comrades made in cramped bunkers, tank turrets, under fire, in strain of responsibility—decisions by people who put their lives on the line—and in some cases lost their lives."[5] The author agrees with every word, especially since he himself experienced the war firsthand, not from the lofty distance of a scholar or a military commentator.

1

Development of the Defense Concept in Western Sinai

The concept of defense in Western Sinai developed according to circumstance and need. It began with routine operational drills when fighting resumed on the Suez Canal in July 1967 and evolved as Egyptian hostilities intensified and the number of Israeli casualties climbed.

The War of Attrition and the construction of the defensive line (strongholds) on the banks of the canal were a turning point in the IDF's war-fighting concept. As military and political circumstances changed and troop deployments shifted, that concept transformed from a classic offensive doctrine to a predominantly static, defensive one. Short- and long-range raids into Egypt and deep-penetration air strikes forced the Egyptians to establish an air defense layout that severely hampered Israeli air activity by the end of the War of Attrition.

The cease-fire (August 8, 1970, to October 6, 1973) dulled the Israeli planners' senses with regard to the nature of the next war with Egypt. Would it be solely defensive and static, or would the IDF have to cross the canal to the western shore at the outset or conclusion of a short, decisive defensive battle? During these years, the Bar-Lev Line deteriorated, but no alternative defense plan was prepared.

Because the nature of any future military confrontation remained unknown, the IDF would have to be ready for a wide range of scenarios: from local raids on the strongholds to battles like those in a war of attrition; from a limited Egyptian thrust to gain a foothold on the eastern bank to full-scale war. The scope of the next war was the subject of debate. Some planners foresaw a very limited Egyptian move—seizing the eastern shore and capturing the Bar-Lev Line. Others thought the Egyptians would try to retake Western Sinai up to the mountain passes, and some weighed the possibility of an Egyptian attempt to recapture the entire Sinai Peninsula. There was consensus on the need to maintain a military presence on the canal to implement the government's unwritten directive of no territorial gains for Egypt, but the planners disagreed over the optimal way to safeguard the canal: mobile or static defense. The complex, often acrimonious debate continued until war erupted. Lacking a clearly defined defensive battle plan, the military was left with a vague directive—the regulars will hold—that failed to address the key question: how to fight a defensive battle with limited air support in the event of a surprise attack.

The Dovecote plan—the deployment of regulars on the canal in the event of a renewal of hostilities—assumed that these troops would be able to block an all-out assault until reinforcing divisions arrived. According to the Rock (in Hebrew, *Sela*) plan, these divisions would counterattack and transfer the fighting to the western bank. Dovecote was ill-defined, however, and this ambiguity would have far-reaching consequences in the first days of the war, when 252nd Division was thrown headlong into furious combat and given impossible tasks. In the opening days of the war, the Egyptians fought according to an organized doctrine based on their study of IDF behavior and operational solutions for clearly defined missions. They adapted the Soviet war-fighting doctrine to the IDF's pattern of ground fighting and succeeded in neutralizing its acknowledged advantage in armor and airpower.

Defense and Offense in Israel's Security Concept

For several years, discussion of defense-related issues in GHQ had been inadequate and generally accompanied by a depreciatory attitude, although it was evident that an in-depth discussion was required at the national level. For years, Israel had prepared for the next war, which, according to the pattern of the Arab-Israeli conflict, would be fought on the cease-fire lines of the last war.

At the end of the War of Independence and in the early 1950s, David Ben-Gurion, Israel's first prime minister and defense minister, laid down the basic principles of Israel's defense strategy and security concept:

1. Each war is a war of survival.
2. Since an unconditional victory is unattainable, the Arab-Israeli conflict cannot be solved by military means alone.

3. An Arab victory means the end of the conflict.
4. Israel cannot rely on overseas support. Security must be based on the IDF's strength.
5. The IDF will be employed only for strategic defensive goals to secure the status quo attained at the end of the War of Independence.
6. On a practical level, the following principles are self-evident:

- Israel lacks a natural strategic depth; therefore, it has to create an artificial one by carrying the war onto the enemy's territory.
- Israel's limited resources preclude it from maintaining a large standing army; therefore, it has to base its defense on a small force of regulars led by a professional career core and backed by a well-trained reserve framework.
- The fighting theater does not allow Israel to engage in a prolonged war or wait for foreign assistance. Thus, the war must be quick and decisive. Since an unconditional victory is impossible and the attainment of political objectives is possible only in war, Israel must aspire to destroy the enemy outright, terminate the fighting in conditions convenient for it, and stave off the next war for as long as possible.[1]

In general, these were the directives that shaped the IDF into an offensive army whose defensive outlook was unsatisfactory and shallow at the strategic level and especially at the applied and doctrinal levels (weapons, training, commander instruction, war-fighting doctrine, and so on).

Thus, doctrinal ignorance and a devaluation of the defensive battle (partly because of the proven success of the offensive battle until after the Six-Day War) characterized the IDF for years. This attitude was revealed in all its shortcomings—both in wartime and during periods of relative quiet—in drills and exercises at all levels. The attack was considered the key to military thinking, as expressed in joint operations at the GHQ level and in ground combat team training.

The IDF's attempts to convince formations and training bases to incorporate defensive exercises into their units' drills and training schedules came to naught. The defensive stage, if included at all, was usually abridged or glossed over, and the lessons that should have been learned were squandered. The offensive battle (especially the breakthrough stage) dominated IDF exercises. The disparaging mind-set toward the defensive battle was echoed in statements by researchers, senior IDF commanders, and the defense establishment.

Planning a defensive battle at the operational and tactical level is an extremely complex task that involves innumerable details: defining the modus operandi of mobile and stationary forces (including territorial defense forces, when possible); creating fire plans for warplanes, helicopter gunships, artillery, tanks, precision-guided munitions (after 1973), and antitank weapons within and beyond the killing grounds; identifying vital areas; planning and marking withdrawal lines, holding lines, and the rear defensive line; setting up obstacles integrated with canalizing and destructive fire; constructing fortifications in vital areas, open areas, and dominating areas; planning the local and main counterattack with fire support; collecting intelligence; logistics; and so forth. Such defensive planning calls for a commander with a highly developed operational imagination and superlative professional control of available forces. It entails advanced training, planning for both deliberate and hasty battle procedures, and preparatory drills for headquarters and troops, all of which the IDF lacked at noon on October 6, 1973.

Only Offense Can Win Wars

Several Israeli military leaders have stated their preference for the offense. Moshe Dayan, chief of staff during the 1956 Sinai Campaign, wrote that an artificial strategic depth (consisting of obstacles and regional defense) and defensive measures can succeed only in delaying the enemy; they cannot provide vital infrastructure with sufficient defense. Thus, the offensive is the only form of combat that wins wars. In Israel's case, the enemy cannot be defeated unless the IDF initiates an offensive and captures strategic objectives in the enemy's territorial depth.

Major General Israel Tal, deputy chief of staff in 1973, stated that the defending side cannot put up an effective defense under quantitatively inferior conditions because its theoretical advantage is eroded as a result of the need to divide its forces.

In reference to the Sinai Campaign, Major General Meir Amit (Ret.) wrote: "We knew that the IDF did not excel in defense. We trained solely for a mobile war and transfer of the fighting onto the enemy's territory. Only offensive moves can undermine the enemy, seize the initiative, and throw him off-balance."[2]

Yitzhak Rabin, chief of staff during the Six-Day War, also endorsed the offensive, avowing that a defensive battle stymies a quick victory. In addition, it was unsuited to the IDF's frequent need to fight on a number of fronts simultaneously and achieve a swift operational decision on one front in order to concentrate its forces on the others. "The defensive concept impairs the fighting force, leads to cognitive stultification, and further erodes the IDF's relative advantage in initiated, improvised, mobile combat," noted Rabin.[3]

It should be mentioned that after the War of Independence, both Dayan and Rabin led the IDF in successful offensive campaigns from borders that were incapable of withstanding a concerted enemy attack. Given the constraints of Israel's borders, the security concept formulated by Ben-Gurion after the War of Independence had to be applied: a national defensive strategy and offensive doctrine that transferred the fighting at the operational level to the enemy's territory.

The "Attack Reflex"

If Dayan's and Rabin's statements seem tailor-made for the realities of 1956 and 1967, the views of Lieutenant General David "Dado" Elazar just prior to the Yom Kippur War are disconcerting: "to win we have to attack—and the faster we attack, the better."[4]

The claim that the defensive battle saps improvisation and stifles creative thinking and fighting capability is nothing new and was certainly not unique to the IDF. Other armies, too, have been hard-pressed to find the optimal balance between defense and offense. Regarding the ethos of the offensive in Europe, renowned British strategist and historian Liddell Hart believed that whereas armies tend to see the attack as a panacea, the sands of history are strewn with the debris of kingdoms that embarked on the offensive.

In Israel's case, the security concept had to take into account the enormous quantitative gap between the IDF and Arab forces. Yet fixation on the attack and the ethos of the offense led the IDF to execute some rash and reckless operations: the ill-prepared counterattack in Sinai on October 8; the overhasty plan for crossing the canal; 143rd Division's movement on the western bank in the direction of Ismailia; and entry of 500th Brigade, 162nd Division, into the city of Suez on October 24. The cult of the offensive spawned the conditioned reflex to attack. Major General Avraham Adan admitted, "We were slaves to the doctrine we'd been reared on that an attack had to be carried out as soon as possible and the war transferred to the enemy."[5]

A survey of the main engagements in Sinai shows that the IDF's defensive battles succeeded and saved lives in both relative and absolute terms. This occurred after the defensive line stabilized on October 9 and the IDF internalized, at least in part, the errors of the first three days of the fighting. The outstanding example is the breaking of the Egyptian offensive on October 14, which caused heavy damage to the enemy. The Egyptians' loss of 200 to 250 tanks and the overall failure of their offensive marked the turning point in the war in Sinai. Behind these Israeli achievements lies the fact that the IDF entered the war unversed in modern defensive combat; it had not studied the application of defensive principles since 1948, including the use of airpower for defense. This lack of experience led to misjudgment in terms of the balance of forces needed to withstand a surprise attack and miscalculations in the size of regular units, number of formations, and amount of time needed to hold the line until the reserves arrived.

Why did the IDF decide to forgo a defensive battle? Given the numerical imbalance of forces, it chose to base its doctrine on the offensives of 1956 and 1967, especially in light of its limited ability to fight defensively. Even when defensive deployment against a full-scale Arab offensive was discussed, it was perceived not as a strategic option but as a short-term tactical answer—a preliminary stage to the immediate follow-up of the main attack. As Generals Gonen and Hofi, commanders of the two regional commands, stated in their testimony to the Agranat Commission, the attack was the quintessence of IDF strategy.

Major General Yeshayahu Gavish (Ret.) admitted that the IDF never considered how to set up a defense: "This was a serious oversight on the eve of the Six-Day War when we realized that fortifications and a defense system were lacking. There was no defensive concept because we never thought in strategic terms about how to protect the state."[6]

Chief of Staff Elazar stated his unequivocal position on defensive combat in April 1973: "I don't intend to discuss the concept of standing defensively on the canal and fighting a defensive war. I don't suffer from this trauma and I don't want a defensive war on the canal. I believe it would be a disaster."[7] Given the chief of staff's definitive attitude, it is little wonder that the entire army rallied around the offensive, abandoned and scorned the defensive battle, and invested neither time nor energy in devising tactics to engage in it.

A month later, Elazar presented his plans to the prime minister and emphasized his intention to avoid a defensive war and launch a counteroffensive on the canal in the event of a surprise attack. Of course, this position, which was adopted by the IDF's senior command, was decisive in shaping the army's war-fighting plans. Offensive plans were thoroughly prepared, but plans for a defensive battle were given short shrift, and the defensive elements constructed in the depths were insignificant. As a result, many units and commanders were insufficiently trained and psychologically ill prepared to fight a defensive battle. In reality, Southern Command's fear that the main line would collapse and its knowledge that there was no second line of defense to fall back on had a powerful impact on the command's thinking in the initial stages of the holding battles.[8]

In principle, the IDF combat doctrine assumed a balanced approach to battle, but in practice, more resources were always allocated to the offensive battle. A careful look at the 1973 training schedule reveals that of the twenty-eight main lessons planned for 252nd and 143rd Divisions, only one dealt with defense; for 146th and 210th Divisions' training exercises, not a single defensive lesson was planned. Brigade exercises included one lesson in organizing a hasty defense (but this allotted time was usually frittered away).

The Role of the Reserves

After the 1956 Sinai Campaign, the IDF realized that an offensive move depended on mobilization of the reserves. In the wake of the Six-Day War, when Israel acquired the strategic depth of Sinai, the question arose whether an urgent call-up of reserves was necessary in the event of an alert. At the time of the "Blue White" alert in Sinai in April–May 1973, only one reserve brigade was mobilized.

This was the backdrop to the debate between Chief of Staff Elazar and Defense Minister Dayan on the morning of October 6, 1973, which revealed the basic divide between the military sphere and the political sphere: the chief of staff urged a general call-up of reservists, but the defense minister wanted to limit mobilization of the reserves to the minimum needed for the regulars to fight a defensive battle. The chief of staff and the defense minister saw eye to eye on the role of the reservists—for attack, not for defense. However, they ignored the fact that the reserves were essentially a militia, not a rapid-response force. In addition, their supply units were located far from the canal, posing serious logistical problems, especially in the event of a surprise attack. Failure to recognize the reservists' limitations, failure to acknowledge their part in the IDF's defense structure, and ignoring (even at the most basic level of planning) the likelihood of a surprise attack were fatal mistakes.[9]

Crystallization of the Defense Doctrine in Sinai

At the end of the Six-Day War, the IDF deployed on advantageous defensive lines far from the international border and Israel's population centers, but the security concept that canonized the offensive battle (the result of the dazzling six-day victory) remained inflexible. The implications of the new geostrategic reality were only superficially analyzed. Israel's sense of strangulation, which had demanded an overwhelming response (either a preventive war or a preemptive strike), had faded. At the same time, a new situation had developed: a very large Egyptian army sat on the western bank of the Suez Canal directly across from Israel's whittled-down forces on the eastern bank. This was a surefire indication of trouble.

Thus, the IDF found itself dragged, largely on its own initiative, into a doctrinal position that jettisoned the classic mobile battle in the area between the canal and the mountain passes and remained stubbornly tied to the dictum of no territorial gain for Egypt. As fighting on the canal escalated, the hasty deployment on the waterline in June 1967 grew into an increasingly entrenched fortification, and the Bar-Lev Line became the de facto rear defensive line.

The diluted regular force, which was supposed to deploy on the canal in case of an emergency (according to the Dovecote plan), was not intended to hold off a massive canal crossing for a lengthy period, even with air support. Fully aware of this, the IDF drafted the Rock plan to reinforce Sinai with two reserve divisions that would arrive, after concentration, within 180 hours. These divisions were not supposed to strengthen the defensive structure; their goal was to counterattack, cross over to the western bank, and destroy the Egyptian army. In reality, the idea mutated into the operational directive "the regulars will hold"—a concept that left 252nd Division to fight a single-handed battle of attrition on October 6–7, the first two days of the Yom Kippur War.

Knowledge of the Six-Day War's cease-fire line is essential for understanding how events developed in the Yom Kippur War and Israel's defense doctrine. The IDF reached the canal in a "rolling operation" on June 9, 1967. The chief of staff, Lieutenant General Yitzhak Rabin, ordered a halt twenty kilometers from the waterline, but due to continued fighting and American intentions to pass a UN Security Council resolution for a cease-fire, the decision was made to press forward and reach the canal.

According to Major General Gavish, head of Southern Command during the Six-Day War, Defense Minister Dayan initially opposed stopping on the waterline; he believed that if the IDF reached the canal, Egyptian president Nasser would reject a cease-fire, and the war would drag on for years. But to everyone's surprise, Dayan suddenly changed his mind and countermanded his own order to stay clear of the waterline. His explanation was that holding the canal line would enable the IDF to withdraw after the UN decision, and no matter where the IDF halted in Sinai, the Egyptians would insist on continuing the war rather than agreeing to a cease-fire. According to this logic, by sitting on the entire length of the Suez Canal, Israel could apply pressure to Egypt. If the Egyptians opened the canal to international shipping, they would be unable to compel Israel to pull back, and Israel could remain safely on the eastern bank. But if Egypt chose not to open the canal, it would lose sorely needed revenue and would be forced to negotiate with Israel. Israeli leaders believed that if the IDF withdrew under pressure of Egyptian fire, this would only invite further pressure; therefore, Israel had to bite the bullet and hold on to the canal, even if it meant a war of attrition, until the Egyptians realized they were incapable of forcing Israel to withdraw under fire. At that point, they would start negotiating. Even more than its symbolic and strategic value, the canal was an antitank obstacle that, the IDF assumed, could not be crossed by large forces. All these factors combined to convince Dayan to order the IDF to remain on the waterline, providing the government with optimal conditions for negotiations.

Beginning in June 1967, Israel's security concept shifted from deterrence to defense—from avoiding war by convincing the enemy of the dire consequences of initiating hostilities to implementing a force buildup that would prevent the enemy from gaining any ground in the event of war. The government realized that the new, strategically favorable borders meant that no additional territory would have to be captured. War could be prevented without "red lines" being drawn. The new situation led to a number of major changes in the security concept. First and foremost, the importance of a preemptive strike abated, and dependence on the United States increased.

Despite the radical change in the security reality and extension of the strategic depth, the IDF's structure remained the same as it had been in the War of Attrition. Although the number of regulars rose, this increase could not offset the Arab troops on the contact line. Furthermore, there were no buffer zones separating the armies. Paradoxically, the concepts of *defendable borders* and *no territorial gain*, which the IDF had uncritically adopted as part of the status quo, negated the operational depth and undermined the strategic depth.

Failure to Exploit the Strategic Depth

Major General Avraham Adan believed that the newly won strategic depth afforded an invaluable early-warning system against enemy aircraft intending to bomb population centers and military targets in Israel. The strategic depth also enabled Israel to conduct a delaying battle and cede territory in exchange for the time needed to mobilize the reserves.

In contrast, Major General Israel Tal argued that the IDF was not exploiting the strategic depth or adopting a flexible defense doctrine—the optimal and most efficient system in the art of war. From the military point of view, Israel's policy could be flexible: stay on the defensive and later shift to the offense. But according to Tal, developments on the ground nullified the strategic depth. Instead of exploiting the depth for a flexible defensive maneuver to crush the Egyptian forces entering Sinai once they advanced beyond the range of their artillery and antiaircraft cover, a line of fortresses was being built along the entire canal for a determined defense in the event of a full-scale war or war of attrition. Israel had distanced the enemy from its border but, ironically, found itself within range of Egyptian observation posts, heavy artillery, and light weapons fire.[10] The IDF saw the vast spaces in Sinai as a force multiplier, a strategic security guarantee, and he accepted the unfavorable force ratio because he believed that depth would enable the IDF to emerge victorious in a war of survival. However, strategic depth is irrelevant if it is not exploited, and it was not exploited in Sinai because of the need to maintain a rigid defense on the canal and on its line of fortifications.

No Territorial Gain for the Enemy

Were the concepts of "not one step" across the canal and "no territorial gain for the enemy" really dictated to the army? According to Tal, these were unequivocal, unwritten directives from the government. The army understood them to mean that the line of fortresses had to block a canal crossing and that there would be no retreat or loss of territory in the north (Golan Heights) or the south (Sinai). Tal saw this as part of the heritage of the Hagana (the prestate underground paramilitary organization) and the territorial defense doctrine: Israel does not yield ground to the enemy.

Gavish, however, claims that when the Six-Day War ended, there was no specific definition of what should be done on the morning after; no order was ever given to build a defensive line on the canal's banks in furtherance of the "not one step" policy. In other words, the IDF's presence in Sinai and on the Suez Canal was an open issue (notwithstanding the government's announcement that it was prepared to return land in exchange for peace). It was obvious that if Israel reached the canal, it would have to defend it; therefore, there was no reason to retreat to a line farther back. The GHQ order was to hold the canal, prevent shipping (except for supplies to the moored vessels), and so forth. No one addressed the question of how the canal was to be held. Was this a final decision? Gavish has his doubts but insists that everyone interpreted it as meaning that the IDF had to deploy on the canal. He claims that the political echelon never issued a specific order; nor was there ever a written military command. Things just developed. Still, the "not one step" dictum was the key element in the IDF's operational concept from the end of the Six-Day War until October 1973.

Indeed, no government document has been found that contains an official order to this effect. Nevertheless, the IDF developed a mind-set that an Egyptian force (even one as small as a company) would be impossible to dislodge once it was established on the eastern bank and protected by hundreds of artillery pieces and a thick surface-to-air antiaircraft umbrella. Therefore, the IDF had to prevent such a scenario from occurring. The army was fully aware of the political consequences of territorial gains by Egypt.

The IDF identified maneuver areas, defensive lines, and vital areas east of the canal. These included the western openings of the Mitla and Gidi passes, the range of dunes on the Tasa-Refidim Road, and the Ras Sudar–Abu Rudeis oil corridor. But even the correct identification of these strategic areas did not stop the IDF from adopting the "not one step" policy, viewing the canal as the rear defensive line, and sanctifying the concept of holding the line at any price, even in areas whose value was negligible. On October 10, 1973, when Dayan proposed withdrawing from the passes to Um Hashiba and waging a prepared defensive battle of counterstrikes, the military was vigorously opposed.

The concept of "not one step" did not necessarily mean fighting a stubborn holding battle on the eastern bank. The same results could have been achieved in mobile fighting. However, the IDF became entrenched in its defense concept. In late 1970 Dayan broached the idea of an Israeli-initiated withdrawal from the canal, even though this ran counter to the "not one step" concept. Israel would move back fifteen to thirty kilometers in exchange for an Egyptian commitment to open the waterway to international shipping. In response, Egypt stipulated that 700 police officers (a trifling number) would be deployed on the Israeli (eastern) side after the withdrawal. Golda Meir, Israel's prime minister, rejected Nasser's condition, and Dayan capitulated because of opposition from a small number of ministers—Meir's hard-line supporters.

Transition to a "Hot" Front

The euphoria following the Six-Day War was best expressed by *Life* magazine's cover in June 1967: the grinning face of Lieutenant Yossi Ben Hanan, soaking wet in the Suez Canal, clutching a Kalashnikov in one hand. This elation soon gave way to the reality of a live-fire front in Sinai. The early shooting incidents on the canal (the first was at Ras al-Eish on July 1, 1967) required a rethinking of the defense concept and improvement of the fortifications. The flimsy protection for the troops consisted mostly of trenches and Egyptian iron hoops scattered in the area. Immediately after the first sign of hostilities, Southern Command prepared a strengthening plan based on building new fortifications, advancing the artillery, and establishing a new regular army tank brigade (the 401st). Thus the IDF's defense became entrenched on the canal line.[11]

On his first day as chief of staff (January 1, 1968), Lieutenant General Haim Bar-Lev met with GHQ staff and set forth his views on the defense of Sinai and how the next war would develop. The Egyptians, he said, would launch an assault. The IDF, including the air force, would take the blow, thwart the advance, break the Egyptian army, and carry the war onto enemy territory. If conditions were propitious for the air force, the IDF would go on the offensive. But even if air conditions were not favorable, the IDF would not pull back. Bar-Lev believed that well-trained, well-equipped, and strongly entrenched forces could repel an Arab attack without the air force.

Formulation of the Defense Concept: November–December 1968

Relative quiet prevailed on the canal between October 1967 and September 1968. When Egyptian shelling intensified in September 1968, the IDF's fortifications proved vulnerable to 160mm shells with delay fuses. Nevertheless, the defense strategy remained unaltered. The IDF embarked on a massive fortification operation and improved protection for the troops; it also began construction of a reinforced static design as the renewal of hostilities approached. Bar-Lev led the thinking on the new defense system while the IDF continued to hold the waterline.

On the night of November 1, 1968, as forces returned from Operation Shock (Helem)—an Israeli commando raid on Nag' Hammadi that blew up bridges and a power plant on the Nile—the chief of staff asked to see Tal and his deputy, General Adan. Bar-Lev told them, "Since we've decided to bring another armor brigade into Sinai, I want one of you to go there and report on what's happening and where improvements have to be made. There's a feeling that something's not right."[12] Adan left for Sinai and prepared a comprehensive defense plan—the Stronghold (Ma'oz) plan—based on two assumptions: (1) The IDF had to be prepared for a long stay on the canal that would entail around-the-clock activity. Therefore, a three-month rotation sequence would have to be organized for the units, consisting of operational deployment on the front and training in the rear. (2) Although no instructions from the government or written orders from the chief of staff had been received, the army had to deploy on the eastern bank of the canal and prevent any Egyptian territorial gain, even a temporary one, lest it be accompanied by a cease-fire, which could have negative military and public relations repercussions for Israel.

Because of the historical and operational importance of three discussions that took place at GHQ in November–December 1968, the main points are discussed here. The chief of staff's conclusions on December 19 and 26 would influence the IDF throughout the War of Attrition and the years of the cease-fire. These discussions were the genesis of the operational doctrine for defense of the canal and the defensive battle that began the Yom Kippur War.

The first discussion: November 21, 1968. During this meeting, GHQ heard assessments of the defensive doctrine in Sinai for both routine operations and emergencies and an evaluation of the steps being taken to counter an Egyptian attempt to cross the canal. The head of military intelligence, Major General Aharon Yariv, reviewed the Egyptians' most likely modus operandi and estimated that they would be satisfied with a strategic objective, such as capture of the mountain passes. In his opinion, the offensive would be supported by a powerful antiaircraft and surface-to-air missile system on the canal. He also pointed out the potential crossing areas (the Kantara opening, Firdan-Ismailia, Dwersuar, and north and south of Kubri) and the possibility of an amphibious operation on the lakes.

Brigadier General Benny Peled, the air force commander in the Yom Kippur War, reckoned that an Egyptian attempt to bridge the canal without neutralizing the IAF (attacking its airfields) would end in catastrophe for Egypt. He assured GHQ (in answer to Dayan's question) that the air force could carry out nighttime operations against a bridging attempt. He warned of the antiaircraft threat on the canal but attested that the IAF was willing to pay the price. He also noted that the Egyptians were mistaken if they thought weather conditions would stymie Israeli air operations.

Gavish presented the principles of force deployment and holding the line—the essence of the Dovecote and Rock plans. This entailed defending the canal line, preventing a crossing where the IDF was situated, and alerting the mobile forces where the IDF was not located to counter any local incursion or large-scale operation. Gavish stated that the IDF's position on the canal was the result of a political decision (the "not one step" policy) and a military consideration (sitting on the waterline gave the IDF an advantage over the enemy's crossing forces while they deployed on the western bank and entered the water). He underscored the fact that the canal was a superb defensive obstacle that had to be exploited to prevent a crossing. Toward this end, some of the tanks would assist in defending the fortresses, and others would maneuver between the front and rear lines.

Gavish also stressed the need for static defense on the rear line (Mitla), from which forces could be sent forward. Since Egyptian artillery could reach twenty kilometers beyond the eastern bank, Israel's mobile forces had to be situated outside this range and, at the same time, be close enough to serve as reserves in the crossing areas. He outlined the plan for defending the canal in an emergency: a tank brigade stationed on the front would be responsible for the southern sector, a brigade in the rear would be responsible for the northern forces, and the tank battalions of the nascent 252nd Division—170 tanks manned by regulars—would be deployed accordingly. Until reserves arrived, the first stage would consist of five or six artillery batteries. Within thirty-six hours of receiving an alert, a force from the armor school would arrive (a brigade headquarters and three or four tank companies) and take responsibility for the northern axis and landing beaches. Within twelve hours, 35th Paratroop Brigade would arrive and hold the second defensive line: a battalion at Mitla, a battalion at Gidi, and a battalion on the Ismailia axis (until the brigade arrived, an armored infantry battalion in the division's sector would hold the mountain passes or reinforce the line). Under the Rock plan, the order of battle would be made up of reserve reinforcements: a tank brigade of Centurions and a mechanized brigade of Shermans deployed between the Gidi and Mitla passes within forty-eight hours for divisional counterstrikes, with or without forces from the front line.

The defense minister approved the idea that defense had to take place on the waterline and emphasized the importance of completing preparations to counter an Egyptian attack by March–April 1969. Dayan realized the Egyptians might acquire some additional territory before reinforcements arrived ("assuming they fail on the first night, they'll try again on the second").[13]

Bar-Lev envisioned three necessary elements:

1. A ground force as firmly entrenched as possible in the right place, protected by obstacles and special means.
2. Strong armor reinforcements for a company-size counterattack within thirty to sixty minutes and two battalions within three hours.
3. Day and nighttime air operations against enemy concentrations and bridges.

Even if only two of the elements worked, the plan would still be feasible. "The Egyptians were, after all, Egyptians!" said the chief of staff.[14] He believed in the IDF's ability to halt the offensive at the waterline but noted that if it failed and enemy artillery made it impossible to counterattack effectively on the first line, the troops would have to make a stand on the second line. Summing up the discussion, Bar-Lev stressed the importance of intelligence warnings to enable the IDF to concentrate tanks in Sinai. He also expressed the hope that the operation could be accomplished quickly: twenty-four or forty-eight hours could make the difference between success and failure.

The defense minister concluded the meeting, stating that war with Egypt was inevitable. From an operational point of view, he considered the first forty-eight hours critical. The Egyptians would open with an artillery barrage in the afternoon, which would continue throughout the night and into the next day and night. Whatever forces and equipment Israel failed to concentrate in the first forty-eight hours of battle would be missing at the critical stage. Therefore, every effort had to be made during these forty-eight hours, no matter what the cost.

Based on his discussions with the chief of staff on November 1 and 21, Adan was appointed commander of the armored forces in Sinai (252nd Division—the IDF's first permanent division) and promoted to major general. As noted earlier, Bar-Lev ordered him to present GHQ with a plan for improving fortifications on the canal.[15] Adan thus assembled a team of commanders from the professional branches and devised the Stronghold plan. It called for the establishment of thirty-three strongholds along the canal within four months; some of them already existed, but others would have to be built to fill in the gaps between them. In addition, seven new artillery batteries would be created and the existing twelve batteries should be fortified.

The first GHQ discussion of the Stronghold plan: December 19, 1968. On December 19 Adan presented GHQ (Major General Elazar was not present) with his basic assumptions underlying the Stronghold plan and his views on the Egyptians' most likely modus operandi. He described in detail the location of the thirty-three proposed strongholds along the canal (sensitive areas would have clusters of strongholds) from the Traklin fortification on the Mediterranean coast in the north to Hamezach in the south (all the names of the strongholds, roads, and so forth mentioned in this book are based on the Sirius map codes; see maps 1–3).[16] The area would be divided into three battalion sectors: the southern sector up to the northern strait separating Little and Great Bitter Lakes, the central sector up to the middle of El-Balah Island, and the northern sector. Each battalion sector would have two tank companies either in the strongholds or adjacent to them and one tank company in one of the rear assembly areas (Baluza, Tasa, or Mitla). The tanks in platoon- or company-size formations (including those in the strongholds) would be available for immediate counterstrikes within sixty to ninety minutes. They would be positioned next to the strongholds or one to two kilometers from the canal in areas overlooking the western bank. A concealed lower road with ascents to firing ramps for the tanks would be built along the dirt embankment, as well as an upper road for daily security patrols by half-tracks. Electronic warning devices would be installed.

The Stronghold plan visualized four basic conditions for activating the force:

1. A reinforced brigade on the line, and two mechanized infantry companies and two tank companies in each of the three sectors.
2. Two brigades forward and rear (from 252nd Division) on the line. Adan differentiated between a warning-based situation and a "rolling" incident or surprise situation. To reinforce the forward brigade, the rear brigade would assume command of the southern sector, and the brigade on the line would take responsibility for the central and northern sectors.

3. The armor school links up with two tank battalions and takes responsibility for the northern sector.
4. The Rock plan—that is, 35th Brigade arrives first and assumes control of the Gidi and Mitla passes. It is later joined by 200th Tank Brigade (Centurions) in reserve, which sends a mechanized infantry battalion forward to the delaying action. The 8th Brigade replaces the 35th and deploys a tank battalion in the passes.

Adan described the proposed strongholds in detail: fifty to seventy-five meters long, with two- and three-directional positions forward and rear, mutual assistance between the positions, and an open communications trench encompassing the perimeter. The strongholds would be built on the waterline and dominate the canal with fire. They would be self-sufficient in ammunition, food, water, and services and would have sophisticated electrical and communications systems. Each stronghold would be supplied with a half-track and manned by fifteen to twenty-two combat troops, a driver, a medic, a forward artillery observer, and an electronic equipment operator. The strongholds would be spaced at ten-kilometer intervals. Antitank mines would be planted between each stronghold and the canal road, and a fenced area with antipersonnel mines would be set up along the entire length of the canal, with barbed wire coils laid out in the water. Antipersonnel and antitank mines would be buried in potential crossing areas. The gap between the strongholds would not be mined, nor would the Gidi and Mitla passes; the landing beaches would be mined in the future. The areas between the strongholds would be patrolled. Patrols would be accompanied by on-call artillery cover, and a road would be constructed (later known as the Artillery Road) for artillery movement. Observation towers would be erected four to five kilometers from the canal, up to a height of forty-three meters. Joint combat exercises would be held with tanks, mechanized infantry, artillery, and air support for pursuing and destroying penetrations, landings, and airdrops on the line and in the depths.

GHQ agreed that the Stronghold plan was the best concept for defending the canal from within the strongholds and for deploying forces in the area. Comments were minimal and dealt with specific items rather than basic assumptions. This point is crucial because, over the years (and especially after the Yom Kippur War), a disproportionate amount of commentary has emerged regarding what was said during that discussion. Some of the postwar literature claims that the debate revolved around static versus mobile defense, or rigidity versus flexibility. However, this had nothing to do with the constraints of the period, the positions expressed on December 19 and 26, 1968, or the chief of staff's assessment of the Stronghold plan.

General Tal, commander of the armored corps, perceived Stronghold as the ideal solution for routine security and limited war. He reiterated his November 21 position regarding the need for two tank brigades of regulars (including 7th Brigade) in the rear; this was necessary because the reservists would not reach the front until after the battle had been decided (unless the warning of an all-out attack was received more than twenty-four hours before it began). He emphasized the importance of concentrating the force and dispatching it en masse to points where the enemy had succeeded. The secret of victory is to concentrate armor in the right place at the right time: dispersed armor will not be able to join in the counterattack, he warned. Therefore, he stressed that the IDF's answer to Egypt would be the two brigades in the rear. Tal agreed with the concept of the strongholds' location on the waterline, stating, "I too believe that the defensive battle must be on the water line, but that doesn't mean concentrating all the forces there."[17] He suggested dispatching patrols and ambushes to the gaps between the strongholds and sending half-tracks to ensure superiority wherever there were indications of penetration. In the event of a breach, the forces in the rear serving as a mobile reserve (up to brigade level) would deal with it. As for the high cost of defense, there was no alternative. The lives of the soldiers had to be protected, he stressed, and the number of people manning the waterline had to be kept to a minimum.

General Ariel Sharon's position is also important, given his later statements about the Bar-Lev Line and its method of defense in the War of Attrition and Yom Kippur War. In the December 19 forum, he focused primarily on the strongholds' structure and protection, without elaborating on the general defense concept. "The planning of the strongholds is an excellent example of dealing with a subject meticulously."[18] As for the concept's limitations in the event of a penetration, Sharon stated that the stronghold's only purpose was to sound the alarm. During a bombardment it would be rendered sightless, unable to observe a crossing taking place a few kilometers away. Its fire would be ineffective at the critical moment of the crossing because it would be engulfed in smoke and under constant barrage. Sharon believed the strongholds' inability to provide effective fire was a major shortcoming. He was also against the introduction of more troops to the front in the event of war. "The strongholds' value for sounding the warning is negligible. It will be Israel's tank concentrations that break the Egyptian offensive."[19] Sharon, like Tal, warned against dividing the tank force into smaller formations.

Summing up the discussion, Chief of Staff Bar-Lev said that although he approved the proposal, there were political and military limitations. He noted the IDF's current unpreparedness for coping with a crossing and said the question of expenses must not deter the IDF from building defenses to protect the troops. He rebuffed Sharon's and Tal's arguments, stating that fire is not returned during a bombardment. Regarding the defense concept, he admitted that the regulars would have to hold until the third brigade or a reserve brigade arrived; the reservists, however, would be needed for offensive operations. In other words, if a catastrophe occurred and the army failed to break the Egyptian attack, it would have to continue fighting.

The second GHQ meeting: December 26, 1968. This meeting is important mainly as a historical record of the defense concepts of Generals Sharon, Tal, and Bar-Lev (Elazar was again absent). Sharon favored defense of the waterline but believed it should occur ten kilometers to the east. He saw nothing wrong with fighting a defensive battle even twenty kilometers east of the canal. He was much more critical than he had been on December 19. In his opinion, the fortifications under construction were better suited for peacetime; they were useful only to establish a presence and for observation. Their value in wartime, he believed, was zero, as only tanks and planes could break an effort to cross the canal. He outlined the doctrine he was trying to implement as general of Southern Command: build a second line of fortifications (*ta'ozim*), and gradually shut down the strongholds on the canal. If war broke out, all the strongholds would have to be evacuated immediately, and any decision would be achieved by the mobile reserves. He realized that, for political reasons, Israel had to control the canal, but he suggested taking a hard look at the enormous sums about to be invested in erecting the strongholds and consider building something different.

Tests of the bunkers' ability to withstand direct laying fire from cannon had proved them unsatisfactory, he noted. (Bar-Lev countered that Israeli tanks could knock out the enemy guns. When Sharon disputed this, Bar-Lev shot back that they would wait for war and meet afterward.)

General Tal also outlined his defense concept. The line's purpose, he said, was to allow freedom of action, provide warnings, obstruct enemy penetration and sabotage, and allow routine operational assignments, patrols, and observation to be carried out without fear of shelling. This was necessary if Israel wanted to hold the line on a full-time basis. But, he added, the units manning the strongholds and the tank force deployed on the line must not be expected to stop a crossing effort. Their role was to sound the alarm and provide the army with twenty-four hours to make sense of what was happening. According to Tal, when the Egyptians attacked, the forces stationed on the canal would be of no value except as a fire screen. No stronghold could block a canal crossing. Not a single bullet would be fired from the strongholds once the crossing commenced because Egyptian artillery concentrations would have already destroyed them. The battle would be decided by the mobile forces, which Israel should concentrate as close as possible to the main Egyptian effort. Tal proposed a minimal investment in building the strongholds—just enough to allow them to fulfill their purpose. In the event of an attack, they would come under suppressive fire in the crossing sector or direct laying fire in the main effort; in either case, they would end up a mass of twisted rails and charred walls, with the troops dead, wounded, or traumatized.

Gavish, who adopted the Stronghold plan, enumerated the outlay: 400,000 Israeli pounds ($1.6 million) per stronghold, for a total of 13 million pounds ($53 million) for thirty-three strongholds. He announced that twenty-six strongholds would be completed in the first phase by mid-February 1969, and the rest would be finished by mid-March.

The chief of GHQ, Major General Ezer Weizman (IAF commander from 1958 to 1966), supported Adan's plan and recognized the need to have the IDF based on the waterline in periods of quiet and especially in wartime.[20] But he had no illusions about the strongholds' abilities. In the end, armor and the IAF would decide the outcome.

Chief of Staff Bar-Lev approved the Stronghold plan but put his finger on two drawbacks: the lack of surveillance and the inability to provide fire on the front. For the enemy to gain control of a stronghold, he would have to fight his way through its formidable system of communications trenches after the shelling ceased. Bar-Lev counted on four elements to break the enemy's attack before any significant gains were achieved: (1) static deployment along the length of the canal, including a tank battalion dispersed among the strongholds; (2) mobile armored forces; (3) artillery fire; and (4) airpower. Responding to Tal's criticism that a massive barrage would render the troops dead, wounded, or in shock—and thus incapable of firing a single round—Bar-Lev said, "Maybe yes, maybe no. It's outside our experience."[21] Israel's investment in reinforcing the line, he argued, was reasonable, and the integration of all elements of the defensive battle would succeed in breaking the attack. Depending on circumstances, each element could be altered. The line—not the individual stronghold—had the strength to withstand an enemy assault. The presence of tanks and observation posts alone would only whet the Egyptians' appetite for an attack. Reinforcing the strongholds, the chief of staff explained, would not come at the expense of other elements in the defense concept (including their budgets).

Summing up Adan's proposal, Bar-Lev approved the establishment of thirty-two strongholds (the thirty-third would remain unmanned) at a cost of 13 million pounds. He believed it was the best solution to protect against enemy raids, crossing attempts, and artillery barrages. The completion date was set for March 31, 1969, while relative quiet prevailed.

Interestingly, Defense Minister Moshe Dayan, a key figure and an authority on security matters, did not participate in the GHQ discussions, although he agreed with the conclusions. He later wrote that the massive Stronghold project began during the November 1968–March 1969 truce. In the spring of 1971 the second line of fortifications was established on the range of hills east of the canal, ten kilometers from the first line. This, in essence, resolved the two competing defense concepts dividing the GHQ. This is Dayan's only mention of the discussion, which strengthens the claim that the intensity of the debate, especially the arguments of Tal and Sharon, was exaggerated; the description of "fists banging on the table" was an embellishment added later.[22]

Subsequent Debate on Defense of the Suez Canal

Participants in the GHQ discussions in November–December 1968 realized that the armored forces between the canal and the Mitla and Gidi passes would have to conduct a mobile battle. However, they also understood that unless the IDF was dug in on the banks of the Suez Canal, it would be politically and militarily difficult to dislodge the Egyptians if they established a toehold on the eastern bank, owing to the forced cease-fire.

The literature on the GHQ debate over the defense method highlights the varying opinions and downplays the points of consensus. It fails to mention that the Stronghold plan was designed to protect the troops in the bunkers against Egyptian artillery fire during routine security operations, limited fighting, and full-scale war. The strongholds' role was to warn of an impending attack and block an Egyptian crossing effort while waging a delaying battle until the reserves assembled (according to the Rock plan), counterattacked, and crossed the canal.

The stronghold line was defined as the forward line, but it was never officially defined as the rear defensive line where the Egyptians would be held to the last bullet. Nevertheless, the understandings, agreements, and often vague statements by Bar-Lev and his successor, Elazar, created (intentionally or not) a situation in which the canal's eastern bank became the de facto rear defensive line. However, maps show that the line linking the western exit from the Mitla and Gidi passes to the dunes overlooking the Tasa-Ismailia Road east of the Lateral Road was the correct rear defensive line for defending Western Sinai. This eastern line was never officially identified as the rear defensive line, and the equivocation persisted until the war.

All the participants in the November–December 1968 meetings estimated that when war broke out (in March 1969 at the earliest), Egypt would launch three full armies across the canal, and Israeli armor with air support would engage them between the canal and the passes. No one actually believed the strongholds could halt a full-scale crossing. At best, they would send reports from the front, maintain observation, obstruct the enemy's plans, and direct artillery fire and air strikes until the reservists arrived and the IDF concentrated enough strength to cross the canal. No one doubted that this was a necessary step.[23]

Given the political situation, Bar-Lev realized that Israel could not allow the Egyptians to reach Bir Gafgafa or Tasa. Unless the Egyptians were stopped on the waterline, they would recapture the eastern bank before the cease-fire went into effect and the IDF had time to drive them out.[24] It should be noted that Bar-Lev stuck to this view during the war. Indeed, it cannot be denied that an IDF retreat eastward would have led to an Egyptian pursuit in the same direction, accompanied by artillery fire, as well as raids and ambushes farther east. This might have happened if Israel had withdrawn (as Dayan suggested during the War of Attrition), and in fact it did happen to a small degree during the Yom Kippur War.

After the collapse of the stronghold line during the Yom Kippur War, the professional discourse on the defense of Western Sinai became a rancorous debate marked by personal recriminations (typical of public controversies in Israel). Mobile defense was associated, unjustifiably, with innovation and creativity, whereas static defense was linked with unoriginality and obtuseness. What the critics lost sight of, however, was the fact that the supporters of mobile defense favored Israel's determined presence on the canal line. Gavish testified that the GHQ forum never argued over flexibility versus rigidity or static versus mobile defense, as it was presented in the literature.

In reality, a middle ground was reached between a rigid and a mobile defense doctrine, although neither withstood the test of war. For all practical purposes, the IDF employed a static defense with the mobile forces until the late hours of the morning of October 7. This was the solution decided on, although there was no case in military history in which a static defense line had stood its ground, and it was questionable whether the Bar-Lev Line would hold. Bar-Lev himself doubted that the strongholds alone could seriously interfere with a crossing, but he refused to base the canal's defense solely on mobile forces, fearing that they would be targeted by Egyptian ambushes. Thus he ordered the construction of strongholds capable of withstanding Egyptian artillery to serve as one element in a defense system that included armored forces close to the front line and mobile reserves in the rear tasked with breaking the attack.

The result was the creation of a conceptual absurdity. The unwritten order to allow no territorial gain for Egypt transformed the waterline (the cease-fire line) into the rear defensive line and gave the small force of regulars the impossible task of blocking an

power and surface-to-air missile batteries. Try as they might, and at
an exorbitant cost, 252nd Division failed to dislodge the Egyptians.
Some of the Rock forces counterattacked, but they were unable to
ust the enemy.

The only way the IDF could have accomplished its missions was
mmediately pull out the stronghold elements on the evening the
broke out or, at the very latest, overnight on October 6–7 and
ct a delaying battle until the Rock forces arrived. The reasons
is was not done are many and diverse.

f the Bar-Lev Line: Invitation to a War of Attrition

e Stronghold plan—the colossal fortification project—
in late December 1968. By January 1969, thirty-two
ad been erected along the entire 150 kilometers of
a dirt embankment running alongside it, and along
f the Mediterranean coastline. In addition, ammu-
ics bases, infrastructure for water supply, hospi-
and so forth were established. By March 1969,
Israel's largest engineering and logistical oper-
e of the most publicly criticized enterprises
profits reaped by the building contractors)—
But the rise of Israel's defensive line—a per-
tructure designed to perpetuate the status
gyptians' appetite for war, and the fighting

ted a four-stage plan for the resumption
the known advantages of static war-
create a situation that would allow a
the recapture of Sinai by force. They
not undertake a countercrossing to
were as follows:

800 artillery pieces (compared
strongholds.
n the eastern bank (to build
apability).
rn bank.
reas on the Israeli side and

Egyptian breakthrough along a 160-kilometer front.[25] De'
on the terrain and the canal, as important as it was, de'
the freedom to maneuver and forced the IDF to res-
and place determined by the enemy's initiative. T'
directive was the antithesis of a concept base'
a delaying battle, and the tactical yielding c'
enemy on the rear defensive line. The corre
offensive moves and channel the enemy
main counterattack takes place.[26]

Foreign scholars, too, have s'
ing Sinai. German historian H
Lev Line was an external lin'
mutual covering fire and '
warnings, thwarting er
and buying the time
defense plan on th
Bar-Lev Line s'
was not buil'
the constr'
than jus'
tactic'
th'

to '
war
cond'
why t'

Rise '

Work on t'
commenced
strongholds '
the canal, with '
20 kilometers o'
nition and logis'
tals, access roads
the project—one o'
ations (and also o'
because of the huge
was nearly complete.
manent, impregnable '
quo—also whetted the '
resumed on March 8, 196'
The Egyptian army dra'
of war with Israel, based o'
fare. The Egyptians hoped to
large-scale canal crossing and
were confident the IDF would
the western bank. The four stage

1. Artillery fire—concentrating
   with Israel's 20) to destroy the
2. Small-scale commando raids
   self-confidence and operational
3. Wide-scale operations on the east
4. A full-scale canal crossing to seize '
   break the political deadlock.

a
forc'

Egyptian breakthrough along a 160-kilometer front.[25] Dependence on the terrain and the canal, as important as it was, detracted from the freedom to maneuver and forced the IDF to respond at a time and place determined by the enemy's initiative. The "not one step" directive was the antithesis of a concept based on early warning, a delaying battle, and the tactical yielding of territory to block the enemy on the rear defensive line. The correct use of depth can enable offensive moves and channel the enemy into killing zones where the main counterattack takes place.[26]

Foreign scholars, too, have studied Israel's plans for defending Sinai. German historian H. Töpfer wrote that, at best, the Bar-Lev Line was an external line of strongholds that lacked depth and mutual covering fire and was multitasked for observing, sounding warnings, thwarting enemy patrols, offering decoy and deception, and buying the time needed to complete preparations for the main defense plan on the first and second lines. According to Töpfer, the Bar-Lev Line suffered from serious conceptual shortcomings and was not built according to the rules for defense, which emphasize the construction of various layers. The primary framework is more than just a strategic and operational concept; it exists primarily at the tactical level and is characterized by a depth relative to the needs of this level. The doctrinal and actual failure of the line exacted a very heavy price. Töpfer concluded that Bar-Lev chose a static defense mainly because he feared the Egyptians would seize an area on the eastern bank that the IDF would be unable to recapture. The entire rationale of the plan was strongholds, tanks on the line, and mobile reserves in the rear. But even the most rudimentary analysis reveals that the IDF would find it impossible to "brush off" an Egyptian territorial gain—even one held by a small Egyptian force—once it was protected by massive artillery cover and the surface-to-air missile umbrella on the western bank.[27] Recall that this was the argument raised by Tal and others during the discussions of December 1968 and afterward.

The December 1968 defense plan, which detailed the principles of deployment and response, assigned the task of holding the line to the regulars and assigned the Rock counterattack to the reservists. However, not even a fully equipped stronghold framework, let alone a thinly manned one, could maintain an effective delaying action or prevent a canal crossing by five infantry divisions reinforced with antitank units and backed by massive artillery firepower and surface-to-air missile batteries. Try as they might, and at an exorbitant cost, 252nd Division failed to dislodge the Egyptians. Some of the Rock forces counterattacked, but they were unable to oust the enemy.

The only way the IDF could have accomplished its missions was to immediately pull out the stronghold elements on the evening the war broke out or, at the very latest, overnight on October 6–7 and conduct a delaying battle until the Rock forces arrived. The reasons why this was not done are many and diverse.

Rise of the Bar-Lev Line: Invitation to a War of Attrition

Work on the Stronghold plan—the colossal fortification project—commenced in late December 1968. By January 1969, thirty-two strongholds had been erected along the entire 150 kilometers of the canal, with a dirt embankment running alongside it, and along 20 kilometers of the Mediterranean coastline. In addition, ammunition and logistics bases, infrastructure for water supply, hospitals, access roads, and so forth were established. By March 1969, the project—one of Israel's largest engineering and logistical operations (and also one of the most publicly criticized enterprises because of the huge profits reaped by the building contractors)—was nearly complete.[28] But the rise of Israel's defensive line—a permanent, impregnable structure designed to perpetuate the status quo—also whetted the Egyptians' appetite for war, and the fighting resumed on March 8, 1969.

The Egyptian army drafted a four-stage plan for the resumption of war with Israel, based on the known advantages of static warfare. The Egyptians hoped to create a situation that would allow a large-scale canal crossing and the recapture of Sinai by force. They were confident the IDF would not undertake a countercrossing to the western bank. The four stages were as follows:

1. Artillery fire—concentrating 800 artillery pieces (compared with Israel's 20) to destroy the strongholds.
2. Small-scale commando raids on the eastern bank (to build self-confidence and operational capability).
3. Wide-scale operations on the eastern bank.
4. A full-scale canal crossing to seize areas on the Israeli side and break the political deadlock.

Many Egyptian units participated in the first three stages, which were designed to overcome Israel's defense structures and provide answers at the operational and tactical levels.[29]

Egyptian activity also included concentrated artillery shelling, harassing mortar fire, air sorties against strongholds and installations close to the line, ambushes, sniper fire, helicopter assaults, and night bombings. In addition, commando units and frogmen operated in the Port of Eilat.

In view of Egypt's aims, Bar-Lev formulated the IDF policy: prevent the enemy from achieving any territorial gains on the stronghold line, and pressure Egypt to sue for a cease-fire. But after the resumption of hostilities in March 1969, the stronghold line was bombarded daily by thousands of shells.[30] This situation demanded a reevaluation of the defense and war-fighting doctrine in Sinai. Bar-Lev realized that without IAF involvement, the line would collapse due to heavy losses, and the Egyptians would never agree to a cease-fire. Beginning in July the air force entered the fighting, targeting the forward line of artillery batteries and army bases. In January 1970 it began to attack Egypt's depth. Bar-Lev also ordered numerous large-scale commando raids (perhaps more than any other chief of staff) that were planned and controlled by the participating commands and branches. (Despite the magnitude of the operations, he refused to establish a special forces headquarters.)

The fighting routine in the War of Attrition—shelling, ambushes, raids, sniper activity, abductions, and so forth—hastened the IDF's development of combat drills in the units on the line. These drills involved stronghold defense, artillery support, use of tanks, patrols, ambushes, and the opening of roads. The 252nd Division, which was responsible for the line, revised its drills based on lessons learned from numerous fire incidents. The armored corps circulated the conclusions to the three territorial commands. By the time the Yom Kippur War erupted, these drills had become the mainstay of divisional activity.

The Linkup Drill

The most important drill involved linking up with a stronghold that was being overrun from the north, south, or east and was signaling for help. A nearby tank force (generally a platoon) would scramble and employ its light weapons and cannon against the enemy assaulting the stronghold. The tanks fired autonomously or in coordination with the stronghold at targets on the fences and openings, starting at a range of hundreds of meters. Then, usually a single tank entered the compound to boost morale and evacuate the wounded.

The division held the canal front with less than 100 tanks (about 30 of them in the strongholds) against 700 Egyptian tanks on the western bank. The Israeli tanks were concentrated in thinned-out companies next to Artillery Road. They were supposed to reach the areas being attacked within minutes and provide assistance at critical or more distant points. The tanks also accompanied patrols, provided fire support, and deployed in platoon-size night parks next to the strongholds for immediate assistance in case of an enemy incursion.

The linkup drill demanded that tank commanders be familiar with the roads leading to the strongholds and the adjacent ramparts, so as to avoid sinking in the marshes or entering the minefields protecting the strongholds. The artillery batteries spread out along Artillery Road also took part in the drills. Every evening they positioned their guns on predetermined coordinates, ready to provide immediate illumination or explosive fire support.

The linkup was a complex, vital, and effective maneuver. It was often implemented during the War of Attrition and was especially useful in repulsing night raids. It was practiced (though rarely, and in only a skeletal format) during the cease-fire. Usually one company-size drill was carried out each week, and battalion- or brigade-level drills were performed once during a three-month period. Linkup drills of larger formations, with the rear brigade reinforcing the forward brigade, were very rare. The last one prior to the Yom Kippur War occurred in November 1972.

Although the drills sharpened the units' defensive capabilities, there were drawbacks. The drills used open radio networks and were carried out in plain view of the Egyptians. Signage on the ground, road markers with code names printed in large letters, and corresponding code names on maps that were left behind made it simple for the enemy to decipher the IDF's tactical and operational plans for defending the canal line and devise the appropriate solutions.

During this period, the strongholds came under heavy bombardment on a daily basis. Egyptian commandos attempted raids and abductions. Solo air sorties dropped 250-kilo bombs on the Bar-Lev Line that seriously damaged the strongholds' defenses. The IAF

retaliated by attacking Egyptian artillery positions near the canal, but the fire continued.

Lieutenant Colonel Avraham Rotem, 252nd Division's G-3, expressed the defense concept in May 1970 as not yielding one step on the canal and holding it with a minimal force. This force was supposed to block a canal crossing of two to three Egyptian divisions while Israel's reservists were mobilizing. The strongholds' task was to hang on until the armored force arrived and destroyed the enemy; they would provide fire to protect the flanks and impede the enemy's entry into the sector. Rotem stressed the importance of Israeli armor, but he also warned of the Egyptians' overwhelming firepower and the ease with which the Egyptian infantry could cross the canal and lay an ambush. Regarding a full-scale Egyptian crossing, the G-3 summed up Israel's defense doctrine on the front, avowing that, unlike the situation a year and a half earlier, the idea of a crossing was passé. No enemy general was threatening to invade Israel. As for the antiaircraft missile batteries, he was sure that they could be dealt with.

The IAF Attacks Egypt's Depth

Despite Rotem's optimism, Egyptian surface-to-air missile batteries continued to pose a serious threat to IAF activity. On December 25, 1969, Israeli fighters carried out the largest air operation since the Six-Day War, silencing the Egyptian artillery and destroying the SA2 missile batteries along the canal in order to gain air superiority. But the attack failed to end the heavy shelling or reduce casualties in the strongholds. In January 1970, as the fighting escalated and the number of Israeli dead and wounded mounted, the government made one of the most crucial decisions in the War of Attrition: the air force would commence deep-penetration attacks to ratchet up the pressure on Nasser. Dayan opposed the decision but capitulated (as was his wont) in the face of the hard-line supporters: Golda Meir, Ezer Weizman, Yigal Allon, and Yitzhak Rabin (Israel's ambassador to the United States, who flew in specifically to report that the Americans supported the bombings as a springboard to eliminating Nasser). Foreign Minister Abba Eban sided with Dayan and warned of Soviet intervention.

The in-depth strikes deterred the Egyptians, undermined their strategy of attrition, and shocked their leaders. Nasser dashed off to

Moscow to ask for assistance, which was immediately granted. The Soviet Union promptly dispatched Russian forces to Egypt: three divisions of advanced surface-to-air missiles (SA2s and SA3s) and ninety-five top-of-the-line MIG 21s (including commanders and pilots). In February the Russians assumed overall command of the antiaircraft bases down to the individual unit level. Russian naval vessels anchored in Port Said. Although Israel's deep penetrating attacks forced the Egyptians into a cease-fire in August 1970, they also induced the Egyptians to establish a sophisticated antiaircraft missile framework that would severely disrupt the IAF's efforts to support the ground forces in the Yom Kippur War.[31]

Until April 13, 1970, Israeli planes (the recently acquired American Phantoms) pummeled targets in Egypt's depth. In June an American effort was under way to bring about a cease-fire, and the Egyptians did not reject the initiative. In July, however, they began to advance an air defense division to the canal under the shield of Soviet missiles, the goal being to prevent the IAF from coming to the aid of the strongholds. The Egyptian air defense umbrella extended from the western bank of the canal twenty kilometers eastward into Sinai. The division's move paralleled the escalation of artillery fire on the strongholds. The IAF began to hit Egyptian artillery positions and missile dugouts on the western bank, but it incurred heavy losses. On June 30 two Phantoms went down while attacking surface-to-air missile batteries; another Phantom was shot down on July 5. The situation on the canal had radically changed. The Egyptians' antiaircraft defenses were continually being enhanced and inching forward. The rate of successful IAF sorties plummeted.

Given the relentless pressure on the strongholds and the mounting Israeli casualties, a political-military situation assessment had to be made and a new ground and air modus operandi formulated. A meeting was held at GHQ on July 19, with the defense minister in attendance. The views voiced and the decisions made there had far-reaching ramifications for the August 1970 cease-fire and the Yom Kippur War three years later.

The defense minister was apprehensive about Soviet involvement in the Middle East and doubted Israel's ability to take out the Egyptian missile structure. He also questioned the value of eliminating it, equating such an action with pulling out weeds: they invariably grow back. Sharon, the general in charge of Southern Command since January 1970, proposed capturing a thirty-kilometer

strip on the western bank and ramping up the pressure on the Egyptians and Russians. The IAF commander, Major General Moti Hod, suggested attacking Egypt's missile dugouts, but he opposed hitting the missile structure itself because of the exorbitant price the IAF would have to pay. Hod proposed temporarily halting the deep-penetration sorties until the IAF could study the problem and procure new technological means.

Bar-Lev acknowledged that the only way to prevent an erosion of Israel's strategic situation was to continue to hold the waterline with the strongholds. At the conclusion of the meeting, he ordered the air force to try to eliminate the first line of missile dugouts and artillery batteries at ranges that did not entail undue losses and to attack the sites of possible surface-to-air missile ambushes, airfields, hangars, and so forth. Despite the risks and the potential losses, the IAF was ordered to attack with "sensitivity" the forward batteries and weak points on the western bank every two or three days. This was part of the air force's concerted effort to arrest the deteriorating situation on the canal and acquire combat experience. Bar-Lev did not dismiss the possibility that if ten or twenty Israeli troops were killed over a three- or four-day period, he might order a pullback from the canal. Therefore, a second line had to be prepared.[32]

Summing up the discussion, Dayan said that the Egyptian batteries' advancement had gone unnoticed and, in his opinion, the IDF should prepare for an Egyptian crossing in the summer of 1970. He stressed the importance of talks with the Americans and noted that Israel could live with American restrictions on its activity. Although he predicted that the Egyptians would escalate the pressure on the strongholds, he saw no alternative to sitting on the waterline. He spoke in only vague terms about a second line west of where the battle would be fought.

Fearing the Russian Bear and the American Eagle

The difficulty of overcoming the Soviet-supported and -operated missile system and fear of a direct confrontation with the Russians (five Russian-flown MIGs were shot down on July 30, 1970) invited American pressure for a cease-fire and a dialogue, despite Israel's opposition. Israel's dependence on American aid hampered its freedom of action in this situation, which involved the threat of a military confrontation between the superpowers. Years later, Weizman mustered all his rhetorical acerbity and venom when he stated that the minute Israel accepted the assumption that it could not eliminate the Russian missiles without American equipment and technology, it ceased being an independent state and became an American satellite. "Intrinsically we feared the Russian bear, the American eagle, and even the Arab snake, but we couldn't unleash the Israeli lion."[33] By avoiding a military decision, Israel weakened its political and strategic position.

Israel's decision not to destroy the Egyptian air defense system neutralized its air superiority and rendered the Bar-Lev Line practically indefensible, as events in the Yom Kippur War would prove. Even after Egypt advanced its missiles, Dayan and senior IDF commanders still avowed that the military status quo remained essentially intact. And even though the IDF devised no solution to deal with this problem, it was certain the air force could destroy the Egyptian air defense system.

As the cease-fire went into effect on the night of August 7–8, the Egyptians immediately began to advance surface-to-air missile batteries to the canal. Israel bowed to American pressure and staved off a confrontation; in exchange, it received Shrike air-to-surface missiles and sophisticated electronic warfare equipment.[34] Bar-Lev stated that Israel had grudgingly turned a blind eye to Egypt's moves in order to receive military supplies from Washington, and it decided not to renew fighting on the line before the fortification work was completed, lest it appear that Israel had violated the cease-fire and torpedoed a political move.

The fear of Soviet intervention forced Israel to accept a cease-fire that lacked any mechanisms to prevent the Egyptians from making military advances. The unprecedented sum of American aid (half a billion dollars during the cease-fire) allayed some of Israel's frustration over the missile situation, and there was even a sense of relief that the War of Attrition was over. The Egyptians perceived the cease-fire as a golden opportunity to build up a sophisticated air defense system and prepare for the next war, especially since, in their view, the War of Attrition had ended in a draw.

The IDF's Lessons from the War of Attrition

The question of who won and who gained the most in the War of Attrition is still debated. The subtext of Bar-Lev's farewell address as chief of staff in late December 1971 reveals the uncertainties and dilemmas surrounding the canal front. The outgoing chief of staff noted the Americans' deepening concern about confrontation with the Russians. He remained convinced that the IDF's methods were justified, including the deep-penetration sorties. He repeated that the Egyptians would gain nothing in a war. The Americans, he opined, were deluding themselves if they thought a solution could be attained based on the 1967 borders, and even they realized that the chances of a diplomatic breakthrough were infinitesimal. The lesson from the War of Attrition was that Israel had to hold fast to the waterline and not be lured by dramatic propositions such as deploying in the rear and abandoning the strongholds. As for the price paid by Israel (270 killed in seventeen months of fighting), Bar-Lev admitted that it had been costly, but he believed those losses should be seen in a broader perspective: 529 civilians were killed in traffic accidents in 1970.

Tal was sharply critical of the Bar-Lev Line, saying, "The stronghold line failed in the War of Attrition, incurred casualties, did nothing to deter the Egyptians from carrying out daring, deep penetration raids, and served as a static target while demonstrating to the Egyptians the importance of their firepower. The IDF's success in the War of Attrition can be attributed to the air force alone. The line created a desperate, exhausting, static, and unprofessional defense incapable of achieving victory while it left the army in contact with the enemy at all levels."[35] Nevertheless, he believed that Israel had won the War of Attrition. If victory is defined as achieving one's goals, then the IDF had indeed been victorious: it had not budged one step from the waterline.

A contrary view was held by Weizman, who stated categorically that Israel had lost the War of Attrition. According to Weizman, it was ludicrous to claim that Israel had won. Despite the Egyptians' losses, they had succeeded, whereas Israel's blunders from March 1969 to August 1970 (and later) paved the way for the Yom Kippur War.

Even after a rotation of command—David Elazar became chief of staff, Israel Tal became head of GHQ and deputy chief of staff, and Ariel Sharon became head of Southern Command—no changes were made to the defense concept, and daily operations continued as usual. After such huge sums had been invested in fortifying the canal, the motivation to amend or rethink the defense concept was weak. Although the IDF suffered many casualties on the line, it sank into political and military complacency. The defense concept stood intact: the strongholds would provide an early warning, and Israeli armor would smash an Egyptian canal crossing.

Egypt's Lessons from the War of Attrition

The Israeli government did not internalize the political and military lessons of the War of Attrition (perhaps because there was too little time before the Yom Kippur War broke out), and the army made no formal study of the lessons of the war (perhaps because it assumed the front would soon heat up again). The Egyptians, in contrast, made a supreme effort to learn the lessons of the War of Attrition (and the Six-Day War), and this was a key factor in their doctrinal and operational planning as the Yom Kippur War approached. They courageously and professionally identified their own weaknesses (and designed bold solutions to overcome them), as well as the strengths and deficiencies of the Israeli soldiers, both as individual fighters and as members of the greater IDF framework.

The Egyptian soldiers gained experience dealing with their Israeli counterparts, which strengthened their self-confidence and trust in their equipment and commanders. The War of Attrition taught the Egyptians how to prepare for a full-scale war with limited objectives. They identified the IDF's advantages and their own shortcomings and came up with answers for both.

The War of Attrition showed the Egyptians that they were capable of crossing a wide water obstacle, and they identified the Bar-Lev Line's weak points: isolated strongholds with ten-kilometer gaps between them that were thinly manned since the cease-fire went into effect. They correctly interpreted Israeli armor's modus operandi on the line: a tank platoon would rush to the rescue of a stronghold under attack. The Egyptians countered this by arming the infantry with antitank weapons and mines and covering the force with antitank fire from ramps on the western bank. The Egyptian infantry's advanced antitank weapons (which were lightweight, low signature, difficult to spot, and hard to hit) were a key element in its war preparations and its organization of infantry divisions for the crossing operation.

The Egyptians recognized their inferiority in armor and mobile warfare (Egyptian tanks saw almost no action in the War of Attrition). Therefore, armor played a limited role in the initial stages of the crossing and fighting; this consisted mainly of providing fire support from tank ramps on the western bank. Most of the tank divisions stayed on the western bank for the duration of the war. The Egyptians also recognized the importance of artillery fire in the offensive stage, especially in support of the crossing forces and defense of the bridgeheads. They identified the strategic importance of air defense (the "missile wall") for challenging Israel's uncontested air superiority and protecting the crossing forces (the infantry and, to a lesser extent, armor) at the bridgeheads and in the depths. They made maximum use of their experience in the War of Attrition to plan the bridgeheads' defense against Israeli armor.[36]

Development of the Defense Concept during the Three-Year Cease-Fire

Fearing that hostilities would resume shortly (both sides had agreed to a three-month cease-fire), the IDF's immediate task was to improve its endurance and fighting capability on the waterline. Reconstructing the destroyed strongholds and improving the fortifications received top priority. Contractors were quickly found to carry out the work. Although the possibility of an Egyptian crossing at the end of the cease-fire was considered, no one really believed that full-scale war was on the horizon. Therefore, no orders were issued to prepare a defense plan for such a contingency.

In the event hostilities resumed, Bar-Lev defined the IDF's goals as attaining another cease-fire within a short time and preventing Egypt from gaining any territory. He ordered the following priorities:

- The air force would formulate war-fighting techniques for neutralizing the Egyptian missile arrangement.
- The line would be reinforced with special means.
- The strongholds would be strengthened.
- Weapons would be procured, and a combat doctrine would be devised.
- Operational plans would be drawn up for all the sectors in every situation, including training and exercises for a canal crossing.

The IDF quickly set to work improving deployment on the line and in the depths. In addition to buttressing the strongholds, construction began on eleven fortifications in the vicinity of Artillery Road. Minefields were laid, the dirt embankment along the canal was elevated to serve as an obstruction for armored vehicles, barbed wire fences were put up, the "plastic" roads were paved through the marshlands in the northern sector, other roads and airfields were upgraded, and ammunition, water, and oil storage depots were built. The IDF also began constructing firing ramps for tanks in the rear of the strongholds.

The three-month cease-fire ended, and silence prevailed on the canal front. After Nasser's death in September 1970, Egypt's new president, Anwar Sadat, focused on stabilizing his regime, and tension on the canal gave way to routine security operations. As long as quiet reigned, the IDF estimated that 252nd Division (with IAF support) and the improved strongholds would be able to counter the Egyptians if fire erupted and thwart any attempted canal crossing. This assessment—the regulars will hold—defined the stages and objectives of the anticipated fighting: a brief holding battle with air support, the Rock divisions' transfer to the western bank, and the enemy's defeat.

Like the Israelis, the Egyptians immediately embarked on a massive fortification project that continued uninterrupted until the outbreak of hostilities on October 6, 1973. They cut through the embankment on the western bank and built landing descents into the water for amphibious and bridging vehicles; then they mined the shoreline and erected fences. Especially important were the newly constructed, thirty-meter-high ramps overlooking the Israeli strongholds, road openings, and tank ramps.[37] The 252nd Division failed to comprehend the purpose of these ramps until war broke out. The Israelis assumed they were firing positions for Egyptian tanks, but they were actually launching sites for Sagger antitank missiles.

The cease-fire reinvigorated debate in the IDF about the rationale for maintaining a static defense on the canal. Feelers were sent out to test the response to the idea of a pullback. Dayan thought forces could be withdrawn a short distance from the canal, and the Americans submitted a similar proposal to the UN Security Council, but nothing came of it. Dayan, who loathed power struggles in the government, summed up the matter: "If Golda's against it—then so am I."[38]

Commanders at all levels expressed their dissatisfaction and frustration over the IDF's ongoing situation. They complained that static fire was to the enemy's advantage and would deny the IDF's ability to attain a decision in a war that was bound to exact heavy casualties. Tal's letter of September 20, 1970, accurately encapsulated this mood. As head of the Tank Directorate but not a participant in the GHQ forum, Tal spoke bluntly about the defense concept; he was especially critical of the strongholds, whose contribution in the event of an all-out Egyptian attack was dubious. He made it clear what the goals of defense were and that the terms *rigid* and *flexible* defense referred to holding on to territory or destroying the enemy force. He focused on the IDF's inability to answer Egyptian fire, which was why administrative activity within its artillery range had to be reduced to a minimum. He emphasized that a small stronghold layout was unjustified and proposed deploying two tank brigades in its place—170 tanks instead of the current 60—and bringing in a third brigade (the 7th) on a permanent basis at the Bir Tmadeh and Refidim (Bir Gafgafa) bases in the rear. The 7th Brigade would also take part in daily security operations and be ready in the event of war. This arrangement was far better than waiting for the arrival of reservists from the middle of the country while the regulars slugged it out in a desperate defensive battle. Tal suggested that mobile activity along the canal be based on mechanized infantry platoons in armored personnel carriers (APCs). Since the strongholds were already built, they could house some of these troops.[39]

Both the minister of defense and the chief of staff opposed Tal's recommendations. They had no intention of surrendering the IDF's physical presence on the water, lest the Egyptians try to annex parts of the eastern bank. In fact, this happened in an abandoned stronghold called Pulchan (Paraguay or Paterson, according to various code maps), south of El-Balah Island, where the Egyptians put up their flag and trained in open view to capture an Israeli stronghold.

Tal was not in a position to demand a discussion, and his suggestions went unheeded, in part because they would have placed a heavy burden on the armor regulars. Also, the cease-fire appeared to be stable, and quiet prevailed on the front. As long as the government adhered to the "no territorial gain for Egypt" dictum, and because maintaining a large number of forces on the canal was unrealistic, the defense doctrine continued to be based on thinned-out forces, with the waterline as the rear defensive line.

Thinning the Strongholds and Building Fortifications in the Rear

On assuming his post as leader of Southern Command in early 1970, General Sharon immediately introduced a radical change in the stronghold layout. This eliminated the need to discuss Tal's proposal, although several elements of Tal's plan were incorporated in the change. Sharon, one of the most vociferous proponents of mobile defense on the canal, suggested abandoning the strongholds and instead employing observation posts, armored patrols, and aggressive actions on the western bank. In addition, a new line of fortifications would be established ten kilometers from the canal, along with a third line located thirty kilometers from the waterway.[40]

Chief of Staff Bar-Lev and Defense Minister Dayan opposed this move but agreed to the construction of a line of fortifications along Artillery Road. In late 1970, in parallel with reinforcement of the strongholds, construction began on eleven fortifications designated for emergency use by the reserve forces—one company in each fort. The structures were not part of the plan for an armored, mobile defensive battle between the canal and Artillery Road, and for all practical purposes, they served as little more than living quarters for the tank and mechanized infantry companies on the line. They were not used tactically during the war, even though the fighting stabilized close to them. It is not clear whether these fortifications were part of Sharon's mobile defense concept.

In early January 1972, after Lieutenant General David Elazar's appointment as chief of staff, and in the face of reduced defense spending, Sharon again broached the idea of closing the strongholds and turning them into tank ramps. Elazar was adamantly against closing all the strongholds, blocking up the communications trenches, and dismantling the fences. He agreed, however, to discuss how to make their maintenance more cost-effective and the possibility of cutting back on manpower "here and there."[41] In late May, the two generals reached a compromise: the number of strongholds would be reduced to sixteen (from the original thirty-two); some would be blocked up, and others would be converted into daytime observation posts. In July, Dayan approved the agreement. Five strongholds were immediately shut down, and eight more closed in October. Sharon ordered tractors to block their entrances and make them impassable—"not even for Jews."[42] Later, some of the strongholds were reopened, not to buttress the defense structure but to reinforce the surveillance system.

Elazar's compromise with Sharon conformed to his perception of the lack of military activity on the line and the public's desire to decrease security expenditures. These factors reduced any reservations about decreasing the number of strongholds and downgrading the quantity and quality of the troops manning them. However, the compromise on the Bar-Lev Line ran counter to military logic, and the line's raison d'être (as a warning system or a defensive line capable of blocking an enemy attack) gradually became blurred. The IDF would pay an exorbitant price in men and equipment for this ambiguity in the first two days of the Yom Kippur War. When the war broke out, there were sixteen strongholds manned by 450 troops (including administrative personnel) and 55 armored crew members with their tanks.

The whittling down of the Bar-Lev Line and the IAF's loss of air superiority after the Egyptian air defense umbrella advanced to the western bank demanded a reassessment of the situation by Israel. Despite the deep gap between operational plans and their execution, no one performed a reevaluation, no one drew the necessary conclusions, and the operational plan remained as it had been. Had a reassessment been made, it would have been clear that reliance on the air force was unfounded—a mental block at both the military and political levels. Likewise, after downsizing the strongholds, the need to shift from a rigid defense on the waterline to a mobile defense would have been obvious. The thinning out of the strongholds neutralized one plan, but instead of drafting a new one, the predetermined defense on the waterline remained the combat doctrine, which required splitting up the tank forces and holding the road junctions.[43] Since GHQ made no situational reassessment, no one issued new orders or did the necessary staff work to replace the personnel in the strongholds with crack troops. In effect, GHQ was captive to the War of Attrition mentality, while the operational doctrine of Southern Command, under Sharon's helmsmanship, was based on word of mouth.

Crossing to the Western Bank versus Holding the Line

Sharon realized that the waterline could not be defended with the current number of forces, so he ordered the building of a second line—the fortification line. His concept was based on an immediate IDF crossing to the western bank to gain victory. He and Deputy Chief of Staff Tal prepared the crossing forces according to this rationale and concentrated pontoons at Baluza and Tasa.

Sharon knew that if the IDF were to cross the Suez Canal, it could not be confined to the waterline. In other words, in wartime, the line would not be defended, but Israeli tanks would be in position at the fortification line, and reinforcements would be directed to the crossing effort. None of these ideas were written down, but according to this concept, the strongholds had to be thinned out and evacuated once hostilities erupted so as not to constitute a constraining factor. Sharon was skeptical about the defensive capability of the forces assigned to routine security operations, so he prepared no defense plan for such a contingency. He undoubtedly would have done so if he had thought it necessary. He viewed Dovecote as a necessary evil for reinforcing the line with regulars, but crossing to the western bank was of the utmost importance.

In contrast, the new chief of staff left the defense plans as they were. During a GHQ tour of the canal in early 1973, Elazar was observing Egyptian crossing exercises at El-Balah Island and was asked what would happen if the Egyptians suddenly crossed the canal. His answer (typical of him): "They wouldn't dare!"

Major General Gonen succeeded Sharon as head of Southern Command in July 1973. Gonen understood orders and proceeded accordingly, but he did not envision how the next war might develop. In his worldview, "the regulars will hold!" meant that the regulars will pay the price. Unlike Sharon, who read intelligence reports, Gonen relied on the assessments of Southern Command's intelligence officers, who estimated that the likelihood of war was low. Thus, in the chaos that erupted on Friday, October 5, 1973, Gonen saw his main mission as holding the stronghold line and reopening the thinly manned strongholds according to the static defense doctrine he was familiar with. This meant not budging from the waterline and keeping the tank companies deployed adjacent to the strongholds. On the morning of October 6, his approach remained the same: "No need to exaggerate. War hasn't broken out yet."[44] He saw no reason to move the forces according to the Dovecote plan for deploying the regulars (i.e., 14th Brigade to enter its daytime parks, and the 401st to move from the rear area to the southern sector).

When fighting erupted, the question became how to employ the force. Should the enemy be allowed to cross the canal so that the IDF could counterattack and then transfer to the western bank—as Sharon envisioned—or should the plan to protect the stronghold line be implemented according to the written order? As expected, Gonen chose the second option, failing to perceive the magnitude of the problem.

Elazar did not explain how the regulars were supposed to defend the line against a full-scale Egyptian offensive. The GHQ had never discussed such a scenario, and no one was prepared to take responsibility for yielding territory in a two-front war (Sinai and the Golan Heights). Thus, the defense concepts of "hold the waterline" and "no territorial gain for Egypt" remained intact. The only person who had planned for such a contingency was Sharon, who realized that if the battle had to be fought in the strongholds, an Israeli crossing would be impossible.[45]

Sharon was correct about the need to evacuate the strongholds on October 6, once it became absolutely clear that war was imminent and the canal could not be defended according to existing plans. Depleting the strongholds without preparing a new defense plan was a grave omission on the part of the defense minister, the chief of staff, the leader of Southern Command, and the commander of 252nd Division. It should be noted that the moment Gonen assumed command, he ordered that plans be drawn up for the reopening of a number of the abandoned strongholds; however, the staff work was still in progress when the war broke out. Due to Gonen's pressure, the chief of staff approved the reopening of three strongholds: Egrofit (southern sector), Lakekan (central sector), and Traklin (northern sector). This activity was completed by the time of the war.

Elazar's Unfamiliarity with the Egyptian Sector

The chief of staff's muddled thinking on the defense of Sinai raises a question: to what extent was it an operational concept or just a mishmash of ideas?[46] General Elazar had not been present during discussions of the Stronghold plan in December 1968. To make matters worse, his involvement in the defense of Sinai was negligible, and his familiarity with the terrain and its unique challenges superficial. He recognized the complexity of the problem only after his appointment as head of GHQ in early 1970, at the height of the War of Attrition. Elazar's insufficient knowledge of the main fighting theater initially discouraged Dayan from appointing him chief of staff (and sidelining General Gavish, who knew Sinai better than any other officer in the GHQ and was the natural candidate for the post). Dayan even suggested that Elazar serve as general of Southern Command for a short time before stepping into the post of chief of staff, giving him an opportunity to fully appreciate the difficulties of the theater. But things turned out differently.

Elazar's unfamiliarity with Sinai can be seen in his approval of Sharon's plan to close the strongholds. He authorized this move before weighing its implications and without ordering a new defense plan that incorporated changes on the ground, including the possibility of fighting simultaneously on the Golan Heights and Suez Canal. The new chief of staff visited Sinai infrequently (he had not been to the southern front since the Blue White alert in April–May 1973), so he lacked an operational understanding of the theater's time and space determinants. His inexperience in Sinai was most evident in his decisions (or lack thereof) during the critical first three days of the war.

Elazar's appointment in the middle of the cease-fire obligated him to present his overall military view and his positions on the defense concept in Western Sinai in various combat scenarios. Occasionally he contradicted himself. For example, he stated that the strongholds were a major contributor to Sinai's defensive structure by limiting the number of possible crossing points, yet in the same breath he ordered a study of the feasibility of closing the strongholds and adding an armored brigade. He accepted the analysis of Major General Eli Zeira, the chief of intelligence: the Egyptians' operations would include a canal crossing and advance to the mountain passes, raids in Sinai and along the canal, shelling, and combined shelling and raiding parties. He completely concurred with the addendum to this intelligence analysis (which would later be bitterly criticized), which stated, "All this was low probability. The lowest being an Egyptian canal crossing and the highest the raids, perhaps some shelling here and there."[47]

In every forum and at every opportunity, the chief of staff espoused his concept of stopping the Egyptians in their tracks, although he probably knew there was no way to prevent some sort of territorial gain. He stated his views straightforwardly in operational discussion groups and at meetings with the political echelon, such as when he approved plans during the Blue White alert. The principle of stopping the enemy on the obstacle line dominated planning in the Northern and Southern Commands, as evidenced by their presentation to the prime minister on May 9, 1973: "We're not looking for brilliant military exercises that lure the enemy into a trap and then destroy him. We plan to stop the enemy in his tracks on the Syrian and Egyptian fronts. For military reasons we believe this is the right solution, and for political reasons we don't want them to achieve even a partial gain. . . . Therefore [our plans are] to stop them in their tracks."[48]

Elazar stressed that the best results would be achieved by having the Rock divisions immediately go on the attack. The 252nd Division, also tasked with defense and blocking the enemy from gaining any territory, would immediately execute the Zefania and Ben-Hayil offensive operations for a canal crossing (see map 4). However, there are glaring discrepancies in Elazar's postwar statements regarding the defense of the canal; he seems to have forgotten how and under what conditions the regulars had to fight according to the Dovecote plan.

Conducting War Games and Exercises

During the three years of the cease-fire in Sinai, Southern Command conducted a number of war games and exercises that tested operational doctrines in plausible scenarios (as well as in extreme cases and special operations). The scenarios were based on the warfare doctrine and the level of Egyptian and Israeli weapons and forces. The games were carried out according to operational plans designed to address the enemy's probable actions; the scenarios were presented by the intelligence officer and approved by the officer in charge and all command levels. War games are an important tool for identifying the Achilles' heels in planning and assessment and for highlighting risks and devising optimal solutions. The responses of the officers participating in the exercises and the solutions they come up with offer insight into commanders' thinking—of both those taking part in the exercises and those at higher levels. The chief of staff's summary of the war games confers official and binding authority to perceptions, plans, orders of battle, assessments, and so forth.

The representations of the Egyptians' actions in the war games corresponded very closely to their actual moves in the Yom Kippur

War. This was true for both the 1970 war game (during the War of Attrition), when Brigadier General Motta Gur simulated an Egyptian commander, and for the Mahaluma (Strike) war game in January 1971, when Brigadier General Musa Peled represented the Arab armies and Brigadier General Benny Peled their air forces. The officer conducting that exercise was Major General Yitzhak Hofi, head of the training branch; he presented a case of 750 Egyptian tanks on the eastern bank but found it difficult to convince Bar-Lev that such a far-fetched scenario was worthwhile. The conclusions were as follows: the enemy was capable of making territorial gains, at least in the initial stage; H hour would be 14:00; defense did not constitute a serious problem requiring a solution; and the air force would be ordered to attack the missile batteries as early as possible.

In the Oz (Courage) exercise in March 1972, defensive action was given short shrift, and the IDF overcame the "enemy" in a hasty defense. In June 1972 the new head of the IDF Doctrine and Instruction Department, General Gonen, held the Iron Ram (Eil Barzel) war game. Ariel Sharon, commander of Southern Command, participated in that exercise, which reflected the IDF's operational doctrine at the time. In the simulation, the Egyptians attacked from their emergency deployment; crossed the canal with five infantry divisions and 380 tanks at three bridgeheads, followed by two additional armored divisions; and then advanced to Lateral Road, Baluza, and the openings of the Tasa and Mitla passes.[49] IAF aircraft were scrambled and began bombing their targets (including bridging equipment) along the canal. The regulars launched a counterattack two hours after the crossing and engaged the enemy forces, beating them back to the western bank. The reserve divisions arrived on the third day of the fighting and crossed only at the northern sector. The opening scenario left too little time to mobilize the artillery reserves and implement Bendigo (a joint artillery–air force operation designed to neutralize the missile batteries), and Gonen regretted that an important lesson from this part of the exercise had been lost (he would return to this omission, justifiably, during summaries of the Yom Kippur War).

When the exercise was summarized on August 3, 1972, Major General Dan Laner, commander of 252nd Division, warned of overoptimism and the problem of integrating nonorganic units into the battle. It was a mistake, he noted, to have reservists carry out the canal crossing, mainly because they lacked the training of the regulars. Sharon made it clear that Israel could not afford to end the war with an unacceptable number of IDF casualties and no major gains—not necessarily territorial conquests, but destruction of the enemy in a way that shattered his morale and wrecked his self-confidence for a long time. This would be possible only if the IDF was willing to allow 1,500 Egyptian tanks to cross to the eastern bank and then annihilate them. The officer conducting the exercise, General Gonen, believed that the regulars in Sinai were sufficient to block the enemy (but not to carry out a counterattack).

The chief of staff summed up the exercise but was still vague on the question of air support in the land battle. His ambiguity would prevail up to and even during the war. He regarded air superiority as the sine qua non for a successful outcome and believed that, with sufficient warning, the armored brigades would be able to engage and hold the enemy with less artillery support than planned and without air support. According to his line of thinking, the army would have to hold the enemy at bay for a few hours, followed by a massive air strike on Egypt's missile system, which, he assumed, would obliterate the missiles in a matter of hours.

The chief of staff's estimate of "a few hours" was, of course, totally unsubstantiated. Although he believed the air force could contribute in some way to the initial stage of defense, he expressly stated that no matter how the war began, the IDF's main goal was to neutralize the missiles to attain freedom of action in the sky. If the fighting was renewed, he saw two options for the IDF—the preferred one being a canal crossing to cause severe damage to the enemy (though not as far as Cairo) and create an advantageous bargaining position for a political settlement. Three divisions and an infantry brigade would suffice for defense, and the outcome would be decided on the western bank.

The Iron Ram war game revealed the problem of a short-term warning (a few days). According to Brigadier General Dov Tamari, deputy commander of 162nd Division in the war, the IDF had three ways to respond to an Egyptian attack: (1) change the balance sheet by launching its own attack—that is, an immediate canal crossing with the regulars—but the chief of staff doubted its feasibility; (2) wage a battle of annihilation against the crossing forces; or (3) engage in a head-on confrontation between the two armies (the option eventually chosen). Despite doubts over the IDF's ability to carry out a crossing while the Egyptians were attacking, the

IDF acquired bridging equipment for an amphibious assault and deployed it at Baluza and Tasa.[50]

In the game's defensive stage, nine hours was sufficient time for the IDF to destroy the Egyptian army on the eastern bank, execute a counterattack, and cross the Suez Canal once the reservists arrived. A short, forty-eight-hour warning was considered an extreme case (in reality, the alert for the Yom Kippur War would be much shorter). No one analyzed the Egyptian crossing method: infantry reinforced with antitank weapons, no concentrated effort, and no operational halt. Nor did the exercise take into account the imbalance of forces, which weighed heavily against 252nd Division, or the division's debilitating exhaustion in the first twenty-four hours of fighting.

The Dovecote Plan: Response to the Resumption of Hostilities on the Canal

The Dovecote plan devised by Southern Command and 252nd Division—GHQ termed it the Chalk (Geer) plan—laid out in detail the deployment of the regulars on the canal front, including tank reinforcements for the isolated strongholds, in the event of renewed fighting in any form. The plan, which was designed to provide an initial answer to an Egyptian attack with minimal warning, was drafted during the cease-fire, although its main features had been defined at the start of the War of Attrition. With the chief of staff's approval, the plan called for two tank brigades of regulars and a regional brigade to be deployed on the canal line, with an additional tank brigade of regulars held in reserve in the rear. This arrangement was considered sufficient to hold the line and create a convenient opening situation for a counterattack and canal crossing by the Rock reserve divisions. In the wake of the Blue White alert, the tanks intended to reinforce the regulars had been put in reserve logistics units in Wadi Mlez and Bir Tmadeh.

The plan specified that the tanks of 275th Regional Brigade and the tank brigade on the line would be dispersed in the strongholds: two tanks in Budapest and two in Orkal in the northern sector, a platoon in Botser, a platoon at Ras Sudar, and two tanks in Hamezach in the southern sector. At the same time, the reduced tank companies were supposed to leave the fortifications, enter the adjacent daytime parks, and, on command, take up their positions—natural ones where possible, and man-made ones (ramps and fins, as they were termed in the northern sector) at the main junctions on Canal Road and in the strongholds' rear area 1,000 to 1,500 meters away.

Dovecote divided the canal sector into three parts. The rear area brigade would command the southern sector, including the brigade's tank battalion deployed on the line there. In addition, it would reinforce the line's southern sector with one of its tank battalions and leave a second battalion to counterstrike while it concentrated in the vicinity of Artillery Road (or remained ready to assist the line itself). The third battalion of the rear area brigade would join the line brigade in the central sector and concentrate on the junction of Artillery Road and Tasa-Ismalia Road to deliver counterpunches. The division's third tank brigade was kept in reserve between Refidim and Tasa. The plan made no allowance for tank reinforcements in the northern sector.

The plan envisioned two types of tank deployment: Little Dovecote—the deployment of tanks only from the line brigade and regional brigade—and Large or Expanded Dovecote—moving the rear area brigade forward, with or without advancing the reserve brigade. In November 1972, on Sharon's initiative, a combined Dovecote plan was drafted. Stage A consisted of the former Little Dovecote plan (reinforcing the strongholds by tanks on the line, without the rear area brigades moving forward); this was supposed to be completed by K+3 (K being code for the start of the reservists' mobilization). Stage B was the former Large Dovecote plan. Thus, to move the rear brigades, it was not enough to order "commence Dovecote." Southern Command had to issue an explicit order.

Although the uniform, amended terminology was published by Southern Command in late 1972, the terms Little Dovecote and Large or Expanded Dovecote remained in use in correspondence between the commander of 252nd Division and his brigade commanders, rather than Stage A and Stage B. However, these terms were not employed at the higher levels of the chain of command, which contributed to confusion and erroneous interpretations in GHQ, Southern Command, and the division itself when war broke out. It should be noted that this confusion had nothing to do with the blunder of not implementing Dovecote.

The Dovecote order did not depend on the Rock order, whose main purpose was to mobilize reserves for the counterattack. The armored regulars would be unable to stop the enemy once he crossed the canal and began setting up a bridgehead; this task would require a concentrated force. Major General Albert Mandler, commander of 252nd Division, also regarded Dovecote as a plan for maximum deployment in the event of an infringement of the cease-fire or as a transition stage to an attack.[51]

An analysis of Dovecote shows that the Suez Canal was essentially only a limited obstacle because of the lack of dominating tactical fire and the absence of lookout posts along its length. A water obstacle of its size could not serve as an effective barrier against an invasion and could not provide the defending force with the time needed to mobilize its reservists. According to the warfare doctrine, a plan designed to prevent penetration must have a system of positions and fortifications in a prearranged protected area located in the depths, close to the flank or even in front of the enemy's likely routes of advance. These positions had to be held (mainly by an armored force) when the attacker advanced to the sector depth where the antipenetration structure was located.[52] In other words, Dovecote had no chance of accomplishing its mission. It was based on a small number of forces, and it lacked the depth and protected fortifications needed to delay the enemy and gain time for a concentration of powerful forces to attack in another sector.

The plan also failed to define the air force's missions and provided no definitive operational answer for dealing with an attacking force of two entire armies, as happened in the Yom Kippur War. The deployment of the forward brigade at the junctions, according to the plan, left yawning gaps, especially in the central sector. But this omission, it turned out, did not trouble anyone.

Gonen said that, upon assuming his post in Southern Command, he dealt almost exclusively with operational planning for an attack (not defense). He knew that Dovecote was based on the regulars, with 7th Brigade as reinforcement, but he was unaware of the difference between Little and Large Dovecotes. He assumed there would be nine or ten companies on the canal line, when in reality there were only eight, and, like his predecessor, he believed that Dovecote plus the IAF would hold the enemy until the reservists mobilized.

The first stage of the plan was ambiguous and erratic. On the one hand, it ordered that the Egyptians be stopped on the waterline; on the other hand, it recognized that they had to be blocked until the reservists arrived. In effect, the plan was no more than a tactical response (deploying the force that carried out daily security duties) to an operational situation (all-out war). Thus, two tank brigades were thrown into battle based on a strategy that was unsuited to the Egyptian battle plan. The price paid by the brigades was high: after the first morning, only 110 of the division's 283 combat-capable tanks remained.

Dovecote's basic inconsistencies were quickly revealed, especially its unsuitability for a full-scale defensive battle. The absurdity was that 252nd Division's brigades were ordered to prepare for operations on the western side of the canal, based on the mistaken assumption that the holding stage would be short. In reality, all the elements of the plan collapsed because it lacked realistic, viable answers to ground developments, in addition to the fact that the division's reserve brigade—the 460th—was not held in reserve. There were conflicting interpretations of the Dovecote order between Southern Command and 252nd Division regarding the reserve battalions of the rear area brigade, which were supposed to deploy between Lateral and Artillery Roads for sectoral counterattacks. Instead, they were ordered to assist the forces in the strongholds on the waterline.

In defense of the Dovecote plan, Major General Yona Efrat, who served as deputy head of GHQ until six days before the war, stated that neither Southern Command nor GHQ thought that Dovecote would be able to defend for thirty-six hours. Dovecote was an alert plan that would scramble the forces and deploy them when hostilities erupted. It was geared toward the resumption of hostilities according to the pattern in the War of Attrition—not a full-scale war.

Gonen emphatically affirmed that no one—not in the recent past or the distant past—had ever considered Dovecote a plan for defending the Sinai Peninsula; rather, it was a plan for deploying the regulars. The defense plan was Rock, and it was based on the full might of the air force and a four- to five-day warning, during which time the entire reservist framework would be mobilized. Gonen mistakenly stated that Dovecote was based mainly on the addition of the reservists.

Given Dovecote's inherent ambiguity, Gonen was not the only one who failed to discern its exact objectives. Even the chief of staff uttered irreconcilably conflicting statements before and after October 6, 1973, regarding the regulars' mission and the plan's dependence on the IAF. In testimony before the IDF's Historical Branch, Gonen recalled the words of his predecessor, Sharon, when he presented Southern Command's plans on May 8, 1973. The thrust of Sharon's argument had been: if there is no plan to cross to the western bank, then the Rock plan is not necessary. In other words, Dovecote would be capable of holding the line with 300 tanks.

The inherent weakness of the Dovecote plan was the unexplainable belief that the Egyptians would not dare to cross the canal and launch a major war. The IDF expected a resumption of raids, battles, and attempts at a land grab on the eastern bank, and based on that, it believed, justifiably, that the Dovecote plan could handle the situation. If the army had to cross the canal to achieve a military decision, it would mobilize the Rock (attack) forces.[53]

The 252nd Division's lower-level units (brigades, battalions, companies) also understood that Dovecote's purpose was to reinforce the line and come to the aid of strongholds being attacked in an attrition scenario. This explains the wide dispersal of the tank battalions. According to Adan, there was operational logic behind the tactical deployment and formation of the regulars. But the plan was not implemented in the Yom Kippur War because grave mistakes were made and because the surprise attack left no time to reinforce or replace the infantry in the strongholds, bring in additional artillery, move the line tanks into position, or shore up the rear with the mobilized Rock units. The IDF had no contingency plans for the regulars to fight an all-out war alone. It always assumed there would be an early warning.[54]

Due to the surprise attack and the lack of an alternative plan, the regulars' deployment plan was used as a defense plan. Under these circumstances, they had to provide an immediate answer to an unexpected situation, during which time the shortcomings of holding the line and waging a forty-eight-hour delaying battle (until the reservists arrived) became agonizingly apparent. Thus, the division was ordered to hold the rear defensive line—the waterline—without taking full advantage of the depths, evacuating the strongholds, or conducting a delaying battle. This was mission impossible, and the heroic effort to carry it out led to debilitating battle exhaustion under conditions dictated by the Egyptians.

Even when the situation changed, Gonen remained committed to the Dovecote plan because it was the one the forces were familiar with—although in practice, he prevented it from being implemented on October 6. The division commander, too, stuck to the existing plan, and herein lies the discrepancy between the deployment plan for daily security operations and the knowledge that war was going to erupt in a matter of hours.

The Rock Plan: Force Concentration for a Counterattack and Canal Crossing

The Rock plan, devised by GHQ, was first distributed to the regional commands in 1967 after the Six-Day War. Its principles expressed the defense concept for Western Sinai:

1. The defense of Israel's territorial integrity must be uncompromising: not yielding any ground.
2. The defense has to block the enemy's attack, sap his strength, and destroy a large part of his army to enable a rapid shift to the counterattack beyond the state's borders.

Force deployment entailed physically occupying natural obstacles along the cease-fire lines, blocking the main attack routes, ensuring depth in the holding area, concentrating armored forces for a counterattack, protecting the reserves from enemy commandos, and deploying GHQ reserves to enable their rapid entry into action.

Basically, the Rock plan dealt with the IDF's full deployment of 143rd and 162nd Divisions in Southern Command, in addition to 252nd Division, which was already deployed on the canal line in the Dovecote formation. One of the additional divisions would be concentrated in the northern sector, and the other in the central sector, prior to executing Desert Cat (Hatul Midbar)—a two-division crossing to the western bank upon conclusion of the counterattack. The force's total strength would be 1,036 tanks and 54 artillery batteries (216 tubes).[55]

Changes and updates in the plan that appeared in the commands' files received no written expression at the GHQ level, even though the chiefs of staff routinely approved them. This recalls the debate over the Dovecote and Rock objectives after the war, when various interpretations were voiced.

Since the Rock plan involved reservists, the quartermaster general was responsible for their transportation. This branch presented an operational plan in which the main Rock forces would be transported in three days, with the entire order of battle transported in five days for a hasty deployment or eight days for a deliberate deployment. The plan also noted that until the force concentration was completed, the regulars would have to hold the line alone, and although the enemy would likely gain some minor ground temporarily, this would not counteract the ultimate defensive mission. Sharon's May 1973 defense plan was based on the assumption that the Rock deployment would take five days. The 1971 Rock plan assumed that Egypt's operational objective would be to capture the western flank of the Mitla and Gidi passes in the south and then dig in for the defense, without advancing any farther east (see map 5).[56]

The Rock plan reflected a lack of defensive awareness and thinking in the IDF. It was not a defense plan, although there were those who perceived it as such. It contained no details on the method of conducting a defensive battle, the location of rear defensive lines or intermediate lines for delay and withdrawal, killing zones, counterattack routes, fire support, and so forth. In essence, Rock was only a schematic outline of force concentration: 162nd Division in the northern sector, and 143rd Division in the central sector. In case of a crossing in the northern sector, the Zefania and Ben-Hayil plans would be implemented. This was how the divisions were concentrated in the war, and to a large degree, their location dictated the execution of the counterattack in Egyptian Second Army's sector, which had achieved greater success.

When the Rock plan came up for approval in Southern Command in 1972, the chief of staff stressed that a rapid shift to the attack was vital to achieve significant gains. He emphasized that if 252nd Division were deployed for defense, this would allow an immediate shift to the attack (with the Rock order of battle); he also stated that a decision in the air was of primary importance. Not a word was mentioned about the defensive battle.

In other discussions in Southern Command in the first half of 1973, the chief of staff enumerated Rock's principles:

- Protect the territorial integrity by defending the canal line.
- Hold the line: 252nd Division (three brigades) would have to hold the line single-handedly for sixteen hours until support arrived from 162nd and 143rd Divisions. (This was the only time Elazar mentioned the possibility of assisting the 252nd with reserve divisions in a defensive battle, but the idea did not filter down the chain of command or become an operational plan or order.)

- Counterattack: 143rd and 162nd Divisions would arrive in Sinai within seventy-two hours on transporters or on their own tracks, while the 252nd held the line alone.[57]

It is unclear why the chief of staff first stated that the 252nd would have to fight unaided for sixteen hours and then revised his opinion to seventy-two hours. The ramifications of this change were neither examined nor appreciated, and it was not interpreted as a plan for effective deployment.

Rock's vagueness left fundamental questions unanswered: Were the regulars supposed to hold the enemy on the waterline at all costs or carry out a delaying battle in the rear? Would the strongholds be reinforced or evacuated? At what point was the division supposed to shift to the counterattack? Would the defensive line have to be stabilized before the crossing, or would the crossing be made immediately? Any approach that relied on the attack obviously made no attempt to study in detail the question of defense and the shift from Dovecote to Rock. The chief of staff admitted that if a warning had been received, the IDF would have organized according to Rock, but he never defined Rock as a defensive plan or issued a binding order before (or after) the war on the link between the two plans. This ambiguity resulted in divergent interpretations that exacted a heavy toll in IDF lives.

Before the war, the IDF assumed there was little likelihood of ever implementing the Rock plan. Indeed, planning was general and limited to timetables, headquarters sites, and assembly areas in Sinai. By May 1973, Southern Command had not conducted any drills for Rock or published general orders. Although Gonen stressed the importance of coordinating Rock's deployment, he did not check to see that it was carried out. Despite the fact that GHQ issued the Rock plan, no one imagined that it would actually be needed, so no one dealt with it. Thus, when the war broke out, 162nd and 143rd Divisions were thrown into a hasty defense to support 252nd Division as it struggled to carry out its mission.[58]

Southern Command believed it would have sufficient time to mobilize the Rock divisions for an immediate attack. As Gonen declared, Rock was not a defense plan but a plan for shifting to the offense. As for the level of planning, less was invested in Rock than in Dovecote. Gonen found no material on Rock in Southern Command—no files, no orders, not even a map. He realized that Rock may have been a GHQ plan for general defense, but if so, he never worked on it when he was in charge of Southern Command in the months before the war, and neither did his predecessor Ariel Sharon. According to Gonen, Rock was an example of muddled orders that were not implemented in the field as an operational plan. Dovecote, in contrast, was drawn up in detail, down to the company level. Rock was intended for divisional deployment, not for defense.

Gonen took responsibility for failing to do everything necessary. He recalled that the Iron Ram war game had been based on the Egyptians capturing large swaths on the eastern bank. As the officer conducting the exercise, he had managed to squeeze this scenario into the war game only after a heated argument with the head of intelligence, who contended it couldn't happen. This explains why Iron Ram opened with the Egyptian seizure of only a few pockets rather than the entire eastern bank.

After the war, Gonen stood before the IDF History Department and testified that when shifting from a holding maneuver to the defense in the counterattack, the IDF lacked an appropriate term for "a battle before the main defense battle. In the absence of such a term we called it 'holding' even though no such term appeared in military manuals. 'Holding' meant putting up a stiff defense until the reservists mobilized and then shifting to the defense. At the GHQ level 'Rock' was essentially a defensive battle, but it failed as such when GHQ's intention was translated into the command's plan."[59] The following statements illustrate the confusion surrounding Rock. The first, from Gonen, is candid, straightforward, and to the point: "In the end the 'Rock' deployment plan was not carried out because the divisions went directly into a defensive battle." The second statement, from the chief of staff, is convoluted, ambiguous, and cryptic: "The proper preparation for a war situation was 'Rock.' There were also other operative plans that we considered suitable to warnings for situations less than total war. If we had received the warning in time, we could have organized according to the 'Rock' plan since it was designed for full-scale war."[60]

Tal, deputy chief of staff during the war, saw things in an entirely different light from Elazar, Gonen, and Sharon. In the 1972 situation assessment, he described the force buildup for the defense of Sinai. According to Tal, the Rock plan had two objectives: holding the line at all costs, and enabling a shift to the attack with the entire order of battle. He noted that the IDF's plans and orders never assumed that one division alone would be enough to defend Sinai. Three divisions would be needed.

According to IDF doctrine, even if a counterattack with the Rock order of battle had been part of the defensive battle, in reality, it was only a plan for transporting 162nd and 143rd Divisions to assembly areas in Sinai. It contained no details (other than a general assertion) regarding the divisions' assignments in the offensive battle or in the crucial defensive part of the counterattack. No mention was made of the two divisions' integration in the battle.

Five Plans for an Attack across the Canal

As the IDF's attack plans in Sinai began to take shape in late 1968, they reflected the traditional security concept: decision in a war can be achieved only by transferring the fighting to enemy territory as quickly as possible. Although the canal was considered an ideal cease-fire and defensive line, as the fighting intensified, GHQ realized that without an offensive, a battlefield decision would be impossible (even if Israel forswore the capture of additional territory on the western bank).

All the offensive plans, with the exception of Green Light (*Or Yarok*)—a joint landing of forces from the sea and by helicopter on the western shore of the Gulf of Suez—were based on a canal crossing. But the dearth of bridging equipment rendered these plans wishful thinking. In the wake of the Blue White alert in April–May 1973, however, huge investments in procurement, construction, combat exercises, and crossing equipment led to a turnabout that enabled the IDF to cross the canal.

The crossing plan was intended to be the opening move in the offensive once the IDF regained control of the eastern bank either immediately or after destroying the Egyptian bridgeheads. But the ground situation did not develop according to plan, and the IDF had to break through the Egyptian 16th Division in a hard-fought battle on the night of October 15–16 to reach the crossing point at the Matsmed stronghold. The crossing equipment—except for the motorized pontoons ("crocodiles"), the only equipment suited for a crossing assault—was supposed to be assembled close to the waterline or towed a short distance and then launched in the water to form a continuous bridge from bank to bank. The pontoons were launched at 07:15 on October 17 and assembled as a bridge at 16:30.

The heavy, cumbersome roller bridge sections were supposed to be assembled without interference near the Israeli embankment, but in reality, they had to be towed a great distance, and the bridge came apart several times during the towing. As a result, the first tanks did not cross on it until 04:00 on October 19.[61]

Two crossing areas were marked on the attack plans: the first, north of Kantara, was intended to threaten Port Said; the second, in the central sector north of Ismailia and Dwersuar, was designed for a quick penetration to the maneuverable areas on the western bank. No fewer than four crossing offensives were planned: (1) Zefania, in which the regulars would establish a bridgehead north of Kantara within thirty-six to forty-eight hours of the beginning of the war (see map 4); (2) Ben-Hayil, an extension of Zefania in the direction of Port Said; (3) Desert Cat, in which two divisions would cross at the conclusion of the counterattack—one north of Ismailia and the other at Dwersuar; and (4) Stout Knights (Abirei Lev), in which two divisions would cross at Dwersuar. The plans were presented to the chief of staff in early September 1973, leaving no time for systematic preparations. Eventually, Stout Knights was carried out during the war.[62]

Was There a Defense Plan for Western Sinai?

The Dovecote plan was not a defense plan. It was a deployment plan for company-size combat teams of regulars until the reservists and the air force arrived. Rock was not a defensive plan either. It was a plan for shifting to the offense—one division in defense and two in rear-based concentrations. As for the defensive battle and mobile defense between the canal and the mountain passes, Southern Command had no plan.

After the war, the commanding officer of Southern Command, Major General Gonen, discussed his own mistakes courageously, honestly, and clearly in every possible forum. According to Gonen, the operational concept was clear: when the Egyptians attacked, Southern Command would deal with them—a blow here, a blow there. There was nothing even approaching an organized defense plan—not even mobile defense for the capture of identified localities or the movement of mobile forces to save time, even if it meant yielding territory. A rear defensive line at a depth of fifteen to twenty kilometers was missing. The drills for a defensive battle consisted only of linkups with the strongholds; an APC practiced reaching them, and with that, the problem was considered solved. Gonen emphasized that he found no plans for company, battalion, or brigade counterattacks from Refidim. "It wasn't that I didn't find any—there were none!" He admitted that on assuming his post at Southern Command, he focused on offensive plans, not defensive ones. "For better or worse, that's the truth!"[63]

Similar statements were made by other Southern Command senior commanders, such as Major General Yeshayahu Gavish, Ariel Sharon's predecessor. The 252nd Division's G-3 officer in the war, Brigadier General Gideon Avidor, harshly criticized the thinking in the division, in Southern Command, and in the IDF in the pre–Yom Kippur War period. According to Avidor, there was no organized defense concept in Sinai. The plans for the Yom Kippur War were merely the continuation of those for the Six-Day War—the same concept and the same triumphant commanders. This kind of defense was a bluff. The entire defense establishment from Dayan down was beguiled by the "not one step" mission on the waterline and the transfer of the war to the other side. Their mantra was: "maintain the daily security operations and we'll cross the canal." Defense was not taken into account; in its place, the term *holding* was coined. Throughout the war, not a single defense battle was fought—there was only a withdrawal to Artillery Road. "We didn't understand defense and didn't know how to implement it," Avidor admitted.[64] This was also the opinion of General Harel, the 252nd's deputy commander during the war.

The IDF had no bona fide defense plan for all-out war and conducted no defensive exercises at the operational level. Regardless of the near-axiomatic assumption that a defensive line will always be broken, Gonen had no operational defense plans for the three divisions. There was only a general expression of Southern Command's defense of the canal and the marking of divisional assembly areas for the implementation of Zefania and Ben-Hayil. When the command presented its operational plans to the chief of staff in May 1973, Dovecote and Rock were referred to as defense plans, even though they were nothing of the kind.

Before the war, Israel obtained Egypt's plans for a full-scale crossing and offensive in Sinai. The area that had to be defended between the canal and the mountain passes (including the line of hills at Artillery Road) was well known, especially to the commanders in Sinai and certain GHQ officers. Most of the field commanders, too, were familiar with the combat doctrine of the defensive battle. In operational discussions and lengthier talks in November–December 1968 and later, the participants held serious conversations on issues related to defensive fighting, such as static versus mobile defense in the area between the canal line and the passes and the role of the mobile forces and strongholds in the event of war.

Be that as it may, knowledge of the problems did not translate into a methodical defense plan for Western Sinai based on situational assessments, systematic planning, and the necessary tools to train and prepare. Maps containing a battle outline and a written order with professional addenda should have been circulated to all levels. There should have been a deliberate defense plan in writing that covered withdrawal and delaying lines, a rear defensive line, routes for counterattacks, killing zones, and dominating fire positions that had been identified and marked with signs in the field. Detailed, written plans were needed for artillery fire and air support; dominating areas and vital areas should have been earmarked, where static and mobile forces would be deployed against possible enemy moves; the level of the enemy threat should have been estimated; and the forces required for defense should have been defined. Also required were fortification works in the field, certainly on the rear defensive line as well as the intermediate lines. None of this was done. Indeed, Sinai lacked a defense plan and major fortification works, with the exception of a few shallow trenches in the western ranges of the mountain passes overlooking the Mitla and Gidi Roads.

Had GHQ's and Southern Command's situational assessment of the defense of Western Sinai been implemented, based on the IDF's knowledge of the Egyptians' probable actions, this would have exposed the regulars' inability to block an all-out attack and their critical need for reinforcements (the Rock divisions) for defense. But even if such an assessment had been made, it would have been superficial and misleading because the Rock forces were never planned as reinforcements for the 252nd's defensive line. Thus, on October 7, in the absence of any plans, the reservists were ordered to rush to the assistance of 252nd Division, which was struggling to stabilize a new defensive line along the hills of Artillery Road. But by then, the Egyptians had attained their limited objectives: capture of the Bar-Lev Line and penetration into Sinai by about five kilometers. Despite their limitations and the IDF's strategic position on the western bank at the end of the war, these two successes began the long, complex political process that led to the Egyptians' attainment of their ultimate goal: retrieval of the entire Sinai Peninsula.

The first and only time some sort of hastily formed planning group met to discuss the defense of Western Sinai was during the defense minister's visit to Dvela (Southern Command's headquarters at Um Hashiba) before noon on October 7. The divisional commanders were not present, and no GHQ representative was in attendance. Dayan issued general instructions for planning and, as required in a democratic society, received governmental approval of his ideas that night—in this case, from the prime minister. All these tension-ridden, hastily patched together measures should have been in place years before October 7, 1973.

The basic reason why there were no plans or written orders for the defense of Western Sinai lies in the IDF's smug attitude toward the defensive battle and the tendency to apply an oral doctrine rather than a written one (e.g., holding rather than defense). But another reason is rooted in Israeli society.

The IDF had sufficient time to plan and exercise a defense plan for Western Sinai but squandered the opportunity to do so. The fighting force, made up of the regulars and reservists, was caught by surprise and flung into the inferno of a full-scale war. Their only defensive tools (other than their own gallantry) were a handful of drills from the War of Attrition and the Dovecote plan for the regulars' deployment on the line for routine security operations.

The lack of a defense plan had fatal consequences in the ensuing battle, especially in the first days of fighting. This omission was the chief reason for the Egyptians' territorial gains, for the failure to implement a defensive mission on the waterline, and for the heavy loss of lives and armored vehicles, which in some cases was absolutely unnecessary. Without a written plan that had been studied, drilled, and analyzed according to the most likely scenarios, decisions were hastily made by the chief of staff, Southern Command, and combat units. Some of these decisions were pivotal but unsound; some were based on intuition, caprice, ignorance, or just plain inept thinking. These blunders, beyond the inevitable margin of error in any war, greatly exacerbated the IDF's predicament during the first three days. According to Gonen, the IDF's problem in force application during this time was not the lack of doctrine: "The problem was that we failed to carry out our own doctrine. . . . The ground and air forces planned for one type of war but had to fight another type that the doctrine didn't provide answers for."[65]

Western Sinai's Defense Concept: The Regulars Will Hold!

The IDF's vague operational concept for waging a defensive battle was encapsulated by its optimistic aphorism: the regulars will hold! The meaning was clear: the regulars had to hold the contact line until the reservists arrived. The chiefs of staff—Bar-Lev and especially Elazar—made wide use of this concept when approving plans at the conclusion of exercises, war games, and so forth.

The origin of the concept can be traced back to Ben-Gurion's instructions to the IDF on November 27, 1948, six months after the founding of the state of Israel. It crystallized in 1949–1950 into the axiom that the IDF is basically an army of reservists. The regulars would have to block the first wave of any attack until mobilization of the reserves; after the reserve units arrived, they would be tasked with leading the attack and transferring the fighting onto enemy territory. This meant that the regular army had to be capable of bearing the brunt of the first blow for a short period—seventy-two hours at most.[66] During the War of Attrition and until the outbreak of the Yom Kippur War, that operational concept was translated into the regulars' deployment on the contact lines, and it dictated their modus operandi when war broke out. However, the concept failed to address certain key issues: What does "holding" mean? What are its aims and timetable? What are the conditions for its implementation? And, most important, what are its chances of success in the event of a surprise attack and the enemy's overwhelming numerical superiority?

The term *regulars* included all the regular ground forces performing routine security assignments in the confrontation sectors, as well as the reservists who supplemented them in those sectors. The doctrine of "the regulars will hold" was invariably followed by the appendage "with the air force's support," which was also based mainly on regulars. The nondoctrinal term *holding*, which the IDF adopted in place of *defense*, served as a synonym for the rigid defense of the "not one step" concept. In other words, the contact line was identical to the rear defensive line, and the enemy had to be prevented from achieving any territorial gains (which had far-reaching implications for the method of defense on the canal line). The way the chiefs of staff, particularly Elazar, used these terms had a major impact on the field commanders' way of thinking and verbal expression and on the low level of defensive battle planning, especially in Sinai, since these were patently vacuous terms rather than a systematic doctrine.

The armored formations' victories in the Six-Day War undoubtedly contributed to the assumption that if certain basic conditions (deterrence, warning, and the massive use of the air force) were met, the regulars would be able to hold even if they were vastly outnumbered at the outset. Following the Six-Day War, General Gavish declared that since an IDF armored brigade or division could break through anything, deception and maneuvering were no longer needed. Although the War of Attrition subdued this sentiment to a great degree, it persisted.

In his summary of Iron Ram, General Gonen said, "I think the regulars alone will be able to hold and Southern Command's order of battle can do it. The counterattack, though, will need more troops."[67] Later, General Shai Tamari would say that the exercise proved the forces were insufficient to hold, but the assumption remained that the Egyptians were incapable of crossing the canal and occupying the eastern bank. The chief of staff's summary of the war game was that the ground force regulars would be able to hold for a few hours, even if there was less artillery than necessary and without air support, until the missile system was eliminated. Then the air force would provide massive assistance to the ground troops in both the defense and the attack. These statements about Rock's designated assignment (the counterattack)—which were addressed to Gonen and the defense minister on the morning of October 6, when the 252nd was the only division in Sinai—contradict what Elazar said in his summary of the combat exercise.[68] Obviously, the three of them believed the regulars alone could hold.

In a GHQ meeting on February 14, 1972, Elazar outlined his concept: armor would hold in the first stage, and the air force would operate on two fronts. A year later—May 9, 1973—he told the prime minister, "We're quite confident in our ability to block the first blow. . . . We're built to hold the Syrian and Egyptian fronts unconditionally, not to destroy the enemy in a later maneuver, but first of all— to stop him from entering [Sinai]. . . . We regard the air force as the primary factor in defense and offense."[69] The chief of staff's plan consisted of the following: the regulars and the IAF would be the holding force in a surprise attack, and they would have to be prepared to avert a catastrophe. He was aware that this was not the desired or the best method, but it enabled a rapid response (in a matter of hours) in the event there was no warning. "The enemy," he said, "has to be killed on the Suez Canal and not in the depth."[70]

With regard to the size of the regular forces needed for the holding assignment, General Tal stated on May 19, 1972, that in addition to 252nd Division, the entire 7th Division would have to be stationed in Sinai. In his opinion, a decision by the regulars could not be based on reinforcements from the middle of the country. Also, the situation in the air might not be in the IAF's favor.

There were various estimates of the time needed to mobilize, organize the reserves in their logistics units, and transport the troops to the front—from forty-eight hours to seven days—depending on the location of the logistics units and the combat zone, the method of transportation (using transporters or their own tracks), and so forth. Because the reservists sensed how precarious the situation was, the timetable was shortened dramatically, especially for the tank brigades. The first units of 162nd Division arrived in the northern sector on the afternoon of October 7. But the slapdash departure and wear and tear on the armored vehicles moving on tracks created enormous problems in the logistics units, as did missing equipment and damage to the armored vehicles during the long drive. Nonetheless, the reservists' contribution was invaluable to the stabilization of the defensive line and the assessment (albeit insufficiently substantiated) that a counterattack would be possible the following day.

Unlike his earlier optimistic estimates of the regulars' ability to hold, the chief of staff was much more prudent and sober on October 3, 1973. In a military-political consultation in Jerusalem, he admitted that the defense had never been based on a force capable of totally preventing Egyptian territorial gains and sealing off Sinai. He assumed that a sufficient warning would be given to mobilize the reservists for the holding stage.[71] Thus, he negated previous statements on the regulars' (252nd Division's) ability to hold the line. At the same meeting, Dayan, beaming with confidence, described the futility of an Egyptian offensive: "If they're planning on crossing the canal under their missile umbrella, they'll find themselves in a very uncomfortable situation after the first step." The prime minister added this fatuous observation: "The Egyptians can cross the canal but they'll be further from their bases. What will they gain by that?"[72]

On October 5, the day before the start of the war, the chief of staff still radiated confidence. Despite his cautious statements on October 3, he decided not to call up the reserves but to place the entire burden on the regulars. He said he was considering a preemptive measure if the unexpected happened, which he thought unlikely. He was convinced that the air force and 500 tanks manned by the regulars in Sinai could hold the line and give the reservists time to mobilize. (It is strange that the chief of staff was unaware that the maximum number of tanks in 252nd Division was 283, only 88 of which were on the canal; the rest were in the rear.) Elazar reiterated his position in a GHQ discussion at 13:30 the same day: "In the worst possible situation—a full-scale war without any warning—the regulars will have to hold the line, with the air force, naturally, and all the forces available."[73] Thus, on the eve of the war, the chief of staff still believed in a rigid defense on the waterline with the regulars and the IAF, and he delayed mobilizing the reservists, not even ordering a partial call-up until there were further indications of the enemy's H hour. Elazar was certain that even a twenty-four-hour warning would allow sufficient time to organize and mobilize the reservist forces for a counterattack—not for a defensive battle.

At a meeting with newspaper editors that day, Dayan was asked whether the regulars alone could deal with an Arab attack. His reply: "The best they can do with air support is to prevent a collapse if the Arab attack comes as a surprise."[74] Even on October 6, two hours before the Egyptian invasion, there was no doubt that the regulars would hold. In a government meeting at noon, the defense minister explained that armor's job, with some air assistance, would be to hold the Egyptian front the first night. He confidently predicted that an attempted canal crossing "would prove a 'reckless gamble' for the Egyptians even if they managed to establish a number of bridgeheads and part of their forces advanced a few kilometers, since Israeli armor would eventually annihilate them. And we always have the air force." Dayan saw no reason to fret over a war on the canal: "Egypt is the enemy but we have a natural barrier—the Suez Canal plus the desert and there are no Israeli settlements there. If war breaks out there—then so be it."[75]

The declarations of the chief of staff and the defense minister rested on three main elements:

1. Deterrence—the IDF's military strength will deter the Arabs from launching a war.
2. Warning—there will be sufficient warning of at least a few days.
3. Air superiority—the IAF will destroy an Arab offensive at its inception and stop the enemy from making any gains.

All three elements failed the acid test of reality.

Deterrence

Deterrence depends on the enemy's awareness that, based on the balance of forces, he has no chance of achieving his goals. But deterrence works only if it is accompanied by proper deployment. For the IDF, the deciding factor in both defense and offense was the ability to immediately activate and mobilize the reservists along with the regulars, especially when the enemy was prepared to sacrifice millions of lives. Otherwise, the effect of deterrence would be nil. In the spring of 1973, the chief of staff and the head of intelligence estimated that Israel's deterrence was working, based on the enemy's assessment of the balance of forces. But they were also aware that deterrence could lose its effectiveness if the enemy acquired weapons systems that mitigated Israel's threat. On October 6, deterrence failed.

Warning

In Israel's security doctrine, the term *warning* was never defined as a warning of intentions; rather, it was the sounding of an alarm based on an imminent threat. The rationale was that, without strategic depth, it was too dangerous for Israel (whose land army was largely unmobilized) to base its national security on the subjective assessment of intentions; if it did, the approach to national security would become more of a gamble than a calculated risk. When a military threat appeared on the horizon, the IDF had to prepare for it according to its gravity in terms of time, space, and the balance of forces. GHQ and the government—not the intelligence agencies or the chief of staff—were responsible for dealing with the challenge and taking the appropriate steps, deciding on the magnitude of the cal-culated risk the state was willing to take, and determining the level of national alert. Each time the balance of forces tilted in the Arabs' direction and the threat increased, the army had to prepare to mobi-lize and meet the menace as the balance of forces allowed.[76] In 1956 and 1967, the distance between the Suez Canal and the green line (Israel's 1948 borders) provided, theoretically, a few days' warning to mobilize the reserves. On the eve of the Yom Kippur War, the IDF erred in assuming that it would receive a similar warning. Because there were two Egyptian armies on immediate standby, reinforced with antitank weapons and surface-to-air missiles, the warning ele-ment was entirely absent in 1973.

The IDF presumed there would be a four- to six-day warning, even for a limited Egyptian action. In April–May 1973, during the Blue White alert, the head of intelligence had reaffirmed that Israel would have prior knowledge of Egypt's intention to cross the canal and would be able to signal both a tactical and an operational alert a number of days before the attack. When the prime minister asked how Israel would know this, the chief of intelligence assured her that "Israel would have the information based on tours of the area by Egyptian commanders, the forward movement of forces, the rein-forcement of batteries and the air defense array, and the cleaning of long neglected dugouts along the canal. In short, we will know when the entire Egyptian army is going into action."[77] He repeated the same lines to the Knesset's Foreign Affairs and Defense Com-mittee on May 18, 1973. The chief of staff spoke in like fashion when he presented the IDF's plans to the prime minister on May 9: "I con-sider 48 hours before an attack to be a short warning. But because I take the intention seriously, even with a 48-hour warning we'll be able to get off on the right foot." He made similar statements in the weekly meeting with the defense minister on May 17, when he esti-mated that a twenty-four-hour warning, in which case "we know the day but not the hour," would be the worst-case scenario.[78]

What would have happened if the IDF had received a forty-eight-hour warning before the fighting erupted? Gonen was certain of the results: the situation would have been entirely different. The reservists would have had time to mobilize and reinforce the line, plan or no plan; the divisions would have entered the battle and implemented Dovecote; and the lead units of the divisions would have arrived. The fact is that when the divisions arrived, the attack halted; that is, three divisions stopped the Egyptians. If there had been an alert of a few days, if Bendigo had been executed as planned (artillery support for the IAF's attack against the missiles), if the enemy offensive had occurred on only one front, and if the defensive framework had held as planned, then the order of battle might have been sufficient. But neither the air force nor the ground forces were prepared for the Egyptians' move. A forty-eight-hour warning before the enemy's H hour was critical for air operations (see below). Naturally, the concentration of forces had to begin before the opening salvo, not at H hour. If the order to mobilize the reservists occurred at H hour, then Southern Command needed a minimum of seventy-two hours to carry out Rock in its entirety.[79]

Since the IDF was certain of an early warning, it believed the reservists would have sufficient time to mobilize, be outfitted for battle, and deploy. A one-week warning was considered feasible, five to six days realistic, and forty-eight hours the barest minimum; anything less than that would be considered a catastrophe. But even with a twenty-four-hour warning, a large reinforcement of reservists could have reached the front in an orderly fashion and stabilized the line west of Artillery Road at a lower price than was paid. Elazar, however, did not see the warning as a "bell" that started a countdown to war; at best, he saw it as a tool for discussion and situational assessment. The nexus between warning, assessment, and the making of crucial decisions was not inherent in the forty-eight-hour plan. The assumption that the regulars would hold emptied the term *warning*—the key element in the timely mobilization of the reserves—of meaning. If the regulars held, the reservists would be directed to the attack, and the problem would be blunted.[80]

On a practical level, the failure to mobilize the reserves was due primarily to the chief of staff's reliance on the head of intelligence's assurance that, in the event of a crossing and full-scale war, Israel would be warned in time. The wavering by Dayan, Israel's security oracle, between war and no war also contributed negatively to the defense system's awareness of developments across the border.

Air Superiority

Dayan made it clear in the GHQ meeting on May 14, 1973, that the solution to the gaps in the order of battle depended not only on the balance of ground forces but also on military intelligence and the air force, with its overwhelming firepower and rapid intervention capability. When presenting plans to the prime minister on May 9, the chief of staff said, "In any case we regard the air force as the primary factor in both defense and offense. . . . The fact that the balance of the ground forces are as I've shown them to be and the fact that we dare not mobilize the reservists is because we believe in the air force's ability to enable the line to be held if we're attacked on one front and we trust in the air force to preempt any enemy ground plan. The IAF's primary task is to achieve air superiority."[81] This was the chief of staff's assessment and modus operandi on the morning of October 6, even though he knew there were insufficient regulars and that their deployment was flawed.

After the war he espoused a different interpretation: "The idea that the air force and the regulars alone could thwart an attack was only in the case of a surprise and imminent catastrophe. It was never a goal and we never thought that the mission of the regulars and air force was to defend the State of Israel by themselves."[82] GHQ accepted without argument the IAF's assessment of when it would be free to assist the ground forces, but in reality, those estimates were far from realistic (see chapter 4). The planners failed to microanalyze the details of the IAF's timetable but trusted in its capabilities to support the ground forces. They relied on the unsubstantiated conviction that the IDF would achieve a decision by the air force and the regulars, either by ousting the Egyptians from the eastern bank or by blocking an all-out Egyptian effort to capture the line of mountain passes.

The mystical belief in the IAF's mastery of any situation, its ability to solve every problem and foil any attack, was deeply ingrained in the field commanders and up to the head of Southern Command. But the air force and the chief of staff failed to take into consideration that the IAF also needed at least forty-eight hours' warning, a factor that appeared in none of the IDF's operational commands. This represented a collapse of one of the mainstays of the security doctrine and resulted in the abandonment of the small force of regulars. After the war, Gonen admitted that even with air support, the regulars could not have held the line. Thus crashed the third linchpin of the operational assumption that the regulars would hold.

The chief of staff did not dismiss the possibility of a surprise attack, but he reckoned that the regulars and the IAF would be able to cope with it. He believed that Sea Sand (the plan for the Golan Heights) and Dovecote in Southern Command would be able to answer a two-front attack with the regulars and reservists on operational duty, backed by air support. They would constitute the blocking force in case of a surprise attack. However, as Elazar acknowledged, this was not the optimal solution; it was only a contingency plan to avoid a catastrophe. He expected to receive sufficient warning of an attack, which is what the plans and decisions were based on. Nevertheless, he was confident the IDF could handle the enemy in the event of a surprise.

Likewise, the defense minister was not overly distraught by the possibility of a surprise attack. In a government meeting on October 6, just two hours before the opening barrage, he professed that even if the Egyptians managed to establish a number of bridgeheads and advance a few kilometers, IDF tanks (without the limitations of surface-to-air missiles) could pursue any force. There were hundreds of Israeli tanks in Sinai, he said, not to mention the air force. During the meeting, the government vetoed a preemptive strike. Dayan's overriding self-confidence—which was shared by senior officers— was anchored in the Six-Day War model: in a surprise attack, the Egyptians would make some local land grabs on the eastern bank, but Israel would "kick them the hell out."

The Balance of Forces on the Eve of War

By any standard of military science, the balance of ground forces in the opening stage of the war was lopsided (see map 6), but despite the Israelis' awareness of this discrepancy, there was no pressure from below to mobilize even part of the reserves. The ratio of ground forces alone could have determined—and indeed, did determine— the results of the defensive battle in the first stage of the fighting. Only when the first units of 162nd Division reached the northern sector on the afternoon of October 7 did the balance of forces begin to change in certain respects, especially with regard to tanks, artillery, and mechanized infantry, but the IDF remained substantially inferior to the enemy throughout the war.

At the outset, the regulars numbered 115,000 (87,000 ground forces). During the course of the war, 260,000 reservists were called up. The IDF had 2,100 tanks, 867 artillery pieces (not including anti-aircraft weapons), and 358 combat aircraft. In Sinai there were 10 infantry-reconnaissance-mechanized companies at the beginning of the war, 12 artillery batteries (52 tubes), 283 tanks, 2 Hawk missile batteries, and 6 antiaircraft batteries (see appendix 1), along with 16 manned strongholds and 4 observation strongholds (see appendix 2).[83] Facing the 252nd on the western bank were 2,300 Egyptian tanks, 2,200 artillery pieces, 400 combat aircraft, 10 infantry brigades, 8 mechanized infantry brigades, 10 armored brigades, 3 airborne brigades, 1 amphibious brigade, and 1 surface-to-surface brigade of Scud missiles (see appendix 3).[84]

The 252nd Division had to stop five Egyptian infantry divisions reinforced with armor and antitank troops. On October 6 the Egyptian force on the canal numbered over 200,000 troops; 130,000 of these were first-echelon operational forces, approximately 40,000 of whom crossed the canal between the strongholds and seized the eastern bank by the evening of the first day. This vast order of battle was organized for direct engagement at the first and second operational echelons. All the infantry divisions that crossed the canal deployed in operational formation to meet the expected resistance. The Egyptians invested an enormous effort in force buildup and unit training, especially in the first operational echelon.

The IDF had 10 combat troops per kilometer against Egypt's 300. In artillery, the ratio was 1:40; in tanks, it was 1:14. However, the theoretical armor ratio at the beginning of the war—1,200 Egyptian tanks on the western bank against 88 Israeli tanks on the eastern bank—did not accurately reflect the operational situation, since the Egyptian tanks were used minimally in the beginning of the war and only gradually joined in the fighting. In addition, the number of IDF tanks increased significantly with the arrival of 162nd and 143rd Divisions and other units. But Egyptian tanks were not the IDF's real problem. The Israelis' major nemesis was the Egyptian infantry with its massive number of antitank troops and artillery guns, which Egyptian planners had strengthened to ensure an advantage over the IDF.

Three tank battalions of 14th Brigade and 275th Regional Brigade, each on a forty- to fifty-kilometer-wide sector, had to hold off one or two Egyptian infantry divisions. In the southern sector the ratio was even more disproportionate: 52nd Battalion, in the sector from the center of the lakes to a point fourteen kilometers south of Ras Masala on the Gulf of Suez, faced off against the entire Egyptian

Third Army (7th and 19th Divisions and a marine brigade at Little Bitter Lake).

Without a doubt, a more equal balance of forces could have been created if the reservists had been mobilized earlier, although they probably would have been assigned to the counterattack rather than being integrated into the defense. At any rate, their presence in Sinai likely would have deterred the Egyptians and lessened their territorial gains. Unfortunately, the defense minister and chief of staff failed to recognize the need to mobilize the reservists, even partially, for defense on the morning of October 6. The outrageous imbalance of forces would have justified the permanent mobilization of Israeli reservists to deter an Egyptian crossing, but Israel's resources could not bear such a burden. Thus, unbounded faith developed in the IAF's ability to close the gap between mobilization time and the order of battle.

The problem of the regulars' ratio in Sinai vis-à-vis the Egyptians was known to Israeli decision makers. Elazar spoke of a five-day warning for mobilizing and deploying the Rock forces, but he was concerned about the time and set a low threshold of forty-eight hours' warning. Thus, a discrepancy was created between the goal of the war (preventing an Egyptian gain) and the high command's wishful thinking that the regulars would hold. Dayan, too, was a partner in the erroneous belief that the regulars would hold, even though he knew the air force would be busy taking out the missile system. Despite his political and military experience, he never anticipated the serious problems the ground forces and the IAF would face.[85]

2

Initial Blunders

The IDF units that were hurled headlong into the fighting at midday on October 6, 1973, and the other units that joined them later bore the burden (whether they were aware of it or not) of the initial blunders that influenced the defensive battle and ultimately the whole campaign. Some of the mistakes had been present in the IDF since its founding; others surfaced in the interval between the Six-Day War and the Yom Kippur War, especially in the weeks, days, and even hours before hostilities erupted. They permeated all areas of the IDF and the defense establishment on the strategic, operational, and tactical levels. Other errors were intrinsic to the ethos and cultural norms of Israeli society. Pinpointing the impact of each of these initial failures is an elusive task, but they undoubtedly contributed to the IDF's difficulties, Egypt's territorial gains, and the outcome of the war.

General Failures

The Agranat Commission cited a number of general failures in the Yom Kippur War.

Lack of discipline. The low level of discipline between 1967 and 1973 was a major factor in the failure of the defensive battle. The generals' turf wars, the frenzied pace of officer promotions and rotations, and the shortage of technical and administrative manpower all contributed to an unacceptable level of discipline.

Lack of preparation. The IDF failed to prepare each element to respond automatically and confidently under fire in "normal" combat operations as well as in unusual situations.

Directionless military thinking. Numerous flaws in military thinking were revealed as the concepts of force application and the defensive battle were formulated. Just three days before the war,

General Tal accurately described the dominant trend in a lecture to command and General Staff course instructors. The IDF, he said, was headed in a mechanistically professional direction rather than operating according to command and staff doctrine. Decision-making processes were nonexistent, and cognitive performance was equivalent to the art of improvisation.[1]

Oral doctrine and ambiguous orders. Beginning in the early 1960s, the IDF developed an oral doctrine and neglected the written one.[2] The oral doctrine evolved in exercises, war games, and doctrinal discussions and provided ad hoc solutions to problems at different levels. However, by its nature, it was less binding than written doctrine, it allowed for various interpretations, and its relevance was limited to time and place—that is, it existed only where it was taught or circulated and only for as long as it was remembered. The advantage of the oral doctrine lay in its flexibility and capacity for generating original thinking, but these attributes vanished as soon as consensual opinion took over, at which point only its shortcomings prevailed.

Oral doctrine undermined military terms and command language by transforming them into a misleading and opaque jargon. Instead of *locality, fortification,* and *demarcated area,* the terms *line* and *stronghold* were used; instead of *defense, holding* became the preferred expression. Terms such as *killing zone* and *vital area* disappeared, and in place of the enemy's probable modus operandi one spoke of *options.* No distinction was made between *preventive attack, preemptive strike,* and *parallel attack.* The Agranat Commission, for example, scorned the expression "exert a little pressure forward." Did that mean exert a little pressure or advance a little bit forward? Orders such as "catch a lift on the bridge" and "proceed cautiously" were used only by commanders who had lost control of the situation. The order "fight without losses" ran counter to the IDF ethos of devotion to mission accomplishment. If losses were not acceptable, then what was the sense in fighting for an objective? One example of a vague, befuddled order was Southern Command's to 252nd Division at 13:30 on October 6, 1973: "Enter standby for entering 'Large Dovecote.'"

Early Failures at the Strategic Level

Failure to update doctrine and concepts. No one updated the combat doctrine, orders of battle, or concepts of warning and decision making to reflect the post–Six-Day War reality. No adjustments were made to address the changes in the enemies' armies.[3]

Failure to mobilize the reserves on time. The lack of an early warning and the fear of escalation, in addition to the ambiguity of the Rock plan for reinforcing Sinai, led to the debacle. Since the chief of staff, Lieutenant General David Elazar, was absolutely convinced that the regulars would hold the line and the reservists would have enough time to mobilize for a counterattack, he saw no need to order even a partial call-up. Under these circumstances, and especially because the Israeli forces were significantly outnumbered, he should have recommended at least a skeleton mobilization on October 1, when the Egyptian "exercise" began, or on October 5 at the very latest. But blind reliance on an intelligence warning worked against prudence in this case. Elazar had exhibited a reluctance to trigger an escalation ever since the Blue White alert. The assumption was that the reservists should not be mobilized until irrefutable information was received from a secure intelligence source that an attack was imminent. But this was a high-stakes gamble, especially as the information might not arrive in time and, in extreme cases, the risk might have to be reduced.[4]

The chief of staff believed that initiating a C-level alert (the highest level of alert preceding the outbreak of war) and sending the Armor School Brigade to Sinai were sufficient precautionary steps. But the situation that developed in the ten days between Rosh Hashanah (the Jewish New Year) and Yom Kippur (the Day of Atonement) clearly warranted further consideration, especially after Soviet advisers and their families abruptly left Egypt and Syria on October 4–5. The chief of staff should have called up some of the reservists rather than waiting for a "foolproof" warning. The defense minister approved the chief of staff's rationale and his refusal to mobilize the reservists on October 5: "Everything you did is in perfect order."[5] Thus, the IDF had to make do with nonorganic forces and units, some of which lacked equipment, and exhausted troops and impaired weapons because of the long drive to the front. The situation should have been reassessed based on up-to-date intelligence (one week before the war) and a comprehensive picture of the enemy's deployment and critical equipment, as occurred in Operation Rotem in February 1960 and in the Six-Day War.[6]

The reluctance to call up the reservists can be attributed to three misconceptions: (1) that the IAF would succeed in destroying the missiles, (2) that the IDF would obtain information about the exact time of a surprise attack, and (3) that the balance of forces was tolerable. Thus, if there was no risk, as the chief of staff put it, "What was all the fuss about?"[7]

Dayan and Elazar agreed that the regulars could deal with the situation, but even if the reserve divisions had been mobilized, they probably would have been earmarked for the counterattack and canal crossing. Although Dayan gave Elazar the green light to mobilize two reserve divisions for defense—one in the north and the other in the south—on the morning of October 6, the chief of staff refrained from doing so because he judged the step unnecessary for the defense. Thus, the decision to mobilize was delayed by four hours. Elazar's play for time and the reservists' delay in reaching the front were fatal errors in the IDF's plan and impacted the entire campaign. The reservists were thrown into the defensive battle —not only the counterattack—without any plan.[8]

The failure of the chief of staff and the defense minister to correctly calculate the balance of forces on the front was a greater oversight than the blunders made by military intelligence (MI). According to Brigadier General Dov Tamari (Ret.), while inspecting the canal during the Blue White alert, the chief of staff told him—in response to growing concern that the imbalance of forces could lead to war—there was reason for anxiety, but Israel would have ample time (a four-day warning at least) to send the Rock order of battle into Sinai. Elazar did not accept MI's assessment in its entirety, but he also deferred mobilization until the morning of October 6. An army cannot be given thirty-six hours to mobilize and seventy-two hours to deploy and then be told that war is going to erupt that very afternoon.

Unclear and unachievable war aims. Israel's security concept was based on avoiding war; therefore, if hostilities broke out, they would be the result of an Egyptian initiative. From Israel's point of view, the first stage would entail a defensive battle and counterattack on the eastern bank, followed by an Israeli canal crossing and destruction of the enemy on the western bank. Thus, the war aims should have been clear, including specifics on what the IDF needed for defense and offense. Yet no documents from the chief of staff containing carefully laid out instructions or meticulously drawn up plans for the next war and its objectives have been found; nor is there any written documentation from the government to the military on war aims. Only general declarations were made by the defense minister and the chief of staff during staff discussions, GHQ presentations, situational assessments, and political and military consultations.

On April 22, 1973, Elazar set forth the military's war aims: first, ascertain that the enemy scored no military gains; then, annihilate his forces and destroy his military infrastructure. This would provide Israel with major (long-term) military advantages in the balance of forces and the location of cease-fire lines. Elazar stressed that the war must not end in a way that could be interpreted ambiguously, as this would be tantamount to defeat for Israel. Dayan declared that in the event of war, Israel would have to capture new territory in Egypt. As he explained to the prime minister on May 9, 1973, this would entail the following:

A. Gaining control of Port Said and the entire western bank.
B. Capturing the bridgeheads . . . which would enable the
    ground forces to neutralize the Egyptian missiles and thus
    provide the IAF with freedom in the air that would inhibit
    Egyptian ground and air attacks against the strongholds.[9]

According to Tal's testimony before the Agranat Commission, the IDF lacked a defined war aim if hostilities resumed on the canal. There were operational plans but no strategic ones. In other words, planning was not based on war aims. Gonen added that "no one told the heads of the territorial commands that if war broke out they had to finish it gaining A, B and C. . . . Nothing approaching this appeared in any of the orders. A lot of words and palaver, but a practical summary of a GHQ order was non-existent."[10]

The IDF believed that deterrence would prevent a war, but if war *did* break out, it would have to stop the Arabs from gaining any territory. This could be accomplished with IAF air superiority and the elimination of enemy surface-to-air missiles, the destruction of enemy forces, and the capture of enemy territory. The Arabs' military objectives were to neutralize Israel's airpower with surface-to-air missiles, knock out its armor with antitank weapons, and execute a simultaneous two-front attack that would inflict heavy losses and stymie the IDF's ability to maneuver rapidly between the fronts.[11]

Failure to integrate defensive and offensive plans. The IDF failed to develop an overall operational concept for a two-front war with a short-term warning, even though it acknowledged that such an event could happen. The IDF remained stuck in the mind-set of no territorial gain for Egypt, in which case a massive Israeli counterattack (following a short warning) would have to destroy the enemy's forces on the western bank. Failure to prevent an Egyptian territorial gain meant that a forced cease-fire might leave parts of the eastern bank in Egypt's hands; thus, the enemy had to be destroyed on the western bank. But because it was assumed that the Egyptians would initiate the war and might succeed in reaching the eastern bank, other plans had to be devised. Thus, Elazar gave assurances that the enemy would be annihilated on the eastern bank, contradicting the "no gain for the enemy" policy. Because these two plans (one defensive, the other offensive) were not integrated, they were unachievable.

Leaving the initiative in the enemy's hands, while setting goals that were incompatible with the "not one step" and "annihilation of the enemy" directives, was guaranteed to produce an operational failure, especially when the enemy's forces were just 180 meters across the waterway. The IDF was capable of a frontal attack only because of the Israeli soldiers' determination—not because of any original military thinking. But tenacity alone could not redress the imbalance, and the IDF's war aims were not achieved.[12]

Lack of stamina. The IDF was not built for long-term conflict; it was designed to fight a short, decisive war. Although the war lasted only eighteen days, its intensity and the cost in lives and equipment greatly exceeded IDF predictions.

Faulty assessment of the enemy. The IDF never imagined that the Arabs would pose a serious military challenge, so no one ever made a sober evaluation of their ability to do so. In the June 1972 Iron Ram war game, a nine-hour defensive battle "succeeded" in clearing the eastern bank of enemy forces, followed immediately by an Israeli attack and canal crossing. Smugness characterized the Israelis' summary of the exercise: "Two Israeli tanks companies sufficed to 'wipe out' an Egyptian division" and immediately exploit the success.[13] The IDF clearly underestimated the Egyptian soldiers. No one dreamed they were capable of penetrating the dirt embankment or reaching the Televizia fortification and the Chinese Farm. This type of thinking effectively negated the need for an in-depth discussion of the gap between the Purkan and Matsmed strongholds.

Lieutenant General Ehud Barak (battalion commander in Sinai during the Yom Kippur War, chief of staff 1991–1995, prime minister 1999–2001) acknowledged that "undervaluing the enemy and overestimating Israel's strength created cognitive dissonance in the IDF's encounter with the enemy. The source of the illusion lay in overlooking the fact that the Six-Day War victory was the result of IDF initiative, pulverization of the Arab air forces, and failure of the Arabs' responses. There was an abiding belief that Israel's professional DNA was the wellspring of its victory over the enemy's inferior genetic code, and lo and behold six years later the Arabs launched a war and Israel was chasing after its own tail."[14]

It must be noted that the conceit that prevailed in much of the IDF high command after the Six-Day War was generally not shared by the field units. They were anything but complacent. They trained hard and prepared intensively. Still, the most common scenario envisioned blocking the Egyptians on the waterline rather than taking defensive action. The possibility of an Egyptian crossing on a broad front, which would involve bridging operations and breaking through the embankment (a move that would take several hours), was never considered, not even by the 252nd Division at 08:30 on October 6.

Decision makers' obtuseness and disregard of ground events. MI's main belief was that the Syrians would not attack on their own, and Egypt would avoid war unless it had the airpower to attack Israel's depth.[15] This concept represented fertile soil for inflexible thinking and even blindness on the part of Israel's decision makers.

Because the chief of staff and the defense minister were warier of Egypt's motives than the head of intelligence was, new units had been organized during the Blue White alert, and their equipping had been reinforced. But in this case, they believed the intelligence chief was right. As a result, he was unchallenged when, on the day before the war began, he declared that an Egyptian-Syrian attack was highly improbable. Despite the chief of staff's cautious wording, he did not propose mobilizing the reserves; instead, he issued a C-level alert.

According to Barak, while 7th Brigade was climbing the Golan

Heights and 460th Brigade was entering Sinai, two reserve divisions could have been outfitted. However, they were not mobilized because no one doubted MI's assurance of a low likelihood of war. In the fateful days before the eruption of hostilities, a combination of intelligence inattention, operational oversights, and the arrogant sociopolitical climate led to the presumption "We're much stronger [than the Arabs] and no matter what happens we'll still be able to clobber them."[16]

Israel's two biggest errors were its blind trust in MI's guarantee of an early warning that would allow the reserves to be mobilized and deployed and its die-hard belief that the regulars and the air force could hold the line despite the limitations revealed in the summer of 1970. No serious dialogue was held at any level over the shape of the next war, and only the arrival of meager reinforcements one day before the war saved the line from total collapse.

No ministerial security committee or defense ministry forum examined the alternatives. State-salaried journalists readily cooperated with the authorities and the censor to withhold the truth from the public. The mounting tension in the north was revealed only on October 1, 1973. The Jewish people may have been caught by surprise, but Israel's leadership certainly was not—it only pretended to be.[17]

Ignoring of field intelligence by GHQ and Southern Command. There was no lack of field intelligence on Egyptian intentions. Southern Command accumulated a vast amount of information from observers and aerial photographs that should have kept the general of the command awake at night. But until Saturday, October 6, Gonen held fast to MI's assessment that the Egyptians were only planning a military exercise and that the likelihood of war was low.

The observation posts reported openings in the descents to the waterline; repairs on the crossing platforms; unusual movement of vehicles, artillery batteries, and heavy equipment; intense construction under way opposite the strongholds and observation posts; nighttime vehicular activity; testing for mines and their removal at the descents; and the stockpiling of ammunition crates. Yet, even in the face of this growing evidence, Gonen made no effort to formulate his own analysis of the reports or visit the area himself and assess it personally. The G-2 insisted that everything in the canal sector was normal. On October 4 GHQ instructed Southern Command to cancel the special alert that had been announced two days earlier.

The story of the S-526 aerial photograph deserves special mention. On October 1 a photo reconnaissance sortie was approved (to avoid escalating tensions, reconnaissance flights had been canceled since September 26). The sortie was carried out on October 2, but the camera's shutter failed to open. At 13:40 on October 4, a second attempt was made; this time, the canal sector was photographed to a depth of thirty kilometers west. The photograph was interpreted the same night, and the results were published in an intelligence report entitled "Egypt, Emergency Deployment in the Canal Zone." According to the decipherers, "The findings provide conclusive evidence that the Egyptian army is engaged in unprecedented emergency deployment on the canal front. The main findings are the addition of 56 artillery batteries [300 tubes], a total of 194 batteries in the forward area numbering 1,100 tubes compared to 802 tubes discovered by photo sorties on September 26. Most of the concentrations seem to be designed for crossing and/or bridging equipment and were partially exposed. The parks of most of the tank firing ramps contained one tank platoon (2–3 tanks) and concentrations of armored combat and lighter vehicles" (see appendix 4).[18]

"The Egyptian arrangement resembled a tiger ready to pounce," recalled Lieutenant Colonel Oded Kam, Southern Command's interpretation officer in 1973.[19] On the morning of October 5, Dayan was handed the report and said, "the numbers alone could induce a stroke." Nonetheless, intelligence stuck to its view that the activity was "just a military exercise."[20] In Southern Command's staff meeting on October 5, Zefania—not Dovecote—was discussed. No attempt was made to reinforce the troops in the strongholds; nor did Southern Command press for at least one reserve division to be sent to strengthen the regular division on the line.

The Lieutenant Simantov affair is also worth relating. The intelligence officer at Southern Command deleted Simantov's pertinent questions and critical comments that contradicted intelligence's assessment of the Egyptian "exercise": the cancellation of Egyptian army courses, the rising war atmosphere, the quantity of bridging and crossing equipment, the openings in the sandbag walls at about forty descents to the water in the southern sector, and the sudden appearance of tanks in the northern sector. Also expunged was Simantov's incisive observation that "we can't ignore the possibility that the concentration of forces in these large-scale maneuvers will shift to a real operation." He asked a number of important questions—Why had the Egyptians gone to such lengths to prepare for just a short exercise? Why wasn't the Egyptian air force taking part? Why were the Egyptians amassing their ammunition and engineering equipment?—but they never reached Southern Command for Gonen's perusal.[21]

Failures of the chief of staff. During the Blue White alert, Elazar's assessment that war was likely had contradicted MI's, but unfortunately, the chief of staff did not act on his independent judgment in early October. He testified that on September 30 a Southern Command intelligence officer had reported routine activity in the canal sector throughout the day. However, Elazar asserted, "In no way was this routine! . . . There was a stack of evidence against it, some of it very significant, such as breaking through the canal wall, leveling the crossing platforms . . . [but] I never laid eyes on this material." He also stated that Gonen failed to focus on Egyptian activity. "As far as I was concerned, October 1–6 was a normal week in Southern Command. I didn't notice anything out of the ordinary. Proof of this was that I planned to replace [General] Albert with [General] Kalman [Magen] on October 7."[22]

Intelligence, however, did convey a report of Egyptian activity to the chief of staff's office in a "military-technical collection" document. Elazar's aide, Lieutenant Colonel Shalev, told the Agranat Commission on February 24, 1974, four months after the war: "In pursuance of the chief of staff's testimony [of January 24, 1974] the chief of staff wished to acknowledge that after an examination, it turns out that this 'collection' was not circulated and did not reach the chief of staff's office, though some of its material was published in a separate collection. These collections reached the chief of staff's office on a regular basis and were destroyed after reading. The chief of staff did not always see all of them."[23]

The chief of staff's explanations and those of his aide are constrained, and Elazar's unawareness of what was happening in these critical days still reverberates. In a senior command conference, Elazar spoke vaguely and meanderingly, using expressions remarkably similar to Dayan's: "The shift from understanding the process taking place in Egypt and Syria to its translation in the amount of forces needed to hold the lines—this was the mistake."[24]

Early Failures at the Operational Level

Cutbacks in length of military service and the order of battle. Less than one month before the war, the IDF was in an advanced stage of staff work designed to shorten the length of military service. It also agreed in principle to cutbacks in the order of battle because of the shortened period of service, as well as for economic reasons, given the public's expectations during the cease-fire.

Significant reductions in the regulars' order of battle were supposed to include the disbanding of 14th Brigade (initial steps had already been taken); limiting to two the number of tank companies in 184th Battalion (14th Brigade) and 79th Battalion (401st Brigade), which involved reducing the number of companies of new recruits; converting the 209th's regular artillery formation (252nd Division) into a reserve formation; and converting 252nd Division's headquarters into a reserve headquarters. The idea was also broached to completely disband the division and transfer control of Sinai to Southern Command by means of two territorial brigades.[25] The seriousness of this belt-tightening not only had implications for the IDF's defensive and offensive abilities; it also illustrated Israel's blindness to the war preparations being pursued by Egypt and Syria.

Shortage of forces for a simultaneous two-front decision. Before the war, no in-depth study was made of the IDF's ability to move between the fronts. The great distance between the Golan Heights and Sinai and the limited number of tank transporters reduced the mobility advantage, especially as the war was being fought furiously on two fronts. In reality, the Golan Heights received priority, even if this meant a small pullback in Sinai until troops could be transferred south. But the war was conducted separately on both fronts, with no concentration of forces for a decision on either one. The chief of staff's decision at dawn on October 7 to send 146th Division (commanded by Brigadier General Musa Peled), GHQ's only armored reserve, to the Golan Heights determined, in effect, the outcome of the war: driving the Syrians back beyond the purple line (the 1967 cease-fire line on the Golan Heights) and penetrating new territory east of the line. On the Egyptian front, however, the IDF failed to attain an indisputable decision. Due to the shortage of forces, secondary efforts in Sinai, such as capturing Port Said and Port Fuad, were impossible. Although a small number of troops were transferred from the Golan Heights to the fighting in "Africa" (the western bank of the canal) in the last stages of the war, they were insufficient to create the critical mass needed to defeat Egyptian Third Army on the eastern bank and achieve a decisive victory.

Gonen's ignorance of the Egyptian offensive plan. MI was fully aware of Syrian and Egyptian offensive plans. On April 11, 1972, it published the Egyptian plan for crossing the canal and capturing Sinai as a special intelligence survey entitled "An Egyptian Headquarters Exercise for Capturing Sinai" (which turned out to be very similar to the actual operation in the Yom Kippur War). But the IDF failed to follow up on this information and deploy troops at the Egyptian crossing sectors. This would have been vital at the outset of the war, especially since Israel's strategy was not to destroy the enemy in a battle of annihilation but to stop him on the waterline. But Gonen claimed he never saw the Egyptian crossing plan, and when asked how he could make a situational assessment without studying the plan, he answered that he had "remembered" the enemy's likely method of operation for two main efforts (in the south and the center) and for two secondary ones.[26] The fact that Southern Command did not acknowledge Egypt's offensive plans led to misunderstandings of events on the ground and gross errors in battle procedure.

The defense establishment failed to identify the Egyptian strategy: all-out war with limited goals. Before the war, various intelligence sources conveyed the details of such a scenario, so steps to counter Egyptian intentions could have been taken; however, the necessity of doing so never entered the minds of Israel's decision makers.[27] There were also flaws in the interpretation of the material. MI first identified the possibility that the Egyptians were engaged in a limited offensive on October 8, after the debacle of the Israeli counterattack. The next day the director of Mossad (Israel's equivalent to the CIA), Zvi Zamir, told Lieutenant General Bar-Lev that Israel's forces were "running up against the wall" and he did not understand why; the Egyptian war plan had been figured out many months earlier, and if the IDF had seriously reviewed this assessment, it would have concluded that this was exactly what the Egyptians wanted. Zamir left the meeting with the impression that the IDF was unfamiliar with the Egyptian plan.

Failure to inform forces in the field that war was imminent.
The chief of staff received a communiqué at 04:30 stating, "War this
evening!" But the forces in the field—especially in Sinai—were not
informed. When the warnings were finally sent at noon, they were
ambiguous and referred to possible hostilities in an attrition scenario. Thus, when fighting broke out, the forces in the field were
caught by surprise. The sudden shift from routine operations to war
mode was so jarring that it made IDF actions seem improvised, and
the Israelis ran the risk of defensive attrition and loss of strategic
and operational equilibrium.[28]

Colonel Dan Shomron (chief of staff, 1987–1991), commander
of 401st Brigade during the Yom Kippur War, testified that even
though he had heard that full-scale war was probable, he thought
it unlikely. "Psychologically we were unprepared for all-out war
although the information indicated that it was in the offing."[29] The
commander of 14th Brigade, Colonel Amnon Reshef, said that the
readiness for war was technical rather than mental.

Inadequacies of the canal's warning system. The distance
between the strongholds, the vast spaces, and the infrequency of
Israeli patrols enabled Egyptian teams to cross freely to the eastern
bank during the War of Attrition (one of their forays was to El-Balah
Island, in the gap between the Purkan and Matsmed strongholds).

Elazar's unfamiliarity with Sinai. Chief of Staff Elazar felt at
home in Northern Command and the Golan Heights, but his familiarity with Sinai was minimal; he had visited the peninsula infrequently and the canal even less. His last tour of the canal had been
in May 1973 during the Blue White alert. Even when tensions escalated in the ten days preceding Yom Kippur, he did not go to Sinai.
Had he devoted even one day to a helicopter tour of the three canal
sectors, listened to the local commanders, and witnessed the Egyptian military concentrations and intense activity on the western
bank, he might have questioned MI's assessment that the Egyptians
were only planning an exercise.

Elazar had no time in his schedule for an inspection of the
southern front mainly because he did not consider it vital. Later,
he explained that urgent discussions had delayed his visit. Other
senior officers—including the deputy chief of staff and the head of
intelligence—also failed to visit the canal line during this period.

When the head of MI, Major General Eli Zeira, was asked why he had not flown to Sinai to get a firsthand impression, he replied that he did not consider it necessary because he received regular reports on developments there. Even Gonen, the head of Southern Command, had visited the canal line only once during the ten days between Rosh Hashanah and Yom Kippur—and then only to inspect the thinly manned strongholds and determine the possibility of opening them.

The Agranat Commission commented: "It is hard to fathom why the chief of staff did not make an effort to check the situation on the Egyptian front by studying the report of Southern Command's G-2 and the technical-military collections and by embarking on a personal tour of the front. The chief of staff did not even take the trouble to go there during the period of tension in the last week before the war to observe with his own eyes what was happening and get an informal first-hand impression of the warning signs that the observation posts had discovered, consult with local commanders, and glean information directly from them." Regarding the chief of staff's heavy schedule, the commission noted, "On Thursday, October 4 he devoted the GHQ meeting to matters of military code and discipline. An intelligence review on the situation never came up for discussion." Elazar explained that he had more urgent things to do, although he admitted that he should have visited the canal that week. He had intended to, but because of the alert and the high-priority discussions, he had canceled the visit.[30] Thus, the chief of staff remained ignorant of the precarious situation in the south. Elazar's unfamiliarity with Sinai—which had dire consequences in the bungled counterattack on October 8—may have contributed to his complacency. As Barak noted, "People who grew up [spent most of their military career] in the north didn't really understand the south and its unique problems."[31]

Belief that the Egyptians would fight a war of attrition. The 252nd Division entered the war assuming that it would be fighting a war of attrition and that IDF tanks should be deployed in tank parks, not in their firing positions.[32] These were the orders issued on October 6, just prior to the Egyptian attack. The 252nd's brigade commanders were informed on the morning of October 6 that they could expect either an expanded war of attrition or a limited crossing. The information that a full-scale war was about to erupt was not relayed, even though GHQ knew about it. If all-out war was mentioned as a possibility, it did not penetrate the consciousness of the senior commanders and officers in the field.

Thus, the 252nd's deployment plan was geared toward a war of attrition rather than all-out war. It was a rational preparation for a battle day or a limited war, but as a partial plan for a full-scale war, it was disastrous. Southern Command was expecting a "battle day with raids—some large, some small."[33] Even though the command possessed the enemy's offensive plans and was warned of a general attack in the evening, deployment and military thinking continued to be based on "fire," "battle day," and "attrition." The Israeli military was preparing "for something they had their own ideas about . . . instead of intelligence-based planning that it most definitely possessed."[34]

Raising and lowering of the alert level. In early October, despite threats on the ground, GHQ and Southern Command made desultory moves that culminated in "anemic" orders to raise and lower the level of alert (Assyria 1 and 2). These were empty moves in the face of imminent war, and they contributed nothing to improving the IDF's situation (except for the crucial move of sending 460th Brigade to Sinai to replace 7th Brigade on the night of October 5–6).

The Assyria 1 alert, issued on October 1, canceled leaves for tank and artillery crews but did not order soldiers who were already on leave to return to their units. The leave rotation in the strongholds continued. An entire mechanized infantry company of 401st Brigade was on leave, and three companies of raw tank crews in 14th Brigade, who had recently completed basic training, were sent on vacation on October 4 when the October 1 alert was canceled. The alert was reinstated on October 5, and the companies were called back, only to be sent home again (excluding replacements for absent crew members).

The orders to heighten the alert on the line without executing actual changes in deployment were meaningless (see appendix 5). Ordering tank crews to sleep with their overalls and combat boots on, on a five-minute standby, was pointless. Brigadier General Baruch Harel queried: "What was the soldier in the stronghold supposed to do—strap on his helmet?"[35] The alert orders dealt with trivialities instead of essentials. Actions that might have had a positive influence, such as the following, were not taken:

- Leaving 7th Brigade in Sinai and sending the Armor School Brigade to the Golan Heights. If this move had been carried out deliberately rather than hastily, the brigade might not have paid such a heavy price in the first night of the war.
- Reinforcing the strongholds with combat soldiers or replacing the infantry with crack troops.
- Removing the "snag" in the division's rear, such as advancing 401st Brigade (the rearward brigade from Bir Tmada). Because the 401st was not under 252nd Division's jurisdiction, its advance required an order from GHQ. Due to this administrative entanglement, 401st Brigade did not arm its tanks until October 6.
- Commencing Dovecote early.
- Partially mobilizing the reserves.

Although alert level C was announced on the afternoon of October 5, and the Assyria 2 order was issued to Southern Command that evening (with complex standby arrangements because forces had already been dispatched to the Golan Heights), the forward line remained as it was—that is, deployment corresponded to daily security operations with a reinforced rear and no Dovecote. Only the airlift of tank crews from the Armor School to Sinai on the night of October 5–6 reduced the manpower gap, and the number of manned tanks rose to 283 (not 300, as the orders stated). The IDF was definitely not operating as though war was about to break out the next day. Assyria 2 failed to define the nature of the alert (attrition, abductions, battle day, or all-out war), the preparations that should be undertaken (mobilizing reserves, enlisting the echelons, outfitting and arming the tanks in the reserve logistics units), or the system of reports and controls to confirm implementation of the alert.[36]

The 252nd Division's failure to grasp that war was imminent. Major General Albert Mandler (hereafter referred to as Albert) was scheduled to step down as commander of the 252nd in the second week of October. An experienced officer who sensed what was on the horizon, Albert expressed his apprehension during his round of farewells to the division's units in late September and early October, but no practical steps were taken to heed his admonition. As a disciplined soldier, he avoided making waves or questioning Southern Command's orders. He did not protest the appraisal that this was an Egyptian exercise, he did not order 79th Battalion to seal the gap in the line (the hole between Purkan and Matsmed), and he did not bring the rear artillery forward; nor did he disperse tanks on the line, as his estimate of Egyptian intentions would have required. His diary entry for October 1 read: "Unbelievable! The 05:15 intelligence report is war tomorrow . . . so much for my replacement."[37]

Brigadier General Benny Taran (Ret.), deputy commander of 184th Battalion during the war, recalled the instructions he received from the commander of 14th Brigade regarding preparations for Albert's farewell party: "Which cake to fly in from Israel and which fish to bring from Lake Bardawil. . . . This is what occupied them on October 4."[38]

On October 4 the deputy division commander, Brigadier General Baruch Harel, suggested that Albert order the forces out of the camps and into their positions. Brigadier General Magen, who was designated to replace Albert on October 8, supported Harel's proposal, but Albert refused; he believed doing so might arouse Egyptian suspicions and be interpreted as an Israeli escalation on the front. When Harel suggested that he, as Albert's deputy, give the order, Albert threatened to dismiss him. On October 5 the division requested reinforcements for Dovecote—additional infantry for the strongholds and mountain passes. Southern Command's answer was negative, with the explanation that, according to GHQ, the Egyptian exercise would end in two days.

"The outrageous blunder was first and foremost at the divisional level," said Harel. "They did nothing despite the new information. They didn't set up a divisional planning group; they didn't review the enemy's possible modus operandi; they didn't convene an orders group; they didn't reassess the situation. They remained fixated on the asinine 'Dovecote' Plan. The catastrophe occurred in the time slot between the morning's orders group and 14:00. For all practical purposes, deploying in 'Little Dovecote' meant doing nothing. Precious time was wasted instead of exploited." Harel acerbically described his commander: "Albert was all spit and polish without doing anything. He was like an engine racing in neutral on 'full revs.'" According to Harel, Albert did not know when to ignore an order. He had no experience in initiating moves before the war.[39]

Even on the morning of October 6, when Elazar knew that war

would erupt that evening, Gonen relayed only a vague message to Albert by telephone that H hour could be expected at 18:00, without elaborating on the nature of the impending attack. Thus the fateful information passed down the chain of command fragmentarily and sterilely. Gonen understood the gist of MI's situational assessment—a low probability of war—and he wanted to avoid heating up the front, which is why he refused to allow forces to advance to the line. Further, alert level C on Friday (Assyria 2 on October 5) provided no instructions on what to do and no order to execute Dovecote; it dealt only with preparations to move. For the line units, Yom Kippur was a routine day until noon, intensifying the mental jolt when hostilities resumed.

  Retention of headquarters and command groups in the rear. The head of Southern Command was absent on the critical night of October 4–5 and did not deem it necessary to send the command group from Beer Sheva to Um Hashiba (south of the Gidi pass) to prepare the facility for hostilities. Instead, when war erupted, the command group was hastily thrown together, which led to control mix-ups and numerous breakdowns. The 252nd's headquarters was not deployed ahead of time to the tactical operations center at Mitla, and the 401st's command group, which could have advanced to Mitla to observe the situation up close and take command of the southern sector, was not sent there either.

  Absence of a headquarters for the ground force buildup. The need for such a headquarters was known before the Yom Kippur War, but responsibility and authority for the training, organization, manpower, and outfitting of the ground forces were characterized by bungling and misunderstanding.[40] The war revealed countless shortcomings. Had such a headquarters been present at the outset, it would have incalculably improved the level of the ground forces' fighting.

  Failure to update GHQ orders. There was no file with operational orders at the GHQ level in October 1973, excluding the December 1969 Rock master plan for defense (which had been updated in the summer of 1972) and the March 1972 order for Operation Ben-Hayil. The IAF's plans were based on the air force commander's guidelines, which were essentially operational assessments dated August 28, 1973, and were circulated only among IAF elements.[41]

Failure to assess the reservists' readiness. No nationwide mobilization exercises were held between 1967 and 1973 to test the troops' arrival at reserve logistics units (apparently due to budgetary constraints) or assess the IDF's preparedness for war. The process of outfitting and transporting divisional units was never drilled, and no one ascertained whether mobilization orders would reach the reservists in time. There was a dearth of supplies in the reserve logistics units because of the requisitioning procedure, which wasted critical hours in the first stages of the battle. Core reservists were not called up to prepare the reserve logistics units to absorb the main body.

Transportation limitations and other logistical failures. Plans may have called for the Rock divisions to be integrated into the defense, but this was impossible on October 6, mainly due to transportation foul-ups. Only one armored division could have been transported to Sinai, requiring a prodigious effort, in the first twenty-four hours. Transporters carried 309 tanks to the two fronts, while more than 1,400 traveled on their own tracks. The result: mechanical fatigue and exhausted troops.[42] The reserve logistics units were critically short of equipment for sustained fighting, including tank and artillery ammunition. This was one of the factors that led to pressure at the political level for a cease-fire on October 12.

Military intelligence's loss of standing. The disdain MI displayed toward field intelligence reports did not go unnoticed by the soldiers manning the observation posts. The assessments received by political leaders and the high command were based solely on research sources that spurned the bulk of the field intelligence data and failed to cross-reference that information with other sources. In a postwar mea culpa, the director of intelligence himself, General Zeira, admitted that when he debriefed the observers, some of their findings were not accorded the proper weight. None of the field intelligence reports reached the highest military level, nor did they go through the pipelines from the general of Southern Command to the chief of staff or from the command staffs to General Staff Operations (GSO).[43]

The analysis of enemy activity reported from the observation posts beginning in early September showed the Egyptians hard at work: elevating ramps on the western bank, completing a dirt embankment between the ramps, paving new roads, blasting the sides of the canal, preparing descents to the water, improving crossing platforms, and bringing crossing equipment up to the forward line, all accompanied by major vehicular movement from the rear. A comparison of these developments and a list of preparatory activities for war should have set off bells in the IDF, but it did not. In total, there were thirty to forty-five signals on MI's list that pointed to an approaching war.

Defects in the buildup of the ground forces. The regular units of 252nd Division that were flung into war at noon on Yom Kippur suffered from a dire shortage of infantry, mechanized infantry, mortars, and artillery. This oversight had grave results until October 9, when the Rock order of battle grew in size, adding artillery formations and mechanized brigades such as the 875th and 204th, which alleviated the shortfall to some extent. Paradoxically, the structural imbalance of the armored divisions was, to a large degree, an outgrowth of the armored formations' successes in the Six-Day War, achievements that had strengthened the importance of the tank.

The replenishment plans between 1967 and 1973 did not assign the proper weight to other vital combat elements. Instead, they called for dissolution of the divisions' mechanized brigades and disbanding of the tank brigades' mechanized infantry battalions, so that only mechanized infantry companies remained in the regular tank battalions; they later became reserve companies.

The air force was christened the "flying artillery" after it damaged the Egyptian artillery in the War of Attrition, but this was before the Egyptians upgraded their air defense on the western bank. The IAF's dubious title enabled some of those responsible for the framework and organization of the ground units to minimize the field artillery without taking into account the air force's limitations in a zone defended by surface-to-air missiles.

Between 1967 and 1973 the infantry structure was reduced from twelve brigades to four. The artillery order of battle, despite minor qualitative improvements, grew only slightly—from 536 tubes in 1967 to 550 in 1973. In the same period, armor's order of battle improved both quantitatively and qualitatively— from 1,050 tanks organized in six tank and three mechanized brigades in 1967, to 2,030 tanks in fourteen tank and six mechanized brigades organized into six divisions in 1973. What had once been a multibranched division now became a tank division because of the belief that the next war would be primarily a battle between huge tank formations. Thus, the balance among the various combat elements, especially infantry and artillery, changed.

The Six-Day War had been a test of the offensive battle carried out primarily by armored divisions; the IDF had not fought any defensive battles geared toward protecting territory, and infantry and mechanized infantry activity had been limited. General Tal assumed that the scenario of future wars would be different from that of the Six-Day War. For one thing, Israel would have to execute infantry and nighttime attacks in closed areas with both standard infantry and mechanized infantry in conjunction with tanks. This meant that an armored brigade would have to be built with an equal proportion of infantry and tanks; the number of mechanized infantry or reconnaissance companies would have to be identical to the number of tank companies in the brigade. But this concept was later changed without justification. The infantry and mechanized infantry weapons that had been mustered out were sorely lacking in the Yom Kippur War.[44]

The first standing division, the 252nd, had been established in 1968. It was supposed to have a motorized brigade as well as a mechanized infantry battalion in each armored brigade (which consisted of two tank battalions and one mechanized infantry battalion), but the accelerated procurement of tanks created a manpower deficit, and the mechanized infantry's manpower was transferred to the new tanks in the organic tank brigades. Mechanized infantry companies, however, still remained in the tank battalions.

Responsibility for the mechanized infantry jostled back and forth between the armored corps and the chief infantry and paratroop officer's headquarters, which added little to its operational capability and reflected a lack of understanding of its roles. Infantry fighting is essential in nighttime combat and in flanking, deception, and the simultaneous application of secondary units when the main force is numerically inferior to the enemy, as in the case of the IDF. In contrast, a large concentration of armored forces engaged in movement and fire and capable of overwhelming the enemy through shock and a direct breakthrough is suited to a force with a numerical advantage. Between the Six-Day War and 1973, the emphasis shifted to armor, even though the IDF was numerically inferior.

In a symposium held on June 25, 1973, to formulate a new concept of ground force buildup, all the speakers (with the exception

of General Tal) supported terminating the division's organic mechanized infantry units and transforming the division from a multibranched, multipurpose force into a tank division without an
infantry brigade and with only minimal artillery support; its main
support weapon would be the 81mm mortars of the mechanized
infantry companies in the tank battalions only. The defense minister approved the new framework after being shown that the proposed configuration would save a total of 228 troops per battalion.
The IDF's Doctrine and Instruction Department did not back up this
restructuring with written material, as required, so these changes
remained in the realm of oral doctrine.

Because the division would have minimal artillery and no
mechanized infantry, it would be dependent on air support and
exposed to enemy infantry equipped with antitank weapons. In
addition to removing the mechanized infantry battalions, it was
decided to mothball or drastically reduce the division's 90mm antitank cannon, 20mm cannon, demolition elements, and 120mm mortars. Although the antitank cannons were outdated and unsuited for
battlefield conditions in 1973, the removal of the mortars—an essential and effective weapon—was a grievous mistake, and they were
sorely missed in engagements with enemy antitank teams. Despite
the serious reduction of the division's infantry and mechanized
infantry, resources were not allocated to dieselizing the half-tracks,
which meant that the mechanized infantry's mobility was inferior
to that of the tanks.[45]

The armored divisions' attitude toward mechanized infantry—
that it was second rate—affected their assignments, level of training,
vehicles, weapons, and so forth. Thus, in the inexorable misreading of the map of the coming war, the armored divisions found
themselves thrown into the fighting practically devoid of infantry
or mechanized infantry. The mechanized infantry units in the few
motorized brigades that survived the reorganization were mounted
on World War II–vintage half-tracks, and the regular and reserve
units on M113 APCs were inadequately trained. Part of the reserve
force lacked mobility and weapons suited to combat in Sinai, mortars had been removed, and the artillery formations were insufficient to provide a decisive response.

Lack of a higher level of headquarters. The lack of a forward
command seriously detracted from Southern Command's ability

to direct the defensive battle being waged by the three divisions. The absence of control was acutely felt in the October 8 counterattack and in the October 15–18 crossing battle and expansion of the bridgeheads.

Early Failures at the Tactical Level

Tanks' inability to counter antitank weapons and other shortcomings. The ground forces' "flagship"—the tank—suffered from numerous shortcomings that reduced its ability to cope with Egyptian infantry reinforced with antitank weapons:

- The tanks' ability to employ machine gun fire against enemy infantry was only medium to low because the 0.3 Browning used woven cloth cartridge belts that tended to misfire, and the tanks were unable to fire light arms on their left side.
- The inability to create a smoke screen decreased the tanks' survivability in an environment teeming with infantry armed with antitank weapons and hindered their ability to perform evasive tactics.
- The tanks lacked sufficient mounted mortars to repel infantry and antitank teams.
- The shortage of special 105mm anti-infantry ammunition became acute during the war. For ranges beyond the machine guns' capability, tank crews improvised by employing high-explosive squash-head and hollow-charge ammunition, which was often in short supply because of its intense use in antitank fighting.
- The tank array included antiquated Shermans.
- Insufficient armor protection against the hollow charges of Sagger missiles and rocket-propelled grenades (RPGs) resulted in heavy damage.
- Tank crews had not been thoroughly drilled and lacked basic know-how, such as how to administer first aid.

Shortfalls and obsolete equipment in infantry units. Outdated weapons and lack of mobility were the major problems:

- The Israeli infantryman's weapon was the FN self-loading rifle—a heavy, obsolete, 7.62-caliber weapon.

- The infantry's webbed combat belt was antiquated, cumbersome, and uncomfortable.
- The Israeli infantry had been without organic antitank weapons for years; the obsolete, limited antitank grenade launcher and bazooka (American 82mm and French 73mm, respectively) were the main antitank weapons in 1973.
- Infantry mobility was deficient and in short supply. Some units had no means of transportation at all, while others traveled on benzene-fueled World War II half-tracks; only a few units had diesel-fueled half-tracks. Some units, mostly regulars, had M113 APCs with automotive improvements, but their ballistic protection was extremely limited.

Shortcomings and deficiencies in other combat frameworks. In general, the ground forces' assault, assistance, and combat support units were hurled into the war only partially equipped with obsolete weapons unsuited to the fighting conditions. The artillery consisted of obsolete cannons with mechanical problems, and ammunition for the 155mm cannon was notorious for its inaccuracy and short range. The basic problem of the combat engineers was transportation—even in the regulars' battalions. There was also a shortage of tank transporters.

In addition, there were flaws in the combat doctrine and framework, as well as critical shortages in equipment, especially in the reserve units. Some of these shortages were known beforehand because of the drastic budget cutbacks; others became apparent during the course of the fighting. Israel failed to take advantage of advanced technologies and acquire desperately needed equipment such as communications systems, modern guided missiles, night-vision gear, artillery fire control systems, APC protection, multi-engine supply vehicles, and so forth.[46]

Failure to reinforce or replace infantry troops in the strongholds. Four days before the war, the head of operations decided that if tensions continued to escalate, two regular infantry brigades— the Paratroop and the Golani—would suffice to hold the sensitive lines. But things did not work out that way. Golani (1st Brigade) was sent north to the Golan Heights after the war broke out; 35th Brigade's headquarters, along with 890th Battalion and brigade units, was flown to Ras Sudar, south of the canal on the eastern bank of the Gulf of Suez; and 202nd Paratroop Battalion was assigned to 252nd Division. During the operational discussion group that convened at midnight on October 5–6, the head of operations concluded that, "Given the current alert status, the infantry doesn't have to be brought to the front lines. We'll keep it concentrated so that IDF will have a core force available for offensive actions or special operations. Also taken into account was the possibility that if the situation deteriorated the reserve infantry units on the canal line would have to be replaced with regular units from the Gaza Strip."[47] But preparations to replace troops in the strongholds with regular units from the Gaza Strip or with officer cadets from Training Base 1 were not carried out.

In the summary of the war, Gonen recalled the need to replace 16th Brigade's reservists on the canal with crack infantry troops but stated, "This didn't happen because the timetable was too short." During the Blue White alert (April–May 1973), the commander of 252nd Division had raised the issue of replacing the troops and reinforcing the strongholds and was promised that paratroop regulars would relieve the reservists. There is no rational explanation why this did not occur. The Agranat Commission deemed it an outrageous failure on Gonen's part. The 16th Brigade reservists in the strongholds were unsuited to hold the line in wartime, and on September 25 Southern Command requested an infantry battalion from the GHQ operations branch, but it never received a reply. Just one day before the war, when Southern Command's G-3 asked the head of operations to replace the infantry, he received a negative reply. Gonen did not refer the matter to the chief of staff. The GHQ's head of operations claimed that when the C-level alert was issued at 10:45 on October 5, the decision was made not to replace the troops on the line, lest it create unnecessary upheaval during a state of high alert. According to the chief of staff, replacements were not brought in because there was not enough time to transfer the units, and the matter had not been referred to him.[48]

If the chief of staff had been more involved in the details of his regular forces' deployment at the outset of tensions in the two sectors—especially at the start of the troop movements, such as 7th Brigade's transfer to the Golan Heights—he would not have waited for requests from Southern Command. He would have personally dealt with the low combat readiness of the *shlav bet* troops in the strongholds.[49] (The 68th Battalion/16th Brigade had undergone only cursory training, and many of its troops were *shlav bet*. The 904th Nachal Unit, whose soldiers served mostly on agricultural settlements, also received only minimal training.) The quality of the infantry in the strongholds played a decisive role in the defensive campaign on the canal.

Shortfalls in 252nd Division's order of battle. The 401st Brigade was short one reconnaissance company and one mechanized infantry company in 195th Battalion and one tank company in 79th Battalion. The 14th Brigade lacked two mechanized infantry companies in 9th and 52nd Battalions and a tank company in 184th Battalion. The 460th (Armor School) Brigade lacked headquarters companies (composed of reservists) in the regular battalions, two mechanized infantry companies, a signal company, mortars, reconnaissance, and vehicles for echelon transportation.

Problems with the IDF's embankment and ramps. On the canal's eastern bank, the IDF had built an embankment with tank positions along its length to serve as an obstacle against an Egyptian crossing, but it proved to be a liability because it blocked long-range (two- to three-kilometer) tank fire in the direction of the waterline. Since the tank positions on the embankment were exposed to short-range small-arms and antitank fire, ramps had been built for ranges of 1,500 to 2,000 meters in the Hakfar area, Hamezach, and Mefatseyach. This should have been done along the entire length of the canal wherever natural positions were lacking, but it was not.

Gonen recognized these problems and, upon assuming command of Southern Command in July 1973, proposed building tank positions three and a half kilometers from the embankment, high enough to dominate the waterline. But due to time constraints, this was never carried out. If such positions had been in place, he said, the forces could have held on much longer.[50] Gonen's proposal was tactically correct, but the cost of carrying it out would have been exorbitant. Opening a line of fire would have entailed tearing down the embankment along the entire length of the canal and building a large number of tank ramps. Moreover, the IDF was opposed to the initiative because the embankment was perceived as a suitable obstacle to an Egyptian crossing, and even if the embankment were removed, the tanks would still lack a clear field of fire at ranges of three and a half to four kilometers, since the stony incline on the eastern bank created a dead space. Sharon was against the construction of positions and advised that, wherever possible, the natural lay of the land should be exploited. "The enemy didn't have to know two years before the war where our positions were."[51]

The Israeli ramps on the eastern bank, situated 1,500 to 2,000 meters from the canal, were completely dominated by Egyptian tanks and missiles on the giant ramps on the western bank and suffered heavy armor losses. The Egyptian infantry captured the artificial tank positions (ramps and "fins") immediately after crossing the canal, but wherever there were natural positions, such as in the Lituf stronghold area, the Israeli forces were safe and did not attract antitank fire.

Misperception of the Egyptian ramps. During the cease-fire (1970–1973), the Egyptians built immense ramps that dominated Israel's tank positions on the roads leading to the canal. The IDF failed to discern the ramps' real purpose and disparagingly called them the "pyramids." The 252nd Division thought the ramps were designed for tank fire and believed the IDF's tanks could deal with them. This was tested by the division in January 1973, when tanks from 401st Brigade accurately hit turret-shaped targets at 3,000 meters. When the war broke out, the Egyptians did deploy a pair of tanks on each ramp, but the ramps' main purpose was to serve as launching sites for Sagger missiles at approximately 2,000-meter ranges against Israeli tanks on the eastern bank. The missile fire was effective, and its source was difficult to spot because of the very low profile of the launcher teams and the smoke and dust from the battle. Visual conditions were also in the Egyptians' favor: the afternoon sun shone directly in the eyes of the Israeli tankers.

Enemy observation of Dovecote deployment. During the War of Attrition and the cease-fire, units of 252nd Division carried out day and night exercises that entailed linking up with the strongholds and capturing positions on the embankment and the ramps along Canal Road. No attempt was made to conceal these exercises from Egyptian observation and eavesdropping. To make matters worse, signposts were put up in the area with the roads' code names and position numbers to facilitate the tank crews' and especially the reinforcements' navigation. The large signs were clearly visible from the western bank. All this blatant clumsiness helped the enemy assess the IDF's deployment and devise a plan to gain a unique advantage in the first stage of the war, far exceeding what would have been possible based on the balance of ground forces.[52]

In addition, code maps that had been lost over the years aided the Egyptians in deciphering the regulars' order of battle in the Dovecote deployment. The identification of areas devoid of tanks in Dovecote—especially in the gaps between the strongholds—allowed Egyptian planners of the armored crossing to select breakthrough areas not yet dominated by IDF tanks. This was a wise move because, until 10:00 on October 7, the 252nd's tanks were still in their primary positions, engaged mainly in a static battle.

Failure to protect the rear defensive line at the mountain passes. After the Six-Day War, the western outlet of the Gidi and Mitla passes was correctly identified as the line where the defensive battle would be fought in the event of a pullback and delaying maneuver. Even though it was considered a third line (the strongholds on the canal were the first line; the line of hills above Artillery Road constituted the second line), it was not officially called a rear defensive line, and fortification construction was neglected, except for the random dispersal of concertina wire and some shallow foxholes with chest-high mounds of local rock (which guaranteed ricochets). This was a far cry from the fortifications needed for a rear defensive line. To add insult to injury, most of the positions were located on the crests, which rendered them incapable of dominating the road below with concentrated fire.

Indifference toward the massive buildup of Egyptian infantry armed with antitank weapons. The change in the Egyptians' concept of antitank fighting and their buildup of infantry divisions with diverse antitank weapons were intended to neutralize Israel's armor superiority and its ability to quickly destroy any crossing efforts. The IDF would not have been caught by surprise had it made an in-depth study of the Soviet combat doctrine for the defense of infantry installations, which was based on a reinforced antitank missile setup supported by organic tanks and covering fire from artillery concentrations. Furthermore, intelligence reports on changes in the Egyptians' replenishment and procurement had reached the IDF and were already being circulated in 1972. This information included the stockpiling of other antitank weapons in addition to Sagger missiles, but only the Saggers got any attention.

The IDF knew the Egyptian plan was based on a canal crossing and the securing of bridgeheads in the first stage, with fire assistance from the western bank and the backup of hundreds of Sagger anti-tank missiles mounted on amphibious combat vehicles. The intelligence collected in 1972 and 1973 had detailed the buildup of antitank weapons in infantry companies and battalions, the introduction of Saggers in motorized brigades, and the increase in armored vehicles carrying Sagger missiles.[53] If the IDF had made a preliminary analysis of this information, it would have identified the need to integrate mechanized infantry units, mortars, and artillery, and it would have recognized that its entire tank concept—based on a rapid crossing in an area bristling with antitank weapons and artillery support—was deadly wrong. But no such analysis was made, and as a result, the makeup of the battlefield—where the enemy infantry was heavily armed with antitank weapons—was misapprehended, and an operational answer based on combat doctrine and the necessary drills was neglected. The armored corps practiced evading Sagger missiles "instead of perceiving the enemy's antitank weapons as a joint, well-orchestrated antitank effort of various concentrations at varying ranges applied to killing zones against our tanks."[54]

Despite the IDF's familiarity with the Shmel antitank missile from the Six-Day War and the War of Attrition and the Sagger missile from the Golan Heights and end of the War of Attrition in Sinai, the significance of the massive use of antitank missiles was lost on it. As a result, the trauma of encountering the Saggers was overwhelming (even greater than the devastation from enemy tanks). Given the IDF's initial obliviousness to the enemy's capabilities, the surprise was twofold: first, that the Egyptians and Syrians were able to pull off a surprise attack; and second, their method of antitank fighting.

Reinforcements' unfamiliarity with the canal sector. Frequent replacements in the regular units made it imperative to refresh orders, carry out operational drills, and familiarize the newly arrived conscripts and commanders with the daily security sector. The canal sector was complex terrain crisscrossed with access roads in the Canal Road area and sand dunes that necessitated meticulous driving, lest the tank tracks come apart (this was a problem mainly, but not solely, in the northern sector). The area was filled with open and hidden swamplands along the canal, so crossing demanded intimate knowledge of the area. Antipersonnel and antitank mine-fields surrounded the strongholds, with tank paths cutting through them in the direction of the strongholds and firing positions on the eastern embankment. The northern sector posed a special problem, especially north of Kantara, where narrow "plastic roads" traversed the marshes from east to west on delineated lanes that offered no opportunity for maneuvering. Navigating these geographic challenges (dunes, swamps, and minefields) required a high degree of expertise that could be gained only by frequent exercises by the officers and the rank and file.

The two regular brigades of 252nd Division rotated on the canal line every three months, so they acquired vast knowledge and experience in the area; naturally, the brigades on the line were more updated on changes than was the brigade in the rear. However, for the reinforcing brigade—the Armor School (460th) Brigade—which arrived on the night of October 5–6, the area was practically terra incognita. To make matters worse, the brigade had instantly metamorphosed from a training school to a combat brigade and had not participated in combat drills at any level. And except for a brief commanders' tour of the sector that was cut short on Saturday morning, 460th Brigade had no time to become acquainted with the fighting sector. When it was suddenly flung into battle on Saturday night (October 6–7) in the northern sector, near Kantara and the Mifreket stronghold, many tanks detonated IDF mines, threw their tracks, or sank in the marshland because of the commanders' unfamiliarity with the area.[55]

Gap between Purkan and Matsmed. The lack of a permanent Israeli presence between the Purkan stronghold (opposite Ismailia) and the Matsmed stronghold (close to the northern coast of Great Bitter Lake) opened a twenty-kilometer gap in force deployment that the enemy readily identified. On October 6 the Egyptian 16th Division crossed the canal through this gap without encountering any resistance and quickly gained control of the Chinese Farm. At 16:00 its motorized force attacked the Televizia fortification, which was empty because of the mechanized infantry's evacuation to Tasa, according to the Dovecote order.[56]

No tank order of battle was available in this unguarded sector. The 184th Battalion had been reduced to only two tank companies for the last year and a half, and the third company arrived from 460th Brigade only on Saturday evening. There is no doubt that the presence of an Israeli tank force between Purkan and Matsmed as part of Dovecote would have impeded Egyptian 16th Division's crossing and prevented it from gaining any significant ground on the first day of the war. These territorial achievements exacted a heavy toll in lives from Israel's 14th Armored Brigade and other units during the breakthrough for the canal crossing.

The IDF was aware of the gap between Purkan and Matsmed (as well as other gaps), but it did nothing to remedy the situation. At 16:00 on October 6, Southern Command ordered the division to prepare to cross the canal according to Zefania or Ben-Hayil, which explains why no one was unduly worried. Despite the mounting prewar warnings, there were no plans of any kind to close the gap.[57] If Dovecote's two-in-front deployment had been carried out, 79th Battalion/401st Brigade could have sealed the gap. In that case, one company could have been deployed west of Missouri (code name for the area north of the Chinese Farm), and two companies and the battalion headquarters could have been deployed in Talisman 21 (code name for the Tasa-Ismailia Road) as the brigade's sector reserve. Had the central sector been reinforced with two tank battalions—79th/401st Brigade and 196th/460th Brigade—on the first night of the fighting (as it later was), a reduced battalion could have been deployed west of Missouri, with two companies in position and one in reserve in Talisman 21.

There was also a gap in Israeli surveillance in the Purkan-Matsmed section. Tank crews of 184th Battalion had been carrying out long-range observation in the Havraga, Televizia, and Kishuf fortifications and the Nozel high-ground area, but when the level of alert heightened on October 3, 14th Brigade had to withdraw the observation posts and return the crews to their tanks. At 13:30 the observers on the waterline, who were also ordered to beat a hasty retreat, reported nothing, mainly because they were in the process of pulling back when the opening rounds of the war occurred.[58]

Had the 79th been ordered to close the gap before the war, it would have made the Egyptian 16th Division's task on October 6 much more difficult. In the afternoon, evening, and night of the first day, 14th Brigade endeavored to close the gap and obtain a picture of what was happening.

GSO's failure to comprehend the importance of the order of battle. On the evening of the Day of Atonement, the regular 35th Paratroop Brigade was on leave, and 875th Reservist Brigade's tank battalion (which had completed combat exercises the previous day) had been discharged. Also just discharged was a reservist tank battalion in Northern Command that had been called up and sent to a reserve logistics unit on a routine mobilization exercise.

3

Ground Forces in the Defensive Battle

On the morning of Yom Kippur, none of the 436 men and officers in the sixteen strongholds on the Bar-Lev Line or the troops of 14th Armored Brigade holding the line could have imagined what the day would bring. It began with routine quiet on the canal. Patrols went out; observers were posted; the dirt roads were checked, as they were every morning, for suspicious tracks. There was no indication of what would happen in a few hours.

The Element of Surprise and the Cost of Delay

The commanders of the tank battalions (14th Brigade on the line and 401st and 460th Brigades in the rear) received no warning or report of irregularities, even though GHQ knew about H hour since early in the morning. Only at 07:20—three hours after the chief of staff received the news—did the general of Southern Command telephone the commander of 252nd Division and inform him that H hour would be at 18:00. Albert, the division commander, met with the divisional orders group at Refidim and at 08:50 was privy to information regarding H hour, including the standby for Dovecote, but this was not conveyed to the battalions. In fact, the division did not know if H hour referred to the conclusion of the Egyptian exercise, a renewal of the War of Attrition, or an all-out war (which seemed the least likely scenario).

The 14th Brigade's battalion commanders first heard that 18:00 was H hour at the noon meeting of the brigade orders group at Tasa. Toward the end of the meeting (around 12:50), a frantic order was received from division to execute Dovecote at once—tanks were to enter the day parks outside the fortifications (the second string of strongholds). This order was the result of an intercepted UN communiqué that explicitly confirmed Egyptian preparations to open artillery fire immediately. Although the battalions' state of readiness and alert was high, the officers and men needed time to adjust psychologically, and when war did erupt—at 14:00—it fell on their heads like a bolt of lightning (see map 6).

But was it really a surprise? Unlike the forces in the field, the political and military leaders were not caught off guard. According to former chief of staff Lieutenant General Ehud Barak (Ret.), the surprise was in the Arabs' ability, in the technical-tactical sense, to launch a two-front campaign. The field commanders in Sinai also agreed that the attack was not a total surprise. The surprise was mental, especially in the southern front, where H hour was assumed to be the start of a "battle day" or the renewal of a war of attrition; the possibility of all-out war was not even considered. The surprise was also in the timing—beginning at 14:00 rather than 18:00. Finally, the IDF was familiar with the Egyptians' weapon systems, but the surprise was in the quantity; as proof, once the front stabilized, events began to move in the desired direction.[1]

According to Brigadier General Yiftach Spector (Ret.), a combat pilot and commander of a Phantom squadron during the war, the war did not catch Israel by surprise. On the morning of October 6, his squadron was already on war footing; the only missing factor was the time. "The air-raid sirens that went off . . . at 14:00 broke the waiting spell. There was no surprise."[2] If anything, the surprise lay in the time of the opening round: 14:00, not 18:00. If the military—GHQ, the commands, and the field units—had known that fire would commence at 14:00, some of the steps taken to prepare would have been carried out four hours earlier. Thus, regardless of Gonen's fear of the Egyptians' response to "Israeli escalation," 401st Brigade would have started moving four hours earlier and, by 14:00, would have deployed in the canal area with the assistance, in daylight, of 52nd Battalion in the southern sector. The 79th Battalion could have assisted the central sector in daylight, and some of the problems 460th Brigade encountered in the northern sector (tank tracks being thrown and tanks sinking in marshlands) might have been avoided. Also, the change of armaments in the warplanes would have been unnecessary.[3]

In addition to the psychological element (the surprise within the surprise), the quality of the regulars' response in the opening hours of the war was crucial, especially in Sinai. Some officers at headquarters succumbed to shock and sought shelter in the bunkers, and the battles were run by junior officers.[4]

The first MI communiqué warning of the possibility of war that day was based on a message from the head of the Mossad, who reported that the Egyptians were planning to open fire, but the exact hour was vague and the head of MI did not bring this information to the chief of staff's attention. Had it not been for this snag, the decision makers might have acted differently. How the message "war today at sunset," which was conveyed by the head of the Mossad in London at 02:40 on Saturday, got entangled remains an unsolved mystery. Even the blue-ribbon Agranat Commission failed to unravel the skein of confusion. The head of MI testified that he had been told that H hour was 18:00, but the Mossad staff member who reported to General Zeira claimed that he read him the message, which stated: "at sunset or before nightfall but not 18:00." Sunset that day was at 17:20; thus, "sunset" could have been any time after 16:00. At the 07:15 meeting of the operational discussion group, when the head of MI announced that "an attack is planned at sunset," Chief of Staff David Elazar said tersely, "We'll proceed on the assumption that the attack will be at 18:00 tonight." An hour later, after consulting with the prime minister, he repeated, "Everything points to war breaking out at 18:00 today."[5] This was the communiqué that Southern Command received at 09:06 on Saturday, but there is no mention of it in 252nd Division's operations log.

As far as we know, the only question asked in the government meeting at 12:00 regarding the timing of the Egyptian attack came from the justice minister, Yaakov Shimshon Shapira: "How can you be certain they won't advance their options? We're expecting them when it gets dark but what if they begin earlier?" The defense minister's reply: the air force had been patrolling the area since noon.[6] The Agranat Commission asked the chief of staff whether, at any point, he had considered the possibility of the enemy attacking in daylight. Elazar answered that no one had ever brought up the idea.

Valuable time was lost because of communications problems. The head of Mossad met in London with an Egyptian agent at 22:00 on Friday, but the crucial message was not conveyed to Mossad in Israel until 02:40 on Saturday. As stated, the chief of staff received the message only at 04:30. More than six hours were wasted.

Another question is: once the chief of staff knew that war would break out at 18:00 on Yom Kippur, why did he not act immediately? Why did he not convey that information to the forces in the field, and why did he fail to call up the Rock order of battle—the two reserve divisions that were designated to counterattack but could have reinforced the regulars holding the line? The meeting between the chief of staff and the defense minister in the early hours of Saturday did not produce even a partial mobilization, as Dayan had suggested. (Dayan was worried about what the Americans would say and what the reservists—"who'll be scampering around under our legs"—would do.)[7]

The chief of staff wanted the entire force mobilized for a counterattack. At the meeting, he proposed "ordering a general call-up so that the whole world knows that we're prepared for war." Dayan replied, "We could let the whole world know this without ordering a full mobilization—but for what? For a war that hasn't begun? For this we have to mobilize for a counterattack? I don't think so. Calling up the reserves for defense will only throw the Syrians into a panic."[8] Also present at the meeting was the chief of intelligence, who, even in the early-morning hours of Yom Kippur, still insisted that everything was quiet and war would not break out. General Zeira's assurances were a major factor in Dayan's approval of a limited mobilization of the air force and one division for the north and one for the south. He decided to wait and call up "the GHQ reservist divisions in the evening after the first shot's fired."[9]

Even after the defense minister approved the call-up, the chief of staff took his time mobilizing the two reserve divisions, losing four more precious hours. Dayan claimed that he was unaware of the delay. Since his conversation with the chief of staff had ended without an agreement, it was decided: "We're going to Golda [Meir]." At the 08:00 meeting with the prime minister, Dayan expressed his reservations about the chief of staff's demand for a full mobilization and stated that his own proposal for one division in Sinai and one on the Golan Heights seemed adequate. If the situation deteriorated and the Egyptians resumed hostilities, a full-scale mobilization could be ordered. Dayan said:

> If I thought there was no alternative, I'd order a full mobilization. The limited mobilization . . . would be ready for action by the next morning. If we want to order a call-up tonight—we will. . . . I won't resign and I won't lie down on the road if you decide on a full mobilization. I just think it's unnecessary. They'll say that we're the aggressor and that

we mustered our forces before the first shot was fired. This has nothing to do with domestic considerations. . . . Despite some serious obstacles, I think we should begin from the best possible international position. We aren't as free as we were in 1967. Tonight it doesn't matter.[10]

Dayan, of course, was wrong. Although a mobilization on the morning of October 6 would not have changed the battlefield situation that night, it would have made a big difference on Sunday. Dayan also erred in estimating the amount of time the reserves needed to organize for combat, and his fear of international condemnation was greatly exaggerated. Elazar, too, misled the prime minister when he told her, "The regular army is deployed at maximum strength." He assumed that the reserve divisions would mobilize and join the battle on Sunday morning (which was true on the Golan Heights but not in Sinai). He also demanded that the prime minister approve the mobilization of reserve combat units, supplements for the regulars, and a call-up of air force reservists. He believed that unless these forces were mobilized immediately, they would not be able to take part in the fighting the next day. "We can hold defensively [without the reserves]," he said, "but we'll be limited to defensive operations. If we have more forces, we'll be able to counterattack." Meir approved the mobilization and stressed her desire to keep IDF casualties to a minimum. "If it means we're in a better situation," she said, "then I prefer them [the international community] to be angry with us. We have to be in the best position possible." The prime minister granted the chief of staff permission to mobilize as he saw fit. Her approval, conveyed to the head of operations at 09:20, was later praised by the Agranat Commission.[11]

Shimon Peres, the communications minister in Meir's government, later recalled that he had spoken with Dayan that morning about summoning the reservists. Dayan's position was: "Let *them* begin." According to Peres, the defense minister was afraid of being accused of political manipulation on the eve of elections; he wanted Israel to appear to be the victim of aggression and therefore wanted to avoid any provocation. Dayan also assumed that the IDF was fully prepared for war and that the regulars could bear the strain of the difficult opening battle.[12]

Approval for full-scale mobilization was given at 09:20, but more than three and a half hours were lost after the Elazar-Dayan meeting. The importance of the rapid arrival of 162nd and 143rd Divisions on the afternoon of October 7 to stabilize the defensive line in the south cannot be overestimated. An additional three and a half hours (not to mention five, if the counting had begun at 04:30) could have contributed to the battle in general and to 252nd Division in particular, preventing the bitter fighting and heavy losses in the following days.

The Dovecote Fiasco

The Dovecote order for deploying the regulars' order of battle on the canal in an emergency was based on a two-stage concept. Stage 1 (Little Dovecote) involved the egress of tank companies from the brigade on the line (14th Brigade in October 1973) to daytime parks outside the fortifications. Southern Command forbade the execution of this move on October 6, lest it appear to be an Israeli escalation. Stage 2 (Large Dovecote)—advancing the reduced 401st Brigade from the rear to take command of the southern sector and deploy in a "two-in-front" formation (two brigades forward and one in the rear)—was delayed for the same reason. Thus, when the Egyptians opened fire, 14th Brigade's tanks were in the camps and fortifications, which were bombed (except for G Company/184th Battalion, which managed to deploy in a day park). As the tanks approached the canal, they discovered that Egyptian infantry had overtaken their positions. The 401st Brigade's camps in the rear were also bombarded. This fiasco, among the worst in the war, had immediate and long-term catastrophic consequences caused by the loss of tanks and crews on the first day and night of the war and territorial gains by Egypt. On Sunday morning, 252nd Division was left with 114 operable tanks out of its original 283 (see appendix 7), and it had lost more than 300 soldiers killed in action.

Although Dovecote was not the answer to a large-scale crossing, had the forces been fully deployed according to the original plan, they would have been in a much better position to counter the first wave of Egyptian infantry. Instead, the Egyptians were able to gain control of Israeli tank positions and ambush the approaching tanks with RPGs and small-arms fire at short ranges, supported by anti-tank weapons, Sagger missiles, and tanks from the elevated ramps on the western bank.

In some areas, such as the Mitla opening in the southern sector, 52nd Battalion/14th Brigade's tanks and APCs succeeded in retaking its positions after a bloody battle with Egyptian infantry. In other areas, especially in the sector north of Kantara, 275th Territorial Brigade was unable to recapture its positions. The failure to execute Dovecote on time was a major factor in the initial shock to the three regular brigades. That night, the rear-based 401st Brigade and reserve 460th Brigade hastily and in piecemeal fashion entered the battle raging between the canal and Lexicon (Canal Road), while they struggled to link up with forces on the line that were incurring heavy losses. The 460th Brigade's combat effectiveness was severely hampered by its unfamiliarity with the sector; this led to the loss of many tanks due to thrown tracks, land mines, and sinking in the swamps.

Given the regulars' grave situation, the two recently mobilized reserve divisions left the emergency storerooms at breakneck speed and raced to the front. The price of this slapdash departure was missing equipment and disorganization. Also, the acute shortage of tank transporters meant that many armored units had to travel on their own tracks, which caused material fatigue and crew exhaustion. The 162nd and 143rd Brigades arrived in the combat theater with insufficient intelligence updates and not even a general picture of the battlefield. They joined the fighting in wrecked formations and without artillery support (which arrived twenty-four hours later). Nevertheless, their immediate entry into the fray proved to be a decisive factor in stabilizing the line and breaking the Egyptian momentum.

In addition to the deployment of tanks, the Dovecote order contained secondary moves that were not implemented, such as reinforcing the soldiers in the strongholds or replacing them with crack infantry troops; advancing a rear artillery battalion; and reinforcing 252nd Division's artillery forces with 214th Reservist Artillery Group/143rd Division, which was supposed to have mobilized first, to provide fire support and carry out Bendigo (a combined artillery-IAF operation to neutralize the enemy's missile defenses). Also, the forward observers were ordered to pack up and withdraw. Thus, in the chaos of the opening round and the first critical minutes, Israeli observation on the canal was nonexistent. The observers in the strongholds were ordered off the towers, and the APC patrols on the embankment were sent to the rear. Only the long-range surveillance remained, but its capabilities were nugatory.

Failure to execute Dovecote was the responsibility of the chief of staff, the general of Southern Command, and, to a certain degree, the commander of 252nd Division. Because of this failure, the regulars were not deployed according to the plan—two-thirds forward in the canal area and one-third in the rear. Instead, they were deployed the other way around. Furthermore, until the renewal of hostilities at 13:55, the general of Southern Command kept 401st Brigade tied to the rear and forbade the forward force to deploy near the canal.[13]

Elazar's Role

Chief of Staff Elazar's role in the Dovecote fiasco began at the meeting with the generals of the commands on Friday, October 5. The noon discussion was characterized by Elazar's irresolute orders and his overriding view that certain preparatory measures were sufficient because he did not think war would break out. He did not discuss with General Gonen, the head of Southern Command, either the fighting method or the key points of the regulars' deployment on the line until the Rock divisions arrived. They only reviewed the deployment of forces in the rear bases. Had they focused their attention on essentials, and had the chief of staff issued an operational order to execute them on Friday, there would have been no need to convene the generals again the next day.

In fact, Elazar called two meetings the following day—one in the morning and one at noon. It is not clear why the generals had to leave their command areas for a second time for the noon meeting. New instructions, if there were any, could have been conveyed via the standard channels or by telephone. Thus, additional critical hours were wasted; when hostilities resumed, the commander of Northern Command was in flight to the north, and Gonen arrived from Beer Sheva only a few minutes before the war erupted. According to General Tal, "The chief of staff's double summoning of Gonen and Yitzhak Hofi (the commanding general of Northern Command) reflects his insecurity." The deputy chief of staff referred to this as "needless pestering."[14]

Even on Saturday, the chief of staff neglected to check the deployment of forces in the south. The Agranat Commission found that "in the perilous situation created that morning, the chief of staff should have reviewed the details of the force concentrations in the field with the generals of the commands and insisted on the optimal deployment of the forces as soon as he obtained the warning. That would have given the generals enough time to carry out his instructions."[15]

The chief of staff's actions on Saturday morning. Elazar did not deal with defense, the most pressing matter that day. Instead, he was busy convincing the government of the urgency of carrying out a preventive strike, mobilizing the reserves, and issuing orders to the generals of the commands, with an emphasis on the counterattack after blocking the enemy. He later stated that Dovecote was not a critical concern that morning; he had much more demanding issues to deal with. In his opinion, the deployment of forces in Sinai was Southern Command's problem.

The chief of staff should have asked Gonen one simple question: had he deployed the regulars according to plan? Elazar's aide recorded in Saturday's log: "Gonen outlined the plan in detail and the chief of staff issued the following instructions: This evening [October 6]—holding [Dovecote is not mentioned]; October 7—holding and 'Zefania' possible to execute in the evening; October 8—'Ben-Hayil'; October 9—'Desert Cat' [a two-division crossing to the western bank at the conclusion of the counterattack]. 'Bendigo' can be executed in the afternoon of October 7 or 8."[16] An hour and a half before the Egyptians opened fire, Elazar and Gonen were busy with plans for crossing the canal and gave no thought to defense. Bendigo, a key element in the war plans, could not be implemented because it was apparently forgotten, and the artillery order of battle for the operation was unprepared.

Gonen recalled that Elazar asked him, "Is it true, Shmulik, that there's going to be an attack this evening? Must we be prepared to hold?" Gonen answered confidently, "We'll hold!" Elazar then queried, "We'll hold, OK, but what about the counterattack?"[17]

Lieutenant Colonel Avner Shalev, Elazar's aide, testified before the Agranat Commission that it was not the chief of staff's business to get involved in details; he was busy planning for the next day. The general of Southern Command would do what was required of him. "The chief of staff doesn't deploy troops and doesn't tell him which routes to take. That's not his job."[18] Elazar said the same thing when he tried to explain why he failed to ascertain whether Southern Command had deployed according to Dovecote: "Before the war I didn't regard these meetings as an orders group. I was satisfied with the general picture I received from the generals of the commands. I didn't go into the details of how each brigade and battalion was deployed. I didn't think it necessary because the general of a command is the highest authority to deploy a force. . . . In 1967 no one told me how to deploy or capture the Golan Heights. The same in this war. I always examined the overall plans of the command generals but didn't delve into details, not even in later stages."[19]

But on October 6, the chief of staff's focus should have been learning the details of the deployment and checking with the generals of the commands on the timetable and exact method of distributing the thinned-out regular forces for the defense in two sectors. This was not the same as in the Six-Day War, when the IDF had the luxury of a three-week waiting period to reevaluate plans. The chief of staff's line of thinking reflected his disastrous management style, which he repeated several times during the first days of the war.

Failure to warn the generals. The chief of staff erred in not telephoning the generals of the commands on the morning of October 6 and informing them of the "war this evening" message immediately after receiving it at 04:30. If he was convinced that war was imminent, why did he not explicitly order them, either personally or through the General Staff's operations branch, to prepare immediately and deploy according to the plans for all-out war (Dovecote in the south; Chalk in the north)?

On the failure to exploit the small window of opportunity to deploy the regulars' order of battle on the morning of October 6, Dayan admitted that Israel did not take advantage of the time available, no matter how short it was, to prepare the forces on the line. "The reserves could not have been mobilized in twelve hours, but the order of battle could have deployed in its designated positions. I don't take a twelve-hour warning lightly, not a ten-hour, five-hour, or even four-hour one," asserted Dayan. As a strange afterthought that illustrated his naïveté or misunderstanding of the Dovecote fiasco, five months after the war he said, "I'm not criticizing where the vehicles [tanks] were. Perhaps some of them, maybe not all of them, or maybe all of them, were deployed where they should have been. If they were or weren't I can't say."[20]

Elazar's unfamiliarity with Dovecote and miscommunication with Gonen. The Rashomon-like conversation between the chief of staff and Gonen on October 6 has yet to be fully pieced together, but it appears that neither general completely understood the Dovecote order, which rendered their communication a dialogue of the deaf. Elazar was unfamiliar with Southern Command's deployment plan but did not ask for clarification. He believed that Gonen was going to deploy immediately; he did not realize that Gonen had no intention of deploying his tanks (14th Brigade) in their forward positions (fearing the appearance of escalation) and would only allow them to leave the fortifications and move to the daytime parks at 16:00 (the hour had been moved forward from 17:00 because of pressure from Albert, the commander of 252nd Division).

On the miscommunication between Gonen and himself, Elazar claimed that Gonen had told him that morning that one brigade would be deployed in front and two in the rear, with the two rear brigades advanced as the situation dictated. Gonen had not yet worked out the exact details of their advance because he was still traveling, but he would finalize the plan with Albert and then inform Elazar.[21] Based on Gonen's information, Elazar told the defense minister at 11:00: "We'll have three brigades deployed in Sinai. One spread out the length of the canal with tanks at different points to meet any situation. Two concentrated brigades will be on standby for the commander's decision to move out." Elazar added: "When he [Gonen] returned at noon he reported to me on the 'Dovecote' deployment."[22]

Shalev, who was present at the morning meeting, testified that this meeting had nothing to do with Dovecote—it was only about a holding operation. According to Shalev, Elazar approved only the Dovecote deployment. Shalev's impression of Elazar's familiarity with the code names and operational plans is illuminating: "Did Elazar take 'Dovecote' out of the drawer this morning? Of course not! That's absurd. I'm not willing to swear under oath that Elazar remembered in the morning that 'Dovecote' was a defensive plan. Elazar didn't remember code names."[23] Shalev also stated that Elazar thought Gonen's deployment proposal was a good idea: one brigade spread out thinly everywhere, and the other two in the rear on standby for immediate deployment wherever they were needed. Elazar never thought for one moment that anyone would hold back the command's regular deployment. Shalev reconstructed what Elazar had told him on the morning of October 6: "What's happening today is out of my hands. Let's think one step ahead. I'm the only person in this mess who's trying to think ahead a day or two and put the war in a framework."[24]

This, of course, was correct. But it did not absolve the chief of staff from ascertaining that things were proceeding as planned. His attitude was absurd. How was it possible to approve both the Dovecote two-in-front deployment and the deployment of one brigade in front at the same time? With a stretch of the imagination, one could say that the chief of staff, who was not familiar with the details of the plan in the south, related to it in concrete, tactical terms— "one in front," "fists" (concentrated brigades), and "holding"—and not in the division's terms (and that Shalev was trying, retrospectively, to put Elazar's thinking in a positive light).

To summarize the Elazar-Gonen meeting: one tank brigade (the 14th) would be dispersed along the canal, and two additional brigades (the 401st and 460th) would be concentrated in the rear. This was the one-in-front deployment that Gonen was supposed to verify with Albert and update Elazar on afterwards, before determining when to execute Dovecote. From this point on, opinion is divided as to whether the deployment was supposed to be carried out immediately or later according to Dovecote. Gonen contended that the chief of staff gave him permission to carry out the Assyria 2 order—that is, one in front.[25]

As noted earlier, Elazar informed the defense minister: "We'll have three brigades [in the south]. One deployed the entire length of the canal with a few tanks in various points capable of responding to developments, and two brigades concentrated towards the west, according to the commander's situation assessment."[26] It appears that Elazar did not know that Dovecote meant two in front. If he was aware of it and unilaterally reversed the two-in-front deployment at a critical moment without informing anyone, that would be very serious. And if he stuck with GSO's Assyria 2 order—one in front—even though the forces in the south had been drilled in the emergency deployment according to Dovecote's two-in-front plan, that would be no less serious.

The fact is that when hostilities erupted, the forces in Sinai remained where they were. Although Dovecote was specifically a two-in-front deployment, Elazar and Gonen beat around the bush and made meandering statements, as neither of them was acquainted with the details of Dovecote. In general, the chief of staff's interpretation of his misunderstanding with Gonen arouses an uncomfortable sense of whitewashing, irrespective of Elazar's opinion that it was not his role to deal with details. Elazar was also hard-pressed to explain whether, at the morning and noon meetings, he meant that Southern Command would execute Dovecote or that it would be on standby to execute Dovecote, perhaps after dark. The chief of staff's cumbersome style of command was a major problem and not only on October 6, when clear and distinct orders—not sophistry—were needed.

Elazar's explanations. When the IDF History Department questioned why the chief of staff met with Gonen twice on Saturday, in the morning and at noon, his answer was that Gonen had been unprepared in the morning. "I didn't finalize with the general of Southern Command that morning his method of deployment. He said that he'd talk with Albert . . . and I knew that he'd deploy in the best way possible and that I'd be hearing from him."[27] Sadly, this is hogwash. What exactly does "the best way possible" mean? Elazar insisted that by noon, he was aware that Southern Command would be deployed in Dovecote. The Agranat Commission's report harshly criticized his vacuous testimony on the two meetings with Gonen: "What did you have to sum up with the general of the command that morning? If there was a plan, you should have told him to proceed according to 'Dovecote,' which meant holding [the line] as best as possible. Why did he have to come to you if at this stage he told you that he was still with one brigade in front, which is what you reported to the defense minister at 11:00? The best possible holding from a 'one in front' situation, according to the GHQ and Southern Command plan, was two brigades in front. What was there to sum up?"[28]

"In reality," Elazar replied, "plans change and have to be examined as the situation develops." The Agranat Commission pursued its questioning, reminding him that Southern Command had carried out a review of orders on Friday, and asked, "Why didn't Gonen come with a prepared proposal?" Elazar answered, "I still didn't know exactly when the war would break out. On Friday this deployment seemed good. Proof of this is that I recommended it to the defense minister on Saturday. In other words, this deployment offered maximum flexibility. But on Saturday noon, when we finished preparing for the renewal of fire we agreed on the two in front deployment."[29]

At 04:30 on Saturday, Elazar already knew that war was about to break out; therefore, his praise of one in front on Friday (before he knew that war was imminent) was already outdated when he presented it to Dayan at 11:00 on Saturday. Furthermore, Gonen mentioned Dovecote but said nothing about one in front. Elazar failed to explain the difference in employing the regulars on Friday and Saturday and what had to change. His answer—"now we knew that war was about to erupt, and we could come up with ideas"—does not hold water.[30]

Unlike the banal discussions with the general of Southern Command, the chief of staff delved into details with the general of Northern Command, such as specific orders for reinforcing the strongholds on the Golan Heights. When asked why he had not done the same in Southern Command, his astonishing reply was: "Southern Command didn't receive such an order because I remembered that the strongholds were stronger [on the canal]. Here [the Golan Heights] the strongholds were manned by twelve men or less; that's why I ordered their reinforcement."[31] Obviously, the chief of staff was knowledgeable about what was happening in the north, but he apparently found it difficult to admit that he was not familiar with the situation in the south and ask Gonen for details. Elazar did not order the general of Southern Command to deploy in Dovecote—the only plan that had been approved and drilled for such a situation—and he did not even clarify the timetable with him. The timetable was a critical issue, since it was foolish to rely on the warning that the attack would begin precisely at sunset. The chief of staff should have taken into account that the attack (from the air, at least) might begin in broad daylight.

The disconnect between Elazar and Gonen on the deployment of Dovecote was evident in the operational discussion group at 18:35 on Saturday, after the Egyptian attack had begun. "We're well deployed for the first stage," Elazar stated. "One brigade is very thinly spread out with two concentrated fists. But now I don't like it. If he had 300 tanks we could form four brigade-size combat teams. This can still be done tonight."[32] By his own admission, the chief of staff obviously knew the war would begin with a one-in-front deployment, even though he and Gonen had agreed on Dovecote's two-in-front deployment at noon. How could he say "we're prepared . . . as required" if 401st Brigade was still in transit and 14th Brigade was slugging it out alone, unless he had given Gonen permission to retain the one-in-front deployment—one that was well suited for the shift to Zefania (an operation that both men were keen to implement)? And if this deployment was so good, why change it at noon?

The chief of staff explained that he did not intend for the concentrated brigades (two fists) to be eighty kilometers away in the rear base camps; he expected them to concentrate closer to the canal at a distance that enabled the general of the command to send them into battle as events developed. But two fists in the rear was not the Dovecote plan that he had given Gonen permission to carry out at noon. And if it was such an optimal deployment, why did he not confirm its implementation with Gonen at the morning or noon meeting? Apparently, when the Egyptians opened fire, Elazar was unaware that the two fists were still in the rear. Since he did not ask Gonen, he did not know the timetable for advancing 401st Brigade. In the GHQ meeting after the war, Elazar had this to say about Dovecote: "In the beginning of the war there were two unfortunate phenomena . . . one was 'Dovecote' and the other Southern Command's first night. . . . I know where the short-circuit lay. It was in not implementing 'Dovecote.' In GHQ, the general of the command and I thought on Saturday that we're going prepared into 'Dovecote.' I know that somewhere along the line 'Dovecote' became 'Little Dovecote,' and until 16:00 'Dovecote' was not executed."[33]

This was an astounding revelation. The source of the short-circuit can be traced directly to the Saturday discussions between the chief of staff and the general of Southern Command and to the fact that Elazar was ignorant of the Dovecote order. In the summary of Southern Command's actions in the war, the chief of staff admitted that he was unfamiliar with the distinction between Little Dovecote and Large Dovecote. He also said that although it was not the best deployment, "this is what we had at the time." In 1976, two and a half years after the war, he squirmed in his chair as he tried to explain the Dovecote fiasco:

The brigades had to move forward during the day, I mean that the two brigades had to remain in the rear where they could deploy according to "Dovecote." But since they were moving in concentrated formation prepared to be sent into battle, this provided the commander with flexibility in their application. I'm not describing operative planning. The fact that we were caught with two concentrated brigades in the rear and far from the canal was not the result of anyone's planning but the result of the enemy attacking at 14:00. That's what caught these brigades at the start of their movement, and later they were advancing to the canal, engaged in combat, and not traveling to the canal for preplanned deployment.[34]

Confusion and ignorance of the facts. The rear brigades received no order to set out from their permanent bases. Only after 401st Brigade was bombed there did they begin to advance. By Elazar's own admission, he did not determine the brigades' location (although the plan specifically designated it), but he believed they had to move forward. Elazar did not distinguish (as he should have) between 401st Brigade, which had to participate in Dovecote in the southern sector and take an active part in the initial fighting, and 460th Brigade, which was being held in reserve for the decisive battle whenever the division decided to call it in. (To gain time, it should have been advanced earlier to Lateral Road.)

Adding to the confusion was the Assyria 2 order issued by the GSO on Friday evening for a one-in-front deployment. The answer to the question of whether Elazar and Gonen agreed to change the deployment from one in front (Assyria 2) to two in front (Dovecote) at their noon meeting remains elusive. Both officers testified before the Agranat Commission that at the conclusion of the meeting at 12:20, they agreed on Dovecote. The records do not mention what that entailed. However, the fact is that the brigades stayed in the rear. According to Elazar, he believed they would move out and advance once the enemy's efforts had been identified.[35]

Elazar stated that, at the end of his second conversation with Gonen, he understood that Southern Command was prepared to implement Dovecote. He did not discuss the timetables for the various units; he assumed that they were moving and that everything would be ready by H hour. He emphasized that in his discussions with Gonen, he realized that the next hours were out of his control. The orders had been issued, and the brigade commanders were on the move. This was Elazar's style. He dealt with things on a grand scale without going into the minutiae, without asking questions, without studying matters independently, and without drawing his own conclusions. In his testimony before the IDF History Depart-

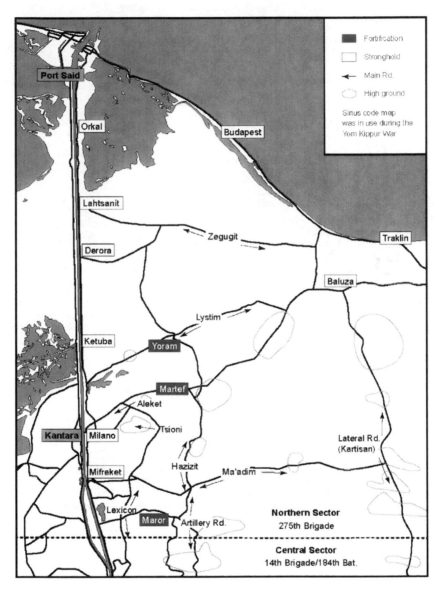

Map 1. "Sirius" control code map—northern sector.

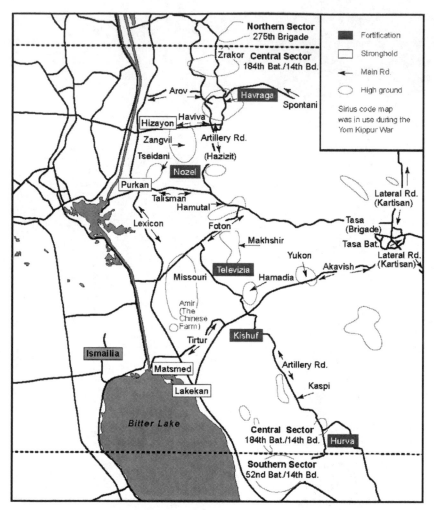

Map 2. "Sirius" control code map—central sector.

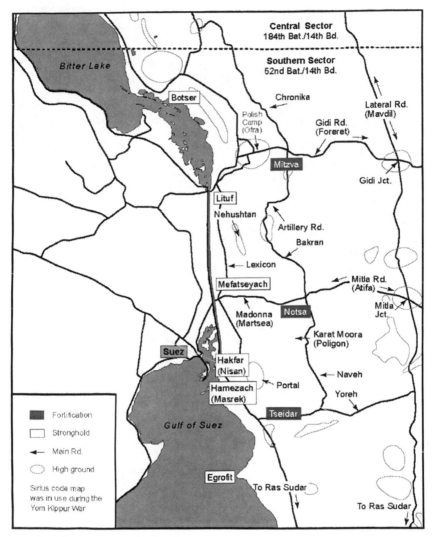

Map 3. "Sirius" control code map—southern sector.

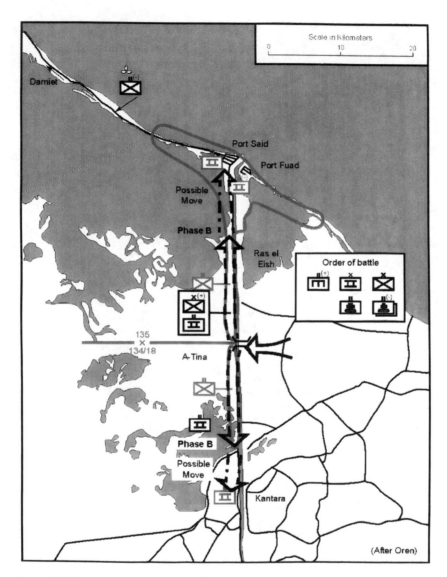

Map 4. Zefania: plan for canal crossing in the northern sector.

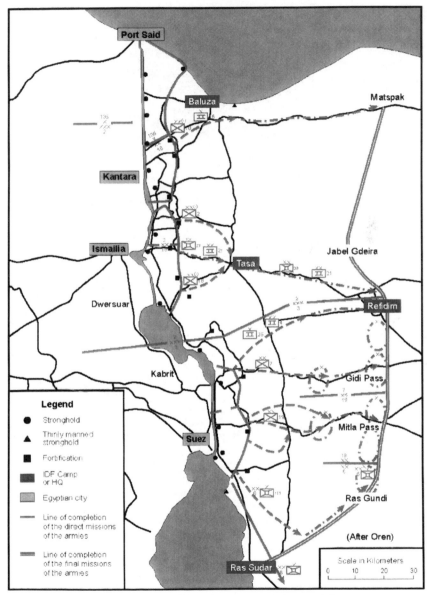

Map 5. Egyptian attack plan and final mission: Refidim and the mountain passes.

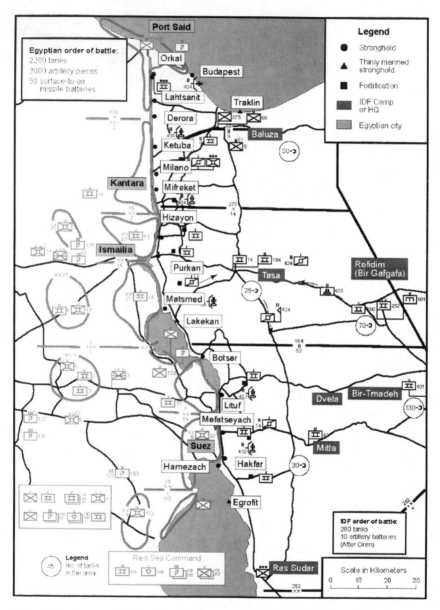

Map 6. Deployment of the Egyptian army and the IDF, 14:00 on October 6.

Course of battle:

0615 – Egyptian tanks start crossing.

0710 – A. Bat. at Km. 137 suffers 90% losses and retreats. B. Bat. crosses at Km.141 and suffers 60% losses. A. and C. Cos. from the 46th Bat. lose 7 tanks. B. Co. from the 52nd Bat. loses 4 tanks.

0715 – Divisional Tank Bat. crosses at Km.137.

0720 – B. Bat. retreats at Km.141, suffering 75% losses.
A. and C. Cos. from the 46th Bat. engage the Divisional Bat., which loses 6 tanks. Sagger missiles on the ramp are destroyed by artillery.

0725 – C. Bat. crosses at Km. 141.

0830 – The Divisional Bat. is destroyed at Km.137. At Km.141 Egyptian C. Bat. loses 50% of its tanks. B. Co. from the 52nd remains with 4 tanks.

0915 – Egyptian C. Bat. with the remains of B. Bat. is destroyed at Km.141.

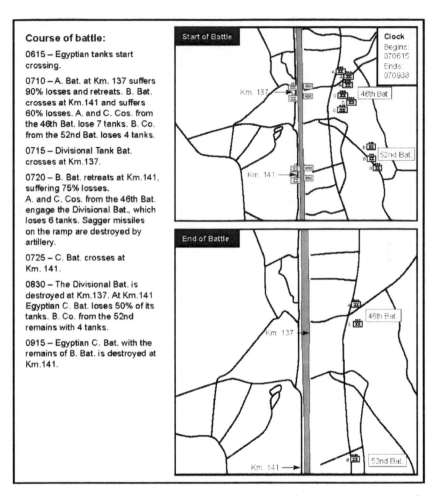

Map 7. Virtual scenario of tank operations in the southern sector, morning of October 7.

Course of battle:

0615 – Egyptian tank battalions start crossing the bridges.

0710 – A. Bat. loses 80% of its tanks and starts a retreat on Tuson bridge. In each of A. & B. Cos. in the 79th Bat., 3 tanks are damaged. B. Bat. loses 75% of its tanks on the Sarafeum bridge and starts retreating. Sagger missiles on Sarafeum ramps are destroyed by IDF artillery.

0740 – Divisional Tank Bat. starts crossing on Tuson bridge. D. Tank Bat. starts crossing on Sarafeum bridge.

0745 – A. & B. Cos. from the 79th Bat. start engaging the Divisional Bat. on Tuson bridge and C. Co. engages the D. Tank Bat. on Sarafeum bridge.

0815 – The Divisional Tank Bat. loses 50% of its tanks. Each of A. & B. Cos. loses 3 more tanks. D. Tank Bat. on Sarafeum bridge loses 50% of its tanks. C. Co. that engaged D. Bat. loses 60% of its tanks.

0840 – The remaining 4 tanks of the Divisional Bat. retreat on Tuson bridge. C. Co. of the 79th Bat. is totally destroyed opposite Sarafeum. D. Tank Bat. crosses on Sarafeum bridge with 4 tanks.

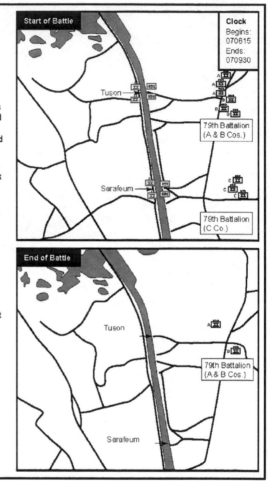

Map 8. Virtual scenario of tank operations in the central sector, morning of October 7.

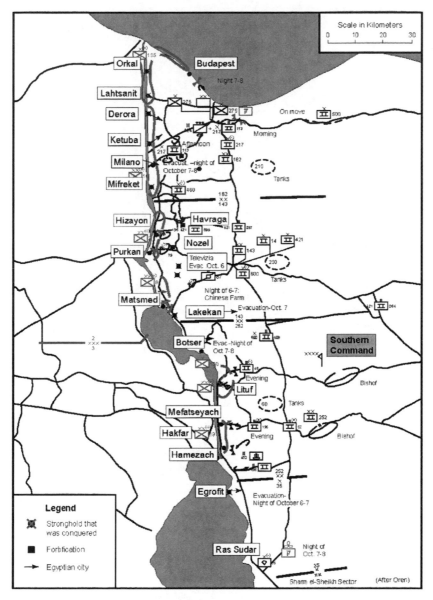

Map 9. The situation along the canal, evening of October 7.

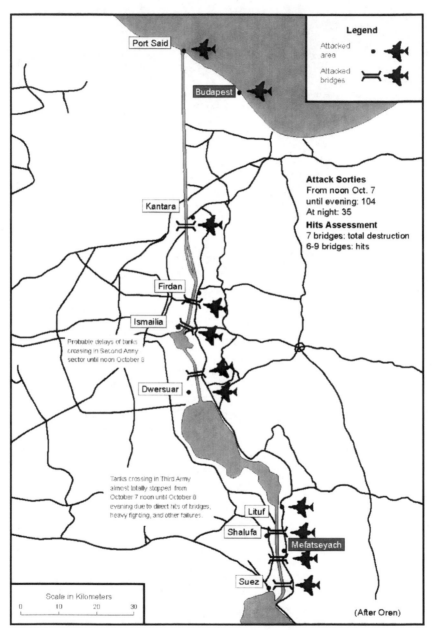

Legend

Attacked area

Attacked bridges

Port Said

Budapest

Kantara

Attack Sorties
From noon Oct. 7
until evening: 104
At night: 35

Hits Assessment
7 bridges: total destruction
6-9 bridges: hits

Firdan

Ismailia

Probable delays of tanks
crossing in Second Army
sector until noon October 8

Dwersuar

Tanks crossing in Third Army
almost totally stopped from
October 7 noon until October 8
evening due to direct hits of bridges,
heavy fighting, and other failures.

Lituf

Shalufa

Mefatseyach

Suez

Scale in Kilometers

0   10   20   30

(After Oren)

Map 10. IAF attacks the bridges on the canal, October 7.

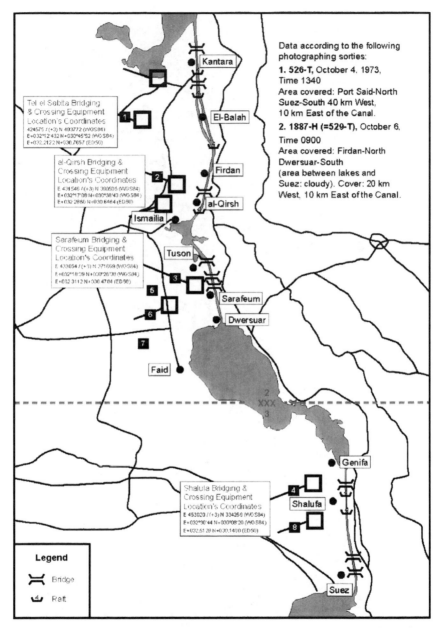

Map 11. Deployment of Egyptian bridging and crossing equipment along the canal, October 4–6, 1973.

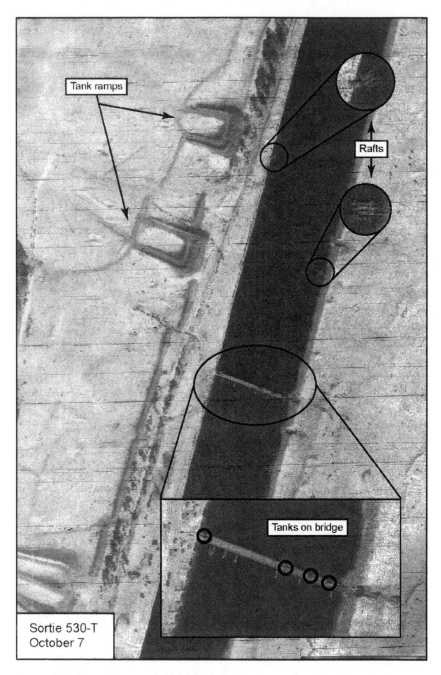

Figure 1. Egyptian forces crossing into Sinai on a unifloat bridge in Sarafeum, sector of 16th Infantry Division.

Infantry Division No. 2 Sector
Sortie 21, October 12

Figure 2. Unifloat bridge and two surface-to-air missile batteries north of Firdan.

A convoy near the bridge, south of Shalufa, October 7, 1973

Figure 3. The "funnels."

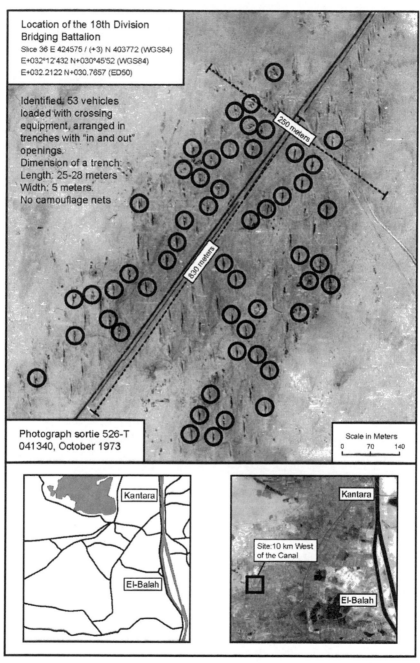

Location of the 18th Division
Bridging Battalion
Slice 36 E 424575 / (+3) N 403772 (WGS84)
E+032°12'432 N+030°45'52 (WGS84)
E+032.2122 N+030.7657 (ED50)

Identified: 53 vehicles
loaded with crossing
equipment, arranged in
trenches with "in and out"
openings.
Dimension of a trench:
Length: 25-28 meters
Width: 5 meters.
No camouflage nets

250 meters

830 meters

Photograph sortie 526-T
041340, October 1973

Scale in Meters
0   70   140

Kantara

El-Balah

Kantara

Site:10 km West
of the Canal

El-Balah

Figure 4. Concentration of bridging and crossing equipment of 18th Infantry
Division.

ment, he made it clear that his conversation with Gonen, which lasted until 13:10, revolved around plans for the post-holding stage. "As the chief of staff, I have to think what we'll be doing the day after. Gonen didn't raise any problems that required my attention."[36]

Gonen's Role

Regarding the Rashomon scenario on Saturday noon, Gonen's memory was sketchy. He testified that he could not remember if he informed the chief of staff of the changes he and Albert had agreed on for the Dovecote deployment at 16:00, he could not recall if the chief of staff asked him about the timing of the deployment, and he was not sure if he updated the chief of staff on the situation. But he did remember that they discussed an attack and Elazar said: "'Today is the acid test. Let's check the timetable for offensive operations.' During the noon meeting we decided to execute 'Dovecote.'"[37]

Based on Gonen's statements, at 10:00 he ordered 252nd Division to execute Dovecote by 17:00 (as noted earlier, at Albert's urging, the time was moved up to 16:00, so the order became "stand by for execution"). In Gonen's opinion, Dovecote was not a good plan, but he approved it because his troops had trained for it, and they were unfamiliar with the one-in-front plan that he and the chief of staff preferred. Gonen did not update the chief of staff on the 252nd's change in timetable.

Like Elazar, Gonen was unversed in the details of Dovecote. His testimony before the Agranat Commission was inconsistent on a number of key points (tank deployment on the line, reinforcements, the tanks' timetable for exiting the fortifications, and so forth).

The 252nd's failure to deploy on time. There is no single reason for this critical failure. One possible explanation is Gonen's fear of escalation and his expectation that the Egyptians would renew hostilities at 18:00. Also, he may have wanted to preserve the option of carrying out Zefania (discussed later) and breaking through to the west. As he told the IDF History Department, he believed the 252nd would be deployed at 18:00 at the latest. He ordered the shift to the Dovecote standby based on his morning conversation. He telephoned Southern Command's G-3 and issued those instructions but warned him not to let the Egyptians observe this movement, in order to avoid premature discovery or provocation.

At the IDF senior staff meeting in February 1974, Gonen claimed that neither he nor the GSO were aware of 252nd Division's terminology that differentiated between Little Dovecote and Large Dovecote. (For all practical purposes, this distinction was irrelevant.) In Southern Command's summary meeting on the war, Gonen stated that he switched to Dovecote and decided to move 460th Brigade from the rear to Pudriya (code name for the area east of Tasa); he gave the order to the division commander, but he did not say whether he updated the chief of staff. According to Gonen, nothing had been decided in his noon meeting with Elazar regarding the Dovecote deployment: "I informed him that I intended to implement 'Dovecote' toward evening."[38] The team from the IDF History Department read what the chief of staff's aide had written in the log: "The chief of staff talked about holding. The general of the command reported on the situation." Gonen replied, "I don't remember."[39]

The catastrophic delay in the tanks' deployment on the line and 401st Brigade's advance to the southern sector was the direct result of Gonen's decision (for which he took sole responsibility). He explained that he feared the forces' early forward movement would provoke the Egyptians and escalate the situation, leading to a war the Egyptians did not intend. The source of Gonen's restricting order is not clear; nor is it clear why the general of the command assumed responsibility for such a crucial decision.

The decision makers were aware of the danger of unintentional escalation resulting from the movement of Israeli forces. According to an MI collection (labeled "Superpowers"), the Americans were "likely to assume that a situation of uncontrolled military deterioration could develop in the Middle East. In this case the Americans would probably see the increased likelihood that Israel initiates preventative activity."[40] The defense minister, too, referred to this point when he vetoed the request to mobilize the reservists on Saturday, but this was the responsibility of the government, not the general of Southern Command. Since it is unlikely that Gonen read this intelligence collection, its contents would not have influenced his decision to delay deployment.

At 06:50 Saturday morning, the head of MI had a "hallway conversation" with the generals who were waiting to meet with the chief of staff. He reiterated his belief that war would not break out but noted that moving the Israeli forces forward could ignite hostilities. Perhaps this is what Gonen understood. It is absolutely certain that neither the government nor the chief of staff issued instructions not to advance forces before a certain hour. Nevertheless, Gonen claimed that at 07:15 he received an explicit order from the chief of staff not to deploy forces before 17:00, lest it exacerbate the situation. But during the GHQ operational discussion group, it was stated that the forces were supposed to be deployed by 17:15.[41]

At both the morning and the noon meetings, Gonen refrained from apprising the chief of staff of his fear that advancing the forces could lead to an escalation in the situation. Elazar assumed that such a conversation had taken place on Saturday morning between Gonen and Albert and that the two generals had agreed on a timetable that the chief of staff was not privy to. By making the decision on his own, and without the prescribed deployment of the armored force according to Dovecote, Gonen committed a grievous error and failed to rectify it with the forces available to him, which could have broken the enemy attack.

After his first meeting with the chief of staff, Gonen telephoned the commander of 252nd Division, presumably at 07:20, and discussed the Dovecote standby. He advised Albert to prepare the forces as required but, in the same breath, warned him (and also notified Southern Command headquarters) not to expose the activity to the enemy. Gonen had a similar conversation with Albert at roughly 08:50 (while the 252nd's commander was in the midst of a divisional orders group). Neither conversation was recorded. The generals discussed the Dovecote standby and emphasized that movement and tank concentrations must not be revealed too early, lest the Egyptians attack them with planes and artillery. Gonen used the phrase "to execute Dovecote," but for all practical purposes he was referring to a "standby for execution." He later stated that if the line had been taken only one hour before 18:00, the anticipated H hour, the Egyptians would have had difficulty changing their master plan at such short notice. He approved Albert's request that afternoon and moved the time up to 16:00. Gonen testified that the idea to deploy at 17:00 was Southern Command's—definitely not the chief of staff's.[42]

The word *escalation* hovered in the air on Saturday morning and also came up at noon in 14th Brigade's orders group at Tasa. When the commander of 52nd Battalion, who was responsible for the southern sector, asked whether 401st Brigade was moving toward his sector—the brigade officers knew that, according to the Dovecote deployment, the 401st was supposed to reinforce the southern sector—the commander of 14th Brigade, Colonel Amnon Reshef, replied, "Negative." There was considerable concern over a possible escalation if the Egyptians observed columns of dust rising from the tanks as they moved west; therefore, 401st Brigade remained in its rearward camps.

Colonel Hagai Golan (Ret.), the G-3 in 275th Territorial Command, recalled the incongruence between the general alert and preparations on the ground: "The highest level forced us to avoid escalation."[43] During Saturday morning's orders group, Colonel Dan Shomron, commander of 401st Brigade, asked the division commander why he wasn't advancing the forces if H hour was known. The answer: if the Egyptians observed the movement of a tank brigade, it might precipitate a flare-up. Gonen hoped that by delaying the movement of forces until dusk, he could prevent the deterioration he so feared.

The contradictions in Gonen's claims defy comprehension. If he and Albert agreed in the morning to deploy at 16:00, why was 401st Brigade not ordered to move out until 14:45, forty-five minutes after its camps had been bombed? (Even a later deployment at 17:00 would have required leaving the rear bases between 12:00 and 13:00.)

On Saturday morning, MI foresaw two scenarios if the rear brigades' movement was observed: H hour would remain the same, or it would be advanced. Gonen may have believed that war was still unconfirmed and that the front was liable to deteriorate if the forces advanced. He reaffirmed that the decision was his. When General Adan noted that "a modest deployment could have been carried out before 17:00," Gonen replied, "I was given the hour 17:00 as a fact and ordered the units to deploy proximate to 17:00, that is, to set out with the rear brigade to the strongholds around 14:00. The war began at 14:05. This is what happened."[44]

In his testimony before the IDF History Department on February 17, 1976, Elazar stated, "Gonen and Albert determined the timetable for deployment. This I learned only after the war. It went against my morning and noon instructions to Gonen that deployment for war had to be executed immediately without a time limit."[45] Elazar's justifiable denial that the fear of escalation came from a GHQ order reveals his problematic method of command. If the chief of staff thought immediate deployment was necessary, he should have ordered Gonen to do so. And it was his duty to check with Gonen at noon (or earlier) to ascertain that the order had been carried out.

The surfeit of orders on Saturday (see below), some of which were contradictory, testifies to the uncertainty that filtered down from Southern Command to 252nd Division, and from the division to the units, regarding whether to carry out Dovecote according to plans. H hour was scheduled for 18:00, but the division was not sure what H hour meant, and the battalions were totally in the dark. Given the precarious situation and the warning of imminent war in the evening, the rear brigade had to move out at noon in order to deploy by 17:00, but Gonen gave an evasive answer about the rear brigade's schedule to egress: "We didn't exactly finalize when it would move, sometime between 13:00 and 13:30."[46]

In a command communiqué to division (registered in command headquarters' log at 10:30 but not sent until 13:30), there was no order to enter standby immediately. Gonen was unable to deliver a convincing reason why the communiqué did not order Dovecote deployment at 16:00 or 17:00. "The order undoubtedly referred to full [Large] 'Dovecote' but it was a general order to be implemented sometime in the future . . . standby for entry without a specific hour. . . . There was no order to carry out 'Dovecote.'"[47] Also, the commander of 401st Brigade and others testified that they received no order at noon to execute Dovecote immediately (in division terminology, Little Dovecote did not refer to the rear brigades). The 401st's commander said that his brigade would have needed six hours if it was to deploy on the line by 16:00. Allocating only three hours for the task, he stressed, was irresponsible because it was impossible.

The commander of 252nd Division was eager to move forward, but Gonen refused permission. The division surely understood the command's orders: "Do not deploy on the front line. Rear brigades to deploy in the rear."[48]

The source of the fatal turn of events was the decision not to deploy the forward brigade in the morning, as soon as the chief of staff received word of "war this evening," and not to move up the rear brigade immediately, so it would be deployed in the southern sector between 10:00 and 11:00. Waiting until 17:00 or 18:00 was disastrous. Gonen agreed: "It would have changed everything. If I hadn't received the hour, I would have moved out immediately."[49] He repeatedly stressed (justifiably, it seems) that he was ordered not to deploy before 17:15, based on conversations in the GHQ operations discussion group that day. As for blunders, Gonen confessed, "I got things wrong twice. Between Friday and Saturday I believed that war wouldn't break out; and later, that it would commence at six on Saturday."[50]

After the publication of the Agranat Commission's first report, Gonen told the commission that he had consulted with Albert, and both of them had come to the same conclusion: another tank brigade (apparently the 460th) did not have to be advanced immediately because movement from the rear to the assembly areas for a counterattack on the forward line would take two and a half hours, and the time needed to prepare for an imminent war, given the spatial conditions of Sinai, was irrelevant (no document exists to verify this conversation). The 252nd's G-3 challenged the veracity of this explanation, claiming that if Albert had been allowed to operate independently, he would have moved the forces out immediately. This seems plausible, given Albert's request that the brigade's timetable be pushed forward from 17:00 to 16:00.

Distrust of the Dovecote plan may have been another factor in Gonen's decision to delay deployment. He admitted that the plan's idea was sound but that the ground was unprepared: the strongholds had been reduced to half or a quarter of the original Bar-Lev Line, the embankment was of dubious efficacy, and, most important, the tank positions were dominated by the Egyptian ramps. He acknowledged that "somewhere he had an aversion to 'Dovecote.'"[51] Gonen stated, "I was full partner to the decision to have one brigade in front and two in the rear. I proposed it. Write this down verbatim: I suggested [to the chief of staff] that instead of 'Dovecote' we have one brigade deployed in front and two concentrated in the rear. That's the truth. I didn't like the 'Dovecote' plan because it lacked a main effort and because of the ground infrastructure. It wasn't for defense. There was nowhere to put the tanks."[52]

But after his first meeting with the chief of staff, Gonen reassessed the situation. Even though he received permission that morning to remain in the Assyria 2 formation (with two brigades in the rear camps), and even though he preferred the Assyria 2 deployment because it allowed two brigades to be concentrated for a divisional attack on one point, he decided to shift to Dovecote.[53] At 08:50 he spoke with the division commander, and they agreed on the Dovecote deployment "because this was what the forces were familiar with."[54] It had been a rash decision on the part of Elazar and Gonen to reverse Dovecote on such a critical day, under such time pressure, and without updating the units of the change, since, despite its drawbacks, it was the only plan the forces in the field had been drilled in.

The Zefania option. Gonen's wish to preserve the Zefania option was expressed in his instructions to Albert and the division commanders on Saturday, after the Egyptian attack had commenced. His interest in Zefania seems to have been another reason for his delay in sending 401st Brigade—which was designated to carry out Zefania—to the line. The one-in-front deployment of Assyria 2 suited the implementation of Zefania (until the situation on the line rendered Zefania a pipe dream).

Gonen's apprehension over possible escalation may have been part of his keen desire to retain the crossing option. The fog surrounding his statements to the chief of staff during their second meeting on Saturday—that he would implement Dovecote even though, in practice, he remained with one in front—may be explained by his wish to preserve this option, at least until the Egyptians renewed hostilities.

His conversation with Albert at 14:03 on Saturday has entered the folklore of the war. Gonen said, "Albert, I think we have to move the brigades." And Albert, who was inspecting tactical headquarters' APCs in the parks, expressed his frustration with the whole saga of Southern Command's orders and the restrictions that impeded 252nd Division when he answered: "Of course we have to move them! They're bombing Refidim!"[55]

Albert's Role

The commander of 252nd Division, General Albert, deserves a share of the blame for the Dovecote fiasco. Known as an overzealous disciplinarian, he had the authority to take the steps necessary to improve the opening situation, but he avoided doing so. Unlike others, he was convinced that war would break out. Nevertheless, he refrained from crossing swords with Gonen on moving 14th Brigade to seal the gap between the Purkan and Matsmed strongholds. He kept the artillery where it was rather than advancing it. He even insisted on pulling back 9th Battalion's tanks, which the commander of 275th Brigade had ordered forward at 13:30.

The deputy division commander stated that on Saturday morning, after the divisional orders group, he implored Albert: "'Let me move the forces from Bir-Tmada. [You can say that] you knew nothing about it, I'll take full responsibility.' The commander of the 275th Brigade agreed. The others remained silent."[56] The division commander threatened to dismiss his deputy and told him in no uncertain terms that Gonen and Elazar absolutely forbade the movement of forces. Even after this dressing down, the deputy commander continued to exhort Albert, trying to convince him that the situation justified advancing the forces, but the answer remained unequivocal: leave the troops under the camouflage nets and avoid escalation. Albert lacked the mettle to override Southern Command's instructions and move 401st Brigade.

The Role of Shoddy GHQ Staff Work

In the hours preceding the outbreak of hostilities, the GHQ did poor work, and the chief of staff neglected to order the GSO to ensure that his instructions had been translated into explicit operational orders. In the briefings to the generals of the commands that day, staff officers and GSO representatives were absent; only aides were present. Elazar recalled that everyone was "running around like crazy."[57] Nevertheless, it is inexcusable that the chief of staff failed to circulate an operational order (to those who needed to know) covering the main points of his instructions to the generals of the commands. The head of the operations department testified that "no GHQ order for executing 'Dovecote' was issued that day, not by this name [Dovecote] or any other."[58]

The deputy chief of staff was busy mobilizing the army, and the head of the operations department was preparing the "Pit" (the GHQ bunker command post in Hakirya in central Tel Aviv—the IDF's main base) for war. It is still not clear why the head of operations was dealing with maps instead of standing by the chief of staff's side. No less serious, it remains a mystery why the Pit had not been prepared on Friday at the latest, as it should have been during a C-level alert.

General Israel Tal, the deputy chief of staff, was asked several times (by the Agranat Commission and the IDF History Department) about the misunderstandings and disagreements (real or imagined) between Elazar and Gonen, between the chief of staff and

Southern Command, and between the operations branch's Assyria 2 order issued at 22:00 on Friday and Southern Command's Dovecote order. Unfortunately, Tal's explanations do little to clear up the muddle, and on some points, they even add to the confusion surrounding the orders on that fateful day. Research on the war has been only partially successful in getting to the root of the disparity between Assyria 2 and Dovecote on Saturday, October 6.

Tal pointed out that during the 11:00 operational discussion group with the defense minister, "the chief of staff presented two brigades to the rear and one in front in accordance with 'Assyria 2.' The question is not whether this was the right move and who was responsible for it. . . . It was enough that the chief of staff presented it to the defense minister at 11:00 to remove responsibility from Gorodish [Gonen]."[59] Tal thought Elazar unconvincingly "jiggled" the facts in his postwar testimony on deployment in Sinai. Tal wisely noted that "if [Elazar] had told Gorodish [in their 12:00 meeting] to move two brigades, he would have informed us. After all, this was two-thirds of the armor force in Sinai."[60] In other words, if Elazar changed the existing order—Assyria 2—at 12:00, it was the result of one of the following (none of which puts the system in a flattering light):

1. The chief of staff had no clue whether Dovecote was two in front or one in front.
2. The chief of staff proceeded according to Assyria 2 (one in front), in complete contradiction of Dovecote (two in front).
3. The chief of staff was certain that this was a temporary situation; therefore, the staff did not have to be updated on the change in Assyria 2.
4. The chief of staff thought Dovecote was one in front, in which case staff approval was not required.
5. The chief of staff knew his order deviated from Assyria 2 but neglected to inform the staff (the GSO representative was absent during Elazar's meeting with Gonen).

Tal added to the confusion when he said that the whole Dovecote deployment mess on Saturday was directly attributable to Gonen. "I was involved in this whole affair. It is the GHQ who decided on that deployment. It did not decide on this deployment [Assyria 2 one-in-front] on Friday in order to change it on Saturday. It was GHQ's operative concept that two armored brigades remain in the rear and one would be brought forward. It was the opposite of 'Dovecote.' . . . This was the chief of staff's call."[61] In other words, if we accept Tal's explanation, Elazar wanted to retain Assyria 2 and organize the forces one in front, but Gonen, on his own initiative and against GHQ's position, reversed the deployment.

Tal's statements contained a number of inconsistencies. He referred to two divisions in the rear that were expected to arrive, according to the Rock plan, after forty-eight hours at the earliest. This meant that the regulars would be deployed alone for at least forty-eight hours, but for the plan to succeed, the brigades had to be deployed two in front. At any rate, Assyria 2 was a GHQ order for one in front, whereas Dovecote was Southern Command's and 252nd Division's order for two in front. The 252nd Division, for its part, knew only of Dovecote's two-in-front deployment. All the ambiguity, misunderstanding, and deviations in the GHQ and Southern Command staff work on the deployment of the regulars in Sinai culminated in a resounding failure during the supreme test of performance on Yom Kippur.

Tal contradicted himself on this issue on more than one occasion. For example, in his testimony before the Agranat Commission, he stated that Gonen's main error was in keeping two-thirds of the force in the rear, but before the IDF History Department, he avowed that Assyria 2 was the correct and necessary move—that is, one in front. "My 'Assyria'—that of the GSO—envisioned two brigades in the rear. At the operations discussion group with the defense minister, they presented this as a clever plan with an ideological basis and everyone thrust it on Gorodish [Gonen]. . . . I state in unequivocal terms that we saw the ideology for waging this war, this battle, in the retention of two brigades in the rear, in the Refidim and Gidi area, to be used as developments warranted. I claim that this was the chief of staff's policy."[62] In other words, the deputy chief of staff admitted that Assyria 2—not Dovecote—was the plan on which the defense of Sinai had been based. This was also the plan that Chief of Staff Elazar presented to Defense Minister Dayan on Saturday at 11:00. To bolster his argument, Tal repeated their dialogue:

DAYAN: Are the tanks advancing towards the canal or are we waiting for the bridges to be assembled?
ELAZAR: We'll have three brigades. One dispersed along

the canal and the other two concentrated in the rear and
prepared to move when the bridges are spotted.

DAYAN: Even at night?

ELAZAR: Immediately when the attack begins [at night].

DAYAN: If the commander thinks he knows where to send the
tanks, will he dispatch them?

ELAZAR: Yes! He'll send the tanks.[63]

With regard to Elazar's testimony to the IDF History Department (February 27, 1976), Tal refuted what the chief of staff said.
According to Elazar, the two rear brigades had been ready to enter
the battle according to the commander's decision, and they were
supposed to move during the day in accordance with Dovecote.
"That's wrong!" Tal exclaimed:

> According to "Dovecote" only one brigade [the 401st] had
> to go out. . . . If Elazar said that the criterion was "Dovecote"
> then he himself admitted that one brigade had to remain
> in either Gidi or Refidim, therefore everything that he said
> about this in 1976—is wisdom in retrospect. It's manipula-
> tion for future reference. The "Assyria" order and its presen-
> tation to the defense minister at 11:00 is what counted most.
> He [Elazar] didn't say a word about moving them [the bri-
> gades]. . . . He said they'd be employed after the Egyptians
> acted. That's all there is to it, pure and simple. No one can
> deny it. They [the brigades] didn't move until the first shot
> was fired.[64]

The chief of staff made no mention of the Assyria 2 order in
any of his statements. Gonen mentioned it once, but no one else
who testified spoke about the discrepancy between Assyria 2 and
Dovecote. Furthermore, Assyria 2, which was also a C-level alert,
did not entail a change in deployment. The deployment of forces
required to execute Dovecote included advancing the rear brigades,
replacing the infantry troops on the line, assuming control of the
mountain passes, deploying tanks on the forward line in daytime
parks, bringing up an artillery battalion from the rear, and deploying an additional artillery group in Sinai. Albert's order to the brigade commanders on Saturday morning was to prepare for Little
Dovecote, not to expand it and bring the rear brigades forward.

This is a flagrant example of the confusion and shoddy staff work on the part of GHQ and its faulty communications with Southern Command, especially the link between the chief of staff and the general of the command. The upshot was that on Saturday, October 6, the regulars on the line were not deployed two in front, as Dovecote required.

Possible Outcomes If Dovecote Had Been Implemented

Can we estimate the impact on the fighting in Sinai on the first day of the war if Dovecote had been deployed as planned?

Deployment of Little Dovecote. Major General Amnon Reshef (Ret.), commander of 14th Brigade, believes that if the brigade's tanks had taken their positions according to Little Dovecote, many lives could have been saved because it would not have been necessary to fight for those positions. And there is no doubt that a better opening situation would have improved the mental acuity of the tank crews. According to Colonel Pinchas Noy (Ret.), commander of 275th Territorial Brigade, had 9th Battalion's tanks arrived on time, the Egyptian infantry would not have been able to reach the ramps on the eastern bank.

The proper deployment of Little Dovecote would have prevented many casualties. Operational estimates by the commanders of the front-line forces in the war—Brigadier General Yom Tov Tamir (9th Battalion commander), Brigadier General Benny Taran (184th Battalion deputy commander), and Major General Emanuel Sakal (52nd Battalion commander)—show that many tanks and soldiers' lives could have been saved in each combat sector. The delay in deploying Little Dovecote resulted in a bitter, unnecessary battle, with many IDF losses resulting from RPGs and small-arms fire while fighting from positions on the eastern bank. The early deployment of Little Dovecote would have prevented, according to these commanders, the loss of sixty-five soldiers killed in action (tank crews and mechanized infantrymen), eighty-six wounded, and twenty-two tanks (one-quarter of the tanks of the brigades on the line, including 275th Territorial Brigade). Had the tanks been in position, their machine guns and cannon could have mowed down the Egyptian infantry approaching across open terrain, and the line could have been held. In addition to being a big morale booster for the IDF, this would have had a major impact on the initial and later stages of the Egyptian crossing.

Deployment of Large Dovecote. In the northern sector—the most difficult combat zone—the results of the fighting could not have been improved significantly without a reinforced tank force.

In the central sector, 79th Battalion would have been able to close a large section of the gap between Purkan and Matsmed in daylight, substantially reducing the gains of Egyptian 16th Infantry Division, which deepened its penetration without interference to the Televizia fortification and Amir and Missouri localities. Had Large Dovecote been correctly deployed—that is, 79th Battalion with three tank companies, including reinforcements from 460th Brigade, between Purkan and Matsmed, and the entire 184th Battalion with three tank companies, including reinforcements from 460th Brigade, in position on time—the Egyptian tanks would not have been able to cross the canal, and the IDF reservists' entry into the fighting would have proceeded in a more orderly fashion.

In the southern sector, 401st Brigade would have reached its area and assumed command in daylight. Its two tank battalions would have deployed on Artillery Road to the rear of the battalion on the line (52nd Battalion/14th Brigade), with 46th Battalion in the western opening of Gidi Road and 195th Battalion in the western opening of Mitla Road or east of Hamezach Junction. Under these circumstances, a sector counterattack would have been possible (like the one 52nd Battalion conducted, for example), and it could have limited—if not completely prevented—the Egyptian infantry's gains and disrupted the crossing of Egyptian armor.

Had Large Dovecote been implemented on time, it would have completely altered the application of the divisional reserve brigade. Commanders were under enormous pressure to come to the aid of the troops in the strongholds, especially in the northern sector. As a result, the reserve brigade—the reduced 460th—was thrown into this sector. A deliberate, full-scale, timely implementation of Dovecote would have significantly relieved the pressure on the strongholds and headquarters. Had 460th Brigade not been split into numerous groups and sent to the Milano-Mifreket section of the northern sector at the outbreak of hostilities, it could have operated as a concentrated force at dawn (on October 7) against the Egyptian crossing effort (which had already been spotted and identified) and especially south of Lituf, opposite Mifreket, or in the Missouri area (where Egyptian tanks crossed that night). From its position on the Tasa-Ismailia Road, it could have been used in a concentrated manner in the central sector as a divisional reserve against Egyptian 16th Division in the Missouri area or against Egyptian 2nd Division in Firdan. In the southern sector, forces of 401st Brigade could have concentrated south of Lituf to block the Egyptian armor crossing.

General Ariel Sharon, commander of 143rd Division, reckoned that even if Dovecote had been deployed on schedule, it would not have been able to thwart the crossing of the Egyptian infantry, but it could have limited the Egyptians' gains and prevented them from capturing territory (excluding a narrow strip on the waterline, possibly up to Canal Road). "Instead of us preempting the Egyptians," Sharon said, "they preempted us."[65]

According to General Adan, commander of 162nd Brigade, if the IDF had deployed in time and according to Dovecote, it would have produced better results: the Egyptians would have suffered heavy losses, their morale would have plummeted, Israel's losses would have been fewer, the Egyptian crossing would have been disrupted, and the time to achieve an Israeli victory would have been shortened. Nevertheless, Israel would not have been able to block the Egyptians from seizing large areas on the eastern bank.

Colonel Shomron, commander of 401st Brigade, also estimated that if more forces had been deployed in the southern sector, the Egyptians would have suffered a serious setback from the outset: "I don't believe we could have stopped the infantry crossing on the first night . . . but if we hadn't been struggling to defend the strongholds and holding [the line], and if the 401st was closer, the Egyptian 3rd Army could have been halted. Our forces in concentrated strength would have set ablaze anyone who tried to penetrate [the breakthroughs in the Israeli embankment]."[66]

Gonen, as expected, thought differently: "We were lucky not to have deployed in 'Dovecote' because this is what spared the second brigade from the fate of the first."[67]

Consequences of Dovecote's Flaws

Most of the senior commanders agree that failure to deploy 252nd Division's tank brigades was a major blunder and one of the costliest errors in the Yom Kippur War. It had dire consequences for the defensive battle in Sinai and for the entire campaign on the Egyptian front. The chain of events that led to this disaster can be summed up as follows:

1. During their morning meeting, the chief of staff and the general of Southern Command neglected to specify when the forces would deploy. They decided on one brigade in front, two in the rear.
2. At 11:00 on Saturday, in the operational discussion group with the defense minister, the Elazar-Gonen position still held sway: the deployment in Sinai, even at this late hour, would be one in front (according to Assyria 2).
3. Gonen did not like Dovecote (for the reasons already stated), and he wanted to remain deployed in a manner that would allow him to execute Zefania. This is why 401st Brigade was not ordered to advance until 14:00 on Saturday (Gonen probably had no intention of advancing it at all). It also explains why Southern Command consistently denied permission for the 401st to move forward and preferred to keep it on standby.
4. During the Elazar-Gonen meeting at noon, the two generals apparently agreed on Dovecote, but without specifying one in front or two in front and without deciding on a timetable for its implementation (Gonen claimed he was told not to deploy until 17:00). The fact is that the 401st remained in place, and the brigade on the line stayed in the fortifications. Elazar and Gonen may have decided on a one-in-front plan with the wrong name—Dovecote (which Elazar was unfamiliar with)—and they retained this plan until hostilities erupted.
5. General Tal, the deputy chief of staff, was probably correct when he said that if Elazar had approved a change to two in front, he would have updated the staff. At any rate, on Saturday the GHQ staff did shoddy work, and no operational orders were issued to Southern Command.
6. Gonen continued to dally until war broke out. The fear of escalation was his excuse for delaying and for keeping the Zefania option for the 401st. Not advancing 14th Brigade was the tragic outcome of his fear of escalation.
7. In the operational discussion group at 18:00, Elazar's comment regarding the opening plan—"this seemed fine to me"—confirms that he and Gonen agreed to stay with Assyria 2 (one

in front) until the outbreak of hostilities. And this is exactly what happened.

8. The 252nd and its units knew nothing of the approaching war or Assyria 2. They knew about the Dovecote plan and its two-in-front deployment and requested permission to execute it (which was denied). The breakdown in communication between GHQ and Southern Command and 252nd Division is inexplicable.

9. Elazar's style of command was not to delve into details. As a result, he was unfamiliar with the plans for Sinai, and the order of battle was not high on his list of priorities that day. Unlike the Golan Heights, with which he was intimately familiar, he ascribed little importance to preparations on the canal.

Before the war, no one assessed whether Dovecote could cope with a full-scale Egyptian attack and not yield one step. The plan did not address how to stop an Egyptian invasion, and the tank deployment did not correlate with the IDF's information about Egyptian plans for a large-scale infantry crossing, which MI assumed would be accompanied by massive artillery support and a huge number of antitank weapons. Dovecote was the only plan available on short notice for an all-out war, and its limitations and inconsistencies were quickly revealed. A deployment plan designed for daily security operations was now tasked with missions that far exceeded its rationale: blocking a full-scale assault and immediately shifting to the offensive.

Had Little Dovecote been executed before H hour, Israeli armor could have caused the Egyptians serious losses. Israel would have attained much better results in both the defensive battle and the entire war, while saving a significant number of lives. The Egyptian infantry could have been halted on Lexicon Road and dealt with later by the air force and artillery.

An orderly execution of Dovecote also would have improved the strongholds' resistance and the reservists' performance when they arrived. The decision regarding the tanks' assignments (see below)—to assist the strongholds or block the crossing—should have been made at an earlier stage, but the Israelis' understanding of events was unfocused until the morning of October 7. By then, the regulars' division had already lost two-thirds of its strength.[68]

With hindsight, it is obvious that the regulars, notwithstanding their courage, were simply insufficient to defend the canal. Had this been recognized in time, they might have been given a more limited assignment, such as a holding and delaying action until the reservists arrived. If their role had been so defined, they might have been able to accomplish their mission. Even if the Egyptians succeeded in crossing the canal and capturing a strip of land a few kilometers wide along the eastern bank, the IDF regulars might have been able to hold them there until the reservists arrived. This would have been invaluable in terms of saving lives and equipment and evacuating the area. But the high command overestimated the regulars' capabilities, and their mission of breaking the attack on the waterline was impossible to accomplish. Furthermore, even if Dovecote had been deployed on the waterline, it could not have repulsed the crossing. The reduced order of battle, limited artillery and mechanized infantry, inhibited air force activity, and shortcomings in performance by some of the regulars ruined any chance of this. At best, the IDF held the enemy and disrupted his timetable. Once the reserve units reached the area, the danger of collapse passed.

The Egyptians' attempt to break through to the east and implement the third stage of their plan on October 14 floundered because they "missed the boat." Part of this delay can be attributed to the regulars' actions on the first day, which later enabled the IDF to cross the canal and end the war on the western bank.[69] Deploying Dovecote's order of battle too late and under fire rendered it a wobbly platform on which 252nd Division tried to do the impossible: defend the strongholds and simultaneously prevent the Egyptian crossing. It failed in this mission, revealing flaws in the tanks' deployment and the strongholds' evacuation.

Tank Battles at and around the Strongholds

According to the Dovecote plan, the tanks would fight next to the strongholds to protect them and stop the Egyptian crossing. Eighty-eight tanks from the forward 14th Brigade and 275th Territorial Brigade were divided into eight companies and dispersed (according to the War of Attrition model) along 200 kilometers—from the Budapest stronghold on a sandbar in the Mediterranean Sea, through Orkal south of Port Said, to Ras Sudar on the Gulf of Suez.

Tanks in pairs and platoons reinforced isolated strongholds

and remote installations, while reduced tank companies remained in either natural or man-made positions (ramps or fins) that dominated the egresses of the main east-west junctions from Central Sinai to Canal Road and the rear of the stronghold clusters. Most of the positions were located approximately 1,500 meters from the water, and some of them on the dirt embankment were designated for tank fire against landing craft in the water. Many tanks reached these positions on Saturday after the war broke out and during the first night, and they managed to fire on boats in the canal despite the high risk of being hit at close range by small-arms fire and antitank weapons.

The northern sector. Tanks from 9th Battalion/275th Brigade (K and M Companies) were sent to take control of the openings of the two roads from Baluza to Kantara (Lystim and Aleket) and the road north of El-Balah Island to the Mifreket stronghold (Tiltul). L Company regularly had two tanks in Orkal, and it now allocated a pair of tanks to Budapest, according to Dovecote. The rest of the tanks were ordered to travel on the marsh roads to the fins (ramps) to the rear of and adjacent to the Ketuba, Lahtsanit, and Derora strongholds north of Kantara.

The central sector. Deployment of the tanks from 184th Battalion/14th Brigade was designed to allow H Company to retain control of the western end of Firdan (Haviva) Road from the Havraga fortification, while G Company held the exit of Tasa–Ismailia–Crocodile Lake (Talisman) Road opposite the Purkan stronghold and two diagonal roads (Akavish Road and the Tirtur dirt road) to Dwersuar. A gap remained between Purkan and Matsmed, and a mechanized infantry company (J Company) of 184th Battalion was positioned in the Televizia fortification.

The southern sector. The 52nd Battalion/14th Brigade deployed from the egress of Gidi Road (Foreret) to the southern part of Little Bitter Lake opposite the Lituf stronghold. C Company assumed responsibility for the area and sent a platoon to the Botser stronghold on the peninsula between Great and Little Bitter Lakes. B Company was given responsibility for the opening of Mitla Road (Atifa-Lexicon Junction), and it sent a tank platoon to Ras Sudar. A Company was ordered to the opening of Yoreh Road opposite

Hamezach Junction, on Lexicon Road, and it dispatched two tanks to the Hamezach stronghold.

The Egyptians had precise knowledge of the brigade's deployment on the waterline, so they selected crossing areas between the strongholds and on the eastern embankment that were not under Israeli observation and fire. The breakthrough in the embankment with high-pressure water jets and bridging works was carried out at night and with almost no interference by Israeli tanks, even though they had reached their positions on the embankment adjacent to the strongholds during the first half of the night. This explains how the Egyptian tanks were able to cross the canal unobserved on Saturday evening in the El-Balah Island area (Egyptian 18th Division) and in the space between Purkan and Matsmed (Egyptian 16th Division). The first tanks of the Egyptian 7th Division crossed the canal south of Lituf early Sunday morning in an area where there were no Israeli tank positions that had to be captured.

The southern sector's depth was based on two tank battalions of 401st Brigade that could be used between Artillery Road and the canal. The central sector faced a dilemma: close the hole between Purkan and Matsmed with the help of 79th Battalion/401st Brigade, or leave the battalion in the rear as a reserve. In the northern sector, no depth had been planned for tank deployment. Furthermore, Dovecote had no contingency arrangements for the northern sector's reinforcement (the possibility of strengthening the sector with 195th Battalion/401st Brigade had been broached by the division commander on Friday at 18:00 but not implemented).

Fighting the Egyptian Crossing Force

In the southern sector, the two battalions of 401st Brigade (46th and 195th) were drawn into the fighting on the canal line on Saturday evening, leaving the brigade without a reserve force. The same happened in the central sector when the commander of 14th Brigade split 79th Battalion, sending part of it to close the gap between Purkan and Matsmed. The northern sector received an improvised tank force as a sector reserve—Force Lapidot—and it too was drawn into the fighting on the contact line.

The division's depth was based on a reserve brigade—the 460th, which reached Sinai on Friday–Saturday night and replaced 7th Brigade, which had been sent north to the Golan Heights ten days earlier. To achieve this depth, the brigade was supposed to advance to Lateral Road east of Tasa and participate in a divisional counterattack. In reality, the brigade had already divided its units on Saturday night: 196th Battalion was sent to reinforce the central sector, and Force Lapidot was sent to the northern sector. All that remained of the 460th was 198th Battalion, which had fought near Mifreket on the first night of the war.

Because of their locations, the Rock divisions—the 162nd in the concentration areas in the northern sector, and the 143rd in the central sector—served, theoretically, as a command depth for 252nd Division. These two divisions were not supposed to take part in the defensive battle (they were designated for the counterattack), but upon their arrival, they were immediately hurled into the fighting to stabilize the defensive line on Sunday, October 7, and counterattack the following day. Although Southern Command envisioned a gradual force deployment that would create depth on Lateral Road, this could not occur until the mechanized brigades arrived: the 204th in the northern sector and the 875th in the southern sector. If the Rock forces had been deployed before H hour, they probably would have acted as a serious deterrent to the Egyptians. Although the reserve divisions were earmarked for the counterattack and canal crossing, they could have been employed to restore the situation to its previous status, while reducing the troops' exhaustion and minimizing Egyptian gains.

The decision to disperse the forward tanks along a great distance, leaving them unable to concentrate their strength, was the result of deploying in accordance with Dovecote's mission: to yield not one step and to defend the strongholds. Thus, criticism of the split-up of the tank units on the first day of the war, contrary to the principle of force concentration, should be directed not at the forces in the field but at the Dovecote operational plan, which had been approved at all levels.[70] The historical literature is rife with inaccuracies on this issue, including the piecemeal arrival of 14th Brigade's tanks. On Saturday, October 6, with the outbreak of the war, the 14th's tank companies (some reduced, others whole, based on their Dovecote assignments) arrived in concentrated form, each to its prescribed area. In practice, there was a discrepancy between the written doctrine—fighting while concentrating the force—and the orders, drills, and oral doctrine that dictated the division of the line brigade.

The need to respond quickly and aggressively to any Egyptian attempt to seize the eastern bank was part and parcel of the operational thinking in 252nd Division. The author was present at a candlelight supper for the battalion commanders held at division headquarters in Refidim in early 1973, where General Albert, the division commander, threatened in his characteristic style: "I pity the battalion commander who lets the Egyptians grab a piece of his section of the canal."

Although the dispersal of the line tanks was unquestionably part of the first stage of the Dovecote order (Little Dovecote), the split-up of the rear brigades—the 401st in the southern sector and the 460th in the northern sector—was the result of the precarious situation on the line and the orders, some of them erroneous, issued by the headquarters responsible for the conduct of operations. Because of the gravity of the situation, 401st Brigade dispatched two of its battalions to assist in the fighting. On Saturday night the southern sector was divided among three battalions: the 46th in the Gidi opening, the 52nd in the Mitla opening, and the 195th opposite Hamezach and Hakfar.

The 14th Brigade ordered the divided 79th Battalion to help in the fighting on the line. Events on the day preceding the war and in the days after it illustrate what can happen when a force is split up:

On Friday night [the 79th] came under the command of the 460th [Brigade]. On noon Saturday its mechanized infantry company was sent to the northern sector. With the opening of hostilities the battalion was ordered to Tasa where it received a third company from the emergency logistics base at Bir-Tmada. While moving to Tasa the battalion commander was ordered to redirect to the southern sector, but before reaching Tasa he received new orders to come under the command of the 14th Brigade. Arriving in Tasa at 17:00 the battalion was divided up: one company with the deputy battalion commander of the 184th went to the Hizayon stronghold; another company was sent to Purkan with the 79th's commander; and a third company headed to Matsmed with the deputy battalion commander.[71]

In the chaos and fog of battle, 401st Brigade, without checking with 52nd Battalion's tactical operations center at Mitla, mistakenly sent three tanks from 46th Battalion to the Botser stronghold, which had already received three tanks from the 52nd's C Company under the Dovecote plan. Thus, in the critical hours when every tank was worth its weight in gold, the six tanks at Botser contributed nothing to the fighting.

At the division level, 460th Brigade, which was supposed to be held in reserve, was split up and thrown into the fighting in the northern sector too early (Saturday night). The brigade commander, Brigadier General Gabi Amir (Ret.), recalled that his force of four tank companies arrived in the north and was divided up on the way. The 198th Battalion was divided in two: one half, led by the deputy brigade commander, went to Kantara, and part of this group became Force Lapidot and was sent to Baluza; the other half was directed to Mifreket. The 196th Battalion remained in Refidim and later came under the command of 14th Brigade. Forty-four tanks of 460th Brigade were tasked with "saving Jews" and were sent wherever there were cries for help. After an hour or two, there were no reserves left for the main effort. With the wisdom of hindsight, the reserve brigade should not have been used in battles on the line until the picture had become clear. Gonen, in an attempt to defend Southern Command's decision, said, "Sometimes you have to 'fire from the hip.'"[72]

By dividing the brigades in the rear, the IDF fell into a trap: it allowed the Egyptians to attack the entire length of the front without encountering a concentrated Israeli effort. The Egyptians not only determined the physical limitations and tactical nature of the battle; they also affected the thinking of Israeli commanders as the campaign developed into a series of grinding clashes between small groups of tanks that lacked room to maneuver and enemy ambushes bristling with antitank weapons. The IDF's concentrated use of tanks began at noon on Sunday, after contact with the strongholds was broken off and 252nd Division realized that continuing the fight with its spread-out units would be disastrous. This was the turning point of the campaign, but only one-third of the division's tank force remained.

Linking Up with the Strongholds

To understand the tanks' modus operandi in the Dovecote deployment from Saturday evening to Sunday morning, it is useful to examine the stronghold linkup drill as it developed during the War of Attrition.

On Saturday night, believing that a war of attrition—not full-scale war—had broken out, individual tanks, tank pairs, and tank platoons fought their way to the strongholds. Contrary to the war literature, linkups occurred in only four strongholds, including one thinly manned one. In the northern sector, a force from 198th Battalion/460th Brigade commanded by Lieutenant Colonel Amir Yoffe linked up twice with the Mifreket stronghold (north of El-Balah Island) and evacuated the wounded at 02:30. The battalion commander's request to evacuate the rest of the stronghold was denied. The 460th's deputy brigade commander, Lieutenant Colonel Shilo Sasson, linked up with the Milano stronghold at Kantara at 04:00. No armor linkups occurred in the central sector (Hizayon was unreachable, and Purkan, Lakekan, and Matsmed did not need to be linked up).

In the southern sector, the commander of C Company/52nd Battalion, Lieutenant Amir Boaz, linked up with Lituf and evacuated the wounded (his request to evacuate the entire stronghold was turned down). The 52nd's battalion commander entered the thinly manned Mefatseyach B stronghold (at the opening of Mitla Road) at 21:00 to look for the Nachal Unit's observation team (which, as it turned out, was not there). Tanks from A Company/52nd Battalion linked up with Hakfar. During the night, linkup attempts became increasingly hazardous as the casualty rates in the tank units started to climb, beginning with 14th Brigade and later 401st and 460th Brigades. By daybreak, linkup with the strongholds became impossible.

Attributing the loss of tanks to these linkups with the strongholds is misleading and a gross exaggeration. Most of the 170 tanks that were put out of commission in the first eighteen hours were in the vicinity of the strongholds, but they were lost by other means: antitank fire on the western bank against positions on the eastern bank during daylight hours on Saturday, fighting against the Egyptian infantry all along the canal, getting bogged down in the marshes, throwing their tracks, or detonating mines in the dark—especially in the northern sector.

On Saturday night, the surviving tanks were concentrated at the junctions of the access roads from the east and Canal Road. Some were in their designated positions for Dovecote (mainly in the southern sector); others (including those that had lost their way) were dispersed in the area. Their primary tasks were evacuating crewmen, defending themselves against Egyptian infantry moving on the ground and firing small arms and RPGs, and towing tanks out of the marshes (especially in the Kantara area and south of it). The tanks entered their positions on the waterline in the three sectors and, wherever possible, fired their machine guns at the Egyptian infantry spotted by the strongholds.

In the southern sector, based on messages from 401st Brigade's tactical operations center at Mitla or the strongholds (which reported the sound of mechanical engineering equipment), the tanks ascended to firing positions and fired on ferries, boats, engineering machinery, and Egyptian forces making their way across the canal (this fire was usually ineffective because the main crossing areas were too distant from the strongholds). In other cases, they fired at the source of direct laying fire on the strongholds. In the latter part of the night, mounting the firing positions became impossible, and attempts to do so ceased.

Colonel Reshef, commander of 14th Brigade, was the only commander who accurately described armor's linkup mission with the strongholds: "According to doctrine, the tanks were supposed to be responsible for the physical link-up . . . in order to evacuate the wounded. . . . Except for that, a number of tank link-ups were carried out in the vicinity of the strongholds. These were not physical link-ups [with the strongholds] but at a distance of a kilometer and a half [from them]. There was no reason or need to enter a stronghold."[73]

Colonel Amir, commander of 460th Brigade, recalled the futility of reaching the strongholds: "There was a link-up with the strongholds but it was in vain because there was no order what to do next. Evacuate? Hold the area? In short, the force was misspent."[74]

Colonel Shomron, commander of 401st Brigade, shared this view: "The line did not fall apart—it slowly eroded and we had to divide the force. In the first night of the fighting we had to overcome the ambushes. Out of 96 tanks in the initial order of battle, including those of the 52nd Battalion, only 23 remained operable the next morning."[75] Of all its tanks damaged during the war, the 401st lost two-thirds on the first night. According to Shomron, the lesson was clear: the war should never have been fought that way, given the results and the high number of casualties. "If a defensive method had been employed and the strongholds weren't the central axis, I think we would have incurred fewer casualties."[76] Twenty years later he added: "We had one artillery battalion and didn't know where to direct it. . . . I'm not even sure we attacked the right places."[77]

The Misuse of Armor

The first night and the following morning witnessed very little Israeli armor movement against the Egyptian crossing areas, although it could have been carried out. Operational obsession with the War of Attrition model, identification of defense of the strongholds and junctions as armor's primary mission (and the associated lack of movement), and failure to recognize that all-out war calls for tank movement along the entire width of a sector to stop the enemy were only a few of the reasons for the situation so aptly described by Brigadier General Baruch Harel (Ret.), deputy commander of 252nd Division: "On the first two days of the war and during the whole first week we misused our armor force. We took our tanks and turned them into bunkers that moved between 500 meters to a kilometer. This is not the way to apply armor."[78] Finally, late Sunday morning, headquarters woke up to the need to change the manner and direction of operational thinking.

There were several mistakes in the application of tanks in the three sectors, but the cardinal sin was a lack of planning and the lack of a defensive plan for Sinai. Had preliminary planning been carried out, the value of dominating ground would have been obvious. Areas such as Karat Moora and Nehushtan in the southern sector; Missouri, Hamutal, and Makhshir in the central sector; and Tsioni in the northern sector had to be held prior to the fighting in a defensive battle or captured during the first night of the war at the latest. Nehushtan, for example, was a chain of dunes that offered excellent observation and fire—beyond the range of antitank missiles on the western bank—on the broad plains of the canal and on Canal Road from Bitter Lake in the north (Lituf stronghold) to Mitla Road in the south (Mefatseyach stronghold). Over the years, armies that had fought in the area recognized its operational value, as evidenced by remnants of trenches and barbed wire fences marked on the Sirius code maps. The IDF, however, failed to carry out a ground analysis for defensive purposes, so this dominating ground, like others, was overlooked, even though 252nd Division's armor and infantry forces could have exploited it to great advantage.

Some of the other problems were as follows:

- The commanders' scant familiarity with the area between the strongholds and its potential for conducting a mobile defensive battle.
- The commanders' acute exhaustion after the first night of fighting, which hindered their ability to recognize the significance of events as they happened. Extreme fatigue is known to blur military thinking and make it all but impossible to devise decisive tactical moves. Therefore, it is the role of stationary headquarters (in this case, 252nd Division and Southern Command) to identify situations and order tactical maneuvers or operational moves if the force in the field fails to recognize the need or the opportunity to do so.
- The tanks' debilitating material fatigue and the commanders' overarching fear of losing more tanks in unplanned and undrilled moves. The commanders preferred to conserve their remaining tanks and assemble them on the roads instead of sending them into battle in the unfamiliar sand dunes. On Sunday morning, 401st Brigade had only twenty-three tanks. Each battalion was left with only eight or ten tanks, and the companies had only three or four. Shomron's sobering words to the author (commander of 52nd Battalion) on the morning of October 7 illustrate the harrowing situation: "Yours are our most important tanks. I don't want to risk them in attacks on the canal line."
- Abiding faith in the reserves and a sense that with the reservists' imminent arrival, the situation would improve and the areas that had been evacuated would be retaken.
- The fear of a breakthrough by Egyptian armored and mechanized divisions. This was one of the main reasons for 401st Brigade's withdrawal to better positions—which were too deep—on the hills of Artillery Road rather than employing the force in a simple maneuver of the highest operational significance: blocking the Egyptian armor's crossing at the outset.

Until Sunday morning, there were no maneuvers of the Israeli tanks, and they remained in their positions in the rear of the strongholds. The only movement undertaken by the 252nd's tanks was to break off contact from the canal and pull back to the high ground to the east overlooking Artillery Road; each sector dealt with its own particular conditions, timetable, and terrain. Thus, the Egyptian armor penetrated, albeit to a limited degree, without any obstruction.

Because there was no tank maneuvering in the southern sector on Sunday morning, a genuine opportunity was lost to block the crossing of Egyptian Third Army, which had only two bridges south of Lituf at the time. This omission had fatal consequences for the defensive battle. Had Third Army's armor been stopped, the entire war might have been different. In the initial encounters with Egyptian armor on Sunday morning, the 252nd's tankers proved their absolute superiority, and wherever a firefight occurred, the enemies' tanks were stopped. Local attacks and maneuvers also blocked the Egyptian advance. One example was the fire and movement maneuver carried out by a handful of tanks led by the commander of 52nd Battalion in the southern sector on Sunday noon, and the return to the "Madonna" (the Queen Victoria statue) on Mitla Road 2,000 meters from Canal Road. In this improvised attack, Egyptian 19th Division's first tanks were knocked out, and the rest were halted in their tracks. The 401st Brigade did not follow up on this success because it had only twenty-three tanks deployed between the Gidi opening in the north and Hamezach Junction in the south.

Attempts to Close the Gap between Purkan and Matsmed

Most of 14th Brigade's activity was in the Purkan-Matsmed sector, while the area between Crocodile Lake and Matsmed remained unobserved. Beginning on Saturday afternoon, the brigade commander, aware of the operational implications of this gap, sent small forces—tank platoons with one or two APCs—to verify the situation.[79] If an Israeli force of reasonable proportions, such as a company or larger, had been deployed earlier north of Matsmed, it would have seriously disrupted or perhaps even stopped the crossing of Egyptian 16th Division's southern flank. But because of the depleted order of battle, the rush of events, and the failure to assess the significance of these junctions, no attempt was made to hold on to them. A company-sized tank force and a mechanized infantry platoon in position at the Lexicon-Tirtur and Lexicon-Akavish Junctions could have whittled down Egyptian 16th Division's territorial gains and prevented a large number of high-cost breakthrough battles fought by 14th Brigade on the night of October 15–16, 890th Paratroop Battalion at the Chinese Farm the following night, and 600th Brigade/143rd Division as it tried to dislodge the Egyptian force compromising the Israeli crossing corridor.

To summarize: when the remnants of 14th Brigade's four forces withdrew to Tasa, no Israeli force remained in the gap between Purkan and Matsmed.[80] Reports on what was happening in this "hole"— enemy movement and concentrations at the Chinese Farm—did not reach Southern Command until Monday morning, at which time Gonen ordered 143rd Division to plan an attack on the Chinese Farm.

By Saturday night, the division had lost between 50 and 60 tanks; by Sunday morning, it had lost 173 in a series of small actions involving a few tanks each, without mechanized infantry or artillery support. As noted earlier, these losses were the result of enemy fire, sinking in the marshes, and throwing their tracks. In the first day of the war, 252nd Division suffered 345 killed or missing in action from Sagger missiles fired from the ramps on the western bank, RPGs fired by Egyptian infantry that had overtaken Israeli positions on the eastern bank, tank fire from the western bank, small-arms fire by Egyptian infantry on the eastern bank, the detonation of mines planted by enemy infantry on the eastern bank, and artillery fire, especially airburst and phosphorescent shells.

Deliberations and Blunders

The tanks on the line were divided up and then deployed in their positions while engaged in furious battles. The two rear brigades were also dragged into the fighting. After about six hours, the orders the fighting forces received from the division, command, and GHQ levels were no longer operationally relevant, as the conduct of operations had become impossible. The desperate attempt to hang on to the canal as a defensive line ("not one step") without infantry, without air assistance, and with only watered-down artillery support against an onslaught of five divisions (not to mention the Israeli forces' mistakes in the opening round) left the regulars no chance to accomplish their mission.

Southern Command had two alternatives (which could have been merged): (1) order the strongholds to evacuate in the brief window of opportunity between dusk Saturday and dawn the next day, or (2) break off contact with the strongholds and the canal line on

Saturday night and conduct a defensive and delaying battle to Artillery Road. The first alternative was squandered because of muddled orders from the chief of staff and Southern Command's refusal to evacuate the strongholds (even though the tank commanders who linked up with them requested it). The second alternative was forced on the division on Sunday morning, after the gravity of the situation became clear: only 110 combat-ready tanks remained. Due to the absence of defensive depth, the command lost its flexibility, maneuverability, and initiative. The previous condition was beyond retrieval, so the division acted on a default plan—a drill—without trying to determine, by a situational assessment, the wisdom of defending the waterline and reaching the strongholds. The upshot was that 252nd Division failed to accomplish its key missions: it did not stop the enemy from breaking through and capturing part of the area, and it did not destroy the enemy.

Later, in a summary of Southern Command's part in the war, Lieutenant General Elazar avoided answering the question: what was the preferred shape of fighting in Dovecote? He was exceedingly noncommittal and did not go into detail with regard to how the forces were supposed to have held the line. He admitted that it was not the best deployment, but it was all they had at the time. And, given the way the war began, he had no illusions that the forces would have to hold the next day too. He said, "We had to begin planning already. The forces were increasing on Monday, Tuesday and Wednesday and we would be able to shift to offensive actions." A convoluted explanation followed: "According to the concept that crystallized . . . we decided that the ceasefire lines had to be held in a defense adjacent to the lines. As for the modus operandi, we would do this with mobile forces but we're talking about iron-clad determination not to surrender any territory."[81]

Gonen's testimony was no less circuitous: "This was a rigid defense with the technique of mobility. The difference between them is that in mobile defense you're allowed to give up areas in order to destroy the enemy. This is characteristic of armor where the areas are such that you can't retain forces in them. . . . When I say a rigid armored defense I mean that the line can't be crossed, but the technique of holding it is mobile."[82]

Despite the strategic depth, the failure to call up the reservists on time, and the rejection of a preemptive strike, the IDF decided to use the canal as the rear defensive line. This created a critical situation that "exploded" in the defenders' faces. Their hands were tied with regard to the modus operandi for a defensive battle; they were stuck with an inappropriate plan that offered no chance of success, with military and political doctrines that contained a surfeit of vacuous slogans and very little operational truth, and with an absurdly limited order of battle that was up against enormous enemy forces following a meticulously prepared battle plan.

"The strongholds were built in the War of Attrition and were suited for the War of Attrition," said Harel, deputy commander of the 252nd. "We erred when we dashed off to the strongholds. They should have been evacuated or been told, 'Look guys, we're not fighting to get you out of the strongholds right now but to push back the Egyptians.'" According to Harel, "If we tried to stop [the Egyptians] on the water line with all the strength that the 252nd could muster on Saturday morning we still wouldn't have been able to stop [them] and would have only incurred more burnt tanks because we had no answer to [their] infantry or missiles. We couldn't beat the Egyptians back along the entire front and shove them into the canal in one blow."[83]

The division's operational log shows that in the first sixteen hours of the war, the orders issued were rife with discrepancies (not including those orders conveyed by radio, which were not recorded). In the absence of instructions on how to conduct operations and how to wage the campaign, the brigade commanders used the War of Attrition model, each one acting in his sector according to the best of his ability. The division commander rarely broadcast on the units' radio frequencies. Instead, he relied on the brigade commanders, who were doing all they could with the defensive plans. When asked what order he received from division, Shomron said, "The reality was . . . do your best."[84] The only defined objective was to stop the Egyptians on the waterline—an order that remained in effect for most of the first night.

At around 19:00 the division tried to organize 14th Brigade's forces based on crossing areas and to prepare for a holding operation while concentrating the rear line battalions: the 9th in the north (for all practical purposes, the battalion no longer existed) and the 52nd in the south; the 184th was not mentioned. The order may have been correct, but it was inapplicable because the forces were decimated, dispersed over a wide area, engaged in combat and unable to break off contact with the enemy, or carrying out rescue operations.

At 22:00, after the division obtained an initial report on casualties, it repeated its order to break off contact with the enemy and pull back to the rear. It finally realized that the situation was complicated and that the forces were being "sucked into" the strongholds. The order, which failed to reach the troops engaged in combat, instructed them not to exhaust their ammunition and to organize in tank parks to be ready to retake the waterline in the morning, block the enemy's armored and mechanized divisions, and gain time until the reservists arrived. Gideon Avidor, the division's G-3, had this to say: "We didn't expect that the 252nd Division would save the Jewish People. The division no longer had any more reserves now that the 460th was involved in the fighting."[85]

At 01:45 the division commander ordered 401st Brigade's commander to deploy along the canal by dawn—that is, to withdraw five kilometers and reorganize. But this order did not reach the forces, was impossible to execute, was issued too late, and was not carried out. The battle for defending the strongholds and the waterline was conducted according to daily security drills. Between 03:00 and 04:00, when the division realized the forces could not break off contact with the enemy, Albert ordered a linkup with the strongholds to rescue the men there, where possible. He also ordered the units to stop the Egyptians from developing the second stage of the invasion—bringing their armored divisions across the canal.

What happens when a headquarters realizes that the situation on the ground is far different from that anticipated in the plan given to the fighting forces? The answer depends on many factors: the level of training, the competence and clarity of command, the credibility of the fighting forces' reports, the type of battle the troops are engaged in (an initiated battle or an encounter), the intensity of the fighting, day or nighttime conditions, and so forth.

In his attempt to conduct operations, Albert probably looked for the enemy's main efforts during the first part of the night (there were none), weighed the possibility of employing the reserve forces (which were applied too early), and contemplated how to ensure that the line would hold by implementing Dovecote. At this point, no one seems to have considered devising a different plan to deal with the Egyptian crossing: withdrawing and conducting a holding action instead of fighting on the canal as a rear defensive line. Since Egypt's war aims were not comprehended, the question of evacuating the strongholds never came up for discussion.

During the night, the chief of staff asked the general of Southern Command whether units could be withdrawn from the waterline to establish four brigade concentrations to be used when the enemy's main efforts were spotted.[86] The chief of staff's queries and orders were detached from the reality on the ground. There was no way that contact with the Egyptians could be broken off during the night. It was inconceivable that four brigade concentrations could be built from the three tank brigades that were fighting on the line. The enemy had not made any main efforts, which the chief of staff should have known by then.

According to the IDF's plan, one reinforced brigade-sized counterattack could have been launched with the sector's order of battle (460th Brigade or another combination), but this force was not sufficient to deal with the situation on the ground, since the units had been split into companies and platoons. No brigade-sized attack was executed anywhere because the whole order of battle had been divided and was engaged on the contact line, and no main Egyptian effort had been detected. Even if a counterattack had been successful in a particular crossing area (perhaps at a heavy price), it would not have prevented Egyptian accomplishments in other sectors. Shifting the counterattacking force to a second attack in another sector would have been absolutely impractical because of the losses already sustained and the impossibility of breaking off contact with the enemy in the fighting zone, not to mention the time and spatial constraints involved in attacking in another sector.[87] A divisional counterattack was out of the question at this point.

From the first day of the war until Sunday morning, the forces fought gallantly and tenaciously, without clear orders or practical instructions from division. They were under the command of junior officers responding to local developments on the ground. As for the division, it could have conducted a defensive battle by making better use of the area east of the canal and taking a line farther west of Artillery Road; instead, its only action was to allocate the few forces that remained. The division commander spoke with the brigade commanders, but no plan was formulated for divisional fighting.

Concerned that the forces were too widely spread out, the chief of staff telephoned the general of Southern Command at 17:55 on Saturday and ordered him to keep the forces concentrated, facing the enemy's main efforts. The intention was correct, but the orders were relayed indistinctly and indecisively; they also partially lagged behind events in the field, certainly regarding the brigade on the line, even though double-quick staff work could have avoided the dispersal of the two rear brigades. But such was not the case. The instructions conveyed by phone at 17:55 and in the operational discussion group at 18:35 were not translated into orders to the forces in the field. In the operational discussion group and again at 20:38, the chief of staff repeated the need to look for the Egyptians' main efforts and position forces opposite them. Elazar also feared the early arrival of Egyptian armored divisions.[88]

Failure to Evacuate the Strongholds

The fall of the Bar-Lev Line and the fate of the soldiers manning the strongholds (killed, wounded, missing, or taken prisoner) left a deep scar on the national psyche, gutted the IDF's perspective on military ethics, and contributed to Israel's sense of missed opportunity, despite its achievements at the end of the fighting. The failure to evacuate the strongholds on the first night of the war remains a painful and controversial subject. Evacuation would have completely altered the opening situation on the line by freeing 252nd Division from close-quarters combat, thus enabling it to conduct a flexible, mobile battle in retrograde and delaying operations. Evacuation would have removed the fetters of the "not one step" directive and eliminated the need to rescue the troops screaming for help in the strongholds. The casualty rate would have been lower, less equipment would have been lost, and Israel's territorial gains would have been more significant.

The political and military leaders' misreading of the gravity of initial conditions in Sinai and the air force's inability to provide assistance created the worst form of limited thinking and inhibited strategic and operational decision making during critical hours. In the first evening of the war, the general of Southern Command had to decide whether to concentrate his forces and counterattack in a narrow sector (a move that would culminate in a canal crossing) or retain the stronghold line at all costs. He chose the latter.

When the grim picture came into focus on Sunday morning, GHQ and Southern Command realized that the strongholds had to be evacuated—but it was already too late. The decision should have been made hours earlier. After the war, Shomron put his finger on the problem: "If the government decided not to call up the reservists, then it should have given the regulars a fighting chance and allowed them to override the order 'not one step' from the water line, including evacuation of the strongholds."[89] There were a number of reasons why the strongholds were not evacuated:

- Political implications.
- Lack of discussion of their evacuation in a full-scale war.
- Presumption that the strongholds would be a major contribution to the battle (observation, reporting, disrupting the enemy's moves, and so forth), making evacuation out of the question.
- Belief by 252nd Division, Southern Command, and GHQ (until midnight) that the IDF had control of the situation and evacuation was unnecessary.
- Elazar's vague statements about evacuation, and unclear responsibility for the final decision.
- Belief that the situation would improve soon after the counterattack (scheduled for Monday morning) and that the troops would reach the strongholds without having to evacuate them.

The Strongholds: Asset or Obstacle?

When comparing the expectations of the Bar-Lev Line during discussions of the Stronghold plan in late 1968 and the strongholds' actual performance in the War of Attrition and Yom Kippur War, it is obvious that the plan's supporters—first and foremost, Chief of Staff Haim Bar-Lev—saw the strongholds not only as a defense system but also as the linchpin of Israeli sovereignty on the waterline. They were designed to impede Egyptian crossing points opposite the main roads on the eastern bank, assist in observation and reporting, provide sites to treat the wounded, and serve as an operations base for action in the gaps on the strongholds' line, while receiving artillery support and armor assistance from tanks in the area. Opponents of the concept, especially Generals Tal and Sharon, perceived the strongholds as expendable encumbrances incapable of serving their purpose and fulfilling expectations. Furthermore, they thought the strongholds would bog down the entire system during rescue operations and divert the forces from their main task—blocking the Egyptian crossing.

After the war, opinion on the strongholds' contribution was split three ways:

1. Supporters of the Bar-Lev Line continued to defend the doctrine. They argued that because it had never been given the chance to prove itself, it was wrong to pin all the blame for the line's collapse on the strongholds rather than on the fact that the elementary conditions of the Dovecote plan had been lacking (an argument with some justification). Bar-Lev himself contended that, according to the original plan, the strongholds were not designed to thwart a massive crossing; they were intended to give a warning and fight as best they could until the reservists arrived. The line, however, had atrophied due to neglect and changes in deployment in the years after his retirement. The number of strongholds was truncated, and the crack troops had been taken out and replaced by second-rate reservists, some of whom had never served in the regular army. On October 6 the Egyptians faced only sixteen strongholds, seven to eight kilometers apart. Until the rear-based IDF armor reached the line, five Egyptian divisions managed to cross the canal, land on the eastern bank, and use missiles and artillery to savage the IDF troops. Tal agreed that because it was never actually tested, the Bar-Lev Line did not collapse; in fact, once the structure began to function as planned and according to the operational concept, the war developed in the desired direction.[90]

2. Others believed that the strongholds contributed to observation, reporting, and delaying the Egyptians' timetable. This was the view of a number of commanders in the south, including the deputy commander of 252nd Division, who thought the strongholds were the only force holding the waterline, obstructing the Egyptian crossing, and continuously reporting on developments. "In areas without strongholds, no one resisted the crossing simply because we didn't know that there was a crossing. Wave after wave attacked the strongholds, and the truth is that until they were surrounded, we didn't cease our attempts to link up with them, and the Egyptians made no advances."[91] Gonen, in a conversation with the chief of staff during the first days of the fighting, said the strongholds justified their existence because their reports

were Southern Command's only source of information about events on the canal. Elazar lauded the strongholds' contribution on a number of occasions, and in an October 8 conversation with the adjutant general, Major General Herzl Shafir, he stated plainly: "They're our eyes. It's another risk you take. One stronghold fell, then another, but out of the thirty or so [there were only sixteen] only two actually capitulated after almost 48 hours [not exactly]." When presenting the defense minister with plans for the counterattack (at 01:00 on October 8), the chief of staff expressed his belief that the strongholds had proved themselves, and he noted that General Uri Ben Ari, Gonen's deputy, was not only against evacuating them but actually wanted to retake them and bring the evacuees back.[92]

3. A third group thought the strongholds contributed nothing and were only a hindrance. Tal explicitly stated this view: "Instead of the strongholds being rock-solid bases that supported mobile fighting that the armor forces could rely on, as their exponents claimed, they were a burden. Their survival dictated the costly moves in the critical first days. The need to secure and assist the strongholds, and extricate the troops inside emboldened the tankers and drove them to carry out suicide missions to get to them."[93]

Many commanders and scholars of the war share Tal's opinion, among them Ehud Barak, who served as chief of staff from 1991 to 1995. "Considering the military forces' combat potential in Sinai, the fortresses were of no value, and they limited the forces both practically and psychologically. From the start, small groups of observation troops could have been stationed on the canal and ordered out at the onset of the real fighting."[94] Shomron, another former chief of staff, averred, "As a result of hanging onto the strongholds many tanks were destroyed. If we'd adopted a different defense method, one in which the strongholds were not the mainstay, we could have done our job with fewer losses."[95]

The author concurs: in the final count, the strongholds contributed nothing to the fighting. They were basically a millstone around 252nd Division's neck, as the following examples illustrate:

- Although some strongholds did spot boats crossing the canal, these reports grew weaker over time. Not a single stronghold reported that the first wave of Egyptian infantry was running up to the tank ramps—not even ramps located 1,000 meters from the entrance gates. As a result, the tanks that approached the strongholds were caught totally by surprise and paid dearly.

- Neither the Botser nor the Lituf stronghold observed any amphibious vehicle movement when Egyptian 130th Brigade began fording Little Bitter Lake a quarter of an hour before the Egyptian shelling commenced. The crossing took about forty minutes, and the first vessels reached a point north of Lituf at 14:36. There was no warning whatsoever from the strongholds or from long-range surveillance because the observers had already pulled out.

- Egyptian artillery pummeled the strongholds with massive shelling, making observation all but impossible (as the opponents of the strongholds foresaw). However, even the strongholds that were spared an artillery barrage provided no reports.

- On the first day of the war, some of the strongholds sent artillery corrections to the batteries firing on enemy bridges and infantry concentrations. Second Lieutenant Rafael Eldan, commander of the Mefatseyach stronghold, proved his mettle. He scored a direct hit on a bridge in the water and kept up a constant stream of reportage until the stronghold fell on Monday. (Eldan received the Distinguished Service Medal after the war.)

- The strongholds' fire against the enemy was generally ineffective. Heavy shelling destroyed sections of the strongholds and paralyzed some of their heaviest weapons (81mm mortars and MAG machine guns), but even the weapons that were still operable were hardly used due to the intense psychological pressure and the soldiers' low level of combat proficiency.

No Discussion of Evacuating the Strongholds

When construction of the Bar-Lev Line was discussed in December 1968, no one brought up the possibility of evacuating the strongholds before a war. In a 1972 meeting on the defense of Sinai, the chief of staff determined that once a stronghold ceased to contribute to the war effort, was not being harassed by enemy efforts, or had been bypassed by the enemy, it could be evacuated. This was an ambiguous directive with impossibly complex conditions. How can one determine whether a stronghold is "contributing"? What constitutes an enemy effort against a stronghold? And if the enemy has circumvented a stronghold, how can it be evacuated? Who has the authority to order an evacuation—the commander in the field, or his superiors? These conditions remained hazy and were not tested in the first night of the war.

The Dovecote order stated that the stronghold personnel would be replaced by or reinforced with crack infantry troops, but the order made no mention of evacuation (let alone under enemy fire), and no drills were ever carried out for reinforcing or evacuating the strongholds. Sharon raised the question of evacuation with the chief of staff on several occasions, and he argued that the time to evacuate the strongholds was the moment large-scale activity began. In a conference in Southern Command on July 25, 1974, Sharon recalled that when he had been in charge, he had wanted to evacuate all the strongholds except those north of Kantara, and he had advocated a reduction in their number. He said that Albert, commander of 252nd Division, and Dan Laner, commander of the division before him, feared for the strongholds if war was renewed. According to Sharon, one of the sanest suggestions was to order their evacuation.

Indeed, such an unwritten order was issued when Sharon was commander of Southern Command, but apparently it was not conveyed to his replacement, Gonen. Or perhaps it was conveyed but Gonen did not fully absorb its implications or did not agree with it. Gonen stated, justifiably:

> Until the postwar summaries, I never came across a plan for evacuating the strongholds, neither in writing nor orally. In the command's "Dovecote" Plan the opposite was the rule. It entailed holding the thinly manned strongholds and replacing the forces at "H" hour + 48. . . . During a GHQ meeting on January 24, 1972 nothing was mentioned about evacuating the strongholds. According to a February 14, 1972 stronghold file, the stronghold was defined as a collecting station for wounded and observation post, tasked with reporting enemy activity, preventing a canal crossing, . . . obstructing the [enemy's] advance, disrupting the enemy's movement in his rear, and so forth.[96]

Prior to 252nd Division's staff meeting at 13:30 on Friday, October 5, the day before the war, Albert jotted down: "Stronghold evacuation alert."[97] But the order to execute was never issued.

Muddled Orders to Evacuate

The fog of war and the difficulty of obtaining an accurate picture of the situation are unavoidable elements in every war. The higher up a headquarters is in the chain of command, the later the reports arrive and the greater the background noise, errors, lack of critical information, and misinterpretations. In the first hours of the fighting, 252nd Division, Southern Command, and GHQ were not immune to these plagues. The erroneous picture was missing two crucial elements: the location of Egypt's main effort, and the circumstances of the IDF forces in contact with the enemy. Although the division's and command's picture of Egyptian territorial gains was wide of the mark, especially in the northern sector (Gonen mistakenly informed the chief of staff at 17:00 on Saturday that Lahtsanit and Mifreket had fallen), the general picture was optimistic.

This overly optimistic assessment was probably the reason for the baffling order to stand by for Zefania, which was issued to 460th Brigade, 275th Territorial Brigade, and the commander of 162nd Division. Some of the overconfidence may have resulted from the IDF's temporary return to and control of the Mitla opening in the Mefatseyach area and the tolerable situation at some of the strongholds, such as Milano in the northern sector and Purkan, Matsmed, and Lakekan in the central sector. Thus, a false picture—one that was accurate only locally and temporarily—took shape: considerable areas of the canal were believed to be under IDF control. Of course, no one could have predicted that the situation would take a sharp turn for the worse during the night, especially since the tank losses and crew casualties had not yet been tallied.

Adding to the sense of control over the situation that first evening (not necessarily misperceived) was the superb fighting of the junior commanders and soldiers of 252nd Division, who engaged the enemy and were determined to carry out their desperate mission of defending the waterline. The units' matter-of-fact reporting, devoid of despair or panic, gave headquarters (which was listening to the operational frequencies) the impression that the situation was under control. Thus, 252nd Division, Southern Command, and

GHQ concluded, at least until sundown on Saturday, that there was no need to evacuate the strongholds. According to Gonen and Elazar, a return to the waterline in a matter of hours seemed likely.

Although permission for a comprehensive evacuation had been denied earlier, it would be wrong to think that the division, the command, and GHQ were indifferent to the strongholds' plight. This denial of permission to evacuate does not refer to explicit requests to evacuate the Lituf stronghold in the southern sector, where tanks from C Company/52nd Battalion came to extract the wounded, or the Mifreket stronghold in the northern sector, where tanks from 198th Battalion/460th Brigade twice entered to remove the wounded and left only five soldiers to hold the fort.

No records can be found of discussions in 252nd Division, Southern Command, or GHQ about evacuating the strongholds either before or after the fighting started. Nevertheless, the log of the command's aide-de-camp contains a significant notation regarding Gonen's order to Albert, indicating that permission to evacuate had apparently been granted and only had to be conveyed: "Send tanks to all the strongholds in the area of the [enemy] crossing and . . . evacuate the force, report to the general."[98]

At the GHQ level, the question of evacuating the strongholds was first brought up for debate in a conversation between Elazar and Gonen at 17:55, but this was only a corollary to Elazar's impractical instructions to leave the force concentrated. "If Ras Masala is marginal—then I'm willing to evacuate it," he said. "If there's a vehicle—they can be evacuated. The chief of staff grants permission." Southern Command's aide-de-camp wrote: "The chief of staff is prepared to evacuate the stronghold so that the forces won't be divided."[99] Nothing in this conversation implied blanket permission to evacuate all the strongholds; it referred only to Egrofit (Ras Masala)—a marginal, thinly manned stronghold (whose location Elazar probably did not know)—although Gonen presumably could have applied the same criterion (marginality) to the rest of the line. An hour later, in the operational discussion group, the chief of staff reiterated the idea of concentrating the effort: "Think where the center of gravity is and concentrate the effort there even if it means that some of the strongholds have to be abandoned. I've informed the general of Southern Command that if a stronghold isn't threatening the enemy's effort, he can evacuate it. I don't want to hold onto any strongholds unless they can seriously disrupt [enemy] efforts."[100]

The chief of staff's order is perplexing. The Egyptians were not making a main effort. All the strongholds (excluding Egrofit and Lakekan) were under artillery fire as well as low-trajectory fire, but they were contributing nothing to the effort to block the Egyptian crossing. Under these circumstances, Elazar should have issued a precise, unequivocal command to Gonen: either evacuate all the strongholds as soon as possible or hang on to every one of them. Another possibility—which the chief of staff apparently intended but was carried out only at Egrofit—was to maintain those strongholds that were a vital element of the defense plan and abandon those contributing nothing to the fighting. While his order was being conveyed to Gonen, Purkan, Matsmed, and Lakekan in the central sector and Botser, Lituf, Mefatseyach, and Hakfar in the southern sector could have been evacuated relatively easily.

The chief of staff's muddled evacuation orders did not escape the notice of the Agranat Commission. Elazar testified that he had explained to Gonen over the telephone that he did not want to keep the strongholds unless they were impeding the enemy's main efforts; when a stronghold lost that capability, it had to be evacuated. The commission pressed him: "In the 401st's sector . . . you heard the units and strongholds. Then this was the night when you had to decide whether or not to evacuate." Elazar's reply: "Let me be clear about this. I didn't want to hold the strongholds, [I] only [wanted] to fight against [the Egyptians'] efforts." Unfortunately, the chief of staff's statements were ambiguous and did not reflect his conversation with Gonen.

Gonen told the Agranat Commission: "I asked for and received permission to evacuate Ras Masala. There was no order to evacuate [other] strongholds on Saturday evening." The commission persisted in its questioning: "No one said there wasn't an order. You received an order to evacuate the strongholds because an order was given to evacuate strongholds where no main effort was being made. Don't say that there wasn't such [an] order. Either you didn't receive it or you didn't understand it?" Gonen, a seasoned officer and a stickler for disciple, understood perfectly well his commanding officer's intention. He answered: "I received no order."[101]

This was the unfortunate result of the chief of staff's vague, convoluted manner of issuing orders. Even his aide-de-camp, Avner Shalev, affirmed that Elazar gave Gonen no definitive order to evacuate the strongholds; instead, he left the decision to Gonen. On that day, it was likely, perhaps even unavoidable, that his statements would be misconstrued as they passed down the chain of command until they reached the field. The same thing happened in his morning conversation with Gonen regarding the Dovecote deployment, and it would happen on the evening of October 7 in Dvela (the command post at Um Hashiba) regarding the rationale for the following morning's counterattack, as well as during the counterattack itself.

Elazar expected Gonen to understand from their conversation about the enemy's main efforts and the evacuation of Egrofit that Gonen had the authority to evacuate the entire line. But this seems absurd. On such a critical matter, the chief of staff should have expressed himself in the clearest of terms. In six areas the chief of staff blundered with regard to the evacuation of the strongholds:

1. There was no follow-up in the form of a written command from GHQ to Southern Command that encapsulated the chief of staff's intention to evacuate strongholds that were "not threatening the enemy's effort."
2. Elazar failed to see that there was no main effort. Therefore, his criterion for evacuating the strongholds was based on a false premise.
3. On such a fateful day, and involving such a critical matter, decisive, sharply worded statements were required, not cryptic declarations.
4. The chief of staff did not understand that the strongholds were contributing nothing to the IDF's efforts and had become an operational liability.
5. The chief of staff was unaware of the problems involved in evacuating a stronghold under fire.
6. His most flagrant mistake was not recognizing the imbalance between the IDF regulars and the enemy and not addressing Israel's severe disadvantage at the start of the war.

It was the chief of staff's duty, as Elazar often stated, to be the key figure in the next day's fighting. Had he planned for the next twenty-four hours, he would have realized that without an immediate order to evacuate the strongholds, disengage the regulars from the line, and change the method of defense, there would be no tomorrow for 252nd Division. As the Day of Atonement drew to a close, Elazar (in consultation with the prime minister and the defense minister) had to decide on defensive tactics to replace "not one step" and defense on the waterline at all costs.

To complete the picture, one can assume that if Gonen had thought it vital to evacuate the strongholds, he would have interpreted the chief of staff's hazy statement as formal permission to do so. But Gonen did not think the strongholds had to be abandoned. At this point, he still believed that they were contributing to the canal's defense, that the situation had stabilized, that Israeli forces would return to the waterline that night or during the coming counterattack, and that the strongholds could hold out until then. If he had wanted to, he easily could have ordered the evacuation of the Lakekan, Matsmed, and Botser strongholds when he evacuated Egrofit.

According to General Adan, when Dayan visited Southern Command's tactical operations center at noon on Sunday, he failed to understand why the strongholds had not been evacuated overnight and why the chief of staff's response had been so indeterminate. Elazar told the Agranat Commission: "It's obvious from my summaries and instructions to the general of Southern Command that I wanted to hold onto the strongholds only if they were actively stalling major efforts. . . . I informed the general of the command at 18:00 Saturday that if a stronghold is not endangered by an enemy effort, he could order its evacuation. The idea was that the strongholds would evacuate themselves—not [that we would] launch an attack to evacuate them." During the IDF senior staff conference he said, "I'm not giving them up at the start of the war. I'm playing with them. When the fighting commences I'll leave them for the main efforts. I'll evacuate all the strongholds in marginal places. . . . This was how I expressed myself at 17:30 on Saturday. The strongholds—only for main efforts. All the 'marginal' ones can be evacuated. The battle didn't begin well and we had to study it."[102]

Adding to the confusion was the fact that the authority to order an evacuation of the entire stronghold line—GHQ's rear defensive line—lay with Southern Command and GHQ rather than 252nd Division, where a much bleaker and more realistic picture was emerging than at the two higher levels. These complications surrounding the authority of command arose precisely because operational decisions (such as linking up with the strongholds) were made at the division level. Albert, however, chose not to put his authority to the test with regard to evacuating any of the strongholds; he deferred to Southern Command and requested permission whenever a call for evacuation came from the field (all of which were answered in the negative).

The belief that the situation would soon improve—certainly after the counterattack—was a major reason for denying permission to evacuate. Shomron recalled that early on Sunday morning he had informed Albert that the strongholds were being held by a handful of soldiers and an immediate decision had to be made whether to evacuate them or replace them with fresh mechanized infantry troops. (Shomron was wrong. It was too late to replace the soldiers in the strongholds.) Albert's answer was unequivocal: bringing in new troops was impossible, and evacuating the strongholds was absolutely forbidden.[103] Thus the situation remained static. Shomron avowed that he had never been issued an explicit order to abandon the strongholds, and Albert had rejected a proposal to evacuate them on foot, since this would have meant leaving some of the wounded behind. According to Shomron, the assessment was that, after the October 8 counterattack, the Israeli forces would be able to reach the strongholds, evacuate the defenders, and replace them with fresh troops. The order he received on October 8 stated: clear the canal line of the enemy and remain in the strongholds (as a follow-up to the 143rd's attack in the southern sector during the counterattack).

The assumption that the IDF would return to the strongholds was not unrealistic on the night of October 6–7. Such a return was actually carried out at Budapest on October 9, and after a few failed breakthrough attempts, the soldiers were replaced by fresh troops. Gideon Avidor recalled that no one intended to evacuate anything that night, and the general feeling was that the situation was under control. "We linked up with the strongholds and evacuated the wounded. Some of them requested evacuation but the division was ordered not to evacuate them because 'everything is under control.' On October 6 only Lahtsanit fell. The answer to the strongholds that requested evacuation was: 'Quit bellyaching, everything's OK.'"[104]

According to Baruch Harel, deputy commander of the 252nd, the basic assumption was that the strongholds had been built to withstand assaults, and their job was to hold the line. An initial check showed that the first day of the war had gone relatively well, and since all the strongholds were still accessible, no one gave priority to evacuating them. At dawn, the bitter reality became known.[105]

Gonen, too, recalled that the stronghold question was not raised on Saturday night. He believed the strongholds had to function as forward observation posts for real-time reportage. He had no reason to believe that the Egyptian attack would be any more successful on Sunday than it had been on Saturday, so evacuation seemed unnecessary. "Why should I have thought on Saturday night that the strongholds had to be evacuated when no one on the ground was calling for it? Why should anyone in Southern Command have thought they had to be evacuated?"[106]

Gonen was mistaken. There were definitely calls for help from Lituf in the south and Mifreket in the north, where linkups had been made twice. (It is possible, but doubtful, that these calls for help never reached Gonen.) Repeated requests to abandon the strongholds were relayed to General Kalman Magen, commander of the northern sector, beginning on Saturday night. All of them were answered in the negative.

In Southern Command's postwar conference, Gonen stated that an order to evacuate the strongholds was issued at 21:23 on Saturday. "At midnight—a second order was issued. The extraction of the men in the strongholds could have been carried out on Saturday night."[107] This is the sole testimony about such an order. It is possible that Gonen was referring only to the evacuation of Egrofit. In fact, in those critical hours, he thought that the situation was under control and that the massive Egyptian crossing had been stopped except in the Hizayon area, which was why the strongholds were not evacuated. According to his account, "By midnight—we had linked up with all the strongholds. At 02:00 we felt the attack had been halted. At 05:00 Sunday, there was a renewal of the Egyptian attack, and within hours we were seven kilometers from the water line."[108]

In a meeting in Refidim on March 5, 1974, Sharon asked whether any order to evacuate the strongholds had been received during the day or evening on Saturday. Harel replied that the division did not request permission to evacuate the strongholds and did everything it could to hold the waterline. "In the southern sector we managed to reach the line and patrol the area between the Hakfar and Hamezach strongholds. . . . Throughout the night until sunrise we believed that we were linked up with the strongholds and that our situation wasn't that bad. Things became worse in the morning when we received the figures on our tank losses and casualties."[109]

In the marshlands north of Kantara, the situation was much

worse. By Saturday night, Israeli units were no longer operating there; only individual soldiers and tank crews remained, and they were trying to escape. For all practical purposes, the regular armor force had abandoned the area from south of Kantara to the southern edge of the northern sector, and if the Egyptians had dared, they could have penetrated deep to the east.[110]

One controversial and sensitive subject is the cries for help coming from the strongholds. The truth is that, in many cases, the troops shut themselves up in the bunkers and goaded nearby tanks with screams of "They're all over us" or "Kill 'em for us." This created intense psychological pressure on the field commanders at all levels, and the tanks persisted in their futile efforts to link up with the strongholds, even when doing so proved counterproductive to the main assignment: stopping the Egyptian crossing. This was the case in the central sector at Hizayon, in the northern sector at Mifreket, and in the southern sector at Hamezach, which the Egyptians had already cut off on Saturday evening with chains of mines and antitank troops. "The strongholds dictated the shape of the battle and interfered with it," one commander complained. "We couldn't ignore the sheer panic in their cries for help. We responded because we thought we were strong enough to knock them [the Egyptians] out on the water line."[111]

In general (as Tal foresaw), the strongholds did not fire their weapons. On the southern sector's radio frequency ("Dahlia"), the commander of 52nd Battalion was heard rebuking the Hakfar stronghold for its exaggerated report of being under heavy fire. "No one's laying down murderous fire on you," he told the troops there, and then demanded that they fire their 81mm mortar at Egyptian infantry in the area. The Ketuba and Derora strongholds were also screaming for help on the radio, but after the war, it turned out that not a single Egyptian soldier had ever approached them. Many of the strongholds were heavily shelled by artillery and came under heavy tank fire from the western bank and the Egyptian infantry that had crossed the canal, but the Egyptian troops generally bypassed the strongholds in the initial stages of the war, preferring to just seal up the entrances and deal with them later.

Which Strongholds Could Have Been Evacuated, and When?

Some strongholds did not have to be evacuated; others could have been evacuated and should have been; some could not be evacuated; and two—Egrofit and Lakekan—evacuated themselves without any assistance.

Northern sector. Traklin (which was not attacked) and Budapest survived the war. The strongholds north of Kantara—Orkal, Lahtsanit, Derora, and Ketuba—could not be systematically evacuated because of the nature of the terrain and the fighting; however, some of the soldiers managed to break through to friendly lines. A force led by the deputy commander of 460th Brigade reached the Milano strongholds at Kantara at 04:00 Sunday and could have evacuated them (some of the troops made it out on their own between Sunday night and Monday morning). Mifreket could have been evacuated during the two linkups on Saturday night.

Central sector. The Hizayon stronghold was in trouble and could not be reached. It is doubtful whether it could have been evacuated during the night. There was no linkup with Purkan on Saturday night. The situation was tolerable there, and the stronghold could have been evacuated. (It eventually evacuated on the night of October 8–9 with the help of 184th Battalion.) Matsmed's situation was satisfactory, and the 184th's tanks in the vicinity could have evacuated it on Saturday if the order had been given. (The next day, Matsmed could have evacuated to Lakekan on foot via a trail along the shore of Crocodile Lake, as the commander of 14th Brigade urged, but the stronghold commander decided to remain in his position.)[112] The 184th's tanks maneuvered around Lakekan on Saturday evening, and the stronghold could have been evacuated. (Thanks to the 14th Brigade commander's exhortations, it evacuated in its own half-tracks on Sunday afternoon, moving out on Akavish Road to Tasa without encountering any problems.)

Southern sector. The Botser stronghold evacuated on its own (there were six tanks in the stronghold) and pulled out overnight between Monday and Tuesday. Tanks linked up with Lituf twice on the first night of the fighting and could have evacuated the stronghold, but permission was denied. The rescue attempt on Sunday morning failed. The soldiers in the stronghold were ordered to flee, under the cover of artillery fire, and try to reach 46th Battalion's tanks, about 1,000 meters from the stronghold. The troops took off, encountered an Egyptian force, and dashed back into the stronghold. The defense minister cited the attempted evacuation of Lituf as a serious blunder.[113] The Mefatseyach stronghold at the Mitla opening was in fairly good shape between Saturday night and Sunday morning and did not request evacuation, although it could have communicated with the adjacent tanks. A Company/52nd Battalion, which had sustained heavy casualties on the ramps east of Hakfar, linked up with that stronghold. Hakfar's situation did not require immediate evacuation, but it could have been evacuated on Saturday night. Hamezach, a large, formidable stronghold, could not be evacuated and surrendered on October 13. As noted earlier, Egrofit, a thinly manned stronghold, evacuated on its own on Saturday night.

As dawn was breaking on Sunday, the division, in coordination with Southern Command, decided that the strongholds had to be evacuated. However, for many if not all of them, it was already too late. Under these circumstances, the painful but unavoidable decision was made to break off contact with the strongholds. This decision from Southern Command, with the chief of staff's approval, was conveyed to 252nd Division at 09:37. There were two considerations: first and foremost, the need to conserve the remaining forces (110 tanks out of the original 283), which would be possible by retrograde and delaying operations west of Artillery Road; and second, the division's assessment that the first stage of the attack had ended, Egyptian armored and mechanized divisions would soon arrive and continue the thrust east, and the smaller Israeli force would be able to deal with them from positions superior to those adjacent to the strongholds. The forces had to be conserved and time gained until the reservists arrived.[114] In the end, the enemy armored divisions did not cross the canal, and the attack halted with the Egyptians' territorial gains of October 7. The IDF disengaged from the waterline and withdrew to the dominating terrain west of Artillery Road and on the road itself.

Based on evidence brought before the Agranat Commission, the defense minister's instructions appear to have been to "let the forces evacuate the strongholds on their own or with the help of tanks." However, Dayan's statement at 08:35 on Sunday seems contradictory: "Do not stubbornly hold onto the strongholds, do not stubbornly hang onto the canal now. Do not evacuate if unnecessary, [only] if there's pressure."[115]

The chief of staff informed Dayan that the previous night he had granted permission to evacuate the strongholds that were cut off. "If they're under pressure—they can leave. A stronghold that's finished its job—can evacuate."[116] This was a far cry from what he had said in the operational discussion group at GHQ and in his conversation with Gonen at 18:00 on Saturday. But Elazar did not explain how a stronghold that was surrounded by enemy forces was supposed to evacuate. The defense minister emphasized the danger of trying to reach them. Instead, a second line had to be stabilized, but he did not go into detail about where that second line would be. Although Dayan perceived the situation much more soberly than others did, he spoke as an adviser rather than a decision maker. Be that as it may, evacuation was already impossible.

At noon on Sunday, Dayan visited the command post (Dvela) at Um Hashiba and announced that a supreme effort should be made at once to evacuate the troops in the strongholds. If they could not be reached, the soldiers inside should break out and link up with other Israeli forces. He added that he would not be demanding their evacuation if he thought a counterblow could be delivered within twenty-four hours and the Egyptian lines broken. But he agreed with the chief of staff: an attack could not be launched until the following morning.[117]

On Sunday afternoon, in a discussion with Elazar, Dayan repeated his position that attempts to link up with the strongholds had to cease: "Whoever can get out on his own—let him get out. The wounded who remain will be taken prisoner; the canal can't be held. We have to decide tonight whether to evacuate them." He informed Elazar that this was exactly what he had told Gonen and then added: "I told him [Gonen] that this was a ministerial opinion, and he [the chief of staff] will contact you and you'll receive further instructions."[118]

Elazar agreed with Dayan: whoever could get out should do so. This was the cold truth and the right direction to take. Unfortunately, it was uttered twelve hours too late. Elazar suggested that the order to evacuate should be issued that night: "Wherever evacuation is possible—we'll pull out. Where it's impossible, we'll leave the wounded. Whoever makes it [to our lines]—is saved. If they [the men in the strongholds] decide to surrender—so be it! We have to inform them that we can't reach them and they have to try to break through [to our lines] or surrender. Hundreds of Egyptian tanks are already on the eastern bank. Any attempt to reach the strongholds will wear out our tanks."[119]

At the Monday morning meeting with the government, the chief of staff's intermediate summary of the evacuation of the strongholds was detached from reality. He stated:

> The question at the outbreak of the war on the canal had been whether to remove the men from the strongholds that were likely to be overtaken, but I thought they were too valuable to abandon. The current balance was quite tolerable: of the thirty something strongholds only two had fallen and ten were successfully evacuated. A disaster had been averted and no stronghold had collapsed because of artillery fire. Several strongholds are still hanging on. Others we might not be able to evacuate. In other words, this is a satisfactory balance for a war. It's not a catastrophe.[120]

The chief of staff's update was far from accurate. There were only sixteen strongholds on the canal, not "thirty something." It was wrong to say that only two had fallen, and the claim that ten strongholds had been evacuated was far from the truth.

In a sorry epilogue, on October 10 (at 18:00), Dayan asked Elazar why he hadn't evacuated the strongholds on Saturday night. And if a warning had been given on Friday night and tank crews flown to Sinai, why hadn't the strongholds evacuated when it became clear that contact with them was going to be broken off? These were incisive questions (which went unanswered), but Dayan should have asked them before hostilities erupted. More important, he should have ordered the evacuation himself.

At 09:37 on Sunday, Gonen told Albert that every stronghold that could be evacuated had to be evacuated. Albert replied, "Evacuation is unfeasible." At 12:06 Gonen ordered the division to extricate the forces from the strongholds, either on their own or with the assistance of armor. (This is the background of 46th Battalion's attempted evacuation of Lituf.) Thirty-five minutes later, Gonen ordered Adan to evacuate Derora and leave the wounded to be taken prisoner.

Of the 505 troops in the strongholds, 126 were killed or missing, 162 were taken prisoner, and 135 were rescued. Sixty-five in Budapest held on until the end (see appendix 6). The tank brigades suffered 279 killed and missing in action on the first day. Of these, 103 were from 14th Brigade's three forward battalions, and the rest were from the six battalions reinforcing the line. The 9th Battalion suffered the largest number of losses—34 tankers and 20 mechanized infantrymen—which was one-fifth of the losses in the tank brigades in the south. In the first day of battle, 252nd Division sustained heavy losses: 345 killed and missing in action. To this number would be added the first casualties of the reservist divisions.[121]

Operational Doctrine

In the war summaries, Elazar outlined his operational doctrine for the strongholds—a vague operational concept that was out of touch with the Dovecote order and the situation on the ground at the start of the war. "I didn't consider the strongholds as a defense line," he said. "If I'd been commanding the 252nd Division and was ordered to hold the canal . . . I would have concentrated the tanks in companies and battalions and held the strongholds, assisting them with tanks and reinforcing them here and there with tank platoons, but I wouldn't have given them up at the outset. I'd have kept them for the main efforts and evacuated them only where there were no battles being fought. The marginal places I'd have evacuated."[122]

The chief of staff ignored the "not one step" concept and the Dovecote deployment, which called for dividing up the brigade on the line; he ignored the lack of an Egyptian main effort and the absence of marginal strongholds (except for Egrofit and Botser). Even at this stage, he may have been unaware of the reality on the canal line during the first two days of fighting. In the Southern Command conference after the war (July 25, 1974), he repeated the deplorable phrase he had used in the command's senior staff meeting in February: "'I'll play with them when the war begins,' that's how I expressed it at 17:30 on Saturday [October 6]."

Dayan could not believe what had happened to the three main elements—armor, air force, and strongholds—that were supposed to disrupt the canal crossing and severely impair the enemy forces. Instead, he noted, the line was held by a reserve unit with very low combat proficiency—a far cry from the paratroopers who were supposed to be manning the strongholds according to Dovecote.[123]

In addition to the inescapable chaos and fog of war, a number of orders that were issued that first evening can only be described as delusional. For example, at 20:00 Gonen instructed the division commander to reach Orkal, then continue the momentum and capture the Egyptian stronghold 900 meters north of Orkal. At 22:00 Gonen ordered the commander to ascertain that 460th Brigade was engaging an Egyptian force that had crossed at Jisr al Hresh.[124] But at the time these orders were given, the roads through the marshes and the paved road on the eastern bank had already been cut off, the decimated 9th Battalion had been removed from the order of battle roster, and 460th Brigade had been split into several secondary forces. At 19:55 Gonen ordered Albert to send 35th Brigade into action on the line and reinforce the strongholds. Obviously, he was unaware that this was no longer possible.

The next morning, Gonen conveyed a palliative message to the chief of staff. Elazar warned him against being optimistic and advised him to prepare for worse to come. The diary entry made by the chief of staff's aide-de-camp at 06:30 on Sunday states: "The situation in the canal sector is between bad and very bad. Danny [401st Brigade commander Dan Shomron] is having a tough time. The situation on the northern sector is bad."[125]

Meanwhile, the Golan Heights strongholds (excluding Mt. Hermon) were held by two regular infantry battalions: 50th Battalion/Paratroop Brigade and 13th Battalion/Golani Brigade. These troops' combat proficiency was incomparably higher than that of the reservists of 16th Brigade manning the Bar-Lev Line down to the Lituf stronghold and of 904th Nachal Unit posted in the Mefatseyach, Hakfar, and Hamezach strongholds. It is undeniable that the quality and combat aptitude of the infantry on the Golan Heights had a decisive impact on the defense of the strongholds there. Had troops of higher caliber been deployed in the strongholds in Sinai, as they should have been according to Dovecote, the results of the fighting on the Bar-Lev Line would have been different, and its collapse could have been prevented. This is a sober professional estimate that is not intended to depreciate the courage of the men on the canal, who encountered extremely stressful conditions. Taking their level of military capability into consideration, they conducted themselves reasonably well. Harel expressed it best: "Had the troops been more tenacious—the strongholds wouldn't have fallen. We could have disrupted the crossing."[126]

With crack infantry troops, the strongholds could have held up and stopped the Egyptians from gaining territorial contiguity on the eastern bank, with its long-term operational implications. By way of comparison, the Botser stronghold, which the IDF abandoned, was captured by a small Egyptian force from the amphibious 130th Brigade. It was repeatedly pummeled but held its position against Israeli forces backed by air and artillery support.

Summary of Mistakes Involving the Strongholds: October 6–7

The wide dispersal of the line brigades' eighty-eight tanks, the premature use of the division's reserves, and the application of tanks according to War of Attrition drills (employing platoons and reduced companies fighting from static defensive positions rather than conducting a mobile battle to smash the Egyptian crossing effort) sealed the fate of the defensive battle and the strongholds in the first two days of the war. The Egyptian army's attack—five infantry divisions reinforced with antitank weapons on the eastern bank, supported by antitank weapons on the western bank—was too much for the small, static Israeli armor force that lacked regular and mechanized infantry units and artillery support. The 252nd Division's strength was exhausted as it fought a heroic but futile war of individual tanks and platoons.

Many shortcomings led to the IDF's initial failure in the war: the absence of an explicit concept of how the strongholds should function in wartime; the lack of a clear picture of the situation in all headquarters up to the GHQ level; the chief of staff's ambiguous and indecisive instructions; and Southern Command's and GHQ's misreading of the battlefield, which necessitated the evacuation of the strongholds overnight between Saturday and Sunday. Elazar should have known that, given the opening conditions and the order of battle, it was impossible to remain close to the waterline and maintain the canal as the rear defensive line. The evacuation of the strongholds and a withdrawal to the east should have been ordered to minimize the regulars' exhaustion and maximize damage to the enemy until the Rock divisions arrived. The 252nd Division was dragged into a ferocious yet pointless battle of attrition and, in the end, was forced to break off contact at noon on Sunday and retreat to Artillery Road.

Certainly, the low combat proficiency of the regular and reservist infantrymen in the dilapidated strongholds, whose number had been vastly reduced from the original Bar-Lev Line, detracted from the forces' ability to conduct a tenacious and effective battle in the strongholds. The strongholds made only a token contribution to the defensive battle, with a few early reports of sporadic attempts to adjust artillery fire on the bridges.

The Withdrawal to Artillery Road

Although the 252nd's disengagement from the canal line on Sunday morning was obligatory, the eastward withdrawal in the southern and central sectors could have been more limited, leaving the IDF with terrain that dominated Canal Road. This would have been of enormous operational significance, and it would have allowed the 252nd to wait on the high ground until the reservists arrived. In reality, the Egyptian army halted on Canal Road on Sunday morning about three kilometers east of the waterline, and wherever it tried to advance, Israeli tank fire stopped it in its tracks—even though IDF forces were greatly reduced.

The order to break off contact with the stronghold line and the canal was painful for many reasons, but especially because it was an admission of the failure of the defensive battle and of the operational concept for the canal's defense. It was an agonizing development for 14th Brigade's battalion commanders, who had direct responsibility for the strongholds in their sectors and were now being ordered to abandon them; they realized they would not be returning in the foreseeable future. But the order was unavoidable when the degree of damage to the tanks became known.

The forces engaged in combat did not convey a sense of emergency, but division and Southern Command understood that disengagement was necessary. Until the reservists entered the fray, the new defensive line had to be held against the Egyptian armored and mechanized divisions that were about to cross the canal (or so it was believed) and continue their push east. A convenient line for establishing a defensive structure was the series of hills overlooking Artillery Road, where deployment required carrying out retrograde or delaying operations, for which the division had never practiced or prepared.

At 09:40 on Sunday, Gonen updated the chief of staff that the division had withdrawn to Artillery Road, although a considerable number of units remained close to Canal Road (79th and 196th Battalions in the central sector and 401st Brigade in the south). The disengagement gave the division an opportunity to conserve its forces and assemble them in companies, battalions, and brigades that could be used for a flexible defense and the mobile armor battle the IDF excelled in. And indeed, those units that were well trained in maneuver and fire quickly adapted to the new situation, and by noon on Sunday, a handful of tanks from 52nd Battalion destroyed Egyptian tanks in a maneuvering battle in the southern sector.

By Sunday afternoon, the 252nd Division's regulars had withdrawn to Artillery Road, and they were joined by 162nd and 143rd Divisions and the 252nd's reserve units beginning on Sunday and throughout Monday. In the northern sector, where 9th Battalion/275th Brigade and 198th Battalion/460th Brigade had incurred heavy losses, the reservists stabilized the line without any regulars.

Disengagement

Disengagement from the Egyptian force that had crossed the canal and advanced east was carried out in four stages.

First stage: keep your distance. At 06:11 on Sunday, Colonel Shomron, commander of 401st Brigade, told Lieutenant Colonel Sakal (the author), commander of 52nd Battalion: "At this stage, don't risk your tanks. Take control of the ramps [along Canal Road]. Employ long-range gunnery and don't get into close range of their missiles. . . . Do not go back to the canal line. Remain in distant positions. As of now, your tanks are our most important weapons and I don't want to risk them in attacks on the canal line."

Second stage: disengage from the stronghold line. At 09:19 Shomron ordered the 52nd's commander to fold up and move out to the Notsa fortification. The battalion commander (nonplussed) asked: "You want me to leave the area?"

Shomron, worried about an Egyptian armor penetration south of Lituf, answered: "Affirmative, there's nothing we can do, otherwise you'll be surrounded. Position yourself in the Notsa area."

The battalion commander responded: "I'm not surrounded yet. Can I wait a bit longer?"

Shomron reconsidered: "Roger. Maybe. But take care not to get surrounded. The minute you see them cutting you off, let me know and I'll order you to reach Notsa."

The battalion commander stubbornly held his position on the

ramps. At 09:55 Major Paz, commander of C Company/195th Battalion, which was reinforcing the 52nd, identified a massive penetration south of the Lituf stronghold: thirty to forty Egyptian tanks moving east in the direction of the Nehushtan area.

Third stage: move east. The 52nd's commander realized that this was the moment of truth: he had to break off contact with the enemy. At 09:59 he gave the most difficult order he had to issue during the war: "All forces move east." The small force disengaged and entered new positions three kilometers west of Notsa and Artillery Road. At the same time, 195th Battalion also disengaged from its positions opposite the Hakfar stronghold and Hamezach Junction and moved out to the Typhoon dirt road. The 46th Battalion did the same and moved east from Lituf to the Polish Camp.

Shomron, who had ordered the deeper withdrawal east to Artillery Road, affirmed at 10:02 the battalion's deployment farther west. Now that the line west of Artillery Road had stabilized, the 401st waited for the newly mobilized reservists. In a burst of optimism, Shomron told the 52nd's commander: "All the people of Israel are behind us. We're not alone. Our problem is that we need a little more time."[127]

Fourth stage: counterattack on Mitla Road. At 12:26 an attempt to evacuate the Lituf stronghold in 46th Battalion's area failed. To create a diversion in the Mitla Road area, a handful of tanks from 52nd Battalion attacked and retook forward positions at the "Madonna," about 2,000 meters from Canal Road, and knocked out a number of Egyptian 19th Division's tanks on Lexicon-Canal Road. There was a feeling that this was a watershed event and that the tide of the war might change. The 52nd's commander reported to the brigade commander at 13:12: "I'm at the Madonna in a fire engagement with enemy tanks. We have successes. If you bring up '3' now [195th Battalion/401st Brigade] on the left flank we can push them back."[128] However, at this point, the 401st was unable to carry out the requisite move, and the sense of local success soon evaporated because of the lack of strength—the greatest obstacle in the regulars' defensive battle.

Shomron described the situation in the clearest of terms: "Permission should have been given much earlier to break off contact with the strongholds so that concentrated counterstrikes could have disrupted the crossing."[129] He also stated that the tanks left the canal line at around 10:00, and wherever the Egyptians had penetrated, the brigade's tanks demolished them. By 11:00, he realized he could no longer link up with the strongholds and informed Albert that further attempts would prevent him from sealing the Gidi and Mitla openings. Therefore, he was requesting permission to disengage, pull back east to Artillery Road, and shift to a mobile defense. The division commander granted him permission.

Reasons for and Consequences of the Excessive Withdrawal

Unlike the crisis atmosphere that pervaded headquarters, the commanders in the field did not sense a state of emergency. The Egyptians had not yet broken through, and the main concern was stopping their eastward advance, conserving the division's strength, and attempting to rescue the wounded.

In the northern sector, Egyptian tanks made inroads four kilometers from the canal line at Kantara (the area 9th Battalion had vacated) and El-Balah Island (the area 198th Battalion had left). In the central sector, the Egyptians penetrated Missouri without interference, and in the south (south of Lituf and Nehushtan), they reached Artillery Road at its bend near the canal.

On Sunday the 401st could have successfully deployed on a line farther west of Artillery Road three to four kilometers from the canal (in the Polish Camp, east of Lituf, in the "Madonna" area, and at the perimeter of the Karat Moora range), beyond the reach of the antitank missiles on the western bank. It could have waited there for 164th and 875th Brigades, maintaining control by firing on the Hamezach–Ras Sudar Junction. Holding this western line could have created a significant operational advantage in the following days by influencing the choice of sector for the October 8 counterattack. Tank fire could have been applied against the Egyptian armor on the canal plain, and artillery fire could have been concentrated against the Egyptian infantry, which had hastily entrenched without cover, causing it heavy damage. The same moves could have been carried out in the central sector with the arrival of the Rock artillery on October 9. The feeling of having squandered an opportunity was accompanied by the fact that at 07:00 on Sunday, 195th Battalion was ordered to vacate its positions on Yoreh Road and opposite Hamezach Junction, despite the absence of pressure from the enemy. On Monday morning 52nd Battalion reentered this area, which was still completely free of enemy forces.

Brigadier General Gideon Avidor (Ret.), the division's G-3, challenged Shomron's statement regarding permission to withdraw to Artillery Road. According to Avidor, even before Gonen ordered Albert to break off contact with the strongholds at 09:20 on Sunday, Shomron had already withdrawn his forces to the east on his own initiative. Albert had not yet decided to move to the Artillery Road line. In fact, the division was thinking in terms of a forward movement—not a withdrawal and delaying action. Shomron claimed he was under pressure in the Hakfar and Hamezach strongholds and that any forward movement there would incur casualties; therefore, there was no sense in reentering them. Because of this, Albert gave permission to fall back a short distance from the canal and organize. However, during the postwar debriefings, the battalion commanders stated there would have been no problem remaining in their positions east of Canal Road.[130] On the baffling withdrawal too far to the east, Captain Yaron Ram, commander of C Company/46th Battalion/401st Brigade, said: "For all practical purposes we abandoned the line of sand dunes overlooking Canal Road even though the enemy wasn't there. . . . We abandoned it because we feared a breakthrough to the south that in the end didn't take place."[131] Around noon the order was given to return to the dunes above Lituf (in a failed rescue attempt).

The 401st commander's fear of having his small tank groups surrounded by Egyptian tanks penetrating from south of Lituf is the reason why he pulled back 46th and 52nd Battalions to the east on Sunday morning. That afternoon, the two battalions headed west again without encountering the enemy. Shortly afterward they returned and withdrew from their dominating positions—the dunes of Lituf and the "Madonna"—an unnecessary move after the failed attempt to extricate the troops at Lituf.

According to David Shoval, commander of 46th Battalion, the Egyptians did not execute an exploitation; therefore, the battalion could have fought with its reduced tank forces from Sunday noon until the reservists arrived, without a massive surrender of territory and definitely west of Artillery Road.[132] The 195th Battalion commander, Lieutenant Colonel Lanzner, also described the pullback from positions opposite Hamezach and Hakfar as too deep. In this area, Yoreh Road was abandoned, and if the Egyptians had wanted to, they could have advanced east on it without interference. Only a reduced tank company defended the junction of Yoreh Road and Artillery Road between October 9 and 12, until 202nd Battalion/35th Brigade sealed it.

Shomron's abiding concern about being surrounded and conserving his enervated forces, even at the cost of ceding a large area, is understandable, given the brigade's order of battle—twenty-three tanks, no support, and no information on the reservists' time of arrival. Only in retrospect can we say that his fears were exaggerated. On October 8–9 the brigade's forces were operating west of Artillery Road, within range of enemy tank fire from Canal Road. The loss of Karat Moora on October 9 necessitated stabilizing the line on Artillery Road in the center of the southern sector, but north and south of the sector, the dominating areas west of the road could have been held.

The Reservists Take Over

On Monday morning, the transfer of responsibility to the reservists in the southern sector was done in an orderly fashion on Gidi Road. The 875th Motorized Brigade assumed control of the Lateral Road–Gidi Road junction. The 164th Tank Brigade (consisting of diesel-powered Centurions), after a backbreaking, fatigue-inducing drive from Eilat on their tracks, assumed responsibility from 46th Battalion for the western side of Artillery Road, including the Mitzva fortification.

In the central sector, 14th Brigade forces held the Arov, Haviva, and Talisman Roads. Although the unit had sustained heavy losses, it halted the expansion of the Egyptian bridgehead and continued to dominate Canal Road in most of the sector until Sunday noon—two kilometers from Hizayon, two and a half kilometers from Talisman-Lexicon, west of Nozel, and as far south as Talisman.[133] Only on Sunday afternoon, after 143rd Division took over the sector at 16:00 and its commander realized that a linkup with the strongholds was no longer possible, did he instruct his forces to disengage in the midst of a long-range firefight and confirm that the Egyptians had not broken through the Talisman, Haviva, and Akavish Roads.

The Egyptians concentrated their effort in the Firdan area. Facing them was 421st Brigade/143rd Division, which had just arrived.

Two battalions of 14th Brigade (the 184th and 79th) suffered many casualties. Lieutenant Colonel Nitzani, commander of 79th Battalion, was hit in the afternoon, and the remainder of the battalion was ordered to Tasa to reorganize and join the better-situated 196th Battalion, commanded by Lieutenant Colonel Mitzna. (From this point on, the 196th was called the 79th, retaining the older battalion's number.) Mitzna was the only battalion commander on the contact line in the central sector, and by Sunday late afternoon–early evening, the Israeli forces had, in effect, disengaged from the enemy in this sector.

Missed Opportunities

From the evening of October 6 to the morning of October 7, tank platoons, pairs of tanks, and bits and pieces of companies from 14th Brigade, 184th Battalion, and 79th Battalion were sent via Akavish and Tirtur Roads to the gap between the Purkan and Matsmed strongholds; they even reached as far north as the Shik-Lexicon Junction at 11:00 on Sunday. This proved that Akavish and Tirtur were clear of the enemy, but the 184th did not advance west from Akavish 52, and no attempt was made to take up positions on the Hamutal and Makhshir high grounds. Due to the small number of forces, the southern part of the central sector had been prematurely abandoned.[134] In retrospect, the Tirtur and Akavish junctions with Lexicon Road could have been held by the fragments of platoons and companies in the area, which could have been combined into two reduced tank companies and a reduced mechanized infantry company, thus becoming a significant force by the standards of October 6–8.

In the central sector, in the Nozel area on Talisman Road, a pullback as far as Artillery Road had not been necessary, and the commander of 196th Battalion emphasized that the enemy had not broken through. This was the situation on Monday when 14th Brigade was suddenly ordered to the southern sector, along with the entire 143rd Division, and hastily left its positions before transferring them to another force.[135] Although the withdrawal to Artillery Road appeared to be too deep, the critical situation of 184th and 79th Battalions must be taken into account. The central sector, like the southern sector, was without air assistance and had only the flimsiest artillery support. There was an obvious need, justified by the conditions that existed on noon Sunday, to safeguard the remaining force, even at the price of relinquishing an area that could have been held. Nevertheless, with the arrival of 143rd Division's reserve units on Sunday evening in the Nozel, Havraga, and Televizia sectors, it seemed that the opportunity to hold on to the terrain dominating Canal Road had been lost.

The situation in the northern sector was different. After incurring heavy losses, 9th Battalion could no longer be counted in the order of battle on Saturday evening. With the departure of the deputy commander of 460th Brigade from Kantara and the withdrawal of the remnants of 198th Battalion from the Mifreket area on Sunday morning, the IDF lost control of the Mifreket-Orkal-Budapest triangle up to the fortifications line. Had the Egyptians wanted to, they could have advanced east without interference up to Lateral Road. But for all practical purposes, excluding their initial penetration to about four kilometers east of Kantara, the Egyptians had halted their advance. Southern Command mistakenly assumed that they had proceeded north as far as Artillery Road. This was the situation until Monday morning, when Major General Avraham "Bren" Adan's 162nd Division led the attack on an area devoid of enemy forces.[136] The northern sector had not been transferred to 162nd Division in a deliberate manner. Adan had assumed responsibility for the sector via radio on Sunday morning. Then, in a meeting with the commander of 460th Brigade, he learned that no units were left in the sector—there were only scraps and a few tanks.

Failure to Disrupt the Egyptian Tank Crossing

As stated, at noon on Sunday, the Egyptians halted their advance and began to dig in on Lexicon Road, with no attempt to pursue even a limited objective such as Artillery Road. Accounts of the Egyptians' operational management by Israeli combat commanders in the three sectors generally stress that the Egyptians made no attempt to expand the bridgeheads beyond the areas they already held. In the few places where they did try to advance, such as the Firdan area, the deputy commander of 196th Battalion stopped the Egyptian tanks in a fire battle as they tried to push east on Haviva Road. The commanders of 79th, 196th, and 198th Battalions and the deputy commander of 184th Battalion all stated that on October 7 the Egyptians made no attempts to attack them, except for lateral maneuvers. On the night of October 7–8 there were no Egyptians in Hamutal and Makhshir.

The Egyptian forces halted their advance primarily for tactical reasons. The only two bridges available for a tank crossing in Third Army's sector were in 7th Division's sector—one at kilometer 137 of the canal and the other at kilometer 141—and both had been bombed from the air and were incapacitated from Sunday afternoon to Monday evening (one bridge in 19th Division's sector was erected only on the evening of October 8). Only three tank battalions of Third Army had managed to cross the canal by Monday evening, and this lack of heavy armor seems to be the main reason why the Egyptians did not advance more than three to five kilometers beyond the bridgeheads. They preferred to wait until they amassed enough strength to resume the armored attack eastward. The Egyptians' fighting to secure the bridgeheads now lacked the tenacity and spirit that had characterized the first echelon across the canal. This rate of development disappointed and worried the Egyptians' General Headquarters.

There was another reason for concern: the Egyptians claimed that the water jets that had punched holes in the dirt embankment in the southern sector had turned the clay soil into mud, which caused the armored vehicles to skid and sink. Thus, their timetable was pushed back much further than intended.

In the central and northern sectors of the canal, Egyptian Second Army's bridging operation was proceeding better than Third Army's, and the first tanks had already rumbled across near Mifreket on Saturday evening. Here, too, there were delays, but less serious than those encountered by Third Army. The Egyptians deepened their penetration to Missouri, which was devoid of IDF forces, and in the northern sector opposite Kantara. Along the rest of the sector, Second Army halted three kilometers from the canal.[137]

Other reasons for the Egyptians' halt was the fierce fighting by 252nd Division's forces against Egypt's first-echelon infantry division from Saturday afternoon until Sunday morning. In addition, Israeli tanks proved their absolute superiority in every armor battle beginning on Sunday morning. This advantage undermined the Egyptians' self-confidence, forcing them to reduce their risks, concentrate their strength, and wait for a stable bridgehead protected by antitank weapons before continuing their thrust east.

Despite the adverse beginning for the IDF, the campaign could have turned to Israel's advantage on October 7, at least in the southern sector. In every encounter between Israeli and Egyptian tanks, IDF armor demonstrated its superiority, and the Egyptians stopped their advance. Had Israel employed its tanks correctly—in maneuvering, not as "bunkers"—beginning at dawn on Sunday, the enemy's armor crossing could have been severely disrupted in many places and brought to a halt.

The fact is that the Israeli tanks did not attempt to maneuver against the armor spearhead in the southern and central sectors, even though it would have been relatively simple to do so in front and on the flanks of the enemy's desultory penetrations. The small number of bridging areas and the limited activity in Egyptian Third Army's sector undoubtedly would have facilitated the success of an Israeli armor maneuver. In the central sector, the Egyptians had put up a large number of bridges, so stopping them there would have been tougher but not impossible if an Israeli force had been deployed earlier.

To examine these scenarios, a virtual condition test was conducted of an Israeli armor combat force facing its Egyptian counterpart on Sunday morning. Hypothetical battles were analyzed involving reduced companies from 46th and 52nd Battalions/401st Brigade in the Nehushtan area in the southern sector (Egyptian Third Army's sector) and 79th Battalion/14th Brigade in the central sector (Egyptian Second Army's sector in the Tuson, Sarafeum, and Sheikh's Tomb areas). Analysis of the virtual results of historical battles is an accepted research tool, but this is the first time the Tactical Numerical Deterministic Model (TNDM) was used for the Yom Kippur War.

In the southern sector, a reduced company from 52nd Battalion and especially 46th Battalion, with four reduced companies (though exhausted from heavy fighting but still with considerable capability), could have been applied on the Archimedean point of the defensive battle on the morning of October 7 to block the Egyptian spearhead south of Lituf in the Nehushtan area. However, this maneuver was not carried out. In the central sector, the gap between the Matsmed and Purkan strongholds was devoid of any Israeli presence when hostilities broke out. The virtual scenario assumes that 252nd Division sent 79th Battalion/401st Brigade to fill in the gap earlier than it actually did. The division had such a plan but failed to employ it.

It can be assumed (as the analysis of the virtual battles shows, although it is dangerous to form conclusions based on it) that the IDF could have blocked the Egyptians' armored crossing in the southern sector, which was initially vacillating and overly cautious because they could not believe their good fortune in finding no Israeli tanks facing them. All the brigade, division, or command needed was a flash of operational insight. This was the one and only chance to turn the tide by commanding the tank units to disengage from the strongholds and deploy in front of the breakthroughs from the bridgeheads. In those fatal hours on the morning of October 7, the IDF lost an unparalleled opportunity in the southern sector to thwart Third Army's armor as it rolled across the only two bridges south of the Lituf stronghold (see map 7).

This was one of the major flaws in the defensive battle and the entire war. The main reasons for Israel's failure to execute such a maneuver were the lack of a general defense plan that incorporated mobile combat; the failure to identify dominating areas; unfamiliarity with the area between the stronghold clusters and fear of entering terra incognita in wartime; certainty that the reservists were about to arrive and that everything would turn out fine; the commanders' reluctance to lose their few remaining tanks in high-risk moves; fear of the Egyptian armored divisions' breakout and the wish to deploy in front of them in familiar, suitable terrain on Artillery Road; and, last but not least, the mental pressure and fatigue felt by commanders in the field. This is what prevented the IDF from identifying the evolving operational situation—that is, the Egyptian armor crossing and the golden opportunity to block it.

The situation in the central sector was different. Unlike in the southern sector, no Israeli force was available on Sunday morning. In other words, there was a wide-open gap between Purkan and Matsmed. This deficiency bordered on operational irresponsibility on the part of Gonen, the general of Southern Command, and Albert, the commander of 252nd Division. The only force available to close the gap was 79th Battalion/401st Brigade, but only part of it was sent to the sector late at night on October 6–7. As the battle simulation in the central sector illustrates (see map 8), Egyptian 16th Division's armor crossing could have been thrown into confusion, halted, and forced to pay such a high price that the Egyptians probably would have ceased the crossing operation after losing two tank battalions on one bridge (in reality, the Egyptians halted when they came up against IDF tanks).

The tank battle simulations and virtual scenarios show that if tactical maneuvers had been carried out on Sunday morning in the southern sector, and if the gap had been closed in the central sector, the tide of the war could have changed. Blocking the armored crossing would have left the Egyptian infantry tightly deployed in shallow positions, without cover on the eastern bank between the Israeli embankment and Lexicon Road, and exposed to fire from three artillery groups of 252nd Division and the Rock divisions beginning on October 9. But tactical maneuvering was not done.

The Picture at Headquarters Darkens

In every war, there is considerable divergence between the reality in the field and the situational picture at headquarters. This was especially true during the first two days of fighting on the southern front, when Southern Command and GHQ were presented with an increasingly bleak picture that was far from accurate.

Although the field reports clearly indicated that the Egyptians were not advancing beyond Canal Road (excluding one deeper tank penetration in each sector), headquarters doubted the IDF's ability to hold the positions dominating Canal Road in the central and southern sectors, beyond the range of antitank weapons on the western bank, until the reserves arrived.[138] This grim estimate stemmed from the reports of heavy losses in 252nd Division, the realization that air support could not be expected, and discouraging intelligence reports. Also, Dayan's disheartening statements at Southern Command on Sunday morning took a toll on morale. Southern Command and GHQ had difficulty interpreting the enemy's situation that morning and assumed that the Egyptians would continue the attack according to the Soviet warfare doctrine: advancing with armored divisions to exploit the success.

Failure to identify the size of the Egyptian armored crossing (first the divisional tank battalions, then the mechanized brigades' tank battalions, and finally the tank brigades attached to the infantry divisions) led to a misunderstanding of the Egyptian armored divisions' intentions and the erroneous announcement that Egyptian 4th Division (minus 3rd Brigade) and 21st Division (minus 14th Brigade) had crossed from their positions on the western bank to the eastern bank on Sunday. This miscalculation had serious implications.

General Tal (whose account contains many accurate operational assessments) realized that things were not as dismal as headquarters thought. He reported his conversation with the commander of 252nd Division, who acknowledged that his present situation was tolerable and that he was four kilometers west of Artillery Road in the southern and central sectors.[139] This important and accurate information did not penetrate the consciousness of the chief of staff, who ordered Gonen to prepare a second defensive line at 07:25 on Sunday (a correct move on its own). He repeated this order half an hour later and spoke of a possible counterattack in three days. Albert's 09:30 report to Gonen—that a breakthrough of scores of tanks had been identified between Purkan and south of the island, north of Hizayon, and in Lituf—was conveyed within fifteen minutes to the chief of staff, who ordered a retrograde and delaying action. Reports to the high command post at 11:45 describing the eastward penetration of approximately sixty tanks from south of Lituf toward the Gidi and Mitla openings added to the feeling that the situation was deteriorating rapidly. These last reports were inaccurate: an armored column that had passed through Egyptian 7th Division's sector was designated for 19th Division (which had failed to bridge the canal and would succeed only on Monday evening) and was moving south on Lexicon Road; a second column had managed to penetrate to Artillery Road. An intelligence summary from 10:00 reported an Egyptian attack along the length of the southern sector, the retreat of Israeli forces to Artillery Road, and enemy armor crossings on three bridges (there were only two). Only at 13:00 on Sunday did the correct picture emerge: the Egyptians had halted. At approximately 15:30 the head of intelligence revised the earlier assessment: "armored divisions have not crossed yet."[140]

Misleading Reports from Southern Command and Military Intelligence

At 12:37 Gonen relayed a bleak report to the chief of staff: he was withdrawing to the passes and hoped to hang on to Tasa until 143rd Division arrived. Appended to this was a somber tally of losses from the air force commander: eleven pilots killed, twenty airplanes lost.

"The situation is very bad—Gonen's pulling back to the passes," Elazar said after receiving the reports.[141]

But Gonen's picture was much darker than the actual situation on the ground. A line of positions could have been stabilized in the central and southern sectors, where tank fire could have dominated the canal plains and Lexicon Road. Had this line been held, forces from the reserve divisions could have reinforced it that evening and contributed significantly to the IDF's situation.

Gonen's pessimism notwithstanding, the chief of staff believed that the southern front had stabilized, and he informed the government shortly after 10:00, "The Egyptians have made a few more gains but they're exhausted and their advance has been blocked. Therefore the situation on the canal was a little better this morning."[142] Tal's report to the chief of staff later that morning was more balanced and based on facts:

1. All the strongholds were surrounded; none could be evacuated (correct).
2. Units from 252nd Division were five to six kilometers from the canal (correct).
3. The Egyptian infantry and 200 to 300 tanks controlled the entire eastern bank (correct).
4. IDF tanks would be hard-pressed to reach most places on the canal (correct).
5. IDF forces were positioned on Artillery Road and farther east (incorrect).
6. The accretion of Israeli forces was proceeding faster than expected (correct).
7. Albert had reported that 252nd Division's situation was satisfactory, and that it was located four kilometers west of Artillery Road.

Tal added: "If the air force manages to hit the bridges—this will be a great contribution."[143]

The reports emanating from the southern front contained inaccurate, dispiriting intelligence updates prepared in GHQ and Southern Command's rear headquarters at Beer Sheva. Although these appendages were groundless, they added an important stratum to the gloomy picture being painted in Gonen's command bunker at Dvela.

Searching in Vain for the Egyptian Main Effort

It is not clear how Branch 6 (the Egyptian department in the IDF intelligence branch) could publish a report at 16:35 on Saturday stating that there were signs of two main efforts: one in the Kantara sector and the other opposite the opening to Mitla Road. Even more baffling, MI documents prepared in 1972 emphasized that "no main effort is expected in the crossing that will be on a wide front the length of the canal." Nevertheless, Southern Command and 252nd Division ceaselessly sought a main effort. Gonen testified that beginning at 14:05 and for the next hour and a half, he asked himself the basic question pondered by every commander: where is the main effort? Only ninety minutes later "did I realize that there was no main effort, that the whole sector was the main effort."[144] The chief of staff, too, erred in the operational group discussion at 18:35 on Saturday when he built his fighting concept on the assumption that there was a main effort.

Another intelligence blunder: where were the armored divisions? The war plan outlined by MI in 1972 explicitly stressed that the armored divisions would not cross the canal in the first stage. The question remains how the intelligence reports, based on surveillance of Egyptian 4th and 21st Divisions, could maintain on Saturday evening, "It can be stated with certainty that the Egyptians are making a divisional effort on Gidi Road and there are continuous warnings that the 4th Division is about to cross."[145] The belief that the armored divisions would follow the infantry attack and the uncertainty of their whereabouts testify to the IDF's ignorance of the Egyptians' offensive plan. This unfamiliarity added raucous "noise" in both Southern Command and GHQ, whose intelligence systems were under intense pressure even without the surplus input. Elazar saw the armor crossing on the Egyptian front as the greatest threat to the entire IDF structure, which was probably the reason for his order on Saturday night to deploy the tanks in four efforts.

On Sunday noon the commanders were still waiting for the armored divisions' breakthrough and assumed it would occur in Second Army's sector. This assessment was backed by two intelligence reports that morning. According to the 10:00 report, "A main effort seems to be underway to transfer [across the canal] the second echelon of the Third Army—the 6th Motorized Division and 4th Armored Division—if they succeed in securing the bridgeheads."

The 11:00 report stated: "Assessment: the two armies are about to transfer the armored divisions to the eastern bank."[146] When colored smoke was sighted in the Mitla opening across from Mefatseyach on the morning of October 7 (thought to be a gas attack), Gonen believed this was the start of the major crossing.

Before the crossing was identified, Gonen's office log noted that the general assumed (overoptimistically) that the Egyptian crossing had failed because the armored brigades were not on the eastern bank. Israeli intelligence, too, reassessed the armored divisions' status. In a conversation with the chief of staff between 14:00 and 15:00, the head of intelligence said, "We're beginning to look into a new assessment—the armored divisions didn't cross." Additional mistakes appeared in intelligence reports during the initial hours of fighting. For instance, an intelligence collection from 22:00 Saturday stated that, based on Egyptian reports, bridgeheads had been established to a depth of six kilometers, and the Egyptian forward forces were twenty-two kilometers deep in Israeli territory and expected to link up with them (apparently, these were intentionally deceptive reports created by the surviving commanders of 130th Amphibious Brigade on Gidi Road). A Southern Command intelligence report from 01:30 Sunday stated that an Egyptian force had reached seven kilometers east of the canal. According to another report from 10:00, armored vehicles had joined the offensive. A report from 13:30 claimed that the Egyptians were continuing to advance on the crossing roads.

If MI's situational assessments had been compared with reports from the forces engaging the enemy late Sunday morning, the discrepancies would have been apparent. Also, Sunday's and Monday's aerial photographs showed that the Egyptian armor concentrations were only a short distance from the canal. Since the infantry's positions and concentrations were not known, it was difficult to determine the exact line the Egyptians had reached (as forces from 162nd Division moved south in the counterattack, they did not encounter the enemy until they turned west opposite the Hizayon stronghold). On Monday, the picture in Southern Command was the same as Sunday's—the enemy had advanced to Artillery Road—when in fact there were no enemy forces east of Lexicon.[147] The wishful thinking that a main effort accompanied by a breakthrough of armored divisions had been identified blinded the intelligence analysts and decision makers.

A conversation with commanders on the ground or careful attention to the radio transmissions of IDF units in the field would have made it clear that the Egyptians had stopped, that the IDF units could remain on the line west of Artillery Road, and that the previous situational assessment had caused 252nd Division's overly deep withdrawal on Sunday. Even in the war summaries, Gonen presented a harsh, mistaken picture of the Egyptian advance, declaring that on Sunday noon the Egyptians had nearly reached the artillery line or a little west of it.[148] The grim view from Southern Command brought the defense minister to the Pit, where he expressed his concern over the situation at 14:25 Sunday:

> This has now become a struggle for the survival of Israel. The Moroccans and Jordanians will enter the war, and I believe the entire Arab world will end up being involved. Our weapons are limited; we'll simply be worn away. I suggest going to the Americans. We'll ask them for tanks, whatever they have in Europe. . . . [But] this will take time. . . . Maybe in the meantime there'll be a ceasefire, but whether or not they bring the tanks there won't be any others, and Israel will have to be defended. I'm not saying that we have to flee at this point.[149]

Hasty Planning for Defense

On Sunday morning the IDF, Southern Command, and 252nd Division had no defense plan or ground analysis of Sinai that could be updated as the situation changed. No plan existed—not even a skeleton one—for a retrograde and delaying operation. No one had performed a preliminary operational analysis for a defensive battle on the second line—Artillery Road—and the rear defensive line had been left undefined. Furthermore, no staff work had been carried out overnight for the 252nd's disengagement or delaying operation to the east, even when it became clear that such a move was in the offing.

Tal claimed that a retrograde and delaying plan was prepared in the Pit, but at 07:20 on Sunday, even before Southern Command's instructions to break off contact with the strongholds, the chief of staff ordered Gonen to plan a second line (not a rear defensive line) in case of an Egyptian breakthrough. He did not mention a rear defensive line or its location (Elazar's aide-de-camp noted in his log: "[we'll either be] standing on a stubborn rear defense line for a rather long time or on a temporary line from which we'll launch the counterattack").[150]

No situational assessment, not even a hastily prepared one for a defensive battle, was carried out, and the fact that the Egyptian attack had halted was not fully appreciated. In general, those hours were characterized by shoddy staff work and an unsystematic conduct of operations at all levels. The chief of staff's orders to the general of Southern Command on the morning of October 7, and from there to 252nd Division, were to plan a second line, organize properly for a defense with two divisions, and not insist on defending the canal and the strongholds. The orders from Southern Command to the strongholds conveyed distress and the intention to deploy the Rock divisions, which had started to arrive in bits and pieces, on Lateral Road but not farther west.

Dayan's visit to Dvela at 11:45 on Sunday was a turning point in the deliberations that day. He assessed the situation and gave official backing to the formulation of a hasty defense plan that would answer the following questions:

- What would be done with the strongholds?
- Where would the second line be?
- Where would the retrograde and delaying lines be?
- Where would the rear defensive line be—Artillery Road, Lateral Road, or elsewhere?
- Should the reserve divisions be integrated into the defense plan as reinforcements for the 252nd or sent to the new rear line from which the counterattack would be launched?

Dayan's position has been recorded in a number of sources, reflecting varying degrees of pessimism. He later said he had insisted that the command prepare a second line, and his suggestion had been Artillery Road. When Gonen stated that he could not hold a line at Artillery Road, Dayan declared that in the present situation he had the authority to order the preparation of a second line, the location of which would be determined by the chief of staff. If Artillery Road could not be held, a line would have to be set up in the passes, but the second line had to be implemented immediately so the Egyptians could not break through and advance along the coast of the Gulf of Suez to Abu Rudeis.[151]

Dayan made it clear to Gonen that he doubted the forces could hold on to the waterline; therefore, the men in the strongholds had to be evacuated in any way possible. He added that the IAF would be diverted to the south to attack the bridges, but there was no guarantee they would be destroyed. Therefore, the waterline would have to be abandoned and another line prepared, and the men in the strongholds would have to break out and link up with IDF forces because the tanks could not reach the canal. As Dayan admitted, if he had believed that an attack could be launched within twenty-four hours and succeed in breaking through the Egyptian line, he might not have thought it necessary to evacuate the strongholds, but he doubted such an attack was possible.[152]

Dayan reckoned that Southern Command would not be able to counterattack the following day, but he changed his mind that evening and authorized the chief of staff to order the attack for Monday morning. Regarding the IAF, he said, "Look what the air force gives you this evening. If there's a miracle [the bridges are eliminated]—then so be it. Even then the canal line is no longer a line. I'm firm on making a new line. Don't exhaust yourselves on the strongholds. . . . Check with Dado [Elazar] about this line—Artillery Road or elsewhere. After you see what the air force accomplishes—you decide."[153]

Later, Gonen claimed that Dayan had told him during the meeting, "Today is not a battle day; it's war for Israel's survival. Leave the strongholds. Withdraw to the mountains."

"I'll withdraw when I have to," Gonen replied.

"This is ministerial advice," Dayan said, and ended the conversation.[154]

In the spirit of Dayan's instructions, Gonen ordered Adan to organize his division on Lateral Road, with secondary forces on Artillery Road. He ordered Albert to remain where he was or, if this was not possible, to prepare a rear defensive line on Lateral Road. Gonen also told Adan and Albert that if they could not reach the men in the strongholds, they should instruct the troops to break out after dark.

At 12:30 Gonen informed the chief of staff that he hoped to hold on to Tasa until 143rd Division arrived, and he had told Dayan the same thing. He reiterated that he believed the 252nd was capable of holding Artillery Road. As he later acknowledged, he updated the defense minister that he had no intention of abandoning the road. "Forces will be assembled. We'll use the air force. We'll see [what happens]."[155] Gonen considered the decision to hold Artillery Road—despite orders to the contrary on Sunday—as one of Southern Command's two cardinal decisions in the war (the second was the Sunday night decision to launch the counterattack the next day).

After Dayan left the command post, Gonen ordered the division commanders (Adan at 12:30 and Albert at 12:35) to make a main effort on Lateral Road and at the outposts on Artillery Road and to inform the men in the strongholds that they had to break out that night if they could not be reached before dark. At 13:06, after Sharon reported that he would have an additional eighty tanks in three hours, Gonen ordered him to concentrate his force at Tasa, take Lateral Road, and deploy small forces on Artillery Road.[156]

At 13:10 Gonen described the deployment to the chief of staff and stressed that holding Artillery Road depended on the swift arrival of 143rd Division with a large force, which would remain at Tasa. Elazar approved the plan, and Gonen suggested Lateral Road as the rear defensive line. In this unrealistically optimistic atmosphere, Gonen laid out three possibilities for a counterattack: north, south, and Dwersuar. Elazar was against employing the 143rd for a counterattack. He explained to Gonen, in his usual vague terms, that the first stage had to ensure the stabilization of the defensive line and the holding of every road that could be held. Elazar decided that 143rd and 162nd Divisions would have to hold Lateral Road as a rear command line that the Egyptians could attack and pay dearly for. "After this we'll shift to the counterattack," he stated. The chief of staff made it clear that he was concerned about the piecemeal pace of force amassment and was opposed to bringing the 143rd forward because he feared its forces would be quickly depleted. He added in his customarily imprecise manner—without mentioning a rear defensive line or where it should be—"I'm not telling you how many tanks, but I want you in a situation where you're positioned as required on the line and whoever is forward, is holding. Let him go by the book for the retrograde and delaying operations. . . . If you reach the line of the passes—that will be the defense line. If you have to, stay there for a day or two until we change the situation. I want to be certain that you form a strong line. Do this with Arik [Sharon] and Albert from Tasa in the south and Bren [Adan] in the north."[157] The chief of staff's aide-de-camp noted: "Let Arik be your rear line. The chief of staff wants a situation in which you're positioned at the passes."[158] On Sunday noon, Elazar thought the first line was holding up fairly well, but "it's like irrigation in a citrus grove, you never know when the water will gush out."

Just as the meeting between the chief of staff and the defense minister was about to begin, the deputy chief of staff held an operational discussion group, and Tal's sharp, straightforward conclusions served as a basis for Dayan's and Elazar's consultation at 14:25: (1) the defensive battle was being conducted reasonably well, and the enemy had not achieved operational objectives; (2) IDF forces were exhausted; and (3) the IDF's goal—to restore balance in the area—would be achieved by stabilizing static defensive lines and assembling fresh forces. Tal also noted that three divisional headquarters were now in contact with the enemy. He suggested that two of them remain in contact and the third deploy to the rear. He assumed, based on his conversation with Albert, that the 252nd's situation, four kilometers *west* of Artillery Road, was still tolerable. Albert reported that Egyptian tanks were packed closely together on Canal Road and were streaming across the bridges; there was danger of a flanking movement that would require the IDF's tanks to break off contact. Tal added, "If we could demolish the bridges, this whole force buildup would grind to a halt."[159]

At the 14:25 meeting, Dayan (just back from Dvela) presented Elazar with his somber impression and expressed his skepticism about the ability to hold Artillery Road. He proposed pulling back in a retrograde and delaying battle to a short rear line and stressed the unfeasibility of trying to reach the strongholds. Earlier, Elazar had informed Dayan that Gonen, fearing the fate of the strongholds, had approved their evacuation. Elazar agreed with Dayan on the need for a second line, but he thought the situation was not as grim as the defense minister depicted it. "There's always time to withdraw," he said. "If we can disrupt the Egyptians, we have two divisions and should attempt a massive counterattack."[160]

Tough questions were raised regarding the continued conduct of the war in the south. Dayan outlined the deployment in three layers: infantry in the rear (possibly at the passes), two divisions in the rear, and 252nd Division forward.[161] In reality, the situation was different. In the end, the 252nd disengaged to Artillery Road without a retrograde and delaying operation.

On Sunday noon, as part of the hasty defense planning, one of the weightiest issues facing Southern Command was how and where to use the reserve divisions. In the end, they were ordered to counterattack and were given responsibility for specific sectors: 162nd Division the northern sector, and 143rd Division the central sector. (After the counterattack's failure on Monday, both were assigned a major role in the defensive battle.)

Sharon testified that since the Egyptians were advancing and the line in front no longer seemed stable—not only in the canal area but also east of the canal—he had been ordered to position his forces on Lateral Road, thirty to forty kilometers from the canal, and was allowed to retain only limited forces a few kilometers forward on Artillery Road. "In the afternoon when I reached Tasa I immediately discovered that the situation was much better than I'd been told and that our forces were much further forward than where Southern Command believed they were. Therefore I requested permission to turn things around: hold our main structure in the Artillery Road area about ten kilometers from the canal, and retain small forces in the rear junctions. Permission was granted."[162] Contrary to Sharon's recollection of events, Southern Command's operational log states that Gonen ordered him to keep the division's main force on Lateral Road and not to engage the Egyptians.

Sunday afternoon was one of the low points in GHQ. This was obvious at the 14:25 meeting between Dayan and Elazar. The chief of staff insisted that the most important matter was to stabilize the line, and for this to succeed, the air force was needed. "I don't know when we'll shift to the counterattack. I don't have enough forces," he told Dayan. "I'm willing to attack earlier but first I have to know where the forces have stabilized. Unless we're stabilized I'm afraid we won't know where to stop or where to concentrate the force . . . so we have to stop, and I don't want to take any risks."[163] Unaware of the IAF's inefficiency, the chief of staff did not determine exactly where the line would be. His statements also expressed his growing frustration with the commanders at the front, who failed to understand him. "The truth is that with two of these commands, either I'm not speaking clearly or they don't comprehend me. This isn't the first time that I said [the line has to be stabilized]. I don't remember when I said it first, [perhaps] this morning. Shmulik [Gonen] didn't do the opposite, but he spoke with me about the opposite."[164]

Dayan presented the assessment of the commanders from the south and his guidelines for a gradual withdrawal under pressure, up to the stable line on Lateral Road—not Artillery Road—relying on

the passes and Ras Sudar. He suggested that the men in the strongholds be ordered to break out under cover of darkness. "Whoever's
killed—is killed. The wounded can remain and be taken prisoner.
. . . We're losing our strength in vain. We have to secure the vital
facilities." In other words, before the IDF could go over to the counterattack and cross to the western bank of the canal, a suitable force
had to be assembled and concentrated, or else the operation would
be doomed. Dayan, the backbone of Israeli security just twenty-five
hours earlier, added, "Let me say, this is the concept. . . . If you buy
it—good; if not—then it's my approach. I'm not saying we have to
flee now."[165]

Dayan realized the importance of establishing a line in the
mountains as long as the Egyptians were not pressing forward. He
was ready to evacuate the oil fields as a last resort, and he expressed
the fear that if the war continued, the IDF would find itself without
weapons. The last line of defense, from his point of view, was Sharm
el-Sheikh and a strip to the west—with or without Saint Catherine.
"Right now I'm worried about Israel for the next fifty years," he
said.[166]

Elazar agreed with Dayan on the need to stabilize a line with
the two reserve divisions on Lateral Road (excluding the evacuation of Ras Sudar). He wanted to shift to the counterattack once the
line stabilized and destroy the enemy on the eastern bank, with the
aim of crossing to the western bank. The 35th Brigade would secure
Ras Sudar.[167] The budding optimism that pervaded Southern Command with the arrival of the first reserve units was the reason for the
urgent demand to counterattack.

The main points of difference between Elazar and Dayan—
which continued to be debated in the GHQ discussion after Dayan
left for the government meeting—involved the timing of shifting
forces to the second line. According to Dayan, it should be done
immediately. According to the chief of staff, the dilemma was that if
the forces went to the second line immediately and left Refidim and
Um Hashiba, it would be difficult to shift to the counterattack later;
therefore, it might be better if the forces remained where they were.
The deputy chief of staff knew there was no second line to withdraw to, and he added that the first thing to do was build one with
the forces in the rear. The forces on the front would hold, and only
if enemy pressure persisted and the line could absorb the forward
forces would it be possible to receive the retreating units.

Dayan addressed the government meeting (which lasted until 16:30) and emphasized the need to stabilize the Mitla line and forgo the canal. He predicted a long, drawn-out war involving the entire Arab world. He proposed concentrating on the line of the mountain passes, thirty to forty kilometers east of the canal, and surrendering Um Hashiba and Refidim. This would be a flexible line, with strategic facilities built behind it, and the tanks would be mobile instead of moored in one place. Under these conditions, he estimated that the IDF could beat back the offensive efforts of Egypt and Syria. He summed up the current situation:

> Regarding the balance of forces, this isn't the time for moral stock taking. I didn't judge the enemy's strength and fighting proficiency correctly and I overestimated our forces and their ability to hold the line. The Arabs are fighting much better than before. . . . They have an enormous supply of weapons. They're knocking out our tanks with personal arms. The missiles are an impregnable umbrella that our air force can't overcome. . . . Neither I, Southern Command, nor the chief of staff sees any possibility of brushing them off the canal even if new forces arrive. Tomorrow may prove that I'm overly pessimistic. Arik [Sharon] thinks that we have to break through, Gorodish [Gonen] doesn't believe it will work.[168]

The prime minister and ministers were shocked by what they heard. After listening to Dayan's misgivings about the army's ability to counterattack the next day, they lambasted him for his long-time opposition to sitting on the canal line and his support for the mountain passes line, inveighing that this was why he was reluctant to undertake an action that could return Israel to the canal. In a painful political-military analysis, Dayan assessed the situation and felt, justifiably, that some members of the government failed to comprehend the asymmetry in size and resources between the IDF and the Arabs. He expressed his fears:

> [There is] enormous risk involved in launching a counterattack and suffering heavy losses without a decision. Our forces would be eroded and end up in the midst of battle without sufficient strength. The Arabs have long staying

power—70–80 million Arabs against less than three million Jews. They have one million troops, weapons from the Soviet Union, resources from the Arab world, and other countries ready to join in the campaign. As for Israel, no one can say if or when we'll receive American assistance in the form of tanks and planes, and no one will fight for us. As the situation seems now, we have to create a new line that can be held without retreating, deploy on it, and continue the war with Egypt from there.[169]

The deliberations in Southern Command, in GHQ, and at the political level were the result of a lack of planning, the absence of an organized plan, and the need to devise a hasty defense under pressure. This was also the background to the chief of staff's presentation to the government—a rough, unsatisfying draft composed in a slapdash manner while under enemy fire, with glaring gaps. At this point, with the ministers, the General Staff, and the fighting forces in the south under tremendous pressure, Elazar set forth three possibilities:

1. Position for defense on Lateral Road, with 143rd Division in the Tasa area and 162nd Division in the northern sector. Hold there, followed by a counterattack in a day or two.
2. Position for defense in the mountain passes, which would entail surrendering Um Hashiba and Refidim.
3. Attack the canal, cross it on an Egyptian bridge, continue from there, and destroy the enemy that had crossed to the eastern bank. (According to Elazar, this was Adan, Sharon, and Gonen's proposal. He considered it a gamble.)

At the conclusion of the meeting, Elazar said he was going to Um Hashiba and would make his decision there. As he stated, the IDF would try to break the Egyptian forces on the eastern bank at dawn with 200 to 300 tanks plus air support; it would then redeploy on the line. "If it succeeds—we'll be in a good opening position, if it doesn't—it won't be fatal."[170]

The idea for the next morning's counterattack crystallized, although it was based on the unsubstantiated assumption that air support would be available to attack the bridges in daylight. It was totally lacking in operational planning and had no relation to the actual situation of Israeli and enemy forces. Elazar seriously erred in assuming that a failed attack would not be fatal, and that crossing to the western bank on an Egyptian bridge would be possible. This mistake would metastasize in the next day's counterattack.

Contrary to Dayan's pessimistic outlook (based on his visit to Dvela), the chief of staff presented Southern Command with an aggressive approach. He rejected the third possibility as too risky, however. He believed the Egyptian bridgeheads had to be attacked, and if this were successful, the forces would be in a favorable position to continue the fight close to the canal. If the attack failed, the IDF would be strong enough to pull back to the passes and deploy for defense. It is obvious from his presentation to the government that Elazar's focus was not on preparing a rear defensive line but on blocking the enemy's offensive and stabilizing the contact line to enable a rapid shift to the counterattack.[171]

Some of the main issues in Southern Command's hasty defense planning were how to deploy the reservist divisions and where to hold the line. Deliberations lasted all day. The fact is, however, the enemy's performance on Sunday was less impressive than reflected by Southern Command's orders to deploy the reservist divisions on Lateral Road (the Egyptian bridgeheads were no deeper than three to four kilometers east of the canal). At 16:25 Gonen granted Sharon permission to deploy on Artillery Road, on the condition that part of his forces remain on Lateral Road. At the same time, he rejected Sharon's proposal to evacuate the strongholds in his sector (Hizayon, Purkan, and Matsmed) on Sunday night.

Following is the deputy chief of staff's assessment of the situation on the evening of the second day of the fighting. It illustrates how things stood at the end of the stage at which the regulars were expected to hold the line alone:

A. In modern warfare with armor and aircraft, the theory that the proportion between defender and aggressor must be 1:3 has been refuted. More are needed for defense.
B. The Arab order of battle, in practical terms, is unlimited.
C. In the air—no gains. The Egyptian missiles remain intact.
D. The number of operational IDF tanks—1880, with 1070 in the south. The problem is the tank crews.
E. Fatigue of the tank crews: absolutely necessary to relieve them with fresh manpower.

F. An all-out effort might deliver a decisive blow to the enemy. At present this is a dangerous gamble. It is our last breath, and failure would be final because this is not a battle—the fate of the war depends on it. Therefore, it makes no sense to concentrate on a last effort. We have to deploy for defense in a way that preserves as much of the force as possible, allowing only a small part of it to engage the enemy.

G. We have to shift to defensive arrangements based on obstacles.

H. There is no practicable line in Sinai between the canal and passes.[172]

Relief of the Regulars

Sunday afternoon the reservist divisions arrived and were allocated to the fighting sectors on the front. The 162nd Division's headquarters reached Baluza at 07:20 and was given responsibility for the northern sector at 07:30. Adan was ordered to assemble in Baluza and to concentrate his tanks, not scatter them to the west. His mission: hold the enemy at bay.

By noon on Sunday, the 143rd had concentrated 100 tanks in Sinai, and at 16:00 it received responsibility for the central sector, including 14th Brigade. Some of its forces deployed on Lateral Road, but most of them concentrated on Artillery Road, thus ending the regulars' stage of holding alone. Beginning on Monday, 252nd Division was reinforced with 875th Mechanized Brigade, the diesel-powered 164th Centurion Tank Brigade, and 274th Tiran Brigade (composed of captured Soviet T54s and T55s retrofitted with 105mm cannon), whose activation required permission from Southern Command. The 252nd's tactical headquarters set off for Mitla.

Actually, the reservists arrived faster than expected. Their immediate entry into the battle made it clear that the postponement of the partial mobilization of two divisions on Saturday morning, not to mention the decision not to order a full-scale mobilization on Friday, October 5, had dire consequences. The arrival of the Rock order of battle three and a half hours earlier (even if only one division)—combined with an understanding that the Egyptian attack had halted with no attempt at a breakthrough by mechanized and motorized divisions to exploit the success—could have led to a turnaround in the defensive battle based on tanks dominating

Canal Road with fire in the central sector (all day Sunday) and in the southern sector (until Sunday noon). The reservist brigades could have reinforced the 252nd's depleted order of battle: 14th Brigade in the central sector at Zangvil, Tseidani, and Nozel, and 401st Brigade in the southern sector on an attainable line—the Gidi Road egress from the Polish Camp, south at the "Madonna" (the Mitla Road opening), and the western folds of the Karat Moora range, a line which had not been overtaken.[173] Thus, a stable defensive line could have been formed that commanded a large part of Lexicon Road, diminished the Egyptians' territorial gains, and done away with the need to withdraw to Artillery Road, all of which would have had a dramatic impact on the rest of the war.

Elazar left the government meeting on Sunday evening and flew to Um Hashiba to choose the defense plan: the lateral line or the passes line. In reality, none of the feverish defense planning was carried out in the field, and the GSO failed to send an order to Southern Command to deploy in a hasty defense. The mountain passes line was held by only Force Bishof from the Officers School, without any fortification; the two reservist divisions held dominating areas on Artillery Road, even though Elazar and Gonen wanted them concentrated on Lateral Road, with only small forces on Artillery Road; and Lateral Road was left undefended except for a force from 875th Brigade in the southern sector deployed at the junction of Gidi and Lateral Roads. The reservists that started amassing on Sunday morning moved west through Tasa and Baluza, which served only as way stations.

The situation stabilized on the evening of October 7 (see map 9) for a number of reasons: 252nd Division stabilized Artillery Road as a defensive line, the reservists arrived earlier than expected, the Egyptians did not break through to the east with mechanized and motorized divisions, and the air force partially succeeded in hitting the bridges spanning the canal.

After the war, the chief of staff claimed he had intended to conduct a holding battle in the area between Canal Road and Lateral Road and did not want to withdraw to the passes unless it was essential. Such a battle did not take place. Despite the Egyptians' halt, their infantry, armed with antitank weapons, swarmed wherever the IDF was absent, and the enemy continued to gain control of the dominating areas the IDF had abandoned along Artillery Road in the central and southern sectors.

The allocation of the canal sectors to the 252nd and the Rock divisions concluded the hardest part of the defensive battle after two days of ferocious fighting. The regulars, who had been holding the line and were thoroughly exhausted, briefly stepped off the stage and transferred responsibility for the next morning's counterattack to the Rock divisions.

The Counterattack: October 8–9

According to the IDF's and other armies' warfare doctrine, the counterattack is part of the defensive battle. Prussian historian Carl von Clausewitz defined it thus: "The defense is the delayed attack whose first stage is attrition and whose second stage is the counterattack, and the swift and powerful transition to the attack—the lightning sword of retribution—is the most brilliant part of the defense."[174]

On the third day of the war, after the IDF had been caught by surprise and ground to exhaustion, it tried to restore the prewar status by means of an initiated counterattack. Some of the commanders, including Gonen, even fantasized about exploiting the success and crossing to the western bank. The original plan involved a graduated two-division attack with 162nd Division first, followed by 143rd Division. In the end, this attack was not carried out. The 19th Battalion/460th Brigade attacked before noon, and 113th Battalion/217th Brigade attacked at the Firdan bridge in the afternoon as part of the plan to seize a toehold on the western bank—a plan Gonen forced on 162nd Division.

The counterattack's failure was the second consecutive blow to the Israeli military, and its self-confidence plummeted. "Israel's military-political leadership lost its balance. It thought it would return after two days, but it didn't. . . . It [the self-confidence] returned only with the crossing."[175]

The traumatic failure made it clear that this would not be a lightning-fast victory like the Six-Day War. The infantry units protected by antitank weapons on the eastern bank would not be easily "brushed away," and the Egyptian offensive had to be stopped so that the IDF could organize, stabilize the defensive line, and figure out the optimal way to continue fighting. Indeed, beginning on Monday night, and especially from Tuesday morning on, the IDF deployed on a defensive line that the Egyptians could not penetrate by either local attempts or an all-out assault (October 14). The enemy's momentum came to a halt. It was from this line that, on the night of October 15–16, 14th Brigade launched the breakthrough battle on the way to a canal crossing.

The IDF incurred heavy losses in the counterattack: nearly 60 tanks were hit, 50 of which were put out of commission. But with the arrival of the diesel-powered 164th Centurion Tank Brigade and 875th Mechanized Brigade to Southern Command's order of battle on October 8, the number of tanks rose to 600. Facing them that Monday were 750 Egyptian tanks that had assembled on the eastern bank after Third Army succeeded in repairing the bridges in 7th Division's sector and putting up another bridge in 19th Division's sector. Although the Egyptian command ordered the armies to complete the "direct action mission"—the first operational stage—on Tuesday, they failed to gain hold of the line on Artillery Road except for two areas: Hamutal and Makhshir in the central sector, and at Bakran 62, seven kilometers from the waterline, in the southern sector. Thus, not one Egyptian division managed to complete its combat assignment.

The failure of the counterattack had political implications as well as strategic repercussions for the IDF's continuation of the war. The results induced Dayan and the high command to leave the Egyptian front temporarily and concentrate on Syria. Gonen, too, admitted that "the outcome of the attack went far in determining the length of the fighting and shape of the battle up to the crossing."[176]

Timing and Planning

Before the war, the operational concept for the timing of a counterattack and canal crossing assumed that the IDF would be in strategic defense mode at the outbreak of hostilities and would cross the canal, transfer the fighting to the enemy's territory, capture that territory, and wipe out his forces, as it had in the 1956 Sinai Campaign and the Six-Day War. Another assumption was that the Arabs would achieve minimal gains and the IDF would embark from the canal line with the eastern bank in its possession. Even when it became obvious that the war would begin with an Egyptian attack and ground gains that would limit the IDF's ability to cross the canal, the IDF did not take into account the connection between the opening defensive move and the counterattack that would enable a crossing and victory on the western bank. No warfare doctrine for an assault crossing—that is, crossing a water obstacle in the midst of battle and assaulting with floating bridges brought up by the advancing forces—had been devised. There was only a plan for crossing from the contact line, and the mobility of the IDF's fording equipment was very limited; only self-propelled rafts ("crocodiles") enabled the assault crossing. The plan also failed to take the main operational issues into consideration, such as the timing of the counterattack in light of the enemy's situation vis-à-vis the IDF's, the optimal sector for the counterattack in light of the terrain, and the enemy's strength in comparison to the buildup of IDF forces. To complete the plan, a detailed accounting of forces and assignments was needed.[177]

The IDF's conditioned reflex and the belief in the offensive's superiority over the defensive had a decisive influence on the premature and insufficiently prepared attack. The Eil Barzel (Iron Ram) war game in June 1972 was a poignant harbinger of these tendencies. The commander of 252nd Division at the time, General Dan Laner, represented a more moderate approach; he thought the IDF should evaluate whether it was wiser to counterattack immediately or to yield ground while amassing forces against the larger enemy and then eliminate him on the Israeli side—in effect, carrying out the attack in an area more convenient for the IDF than for the enemy. Laner was deeply troubled by the manpower "mishmash," as he defined it, the deficient order of battle, and the fact that the reservists would be the crossing forces.

Sharon, the general of Southern Command in 1972, thought otherwise. He demanded an immediate attack to "prevent the Egyptians from feeling they had gained a territorial achievement even for a number of hours. And for us it is vital to execute at least the first stage of the crossing." Sharon called for an immediate attack at every level—from company to division. "Considering the political factor, the Egyptians mustn't be allowed the exhilaration of gain, not even psychologically. They have to understand that nothing is stable."[178]

Unlike Sharon, General Adan, commander of the armor corps, underscored the need for time to complete preparations for the counterattack. Gonen, as head of the doctrine and training branch and director of the Eil Barzel exercise, said that "counterattacks had to be carried out immediately with all the strength we can muster. . . . I don't think we should wait—we should cross."[179] The chief of staff summed up the issue: "It's imperative to carry out such an attack immediately with all the available forces in Southern Command . . . [but] a crossing can't be planned before completing the counterattack and gaining air superiority." To even out the record, he added, "I doubt an order can be issued for our crossing on the following day just twelve hours after the enemy has crossed. . . . The main thing is how to destroy the enemy forces. Everything depends on our eliminating the forces that crossed."[180] To remove any doubt, the chief of staff said he did not envision floundering or being worn down in a dragged-out war of attrition. He stressed the need for early decisions and immediate standby for carrying out the attack.[181]

As Elazar, Sharon, and Gonen saw it, the counterattack on the eastern bank was only the prelude to the real objective: crossing to the western bank. This explains why, from GHQ to the 252nd, an attack on the eastern bank was never planned, either as an independent action or as part of a defensive battle that would include the counterattack.

The chief of staff anticipated an immediate shift to the attack once the Rock order of battle was completed, or even limited offensive operations by the regulars (before Rock was completed) that would be expanded when additional forces arrived. In this light, the wish to execute Desert Cat (a two-division crossing to the western bank upon conclusion of the counterattack) after five days can be understood, as can Gonen's toying with the idea of carrying out Zefania on Saturday evening, just after the war broke out.

In the absence of a plan for a counterattack, the IDF had to formulate one in the midst of fighting under enemy pressure and time constraints. In addition to the time and place of the attack, it had to determine the participating forces and their missions, even though the enemy's situation, intentions, and achievements in the different sectors were unclear.

In Saturday evening's operational discussion group, Elazar said, "Something will have to be done on October 8 that hasn't been operationally planned for: attacking the enemy's territorial holds on the eastern bank with the 700 tanks that are expected to be concentrated in Southern Command by then."[182] It is important to note that the chief of staff recognized the lack of operational planning for the counterattack but believed that October 8 was the most expedient date, even though he pondered the question over the next two days.

The events of October 7 and the uptick in morale were major factors in Southern Command's decision to advance the date of the attack. The fear of armored and motorized divisions crossing the canal and the fog of war that lasted until Sunday afternoon were undoubtedly the main reasons behind the decision to push the counterattack forward to Monday. The chief of staff's aide-de-camp, Brigadier General Avner Shalev (Ret.), claimed that Elazar had a number of goals in mind when he moved up the time: undermining the Egyptians' confidence, halting the transfer of armored divisions, and gaining control of a block of territory in preparation for the crossing.[183] Also, Elazar must have considered the advantages of an early achievement of the real objective—crossing to the western bank—even though he insisted that the present operation was only a counterattack.

Elazar presented an important justification for advancing the attack to Monday: the Egyptians' modus operandi. They were not attacking with their armor in front. Instead, their tanks were proceeding very slowly, with large quantities of antitank weapons in front, and they were likely to continue in this manner as long as they were being reinforced. "Tomorrow there will be mines and the day after small entrenchments. . . . We have to attack them sometime. The question is—when. When they're even better organized with more tanks or much less organized with fewer tanks?"[184]

When he addressed the government meeting on Sunday morning, Elazar still had not made up his mind. Minister Yisrael Galili, one of Golda Meir's top advisers, feared a UN Security Council decision and asked about the minimum time required to repulse the enemy. The chief of staff answered that these were the most trying hours, and he hoped the forces would get over the slump that night and recover by the next day. The reserve divisions had to assume control of the forward line (an operation for which there was no plan) so that the forces holding it could withdraw and stabilize a second defensive line. At this stage, he still believed it would take two days to shift to the attack in the two sectors: "There's a chance that on Tuesday or Wednesday we might be able to counterattack in the canal sector. If [the Egyptians] attack, we'll bring in air support and demolish them. Afterwards it will be easier to shift to the attack. I'm ready to attack earlier if conditions are right, but first I've got to know where my forces have stabilized."[185]

Based on these statements, the chief of staff obviously did not foresee a counterattack the next day (October 8). Later that day he met with Dayan, who had returned from his disheartening visit to Dvela. Elazar told him, "The Golan Heights Monday, the canal Tuesday."[186] At the 14:30 meeting with Dayan, Elazar admitted he was still unsure "when we'll shift to the counterattack. I don't have the forces. There has to be a [defensive] line." He stressed that the tank crews had to "sleep, refuel the tanks, and most important, stabilize a strong defense line."[187] In the war summaries, too, Elazar stated that he was certain that Sunday would be spent holding the line, but preparations had to be made so that when the reservists arrived on Monday, Tuesday, and Wednesday, the IDF could shift to offensive actions, "with the possibility of crossing on Wednesday."[188]

In the meeting with Elazar, Dayan expressed his concern over failure accompanied by heavy losses. He was skeptical that a successful attack could be mounted in twenty-four hours: the reservists would have to be assembled on October 8 or 9, a withdrawal would have to be made to a second line, and Israel would have to receive weapons from the United States before it launched a counterattack. He presented Sharon's recommendation to attack at once, but Elazar said that with only two divisions in the field, it was too risky: "I won't gamble on the only two divisions that I have separating Sinai from Tel Aviv. If I had five divisions I'd be willing to gamble on one or even two of them."[189]

A synopsis of Dayan's thinking after his meeting with Elazar also appeared in the log of the latter's aide-de-camp: "The defense minister favors a delaying battle and postponement of the withdrawal to the rear defense line, but does not believe that the current balance of forces enables foreseeing a date for a counterattack. At this stage we have to strengthen by planning and stabilizing the defense lines."[190] Dayan was right, but as usual, he did not impose his view on the military. In a pessimistic mood, he reported to the prime minister and the government on Sunday afternoon that neither he nor Southern Command nor the chief of staff believed it possible to "brush off" the Egyptians from the canal.

Shalev's log, apparently written while Dayan was in the government meeting, also summed up Elazar's position: "Tomorrow launching the counterattack in our areas to repulse them from Sinai and the Golan Heights. [Possible] only if pressure abates."[191] The same entry reiterated the importance Elazar placed on stabilizing the line and conducting a delaying battle, in the hope that a determined stand by the ground forces, with air support, would deter the Egyptians from attacking the line. Thus, the balance of forces would be redressed, and the IDF could execute a massive counterattack.

What caused the chief of staff to alter his position and decide to attack on October 8? After 13:00, Southern Command finally realized that the Egyptians had halted, the armored divisions were not about to attack, and the Israeli reservists were arriving earlier than expected. In this upbeat atmosphere, Gonen suggested to Elazar that a counterattack, and perhaps even a canal crossing, be launched immediately. Elazar politely rejected the suggestion, but after speaking later with Sharon, who also recommended an attack and a crossing, he changed his mind and decided to go to the Um Hashiba command headquarters that evening. According to updates by the head of MI, the enemy armor that had crossed to the eastern bank was not an armored division but two mechanized divisions, each reinforced with a tank brigade. The air force commander's optimistic reports that aircraft had destroyed eleven of the fourteen bridges (a far cry from reality) also had a strong bearing on the decision. At 19:15 the IAF intelligence chief, Brigadier General Rafi Harlev, reported that an enemy communiqué had been intercepted stating that the Egyptians had called an operational pause because of damage to the bridges.[192] Finally, another reason to advance the date was that Elazar believed an early counterattack would save the besieged troops in the strongholds.

Encouraged by developments in Southern Command and by the intelligence assessments, Elazar presented three possibilities at the government meeting held at 16:00:

1. Deployment on an impenetrable defensive line (Dayan's recommendation).
2. Deployment on a line farther forward (Lateral Road or Artillery Road?) and, with air support, an attempted counterattack on the eastern bank in a day or two.
3. Crossing of the canal (Gonen and Sharon's recommendation).

At the same meeting, Dayan conveyed his grim impression that a counterattack and a crossing were unrealistic at present—not even an attack against the enemy on the eastern bank was advisable. But in light of the air commander's glowing reports of the sorties against the bridges, Dayan suggested that the chief of staff should decide in Dvela whether a counterattack on the eastern bank was feasible, even though Dayan doubted it was.[193]

Elazar was an ardent believer in seizing the initiative, attacking, and throwing the enemy off balance as the key to victory. In this spirit, he mused over the timing of the attack on October 7. He wanted to be certain he had enough forces, and the early arrival of the reservists was the deciding factor. Since the Egyptians' bridgeheads had not been secured and the armored divisions had not been sent into battle, Elazar judged that this might be a window of opportunity, even though the defensive stage had not been completed. Discussions of the counterattack's timing revealed the confusion created by the lack of planning, especially concerning completion of the defensive stage. Should the IDF wait for the Egyptian armored divisions to cross and then contain and destroy them, or should it take preemptive action to thwart the Egyptians' deepening hold on the eastern bank?

In reality, no serious discussion was held at Dvela on the timing of the attack or its postponement until Tuesday, October 9. Elazar had already decided to attack on October 8. According to Adan, the commander of 252nd Division proposed a crossing in the southern sector, but not until noon on Monday, when two divisions could attack in the narrow sector and one of them could cross to the western bank. Adan pointed out that his artillery would not arrive until Monday evening or Tuesday, and currently he had only ten cannon. The 11th Brigade, with infantry and mechanized infantry, was expected at noon the next day. Considering the mass of Egyptian infantry and antitank weapons, if the IDF wanted to approach the canal, two divisions would have to be concentrated in a narrow sector with abundant artillery and air support. None of this could be ready before Monday noon. Conversely, unless action was taken, the enemy would retain the initiative, which could have dire results. Adan doubted the feasibility of crossing or even approaching the canal. He also cited the IDF ethos, which implied an obligation to try to rescue the strongholds. "If the offensive fails, the strongholds won't be saved and we'll suffer heavy losses."[194]

Assembling the Necessary Reservists, Tanks, and Artillery

The reservist divisions were absolutely necessary for the counterattack, but they were not a rapid-reaction force capable of immediate activation. Also, the abysmal shortages in the emergency storerooms exacted a heavy price. Before the war, Southern Command had defined the buildup of the reserves for a counterattack as dependent on the allocation of semitrailers from the quartermaster general, completion of preparations in the emergency storerooms by K+24 (K being the time the order was given to mobilize the reservists), and completion of a force concentration in six to seven days. However, this timetable was unacceptable in view of recent developments. Southern Command's lack of control over the traffic to Sinai by means of military police posts detracted from its ability to collect organic, balanced reservist forces.

At 11:00 Monday, the deputy chief of staff informed the chief of staff (who was in the government meeting) that the Egyptians controlled a strip of land ten kilometers east of the canal (this was incorrect) and that, upon completion of its force amassment, the IDF would have 837 tanks in the south (he neglected to mention that 190 of them had been destroyed or put out of commission on October 6). The chief of staff prioritized the buildup of the reservist order of battle in Sinai: tanks before artillery. Thus, 162nd Division's artillery group, which was supposed to be a key element in the counterattack, was stuck in the rear in traffic jams. The first vehicles from the self-propelled heavy mortar battalion reached their destination only on Sunday night—after the division's forces had started moving to their positions for the counterattack—and did not take part in the fighting. The 162nd's only artillery support was two reduced batteries of 404th Battalion/252nd Division, which had been on regular security duty when the war broke out. Each battery consisted of three cannon that were deployed in the northern sector on Saturday. The 162nd Division also lacked mechanized infantry and APCs. Adan did not hide his dismay over the lack of tanks and artillery.

The high command estimated that 650 to 700 tanks would be needed for Monday morning, while Southern Command expected 530 to arrive. The actual number on the morning of October 8 was only 433: 163 in Adan's 162nd Division, 240 in Sharon's 143rd Division, and 30 in Albert's 252nd Division (all of them from 401st Brigade). (The 252nd received reinforcements from 164th and 875th Brigades all day Monday.) There is some disagreement in figures from the various sources on the amassment of 162nd Division's tank order of battle. However, for our purposes, we will assume that 217th Brigade had 77 tanks; 500th Brigade, which arrived in Tasa late Monday morning, had 62 tanks; 460th Brigade had 25 tanks;

and 26 tanks came from 19th Battalion/204th Brigade/252nd Division, for a total of 190 tanks. After allocating the tanks to their various assignments, Adan claimed he was left with only 163 tanks. By noon on Sunday, 143rd Division had assembled only 100 tanks, but it managed to concentrate a sufficient number by evening.

Infectious Optimism, Overconfidence, and Unpreparedness

After the chief of staff wrapped up plans for the Monday morning counterattack and updated Dayan, the defense minister presented his views in the government meeting at 21:00 on Sunday. This time, he sounded overly optimistic. The air force was dealing with the bridges, the ground forces had been amassed and were prepared for action, and the Egyptians on the eastern bank could expect to encounter stiff resistance and incur heavy damage. Dayan estimated that if the counterattack succeeded, the IDF would destroy everything the Egyptians had and push them back to the western bank. Dayan did not believe that IDF armor and aircraft were inferior to their Egyptian counterparts. He later explained, "Until now the balance of forces was considered impossible by international standards. We wanted to incapacitate the bridges until we brought up the reinforcements, and we were losing planes. The results of these battles were most unexpected for us. Things didn't go as we thought. I was infected with the chief of staff's optimism regarding the importance of a counterattack and the need to try to smash the Egyptian armor at as early a date as possible and shatter the new myth beginning to crystallize that the Arabs had become superlative fighters."[195]

Unlike the IDF's intelligence blunders, the Egyptians correctly assumed that, starting on Monday morning, the IDF would launch a powerful counterattack made up of at least one armored brigade and one motorized brigade opposite the sectors where the crossing forces had achieved the greatest success. In retrospect, it turned out that the Egyptians were accurate about the exact time and place of the IDF's counterattack: opposite the Egyptian Second Army.

An analysis of the counterattack's failure reveals the IDF's flagrant unpreparedness, especially 162nd Division, mainly due to the shortage of artillery and mechanized infantry. Adan said, "In retrospect the question could be asked whether we should have called off the October 8 attack. Had we known that the Egyptian plans entailed an 'operational pause' it would have been better to wait and complete the concentration and organization of the forces with the crossing equipment. But we didn't know this then."[196] Adan was convinced that the attack had to be made on October 8, even if his division's situation was unfavorable. None of the commanders at the meeting suggested a delay. The prevailing feeling was that the initiative had to be regained, the enemy's moves had to be disrupted, and conditions had to be improved for a transition to the primary counterattack, which would include a canal crossing and a decision.[197]

After the war, Adan astutely observed that Elazar may have perceived the October 8 attack in terms of more limited goals. In this case, the IDF's fighting from October 15 on could be considered the main counterattack, which was a spectacular success. The IDF broke through, crossed the canal, fought on the western bank, and defeated the Egyptian army before the arrival of weapons from the United States.

Why did the IDF precipitate a counterattack on October 8? Had all the possibilities been taken into account before deciding on the time and place, or was this a case of misguided overconfidence? Did the decision stem from fear that Egypt would pursue the offensive eastward? Was detailed, updated intelligence available when the decision was made? Were there alternatives to an October 8 counterattack? Why didn't GHQ consider the possibility of successive efforts on the fronts in coordination with air support: first the Golan Heights, then Sinai? After the war, Elazar explained that a consensus of opinion existed among the division commanders, the general of Southern Command, and himself for an attack on October 8. He believed that the decision to attack on two fronts was one of the most critical and wisest decisions of the war.

In contrast, some observers believe the overemphasis on the offensive led to unrestrained activity in the counterattack in Sinai. The haste with which 162nd Division (a reservist division) was flung into the war left no time to convey the regulars' hard-won lessons from the first two days of fighting, especially regarding the Egyptian infantry, which was armed to the teeth with antitank weapons. The Agranat Commission, whose raison d'être was to investigate the failed counterattack, devoted much time and energy to the timing of the attack and determined that, on the morning of October 8, 162nd Division lacked vital elements, particularly artillery and mechanized infantry. The commission questioned whether the chief of staff had taken this into consideration: was the 162nd capable of tackling the Egyptian infantry? Elazar answered that, in his opinion, "Despite the shortages, the timing was right; though the matter of shortages had not been examined. The question might have been relevant if the attack had been on the divisional level . . . [if] the entire force had been concentrated for the attack. [But] this was not the case therefore it's not a question of whether the 162nd executed a divisional attack as planned and its force was insufficient." According to Elazar, when he consulted with the division commanders and Gonen on October 7, nobody said, "Sir, we can't attack. Give us another day." Elazar claimed that if he had been told, "'Your plan's excellent but not doable'—it seems logical that I would have said okay. So, that was the plan. Preparations had to be made for the decisive battle the next day. Strength accumulated and organized. We'd attack on the ninth [of October]. . . . No one claimed they couldn't. They received the order and said they'd attack. This was clear."[198]

Despite the desire to prevent the Egyptians from establishing a hold on the eastern bank, despite the unawareness of the enemy's intention to execute an operational pause, and regardless of the paramountcy of the offensive approach and the IDF's preference for it, the major counterattack on October 8 was launched prematurely. The 162nd Division lacked vital fighting elements—artillery, infantry, and air support—and the 162nd's commander, the general of Southern Command, and the chief of staff should have recognized this shortfall. They should have been aware of the seriousness of the situation, especially in light of the regulars' experience in the first two days of the war. The Agranat Commission determinedly investigated the premature timing of the attack. It found that the decision to commence the attack on October 8—before the necessary strength had been built up and before 162nd Division's readiness had been ascertained by the general of Southern Command—deviated from IDF combat doctrine.[199]

Determining Which Sector to Attack

Before any counterattack, a situational assessment should have included, as part of battle procedure, a comparison of the two Egyptian armies' operational status and ground achievements—bridging, order of battle amassed on the eastern bank, and bridgehead depth—as well as the IDF's position and status in the two sectors, the counterattack's objectives, and the optimal spot on the eastern bank for its development. No such assessment was made.

No one in the chain of command, including the chief of staff, ordered a comparison of the Egyptian armies' strengths. Reports from the forces in contact with the enemy (especially in the central and southern sectors), from the still operational strongholds, and from pilots who had attacked the bridges could have supplied a picture of the two armies. Had such reports been carefully studied, it would have been apparent that Egyptian Second Army was superior to Third Army in terms of bridgehead depth, number of bridges capable of bearing armored combat vehicles, and order of battle on the eastern bank. If a methodical situational assessment had been made, it would have been clear that, based on ground conditions and the enemy's status, the southern sector was preferable for the counterattack, facing Third Army's limited bridgeheads and unprotected flanks.

Since early morning, Southern Command had known about Third Army's delay in transferring its tanks and the disproportionate concentration of forces between the two Egyptian armies; it knew that the Egyptian armored divisions would not be crossing the canal. Nevertheless, none of this information was presented at the Dvela meeting; nor was it used to determine the counterattack's location. Third Army's relative weakness was not understood or not emphasized (or both). This failure was especially galling, given that a number of attempts were made on October 7 to quantify and identify the armored forces that had crossed the canal. Four hours before the attack, Southern Command's intelligence reports contained not a word about the location of enemy units on the eastern bank, and nothing could be gleaned about the Egyptians' probable modus operandi.

In an ad hoc planning group that afternoon, the head of MI estimated that Egypt's 21st Division was still on the western bank, which meant that only 250 enemy tanks had crossed to the eastern bank. This information was crucial for assessing the value of a counterattack, and it influenced the deputy chief of staff to make an incisive observation whose significance was not understood at the time: "Perhaps in this case, without all these forces, the Third Army area will contain only one mechanized division [the 23rd] and armored brigade [the 25th with T62 tanks] or about 250 tanks. So it might be worth the effort to counterattack these tanks."[200]

The difference between the two Egyptian armies increased the next day. Both GHQ and Southern Command realized this on the morning of October 8, but by then, it was too late—162nd Division had already moved out.

Gonen's attempt to redress the situation by sending the 162nd against a stronger enemy can be inferred from Elazar's testimony regarding the order to send 143rd Division south: "He [Gonen] explained to me . . . that in his opinion . . . the Third Army's position was weaker." In the war summaries, commanders from 252nd Division stated that they were certain the counterattack would have been more successful if it had been launched in the southern sector, from Ayun Musa north or from Lituf south.[201]

Why, then, was the military leadership fixated on a counterattack in Second Army's sector? There is no logical or operational explanation. The answer may lie in the realm of the irrational and the personal: the desire to get to the real objective—crossing to the western bank—as quickly as possible. This may have influenced the chief of staff's decision on the sector for the attack, since the IDF already had crossing plans: Zefania north of Kantara, Ben-Hayil as the development of Zefania, and Desert Cat (two divisions crossing north of Ismailia and Dwersuar). Although not specifically stated, the chief of staff may have found the southern sector, which was not involved in the planned crossing, less attractive for launching the counterattack, even though the Egyptian force was much weaker there.

Another reason for his choice may have been Gonen's turbulent relationship with Sharon, which was far different from his relationship with Adan. Gonen held Adan, his former commander, in the highest esteem. Gonen may have felt that Adan's temperament was more conducive to understanding and compliance. A third reason may have been the breakdown of the staffs, as the deputy chief of staff defined it, at Southern Command and GHQ. Had systematic staff work been conducted, the staffs might have recommended shifting the counterattack to the southern sector or postponing it by a day.

The Dvela Meeting

By the time Elazar arrived at Dvela, he had already made up his mind to attack the next day (October 8), even though the reason for his flight to Sinai was to gain a firsthand impression of the situation from the commanders and formulate a decision for action. Elazar knew that 143rd Division could operate as the main effort against Second Army in the central sector (in the Matsmed area) or against Third Army in the southern sector (south of Lituf). This option appeared in the Dvela summary but was not carried out. At any rate, the concentration of Rock forces enabled a counterattack in all the sectors. In the absence of a meaningful discussion of the optimal sector and the relative strengths of the two Egyptian armies, the underlying goal of a crossing may have driven Elazar to decide that the counterattack should be launched in the northern sector (south of Kantara) and proceed from there to the central sector.

The Dvela meeting cannot be called a group planning meeting or an orders group. At best, it was a consultation through which a main idea was hammered out. Without a representative from GSO present, no written summary of the meeting was made and no report was published. The chief of staff's aide-de-camp attended the meeting but left no written record that could be called a summary of the plan. A reconstruction of the opinions voiced at the meeting—the chief of staff's conclusion and its interpretation by the commanders—is critical for an understanding of the events that followed.

The following order of battle was presented for the next morning: Sharon, 200 tanks; Adan, 200; Yoel (commander of 274th Tiran Brigade), 200; Albert, 50 to 60. Gonen and Albert proposed attacking in the center with two divisions and then crossing immediately (Desert Cat). Albert expressed concern over heavy losses, given the massive enemy infantry in the El-Balah Island area. Adan and Gonen's deputy, Brigadier General Uri Ben Ari, wanted to attack the forces that had already crossed and thus avoid an IDF crossing. Albert objected and said he was not happy about waiting another twenty-four hours. Sharon was not present at the meeting. The official reason for his absence was a problem with the helicopter that was supposed to transport him to Dvela.

The chief of staff's plan, according to the minutes taken by his aide-de-camp, was as follows: "Possibility A: A one-division attack in the morning—very likely. Albert holds. Arik [Sharon] goes [south] and destroys [enemy]. Possibility B: [Elazar] agrees with Adan's concern over getting stuck in the marshes in the northern sector. Adan attacks in the center—is prepared to do both. Gradually breaks [enemy] armor, which is better deployed and then we'll see what happens. An attack [with] meager results [means] no crossing. [I'm] not against a crossing after the attack if there's a bridge [to cross on]. Not a simultaneous attack. The two divisions have to plan." The minutes conclude: "The idea behind the operation: Albert, doesn't matter if he pulls back in a delaying action. Albert holds; Sharon attacks. Two basic [plans]. Adan attacks [and] Sharon shifts to an attack below [in the south]. Stabilization [to be achieved] after the two attacks. Continuous air support [to be supplied]. The strongholds make a limited contribution . . . highly unlikely [with] . . . 14 men [in them]. We'll do what we can to save them wherever possible."[202]

Elazar's plan, if it can be called that, was muddled in the extreme. It was a half-baked text open to multiple interpretations, a syntactical jungle of disjointed sentences and misplaced punctuation that threatened to radically alter the operational meaning of what had been discussed. The confusion was atrocious, but at the end of the consultation, in Sharon's absence, the chief of staff summed up the two sequential attacks:

1. The 162nd Division in the northern sector attacks from north to south. The 252nd and 143rd hold.
2. The 143rd then attacks in the southern sector, and the 162nd and 252nd hold.

It was decided that if enemy forces strengthened in the northern sector, the first stage would be adjusted: the 162nd would hold and the 143rd would attack in the northern sector in a westerly and northerly direction. This change would require the chief of staff's approval.

Immediately after the meeting in Southern Command, the chief of staff returned to Tel Aviv and conveyed the main points of the operational concept to the defense minister by telephone: The 143rd was to attack in the southern sector, the 162nd was to attack in the northern sector, and the 252nd was to hold in its sector. These two- or three-division attacks did not entail a crossing, certainly not one simultaneous to the attack. Great care would be taken that when one division attacked, the second held. Elazar reported that the Egyptians had 500 tanks in two or three concentrations. H hour would probably be before noon and would have to be coordinated with the attack on the Golan Heights. There were crossing plans, but these would be implemented at a later stage, depending on the results of the two attacks.[203]

After Elazar updated Dayan, the head of MI, Major General Eli Zeira, and Deputy Chief of Staff Tal held an impromptu discussion during which Tal expressed his belief that an armored battle would develop the following day when Israel had the advantage. However, Zeira warned prophetically, "If we counterattack tomorrow and run headlong into the same infantry and embankment and same canal, who can guarantee that the same scene won't repeat itself? They'll rush headlong into the enemy's artillery and missiles."

Tal replied, "Who says we have to enter their missile zone? We're talking about an armor battle."

Zeira countered, "But the chief of staff said that he intends to reach the water and perhaps cross [the canal]."

"That depends on your decision," said Tal.

Elazar's Muddled Plan

Elazar presented his prognostications: The Egyptians would advance their infantry, reinforced with antitank weapons, while deepening their hold on the ground. It would be better to attack before their forces were completely organized. He summed up his operational concept for the counterattack: avoid approaching the eastern embankment; get rid of the bridgeheads and their 200 to 300 tanks; attack with two divisions while one holds (a departure from his summary at Dvela); open the attack with 162nd Division, and if it is successful, send the 143rd south; and carry out the offensive in a wide deployment, employing artillery and heavy air support so that many tanks will be destroyed by the time the bridgehead is broken. "If I knock out these two bridgeheads tomorrow—then we've changed the situation," he said. As for H hour, he estimated it would be 10:00 or 11:00.[204]

At about half past midnight, Elazar presented the plan to the operational discussion group. That presentation is important for understanding his intentions and overview of the battle: The southern and central crossing areas—not the northern—would be attacked the next day sequentially, depending on what happened overnight, especially in terms of the enemy's amassment and deployment and the coordination between Israeli forces. The 252nd would not take part in the attack. The attack by 162nd and 143rd Divisions could be carried out in a number of ways, but the 162nd would most likely attack from north to south, avoid approaching the canal because of antitank weapons on the embankment, and focus on destroying tanks and forces east of the canal. Artillery and air concentration would be supplied to each division making the attack, and it would be applied against enemy infantry so that IDF tanks could destroy enemy tanks.[205]

The chief of staff's statements about the direction of the attack by Sharon's division are filled with inconsistencies: "Then, when Arik's [Sharon's] division is here and pressing forward a little, that is, the division is engaging the enemy and advancing, the second division will come up from above. This is one attack. This division deploys and remains in the area. When it deploys here [?] Arik's division will attack this area from south to north by the same method, while Albert holds here. The attacks will be gradated. Air concentration will be [present] throughout the attack."[206]

Regarding Sharon's division, the chief of staff made it clear that he did not intend for it to reach the canal and embankment, except in the event of a general collapse. He reckoned that one attack would take place before noon and the other in the afternoon. He emphasized that if the enemy's deployment changed and a threat developed from the north, the 162nd would remain where it was and the 143rd would attack in the northern sector from south to north. (This scenario became a real likelihood on the afternoon of October 8, but it was not carried out because of Sharon's opposition.) Elazar hoped to launch simultaneous attacks in Sinai and the Golan Heights on October 8, and he believed the air force would be able to support both efforts.[207]

One problem that was immediately apparent in the counterattack plan was the direction of Sharon's attack. Was he supposed to attack from south to north or vice versa? On at least two occasions, Elazar said the direction of the attack was from south to north when he really meant from north to south. Was this human error? Was fatigue to blame? The Agranat Commission defined it as a slip of the tongue. The chief of staff made the same defense in his testimony before the commission, stressing that everyone understood that he meant from north to south. (His aide-de-camp's log states: "The 143rd Division—from south to north.")

Elazar also referred to his statements in the operational discussion group as an "operational idea" that still had to be developed into a deliberate plan. But no systematic order was given by GSO after the Dvela consultation and the operational discussion group.

Furthermore, Elazar never sent a summary of his ideas to Gonen, as he had intended. In reality, as demanded by GSO, Southern Command issued a summary at 01:30, a few hours before the counterattack was supposed to begin, that deviated from what Elazar had said. Southern Command's summary reached the chief of staff at 05:30; exhausted after two sleepless nights, he approved it without discerning the discrepancies. When asked about this later, he said: "Don't think that I was able to read every slip of paper that came in during a battle. . . . I have no recollection of this document."[208] He also had no recollection of Assyria 6—Southern Command's missions for October 8—that detailed a counterattack with standby for a crossing.

Elazar believed the plan was understood as he intended it. It entailed one attack, not two parallel attacks. The 162nd Division would attack from north to south, and if the enemy's situation seemed amenable to a one-division attack, only then would Sharon attack *from south to north* (a slip of the tongue). Elazar did not give Gonen two options: this was an alternative plan in case the enemy's status necessitated abandoning the existing plan. He emphasized that the summary at Dvela had been his, not Gonen's, and that the plan was based on two sequential attacks: The 162nd Division would attack Second Army in the northern sector from north to south, avoiding the marshlands, approximately opposite Kantara. The 143rd Division would be held in reserve; under no circumstances would it move until Adan had completed his mission. Once the 162nd had completed its mission, the 143rd would attack Third Army in the same way, from north to south, along Bitter Lake and the canal in the direction of the city of Suez.[209]

When Tal was asked whether there had been an earlier GHQ plan for the counterattack, he avowed that the situational assessment had been very comprehensive, and Elazar's summary at Dvela was contrary to what had been decided in the Pit. According to Tal, the situational assessment was based on the following principles: (1) two divisions would attack simultaneously in a concentrated effort from north to south (even though someone had said "from south to north"), and (2) these two divisions would be opposite each other—Sharon from south to north (therefore, Suez had to be reached), and Adan to the south. Tal noted that when Elazar returned to the Pit, he was assailed for presenting a different plan at Dvela. "Elazar was another factor in the October 8 fiasco, in addition to Adan," Tal concluded.[210]

Obviously, there were many possibilities for the attack as the chief of staff presented it at Dvela—perhaps too many. Under the circumstances—the commanders' physical exhaustion, Elazar's muddled conclusions, the absence of a written summary, and the failure to carry out approved plans—misunderstandings of and deviations from the chief of staff's plan were probably unavoidable. They appeared just after midnight. According to Gonen, the chief of staff envisioned a simple attack: one division (Adan's) would attack from north to south, and the second division (Sharon's) would remain in the center as a reserve. The first stage would be executed before noon. There would be a crossing—but only as the exploitation of a successful attack. If the attack failed, Sharon would remain as a reserve in the sector. Gonen was sure he would receive one of three possible orders: (1) Adan attacks from the north to the center, (2) Sharon attacks from the center to the south, or, as a kind of compromise, (3) Sharon attacks opposite Hizayon on the Firdan bridge (since this was his sector), and Adan comes to his assistance.[211] According to Adan, the first two possibilities, as he understood them, meant staying clear of the strongholds, reducing the Egyptian bridgehead if it was wide, advancing, mopping up the area from north to south, and avoiding the marshes and embankments. The third possibility was not brought up in the chief of staff's summaries, although in the operational discussion group, he may have implied that Sharon could attack the bridgehead in the northern sector.

The counterattack, it turned out, was born in haste. It represented a misinterpretation of the chief of staff's plan and a deviation from the IDF's standard battle procedure and war-fighting doctrine. The force was unprepared to carry out the missions, the orders were incorrect, the view of the battle was defective, mechanized infantry and artillery were in short supply, and intelligence was flawed.

Why Did the Counterattack Fail?

The counterattack's failure did not begin at the chief of staff's meeting at Dvela; it was the result of shortcomings that existed long before H hour.

The Rock plan pertained only to the transportation of 162nd and 143rd Divisions to Sinai and their assembly areas. It had nothing to do with the way they would be integrated into the defensive battle or how the counterattack would be carried out. The rapid assembly of the reserve units in the deployment areas was vital for the launch of a counterattack at 08:00 on Monday, but the preparations were poor. There was no prioritization with regard to transporting the forces into Sinai or their assembling and equipping. The lack of coordination between the chief of staff's instructions and Southern Command's order to move the reservists created massive traffic snarl-ups.

No plan had been prepared for a counteroffensive on the eastern bank and its possible continuation as a crossing operation to the western bank. Naturally, the slapdash planning on Sunday evening, October 7, was unable to cope with the rush of incoming emergencies, some of which could have been dealt with by implementing a systematic battle procedure years earlier. The lack of organized planning was the source of endless problems, breakdowns, coordination glitches, and misunderstandings, on top of the inevitable foul-ups that occur in any wartime situation.

The forty-two hours between the outbreak of war and the Israelis' H hour for the counterattack had not been devoted to serious planning, which meant that in practical terms, the counterattack was nothing less than a full-scale encounter battle. It was characterized at all levels by a lack of preliminary planning and battle procedure, an absence of information on the enemy and his force buildup (or at least inattention to it), and a misinterpretation of the mission by Southern Command and the operating forces. The deputy chief of staff found that, at this stage, neither Southern Command nor GHQ was performing staff work according to IDF doctrine and methods. Tal noted that "the brigades and divisions failed to keep their operational logs, certainly not in a systematic fashion. The conditions at Dvela were execrable; it was impossible to work there."[212]

Flawed Battle Procedure

The consultation at Dvela on Sunday evening was the starting point for the creation of a hasty battle procedure for the counterattack, but in practical terms, there was no battle procedure on the key GHQ–Southern Command–division axis. As defined in the IDF warfighting doctrine, a battle procedure requires making a situational assessment, devising an operational plan, distributing it among the forces, and approving the plan. The litany of flaws, even before the counterattack began, was long and frustrating:

- Neither GHQ nor Southern Command issued a warning order to the divisions.
- The chief of staff decided on the counterattack's main goal before checking alternatives.
- The counterattack's objective was ambiguously defined: destroying the bridgeheads east of the canal, and crossing the canal only as an exploitation of the attack's success. When the goals were expanded, misunderstanding prevailed among GHQ, Southern Command, and the divisions.
- No one assessed whether the IDF was capable of "brushing off" a defensive army.
- The Dvela meeting (from 19:20 on Sunday) was a consulta- tion—not a planning or orders group—and the participants had faulty intelligence on both the enemy's situation and the IDF forces.
- Imprecise orders were issued, leading to multiple interpre- tations. For instance, Sharon (who did not attend the Dvela meeting) saw the possibility of linking up with the strong- holds as the main mission. There was neither a GHQ written summary of the Dvela consultation nor a Southern Command summary, and no written order defining the counterattack's missions was issued.[213] Thus, the commanders had to trust their memories and their own understanding. The absence of a written operational order raises ticklish questions.[214] As head of GHQ, Tal assumed responsibility for this oversight, even if it was a Southern Command's plan, not GHQ's. Accord- ing to Tal, Elazar preferred to issue orders over the telephone in the field, but even an experienced commander like Sha- ron needed a written order. The chief of staff had arrived at Dvela without a representative from GSO, but he could have ordered Southern Command's G-3 to write a summary of the meeting, rather than leaving it to his aide-de-camp.
- The 162nd Division did not issue orders to the brigades. The 217th Brigade's deputy commander and G-3 had no informa- tion on the divisional counterattack scheduled for the next day, heading south along the canal. They thought that only a retrograde and delaying operation would be carried out.

- There is no written evidence of any staff work on the plan, intelligence updates, or deliberate orders between 21:00 (the end of the Dvela consultation) and 08:00 (the divisions' order to move). At 01:30 Ben Ari woke Gonen, probably at the behest of GSO, to write a plan and issue a command. Gonen spent about thirty-five minutes doing so and went back to sleep at 02:05.[215] It is therefore not surprising that the plan GSO received bore no resemblance to the chief of staff's plan. For example, it stated that the 162nd's assignment was to mop up the canal line between Artillery Road and the waterline and to destroy the enemy while rescuing the men in the strongholds, extricating immobilized tanks, and standing by for a canal crossing. The Agranat Commission criticized the shoddy planning: "This was neither an operational order nor a 'plan.' The written assignment differed from the chief of staff's summary and the wording was confusing and meaningless."[216]
- The attack was launched before a minimal force buildup was completed (especially artillery). Lieutenant Colonel Shai Tamari, Southern Command's G-3, recalled that no one pointed out to Elazar that the 162nd lacked artillery. After he returned from Southern Command, the chief of staff realized that the attack could not be launched before noon. He should have examined the attacking force's readiness for Southern Command's scheduled H hour—08:00—and he could have postponed the attack until the next morning, but he did not.
- Until H hour, no plan approvals were given, even though they were vital to battle procedure. These approvals, which generally require a face-to-face meeting, were needed to coordinate planning at the lower echelon, issue instructions at the higher level, clarify questions that arose during planning, and solve problems of coordination between neighboring forces, sector borders, and so forth. But no plan approvals were issued from the chief of staff to Southern Command or from Southern Command to the divisions. The command's "plan"—a copy of which was sent to GHQ—was not reviewed according to the IDF's plan approval process and was not compared with Elazar's principles as stated in the operational group discussion. A copy of the plan was submitted to the chief of staff for approval at 05:30 on October 8, but it was

not formally approved by GSO, and comments about the plan and its wording were not conveyed to Gonen. Regarding Southern Command's plan, the chief of staff admitted: "I only looked at the main part . . . that is, the maps. . . . As for Southern Command's wording of the mission, I cannot verify if it was correct . . . but it left the possibility open for misunderstanding."[217]

Gonen did not approve the divisions' written plans, if there were any, and since they were not brought to Southern Command's attention, there was no way to review them. Gonen could have flown to 162nd's headquarters at dawn, where he and Adan could have examined the plan on a map and cleared up any misunderstandings. From there, he could have reached Sharon's division, reviewed the plan, and returned to Dvela before H hour. Alternatively, Gonen could have gone to the 162nd and sent Ben Ari to the 143rd. When questioned why the plan approval procedure had not been followed and why he had not met with the two division commanders, Gonen gave this baffling reply: "Adan was more senior than me and had been my commander for years. Although he behaved with prefect military decorum I felt that it went against his grain to be my subordinate. What I mean to say is that in all honesty I didn't feel I could approve Adan's plans. He'd been a major general much longer than me. When Adan left, I said to him: 'I'm not going to approve your plans.'"[218] The commission pointed out that, despite the issue of "decorum," by not approving Sharon's and Adan's plans, Gonen was not fulfilling his responsibilities as the general of Southern Command. Gonen answered that the problem could have been solved with goodwill.

Southern Command performed slipshod staff work. Its headquarters location was also a contributing factor. The absence of staff work affected not only the battle procedure but also data collection for decision making in the counterattack. Thus, Gonen's impromptu decision was accorded the title "situational assessment," and decisions and plans never became precise orders. The orders that were issued were conveyed orally, tersely, and in muddled language to commanders over the radio. The only written documents related to the October 8 attack plan consisted of a slide that Southern Command sent to GHQ but never reached the divisions, and a note sent to the 143rd's commander via one of his officers.

Unauthorized Alterations in the Chief of Staff's Plan

Because Elazar presented his operational ideas orally rather than circulating a written plan, misinterpretation and confusion were possible, especially in light of the commanders' fatigue and a surfeit of potential actions. Sharon's absence at Dvela added to the misunderstanding. In addition, Gonen deviated from Elazar's operational concept because of ideas he had been nurturing before and after the Dvela meeting, and his instructions to the divisions on the night prior to the attack and the next morning reflect his three operational priorities:

1. Cross the canal and capture the western bank at Hizayon and Matsmed (this entailed a change in direction of the 162nd's attack—to the west rather than the south).
2. Approach the strongholds before the counterattack's success (this too entailed a change in direction to the west).
3. Transfer the 143rd south before the 162nd completed its attack to gain time to cross in the Hakfar area and capture the city of Suez.

Gonen's digressions from Elazar's oral plan began after midnight in his radio instructions to Adan and increased after dawn.

At approximately 06:00 Elazar spoke with Gonen and heard the main points of Southern Command's plan, including the idea of crossing the canal on an Egyptian bridge and exploiting the success at Matsmed. Elazar again warned Gonen not to approach the canal's embankment and expressed his pessimism about crossing on an Egyptian bridge. After this conversation, GSO sent a communiqué to Southern Command stating that a canal crossing would be carried out only with the chief of staff's approval. But the erosion of the chief of staff's main mission—the enemy's destruction at the bridgeheads—only grew in intensity. Southern Command's orders emphasized two missions—liberating the strongholds and crossing the canal—which could be undertaken only after accomplishing the main assignment: destroying Egyptian forces on the eastern bank.[219]

Southern Command's order instructed forces to stand by for transfer to the other side. When Gonen was asked whether the crossing option had been included in his consultation with the chief of staff, he answered in the negative: "This was my plan from

01:30 on. I would call it the crystallization of the plan. The chief of staff summed up a general idea . . . Southern Command formulated a plan."[220] This flagrant deviation from the chief of staff's plan received additional authorization in Southern Command's orders at 04:00, a few hours before the counterattack commenced:

1. The 143rd Division attacks in the direction of the strongholds, liberates them, and returns (to where? why does it have to return?). This takes place prior to execution of the 162nd's assignment.
2. The 162nd Division attacks—*after* the 143rd's evacuation of the strongholds—from the north to Matsmed (a change from Purkan), with the objective of destroying the enemy and crossing in the Matsmed area.
3. The 143rd attacks after the 162nd in the Suez area (Hakfar) and crosses the canal.[221]

Gonen's deviation from the chief of staff's plan may have been based on his wish to overcome, as quickly as possible, the severe setbacks suffered during the first two days of fighting. The strongholds' desperate situation undoubtedly gnawed at him as well. Gonen might have thought that a swift crossing to the western bank would turn the tide of the war, offset the initial blunders, and crown his bruised head with laurels. Thus, Southern Command issued an order to the 162nd by radio, sent via General Kalman Magen, commander of the northern sector—a most unorthodox method of relaying orders: (1) at first light, Sharon goes to the strongholds; (2) prepare to move south to Matsmed (a change from Purkan); (3) if a bridge can be crossed, use it to transfer one brigade and deploy on the Havit Road line (on the western bank). Each of these three points was a radical departure from the chief of staff's summary. Later, when radio contact was established between Gonen and Adan, Gonen reaffirmed and expanded his order: "Head south to Matsmed and destroy the enemy, then cross west at Matsmed with a brigade."[222]

In his conversation with Sharon and Adan (between 04:00 and 04:30), Gonen was still undecided on H hour and who would reach the strongholds, although it was obvious that one of the divisions would. At 05:40 he decided that the 162nd's H hour would be 08:00. At 06:17 he informed the 143rd's chief of staff that the division would attack south at noon for a crossing at Suez, and Southern Command's air force liaison was ordered not to destroy any bridges spanning the canal. This was a blatant contradiction of the chief of staff's order to eliminate the bridgeheads. But if the IDF was going to "hitchhike" across the canal, the bridges obviously had to remain intact.

Gonen's orders to 143rd Division and Southern Command staff at 06:17 were the official authorization for the changes he had first broached in preliminary moves at headquarters and in preparatory talks with Adan. By 04:32, he had already told the command's staff that he needed Sharon in the south and that the main mission was to approach the strongholds. Sharon would liberate the strongholds in the morning and then return.

Throughout the night and even after H hour, Gonen pressed Adan to diverge from the original plan and cross at Hizayon. At 04:32 Gonen asked him whether he could approach Hizayon and Matsmed and make contact with the strongholds while carrying out his mission. Adan answered that he would try to do so when he got there. Gonen said that the 162nd's mission would be to head south, destroy the enemy up to Matsmed, and then cross west to the Havit line. He asked Adan whether he "saw a problem with that." Adan replied, "I'll let you know at daybreak."[223]

All these improvised missions were couched in euphemisms. "Approach" the strongholds ignored the reality of the Egyptians' powerful grip on the area; the "approach" would actually entail a ferocious breakthrough battle. "Go to the other side" downplayed the bitter fighting that would be required to reach the water and cross the canal. These were two major assignments that demanded painstaking planning, a detailed battle procedure, and concentrated artillery fire and air support. They were definitely not ancillary, easy-to-accomplish tasks.

Gonen told the Agranat Commission that he perceived the attack on Hizayon and the capture of a bridgehead on the western bank as minor modifications of the plan; likewise, he considered the three-kilometer deviation south from the division's path as within the boundaries of the chief of staff's order. He explained to the commission that he had spoken with Sharon about approaching the strongholds and returning not in the course of the mission but as an additional task before carrying out the main mission: destroying the enemy in the southern sector and crossing in the Suez area.

Gonen also said that the two divisions in the southern sector were planning the rescue of the strongholds and waiting to see which one would carry out the order. He reckoned the operation would begin at 06:00 or 06:30 and take about two hours. This was a "precursory task" that would not interfere with the chief of staff's main mission. But at 06:17, in a conversation with the 143rd's chief of staff, he canceled the division's approach to the strongholds, fearing the 143rd would get bogged down and fail to reach the crossing at Suez, which he considered the jewel in the crown. "If [the 143rd] fails, there won't be anyone to head south," he said.[224]

An attempt at even a small-scale crossing, before the main mission was completed, deviated from Elazar's plan. Trying to enter the strongholds while the Egyptian bridgehead was still active was asking for trouble. At any rate, if the chief of staff's plan was carried out and the Egyptian force was destroyed, there would be no one to stop the Israelis from reaching the strongholds.

According to Southern Command's aide-de-camp, at 06:04 Gonen informed the chief of staff that the 162nd's H hour was 08:00. Elazar approved. The chief of staff did not try to halt the erosion of his plans and even granted permission for the crossing at Matsmed. "Send only one brigade across," he told Gonen, and mumbled a stipulation: "on condition that there are bridges there, depending on the results between Mifreket and Matsmed and then we'll speak." Elazar accepted the reversal in his plan without batting an eye and admonished Gonen, "Be careful not to get too close to the embankment. Good luck! Permission granted to begin at 08:00 with Adan who should be arriving."[225]

In addition to the confusion over the critical issue of the direction of the 143rd's attack (from north to south or vice versa), there were questions about the attack's mission in the southern sector. Sharon understood that his assignment was to destroy the Egyptians and rescue the men in the strongholds, and he issued the divisional order at 02:00. The Agranat Commission asked the chief of staff whether a change in the main plan was possible because of unexpected developments in the enemy's situation (especially if it posed a greater danger to the 162nd's front) and whether the general of Southern Command had proposed an alternative—Adan defending and Sharon attacking from south to north in the northern sector, not at Suez. Elazar explained that there was only one plan, and the general of Southern Command was not permitted to decide on a different option. A change in the original plan was possible, Elazar admitted, "if changes in the enemy's situation forced him [Gonen] to abandon the agreed upon plan," but it would require Elazar's authorization.[226]

In reality, the chief of staff's plan was not taken as engraved in stone. Major and minor modifications sprang up almost immediately after his departure from Dvela at about 21:00. For the historical record, it should be noted that the deviations stemmed, among other things, from the commanders' intuitive understanding that in times of crisis, they had to act according to their IDF education. The order to "approach" the strongholds naturally contained a strong element of moral obligation to assist IDF troops that were in immediate danger. Divergence from the original plan was the result of the IDF's long-standing offensive approach that, for better or worse, generations of commanders had been reared on. On the morning of October 8, this approach translated into the rapid transfer of the war to the enemy's territory. The chief of staff was aware of the inner drives of the IDF commanders, and had he been present at Dvela during the attack, he might have counteracted the erosion of his plan.

The main plan presented in Dvela on October 7 had at least three drawbacks, all of which influenced the conduct of operations. The first was the befuddlement over the direction of the 143rd's attack (from south to north or vice versa). Gonen claimed that he heard the chief of staff order an attack from south to north, and the 143rd's move south corresponded to his understanding of Elazar's plan. (This is amazingly similar to the Rashomon-like conversation between Elazar and Gonen regarding the deployment of Dovecote in Southern Command: one in front or two in front?) In Gonen's words, "There were precisely two options: one that Arik [Sharon] attacks from north to south and two, he attacks in the opposite direction. . . . I decided from south to north . . . in the southern sector." The Agranat Commission reminded Gonen that "in the command's record of the plan . . . only one option appears, that Sharon goes from north to south."[227] The misunderstanding also surfaced in the war summary. Ben Ari stated that the plan approved by the chief of staff was for the 162nd to attack from north to south and for the 143rd to attack Third Army from south to north. Ben Ari also criticized Sharon's claim that the order to attack from south to north had been given to him by radio at 10:30 (Sharon actually received the order much earlier).

The second problem was that the order to keep clear of the embankment by three kilometers nullified the attack's operational significance. To destroy the enemy deployed on Lexicon, one had to approach him from east to west, but the enemy was not present in the area east of Lexicon. Translating the order to remain three kilometers from the embankment into operational language created an absurd situation in which the 162nd's westernmost tank would be moving four kilometers from the embankment (a one-kilometer safety margin was necessary because of Egyptian missile teams on Lexicon Road, about a kilometer east of the embankment), and the rest of the force would be deployed to the left of it (east, when heading south) in an area devoid of enemy forces. This is exactly what happened when the division started moving.

The warning not to approach the canal was absorbed and reiterated by Elazar and Gonen. Southern Command's log entry for 07:20 read: "The chief of staff is certain that the forces won't approach the canal." At 08:08 it stated: "The general [Gonen] radioed Adan and reminded him not to approach the canal." Perceiving the battle, the 162nd's commander stressed: "Don't pass Lexicon. The 217th [Brigade] is between Hazizit and Lexicon, the 460th [Brigade] is on Ma'adim [heading] south along the canal."[228]

The third problem was leaving the canal crossing as an option. Although the crossing was defined as the exploitation of a successful attack, to be carried out only if everything went as planned, this option was totally unrealistic: the IDF's crossing equipment was not even in the area. And the idea of "catching a lift" on the Egyptian bridge was nothing less than foolhardy. The goal of crossing to the western bank undoubtedly pervaded the tactical operations centers (TOCs). The chief of staff expressed his reservations about this objective in the clearest of terms at Dvela; however, in a later telephone conversation with Dayan, he specifically mentioned the crossing, and Gonen and Sharon also brought it up.[229] Thus, whether consciously or not, the crossing became the main objective for Gonen (and others) and influenced the decisions and calculations made during the counterattack.

A Distorted Intelligence Picture

The situational assessment prior to the attack suffered from a lack of information and hastily devised battle procedures that were not always justified by the circumstances. As a result, the commanders had no clearly defined goals, and the operational forces struggled to execute urgent moves. Effective battlefield intelligence could have provided all command levels with an accurate picture of the enemy at any given time. The Agranat Commission concluded, "The lack of solid battlefield intelligence dominated the moves in the war not only in the days leading up to the war . . . but was decisive in the holding stage. Because of an incorrect situation picture the senior levels, including the political level, sometimes made faulty decisions."[230]

Sunday's intelligence reports on the depth of the enemy penetration were depressing and created the impression that the Egyptians had reached Artillery Road. They were also inaccurate, and the 162nd's counterattack initially encountered empty areas west of Artillery Road. Because the enemy's situation, strength, disposition, and deployment were misread, the entire attack plan was based on erroneous assumptions. Southern Command headquarters was unaware that the Egyptians had deployed defensively to meet an Israeli attack.

The IDF was also mistaken about its tank force. The chief of staff based his plan on obsolete data—that is, the number of tanks available before the war; thus, he claimed that the 162nd had many more tanks (300) than it actually had. The assessment in the Pit was that between 650 and 700 battle-ready tanks would be amassed on the morning of October 8—nearly one-third more than the actual number. Also, the forces' location was unclear. Southern Command assumed the 143rd had a few platoons on Artillery Road, with the rest of the order of battle in the rear; in reality, the situation was just the opposite. Thus, on the evening of October 7, Southern Command's distorted picture of the battlefield situation had a powerful effect on its degree of control during the battles the next day.[231]

It defies explanation why Gonen failed to augment intelligence work the moment the Dvela consultation concluded so that he could identify the bridgeheads; perform an accurate situational assessment; draft a detailed, lucid plan; and issue a written order. Since there were a number of possible moves, the general of Southern Command had to decide which one would be optimal, after acquiring additional data on the enemy's layout and the amassment of IDF forces. But Gonen held no further consultations with the orders groups or division commanders—not even with Adan.

The inattention to the enemy's situation, deployment, capabilities, and modus operandi was compounded by the failure to obtain information from the regulars who had been fighting since day one of the war. The regulars had learned the Egyptians' tactics and had experienced the fatal consequences of initiating a tank attack, without the support of artillery and mechanized infantry, against an Egyptian infantry reinforced with antitank weapons. Unfortunately, when the 162nd's mainly reservist units attacked Hizayon, they repeated the same mistakes the regulars had made.[232]

Flaws in the Conduct of Operations

There were two major flaws in the conduct of the counterattack: poor use of the available forces, and Gonen's obsession with the canal crossing.

Misuse of Forces

Mistakes in the application of 162nd Division. Gonen's desire—at first masked and then glaring—to cross the canal as soon as possible was the driving force behind the 162nd's diversion to the west and the failure of the entire counterattack, including the central event: the attack at Hizayon. From the outset, Gonen planned to use the 162nd to capture toeholds on the western bank, first at Hizayon and then at Matsmed. He even mentioned this to Adan several times shortly before H hour. The 162nd's forces kept their radio frequencies quiet and moved south, west of Artillery Road, without encountering the enemy. This justified Gonen's decision to move the division farther west, seek contact with enemy tanks, and cross the canal. At 09:05 he ordered Adan to halt his movement south and turn west toward the strongholds. At first, the deviation was attributed to the destruction of the enemy; afterward, it became clear that the small crossing (to obtain toeholds) that was supposed to be an exploitation of a successful attack had abruptly become a large crossing at Matsmed.

At this stage, Gonen finalized the idea he had been cultivating all along: bring down 143rd Division earlier than originally planned (after the 162nd completed its mission). At 09:23 Gonen ordered Adan to wipe out "all enemy forces opposite Milano, south to the sector's border . . . and seize one or two small toeholds on the other side, double time south, cross at 'Matsmed,' and deploy on Havit Road [on the western side of the canal]."[233] Gonen regarded the 162nd's precipitous move to Matsmed a key factor, especially since he had already decided to bring the 143rd south and feared leaving its sector exposed.

After consulting with Adan, at 10:15 Gonen told his chief of staff to order the 162nd to seize the bridges. At 10:19 Gonen requested and received permission from Elazar to cross at Hizayon.[234] He continued to pressure Adan, and at 10:21 he repeated his order: "Capture a hold on the other side of Hizayon. When approximately will you begin?" The commander of the 162nd, who had been promised massive air assistance, soon discovered that air support was nonexistent. When he demanded air assistance for the attack on Hizayon, he received a banal reply from Gonen at 10:22: "We'll get it to you. Don't worry. It's urgent that [you take] Hizayon from the other side." At 10:23 Gonen again ordered an expansion of assignments: "Push Hizayon. Reach Missouri from the north at Lexicon. You'll receive an order shortly to capture several holds on the western side."[235]

Had Gonen made the effort to run a quick intelligence check, he would have learned that a huge force from Egyptian 16th Division had been organizing and digging in at Missouri for the last two days, without any interference. Thus, the attack on Hizayon began with no knowledge of the enemy's deployment at Firdan and on the front in general, and the divisions' assignments were quickly and nervously changed.

As opposed to the derring-do spirit in Southern Command, Adan radioed at 10:41: "I don't know what your information is, but in this area things look completely different . . . I need lots of air [support]." Gonen's relentless pressure on Adan since early Monday eventually had its intended effect, and the result was bitter. Without combat intelligence on the enemy's position, and with only tanks (no mechanized infantry, artillery, or air support), one tank battalion attacked an Egyptian infantry structure bristling with anti-tank weapons. The battalion repeated the costly mistakes of the regulars in the first two days of the war and found itself incapable of holding and securing the area in the dark.

Between 11:00 and 11:45, 19th Battalion/460th Brigade attacked alone and came under heavy artillery fire. According to the tankers' accounts, the Egyptian infantry began to flee, and the battalion came to within 1,000 meters of the Hizayon stronghold. As soon as the Egyptians realized there was no continuity to the attack, they halted their retreat. Six or more of the battalion's tanks were hit by missiles and RPGs, and the tide turned. Now the battalion had to conduct a difficult withdrawal battle.

Adan received a report from the 460th's commander that 19th Battalion's situation was critical, and at 11:20 he relayed that information to Southern Command, which had been ignoring him: "We're repeating the drill that those before us did, and we need lots of air [support]." But air assistance was not forthcoming. Between 11:30 and 12:00, the 19th managed to extricate itself from Firdan with heavy losses, and still Southern Command did not recognize the seriousness of the situation. Adan's pessimistic reports were seen merely as demands for air support in the Hizayon area; the necessary conclusions were not drawn regarding the wisdom of bringing 143rd Division south.

At 12:12 Sharon, who was at Tasa, informed Gonen that, based on his own observations, 162nd Division was not advancing and many tanks had been left in the field. Yet Gonen continued to act as though he did not understand the 162nd's predicament. He informed Sharon of his new assignment, and Sharon was happy to lead the attack in the south and proceed to the canal crossing.

The divisional attack (in reality, two brigades) planned for Hizayon was impossible at this stage. The 217th Brigade had to be released from the northern sector, in coordination with General Magen; 500th Brigade, which was still moving south on Lateral Road, had to be added. Only at 10:57 did Adan inform the 217th's commander that he could move to Maror and the map coordinates Segulim 276 and 150 (a two-hour trip). The 217th's limitations notwithstanding, Southern Command could have coordinated a two-brigade attack on Hizayon with 421st Brigade/143rd Division and 460th Brigade/162nd Division, which were available. But this too failed to materialize because of the command's lack of control and understanding of developments in the field, especially at Firdan.

Even when the 460th's commander and the division commander realized that the divisional attack had been canceled, the division still attempted to capture the passes during the complex rescue of 19th Battalion. Between 11:30 and 12:00, as 217th Brigade was moving south, Adan ordered its commander to "gain control of the three passes between Hizayon and Shahaf, and proceed with all due haste."[236]

The 19th Battalion attacked without air or artillery support. The failure of 599th Battalion/421st Brigade/143rd Division to support the attack, and especially its failure to help in the extraction of 19th Battalion, was one of the most regrettable incidents in this operation and perhaps in all of Sinai during the Yom Kippur War. The 599th was at Havraga, two kilometers behind 19th Battalion, and it provided no assistance whatsoever, despite repeated requests and 162nd Division's attempts to coordinate with the battalion, with 421st Brigade, with 143rd Division, and with Southern Command. The 143rd's G-3 testified that 460th Brigade requested assistance about a quarter of an hour after the 143rd had been ordered to move south, "where the situation was very bad." According to the G-3, he recommended that Sharon respond to the request, but Sharon decided: "We didn't receive an order for this from Southern Command and we need the battalion [the 599th] in the drive south."[237] The 143rd's G-3 did not ask Southern Command to intervene. The commander of 421st Brigade, Colonel Erez, and the commander of 143rd Division testified that another reason for their refusal to transfer the battalion to the 162nd (in addition to the order to move south to Mitla, where a "holocaust" was taking place) was that the tanks of 430th Battalion/500th Brigade/162nd Division were behind Havraga, and the men were sitting on the turrets eating.

The 599th's commander met Sharon at Tasa Junction, where he was refueling before heading south, and told him that the whole incident weighed heavily on his conscience. Sharon replied curtly: "Everything that's on your conscience—transfer to me."[238] Later, Sharon was accused of knowing that 162nd Division was in trouble and turning his back on it, preferring to carry out Gonen's order with exemplary obedience and win the glory of a crossing.

In addition to 599th Battalion, 198th Battalion/460th Brigade was nearby. It was moving north from 19th Battalion but had stopped because of heavy Egyptian fire and was returning long-range fire. It did not assist in the attack and rescue. The commander of the 19th harshly criticized the 198th's conduct, but the 198th's commander, Lieutenant Colonel Yoffe, claimed that he was reloading his tanks and had been sent at 15:00 to assist 500th Brigade at Hamutal.[239]

There was also the problem of the air and artillery support that failed to arrive. Following the 162nd's requests, a Skyhawk air formation executed ineffective "loft bombing" on Egyptian ground targets on the eastern bank.[240] Repeated calls for air assistance reached all the way to the deputy chief of staff, who ordered the IAF commander to send support to Hizayon, Kantara, and the Hamezah stronghold. Tal was told that it would take an hour to an hour and a half for air assistance to arrive. Later, the air force explained that the air support center (ASC) knew nothing of 162nd Division's attack, and the IAF was needed on the Golan Heights. As for artillery assistance for the desperate battalion, 162nd Division's artillery support commander said that he had received no instructions and there was nothing he could do because he had no artillery, and permission had been denied to remove batteries from 404th Battalion in the northern sector.

This multiplicity of omissions—the lack of air support in Sinai, the paucity of artillery, and the denial of assistance to 19th Battalion—was, according to the Agranat Commission, "outrageous." It exemplified "the fundamental bungling in the direction of the entire campaign: the lack of information, lack of coordination between the forces, and lack of clarity in orders that deviated from standard procedure."[241]

The 113th Battalion attacked alone at Hizayon. General Adan did not see the connection between 19th Battalion's entanglement and his crossing mission at Hizayon, and he tried to assemble a force for a two-brigade attack (the 460th and 217th). At 11:45 the 217th's commander, who was left with only two battalions after the 126th was transferred to 11th Brigade, was ordered to move on Haviva Road, cross through 460th Brigade, and assume control of the three passes between Hizayon and Shahaf. Although Adan understood the seriousness of the 19th's situation at about this time and reported it to Southern Command, he admitted that he did not question Gonen's order and did not try to convince him to change it. Adan concentrated a large force, and since 19th Battalion had almost reached the waterline, he thought an attack in coordination with air support would succeed in reaching the water. However, he ignored the advice of the deputy commander of 460th Brigade, Lieutenant Colonel Shilo Sasson, who warned him not to attack with just one battalion.

With 460th Brigade unable to participate because of 19th Battalion's plight, Adan tried to build a second attack on the basis of 217th Brigade and the division's reconnaissance battalion—a continuation of the morning's mission that had gone awry. The 460th's commander misunderstood and thought he was supposed to provide covering fire in the afternoon attack (Adan later noted that there was no such thing as a covering brigade), and he assumed 217th Brigade had come to replace him. No divisional battle procedure had been devised for the brigade attack, and there was no authorization for the 217th's plans, not even by radio.

The commanders of the 460th and 217th met at Havraga without the division commander. There are different versions of what took place at this meeting between the two brigade commanders, which was designed to exchange information on 19th Battalion and coordinate the attack. Asaf Yaguri, commander of 113th Battalion, which would be making the attack, knew nothing about the 19th that morning. In his opinion, neither did the commander of 217th Brigade. Yaguri recalled that he warned the brigade commander, Colonel Natke Nir, of the conditions on the ground. On the application of the 217th, Adan said, "I don't believe that I did two such absurd things, that I sent a reduced brigade to attack where one had failed. . . . By the way," he added, "we're talking about a reduced brigade; this was a reduced division."[242]

The commander of the 217th claimed he knew what had happened to 460th Brigade in the morning attack but did not question his assignment because he thought IDF forces had already crossed the canal and the Egyptians were folding up. He realized that a two-brigade attack was taking place on both sides of Haviva Road in an effort to send a force across the canal. After the war, Nir claimed he had not understood at the time why the 460th did not participate in the attack. His G-3 testified that no one questioned the order, neither the brigade commander nor Yaguri.

Yaguri, commander of 113th Battalion, described the attack area as teeming with Egyptian armor, artillery, and infantry. He and his company commanders thought they were on a suicide mission. He assumed that 460th Brigade was attacking simultaneously from the left, south of Haviva, and that air support would be provided. He knew it was imperative to get across the canal. "We'll deploy, organize . . . be given clear orders and proper artillery assistance, and then attack," he thought. Later he testified, "It's hard to believe how anyone could have allowed himself to issue an order unless he assumed that we had a brigade-size force. . . . Three good tank battalions would have been able to open an effort with air support."[243]

Finally, at 14:00, the 113th attacked single-handedly without any intelligence updates, without mechanized infantry, and without artillery or air support. The 217th's northern battalion—the 142nd—halted after a number of its tanks were hit and did not join in the attack. The 430th Battalion/500th Brigade, commanded by Lieutenant Colonel Shimshi, remained in position a distance from the battlefield and did not take part in the fighting. At 14:20 the 217th's commander, who was in a tank behind 113th Battalion, radioed that he was withdrawing. Adan granted permission. Only at 16:00, in a meeting with Nir, did he realize the 113th's failure.

Summary of mistakes. The counterattack on Monday, October 8, was intended to annihilate the Egyptians' hold on the eastern bank of the canal and perhaps—as Gonen and other senior commanders fantasized—culminate in a canal crossing in the central and southern sectors. Events on the battlefield led to a different outcome. Two tank battalions, the 19th in the morning and 113th in the afternoon, incurred heavy losses, and Yaguri and others were taken prisoner. The long list of shortcomings that led to this stinging failure covers almost every stage of the battle:

- Defective control and sloppy work procedures between the forward command group (FCG) and main headquarters.
- Failure to employ two full-strength divisions, with all the requisite support, in the Firdan sector. "Only then would it have been possible to cut through the Second Army's disposition and roll it up on the flanks . . . and perhaps exploit the success for crossing the canal," said Uri Ben Ari, deputy commander of Southern Command. "Had two divisions acted in tandem, the earth would have trembled."[244] The force was not concentrated; nor was a multidivisional effort made to achieve better results. Elazar claimed that he "envisioned at least two brigades simultaneously attacking the area with the third held in reserve for the second wave, then exploiting the success and leapfrogging, advancing and exceeding one another. One passes and the other cuts through it. [But] if one battalion engages the enemy here, a second battalion there, and the bri-

gade is elsewhere, then this is scattering the effort and not a divisional attack."[245]

- Lack of military intelligence prior to the attack. The division commander, his deputy, and the G-3 were in the dark regarding the depth of the Egyptians' penetration. Vital information from the regulars was not conveyed to the reservists. The 217th's commander, who was waiting near Baluza for several hours on October 7, should have used this time to patch together a comprehensive intelligence picture. No one warned the reserve units of the Egyptian infantry's antitank missiles; no information was received from the strongholds.

- Fewer tanks than expected. Adan informed Gonen of this situation in the early hours of October 8. There were 77 tanks in 217th Brigade, 62 in 500th Brigade, 25 in 460th Brigade, and 26 in 19th Battalion—for a total of 190 in the division. In reality, after some of the tanks were allocated to other assignments, the division was left with only 163 tanks for the attack.

- Delayed arrival of 500th Brigade. The brigade got bogged down in a huge traffic jam on El Arish–Romani Road and its westward branches. It started trickling into Tasa at 14:00 and did not take part in the attack or receive any information about what was happening.[246]

- Failure to make maximum use of the force's strength. According to Sharon, "October 8 was the critical day of the war." On that day "we had sufficiently large forces in the sector north of Tasa to smash the Egyptians' northern hold had we attacked in great strength. Afterwards we could have attacked in the southern sector. But this was not the case. . . . Almost nothing was done. First of all, a multidivisional effort was not executed."[247]

- Lack of artillery support. The 162nd's artillery group trundled through Sinai on its tracks, arriving only on Monday evening. The division had no artillery support except for two reduced batteries from 404th Battalion in the northern sector, which had been on regular operational duty at support ranges before the war. The chief of staff ordered full air and artillery support, but this was impossible because he had given the artillery low transportation priority. The 143rd's artillery group was not employed to support 162nd Division, despite the order from Southern Command's chief artillery officer.[248]

- Lack of air support. Since the ASC was not informed of the October 8 counterattack, the IAF reacted accordingly.[249] Dayan states in his autobiography, "as IAF activity in the south did not provide direct assistance, the armored forces that were attacking had to operate almost entirely bereft of air support."[250]
- Lack of control in the various headquarters, commanders in the wrong locations, and a skewed picture of enemy and IDF forces. As a result, reports of an Egyptian counterattack on 162nd Division were accepted without verification, and 143rd Division was ordered to return to the central sector.

Gonen's Obsession with the Canal Crossing

The second major failure can be attributed to the fact that Gonen's obsession with a canal crossing had been rekindled. This was the reason for his rash decision to order the 162nd to cross at Hizayon in the central sector and the 143rd to cross at Hakfar in the southern sector (followed by the latter's frenetic return due to the mistaken belief that the Egyptians were attacking the 162nd on a broad front). Additional problems were related to the chief of staff's whereabouts on the day of the attack, Gonen's repeated requests for changes in the plan, Elazar's offhand style of granting permission, and the chaotic activity in Southern Command and the Pit in Tel Aviv.

Crossing the canal at an early stage of war had been broached as an operational idea prior to October 6 and was part of the IDF ethos that undervalued the defense and sanctified a rapid shift to the offense and a swift transfer of the fighting to the enemy's territory. The crossing was almost a conditioned reflex, inseparable from the counterattack; however, the timetables were unrealistic, and the crossing was intended to occur when the eastern bank was in Israeli hands. Planning for a crossing focused on engineering and technical aspects, and only skeleton exercises had been held (excluding the Oz exercise in March 1972). A scenario in which the enemy held the eastern bank was not envisioned, and if such an idea was raised, it was addressed without any regard for the complexities involved in the difficult breakthrough battle that would be required to reach the canal, as indeed happened.

In the summary of the Eil Barzel war game (August 3, 1972), the chief of staff made it clear that crossing the canal while engaged in a holding battle was contrary to his war-fighting concept, and he doubted that anyone could lead a crossing while the entire effort was directed toward destroying the enemy's forces on the eastern bank. The fording equipment's capabilities, quality, quantity, and location had never been carefully studied in operational plans until the Blue White alert in April–May 1973. Only then was the matter given appropriate attention, on the initiative of Deputy Chief of Staff Tal and General Sharon of Southern Command. It turned out that the troops' training and the equipment's engineering and operational quality were far from satisfactory, and a massive effort was undertaken to improve both. "Crocodiles" (self-propelled rafts originally purchased at junk sales) were repaired, new ones were acquired, roller bridges were constructed, and training exercises were held to hone the troops' proficiency in the use of some of the equipment.

The main operational plans—Zefania and Ben-Hayil—were designed for less than an all-out war. They assumed, as had Gonen and Elazar, that a successful holding would be accomplished quickly and easily, after which full attention could be concentrated on offensive operations and the crossing (in this case, Zefania in the northern sector). Indeed, as we have seen, the offensive plans were the focus in Southern Command and 252nd Division until hostilities erupted.

Although everyone was fixated on transferring the war to the enemy's territory (Zefania), the IDF was totally unprepared for an actual crossing operation. There was no signage in the crossing areas and no gaps in the embankment (except at Matsmed). Before the war, planning for a crossing would have been a rational act, but once the firing began and an attack and counterattack had to be prepared, a water crossing seemed hallucinatory. Gonen's obsession with reaching the enemy's territory was the engine behind the successive orders for a crossing at the start of the war: his order to Albert on Saturday morning, three hours before the battles commenced, to prepare Zefania; and Albert's order to the commander of 275th Brigade, Colonel Noy, after firing began, "to be on 24-hour standby for executing 'Zefania' tomorrow in the Jisr al Hresh area and transferring the forces."[251]

Two hours after the Egyptians crossed, Gonen ordered the commander of 162nd Division to go to Baluza. An hour and a half later he ordered him to plan Ben-Hayil and capture the sandbank (between Port Said and the Budapest stronghold). He expected that the division's crossing would be executed according to the Desert Cat or Stout Knights plan. The chief of staff, too, fantasized about a crossing on Saturday, and the conclusion of his operational discussion group at 18:30 states: "Holding on October 7, 1973. Depending on its results. If the holding is good then the designated operative idea for October 8 is 'Zefania.'" In this spirit, the GSO granted permission according to the Assyria order at 23:30 Saturday: "In the Egyptian sector standby for executing 'Zefania'; 'Ben-Hayil' to commence on Monday October 8."[252]

Attempts to orchestrate an impossible crossing continued on Sunday morning, while Southern Command's main problem was stabilizing the defensive line. In the early morning Gonen spoke with Adan about the possibility of switching to the attack. "We have to find out where the bridges are," he told the division commander (he was referring to a crossing via an Egyptian bridge). He also ordered Adan to concentrate his division in Baluza as a reserve force and not to advance his tanks, which he intended to use for a crossing in the northern sector.

Even at 10:00 on Sunday, after Southern Command had already issued the order to break off contact with the strongholds, an absurd conversation took place between Gonen and Elazar (in the ongoing struggle to coordinate IAF attacks). Gonen conveyed a mistaken report that Egyptian forces had quit Lahtsanit and were also vacating Orkal. Elazar replied that if this was the case, there would not be many Egyptians in the area; therefore, when the 162nd arrived the next morning, it could execute Ben-Hayil or an expanded version of Zefania.

Between 13:00 and 15:00 on Sunday, Gonen believed the situation had stabilized, and he began planning the next day's counterattack with the intention of crossing the canal. Thus, at 13:06 he ordered Sharon (who informed Gonen he would have another eighty tanks within three hours) to assemble at Tasa and prepare to cross at Matsmed (where the necessary equipment was nonexistent). Gonen spoke with Adan two hours later and told him it was vital to know where the crossable bridges were. At 15:09 he again suggested to the chief of staff: "The 252nd goes to Lateral Road, Arik [Sharon] heads south . . . destroys everything on the way, reaches the southern corner, crosses the bridge . . . with Adan . . . executes 'Large Zefania.'" The log of Southern Command's aide-de-camp detailed the crossing options: "Option A: Sharon crosses on Egyptian bridges [Hizayon and Purkan] . . . Adan . . . simultaneously crosses on their bridges and heads north. Option B: Adan does the same; Sharon crosses at Nisan [Hakfar]."[253]

Elazar opposed the plans and told Major General Rehavam "Gandhi" Zeevi, the assistant chief of staff: "And you say that I'm too optimistic! Look what's happening down there." Even after Elazar denied permission, Gonen ordered Adan to plan the crossing at 17:30 and move to Port Said or Ismailia.

Influenced by the optimism permeating Southern Command, the chief of staff raised hope among those attending the government meeting at 16:00 when he stated that the commanders in the south were suggesting a canal crossing. The 143rd and 162nd Divisions would presumably arrive that night, the 143rd would cross on an Egyptian bridge, and Adan would carry out Large Zefania and destroy the enemy on the western bank and then on the eastern bank.[254]

After this, no one (especially not the chief of staff) could claim to be surprised that a canal crossing was a key element in Gonen's plan for the counterattack. On October 8 the idea of a crossing was translated into explicit, albeit unrealistic, orders: "Destroy all enemy forces on the road to Matsmed then cross there, and deploy on Havit Road."[255] The IDF had no crossing equipment in the sector, and if Gonen intended to cross at Matsmed, the counterattack should have been launched there and not at Firdan.

There was no end to Gonen's preposterous commands. At 07:31 on Monday he told the commander of IAF tactical headquarters: "Don't destroy any Egyptian bridges on the canal." At 08:10 he briefed the commander of the regulars' 35th Paratroop Brigade, Colonel Uzi Yairi, who was at Ras Sudar: "If everything turns out as planned, we'll cross." A quarter of an hour later he ordered Yairi to be ready to move north if the attack succeeded. At 08:27 Gonen ordered Southern Command's engineers headquarters to prepare bridging equipment because if Adan succeeded, he would be sent to execute Zefania. At 11:40 he told Kalman Magen to cross with a small force in the Milano area and to clean out all the strongholds north of Matsmed.[256]

Elazar did not hit the roof when he heard of Gonen's intention to cross the canal. After all, he had given him near-total freedom of action. In a conversation with the defense minister in the Pit at

08:29, however, the chief of staff had second thoughts about a crossing that day and estimated its chance of success as less than 50 percent. Ironically, it was Dayan who wanted to capture Port Said in an action that would have entailed a crossing. Elazar thought it unwise to present the crossing operation to the government that day, but Dayan disagreed.

At 09:55 Gonen urged Adan to cross in two places: "Go immediately south, engage the enemy at Missouri and Amir and then cross at Hizayon with a small force."[257] According to Gonen, the Hizayon crossing was only a toehold, a small bridgehead, and did not constitute a change in the original plan, whereas a major bridgehead combined with a crossing would be considered a significant change. Thus, Gonen reshaped Southern Command's entire plan to fit his dream of crossing the canal as early as possible.

At 06:17 the 143rd's chief of staff received an order to stand by for a change of assignment: "The attack won't be in the direction of the strongholds, instead the 143rd will attack enemy in the southern area at noon and 'catch a lift' on a bridge. It will allow a brigade-size force to traverse the bridge." Years later, Gonen's G-3, Shai Tamari, recalled that he crossed swords with Gonen to forestall this move and even tried to get him to see that 162nd Division was not advancing as expected at the start of the attack, but Gonen ignored his advice and was determined to bring Sharon's division south.[258]

Gonen denied that he deviated from the chief of staff's plan when he presented the crossing as a minor operation: "The operation's 'high line' was not the crossing. The operation's objective was to destroy the enemy's forces on the eastern bank. If we found a bridge and could have crossed it, [we would have done so] at Matsmed not at Hizayon or Purkan, not with the entire division but with one brigade. What I wanted to achieve by this was a toehold on the other side [since] I thought that this way we could knock the Egyptians off balance and they'd stop thinking about an attack and begin thinking about defense."[259]

Gonen's obsession with the crossing also drove him to issue orders that made no sense, such as telling the 143rd's chief of staff to "'catch a lift' on a bridge." When Sharon told Gonen that no bridge existed east of the city of Suez (which was correct) and that the location of any other bridge was uncertain, the two generals agreed on "a crossing a few kilometers to the north . . . where there were three bridges."[260] The Agranat Commission revealed the vacuity of this type of order. When the commission asked Gonen whether there was a bridge at Hakfar, he answered, "I knew there was but Arik [Sharon] told me there wasn't. . . . Then I said to him, 'take another bridge. There's three to the north.' . . . That satisfied Sharon who said that he knew about them."[261]

This bizarre dialogue on the existence of bridges in the southern sector took place over the radio at 12:12 (at that point, Gonen and Sharon had not been in direct contact, as the latter apparently preferred not to speak face-to-face with his commander). Gonen gave the 143rd an explicit new assignment: capture the bridge at Hakfar (Nisan) or some other bridge. But at the time of their conversation, there was no traversable bridge in the entire Third Army sector, and there would not be one until Monday evening. Furthermore, to protect the bridges, the Egyptians moved them several hundred meters from their original sites—disassembling them in daylight and laying their sections on the canal banks so they would not become targets for IDF warplanes. Therefore, the Israelis should have realized that no bridges would be intact when IDF forces arrived. Furthermore, the bridges' load-bearing capacity was unclear, which magnified the risk factor and illustrated the irresponsibility of an order to cross the canal on an Egyptian bridge. IDF tanks were much heavier than Egyptian ones—the Egyptian T54s/T55s weighed 36 tons, while the IDF's M48A3 weighed 47.2 tons, the M60 weighed 48 tons, and the Centurion was more than 50 tons. Therefore, the Egyptian bridges could—with limitations—carry an Israeli assault crossing of three to four tanks before collapsing. Taking all these facts into consideration, Southern Command's level of "planning" for the 162nd's crossing missions at Hizayon and Matsmed and for the 143rd's in the Mefatseyach-Hakfar sector was reprehensible and ludicrous.

The decision to bring 143rd Division to the southern sector—perhaps the most crucial move in the counterattack—revealed a number of shortcomings in the command's management and the chief of staff's performance. In addition to the order to "stand by for a change of assignment" that Gonen issued to the 143rd's chief of staff at 06:17, mission creep continued in the field. Gonen informed Adan and his deputy that he intended to dispatch Sharon to the southern sector. The aide-de-camp's 09:37 log entry read: "Situation assessment. [Gonen] wants to bring Arik [Sharon] south for the crossing."[262] A complex move like a mission change should have been accompanied by parallel staff work on battle procedure. But Southern Command lacked orderly work procedures. No staff work was carried out to coordinate the command with the divisions; and, most vexing, the 143rd lacked methodical updating and coordination with the 252nd. The only staff work consisted of a communiqué stating that the 143rd now had responsibility for Lateral Road. The battle was managed like a shot from the hip, and even the Pit failed to comprehend the implications and dimensions of a change in plans. According to Tamari, "No staff work at all was carried out; only continuous conduct of operations."[263]

Tamari was baffled by Gonen's impression that the 162nd's situation was satisfactory and by his belief that Sharon's reserve division could be brought south. He tried to tell Gonen that the 162nd might not be faring well, but Gonen brushed aside his opinion and at 10:45 ordered the 143rd to the southern sector. Had Southern Command's control system been functioning properly, it would have warned of the 162nd's situation before noon, before Gonen ordered the 143rd to move south (Gonen commanded the divisions by microphone, as though they were battalions or brigades). At approximately the same time, 401st Brigade in the southern sector was ordered to leave its positions west of Artillery Road (too early by any calculation of time or space), which dominated Canal Road with fire, and hand over the area to 143rd Division.

Revising the Plan: Gonen Repeatedly Requests Permission, and Elazar Grants It

As a highly disciplined officer, Gonen insisted on obtaining permission from the chief of staff before ordering the execution of the altered plan. Despite Elazar's presence at the government meeting, his physical remove from the rush of events, his ignorance of what was happening, and his failure to meticulously review Gonen's requests, he granted permission with a nonchalance bordering on irresponsibility.

On October 8 the IDF launched two counterattacks—one on the Golan Heights (Northern Command), and the other in Sinai (Southern Command). The deputy chief of staff was in Northern Command, but in the south, in Dvela, neither the chief of staff nor his deputy was present. In the late morning, Elazar's attendance at the aforementioned government meeting proved to be a grievous mistake. Had he (or his deputy) been at Dvela, they might have quickly spotted the digression from his instructions and thus averted Gonen's disastrous misjudgments: redirecting the 162nd to the west, ordering toeholds to be seized on the western bank, attempting the twofold attack at Hizayon, sending 143rd Division south too soon and then ordering it back to the central sector to participate in the battles at Makhshir and Hamutal, and so forth. If Elazar had asked Dayan to excuse him from the meeting, the defense minister would have done so. In such situations, Napoleon said, "a commander who has to view the battlefield through the eyes of others can never command his army as required." Gonen—a brave commander by all accounts—directed the counterattack without once leaving Dvela and going to the tactical headquarters of 162nd or 143rd Division, speaking directly with the commanders, gaining a firsthand impression, exercising control over the troops, and serving as a personal example.

Gonen's changes in the counterattack forced the chief of staff into an impossible situation during the IDF's main effort that day. In effect, Elazar had given Gonen free rein to revise the plan without consulting anyone in GHQ, without reviewing matters with Gonen and the field commanders, and without even looking at a map. By 11:25, when Elazar returned to the Pit, most of the blunders that led to the counterattack's debacle had already been set in motion.

During Monday morning's government meeting, Gonen spoke with Gandhi, the acting chief of staff, by telephone and submitted his requests. Gandhi jotted them down, called the chief of staff's aide-de-camp, and conveyed the details. The aide-de-camp handed a note with the requests to Elazar, who was still in the meeting. The chief of staff wrote down "permission granted" in most cases and returned the note to his aide-de-camp. The latter phoned Gandhi and read him the chief of staff's answers; Gandhi then wrote: "I have permission from the chief of staff," noted the hour, and hurried to contact Gonen and convey Elazar's permission.

This was, without a doubt, an extremely bizarre and inappropriate way to review operational plans and make major decisions during a counterattack. The facility with which the chief of staff granted Gonen permission defies understanding. There was no justification for it, even if Elazar believed the IDF was on the verge of a major breakthrough on both fronts (at 07:30, while in his office, he had fantasized about attacking Damascus via the Beirut-Damascus Road and bringing up a division from Southern Command for a decision in the north). At 09:10, in light of Southern Command's distorted, prematurely optimistic reports on the rescue of the strongholds, the chief of staff gushed, "[It's] too good to be true. What, has he [Gonen] already reached the canal?"[264] When Gonen's requests for a change in plans arrived, Elazar tried to temper the general's exuberance, but later he was lured into believing Gonen's unsubstantiated, groundlessly rosy reports.[265] Contributing to Southern Command's optimism was a dispatch from Brigadier General Shalev of MI, who reported that an Egyptian armored brigade in the southern sector had been ordered to withdraw three kilometers in the direction of the canal.

Southern Command's aide-de-camp wrote in his log at 09:55: "The chief of staff called, and received a situation update and reassessment." At 10:05 Elazar's aide-de-camp relayed Gandhi's report (written at 09:55) to the chief of staff, who was still in the government meeting: "Adan's spearhead is at Hizayon, more or less clean there . . . [there's] a bridge for crossing to the other side . . . he's ordered Adan to reach the Chinese Farm and attack there. He's ordered Albert to engage the enemy and drive [him] to the water . . . Arik [Sharon] is being kept in reserve."[266]

Beginning at 10:15, Gonen sent several requests to the chief of staff, via Gandhi, for permission to consider "options,"[267] but he sent his orders to the 162nd even earlier, before Elazar granted permission. At the same time, Gonen requested permission to capture a number of bridges in the Hizayon area and cross the canal. Elazar stepped out of the government meeting at 10:15 and spoke with Gandhi. He denied permission and ordered Gonen to reconfirm that "the bridge was made of iron." At 10:32 Gonen dispatched another request for permission to capture the bridge next to Hizayon and cross the canal about 200 meters to the west. The chief of staff reemerged from the government meeting and told Gandhi to determine whether this step was too bold and whether the force might be too small and vulnerable. Gandhi conveyed the instructions to Gonen, emphasizing that "in the meantime he [Elazar] denied permission of what I granted you earlier." Gonen persisted. He explained to Gandhi that he was not asking for permission to cross at specific places (except for Hizayon); he was requesting the *option* to cross. Gandhi conveyed this explanation to the aide-de-camp, who passed it on to Elazar. The chief of staff's reply (via the aide-de-camp and Gandhi): "Make sure we're not acting foolishly." According to Gandhi's notes, at 10:35 the chief of staff granted permission to cross the bridges if his conditions were met.

At 10:30 Gonen decided that the time had come to move the 143rd south. Given the chief of staff's instructions not to send the 143rd into battle without his express authorization, Gonen asked, through Gandhi, to move the 143rd south to Gidi Junction in order to save four hours, attack in the southern sector earlier than planned, and cross in the Suez area. Elazar granted his permission.[268]

Thus, at 10:35, the chief of staff, via Gandhi, approved two operations for Gonen: (1) to cross at Hizayon (despite his reservations about the wisdom of doing so), and (2) to send 143rd Division south to Gidi (with no reservations). Gonen received permission at 10:40, but he ordered Sharon's chief of staff to prepare for a crossing south on Gidi Road at 10:37—three minutes before receiving permission from Elazar. At 10:40 the 143rd's chief of staff received an order from Ben Ari (Gonen's deputy): "Go south, destroy everything in your path, and carry out your mission at Nisan [Hakfar]." Gonen personally informed the division's chief of staff—he claimed he was unable to reach Sharon—that "Arik [Sharon] won't attack the strongholds before noon. He'll attack in the south at noon. You're permitted to go as far as the Gidi Road. When you reach Gidi report to me so I'll know if you're ready to engage [enemy] armor west of the southern sector or whether you're heading straight to Nisan for the crossing and that you'll cover the city. Understood? Commence movement and inform me when you get to the Gidi." GHQ's 10:40 log entry states: "A. Arik's [Sharon's] division to go as far as the Gidi Junction. B. Crossing the canal through the passes where there's no resistance and reaching 200–300 meters [from the water on the western side]."[269]

After the chief of staff granted permission, Gandhi contacted the commander of the air force and told him that 162nd Division was approved to cross in four or five places and that the 143rd was heading to the Gidi pass. At 11:00 Gonen made another request: he wanted the 143rd to continue to Suez and then attack from south to north—the opposite of the original plan. At 11:00 Southern Command's aide-de-camp wrote, "Situation assessment: Arik [Sharon] to capture a bridge at Nisan and then smash the enemy to the north." There are several versions of what happened next: (1) Elazar hesitated, expressed his doubts, and in the end approved; (2) Elazar denied permission because of time constraints—he was about to fly north and wanted to study the data; or (3) at 11:05 Gonen requested permission for the 143rd to fight from Mitla south, capture a bridge at Hakfar, and cross in the direction of Suez—that is, attack a bridgehead from south to north and cross at the same time as the counterattack. At 11:22 Southern Command's aide-de-camp logged: "[Gonen] relayed the plan to Gandhi and requested approval."[270]

At 11:25, while 19th Battalion was being chewed up at Firdan, the chief of staff returned from the government meeting and asked Gonen why he had deviated from the north-to-south attack plan. Gonen explained that this would allow the 143rd to immediately capture bridges at Hakfar and proceed to Suez, whereas in a north-to-south movement, the Egyptians would have time to disassemble the bridges. Elazar approved. This totaled three changes to the original plan:

1. Sending the 143rd south to Mitla before the designated time and without ascertaining that the 162nd's attack had succeeded.
2. Attacking from south to north, rather than north to south, in the Suez area.
3. Having the 143rd destroy the bridgeheads and simultaneously cross the canal.

After he granted Gonen's request, Elazar instructed Gandhi to update GSO on the change—a significant deviation from his instructions at Dvela. His report stressed that time was of the essence (given the hours of daylight remaining). "I gave Gorodish [Gonen] permission to bring Arik completely south, to travel on Lateral Road and attack not according to the original plan from above to below [north to south] but directly from below to above [south to north] and capture the bridge there. He wants to capture Suez immediately. . . . He wants to capture the bridge first. Albert won't get in his way. He [Sharon] won't be passing through Albert; he'll pass behind Albert and destroy [the enemy's] tanks. It will be dark in four to five hours."[271]

The chief of staff did not identify (or understand) the difficulties involved in having one force (the 143rd) pass through another (the 252nd). In addition, he was unaware of the 252nd's situation in the southern sector—that is, its units dominated Canal Road with tank fire and were successfully battling the Egyptian armor. The 143rd's chief of staff, Brigadier General Gideon Altschuler, was keenly aware of the need for coordination between the two divisions on the roads his division was traveling—Foreret (Gidi), Atifa (Mitla), and Yoreh (the southern road). As it turned out, Gonen's demands were delusional, and the chief of staff's approvals were utterly irresponsible. They were detached from reality and did not stand up to any critical examination of time and space. "Passing behind Albert" made no sense.

The fact that daylight was ebbing worried the chief of staff. Those present in the room feared that darkness would overtake the attack, whereas an attack from the north—from Lituf south—would allow the division to destroy the enemy on the eastern bank. Against this background, Elazar asked Gonen to reexamine the original (logical) plan—which called for the attack to be made from north to south, from Lituf to Mefatseyach—and to do something before dark: perhaps part of the division could begin the attack from south to north, and the rest could proceed according to the original north-to-south plan. But Gonen convinced Elazar to keep the south-to-north direction of the attack. Elazar concurred: "He [Gonen] is right. A. It seems to me that he's right. B. The moment [time] starts running out let him do what he wants."[272] Regarding the Gonen-Elazar conversation at 11:25, Southern Command's aide-de-camp noted that Elazar was in full accord with Gonen's suggestion to attack from south to north.

The litany of requests and approvals continued when the chief of staff left for Northern Command. At 12:22 he met his deputy at Sde Dov (Tel Aviv airport) and updated Tal, just back from the north, on his authorization of a change in plans: capturing one bridge; seizing a toehold on the other side of the embankment; a full-scale crossing of the canal, depending on the forces' situation; and Sharon's move south. At 12:40 Gandhi collared him with another request from Gonen (submitted at 12:15): he wanted permission to cross between 16:00 and 18:00 and occupy the city of Suez. Elazar gave him the go-ahead.[273] Gandhi conveyed the permission to Gonen.[274]

Why did the chief of staff fly off to Northern Command after his deputy had just been there, and not to Southern Command? There is no rational explanation. Elazar may have felt that the north was his home turf, or he may have believed that his absence in Southern Command would strengthen his role as "observer" on the challenging Sinai front, which he was unfamiliar with.

Gonen seems to have believed that, at this stage, the chief of staff had granted him permission (just as Elazar had approved all his previous requests) to send 143rd Division farther south from Gidi to Mitla, where it would cross in the southern sector and capture the city of Suez. He contacted Sharon at 12:12 (before receiving permission from the chief of staff at 12:40) and "coaxed" him into accepting the alluring crossing assignment. "I'm giving you a more important mission [than serving as a reserve force in the central sector]. There's a tank concentration East of Masrek [Hamezach] . . . I want you there as quickly as possible. . . . Your entire force . . . will go to the area and accomplish two things: capture the bridge at Nisan [Hakfar] or another bridge [Third Army's sector had no bridge] and destroy the armor there. At the same time destroy and capture the bridge."[275]

This, by the way, is the only evidence of a direct conversation between the two generals for hours. Until then, Gonen had been unable to reach Sharon and had been in contact with the division's chief of staff. Sharon had already informed Gonen that there was no bridge at Hakfar, but he knew of three bridges north of the stronghold (as did Gonen) and accepted the assignment. Gonen explained to Sharon that his mission was "to capture the city [of Suez] and stabilize a new line on the western bank beyond the city. I mean the other side [of the canal], Arik. When can you be at Matsmed [?] or Hamezach at the earliest?" Sharon estimated he could be there by 16:00, and Gonen replied, "Let's hope so."[276]

At this point, irresponsibility and negligence came to a climax. During the surreal conversation between the general of Southern Command and the division commander, Sharon accepted the hallucinatory mission: execute a complex crossing operation without IDF bridging equipment on a nonexistent Egyptian bridge, and capture the city of Suez. Sharon displayed surprising obedience to Gonen's orders, seemingly blinded by the glory-bound crossing operation. With this opportunity in sight, the obstacles facing 162nd Division suddenly shrank, and the 143rd's presence in the central sector was no longer required. The division hurriedly abandoned most of the areas it held without waiting for a replacement force (in effect, it had already left the area when it was ordered to leapfrog to Gidi).

In the GHQ discussion that afternoon, the defense minister questioned the wisdom of moving 143rd Division south and expressed concern about the approaching darkness. He spoke with Gonen, who explained that the reason for the change in plans was the large breakthrough of Egyptian armor in the south (there was no breakthrough); in addition, he thought the Egyptians wanted to divert their forces to Abu Rudeis (Dayan considered the "oil corridor" the key), and the 252nd could keep them pinned down until the 143rd arrived. At this point, Dayan proposed halting the 143rd and attacking the next morning. Gonen too began to have doubts about his timetable and the possibility of attacking at 16:00, but Dayan did not intervene or force his will, and Elazar was on his way to Northern Command.

Elazar's Detachment from Reality

When Elazar returned from Northern Command, Yigael Yadin and Yitzhak Rabin (two former chiefs of staff) pointed out to him that, in granting Gonen permission to transfer the 143rd south, he had strayed from his agreement with the defense minister, who wanted Port Said in the northern sector captured. Elazar's reply: "I can send Adan north." The chief of staff's statements in the Pit on the capture of Port Said—like his management of the entire counterattack—lacked any intelligence input or operational preparation, and he was completely detached from the situation on the ground. This typified the chief of staff's and GHQ's disconnect from reality during the decisive hours of October 8.

When the Agranat Commission presented Elazar with a complete list of Gonen's requests and his own gratuitous approval of them on the morning of October 8, he expressed surprise that the permission he had granted to the 143rd to move to Gidi at 10:45 was only the first stage of Gonen's plan to reach Suez. He testified before the commission: "This is material I'm not familiar with but I understand from it that Gonen already planned to attack Suez. He still didn't have my permission. He was taking preemptive action. He allowed them to move, he still hadn't told them the plan [not true]. He spoke to me about it at 11:45 and I thought it would take Adan half a day. I didn't want it [the 143rd's move south] to be before Adan had accomplished his mission. But here . . . at 11:45 the picture that I received was as though everything was going smoothly for Adan." At 11:45 Elazar's permission to Gonen contained two changes: (1) the 143rd would move earlier than intended, and (2) it would head for Suez rather than going south. The chief of staff avowed that this was a very significant change: "The original plan was to go south to the area adjacent to the canal and destroy the Egyptian army. The change meant traveling on the internal road in our area and reaching [the canal] without encountering the enemy." Be that as it may, Elazar tried to construct an operational logic, stating, "the change that [Gonen] requested at 11:45 was to go south in our area without destroying enemy forces, then proceed to the Mitla Road, continue on it, and rapidly attack Suez. The goal was for the division to arrive without having engaged the enemy in combat so that it would be fresh and [able to] attack Suez. There was a good chance [of success] in Suez and this was what had to be done."[277]

The chief of staff also acknowledged that going to Gidi deviated from an earlier decision. According to "the original plan . . . Arik [Sharon] was supposed to begin only after Adan completed [his mission]. Why did I approve of the change after 11:30? Because I saw that the plan was succeeding beyond my expectations [so] I gave them permission to advance faster. The first decision [to go to Gidi] was an early start on the timetable while the second decision [attacking Suez] was a change in plan." Regarding his unfounded optimism on the morning of the counterattack, Elazar said, "I received a continuous flow of information that created an optimistic picture. By the way, I wasn't the only one who saw it this way. The general of Southern Command, who, at 10:30 asked for permission to move Arik, and at 11:30 to take out one division [and move it] to Suez, had exactly the same optimistic picture. The picture was the same in the Pit and in the memos that I received from GSO orally. This provided me with a continuous good picture." When the Agranat Commission pointed out that this favorable picture was distorted, the chief of staff squirmed and said, "It was biased . . . I used all means available but they gave me a distorted picture of the battle. Let me make it clear, a chief of staff running a war on two fronts can't personally verify [every piece of] information [coming in]; he [has to rely on] the general of the command, GSO, and radio frequencies."[278]

Elazar's explanation of his approval of another change in the 143rd's mission—its return north and the attack at the Chinese Farm—proves that he did not receive timely information about the 162nd's failed attack. Whereas Gonen's main reason for returning the 143rd north was his fear of an Egyptian counterattack against 162nd Division, the chief of staff believed, at least until evening, that the change stemmed from Sharon's delay in leaving Tasa. Once

Elazar returned to the Pit, the Egyptian attack was no longer mentioned as a factor in the decision to halt 143rd Division—the 162nd's situation was the major factor. At this stage, a more accurate picture of Adan's situation came into focus, especially on his flanks. "On the one hand, T62s were in Kantara, on the other hand there was a concentration of forces on his southern flank at the Chinese Farm, and it was clear that his gains were not what we thought they were. This is where we began to realize the situation on October 8th."[279]

The decision to send 143rd Division to the southern sector had a number of unfortunate consequences:

- The division's secondary units received no explanation for their rapid departure from the central sector and their race south at breakneck speed. Brigade and battalion commanders thought a catastrophe had occurred in the southern sector—perhaps Egyptian 4th Division had broken through and was storming the central sector. Other commanders interpreted the hasty move to mean that operations in the northern sector had been successful, enabling the division to go south.
- There was insufficient coordination for the 143rd's passage through the 252nd, even though the 143rd's chief of staff had stressed its importance.
- Because of the 143rd's race south, its 599th Battalion/421st Brigade did not come to the aid of Adan's 19th Battalion, which was taking heavy casualties at Firdan.
- There was no provision for handing over the 143rd's vacated sector to another force. The 143rd's chief of staff, Colonel Altschuler, had a serious falling out with Sharon over who would take responsibility for the sector until Adan arrived, and he requested that Adan "properly receive our sector: the high ground at Kishuf, Hamadia, and Makhshir." On the initiative of Altschuler and the division's deputy commander, Brigadier General Even, 600th Brigade and 87th Reconnaissance Battalion held the high ground at Hamadia and Kishuf (but not at Makhshir) until the last minute.[280] This step was of singular importance. When Gonen ordered 143rd Division to move south, he believed that Makhshir had already fallen into enemy hands; therefore, he attributed no importance to the 143rd's request to transfer the sector in an orderly fashion. Gonen hoped that by the time the 143rd got rolling (which

he thought would take considerable time), Adan would have accomplished his mission and deployed in the central sector, and everything would turn out fine.

The IDF Loses Ground, and the Egyptians Move Eastward

While Adan's division was encountering more than it bargained for in Firdan, and Gonen and Sharon were champing at the bit to gallop south and reach Suez by nightfall, the Egyptians exploited the 143rd's thinly spread out deployment to advance and capture more territory in its sector. Between 06:30 and 08:00, even before the division started moving south, Egyptian forces reached part of Makhshir, were very close to Hamutal, and were penetrating large gaps created by 14th Brigade's broad deployment between Nozel (196th Battalion) and Hamadia (manned by remnants of 184th Battalion and later 409th Battalion/600th Brigade).

At 10:45, 14th Brigade's commander was ordered to move to Lateral Road at once and continue south to Gidi Junction. At 11:00, 196th Battalion's commander, Lieutenant Colonel Mitzna, received an order to leave Nozel (a dominating area in the sector's center) and proceed to the southern sector. He interpreted this to mean that there was an emergency there, and he reminded the brigade commander that no force had come to relieve him at Nozel. The answer of the brigade commander, Colonel Amnon Reshef, was clear: "This is an order! Move south."[281] The battalion commander recalled that as he made his way east, he met Centurion tanks from 500th Brigade at Talisman 26–29, but they had not been updated on the situation in the area they were entering. He knew this was wrong, but he had his own problems to deal with.

According to Sharon, when the division began to move south between 10:00 and 11:00, Nozel, Hamutal, Makhshir, and Halutz were still held by Israeli forces. Just as the IDF left Nozel, Hamutal, and Makhshir, the Egyptians were ordered to complete stage C—gaining control of Artillery Road—and 500th Brigade failed to hold these places. At 12:12, while Gonen was explaining the mission to Sharon (cross on an Egyptian bridge in the southern sector and capture Suez between 16:00 and 18:00), the 143rd was already on its way south. Based on Sharon's account, his discussion with Gonen about 162nd Division's difficulties was a "heart-to-heart" talk at best, and Gonen himself did not fully comprehend what was happening. Altschuler remembered that, "at this stage we all thought that things were going smoother, but Arik [Sharon] said . . . the exact opposite was happening."[282] Sharon stated: "When the division returned to the area around 16:00–16:30 . . . the picture was already completely different. The enemy was at Hamutal and Makhshir with tanks and infantry. Nozel was no longer in our hands, Halutz's situation was unclear. We still held Hamadia . . . and we were trying to see what could be done to stabilize what we still held that morning. I admit we didn't succeed. . . . In fact we found ourselves standing on a new line . . . Tsioni, Hamadia, Kishuf, instead of the Nozel-Hamutal-Makhshir line."[283]

Sharon got it wrong. For various reasons, Hamutal and Makhshir had not been held by the division's forces, and the Egyptians were very close to Hamutal, which was not held by any IDF force. Of all the dominating areas the Egyptians captured on October 8, the only place an IDF force held that morning was Nozel, which the Egyptians took after it was evacuated by 433rd Battalion/500th Brigade (according to one version, to join in the attack on Hamutal; according to another version, to avoid encirclement).

Counterattack Epilogue

At 12:44 the chief of staff informed the defense minister of the situation. Intelligence reports, based on communiqué intercepts, indicated that the Egyptian forces on the eastern bank would attack at 13:30, with the aim of establishing themselves twelve kilometers from the canal before dark. A similar attack was expected in the south, but there was no information that Egyptian 4th and 21st Divisions were preparing to move. Just as the MI reports arrived, a report from Southern Command reached the Pit: 162nd Division, which was attacking in the central sector, had come under attack by enemy forces.

The 143rd Division Is Rerouted Again

As before, because of slipshod staff work in Southern Command and GHQ, the report of an Egyptian attack on the 162nd led to a radical change in 143rd Division's assignment. Southern Command requested air support, and Gonen decided to halt the 143rd in its tracks. At 14:15 Altschuler received orders to stop the forces where they were and prepare for a new assignment: the capture of Missouri and Amir. Gonen immediately requested permission from Tal, because Elazar was still at Northern Command. At 14:15, in light of Egyptian pressure on the 162nd, Gandhi suggested that the 143rd be redirected to the central sector instead of attacking in the southern sector.[284] At 14:22 Gonen reported that, as far as he knew, he had revised the division's mission "before it embarked from its assembly area at Tasa." This report testifies to Southern Command's utter lack of control and the absence of updates on its forces' status. At that very moment, 599th Battalion/421st Brigade was already on Mitla Road, and two of the division's brigades were close to Gidi. Only 600th Brigade was still just south of Tasa.

Thus, for all practical purposes, the second part of the planned counterattack was aborted, and 143rd Division (which, until then, had been held in reserve) returned to the central sector to reinforce Adan's division. Sharon received the order at 14:00, and within five minutes he and Gonen were going over the details of a new plan: 600th Brigade and the reconnaissance battalion would capture Hamadia and Makhshir, and the rest of the division would attack via Akavish Road. Sharon reckoned he could commence the attack at 17:00, but the timetable was disrupted when 421st Brigade mistakenly entered Talisman Road instead of Akavish.

In the flurry of activity, someone forgot to order the 252nd to return 401st Brigade's tanks to its positions dominating Lexicon Road—positions it had been ordered to withdraw from before noon. The area had been evacuated to make room for 143rd Division, which was headed for the crossing at Hakfar (Nisan).

The deputy chief of staff, back from Northern Command, spoke with Gonen at 13:00 (or 13:30) and was dumbstruck when he heard that optimism had given way to harsh reality. Gonen described an Egyptian counterattack on the whole sector with artillery and a full-scale crossing (notwithstanding the air force commander's report that the bridges had been knocked out). At 14:02 he requested permission to reroute the 143rd to the Chinese Farm. Gonen erroneously interpreted 162nd Division's two failed attacks on Firdan as the result of an Egyptian counterattack and called for air support. Neither Southern Command nor GHQ had any inkling what was happening on the ground or where the 143rd's units were located. They had no proof of the existence of an Egyptian counterattack, and there was nothing linking the 162nd's difficult situation to such an attack. Had Southern Command and GHQ carefully analyzed the information obtained from listening devices, they would have realized that the Egyptian mission had been tasked to infantry divisions that had already crossed and to armored divisions—and this was explicitly stated—that were still in their positions on the western bank.

Tal asked Gonen to wait for the chief of staff's permission, and to save time, he went to Sde Dov to meet Elazar, who returned from Northern Command at 15:05. Tal explained the situation to him: "Of all the grandiose plans regarding Arik's [Sharon's] move here [south] and attack at Suez, in reality, nothing has come of them. Adan's been hit hard and is losing many tanks, and Arik, according to Gonen, is still at Tasa. In other words, he hasn't moved since the morning."[285] After a brief exchange, Tal said he saw no reason for the 143rd to continue its journey, especially because no one seemed to know whether it was at Tasa or Gidi. Instead, Sharon's division should be redirected to the Chinese Farm, establish immediate contact with the Egyptians, and attack from east to west. This was also Southern Command's recommendation.[286]

At 15:30 the chief of staff approved Southern Command's request to attack the Chinese Farm and suggested that Adan halt and shift his effort to Kantara, to avoid being outflanked. Again, Elazar displayed his ignorance of the location of Israeli forces—this time, the whereabouts of the 143rd's units. He still thought that the change in plan was due to the 143rd's delay in embarking from the central sector and its failure to meet the timetable for attacking Suez, both of which he considered grievous shortcomings. But he accepted with marked equanimity the drastic mission change, which torpedoed any chance of succeeding in a counterattack, and he made no effort to initiate any move other than approving Gonen's suggestion. In the Pit, he noted that Sharon would be at the Chinese Farm rather than Suez that evening: "Too bad, but this happens sometimes."[287]

The timing of the 143rd's mission change was curious. Sharon stated that he received his new orders at 14:00, but by Gonen's own account, he ordered the 143rd to halt at 14:15 and immediately informed Gandhi. At 14:15 he suggested bringing the 143rd back to the central sector and relayed this recommendation to Gandhi at 14:22, "before the 143rd left Tasa." However, reports of the 162nd coming under pressure did not begin until 16:00. Gonen received permission from Elazar at 15:30 (or 15:20, according to another version) to attack the Chinese Farm. Elazar reminded the general of Southern Command that the main mission was to bring Sharon's division south. Gonen, however, presented the 143rd's rerouting to the Chinese Farm not as the cancellation of the order to go south but as an intermediate move. This, of course, was preposterous. The 143rd's hasty change of direction to engage in combat with Egyptian 16th Infantry Division, which had been entrenched at the Chinese Farm for two days and was armed to the teeth with antitank weapons, could hardly be described as a brief encounter before pursuing the main fight in the south.

Gonen gave three reasons for the division's change of assignment: (1) It failed to keep to the timetable. As Gonen stated, "I want to emphasize that Arik's [Sharon's] return was not because of Adan's situation but because of the timetable. (2) "The Egyptians were about to counterattack the entire length of the central sector" (there was no proof of this). (3) "It wasn't going well for Adan."[288] These are dubious reasons. Gonen could have easily changed the timetable. Regarding the Egyptian counterattack, an examination of the incoming information would have revealed that the attack was not threatening Adan's division. As for the third reason, this was already the case at 11:00, and if 143rd Division was needed to assist the 162nd, it should have done so before noon, before the whole division was sent south.

An Absolute Lack of Coordination between the Two Divisions

While orders were being conveyed via the chiefs of staff of Southern Command and 143rd Division, only ten kilometers separated Gonen and Sharon. A face-to-face meeting certainly could have been arranged, clearing up any uncertainty regarding the location of the 143rd's units, and it might have clarified what could (and could not) be done in the remaining daylight hours. But the day's blunders and foul-ups were not over yet.

At 16:55 Gonen reported to the chief of staff that the 143rd was advancing to attack the Chinese Farm. Sharon was waiting for an additional brigade and planned to attack Missouri at 17:00. The reconnaissance battalion and 600th Brigade would seize Hamadia and Makhshir as a solid base, and 14th and 421st Brigades would enter Akavish in the direction of Missouri to engage in a nighttime battle illuminated by the air force (Sharon had requested IAF assistance).

In the neighboring sector, there was a total absence of coordination between the two divisions. As the 143rd returned to the central sector, the 162nd was fighting in two areas: north of Tasa-Ismailia Road, 217th and 460th Brigades were blocking the Egyptian attack; south of the road, 500th Brigade was attacking Hamutal and Makhshir in one of the most controversial battles of the war. At 15:26, 198th Battalion disengaged from 460th Brigade to assist 500th Brigade in its attack on Hamutal, which the Egyptians had overrun earlier that afternoon. Under the command of Lieutenant Colonel Yoffe, the battalion mistakenly attacked Makhshir at 16:30. The attack failed, and as darkness descended, the battalion retreated from the hill that Yoffe believed to be Hamutal.

Meanwhile, 433rd Battalion/500th Brigade was summoned to assist in the capture of Hamutal, and it left Nozel without informing the division. The Egyptians quickly seized Nozel. The attacks on both Hamutal and Makhshir foundered, and the 500th incurred serious losses as it withdrew from the dominating areas. The fighting had been characterized by an utter lack of coordination between the attacking units, the absence of a battle procedure, no recognizable markings on neighboring forces, and a lack of intelligence on the enemy. Professional deficiencies were widespread at all levels, and basic combat values such as devotion to mission accomplishment, evacuation of the wounded, and accurate reporting were sadly lacking.[289]

The 143rd's battle plan fell apart after 421st Brigade entered Talisman Road instead of Akavish due to a misunderstanding by the deputy division commander. Because of the mistake, Sharon changed the battle plan: at 17:05 he ordered the 421st to travel on Talisman, capture Hamutal immediately and then Makhshir, and continue to Nozel. When one of the 421st's battalions mistakenly entered Akavish, Sharon ordered it to turn around and join the brigade for the attack on Hamutal and Makhshir. The 600th and 14th Brigades were ordered to attack Missouri. In the last rays of light, the 421st unexpectedly engaged the enemy at Hamutal after 500th Brigade had pulled back. No radio contact or coordination had been established between the two. In addition, there was confusion in the 421st regarding assignments, such as who was to provide covering fire, as well as flaws in their execution. As the battle drew to a close, the 421st, too, withdrew from Hamutal.[290] In practical terms, the two divisions fought for the same objectives without defining their respective sector borders and without coordinating or updating each other on their assignments. And at the end of the day, both Hamutal and Makhshir remained in Egyptian hands.

Given the enemy's pressure on the 162nd, the misuse of forces, and Southern Command's grim picture (between 17:07 and 17:09) of the enemy attack on the 162nd, at 17:21 Gonen ordered Sharon to halt the attack on Missouri and Amir and called in air support for the entire sector. The IAF commander's response was disappointing, as usual: loft bombing within an hour. Gonen and Sharon discussed whether the 162nd could be helped by sending 421st Brigade to attack from the south. Adan, too, requested this assistance, but Sharon was opposed because he needed the brigade for the attack on Hamutal and Makhshir. Southern Command's aide-de-camp noted that Gonen's explanation for calling off the attack on Missouri was that a large number of enemy tanks were moving out of Firdan, and he doubted that Adan's 217th Brigade could obstruct them. Gonen estimated the enemy's strength at approximately one reinforced armored brigade in Missouri. He ordered the capture of Hamutal and Makhshir, but the attacks failed.

With nightfall, after the 421st had failed to regain Hamutal (although Sharon reported otherwise), 143rd Division began to reorganize: 600th Brigade deployed on Hamadia, 421st Brigade on Talisman Road east of Hamutal, and 14th Brigade, which had been ordered back from Gidi, entered Yukon on Akavish Road.

Did the Egyptians Attack 162nd Division?

Information on the Egyptians' attack came from MI's listening unit and led to Gonen's decision to halt 143rd Division on its way to the southern sector and return it to the central sector and later to cancel the planned attack on Missouri. However, reports from the commanders in the field and a basic debriefing revealed that the attack never occurred. So what really happened? Was there any justification for a deep pullback of 162nd Division's forces from the areas they were holding?

Reports of an Egyptian attack reached the 162nd's headquarters from 217th and 460th Brigades at 16:00, while Adan and the brigade commanders were exchanging updates. When the commanders returned to their brigades, they told Adan they would hang in, and at 16:30 they reported that the attack had been blocked. The deputy commander of the 460th, Lieutenant Colonel Sasson, and a company commander of 113th Battalion, Major Brik, both of whom had observed the area, reported that there was no attack, except for a minor Egyptian force that had moved east and been stopped. At any rate, Southern Command magnified the event as a looming catastrophe, and as a result, Gonen halted the 143rd's attack on Missouri and Amir at 17:12. At 17:20 the commander of 217th Brigade reported that he had thwarted the attack. Nevertheless, 162nd Division ordered a withdrawal, and Adan's dismal reports were conveyed to Gonen, who concluded that if a slight withdrawal was necessary, it would be permitted. Gonen informed Adan that 143rd Division would not be entering from south to north.

At 18:00 the 162nd's units pulled back, evacuated the dominating areas, and withdrew a few kilometers east. At 18:05 the division radioed Southern Command that it had repulsed the Egyptian attack and was organizing, but it made no mention of a withdrawal or its change in deployment, which included the evacuation of Havraga. The 500th Brigade moved seven kilometers east of Hamutal to Talisman 39; 217th Brigade was sent north to Ma'adim Road; 460th Brigade moved east to Spontani 36; and 162nd Division's tactical headquarters relocated to the Spontani Road–Lateral Road junction. No Israeli force moved into the vacated areas. The reconnaissance battalion was ordered to hold the Havraga-Zrakor sand dune line, but this assignment was canceled, and the battalion returned to Spontani Road.

Such a deep withdrawal was unnecessary. It stemmed from the mistaken assessment of a massive enemy counterattack, the lack of accurate information about the situation of friendly and enemy forces, and the failure to thoroughly check intelligence reporters and their locations. Even after IDF forces reported at 17:20 that they had stanched the enemy's advance, the 162nd moved to the rear at 18:00. This pullback, which Gonen had approved and was ostensibly designed for reorganization, was, as Adan testified, the result of the division's bitter combat operations that day.[291]

A Lost Opportunity in the Southern Sector

On the afternoon of October 7, the 252nd's responsibility was limited to the southern sector, where it conducted a defensive battle with thirty-five tanks from 401st Brigade. The next day the brigade engaged in major fire and movement battles against Egyptian 7th and 19th Divisions' armor, which attempted to break through; the 252nd dominated Canal Road with fire and encountered only minimal enemy pressure. This strengthens the conclusion that launching the IDF counterattack in the southern sector against Third Army, which was weaker than Second Army, would have been the right decision. But the golden opportunity to smash Third Army, or at last thrust it back to two limited and separated bridgeheads, was lost.

By late Monday morning, Southern Command had ordered 252nd Division and 401st Brigade to withdraw its forces to Artillery Road. They had to vacate the area to make room for 143rd Division, which was due to arrive from the central sector. Southern Command's G-3 warned the 252nd about this possibility on the night of October 7–8 and stated that the air force would carry out a massive attack on the enemy. The 143rd would move north to south, clean out the whole area up to Hamezach, and attempt a crossing at Hakfar or Lituf. Adan would do the same in the central sector. (As early as the night of October 7–8, it was clear that Southern Command had already been planning to send the 143rd to the southern sector.)

Close to 10:00, the deputy commander of 421st Brigade called from the Gidi Road–Lateral Road junction and said that the brigade's forces would be arriving shortly. Around 11:00, the 401st was ordered to pull back to Artillery Road.[292] Two of the brigade's battalions, the 52nd and 195th, were adjacent to Lexicon Road and had successfully blocked Egyptian 19th Division on Mitla Road and south of it; they received no explanation for the withdrawal. The brigade commander, Colonel Shomron, said, "The [Egyptian] tanks were no longer coming out but remained in positions on the road and close to the canal. . . . Any [Egyptian] tank that emerged—was set ablaze."[293]

The mood in 252nd Division improved when it became clear that the Egyptian attack had been blocked on Mitla Road and did not involve armored divisions. According to Gideon Avidor, the 252nd's G-3, the prevailing feeling was, "We've won the war and now the problem is only time, the reservist divisions will be arriving."[294] At 10:47 Gonen informed Albert that Sharon's division would head south to Gidi on Lateral Road (not Artillery Road). After Sharon's division cleaned up the area, the 252nd would link up with the strongholds, together with 875th Mechanized Brigade. If Sharon's crossing succeeded, Albert's division would follow. Avidor recalled, "We waited for the attack. Our forces actually pulled back. We prepared for an attack that never came. . . . Arik Sharon was on the way . . . but he didn't arrive. . . . We vacated the roads for them. . . . The 252nd didn't know that the 143rd's attack was planned to take place directly at Nisan [Hakfar]."[295]

Following Southern Command's orders, the 252nd returned to Artillery Road without pressure from the enemy, which was in the Canal Road area. According to Avidor: "We waited for the attack at 06:00. They said that things are going extremely well for Adan and [that] Arik [Sharon] is on the way . . . [only] around 14:00–15:00 they informed us that it [the attack] was cancelled. . . . The sector had been left empty the whole time."[296] When asked about Albert's slow responses and the fact that the forces did not return to the positions they had vacated before noon, Avidor offered the following constrained explanation: "Southern Command decided ahead of time not to approve the plans. . . . We'd have been happy with a plan and that we were finally going over to the attack and the disappointment was great. . . . Albert was a highly disciplined soldier."[297]

Gonen and Albert spoke a few times on Monday morning and concurred that the tide was turning and the IDF would soon be able to shift to the attack. At 13:35, after vacating the area, Albert asked Gonen when the 143rd would arrive. Gonen replied that he "hoped as soon as possible. Now everything depends on him [Sharon]."[298] Albert asked for an update so he could get his tanks out of the way for Sharon's division to pass through. But at the time of this strange and pointless conversation, 401st Brigade had already withdrawn to Artillery Road two hours earlier, and Southern Command had decided to send 143rd Division back to the central sector. Later, Gonen told Albert that the 143rd had been ordered back to the central sector because of the Egyptian counterattack there.

Egyptian Third Army's difficulties are revealed in its failure to exploit 401st Brigade's withdrawal and improve its positions to the east after Gonen aborted Sharon's move south. The 252nd Division received no orders to immediately redeploy in the areas it had vacated; nor did it initiate such a move. The next morning (Tuesday), when the 401st's tanks returned to the same (more or less) vacated areas, it was obvious that the Egyptians had made no attempt to advance east—except in the direction of Ayun Musa.

The 143rd Division's Gratuitous Battles

The battles 143rd Division fought Tuesday morning at Makhshir and Hamutal were not part of the planned counterattack, but given their importance and the way they were conducted, they served as the final chord of the October 8 fight and the struggle for the strongholds. On Tuesday afternoon, the IDF began what was intended to culminate in a canal crossing.

Tuesday, October 9, was a turning point in Southern Command's defensive battle. Until then, the IDF had failed to execute a single divisional attack in the defensive battle. The 143rd had plans for 600th and 14th Brigades to attack in the west on October 9, but as it turned out, only two battalions from the 600th attacked, and both incurred heavy losses. The 14th arrived later and held the areas where the 600th had fought.

At 06:30, 421st Brigade ordered its 599th and 264th Battalions to attack Hamutal, with the goal of improving their positions to assist in the rescue of the Purkan stronghold. The attack failed mainly because of the lack of mechanized infantry, tanks, and machine guns, as well as the lack of strength to continue the attack's momentum. An Egyptian brigade's attempt to capture Hamadia also failed, and the force returned to the area between Hamutal and Tsioni to reorganize, leaving the northern part of Hamutal in IDF hands. The October 9 battles reflect slapdash planning, sloppy preparation, and lack of knowledge of the enemy's strength. No attempts were made to obtain information from the ground, and instead of surprising the enemy, the IDF forces were caught by surprise. Although the brigade commanders were very close to the battle zone, the attacks were poorly coordinated and launched with insufficient force concentrations. Some of these errors could have been avoided had the division learned the lessons from the 162nd's battles at Hamutal the day before.[299]

As a result of setbacks and blunders, eighty of Southern Command's tanks were put out of commission—fifty in 143rd Division (eighteen abandoned), twelve in the 162nd, and the rest in the 252nd. Eighty Egyptian tanks were destroyed. Sharon fought initiated attacks (although he had been ordered only to stabilize a defensive line) at Kishuf, Makhshir, and Hamutal, but except for Kishuf, they failed. The division succeeded at Televizia and blocked the Egyptian attack on Hamadia. These were impromptu attacks without divisional planning or an orderly battle procedure, and no instructions were issued to the forces. Sharon called this "maintaining contact" and "reconnaissance activity."

That night, the division's reconnaissance battalion reached the Lakekan stronghold. This was an important move that identified the seam between the two Egyptian armies and would prove vital to the canal crossing the following week.

Summary of the Counterattack's Blunders

Mistakes were made by Southern Command, by Chief of Staff Elazar, and by General Gonen.

Southern Command's Blunders

Southern Command made the following mistakes in the battle procedure:

- No one prepared a detailed operational plan, issued orders to the units, or obtained plan approvals.
- There was no follow-up of force buildup or preparation for the operation.
- There were inexcusable deficits in intelligence prior to the counterattack, including disregard of the relative strengths of the two Egyptian armies and not a word about the enemy's location.
- No lessons were learned from the regulars' two days of tank fighting (unsupported by mechanized infantry and artillery) against enemy infantry that was heavily armed with antitank weapons. None of the regulars' hard-won experience was exploited to devise an operational plan adapted to the ground situation.

The flaws in Southern Command's conduct of operations were as follows:

- The divisions' missions were frequently changed without comprehending the time needed to execute them; without staff summaries and updates on the IDF's and the enemy's situation; without a standby order; and without mission definition, coordination with neighboring forces, delineation of new sector borders, allocation of support, and so forth.

- Deviations from battle objectives, as defined by the chief of staff, proved to be debilitating. These included ordering the 162nd to Hizayon and across the canal without creating the proper conditions, and sending 143rd Division south before the 162nd had completed its assignments, thereby leaving the central sector exposed and exhausting the 143rd before it engaged in battle.[300]
- There were intelligence gaps in the conduct of operations.
- Lucid standing orders were absent in connection with staff work on operations, intelligence, and administration; terms were muddled (e.g., tactical headquarters, main headquarters, command post, rear headquarters); and there was a lack of control according to the IDF's war-fighting doctrine.
- The orders issued were too generalized and indefinite: for instance, the 162nd was ordered to seize a toehold at Hizayon and the 143rd was instructed to reach the southern sector, with no discussion of neighboring forces or the transit of one force through another. All these shortcomings had fatal results: the wrong objectives were attacked, missions were misconstrued, and so forth.
- Attacks were hastily executed, divisions were redirected from one sector to another before their missions were completed, and there was insufficient preparation and coordination at all levels. Activating divisions and brigades primarily by radio compromised field and communications security and impeded the transmission of clear and intelligible orders, the sine qua non for managing large formations.
- Divisions and brigades operated in a timetable better suited to battalions and companies. "Divisions and brigades can't be scrambled, even if there are those who would issue such an order."[301] In addition, Sinai's time and space dimensions were not fully considered.
- The headquarters of Southern Command and the divisions had a hard time maintaining control. Southern Command's control bodies—the rear in Beer Sheva and the mobile and stationery tactical headquarters in Sinai—had been trained to deal with daily security operations, not a sudden all-out

war. The plan to deploy control bodies in Sinai's vastness had already become anachronistic, and Southern Command's new plan was not yet operational. The solution decided on—the command post at Dvela—was unsuitable. At first, the divisions were controlled from the FCGs (the main headquarters was nonfunctional, and orderly staff work was all but impossible). Operational logs were either completely neglected or slovenly kept. Written orders were not circulated.

- Distorted pictures of the situation prevailed in headquarters at all levels because the commanders had no direct contact. When Gonen conveyed a crucial order to Adan via General Magen at Baluza, Gonen had no way of knowing whether Adan received the order and understood its intention. The 143rd Division received its orders from Gonen over the radio, but he had no direct contact with Sharon, who was intentionally not answering the radio. The commanders did not personally meet with their subordinates to give them instructions, and they did not receive the latter's confirmation. The division commanders acted according to their interpretation of the chief of staff's plan at Dvela. But without confirmation of the plan, a succession of misunderstandings developed on the ground; these were aggravated by Southern Command's expansion of the chief of staff's intentions and deviations from his original plan.
- Reports were imprecise, and systems for conveying and processing data were lacking. Overly optimistic reporting and the failure to understand reports' implications repeatedly misguided the command; gave Gonen a distorted picture of the battle; and led him to order a canal crossing in the morning and afternoon, send the 143rd south, and then order it to return and attack the Chinese Farm. Even when Adan reported at 11:48 that several of his tanks were on fire, Gonen did not comprehend the ramifications and continued to press for the Suez crossing. He ordered Sharon to "prepare for a large attack there."[302] GHQ, too, received inaccurate information because Southern Command and the divisions lacked a reporting system. The chief of staff recalled that "the fog of battle was very thick that day and the picture we received was that things were going exceptionally well in the 162nd."[303]

- Commanders were in the wrong places. This was a major factor in the skewed situational assessments and misguided decisions at senior levels. The chief of staff was attending the government meeting, Gonen was ensconced in Dvela, and the commander of the 162nd remained in Zrakor—the wrong place for him to be during the main battle at Firdan, thirteen kilometers from the battlefield and without visual contact.[304]

The Chief of Staff's Blunders

Although the Agranat Commission judged Elazar leniently and placed the bulk of the responsibility on General Gonen of Southern Command—as the initiator of the requests for changes in the plan—the chief of staff's role was definitely more significant than the commission's conclusions indicated and was even greater than Gonen's. The chief of staff approved Gonen's requests irresponsibly and far too hastily without checking them, verifying them, or consulting with other officers at GHQ or Southern Command.

Wrong place. The chief of staff was in the wrong place during the counterattack. He was attending the government meeting when he should have been at Dvela.

Deficient and defective updates. This was the inevitable result of commanders being in the wrong places and not delving into the details of the battle. During consultations at the high command post in Tel Aviv between 05:00 and 06:45 on October 9, Elazar outlined the reasons for the attack's failure: misleading reports that led to his flawed decisions, instructions to the armored forces not to expose themselves to antitank fire, artillery's failure to operate in close support of armor against Egyptian infantry, and 162nd Division's delayed arrival. Although these points were essentially correct, they were not a war summary, and as the following pages show, there were too many other failures he did not mention.

During the government meeting convened at 10:00 on October 8, the chief of staff was detached from the reality of the counterattack and presented extremely inaccurate data on the order of battle: he stated that the 252nd had returned to its capacity of 250 tanks, but at the time, it had only about 35; he claimed the 162nd had 300 tanks, but it had launched the operation with only 163; and he said 143rd Division had more than 200 tanks—also incorrect. In his description of the divisions' assignments—even though he himself had determined the attack's limitations—he spoke of the possibility of the 162nd crossing the canal, perhaps on an Egyptian bridge (this was his idea), and the 143rd moving south in the afternoon. However, he stated, "This depends on Adan completing this [his assignment] by noon and deploying either on this side or the other side." At any rate, less than an hour later, he granted Gonen permission to bring the 143rd south.[305]

His statements on the strongholds, too, were removed from reality. He explained his dilemma: "If war begins on the canal the troops will have to be taken out of the strongholds otherwise they'll probably be captured. Many reports were coming in stating that we had to get them out. I thought that it was worth having the men remain in the strongholds. At the time, the balance was rather satisfactory for a war. Of the thirty or so, two actually fell. About ten were evacuated successfully, the ones with the wounded."[306] There was not an ounce of truth to any of this. It goes without saying that the chief of staff was ignorant of the number of strongholds and their real situation, and not only in the government meeting.

His assessment of the 162nd was totally groundless. He told the government that if the forces reached the canal and captured a bridge intact, they would have to "request permission to cross to the other side and establish our own limited bridgehead. I don't know if this will work. As of now, Adan is requesting an option. He's approaching a bridge and thinks that he's standing on it. The general of Southern Command is already asking for permission. I haven't granted it yet. I want to be certain that this breakthrough isn't too narrow and reckless. I prefer to have the bridgehead destroyed."[307]

Elazar's outline of the counterattack's priorities illustrates his disconnect with reality: "Our first task is to clean up the canal on our side and redeploy in the strongholds and ceasefire line; second, hold, if possible, one or two bridgeheads on the other side; third, we have a detailed plan for [taking] Port Said." Elazar may have been paying lip service to Dayan, who was relentlessly urging him to execute the crossing no matter how preposterous the task. Ultimately, the government decided on the following "mission impossible" for the IDF, mainly because of the chief of staff's delusional optimism:

1. Push the Egyptian army back across the canal.
2. Push the Syrian army back across the cease-fire line on the Golan Heights.
3. Simultaneously smash both enemy armies.

The prime minister and the defense minister were authorized to grant the IDF permission, if the opportunity arose, to capture military holds across the canal (in the north and the south). At the meeting of the Foreign Affairs and Defense Committee that convened the following afternoon (after the magnitude and gravity of the counterattack's failure became known), the prime minister approved this decision. The chief of staff's ignorance of the combat situation was brought up in the government meeting at 21:00, and his explanation of the counterattack's failure was blunt and contemptuous: "Adan's division attacked and destroyed [the enemy] but they [the enemy] brought in more tanks. . . . Arik Sharon's counterattack wasn't executed. I don't know why exactly. He was supposed to be ready for the attack this morning. . . . He received the order at 10:00 but didn't manage to move out. . . . [His division] started moving quite late in the afternoon, conducted a small-scale attack, and didn't have time to block or do much that day."[308]

Even at 21:30, the chief of staff, back in his office after the government meeting, still had not been updated on events. He assumed that 143rd Division had not headed to Suez because of a delay in its departure. His information on the fighting of the 162nd and 143rd was also far from accurate. As far as he knew, the 162nd was deployed two kilometers from the canal, had control of the situation, and was knocking out enemy tanks on the embankment across the bridge. "The information that I received, and maybe what Gorodish [Gonen] and Bren [Adan] also received . . . was that he [Adan] had completed the line and would soon be at Dwersuar."[309]

Elazar explained that his decision to allow Gonen to cross the canal was based on the assumption that the situation was favorable. Therefore, believing that one bridgehead had been destroyed (as in the Six-Day War), he approved sending the 143rd south to eliminate the second bridgehead. He described the contents of the note he received: "'Your approval [is requested] to capture Suez at four o'clock.' A normal person who didn't leave Tasa, wouldn't ask permission to capture Suez. . . . Therefore I have inaccurate information about capturing Suez at four o'clock. 'Your permission is requested.'

I said: 'permission granted.' That is, I understand that this is okay. Later it turned out that first of all Adan hadn't cleaned out the area from top to bottom, but had attacked frontally and may or may not have destroyed [the enemy]. The Egyptians fired on him in response . . . [that's] not important. He did what he did." At this point, the chief of staff realized that "the 162nd is in big trouble. The bridgehead exists. The 143rd did what it did and is on the 162nd's flank." His conclusion: "I didn't accomplish the mission as I wanted to."[310]

The chief of staff's account reflects the absence of a mechanism to ensure he received regular updates on the fighting, no matter where he was. Elazar admitted that until 12:40, Southern Command did not ask him for permission to send the 143rd to the Chinese Farm; it asked for permission to capture Suez. Elazar claimed that he informed General Hofi of Northern Command at 13:35 what was happening in Sinai and about Sharon's movement toward Suez. The timetables show that Gonen came up with the idea to redirect the 143rd to the central sector at 13:35; this is corroborated by his conversation with Albert. Gonen told Tal about the 162nd's problems with the Egyptian counterattack in a conversation at 13:30, and he received permission to bring the 143rd back to the central sector at 14:02. No attempt was made to update the chief of staff or consult with him, even though this was possible while he was in flight and at Northern Command. His subordinates in the GSO may have incorrectly interpreted his style of command and the free rein he gave his subordinates as a system that did not demand his continuous input on key matters. The chief of staff insisted that he had no record of being told about the 143rd's return to the central sector while he was at Northern Command; therefore, as he understood it, the 143rd's assignment was changed by the general of the command either acting on his own or with Tal's permission. By Elazar's own account, he learned of the change only when he landed at Sde Dov upon his return from Northern Command.[311]

Elazar's 15:30 telephone conversation with Gonen when he was back in the Pit shows the huge information gap caused by the lack of updates. He was unaware of the 162nd's situation, deployment, or operations, and he still believed it had 300 tanks (only then did he realize that the number was much lower). His picture of the situation between 16:45 and 17:00 was also wrong, but he made no effort to speak with the division commanders. He thought that the 162nd was progressing well in its tasks and that the 143rd had not left the central sector until 14:00. Dayan too anticipated the Egyptians' collapse, although there were no reports of IDF accomplishments.

Giving advice instead of issuing orders. Elazar's style of command had a negative influence on the development of the war at a number of critical junctures. He tended to speak like an observer and offer advice rather than cut through matters and issue direct commands. This was his style on October 8, and it had disastrous results. On the afternoon of October 8, when it was evident that the counterattack had failed (although the extent of the failure was still unclear) and that the operational concept had to be realigned from attack to defense, Elazar thought it sufficient to give advice. At 15:30 he said to Gonen: "I'm not going into details, I just want to suggest that you prepare Adan for three things: destroy the enemy in the area, avoid crossing if he's deployed opposite the crossing and if he has enough forces—check with him about this—have him divert part of his force towards Milano."[312] This was the chief of staff's advice when the 162nd's situation was unmistakably depressing.

The 217th Brigade arrived at noon with two battalions from the northern sector, where it had been delayed for hours because of fear of a T62 tank force. The 217th was already heavily engaged in battle, and there was no way to bring it back to Kantara (the Milano stronghold). An afternoon attack by the brigade's 113th Battalion had ended in failure. The 500th Brigade was also bogged down in fighting at Hamutal, and 162nd Division could not carry out any of the tasks Elazar suggested to Gonen (except for destroying tanks with long-range cannon fire, which it did). Using simple tools of command—such as getting on the division's radio frequency and speaking with Adan, who was at Havraga, or even visiting him in the field—Elazar could have enlightened himself on the 162nd's situation. Instead, he chose to give unrealistic advice.

The chief of staff cannot be a neutral observer who analyzes the mistakes of his subordinates. It is difficult to acknowledge that Elazar's ignorance of the combat situation led to his approval (almost as an afterthought) of mission changes that were operationally unsound. Speaking in the tone of an observer cannot blur the fact that the chief of staff alone bears the overall responsibility.

Failure to recognize Sinai's time and spatial constraints. The chief of staff's alacrity in blindly approving Gonen's frequent requests also stemmed from his unfamiliarity with Sinai and the time required to move large formations across such great distances. Thus, at 11:25 he allowed Gonen to order the 143rd to break off contact in the central sector and move to Gidi; at 12:40 he approved its move to Mitla to execute a force-through-force maneuver, cross the canal at Hakfar between 16:00 and 18:00, and capture Suez. These approvals had no operational, intelligence, or technical basis whatsoever (and involved crossing on a nonexistent Egyptian bridge). Without realizing it, Elazar approved a timetable of two hours to eliminate Egyptian Second Army! In contrast, he demonstrated intimate and impressive knowledge of the geography of the Golan Heights and its road network. During the October 8 counterattack on the Golan Heights, he spoke on the telephone with the general of Northern Command and went into great detail about which roads should be used. He displayed none of this erudition in Sinai. According to Lieutenant General Ehud Barak, "People who matured in the north [Golan Heights] do not really understand the south [Sinai] and its problems. Many senior IDF commanders [Gonen and Elazar] can't conceive of the 'rhythm' of action of large formations and the command and GHQ systems [there] . . . [of] how long it takes from the moment you give an order until something happens and the inevitable haze created in this situation."[313]

Impetuosity in force concentration. The chief of staff ordered the massive use of artillery against Egyptian infantry, but the 162nd's entry into the fighting without artillery support (except for two reduced batteries in the northern sector) exemplified the impatience and rashness that characterized headquarters activity. Launching a counterattack on October 8 before the forces were ready, instead of waiting another day, was the most glaring expression of the chief of staff's lack of patience.[314]

Gonen's Blunders

Gonen repeatedly whittled down the chief of staff's October 7 plan and countermanded his instructions. The order issued to Adan at 09:05 on October 8—"It might be worth looking for [the enemy] more to the west"—did not justify Gonen's far-reaching decision to attempt a crossing near Hizayon. Because of a misreading of the battlefield picture and the 162nd's situation, along with Gonen's obsession with crossing the canal as early as possible, the 143rd was sent south earlier than planned, the 162nd's distress signals fell on deaf ears, and the division was given the impossible mission of capturing toeholds on the western bank.

Dispatching 143rd Division south before the 162nd had completed its attack was an egregious deviation from Elazar's original plan, and it had painful results. This was a brash decision based on an incorrect assessment of the 162nd's situation. Accomplishment of the 162nd's missions was the cornerstone of the plan. Gonen requested permission to bring the 143rd south because he understood from Adan's reports that everything was proceeding smoothly. In his initial decision (moving the 143rd to Gidi and waiting there), Gonen saw no deviation from the primary assignment— holding the division in reserve for the 162nd. However, keeping a reserve force forty kilometers from the combat zone made no sense, since a reserve has to be located where it can quickly intervene. Gonen explained that the move's rationale was based on time and space considerations and that four hours could be saved. He correctly regarded the chief of staff's summary at Dvela as an idea that he had to work into a plan.

According to Gonen, the decision to dispatch the 143rd to Suez rather than have it attack from north to south stemmed from information that the enemy was weaker there. This was true, but it should have been taken into account in the planning that occurred on the evening of October 7. When asked why he decided to bring the 143rd south so early (09:37), Gonen had no intelligent answer. "I'm allowed to request permission," he said, claiming that, at the time, only part of the 162nd was in contact with the enemy; he reckoned that when the rest of it arrived, the battle would be decided. He waited for the "red line"—the moment when Sharon would have to move—and it came at approximately 10:30. But when he asked the chief of staff for an option, he should have apprised him of the real situation: "Adan is not inside [Second Army's formation]; Gabi Amir [commander of 460th Brigade] is stuck; his tanks are burning and he's looking for a battalion to rescue him—not to help him enter [Hizayon]—and he has one artillery battery."[315] Gonen mentioned none of this to Elazar when he asked for the option at 10:30, and later he could not explain why he had not reported it. According to the plan at Dvela, the 162nd's assignment was supposed to be completed by noon, and use of the 143rd was planned from noon to evening.

Gonen wanted to make the most of Sharon's attack, but he was also worried about employing it too early, in which case he would not be able to take him out. "I did the math," Gonen stated, and the optimal time for Sharon to move was 10:30. "Until [Sharon] arrived another hour and a half or two would pass and it would be 12:00. He'd be in the Gidi between 12:00 and 13:00." (At 12:40 the chief of staff granted Gonen permission, via Gandhi, to bring the 143rd from Gidi to attack at Suez.) Gonen testified that he asked for permission to move the 143rd from Gidi to Suez on the basis of Adan's report and monitoring of Adan's radio networks. In Gonen's opinion, "Adan was optimistic and felt that he was accomplishing the assignment, that he only needed air support and had only six casualties."[316] Gonen explained that he perceived this as a divisional, not a battalion, battle, and six destroyed tanks should be seen from that perspective. As evidence of this, Adan ordered 217th Brigade to seize the passes on the canal.

Gonen's replies to the Agranat Commission's questions were odd, to say the least. The commission noted that "Adan's report of six tanks ablaze shows that the battle was still not over. In fact it was not going smoothly. In other words, at this stage Sharon should not have been removed from areas that would be very difficult to recapture (Nozel, Hamutal, Makhshir and others)." Gonen's reply: "There was enough time to bring [Sharon's division] back. In my opinion, this was the right calculation. Nothing disastrous would have happened if he was waiting or on his way to the southern sector. I could have always brought him back to intercede in the battle."[317]

The two commanders, Adan and Sharon, should have reminded Gonen that sending the 143rd south depended on the 162nd's success. It is not clear why Adan kept silent. As for Sharon, he may have been enticed by the glory of a successful crossing operation. Gonen was certain that the 162nd's forces were already in the positions vacated by the 143rd (or in their immediate vicinity). This was a serious error that resulted from the lack of basic coordination between the two divisions. Gonen hurled the 143rd into the fighting from south to north, and not vice versa, because he preferred to begin the operation with a large mass of forces in the south, rather than ending it there. This was a ridiculous argument, since most of the enemy armor was concentrated in the northern part of the sector, in Egyptian 7th Division.

Sobering Up

The events of October 8 and the failures of the following morning led to a sober reassessment and a realization that this war was different from all previous ones. Both the IDF and the Israeli government decided to change tack: cease the futile attacks in the south, conserve the forces, and organize for defense on Artillery Road, with the aim of amassing strength for further moves—the main one being the canal crossing. The decision to concentrate the effort in Syria, and thus remove it from the fighting circle, and then shift the effort to the Egyptian front was the right decision, even though in its practical application it did not contribute additional ground troops or air support to Southern Command.

The act of sobering up helped stabilize staff work and various systems (intelligence, fire support, logistics, communications, operational planning, and so forth) in GHQ and Southern Command; it also changed the performance of a number of senior commanders, some of whom recovered from the initial shock and were now more prudent, realistic, and pragmatic in their decision making, applying some of the lessons of the first days. On the basis of the October 9 lines, the IDF blocked the Egyptian attack on October 14, and from there, 14th Brigade embarked on a breakthrough battle on the way to a canal crossing.

Early on Monday evening, the general of Southern Command informed the chief of staff that the 143rd would attack not at Missouri but farther north. Elazar figured this would not happen and that the 143rd together with the 162nd would enter a holding position, block the counterattack, put up a defense with the main force on Lateral Road and the forward forces on Artillery Road, and wait until greater strength was amassed. In his typical style, Elazar shied away from forcing a decision on Gonen and advised and cajoled instead: "Keep Arik [Sharon]. Try not to push him into contact. If you push him forward you'll enter two battles both of which might be too big. We have to go over to the defense now. Link up with Adan's flank and together try to block. I'll try to get you air support."[318] (At this point, air support was meaningless, especially at night.)

At 20:00 the picture was still muddled. Gonen was unaware that the 162nd had left Artillery Road and was organizing at Talisman-Spontani. The Pit also received a distorted picture. Elazar thought the Egyptian line was continuous; the IAF commander corrected that misimpression, informing him that the Egyptians had separate bridgeheads.

Southern Command's divisions deployed defensively on Monday night. Magen's force in the northern sector was holding Egyptian 18th Division. The 162nd, after withdrawing on Monday evening, was deployed defensively halfway between Artillery Road and Lateral Road. In the southern sector, the 252nd was holding the Mitzva fortification on Gidi Road, the Notsa fortification on Mitla Road, and the Tseidar fortification on Yoreh Road, while Artillery Road was cut off east of the Nehushtan high ground. On the morning of October 9, the 252nd's 401st Brigade was holding the area of the Polish Camp and the Karat Moora range and its western margins, while it dominated Canal Road and Hamezach Junction with tank fire. In the central sector, 143rd Division lost Nozel, Hamutal, and Makhshir, three dominating areas the Egyptians had captured Monday morning. Hamadia and Tsioni were still in the IDF's hands.

Even after the chief of staff realized the necessity of shifting to the defense, he refrained from intervening decisively. In his conversation with Gonen at 20:25 about the 252nd's deployment, he remarked, "I won't interfere if the tanks are closer to the rear or more forward."[319]

Beginning on Monday evening, the government, the GHQ command post in Tel Aviv, and Southern Command's tactical operations center at Dvela tried to piece together a picture of what had happened, why they had failed, and what moves were required to continue the fight after the heavy losses of the first three days. At 17:15 in the Pit, Dayan asked the chief of staff if the Egyptians were in a state of crisis and beating a hasty retreat to the western bank. Elazar answered that the opposite was true: "It's too early to say that they're broken . . . it's increasingly clear to them that their goal mustn't be over-ambitious [capturing the passes] but based on a line eight kilometers from the canal."[320] Dayan disagreed. In his opinion, the Egyptians would stick to their original plan. He again brought up the idea of Green Light (Or Yarok), a combined-arms operation on the western shore of the Bay of Suez.

That evening, GHQ devised a realistic defense plan for Southern Command. The forces would organize in a forward defense on Artillery Road: the 252nd would deploy defensively on the passes and Artillery Road, the 162nd would spread out on a wide front on Artillery Road, and Magen's force would remain in place. The 143rd, which had engaged in only minor skirmishes that day, would concentrate and organize in the rear and prepare for the following day's counterattack in either the central or southern sector. At 20:25 Elazar and Gonen weighed a number of options: a counterattack in the 252nd's or the 162nd's sector; some kind of an initiated operation, such as Zefania, north of Suez (those present corrected the chief of staff's mistake: Port Said, not Suez); or Or Yarok.

In the government meeting at 21:00 on Monday, the chief of staff understated the counterattack's results, merely acknowledging that it had not been a turning point that signaled the transition from defense to attack. He outlined the attack's development on that miserable day, but his descriptions did not correlate with events on the ground. Even as late as 21:15, after the battles had tapered off, the chief of staff had not been informed of the fate of 162nd and 143rd Divisions. He and Dayan still believed that the day's setbacks did not necessitate an essential change in the plan, only its postponement. Later, at GHQ headquarters in Tel Aviv, in the presence of the defense minister, Elazar expounded on his recommendation for action on the two fronts. In Sinai he saw minimal activity—one kilometer more or less would not make a difference. He stressed the divisions' need to reorganize, build up their strength, and attend to logistics. The air force's job the next day would be "an air effort to lighten the ground forces' burden and provide, if necessary, day and night support." It was too early to launch a decisive battle, and the three divisions had to be deployed to prevent an enemy attack. The IAF would also be tasked with stopping the Egyptians from establishing bridgeheads in the rear. Elazar still had not been updated on the 162nd: "I knew that Adan was about two kilometers from the canal . . . beyond the range of the antitank weapons, but he knocked out all [the enemy's] tanks. Although there's a bridge, whoever's on top of the embankment can make mincemeat out of [anything] and we feel he's in control of the situation."[321]

Employing the Ground Forces: October 9–15

Once the actual situation became clear, Israeli leaders began to discuss how best to proceed.

What Happens Next?

Discussion in the Pit focused on the IDF's next moves. Dayan urged the capture of as many strategic assets as possible before Israel was forced to accept a cease-fire and the IDF had to pull back to the pre-war lines. Major General Zeira, the chief of MI, presented an accurate intelligence assessment of the Egyptians' intention to order a halt. He outlined their two possible moves: (1) if the armies established themselves at a depth of twelve kilometers in the two sectors where they had crossed, the armored divisions that were still on the western bank would join them on the eastern bank and continue the advance; (2) failing that, the Egyptians would dig in where they were (seven to twelve kilometers from the canal) and hold with five infantry divisions, along with armored brigades from the motorized divisions and two independent brigades.

Zeira reckoned that both the Egyptian chief of staff and the president of Egypt believed that the units on the eastern bank had a good chance of holding until the cease-fire, as long as they received support from the western bank and were protected by an antiaircraft umbrella. The Egyptian forces would not be ordered to retreat as they had in 1967. This time, they would fight to the last man, seize the maximum amount of territory on the eastern bank, and hang on to it for as long as possible. Israel's intelligence assessment—unlike on the eve of the war—was that the Egyptians did not intend to advance east into Sinai but would remain close to the canal for a maximum of two weeks. At the same time, they would use Arab oil production as a financial weapon to get the Americans to convince Israel to accept a cease-fire. President Sadat's main objective in this military adventure was political: creating a strategic situation whereby Egyptian troops remained on the eastern bank and U.S. Secretary of State Henry Kissinger drew up a new political initiative. In this scenario, the Egyptian armored divisions might not cross the canal.

In Zeira's opinion, the Egyptians knew they could not defeat Israel and retake all of Sinai, but they figured that by securing the eastern bank with infantry divisions supported by artillery and antiaircraft missiles and reinforced with tanks, they could hold out for an extended period. The IDF, short on infantry, would employ its armor in attacks that could be exhausted by Egyptian infantry, mines, firepower, and missiles, regardless of their losses. According to Israeli estimates, the Egyptians were certain that sooner or later the IDF would realize the futility of trying to dislodge the Egyptians from the eastern bank. The Egyptians were fully aware of Israeli air superiority, but they relied on their 160 antiaircraft batteries on the western bank to neutralize Israel's qualitative advantage. "Yesterday, when Adan and Sharon were moving," Zeira said, "I didn't quite understand what they were supposed to achieve. It isn't like [the enemy] has large armor fists on our side threatening to overrun us, and if we destroy them the game is open. The [Egyptians] have five infantry divisions just waiting for us [to attack]. . . . The question is which strategy to choose. This is quite complicated."[322]

At Dvela, Southern Command's tactical headquarters, there was also a discussion of the IDF's next moves. Sharon argued that if the IDF had attacked with two divisions, not a single Arab would have remained in the canal sector. The Egyptians had no intention of advancing farther east than their bridgehead, he added; they only wanted to retain a strip of land ten kilometers wide and wait for a cease-fire to go into effect. Elazar concurred, stating that a line had to be stabilized that could be defended if a war of attrition resumed. "When the balance of forces changes," he said, "we'll go for the decision." Dayan was the most pessimistic: "Many of the truths that we determined before the war have proven false. We thought our armor would prevent them from establishing bridgeheads. No one imagined the quantity of antitank missiles. . . . We have a lot of relearning to do. . . . They're very strong, we have to accept the fact that there are no magic formulas."[323] For the first time, both Elazar and Dayan realized that the situation offered the Egyptians a clear advantage and that the IDF could not achieve its war objectives as formulated on May 9, 1973: preventing any military gains by the enemy and defeating him by maximum destruction of his forces and military infrastructure.

Elazar concluded the discussion with operational instructions: the IDF would hold the enemy instead of trying to reach a decision; the air force's main effort would shift to the Golan Heights on October 9; and in the south, a relative cessation of hostilities would be sought by avoiding contact. Tank repairs would receive top priority, and as many combat units as possible had to be given time to recuperate and reorganize. Any force that could seize a dominating position and hit the enemy should do so, on the condition that it would not be worn away and no battalions would be moved. Ela-

zar also ordered 143rd Division to prepare for a canal crossing and
Southern Command to plan for the capture of Port Said; however,
the decision whether to cross in the central sector or the northern
sector or to postpone the crossing would be made the following day
as events unfolded. Dayan remarked that the fate of the strongholds
had to be decided, to which Elazar replied that this had been done
the day before: "Any stronghold that can exfiltrate should do so. It's
already too late today since there are only two hours of darkness."[324]

Only at 04:40 the following day, in a meeting with Dayan in the
Pit, did the chief of staff finally digest the abysmal results of the
counterattack: "The situation in Egypt is very bad. I learned that
Adan's attack was a disaster and there were heavy losses. . . . At
least fifty tanks were left on the battlefield. I'm told that losses are
as high as 200—they're afraid to say more. . . . The situation is critical. We entered the war under the worst possible circumstances. The
counterattack was futile. Yesterday I thought it imperative to counterattack; that it might get us out of the rut. . . . But something much
different happened in the south . . . a day of attrition [for us]. . . .
We're hurting. . . . They won't break before we do."[325]

Dayan ordered the IDF to find the most effective line that could
be held even in extreme conditions. The line had to encompass
Sharm el-Sheikh, Saint Catherine, and El Arish; if Refidim and Um
Hashiba were also included, so much the better, but it was not
absolutely necessary. The rationale behind the new line was solely
military: to avoid being worn away. Work on the new defensive
line had to begin immediately, and the enemy had to be held by
the rest of the forces until it was completed. Until that time, no
offensive actions would be undertaken—not in Port Said or any
other sector.

Dayan's summary was clear and incisive, although he was too
pessimistic about the depth of the rear defensive line. On the morning of October 9, the forces were located west of Artillery Road and
could have stayed there and defended their positions. Elazar was
against a deliberate withdrawal from Um Hashiba and Refidim and
agreed to set up a rear line. Dayan presented what he considered
to be the best line, but he made it clear that this was only his opinion and not a government mandate. If Elazar agreed, work could
begin at once; if not, they would have to await a government decision.[326] In his summary, Dayan was also prepared to cede Ras Sudar,
although, according to Tal, he later rescinded that order "because

somebody intervened." Dayan correctly identified the IDF's problem as quantitative, which meant that the lines had to be shortened and the forces not eroded, as they had been on October 6. Dayan astutely noted that if the chief of staff's October 8 reports to himself and the government had been based on information fed to him by Gonen, it proved that Gonen had no clue about what was happening on the ground.[327]

Dayan's caustic comment reflected the dissatisfaction with Gonen's performance felt by Elazar, Tal, and others. Several discreet, top-level meetings were held to find a solution that would not shatter Gonen's pride and cause him to walk out in a huff in the middle of the war. After a complex persuasion campaign on the part of Elazar and others, Gonen assented (with a heavy heart) to the appointment of Lieutenant General Haim Bar-Lev, the former chief of staff and minister of trade and industry, as commander of the southern front and special representative of the chief of staff—a grade above the general of Southern Command. Bar-Lev assumed command on the night of October 9 and almost immediately restored an atmosphere of calm and confidence in the command's staff work. Bar-Lev's experience and quiet composure soon permeated the headquarters and units in Sinai that had been knocked off balance by the stormy events of the last few days.

As part of the reassessment process, Dayan presented the prime minister with a realistic report at 05:00 on Tuesday. The canal line could not be held. The lines had to be shortened and a defensive line established that could be held "forever." In practical terms, the engineering work on the rear defensive line remained frozen, despite talks at Dvela on October 7 and 9. Major General Mandy Meron was appointed officer in charge of constructing the rear defensive line on Tuesday morning, and 440th Division's headquarters was ordered to Sinai for this task, under Meron's command. Neither event got the ball rolling.

During discussions in the chief of staff's office between 05:00 and 06:45 on Tuesday, Dayan and Elazar expressed different views. The chief of staff said that before he withdrew to the line proposed by the defense minister, he "wanted to make one more attempt that may or may not succeed. If it fails, then we'll have enough time to do what you [Dayan] said about withdrawing."[328] Tal, too, was against a hasty decision. He thought October 9 should be devoted to delaying operations and formulating a plan that would combine political and military moves. Tal dismissed the notion that the fate of the war would be decided in the next twenty-four hours. The fact that the Egyptian divisions had not crossed the canal gave the IDF a whole day to eliminate the enemy forces on the eastern bank. Tal recommended—and he maintained this view throughout the war—a mobile battle with controlled retrograde movements to lure the Egyptians out of their secure bases and into IDF killing zones between the canal and the mountain passes. In his opinion, "Our conventional force has to develop a great offensive, but we won't allow it and the air force to be worn down in an area crammed with missiles. . . . Only the air force and the concentrated use of the ground forces could eradicate the hundreds of Egyptian tanks. Because of our setbacks and shortages we've underestimated our current strength."[329]

Summing up the morning meeting, the chief of staff ordered Southern Command to reorganize for defense with three divisions (approximately 600 tanks, according to his estimate), refrain from attacking, build up strength, and hang on. First, Syria had to be taken out of the war, followed by Egypt. Elazar instructed 252nd and 162nd Divisions to remain in defensive positions and not attack. Force Magen would plan the capture of Ports Fuad and Said from the sandbank and the rear; the 143rd would concentrate to the rear of Tasa and remain on standby for a nighttime crossing between Wednesday and Thursday, either behind Force Magen or in the Kantara or El-Balah Island area.

Elazar did not want the 143rd to engage the Egyptian armor that might penetrate the Gidi pass, but if Egyptian 4th Armored Division did cross the canal and conditions were favorable for destroying it, he would order Gonen to grind the enemy down by means of a defensive battle, retrograde movements, and delaying actions.[330] Elazar's instructions were correct and to the point, but at that very moment, units of the 143rd were attacking Hamutal and Makhshir, floundering, and incurring heavy losses.

In the political-military meeting at 07:30 on Tuesday, October 9, attended by Prime Minister Golda Meir and ministers Israel Galili and Yigal Allon, Dayan presented the newly formulated concept of stabilizing a line on Artillery Road and preparing a second line at the mountain passes. He outlined the situation exactly as it was, with no attempt to whitewash the harsh reality. With his characteristic gloom, Dayan noted, "I may be more pessimistic than Elazar;

perhaps because of my age."[331] Then he described the situation in the bleakest terms:

1. The strongholds' situation is desperate—they cannot last much longer, and it is impossible to link up with them.
2. As of now, all crossing attempts have to be postponed.
3. As of now, no attempts will be made to recapture the canal line.
4. A defensive line must be established on Artillery Road. If there's enemy pressure, forces will withdraw to a second line at the passes.
5. This will be a protracted war. Israel will have to enlist Jews from abroad, acquire more weapons, train men of other age groups, and restructure the command systems.
6. There is a chance of knocking Syria out of the war through intensified pressure and deep-penetration strategic bombing.
7. After destroying Syria's forces, offensive plans can be resumed on the Egyptian front.
8. Many truths regarding operational matters have proved false.
9. Regarding Sharon's proposal to cross the canal on an Israeli bridge: this operation is unlikely to change the basic situation, and it is not practical in the near future. If the situation changes, the IDF will try to attack and break through.

The chief of staff also presented an assessment that depicted the blunders of the first three days of the war, as well as the military actions required to continue it. He admitted that he had only recently become aware that the artillery had failed to reach the front and join in the counterattack. He also acknowledged that at this stage, the IDF was unable to dislodge the Egyptians from the canal, although he believed it was possible and tactically sound to capture Port Said that night. He agreed with Dayan's view that long-held truths had proved groundless, yet he noted that some of them had not been put to the test. Because of the surprise attack, Israel's failure to launch preventive strikes, and the armor's hasty mobilization, the IDF had not been able to execute its own doctrine. Unlike Dayan, who accentuated the 162nd's losses, Elazar emphasized the enemy's casualties in the first three days of fighting. At the end of the meeting, Elazar summed up the main activities on the southern front: reorganizing for defense, and shifting as rapidly as possible to facilitate a crossing by Sharon's division. The chief of staff stressed that a crossing might be possible the next day at the earliest, or sometime in the following days. He reiterated his assessment that Egyptian attacks would be repulsed and that continued IDF operations remained an option.

In the next day's government meeting at 10:30, Dayan again portrayed the situation in dark colors: the IDF could not employ its full strength against enemies on two fronts. The situation on the Golan Heights was extremely fragile; if the northern front collapsed, the Syrians would reach the Jordan valley and enter Israel. On the canal, however, Israel's very survival would not be jeopardized if the IDF kept the Egyptians at bay instead of ousting them immediately. The defense minister recommended making a maximum effort—even a brutal one—in the north, until the Syrians were forced to throw in the towel. As for Sinai:

> The current estimate is that we lack the military strength to push the Egyptians back across the canal. . . . In an all-out effort to reach the water line, we'll lose the lion's share of our armor. . . . As of this morning, we can't promise the government that today, tomorrow or the next day we'll fling the enemy to the other side or that we'll get as far as the canal. If, following our operations [in Syria] the situation on the canal improves, [we'll be able] to cross the canal or throw [the Egyptians] back [to the western bank], and we won't hesitate to do so. . . . This is not what we thought yesterday, but this is the reality we have to accept.[332]

Elazar went over the main reasons for the counterattack's failure: misleading reports from the field, which created an inaccurate picture of the situation on the ground, and ignoring the Sagger antitank missiles before the war. He presented the government ministers with his plan for continuing the fighting in the south:

- Smashing the Egyptian armor attack and inflicting heavy losses on the enemy that would put the balance of forces in Israel's favor and leave us the option of attacking again.
- Leapfrogging to the rear because of Egyptian pressure while destroying a sizable portion of the enemy's forces. We may not reach a decision and we may be forced to give

up Refidim and Um Hashiba and ascend the mountain crests. That's the most the Egyptians can achieve. I'm not ignoring the worst scenario of going up the mountains in three places. We're preparing the line there.[333]

This was the first government meeting at which the political leadership had to approve a defensive plan for Sinai that went beyond the one Dayan had submitted to the prime minister on the night of October 7. At any rate, approval was not given.

After the government meeting, Elazar, Tal, Zeira, the IAF commander, and Generals Yariv and Gandhi met and agreed on the following principles:

- Maintaining a defense in the south and ceasing attacks.
- Smashing Syria within twenty-four hours, not withdrawing from the Golan Heights, and commencing deep-penetration bombing in Syria.
- In Southern Command, deploying 252nd and 162nd Divisions for defense. The 143rd would concentrate east of Tasa and prepare for a nighttime crossing between October 10 and 11. Force Kalman (Magen) would remain in place and might be used for the capture of Port Said. The 440th Division would build a second rear defensive line at the mountain passes— the Green Light plan (transporting forces by helicopter and tanks on landing craft to the western shore of the Bay of Suez and outflanking the front from the rear).
- Placing southern Sinai and Ras Sudar under GHQ's control on October 9, and transferring responsibility for the Negev to Central Command.

The American assessment was also presented, according to which Egyptian war aims were limited to holding on to the bridgeheads on the eastern bank.

GHQ estimated that on October 9, the Egyptians would try to deepen the southern bridgehead in the direction of Ras Sudar in order to open a road to southern Sinai. The first stage of the Egyptian plan included the capture of Ras Sudar but was not carried out because of a delay in 19th Division's crossing. At noon GHQ still did not realize that the Egyptians had executed an operational halt. The chief of intelligence reckoned that Egyptian 21st and 4th Armored

Divisions might enter the eastern bank at points where the Egyptian infantry had attained the necessary depth.

In the discussion group in the chief of staff's office that afternoon, the deputy chief of staff described the tank and artillery ammunition situation as critical. Elazar said he had ordered Southern Command to prepare the 143rd to cross the canal between Wednesday and Thursday night, but now he thought that would be too early. During the course of the meeting, the idea resurfaced that Egypt had a limited goal in mind. The chief of staff expressed concern that "the Egyptians will decide that this is what they intended all along, and we'll have to sit and wait until they make the next move."[334] Such a development was fraught with danger, since it would lengthen the war.

The Knesset's Foreign Affairs and Defense Committee also met that afternoon to receive the latest updates and situational assessments. Golda Meir repeated the government summary of October 8:

1. Push the Egyptian army back across the canal.
2. Push the Syrian army back across the cease-fire lines on the Golan Heights.
3. Simultaneously batter both armies.[335]

Southern Command's unsuccessful counterattack represented Israel's bitterest combat experience in the Yom Kippur War; it resulted in the heaviest casualties and the most agonizing disappointments. Nevertheless, both the regulars and the reservists displayed a remarkable ability to recover, and they soon changed the tide of the war, including a successful crossing to the western bank.

A Lost Opportunity in the Southern Sector

Parallel to the counterattack's rearguard battles in the central sector on the morning of October 9, and especially 143rd Division's fighting at Hamutal and Makhshir, large-scale armor battles were being fought independently in the southern sector against Egyptian 19th and 7th Divisions. The IDF outgunned the Egyptians, destroying about sixty of their tanks. An Israeli tank battalion led by Colonel Avraham Baram, commander of 164th Brigade, broke through Artillery Road between the Mitzva and Notsa fortresses in a daring move to assist 401st Brigade. But this important operation had no follow-up. There was no exploitation of the 401st's operational and tactical advantages (dominating Canal Road with fire); nor was the brigade's highly favorable position developed into a major operational move in the southern sector. The main reasons were the lack of reinforcements to maintain the momentum of the attack and Southern Command's view of the southern sector as a secondary effort. IDF armor stood at 600 tanks in the central sector and about 150 in the southern sector.

Likewise, momentum in the southern sector was squandered through a string of IDF blunders and mishaps that enabled the Egyptians to gain control of the Karat Moora range, which allowed observation of most of the southern sector and dominated the immediate environs with fire. Despite the achievements in the southern sector, 252nd Division withdrew its forces to Artillery Road, needlessly conceding areas that dominated the northern (the Polish Camp area) and southern (south of Karat Moora) parts of the sector. The Karat Moora range, held by 46th Battalion, was lost on October 9 after the battalion was ordered to vacate it at 11:00 in preparation for an IAF strike to the west to mark a bombing line—a line west of which IAF planes could attack without coordinating with the ground forces in the area. But the IAF attack was delayed, and when it came, it was anemic and ineffective; the Egyptians lost no time in seizing the empty mountain range. When the 46th tried to retake Karat Moora, it came under antitank fire and was forced to beat a hasty retreat.[336] However, if the battalion had been deployed on the range when Egyptian 19th Division ascended from the west, it could have repulsed the attack easily.

The Egyptian mechanized force that captured the range acted bravely and wisely. Even though 52nd Battalion was on its right flank and 195th Battalion was on its left, and even though both battalions set the Egyptian tanks ablaze on the canal plain, the mechanized force advanced quickly in the wide gap between the two battalions, along the terrain's fold belts and riverbeds, and gained control of the just-vacated range at approximately 13:00. They were probably unaware that the range was empty, in which case their gallantry was commendable. The determined Egyptian attack forced Colonel Shomron to remove his tactical headquarters from the range. He noted that it was unusual for the Egyptians to try to execute a breakthrough, stating, "This is the first time they attacked in a deliberate and organized manner."[337] Shomron asked Albert for an infantry (or mechanized infantry) company for a limited time to try to recapture the dominating areas, but the division commander had no such force.

Had the 252nd possessed a defense plan, it would have been obvious that Karat Moora was a dominating area and that holding it should be a top priority. A force could have been sent there on foot on the morning of October 6, and available infantry or mechanized infantry forces, regulars or reservists from 875th Brigade that arrived on October 8, could have seized it after war broke out. The importance of the range is illustrated by the fact that the westernmost battalion, the 52nd, dominated Canal Road with fire, and within twenty minutes it destroyed at least twenty Egyptian tanks and ten APCs in a classic armor battle, suffering only one of its own tanks lightly damaged. Nevertheless, at approximately 13:00 the battalion was ordered to withdraw east of Artillery Road in the Sportai area and deploy south of Atifa on the new brigade line. Thus, the IDF relinquished fire dominance on Canal Road in the southern part of the sector (Hamezach Junction), and IDF forces lost the area. The commander of 52nd Battalion, Lieutenant Colonel Sakal, had this to say about the inexplicable retreat: "We knocked out twenty of their tanks and received the order to leapfrog rapidly to the rear. Till today I can't figure out that command. I knew that the 46th Battalion had been ordered to pull out. When they returned, there were already missiles and bazookas and other kinds of infantry weapons there."[338]

Since the Egyptians were not exerting pressure, a withdrawal was unnecessary. Shomron admitted as such when the bombing line was cited as the reason for evacuating the mountain range. The 401st Brigade (52nd and 195th Battalions), still with absolute faith in the IAF's ability to destroy the Egyptian force (which was unnecessary), maneuvered to the rear without protesting the order. The upshot of the air force's delayed bombing was that it accomplished nothing. A few planes lamely dropped their munitions against tanks in an open area, and when they were threatened by surface-to-air missiles, they attacked by loft bombing.

The Egyptians Lose Momentum

Beginning on Tuesday, October 9, the situation on the southern front changed for the better. At the next day's government meeting, General Tal informed the participants that the crisis involving the balance of forces had passed, as newly arrived reinforcements exceeded losses. The 252nd Division, for example, which had incurred heavy losses, stabilized with 145 tanks, and in the following days, as the IDF deployed defensively, the order of battle remained more or less the same. The impression in the Pit was that the Egyptians had lost their momentum after incurring immense losses due to reckless assaults against the defenders. At the same time, the IDF concentrated its strength on the main roads and amassed its reserves in the rear.

The chief of staff's greatest concern was a protracted war of attrition. Speaking with Bar-Lev, the chief of Southern Command, Elazar acknowledged that a cease-fire had to be reached by October 14. He wanted to force a cease-fire by all means possible because, even if the IDF smashed the Egyptians, "our situation would continue to deteriorate and not necessarily because of dramatic events. The IDF cannot turn the balance of forces around, but it can prevent a catastrophe."[339] According to Tamari, Elazar examined the possibility of a cease-fire based on Southern Command's gains and the IAF's situation. The air force commander delineated a red line—a term GHQ was not familiar with before the war—and the chief of staff (who was greatly influenced by the IAF commander's views) decided that the optimal date for the cease-fire would be October 13.

The chief of staff, his deputy, and Bar-Lev were not in agreement on the canal crossing. Elazar perceived it as a catalyst that would jump-start the cease-fire, and he wanted it implemented after the Egyptians' armored divisions had crossed to the eastern bank and were eliminated by Israeli armor. Bar-Lev, who believed a crossing was impossible before October 13, wanted to wait and see when the Egyptians launched an attack from their forward defensive line. This correlated with the IDF's interpretation of Egypt's operational doctrine; the IDF estimated that it would be able to block the attack and inflict heavy losses on the enemy. However, Bar-Lev preferred a crossing over giving the Egyptian armored divisions an opportunity to attack. Tal was against a crossing. He viewed it as a gamble and suggested preparing for a decisive armored battle that would enable Israeli armor to exploit its indisputable advantage. "You've got the best tank crews in the world," he told the prime minister. "On that day hundreds of bonfires [Egyptian tanks] will be lit and the Egyptian offensive will come to an end."[340]

Egypt's and Israel's most likely moves were outlined in these discussions. Egypt might renew the attack with armored divisions from the bridgehead, or it might be satisfied with its gains and shift to a war of attrition. The IDF could maintain the status quo and prevent the Egyptians from advancing, even though it had been ordered to limit the erosion of its forces; alternatively, two brigades from 143rd Division could attack Third Army. A third possibility was a canal crossing to transfer the war to the enemy's territory and force him to sue for a cease-fire.

The main dilemma in the crossing option was when to execute it—before or after the Egyptians transferred their armored divisions to the eastern bank.[341] Bar-Lev was very worried about a war of attrition and felt that a cease-fire had to be attained no later than October 14. The estimate was that Egypt had 800 tanks on the eastern bank and 500 on the western bank. Facing them were three IDF divisions and Force Magen, which totaled 500 tanks (that number rose to 750 by October 15). The Arabs' unlimited potential compared with the IDF's limited manpower and equipment tormented Elazar and Bar-Lev. Both had doubts that a successful crossing would force a cease-fire and lead to the collapse of the Egyptian army.

The shift to the defense and the relative quiet on the southern front enabled the units on the contact line to develop drills to evade antitank missiles. One involved a continuous series of tank fire: one tank fired and quickly descended from its position after each round was fired, a second observed, and a third covered the other two (this drill was renewed from the days of the war of attrition in the Jordan valley). Drills also entailed the use of smoke screens to conceal movement in areas exposed to antitank missiles and the use of artillery and mortars to neutralize suspicious areas. In a drill developed by 401st Brigade, mechanized infantrymen secured the tank positions at night when the tanks were in parks in the rear for rest, refueling, rearming, and repairs.

Except for a few instances, the Egyptians made no effort to improve their positions. By sitting tight on the static line, Israel's armor losses and erosion were significantly reduced. Dayan mentioned this to Gonen in the early-morning hours of October 10: "Don't exhaust your forces. This isn't the time for a philosophical discussion, but our great advantage in Sinai is that we can be flexible. This isn't Degania Alef or Ein Harod [two early Zionist collectivist settlements]. Here it's all about doing what's best for us. Don't worry if we lose five dunam [5,000 square meters]—not in Sinai at any rate. If [the enemy] reaches the Temple Mount [in Jerusalem] then we'll deal with the situation differently."[342]

In the spirit of the new policy of avoiding any military adventures, the joint attack by 252nd and 143rd Divisions, planned for October 10 in the southern sector, was canceled.

The Egyptians' Operational Halt

While the troops were recuperating and reorganizing, GHQ and Southern Command tried to grasp the meaning of the Egyptian army's operational halt. Before October 6, conventional wisdom had been that the Egyptian attack would develop in four stages: on D day + 2 they would reach Lateral Road and, after three days of fighting, advance east to the passes. No mention was made of an operational halt. When the Egyptians stopped far west of the line Israeli intelligence assumed they would reach, the IDF was baffled and had no explanation for it. This perplexity was a major factor in the IDF's response at all levels—in the management of the defensive battle, the counterattack, and the timetable for the crossing. Everyone expected the Egyptian armored divisions to cross to the eastern bank, but they did not. The IDF was unaware of the term *operational halt* and described the Egyptians as "establishing themselves on the bridgeheads." By the night of October 7, in the meeting at Dvela before the counterattack, the IDF realized the Egyptians had indeed halted and were digging in on a defensive line based on infantry and mechanized divisions ten to fifteen kilometers from the canal.

Military researchers on both sides are divided over the reasons for the halt. Dov Tamari claims that the Egyptians planned an operational stop line as the final objective of the battle, at a depth of thirty kilometers from the canal—that is, on Lateral Road, not at the mountain passes as the IDF assumed. According to Tamari, Israeli intelligence failed to comprehend the concept of an operational halt, as defined in Soviet doctrine, and erroneously interpreted it as a limited war. On the Egyptian side, Chief of Staff Shazly (who was ousted by Sadat in January 1974) and General Gamasy, head of the Egyptian army's general staff headquarters, were radically divided over the halt. Shazly asserted that, from the beginning, the Egyptians' mission was limited to penetrating ten to twelve kilometers on the eastern bank, a distance based on a sober evaluation of the Egyptians' capabilities. Gamasy, in contrast, thought the Egyptian army's goal was to fight its way through to the passes and capture them. Therefore, he considered the October 8–14 standstill a grievous operational blunder that had catastrophic consequences for Egypt. From Gamasy's point of view, the Egyptian army did not carry out its mission.[343] The two Egyptian generals agreed, however, that the October 14 attack, which was designed to restore the initiative to Egypt and renew the momentum that had fizzled out on October 8, was a deplorable mishap. Shazly defined it as a resounding disaster that turned the tide of battle to Israel's favor. Gamasy agreed, blaming the attack's failure on the October 8 operational halt.

The Egyptians' October 14 Attack

Just as opinion is divided over the reasons for the operational halt, scholars are still debating why the Egyptian army launched its October 14 attack. Did they hope it would alleviate the pressure on the Syrian army? Was it a prearranged stage in the overall plan? Chief of Staff Shazly and the commanders of Second and Third Armies (and probably the commander of 4th Division) opposed the attack and voiced their criticism to Minister of War Ismail Ali, but their arguments were brushed aside, and the attack was only postponed by one day. On October 13 the British ambassador in Cairo submitted a proposal to Sadat for an immediate cease-fire—a proposal Israel had agreed to—but the Egyptian president dismissed it; he believed Israel had been weakened and this was the time to go forward with the attack. By the morning of October 14, the armies on the eastern bank had been reinforced with units from the western bank: the greater part of 21st Division and 3rd Brigade/4th Division. Egypt now had approximately a thousand tanks on the eastern bank and fifteen surface-to-air missile batteries tasked with neutralizing Israeli air superiority as the Egyptian tanks advanced east. Its military goal was to capture the mountain passes, about thirty kilometers east of the canal. The attack commenced with a massive barrage and tank and infantry assault along the entire length of the front.[344]

Third Army's original plan was to advance beyond the Gidi pass, but the effort was diverted south to Mitla Road because the Egyptians thought they had identified a soft spot in 202nd Battalion's sector, not realizing that the battalion had been reinforced with tanks and a mechanized infantry battalion. The armored brigade and another battalion opened the attack in the direction of the Mitla pass, and a mechanized brigade advanced toward the Gidi pass.

In Egyptian 7th Division's sector, 25th Independent Tank Brigade and a force from 7th Infantry Division attacked. Their mission was to break through the Gidi sector in front of the IDF's 164th Brigade/252nd Division.

In Egyptian 19th Infantry Division's sector, 3rd Tank Brigade/4th Division (which had crossed the canal) was ordered to clear a path through 19th Division from Wadi Mabrook to Lateral Road. The brigade was spotted after it penetrated deep into the sector of 202nd Battalion/252nd Division. The 202nd, reinforced with a tank company and together with 46th Battalion/401st Brigade and air support, wiped out most of the brigade.

The IAF and Sharm el-Sheikh sector forces stemmed the advance of Egyptian 6th Division forces and 22nd Armored Brigade (both under the command of 19th Division), causing them heavy losses.

In Second Army's sector (the army's commander had suffered a heart attack on October 13 and been replaced by his deputy), the effort was diverted to Tasa. The 15th Armored Brigade (T62s), which was attached to 18th Infantry Division, attacked Force Sasson on the Kantara-Baluza Road and was blocked about four kilometers west of Artillery Road.

In 2nd Infantry Division's sector, 24th Armored Brigade (originally from 23rd Mechanized Division but now attached to 2nd Division) operated on a wide front in the Firdan sector opposite 162nd Division (commanded by Tamari, the deputy commander, because Adan was in flight and unable to land). The 162nd blocked the Egyptian brigade's attempt to break out from the bridgehead.

In the Egyptian 16th Infantry Division's sector, opposite 14th Brigade/143rd Division between the Tasa-Ismailia Road and the Hurva fortification, two Egyptian tank brigades were operating— the 14th and the 1st (both from 21st Armored Division). Their mission was to break through to Tasa on Akavish, Foton, and Talisman Roads. The Egyptian 14th Brigade had been operating in this area since the start of the war as part of the armor order of battle reinforcing 16th Division; 1st Brigade was the only one of Second Army's three tank brigades that crossed the canal to bolster the attack. This was the only sector where two Egyptian tank brigades from the same division operated on the two flanks of the bridgehead, but they did so without any discernible coordination or concentrated effort.

Egyptian forces trickled into the combat zone and were thwarted by Israeli tank fire the minute they came into range. According to one Egyptian source, two tank brigades attacked in the direction of the main axis (to Tasa), and another tank brigade in the direction of the northern axis (to Baluza). The attack ended in a devastating defeat for the Egyptians, its armor beating a retreat to infantry positions and leaving behind 200 to 250 destroyed tanks. The IDF's losses were twenty tanks hit, with six destroyed. The disproportionately high rate of destruction of Egyptian armor was repeated in battles before and after October 14 on both sides of the canal.

The battles of October 14 again proved two long-held truths: a successful defense causes the enemy heavy losses, and Israeli armor was unequivocally superior to the Egyptians'. The latter was especially true when the IDF tank crews took full advantage of good, natural, familiar positions—in this case, Artillery Road's hill line. In the October 14 battles, Egyptian armor showed its limitations in the application and maneuver of large forces in a mobile battle and in its gunnery capability.

The Egyptians also made several major mistakes in the attack. They failed to complete preparations and bring in all their airborne and armored forces as planned. There was no sign of a concentrated force. The attacks were carried out at brigade-level strength and were not timed to occur at a coordinated H hour. The Egyptians never attained a superior balance of strength in the attack sectors and failed to break through any axis. Their armor moved forward without air support, even where they lacked a surface-to-air missile umbrella. The 3rd Brigade/4th Division advanced on an inferior road (Wadi Mabrook) and became trapped.[345]

The October 14 battles, as well as Israel's October 9 decision to shift to the defensive, signaled the turning point in the campaign. The 14th Brigade's breakthrough battle on the night of October 15–16 and the start of the crossing were defining moments in the war in the south, a turnabout that eventually brought the IDF to Kilometer 101 (101 kilometers from Cairo—the end point of the Israeli advance).

The volte-face in Israel's favor highlighted the long and frustrating list of flaws in almost every move by the IDF in the first days of the war. The commanders were to blame for some of them; others were deeply embedded at the tactical and operational level and in the application of force. The identification of these shortcomings is crucial to the learning process and for the rectification of blunders and deficiencies.

Flaws in the Ground Forces' Defensive Battle

According to the deputy chief of staff, some of the mistakes stemmed from unprofessional work in the various headquarters and from the collapse of staffs, including at GHQ. Staff work was not carried out according to standard operating procedures. Ehud Barak claimed that "the military-political leadership of Israel lost its equilibrium for a few days . . . and had it restored after two weeks when it made the canal crossing."[346] Other deficiencies are detailed below.

Lack of Joint Operations

At first, the tanks fought without artillery, infantry, or mechanized infantry—all of which were in short supply and desperately needed. Mechanized infantry was vital in the holding stage to protect the tanks against enemy infantry; it was also crucial in the attack, especially when the tanks were in firing positions or in enemy localities manned with infantry.

Engaging in tank combat without infantry or mechanized infantry support reflected greater problems than just an insufficient order of battle and mistaken priorities in force buildup. It testified to the combat units' basic ignorance of joint operations as a key element of battle. The IDF of 1973 was not built organizationally or mentally for an absolute commitment to joint operations. The realization of the paramount value of combined-arms combat was one of the IDF's bitterest lessons of the Yom Kippur War, and even today its importance is not fully appreciated. Effective joint operations demand continuous training to achieve a proper, proficient, accessible, and well-organized order of battle with suitable weapons starting at the lowest level—the platoon.

In-depth actions were absent during the land battles. Given the intensity, pressure, and urgency of the fighting, especially in the initial stages of the war, headquarters had no time to listen to suggestions about planning and executing this type of activity, even though the requisite order of battle was available in GHQ and Southern Command. Once the front stabilized on October 9, some actions could be carried out, but they amounted to only limited-depth nighttime penetrations by small paratroop units (ten men with a forward observation officer) and artillery fire on Egyptian nighttime tank parks. More complex actions were not undertaken until the IDF landed a force on Jebel Ataka (approximately 134 kilometers east of Cairo) at the end of the war.

Shoddy Command and Control in the Field

The absence of so many commanders from the front had a negative impact on the first days of the fighting and afterward. This has always been a sensitive and contentious issue. Modern command and control systems create the illusion that the commander sees everything on a map or a screen. The temptation is great—sometimes overwhelmingly so—for the commander to remain in the TOC, where he thinks he can observe, listen, and control events without ever having to go into the field or into the fury of battle. Some brigade commanders on the line continued to control their forces through static systems from the brigade TOCs, as they did for daily security operations or on a battle day. In some cases, it took hours (in the north) or days (in the south) for the brigade commanders to leave the TOCs and take control of the troops, but not control of the sector.

The fact that several unit commanders at all levels remained in the TOCs was one of the main reasons for the unacceptable amount of time it took to perceive the enemy's modus operandi and battlefield achievements and comprehend that this was all-out war. "The entire [Southern Command] staff sat in the TOC. They functioned as though this was the War of Attrition," recalled Colonel Israel Granit (Ret.), the 252nd's chief of staff.[347] At one point, Sharon made it clear to Gonen that he thought they lacked a real picture of what was happening on the ground. "I advised him to order all commanders to leave the TOCs immediately with their command groups and go into the field to learn firsthand what was going on."[348]

Southern Command's tactical command group did not relocate to Sinai even when it became clear that war was fast approaching. Once the shooting began, Gonen commanded the troops from Beer Sheva and then from Dvela. Because of the lack of control equipment at the TOC in Mitla, the 252nd's commander ran operations from Refidim on the first day of the fighting. Only on the following day did he transfer the division's TOC to Mitla and venture out to the brigade commanders with his forward command group.

In the northern sector, the commanders of 275th Brigade, Colonel Pinchas Noy and later Brigadier General Kalman Magen, managed the battles from the TOC at Baluza. On the day the war broke out, the commander of 9th Battalion positioned his APC on a high sand dune south of Martef to allow direct control of his forces. In the central sector, the battalion commander planned to control his battalion not from the FCG in the field but from the "Tasa Battalion," as he would in an attrition scenario or on a battle day. The commander of 184th Battalion, Major Shalev, moved to Nozel when hostilities erupted. He mounted a tank that was waiting for him there, but because of communications foul-ups, he returned to the battalion TOC at Tasa. The deputy battalion commander was also at Tasa, and three of the battalion's companies—G and H Companies (tanks) and I Company (mechanized infantry)—engaged the enemy without the forward command of the battalion commander. On October 6–7 the brigade commander spoke with the 184th's deputy commander because the commander was not in radio contact. Only at 17:00, as darkness fell, did a battalion-level commander arrive in the field: Lieutenant Colonel Moni Nitzani, commander of 79th Battalion, was briefed and drove to the line in his tank.

At 03:30 on October 7, the commander of 196th Battalion, Lieutenant Colonel Mitzna, brought his tank onto the contact line. The deputy commander of 184th Battalion, Major Taran (not the battalion commander, per Shalev's order), ventured out to the Hizayon area to assist the stronghold with remnants of H Company/184th Battalion and F Company/79th Battalion. For all practical purposes, until the morning of October 8, three tank battalions were operating in the central sector without forward control or brigade coordination.

On October 7 the commander of 14th Brigade made a sortie in an APC with his FCG in the direction of Firdan. The next day at sunrise he left Tasa in a tank with his FCG . He commanded his forces this way until the end of the war.

The southern sector was the responsibility of the 52nd Battalion/ 14th Brigade (the 52nd was later attached to 401st Brigade). After the battalion commander, Lieutenant Colonel Sakal, returned from an orders group at Tasa, he made a brief stop at the battalion TOC at Mitla; then, beginning at 14:40, he fought in his tank with B Company at the Lexicon-Atifa junction, commanding the battalion from his tank for the duration of the war. The commander of 14th Brigade did his best under the circumstances to gain control of the southern sector until it was transferred to 401st Brigade at 17:55. On the afternoon of October 6, the 401st's commander was in the Lateral Road area, and from 23:00 he was at the brigade's TOC in Mitla. Communications with the three battalions in the field occurred via the deputy brigade commander at Mitla, not the brigade commander. Shomron was in the field with his FCG on the morning of October 7 but generally returned to Mitla at night rather than remaining with his forces in the field.

Thus, in the first night's battles, eight tank battalions from the division's three brigades (and another impromptu battalion force) fought on the canal line, and in only four of them (plus a fifth near daybreak) was a battalion commander on the fighting line. No brigade (or division) FCG was located in a forward position where it could observe firsthand what was happening in the field and maintain command and control as situations developed.

Commanders were situated in the rear, headquarters did not deploy on time or function properly, and Southern Command failed to transfer its headquarters to Dvela and 252nd Division's headquarters to Mitla in a timely fashion. All this precluded an accurate picture of the situation on the first day of the war and led to the exhaustion of the 252nd. On Sunday morning, when the picture finally came into focus, it was already too late for critical decisions—especially regarding the shift to mobile tank fighting versus static warfare and the evacuation of the strongholds.

The "bunker complex" also prevailed in the later stages of the war, and some brigade commanders did not join their subordinates in the field to command the main effort or during the movement and maneuver and assault stages, when courage and personal example were called for.[349] In the October 8 counterattack, for example, the commander of 460th Brigade was in Havraga, nine kilometers from the battlefield; he had no line of vision on Hizayon, where 19th Battalion was mounting an attack. The commander of 500th Brigade stayed in Tasa while 429th Battalion was storming Hamutal (during which the battalion commander was killed), and he relocated to a jeep east of the event during the battalion's withdrawal. The division commander, General Adan, remained at Zrakor, thirteen kilometers from the battle for Firdan, rather than joining his two brigades engaged in the main effort. Gonen was not in the field either, where he could have at least coordinated and planned the next moves with his two division commanders. "All of these levels were ensconced in various headquarters with maps, radio sets, and telephones and believed they had a grasp on things."[350]

Sharon criticized commanders who directed their forces from the rear. "It's absolutely impossible to command troops in modern warfare, which has become so intensive and involves great numbers of forces, if the commanders or headquarters are not in forward positions. . . . Today a commander must be present with his forces in order to understand for himself what's happening and make decisions."[351] As noted earlier, the chief of staff, too, was in the wrong place during the October 8 counterattack. Elazar attended a government meeting instead of being in Dvela to ensure that the operation was proceeding as scheduled and to convey instructions as the situation unfolded, as a commander is supposed to do. Incontestably, the main foul-ups in the October 8 counterattack stemmed from flaws in control and the lack of face-to-face command. In addition, an excessive number of pivotal decisions were based on impromptu conversations between senior commanders (the chief of staff and the general of Southern Command), without consulting their staffs to obtain updated information.

There are many reasons why so many commanders preferred to stay in the rear:

- The IDF initially believed it was engaged in a war of attrition (which would call for controlling events from rear-based TOCs and bunkers).
- A bunker packed with equipment, radio communications, staff officers, and maps created the impression of being in control of the situation.
- Advanced communications equipment lulled commanders into believing that they would have a clearer picture of events in the field if they remained in the TOC.
- Sitting in a rear-based TOC was preferable to being jostled inside a tank, jerked from side to side in an APC, or riveted to an FCG on a godforsaken hilltop.
- Nighttime visibility was poor, so it was better to be somewhere that at least offered continuous radio contact.
- Commanders had a natural fear of putting themselves in harm's way (command posts are highly vulnerable).

- Commanders received insufficient training in FCG operations.
- The command posts had difficulty navigating in the field, especially at night.
- Commanding troops from the TOC infected all levels of command, from top to bottom, while a key element in combat—personal example—was missing.

Failure to Delegate Authority

In regular security operations, centralization of authority is the norm. In wartime, however, delegating authority is a vital aspect of command because of the inevitable influx of problems. In this case, owing to the surprise start of the war, senior commanders lacked the forces or intelligence sources to assist their subordinate headquarters. Under these circumstances, the senior command level should have delegated authority and responsibility for management of the defensive battle (which happened spontaneously) and focused on the next moves, such as overseeing and updating the reserve units so they could enter the fighting as quickly as possible. Southern Command attempted to control both the fighting on the contact line and the flow of reservists, creating a situation in which both suffered. This was especially problematic in the first two days of fighting, when slipshod mobilization and heavy congestion on Sinai's roads prevented the deployment of forward control points, the stationing of military police, and the building of landline and wireless radio communications structures. The control framework for movement to the front, which was so critical in those fateful hours, all but collapsed, particularly on the northern axis from El Arish to Romani.[352]

According to Tal, "What happened on Yom Kippur, especially in the first three days, was not that the IDF had the wrong doctrines. The problem was that we didn't implement our own doctrines. . . . We made every mistake in the book."[353] Gonen, too, said, "Our war doctrine didn't fail; it just wasn't implemented. In combat conditions that the enemy initiated, the IDF found its fighting capability divorced from the warfighting doctrine so that instead of delivering a powerful knock-out at the onset of hostilities that would have caused minimum damage to our forces, we suffered exorbitant losses."[354]

Professional Shortcomings at the Tactical and Operational Levels

The IDF experienced problems with armor, missiles, infantry, artillery, intelligence, and the air force, as well as the coordination of all these elements.

Armor

Armor was the main element of the IDF's ground forces, and it suffered the brunt of casualties in its fight against Egyptian infantry armed with a vast array of antitank weapons and supported by artillery cover.[355] The "armor shock" concept that had been so effective in the Six-Day War failed in the October 8 counterattack. Also, insufficient armor concentration and the enemy's correct assumption about the direction of the attack excluded an IDF decision.

The reason for Israel's heavy losses was not the piecemeal use of tanks at the start of the war. Poor management at the tactical and operational levels exacerbated the situation in the field and created the following grave problems for the tank units:

- Difficulty spotting enemy antitank teams, short-range RPGs, and especially long-range Sagger missiles.
- The absence of prewar drills for countering antitank missiles (impromptu drills were developed during the war).
- The lack of infantry, mechanized infantry, artillery, and mortars to combat antitank teams.
- The shock effect of the surprise attack.
- Egyptian firing ramps on the western bank that dominated Israel's tank positions on the eastern bank with fire.
- Ineffective protection against antitank hollow charges.
- The misuse of armor in the first days—that is, armor was employed in static fighting because its mission was to defend the strongholds.

On this last point, Tal noted:

> The tank's role was to return mobility to the battlefield, [like] the cavalry. But our tanks entered directly and statically into killing zones packed with antitank weapons. This should never have been done. . . . When a tank is static in a kill-

ing zone packed with antitank weapons, it is destroyed. . . .
Never in history has armor assaulted in fits and starts a killing zone of antitank weapons . . . without being destroyed.
. . . Had there been antitank cannons instead of antitank missiles, the exact same thing would have happened in the first
three days. The problem was not the type of weapon. The
tanks entered the killing zone with insufficient momentum
and no fire support. The mortars had been removed from the
companies and the artillery hadn't been mobilized yet. The
antitank missiles added precision fire but their rate of fire
was less than that of antitank cannons. The missiles added
one kilometer to the range of the antitank cannon, in other
words the difference was not one of essence but of quantity.

The turnabout occurred, Tal avowed, only "after we realized that
the missiles' killing range was three kilometers and that we should
never have attacked intermittently and remained static in the killing zones." Despite the painful beginning, Israeli armor quickly
adapted, amending its errors, devising ad hoc drills, and display-
ing superb recovery. "This is the first time in history that the armor
corps was not wiped out after so disastrous a start," Tal asserted.
"We performed poorly and blamed the weapons."[356]

Sagger Missiles

According to postwar debriefings of commanders and the Recovery
and Maintenance Center's study of 214 damaged tanks in the two
sectors, of all the tanks hit in Sinai, 41 percent were destroyed by
hollow charges from tanks, antitank cannon, recoilless guns, RPGs,
and Saggers. Twenty-six percent of the tanks were struck by Saggers, and 15 percent by other types of hollow charges.[357] The Sagger
undoubtedly had a significant physical and psychological impact
on the armor force because of the tank crews' vulnerability, mainly
in the first days; however, their effectiveness was disproportionate
to the publicity they received.[358] The mechanized infantry's lack of
0.50-caliber machine guns, mortars, artillery, tactical smoke for con-
cealment and evasion, a war-fighting doctrine, and defensive drills
all contributed to the antitank missiles' potency. Gonen insisted,
"The Egyptians concentrated fifty-four antitank missiles on every
kilometer of the crossing. No tank could withstand that."[359] Facing

this massive missile array was the IDF's thinly stretched tank align-
ment, which was incapable of providing an effective tactical answer
and altering the overall battle framework.

The tank units' biggest problem in the initial stage was their
unawareness of the existence of the antitank missiles. In a briefing before the October 8 counterattack, Lieutenant Colonel Haim
Adini, commander of 19th Battalion/460th Brigade, noted, "No one
mentioned that the Egyptian infantry had antitank missiles. So we
had no idea what we were going up against."[360] Within a few days,
impromptu combat drills and the addition of artillery, mortars, and
the mechanized infantry's 0.50-caliber machine guns significantly
reduced the number of tanks being hit by missiles, although they
continued to plague Israeli armor until the end of the war.

Infantry

Southern Command possessed a large number of regular and
reserve infantry units, elite infantry units, and mechanized infantry
units, but few of them were used in combat; most were squandered
on secondary tasks or were not even mobilized. The opportunity
to send them into combat was wasted. Such was the case of 247th
Reservist Paratroop Brigade, which was brought into combat only
on October 15–16 when it crossed the canal.

The background to this grievous shortcoming can be traced to
the chief of staff's decision on Yom Kippur morning to suspend the
replacement of infantry and mechanized infantry brigades on the
lines and not to mobilize the reserve brigades.[361] The official explanation for this nonmobilization was that it exceeded the prime minister's limitation of four divisions, but the chief of staff and GSO
should have recognized the dire need for infantry in a defensive
battle based solely on tanks. They also should have realized that it
was imperative to employ elite infantry brigades for the IDF counterattack, which Elazar wanted to begin as soon as possible. Had
the chief of staff asked the defense minister to include a number of
elite infantry brigades in the general mobilization, the request probably would have been granted. But Elazar made no such request, so
the first days of the defensive campaign and the counterattack took
place without any infantry support.

For the record, there were several infantry and elite infantry
units in Sinai that could have performed the necessary tasks, but

they were deployed in secondary facilities or engaged in auxiliary activities. Thus, the antitank reconnaissance battalion of 317th Reservist Paratroop Brigade sat out most of the war on the Mitla airfield (October 8–18). Another elite infantry unit was kept at the Refidim airfield until October 13, when it was replaced by an ad hoc battalion made up of staff and trainees from 908th Nachal Unit. Other infantry units were assigned minor roles in secondary places instead of being used in vital areas east of the canal. Force Bishof, for example, which consisted of three battalions of infantry and GHQ officer cadets, tanks, and mechanized infantry, was deployed in Um Hashiba and the Mitla and Gidi passes—an inexcusable waste of valuable manpower. The 14th Brigade's reconnaissance company and 184th Battalion's reduced mechanized infantry company were ordered to the rear according to the Dovecote plan (the deployment of regulars east of the canal in case of an Egyptian attack) instead of being integrated immediately into the tank fighting (this happened later). Almost no operational use was made of 875th Mechanized Brigade's two mechanized infantry battalions and 601st Engineer Battalion/252nd Division.

In what was undoubtedly the most flagrant example of squandered opportunity in the war, 35th Paratroop Brigade, a first-class fighting force of regulars, was kept in Ras Sudar. As early as 18:30 on October 6, Southern Command requested the brigade to engage the enemy in the central and southern sectors, but the brigade's 890th and 450th Battalions and an engineer company (202nd Battalion was divided and came under the command of 252nd Division on October 12) were sent to Ras Sudar in case the Egyptians tried to seize control of the coastal base. The brigade mainly carried out hot pursuits of remnants of the Egyptian commando force that had landed on October 6. Crack troops were not needed to perform these tasks, especially after the Egyptians ordered the operational halt on October 8.

The squandering of quality forces in Ras Sudar was especially galling, since the site was outside the range of Egyptian antiaircraft missiles and could have been defended from the north on the access roads or from the Gulf of Suez against landings and air strikes. First-class infantry troops and many other high-quality units were deployed at Ras Sudar: reduced 424th Battalion; an infantry Nachal platoon; a tank platoon from 52nd Battalion, which arrived on the afternoon of October 6 according to Dovecote; seven Sherman tanks from 129th Battalion/875th Brigade, which reached Ras Sudar on October 8–9; and a force of Tirans (Russian tanks converted to IDF use) from the Sharm el-Sheikh sector, which joined them later. Indeed, with such an impressive order of battle, 35th Brigade was hardly needed as reinforcement. In practical terms, the first time 890th Battalion fought was on the night of October 16–17 at the Chinese Farm.

The GSO did not realize the importance of crack infantry troops for the defensive battles being waged by the tanks on the canal line. A whole day of intensive fighting passed in the two commands while the regular paratroop brigade sat on its haunches in camps in Israel and the regular armor force begged for infantry support. Finally, at noon Sunday, Tal agreed to bring the brigade to Ras Sudar, under the command of the Sharm el-Sheikh sector and reservists. Thus, the IDF's best regular paratroop brigade and reservist paratroop brigade were frittered away on nonessential tasks. In general, the infantry was put to negligible use in Sinai. Although this was a relatively large order of battle, in only a few cases was it employed effectively. For the most part, Israeli armor single-handedly fought against five infantry divisions while simultaneously tasked with holding the front line and conducting the counterattack. The regular and reservist infantry, elite infantry, mechanized infantry, reconnaissance, and engineers easily could have carried out key missions, such as replacing and reinforcing the infantry in the strongholds and capturing dominating areas (Karat Moora, Nehushtan, and Missouri), even without mobile equipment. This would have been possible as long as the tanks in the vicinity supported them, and as long as the infantry and tanks teamed up as a joint combat force for the defensive battle. At a later stage, with the arrival of the reservists, many classic infantry missions could have been carried out.

Even if we excuse the initial blundering and blame the frivolous waste of infantry on the fog of battle, the only explanation for the inability to redress these flaws on October 8–9 was a cognitive and operational breakdown.

Artillery

One of the major failings in the war was the dearth of artillery in the first three days of fighting (excluding 209th Artillery Group/252nd Division). At 10:00 on the first day, the GSO discussion group decided that moving artillery units to the canal line depended on whether Bendigo (the joint artillery–air force operation designed to neutralize Egyptian missile batteries) could be carried out. Bendigo was not executed, owing to cancellation of the preemptive strike it was supposed to be part of. In the following days, artillery units received low transportation priority compared with armor. This shortsightedness had severe ramifications on the 162nd's counterattack, on the fighting strength of the entire order of battle, and on the huge number of casualties resulting from Egypt's massive artillery force, which operated freely throughout the length of the canal without retaliation.

The paucity of artillery and the lack of mortars made it impossible to use high-trajectory fire against the Egyptian infantry, which was heavily armed with antitank weapons and operated virtually unhindered for the first three days. Before the war, few believed that artillery's low transportation priority and nonintegration into combined-arms warfare were problems. As a result, the ground forces were at a serious disadvantage when war broke out. Also, viewing the IAF as "flying artillery" contributed little to an understanding of how crucial it was to integrate artillery fire into ground operations.[362]

Field Intelligence

IDF forces entered the battle with minimal and often misleading information about the enemy's deployment, activity, weapons, modus operandi, and limitations. The reservists and even their regular army commanders were frequently unfamiliar with the areas they were fighting in. Other units were thrown into combat before they received basic intelligence tools such as maps, photostats, area files, and updated air photographs. "Instead of interpreting air reconnaissance photos to discover the enemy's deployment, the interpretation focused on identifying types of weapons—mainly tanks—and an inordinate amount of time passed until Southern Command received the results. . . . Interpreted updates of the photos never reached the troops. . . . The interpretations of Egyptian infantry structures arrived, if at all, eighteen hours late . . . while the structures showed, in the first stage of the war, the Egyptians' actual deployment. . . . The air force received the first copy [of the film] . . . interpreted independently [to cover] only matters that it was interested in such as antiaircraft layouts and missiles."[363]

The advantage of receiving intelligence reports from the forces in contact with the enemy was all but ignored, and the information gleaned from listening devices fell far short of what the IDF had collected before the war. In any case, as soon as the Egyptians started to cross the canal, the strongholds came under fire, and reporting practically ceased. The observation posts on the waterline, which were based on reconnaissance teams and mechanized infantry, were ordered to pull back. There was no intelligence collection plan; no one processed the information from the fighting forces into updated intelligence that could have contributed to the accuracy of the picture in Southern Command and GHQ; and no one took responsibility for circulating the information gained from the regulars' early encounters with the enemy. The commander of 198th Battalion expressed it best: "The information on the enemy was exceedingly sparse. We didn't know where he was or how far he had advanced. . . . I don't recall in the brigade's orders group any intelligence officer giving us a review [of] where the enemy was."[364]

A flawed model from the Intelligence Branch dated April 1972 caused grave mistakes in GHQ's and Southern Command's management of the war. On the evening of October 7, the head of MI finally realized that the model was misleading in a number of vital areas:

- It assumed that a war of attrition would precede all-out war.
- It determined that the Egyptians' H hour would be at the last light of day (in reality, the enemy attacked at 13:55).
- It determined that Egyptian armored divisions would cross the canal twenty-four hours after H hour, and operations to capture the passes would be conducted from D day + 2 to D day + 6–7. (Gonen assessed the situation as critical, believing that the armored divisions had started to cross.)
- It envisioned a main effort in which the Egyptians' aim was to capture all of Sinai (in reality, there was no main effort, and the Egyptians had no plans to retake Sinai).[365]

Besides the model's miscalculations, there were numerous other intelligence shortcomings.

The commanders presented an unflattering picture of what they considered extremely shoddy field intelligence. According to Shomron, commander of 401st Brigade, "On the night of October 6–7 we didn't know how to fire the small amount of artillery that we had and what to do with our meager forces. . . . There was no [external] intelligence. . . . The only information that we had came from lookouts in the field." Shomron also recalled the October 14 battle in Wadi Mabrook: "The division didn't know what the dust over there was. A long-range observation team from the reconnaissance company had reported it. Although a large battle was being fought, we received nothing from intelligence. . . . So much information was flooding in that the [distribution] system was probably incapable of digesting it all and relaying the important items to the lower units. In one case we received an air photo that turned out to be two weeks old."[366]

Major General Yehoshua Saguy (Ret.), the intelligence officer in Sharon's division, claimed that before the troops in the strongholds surrendered, some people were "aching" to speak with them because they were the best intelligence source on the waterline, but nothing came of it. There was no intelligence photography, and the information distribution system was worthless. Saguy stated that this was a lesson from the 1956 Sinai Campaign, but as of today (including the Lebanon War in 1982), the problem has not been solved. Brigadier General Dov Tamari, deputy commander of 162nd Division, claimed that the quantitative potential of intelligence collection was not fully exploited in 1973—an inexcusable and costly shortcoming. General Adan summed it up best when he said that, to his deep regret, the war taught him that information had to be carefully corroborated not from top to bottom but from the bottom up: "Although valuable information is received from sources and reaches the divisions and from there to the brigades . . . priority always has to be given to what is reported on the contact line."[367]

The habit of acquiring intelligence from above prevented the forces in the field from employing their own collection units; as a result, headquarters received only minimal information about what they were facing. This insight is invaluable in terms of educating commanders and training units to collect intelligence by their own means, and it highlights the immense importance of "binocular intelligence" in wartime.[368]

The IAF

The ground forces expected the air force to help stave off the enemy, and their faith that such assistance would be provided remained strong in the first days of the war. Eventually, they wised up. There were also operational glitches: interminable waiting for coordinated air support created long delays in ground moves, and vital areas were evacuated to provide the air force with freedom of action west of the bombing line. From the outset, ground commanders at all levels erred in expecting the air force to come to their assistance, and they failed to understand the IAF's priorities and limitations (see chapter 4).

Lack of a Supradivisional Headquarters in Sinai

The lack of a supradivisional (corps) headquarters in Sinai was particularly costly in two cases. The first involved the absence of coordination between 162nd and 143rd Divisions during the October 8 counterattack—the 162nd requested assistance and the 143rd refused—and later when the 143rd returned from the southern sector for its uncoordinated attack on Makhshir and Hamutal. The second involved the crossing battle. Again, the two divisions had no headquarters to coordinate their moves, issue orders in real time as developments necessitated, and slice through the division commanders' egotistical battle for the glory of being the first to cross the canal. A supradivisional headquarters could have united the divisions in a common cause—victory in battle. Southern Command was incapable of doing this from its TOC at Dvela. Thus, innumerable problems in coordination and timing were created as the two divisions engaged in combat at the bridgehead on both sides of the canal. The need for a supradivisional headquarters was recognized during the war. Sharon told Dayan on October 21, "There's no one to talk to. The general of Southern Command hasn't visited us once—not on the bridge, not on the rafts, and not here." In their postwar summaries, both Adan and Sharon repeated their criticism regarding the lack of a supradivisional headquarters.[369]

Flaws at the Strategic Level

Strategically, the IDF made several costly mistakes during the Yom Kippur War.

Link between the Air Force and the Ground Battle

Although providing air support to the ground forces was low on the IAF's list of priorities, it could not be ignored. Still, the planning, resources, and order of battle it entailed exacted a high price and yielded only meager results. It would have been preferable to absolve the air force (except in extreme cases) from providing close air support (excluding interdiction missions, if possible, in areas crammed with antiaircraft missiles). Thus, the IAF should have been allowed to concentrate on its strategic and standard missions, such as neutralizing surface-to-air missiles. In reality, it had a sufficient number of planes to supply close air support without detracting from its strategic assignments, but it viewed assisting the ground forces as a nuisance with a heavy price (see chapter 4).

Failure to Rout Third Army on the Eastern Bank

The Egyptian Third Army suffered some setbacks at the beginning of the war—in absolute terms and relative to Second Army—and its fighting spirit seemingly plummeted. The marine brigade had been clobbered, the divisions' bridgeheads were shallow, and its units made no effort to advance, preferring instead to attack the strongholds. The first time MI presented Third Army's predicament in an intelligence collection was in the early morning of October 7, but this invaluable information was all but ignored when deciding on the sector for the counterattack. Zeira suggested to Elazar that 401st Brigade be strengthened in the southern sector so it could block the weak flank of the Egyptian attack, but Elazar made no comment. Just as in the armor battle simulation on the morning of October 7, had the 401st maneuvered to the Nehushtan area, it could have thwarted the crossing of Third Army's tanks and altered the face of the battle and the entire campaign. At 10:00 on October 7, MI described renewed Egyptian momentum throughout the entire length of the southern sector, and this may have obscured the knowledge that Third Army was experiencing difficulty completing its missions; nevertheless, IDF intelligence reports on the Egyptians' plight continued throughout the day and until daybreak on October 8. Southern Command's intelligence officer later acknowledged that Third Army's problems were known to the command, but apparently not in real time.

One of the main factors that contributed to Third Army's quagmire was the tenacious fighting of IDF units in the southern sector. The 401st Brigade's three tank battalions stubbornly impeded the Egyptian advance on Lexicon Road (except for an Egyptian armor penetration into Nehushtan) and successfully delayed the Egyptians until they were ordered to withdraw east to Artillery Road. Shomron believed that if a concerted effort had been made at any point, the brigade would have been able to control the eastern bank throughout the southern sector:

> If we hadn't been fighting to protect the strongholds, but had evacuated them earlier, and if we'd only been busy holding the enemy at bay, and if we'd been closer to the front in the first stage rather than being at Bir Tmadeh, I am sure the Third Army would not have been able to cross in the sector. The infantry may have been able to, but we would have deployed as a concentrated force and no one could have crossed the canal because it would have required breaking through the embankment. We had enough tanks to meet the enemy and would have set aflame anyone who tried to advance.[370]

If Third Army had been destroyed in an IDF counterattack in the southern sector or crippled so severely that it was forced to pull back to the western bank, the results of the war would have been different, and Egypt's military assets would have been pruned in the political negotiations to lift the IDF's encirclement of Third Army. After the October 9 decision to shift to the defense in Sinai, no one seriously considered attacking Third Army. A trial balloon was floated on October 10 to have the 143rd, in a joint operation with the 252nd, attack south to the southern sector, but nothing came of it.

To present a balanced picture, it should be noted that the crossing was supposed to take place after the organization and force amassment in Southern Command were complete. This move, which required a concerted effort in every field, could have led to a turning point—a decision and a cease-fire. Indeed, the IDF's arrival at Kilometer 101 had an enormous psychological impact on the enemy—perhaps no less than if Third Army had been wiped out. Final judgment on this matter remains elusive. The IAF could not have operated in a massive formation against Third Army unless the missiles on the western bank had been eliminated—a move that was possible because of the ground forces' penetration and advance. However, air strikes on Third Army in the final days of the war did not produce significant results.[371]

In practical terms, the IDF could not have executed a crossing operation followed by an attack on Third Army—certainly not simultaneously, and probably not sequentially either. To do so would have meant transferring a division from the Golan Heights, but this was an unrealistic move at the time. The IDF had reached the "bulge" (newly captured areas on the Golan Heights) and "Africa" (Egyptian territory west of the canal) completely out of breath.

Given the IDF's situation on and around October 24, it is doubtful that it could have attacked Third Army by doubling back forces to the eastern bank and attacking a well-entrenched army. At any rate, the survival of Third Army left the IDF, as well as Israel in general, with the bitter taste of an opportunity lost.

Shortage of Ammunition

The logistics system—the quartermaster branch, transportation corps, ordnance corps, and medical corps—deployed quickly and generally succeeded in supplying fuel, ammunition, food, medical equipment, spare parts, combat vehicle repairs, and medevac services. The IDF's logistical capability in the repair and maintenance of armored combat vehicles had a major impact on the war's direction. The ability to put damaged tanks in working order and return them to the battlefield was crucial. Repaired tanks were a key element in the order of battle and contributed to the IDF's ability to turn the tide of battle. In contrast was GHQ's perception of an acute shortage of tank and artillery ammunition after the first few days of fighting, attributable to ineffective control and a second-rate reporting system. This perception led to excessively pessimistic assessments of Israel's logistical survivability and created an unjustified sense of urgency to receive American aid. Thus, at an early stage, Israel overreacted and revealed its desperation for a cease-fire and its willingness to lift the siege on Third Army.

The problem of the dearth of ammunition first arose in GHQ's operational discussion group on October 9, when Tal outlined the situation and reported that tank and artillery ammunition was in critically short supply. The next day, at a meeting of the heads of various branches, the quartermaster general declared that there was no shortage and attributed the rumors to a lack of control at all levels. The fears were repudiated, and although the IDF overestimated its need for artillery ammunition, it was not far off the mark regarding tank ammunition.

The fear of an ammunition shortage was caused by the breakdown of the quartermaster corps' reporting system at the start of the war, especially in GHQ and the commands, though not in the divisions and lower levels. By the end of the war, there was a surplus of supplies, according to IDF standards, at all field levels, but the GHQ bases were depleted of ammunition.[372]

The Effect of Venomous Relationships and Problematic Orders

Much has already been written about the toxic relationships among the commanders, and the expression "the wars of the generals" has entered the Hebrew lexicon. Undoubtedly, Sharon's disrespectful attitude toward Gonen—such as ignoring his radio calls and countermanding his orders—created distrust and a poisonous atmosphere that exacerbated the tension and confusion.

Some of the orders issued during the war were unethical, unclear, and unprofessional. For example, the GSO order at 22:30 on Yom Kippur, issued in the chief of staff's name, stated that "each command will set up four power fists." This came after the commands' initial orders of battle had already incurred ruinous losses. In other words, orders that were incapable of being carried out were uncalled for and added to the already pervasive vexation.

Incomprehensible orders were also a problem. For example: "press forward a little." How much was "a little"? The orders "catch a lift on a bridge," "gnaw away at the enemy," and "advance cautiously" were also unclear. A conditionally stated order, such as "engage the enemy—but without incurring losses," cannot be followed; if losses are to be avoided, then there is no justification for fighting. Other examples such as "clean up," "sweep out," "wash away," and "brush off" all implied "eliminating" the enemy from a particular area.

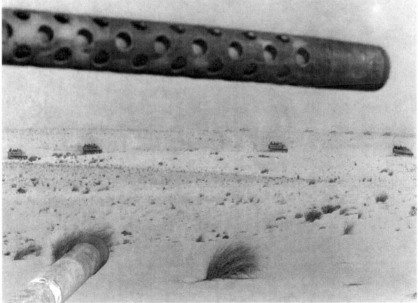

Tanks from 52nd Battalion participating in the defensive campaign in the southern sector of the Suez Canal.

Defensive battles in the southern sector.

Tanks from 52nd Battalion in the southern sector.

Evacuation of the Notza fortification, October 9, 1973.

A tank company commander tells the commander of 52nd Battalion about his company's exploits.

Mitla Road ("Atifa" in the Sirius code map).

The commander of 52nd Battalion, Lieutenant Colonel Sakal, had three tanks under his command on the evening of October 7, the second day of the war.

The FCG of 401st Brigade, commanded by Colonel Dan Shomron, under artillery fire.

Officers of 52nd Battalion on the commander's tank during the battle on Karat Moora, October 9.

A knocked-out Egyptian tank on fire.

Defensive position in the southern sector.

By the bridge, before crossing to the western bank.

Israeli tanks cross the Suez Canal.

The commander of 162nd Division, General Adan (right), explains the
situation to Moshe Dayan, the minister of defense.

Israeli tanks cross the Suez Canal.

Chief of Staff Elazar at the Chinese Farm.

Tanks of 52nd Battalion on the western bank of the Suez Canal.

Fighting on the western bank of the Suez Canal.

The freshwater canal on the western bank.

Surface-to-air missile site on the western bank, destroyed by 421st Armored Brigade. The IAF complained, "The tankers destroyed our missiles."

Coordination of neighboring sectors: 143rd Division.

The 52nd Battalion tank crew. (Lieutenant Colonel Sakal is second from left.)

Commanders of 52nd Battalion at the tank gunnery range north of Jabel Ataka, winter 1973.

Lieutenant Colonel Sakal (commander of 52nd Battalion during the war) receives the Medal of Courage from the chief of staff, Lieutenant General Gur, May 1975.

4

Air Support for the Ground Forces

In the final months of the War of Attrition, the Egyptians built a tight air defense system with Soviet help and advanced it to the Canal Zone during the cease-fire on the nights of August 7–8 and 8–9, 1970. This new reality posed a daunting challenge to future combat operations for the IDF in general and the IAF in particular.

The cease-fire precluded an Israeli attack, but during the three years of quiet on the canal, the IAF carefully studied the problem, developed a combat doctrine, procured weapons, intensified training, and devised operational plans to destroy the Egyptian system. The air force devoted most of its attention during this time to anti-missile warfare. It was aware of its limited ability to provide air support and conduct other missions in the Canal Zone, but opinion on the gravity of the threat was divided.

Success Depends on Air Superiority

The IDF did not take the Egyptian threat lightly, as evidenced by the summaries of operational plans and discussions, the presentations of work plans, and the air force's day-to-day activities. In a situational assessment on June 26, 1972, Major General Tal, the head of GHQ, said, "Regarding Egypt's limited goal to seize toeholds east of the canal, we have the option to flush them out only if the air force carries out a massive attack that pulverizes the enemy's artillery. This, of course, depends on neutralizing all or part of the missile layout."[1]

At the conclusion of the Iron Ram war game in August 1972, the chief of staff made it clear that "gaining air superiority is a precondition for success in the campaign and that 'Bendigo' will have an important part to play in it. The ground forces will be fighting with minimal artillery and no air support until the missile layout is eliminated. . . . They'll have to hang on for a few hours [!] but [the air force] will eliminate the missile layout. Afterwards it will [be free to] assist the ground forces in defensive and offensive operations."[2] In a

GHQ meeting the day before the war, Elazar declared, "In the worst case scenario, let's say an attack without any warning, the regulars will have to hold, that means, with help from the air force and all available forces on the lines."[3]

The entire defense system believed that the IAF was its insurance against any threat. It would provide the IDF with the short-term breathing space it needed to deal with the enemy and buy time for the reservists to mobilize. The air force exuded confidence, as did its commander, Major General Mordechai Hod. At a restricted GHQ meeting on April 19, 1973, during the Blue White alert, Hod stated, "The best solution is to make maximum use of the IAF's inherent capability. This way we can hide the shortage of tanks in Sinai. The air force can cope with every beachhead that crosses [the canal] for twenty-four, even forty-eight hours, and none of our preparations will cost any money."[4] Hod (who had been the IAF commander during the Six-Day War as well) stated emphatically that when the air force was in a state of high alert, it could prevent a surprise attack, facilitate the reservists' mobilization, and safeguard Israel's skies. Armed with Hod's evaluation, Elazar presented operational plans to the prime minister on May 9, 1973, in the presence of Defense Minister Dayan, General Tal, and the head of the operations department:

> Whatever happens, we consider the air force the primary element in defense and offense. In other words, if war breaks out, the IAF will pay back the dividends it owes us on the vast resources (over 50% of the defense budget) we've invested in it. The disproportion between our ground forces [and the enemy's], as I've shown, and the fact that we dare not to call up the reservists prematurely, stem from our belief in the IAF's capability to hold or stop an invasion or crossing on one or two fronts, since we see the air force executing an attack prior to any ground move.[5]

Elazar stressed that by maintaining air superiority, the IAF would prevent the enemy from achieving territorial gains, especially if the Egyptians initiated an attack before the IDF's reservists had been mobilized. Ground defense on the borders was based on thinly spread out forces because of the confidence in the IAF's ability to staunch a ground attack.

When Major General Benny Peled became the new IAF commander in May 1973, he nurtured the same level of confidence among the ground forces. An internal document he wrote on August 29 stated, "The air force was and will continue to be the IDF's main instrument in deterring the enemy from opening fire. This deterrence is based on the IAF's ability to win wars in the region."[6]

For these reasons, when the "Ofek A" multiyear plan was submitted to the government in July, no one questioned the IAF's proposed budget increase. Elazar justified the investment of more than 52 percent of the defense budget in airpower: "The IAF is the bulwark of our strength and air superiority is essential for victory in war. Since the IDF's strength is based on the reservists, this means that the regulars, like the air force that can remain on a high level of alert, will have to make sure that we're not caught by surprise, and enable us to call up the IDF and close the gap for the first 24, 48 or 72 hours, while the IAF protects our skies."[7]

As an "observer," Dayan recalled that, according to GHQ planning, the IAF was to play the main role in the holding stage. Its job was to pummel the enemy so severely that he could no longer expect to make any headway. Tal added an apocalyptic caveat to any would-be aggressor: "Let the Arab states know that any attempt to attack Israel on the ground . . . will be met with devastating air superiority, overwhelming firepower, and the IAF's full destructive capabilities. Let them keep in mind that even before Israel's crack ground troops mobilize and deploy, the IAF's staggering air power can be applied within minutes whether inside Israel, along the borders, or in the depth of their lands."[8]

Thus, the chief of staff believed that reliance on the IAF was a cost-saving strategy that guaranteed the IDF's success. There would be no need for an early call-up of reservists to repel a ground attack because the IAF's air superiority would handle that. No one spotted the fly in the ointment: if it turned out that, for whatever reason, the air force could not provide close air support to the ground forces in the first stages of war, the entire security concept might collapse.[9]

The IAF was perceived as "flying artillery"—a term first coined during the War of Attrition when the IAF dealt with Egyptian artillery shelling of the strongholds. It also justified the low-priority budgeting of the IDF's artillery branch. As flying artillery, the IAF was considered capable of providing air assistance on demand, and it was seen as Israel's ultimate guarantor and protector in the event of a catastrophe.

The IAF's Priorities

Brigadier General Giora Forman (Ret.), head of the IAF Operations Department in 1973, saw the Six-Day War, the War of Attrition, and the Yom Kippur War as a single event—the "Seven-Year War." He noted that before the Six-Day War, the air force regarded support of ground and naval combat as its least important function. According to Hod, the IAF's priorities were as follows:

1. Attaining air superiority and destroying surface-to-air missiles.
2. Attacking airfields.
3. Assisting and supporting the ground forces—the Scratch (Sreeta) plan—even if air superiority was not achieved.[10]

Peled, Hod's replacement, also ranked air support for the ground battle last on his list of priorities presented during the Blue White alert:

1. Protecting Israel's airspace.
2. Destroying the enemy's air forces mainly by neutralizing his airfields.
3. Destroying the antiaircraft missiles.
4. Participating in the ground battle.

The second and third missions were perceived as absolutely essential for providing wide-scale support to the ground forces, and during the war, the IAF operated according to these priorities.

On the eve of the Yom Kippur War, there were three basic beliefs in play:

1. If military and political conditions were favorable, the IDF would deliver a preemptive strike.
2. Since the IDF was not initiating a ground attack, the regulars would have to hold the invader at bay.
3. A situation in which the enemy embarked on war without any warning was inconceivable.

With regard to the third point, a forty-eight-hour warning was thought to be sufficient for the air force to prepare an attack against

Egypt's missiles and airfields. In the first forty-eight hours, the IAF would be engaged in attaining air superiority, so the ground forces would have to hold the line on their own. Afterward, the air force would provide ground support. The dominant feeling in GHQ, however, was that Israel would have more than forty-eight hours' warning and that the enemy's attack would be thwarted by the air force—the main element—along with the regulars on the line until the reservists arrived. This was the belief even though it had been stated unequivocally that the ground forces would receive air support only after the enemy missiles were eliminated.[11]

Airfields versus Missiles

The dilemma for the IAF was which to attack first—the missiles or the airfields. Hod said, "We prefer 'Tagar' [the plan to attack the missiles in Egypt first], [since] airfields can't escape us." Peled (still the second in command at the time), added, "Assuming that the goal is to disrupt a crossing and enable our forces to organize for blocking and immediately counterattacking, then we have to attack the missile layout first." But when he presented the IAF's plans in May 1973, Peled told the defense minister that he envisioned two possibilities:

> One, a preemptive strike, first against all the enemy air forces [airfields], afterwards the missiles, and lastly ground support; and two, [the more likely scenario] would be in response to an Egyptian attack and a situation in which our forces are under pressure, . . . there's an enemy's crossing, and we're extremely concerned about the line's ability to hold . . . we'll want to commence Operation "Tagar," attacking the missiles and relieving the pressure from the line in the first strike. . . . But if the situation on the line doesn't make this mandatory, the IAF prefers to employ all its strength to "take out" the Egyptian air force before going after the missiles, except for dealing with the extremities: Port Said or knocking the batteries out of commission at the southern entrances.[12]

Unlike his previous agreement with Hod's "missiles first" approach, Peled, now as IAF commander, preferred to smash all the Arab airfields in a first strike.

In a GHQ discussion on May 14, 1973, during the Blue White alert, Dayan decided that destruction of the missiles would be the primary mission: "This is good in every sense. . . . If we see the Egyptians crossing the canal, the air force can help the ground forces block the invasion, but responsibility for preventing territorial gains [by the enemy] falls on the ground forces." What Dayan said (in contrast to what Gonen thought) made it perfectly clear that the ground forces were responsible for holding the line. No one considered the possibility that they would be so hard-pressed that the air force would have to rush to their assistance before the missiles were neutralized. A situational assessment in September 1973 stated: "By maintaining and correctly exploiting air superiority, the IAF has to prevent the enemy from ground gains. This is especially true if the enemy launches offensive activity and IDF ground forces haven't the time to deploy."[13]

The air force consistently and deliberately presented an unconditional set of priorities and underscored the fact that, in order to destroy the enemy air forces, it would have to concentrate its strength for forty-eight hours before assisting the ground units. A detailed list of priorities was compiled during the operational planning for Blue White and received the chief of staff's approval, with an emphasis on the following:

1. Defending the skies of the state and preventing the enemy from any gains in the air.
2. Attacking aircraft, airfields, and surface-to-air missile batteries.
3. Assisting ground and naval fighting.
4. Attacking strategic targets.
5. Other tasks: photography and intelligence collecting, medevac, liaison, electronic relaying, electronic warfare (EW), and transportation.

This list shows that the IAF's basic policy was to attain freedom of action in the air within twenty-four to forty-eight hours and then quickly shift to providing maximum assistance to ground and naval combat forces. In effect, missile destruction became the sine qua non for ground support. Elazar followed this order of priorities even on Saturday, the Day of Atonement, leaving ground support third on the list. A number of aircraft were allocated for emergencies, but on Sunday, air assistance was still in third place.[14]

Tagar in Egypt versus Dugman in Syria

The lessons learned at the end of the War of Attrition and during the three-year cease-fire produced two main IAF operational plans for destroying the Arabs' missile arrays: Tagar 4 in Egypt and Dugman 5 in Syria. The Tagar 4 plan, as it crystallized and was presented during the Blue White alert, would be applied in the Canal Zone upon the resumption of hostilities. The Egyptian missile batteries would undergo a concentrated attack for an entire day, consisting of a preparatory aerial attack against antiaircraft cannon batteries on the canal line, followed an hour later by an attack against the missiles at Port Said. The second sortie, which would begin either four hours later or the next day, would attack the central or southern missile arrays. The third sortie, four hours after the second, would eliminate the remaining missiles. The last sortie—a nighttime attack—would employ loft bombing to inhibit the enemy from reorganizing.

As a preemptive strike, the IAF planned a single surprise attack (consisting of two sorties) against the Egyptian missile formations along the entire length of the canal (excluding Port Said) to a depth of thirty kilometers. But even before the war, the IAF realized that the chances of being granted permission to carry out this mission were very slim, so when the strike was canceled on the morning of October 6, it came as no surprise.

Besides Tagar and Dugman, the air force had several other plans. Negiha (Ramming) involved attacking the airfields in Egypt and Syria. Bendigo called for the destruction, with artillery assistance, of surface-to-air missiles on the western bank (either on a battle day or in an all-out war). Bendigo required the early call-up of artillery batteries, spotting and observation units, and air units; coordination among these bodies; and their integration into the combined-arms operation. Bendigo had the potential to reduce aircraft vulnerability.[15] Scratch (Sreeta) was the only plan that included assistance to ground operations. It had been devised in 1972–1973 to provide day and nighttime close air support by loft bombing in all weather conditions, in the event the IDF was caught by surprise or had to single-handedly block an Egyptian offensive. Scratch would be initiated even before the IAF annihilated the enemy's missiles and gained air superiority. It should be noted, however, that no one envisioned a scenario in which the main defensive lines had collapsed and the warplanes had to hold the line while preparing to attack the missiles. Scratch existed during the Blue White alert in May 1973 in the same list of GSO orders that included Tagar 4, Dugman 5, Ramming, and so forth. The plan was never drilled. In August 1973 Peled ordered Scratch simplified to lessen its dependence on external variables.[16]

The IAF's plans notwithstanding, the commanders in Southern Command expected that warplanes would be on hand to assist them once hostilities erupted. They expected the IAF to begin destroying tanks, bridges, and Egyptian force concentrations while providing close support and carrying out in-depth interdiction. In short, the air force would break the enemy's offensive.

The chief of staff's contradictory, ambiguous statements were unmistakably the main reason for the ground forces' certainty that the air force would play a key role in the holding battle, even if it was simultaneously engaged in missile destruction. When Southern Command's operational plans were presented to Elazar in May 1973, he stated that the IAF would take part in the battle because the crossing had to be thwarted at all costs: "First of all an air attack. We've built a large air force and invested in it, this is the time it repays the dividends in the ground battle." But earlier, in the summary of the Iron Ram war game in August 1972, he had said the opposite: the air force would be too busy taking out the missiles, so the ground forces would have to manage on their own for forty-eight hours. Ultimately, when Dayan presented the plans to the prime minister in May 1973, the IAF's primary task was to destroy the enemy's missiles and air force. "In this stage, Arik's [Sharon's] tanks will deal with the invader."[17]

The IAF's Timetable

The timetable for the IAF to attain air superiority remained ill-defined and nebulous—not only in the interface between the air force and the ground forces but also between the air force and the chief of staff. On different occasions, various timetables were put forward. On June 13, 1973, while presenting IAF plans to the defense minister, Peled suggested a nine-hour time frame for eliminating the missiles. Yet three weeks earlier, on May 22, he had stated that an operational decision on the missiles could be achieved within forty-eight hours, but only if he allocated most of the IAF's order of battle to the mission. The air force could allot a number of "four-aircraft formations" from the Skyhawk quota for ground assistance, but it could not engage en masse in the all-out war until after the missiles were eliminated. Elazar summed up that meeting by promising to do all he could to ensure that the air force received the necessary forty-eight hours. Later, in a discussion with the prime minister on October 3, and in the presence of the defense minister, Elazar stated that the air force needed one day to destroy the Egyptian or Syrian missiles. In any event, the prevailing assessment in GHQ was that the ground force regulars were capable of holding the line until the reservists mobilized and reached the canal.

In May 1973 (during the Blue White alert) the air force presented three scenarios that depended on the length of the warning time:

1. With a five-day warning, a preemptive strike could be carried out, immediately followed by support of the ground forces. If the preemptive strike was vetoed, the air force would achieve air superiority within forty-eight hours after the commencement of hostilities, after which it would be able to provide massive assistance to the ground operations.
2. With a forty-eight-hour warning, the IAF would be able to attack Egypt parallel with the enemy's H hour, with or without a preemptive strike.
3. In the case of a catastrophe—less than forty-eight hours' warning—if the ground forces were unable to hold off the enemy by themselves, the IAF would have to attack the enemy and assist the ground units before it operated against the missiles (Scratch).[18]

The IAF's Deployment for War

October 5: thirty hours before the war. In a staff and commanders forum, the IAF commander announced, "Tomorrow war!" But it did not register. Peled was referring to war in the north, which explains why he presented Dugman—the attack against Syria's missiles—and omitted mention of the war on the canal. On the same day at 09:30, the IAF entered alert level C and armed its aircraft with munitions for Dugman. After the war, Peled acknowledged saying that if war broke out on Friday evening, there would not be enough forces in Sinai, and the air force would have to assist the troops before eliminating the missiles.

October 6: nine hours before the war. On the morning of October 6, leaders were still leaning toward a preemptive attack against Syrian missiles and airfields, with no plans for operations in Egypt. At 04:35 the chief of staff ordered Peled to prepare for the attack against Syria, and the air commander said he would be ready at 11:00. In talks with the defense minister thirty minutes later, no one brought up the southern front. Peled later reported that the air force would be ready to attack the airfields and missiles in Syria between 14:00 and 16:00. Dayan vetoed a preemptive strike but gave the green light for a parallel strike (the moment the Syrians opened fire), and the matter went to the prime minister for a decision.

In the GHQ discussion group at 05:30, the attack in Syria received top priority: missiles, the Syrian air force, and the Syrian line. Peled reported that his planes would be ready between 12:00 and 15:00. He was granted permission to mobilize aircrews, antiaircraft crews, and air control crews. As Dugman was being prepared, there were pessimistic weather reports for the Golan Heights (but better weather was expected in Syria). Once again, this discussion involved no planning for an attack on the canal.[19]

October 6: seven hours before the war. In the orders group, Peled stated that aircraft might have to fly on the line to stem the Syrian attack until dark and then carry out loft bombing in Syria's depths. Due to the weather forecast, he decided to replace part of the ordnance and prepare for an attack on the Syrian airfields in the first stage, before going after the missiles. He stated that he would give top priority to attacking the airfields on October 7, too, and had no intention of "messing up" the ordnance arrangement. Regarding the mobilization of IAF crews beyond the chief of staff's approval of a partial call-up that morning, Peled made it clear that "the air force is mobilizing as though for war. There's no way that I'm going to sit around waiting for the government's permission to mobilize. That's all there is to it!"

During the discussion, the possibility of fighting in the canal theater was raised for the first time. Peled thought Egypt would have little success and believed the IAF could knock out the bridges at night. He considered nighttime aerial combat a necessary evil because it entailed the sporadic hurtling of ordnance. According to his conception and the detailed timetables, the forces on the canal would have to wait at least forty-eight hours until the air force could turn its full attention to them. Nevertheless, the IAF commander knew he might have to assist the ground battle with loft bombing. He informed the head of the IAF's Operations Department that if, by 15:00 or 16:00, it looked like "we're not going to attack, then the mission would have to be changed to defense and attacking the crossing forces. The IAF won't have to allocate a lot of planes," he pointed out, and added, "I don't want a situation where you [Forman] will tell me to execute loft bombing on the canal according to a grid coordinate and I don't have any planes."[20]

The IAF's central command post (CCP) did not consider the Egyptian threat serious, even though Peled painted a scenario in which the Egyptians implemented a nighttime transfer of 500 to 700 amphibious APCs from two infantry divisions and began to move bridging equipment across. His conclusion: if they managed to bring across only part of the infantry at night, the bridges would not be ready by the morning, and they would be "up shit creek without a paddle." The head of operations described the "greens'" (ground forces') position in a facetious tone: "I'll take care of those who crossed. You just make sure there aren't any bridges. . . . If there aren't any, then the more [Egyptians] that cross, the more prisoners we'll take."[21]

October 6: four hours before the war. Peled thought the enemy attack would most likely come at 15:00 and would include an air strike. He figured it would come at 16:00 at the latest; therefore, he had to receive the order to attack by 15:00. If the IAF did not carry out a strike, it would have to change its ordnance setup before nightfall. As for the next day, Sunday, a decision would have to be made whether to attack Egypt or Syria and whether the targets were missiles or airfields.

October 6: three hours before the war. In the operational discussion group in the defense minister's office, Peled stressed, "We won't be able to do anything tonight. It'll take us an hour on Sunday [to annihilate] the Syrian air force. It all depends on the right weather. . . . The missiles will be destroyed by noon and then we'll turn to Egypt."[22]

During the course of the meeting, the preemptive strike was finally canceled. The chief of staff granted Peled permission to change the ordnance setup to air-to-air. Peled put off issuing the order until 12:50.

October 6: an hour and a half before the war. For the first time in an IAF operational discussion, questions were raised regarding Tagar's timing and the method of attack on the Egyptian front, which included targeting the crossing forces. Now that the preemptive air strike had been called off, some of the aircraft were assigned to protect the state's airspace, and the rest were deployed for "pop-up" bombing (whereby the pilot executes a low-altitude approach to an identified point, climbs to spot the target, dives, releases the ordnance, and then leaves the area in a low-altitude flight) on both fronts. Peled believed the canal crossing would come late in the day, so the air force would have to conduct loft bombing on the crossing areas at dusk and at night. His orders stated: "Enemy aerial 'H' hour from 15:00 to last light."[23] His plans for the next day reflected his priorities: Syrian airfields first, then the missiles; he added an attack on the Egyptian front, based on developments. Tagar would take only one day, but that could change, he stressed, depending on the ground forces' staying power and the reservists' rate of arrival in Sinai.

Peled repeated his estimate that the Egyptians would not reach the eastern bank before dark and the air force would not have to attack there. If crossing areas were spotted, however, the IAF would attack immediately from first light and at night. He correctly predicted large-scale enemy helicopter activity and the need to hunt and destroy them, but he still believed that the primary target was the Syrian airfields, followed by the missiles the next morning. Then the IAF could turn to the south, where destruction of the Egyptian air force was of paramount importance, followed by the missiles. Peled said nothing about close ground support, enemy bridges, or force concentrations on both banks; these were low-priority issues "unless the 'fuck-up' on the canal is so great that we have to enter en masse to help our shattered forces make it to the Mitla Pass in which case we'll have to execute 'Tagar' earlier than planned."[24]

October 6: one hour before the war. Following the chief of staff's 12:30 announcement that the preemptive strike had been canceled and the air commander's assessment that two and a half hours remained until the enemy's attack, at 12:50 the latter ordered the aircraft's munitions setup changed to air defense and ground attacks so that it could support the ground forces.[25]

October 6: war. The only thing left for the IAF to do was impro-vise.[26] At 14:05 the Skyhawks were scrambled to assist in the hold-ing effort. This was done with unplanned loft bombing, and the air force suffered heavy losses. At 14:30 the chief of staff asked Peled if a parallel strike could be conducted in response to the Syrians' initiation of war. The IAF commander answered that it was too late because the Phantoms—the main force—were engaged in air defense; however, an attack could be organized against other targets in Syria's depths and against Egyptian radar installations on the Gulf of Suez. Elazar gave the green light for this attack, and Dayan agreed, on the condition that it would not compromise the defense of Israel's skies. At 16:00 the chief of staff summed up the next day's priorities: "Action against the Syrian and Egyptian air forces, fol-lowed by an attack on their missiles, and lastly—assistance to the ground forces."[27] At the same time, Peled decided to provide maxi-mum assistance to Southern Command in the remaining daylight because of the harrowing reports coming in from the lines. The IAF extended the number of sorties to include target hunting, since the commands—according to Major General David Ivry (Ret.)—had failed to provide such information.

An agonizing dilemma arose during these discussions: what to do now? Southern Command wanted the main focus to be on the bridges (although no bridges had been erected yet); the chief of staff insisted that the missiles on the canal should be dealt with first. After the Skyhawk losses that afternoon, the IAF commander realized the air force was incapable of conducting operations on the canal as long as the missiles threatened its aircraft. In the opera-tional discussion group at 16:00, attended by the defense minister, Peled stated that if the crossing points were known, a nighttime ord-nance drop on the other side of the canal was feasible, even though the planes risked being hit by missiles. IDF artillery, he claimed, could knock out the SA6s. At 17:16 he gave the okay for ground assistance, but only with loft bombing—a relatively safe but noto-riously inaccurate method—in areas suspected of a major crossing, with the intention of pinning down the enemy as much as possible. (This was a euphemistic way of stating the obvious: the air force was incapable of doing anything that would be more effective.) The head of the IAF's Operations Department avowed that the bridges could not be attacked at night, but Peled replied that just dropping ordnance on a bridge would be sufficient.

At a 20:20 meeting with the chief of staff, his deputy, and the head of intelligence, Dayan suggested making a supreme effort to incapacitate the bridges. At around 20:30 Gonen asked Peled to bomb the bridges (which still had not been established). At 21:00, following Gonen's request, Peled repeated his suggestion that the IAF execute intense loft bombing in areas where a major crossing was suspected. Loft bombings were carried out during the night in a number of places, but they missed their targets. The air force promised to conduct loft bombings throughout the night on the bridges north of Purkan, and Gonen promised Albert air assistance in the northern sector. It soon became clear that this was out of the question, and at 23:15 Southern Command's artillery commander informed Gonen that bombing would cease at midnight.

The IAF's Missions on Sunday

The IAF commander, the chief of staff, and the defense minister faced another, more perplexing dilemma: how to use the air force the next morning. Which sector should be attacked? Which bombing method should be applied? What were the operational priorities? Did air superiority take precedence, as determined before the war, or, in light of the ground situation, should ground support and destruction of the bridges in areas bristling with missiles take priority? The pendulum swing of opinions, proposals, and decisions continued throughout the night until the next morning's decision to reverse direction: cancel Tagar and switch to Dugman. In a five-hour (!) commanders' discussion with Peled between 14:00 and 19:00, no one ordered Scratch, and no serious attack was made on the crossing areas.

Dayan was informed of the IAF's plan of action for Sunday morning: attack missiles and airfields in the south to gain control of the skies and enable greater freedom of action on both banks. The defense minister, however, saw things differently. He thought priority should be given to eliminating the bridges and enemy forces on the canal, even though this ran counter to the chief of staff's instructions to achieve air superiority on the Egyptian front first. But, true to form, Dayan did not force his opinion.

Furthermore, former chief of staff Haim Bar-Lev, who joined the discussion, stated that if a crossing had not occurred, attacking the missiles would be a costly venture. Peled continued to weigh the pros and cons, even after the decision was made: Tagar in the morning. Was it preferable to attack the missiles before the IDF crossed to the western bank—where there would be new missiles to deal with—and before the reservist divisions arrived?[28]

At 01:30 Peled outlined Tagar 4 in the chief of staff's office and estimated that its chances of success were good. The attack would commence at approximately 07:00 and consist of a forty-minute preparatory flight that targeted the antiaircraft cannon batteries along the canal, followed by an attack on eight airfields to render the runways inoperable and keep the Egyptian air force grounded for four hours, followed immediately thereafter by an attack on the missiles. Only then would the IAF be free to give significant support to the ground forces.

Cancellation of Tagar and the Switch to Dugman

The switch to Dugman was, without a doubt, one of the most controversial decisions of the war, and not only for the IAF. The chief of staff's decision came in the wake of the volte-face on the Golan Heights in the latter half of Saturday night. Elazar asked Peled whether operations in the south and in the north could be carried out simultaneously by attacking missile batteries on both fronts. Peled's answer was negative, at which point the chief of staff granted the air force permission to complete Tagar, including the preliminary activity. Still, the possibility of a change in plans hovered in the air and intensified through the night as reports of a Syrian breakthrough in the southern part of the Golan Heights grew more desperate. Because of these reports, Elazar ordered the main air effort transferred to the north.[29]

A few minutes before 05:00, Dayan, who was on his way north, spoke with Peled from Sde Dov and informed him of the critical situation in the north. But twenty minutes later, the chief of staff again granted the Egyptian sector IAF priority, including a flight against antiaircraft defenses and a flight against airfields. He cautioned, however, that the decision whether to attack the missiles or the Golan Heights might change.[30] Elazar asked the IAF commander whether Dugman could be executed that afternoon, and Peled replied in the negative. When he inquired as to the latest possible time to order Dugman instead of Tagar, Peled answered between 07:30 and 0745. At this stage, Elazar decided that the plan would remain as it was, but his questions implied that modifications were conceivable.

At 06:42 Dayan spoke with Peled (the defense minister was in Northern Command and could not reach Elazar by telephone). Dayan made it clear that unless there were four-aircraft formations until noon, the Syrians would break through to the Jordan valley. He said, "The IAF is the only force that can hold them until the tanks arrive." He asked Peled to inform the chief of staff that the entire air effort in the north had been upended (but he did not demand the cancellation of Tagar). Dayan and others have described this important conversation. According to Dayan, he "told [the air force commander] that he had to use IAF warplanes continuously and en masse against the Syrian armor's breakthrough in the Rafid area. Only the air force could [stop them]. There would be more armored forces in the afternoon, but as of now the responsibility was his. If not, we would lose the southern Golan Heights and after that who knows what would happen to the Jordan Valley."[31]

When Elazar returned to the IAF's CCP, Peled updated him on his conversation with Dayan and informed him that the first preparatory Tagar flight was almost over and the second was planned for 07:25. The chief of staff asked if Tagar could be switched to Dugman. Peled answered that it was possible, but someone would have to decide whether it was worth abandoning a large part of Tagar and spending four hours preparing for Dugman. In the meantime, Peled suggested diverting Mirages from air defense to ground assistance on the Golan Heights. Elazar insisted that small-scale sorties would not decide the outcome of the battle, but Dugman could.

The IAF commander emphasized that preparations for Dugman would take four hours, and it would not save the Golan Heights. Seeing no other alternative, he proposed canceling the second Tagar flight ("even though it's a damn shame that we have to cut the momentum short"). Elazar was in a quandary about whether to continue the momentum for another four hours (leaving Northern Command without air support) in the hope that the air force could wipe out the Egyptian army later. He finally decided to cancel Tagar and shift to Dugman, just as the first plane was releasing its munitions. Tagar was halted, and the entire air effort was diverted north. Two Skyhawks had been shot down during Tagar's preparatory flights, while the antiaircraft layout on the canal remained undamaged. In Operation Ramming, seven airfields were attacked, with partial success. Elazar hoped the IAF would return to Southern Command en masse and operate with greater freedom, "but the question was could the guys hold out till noon."[32] They did, although the IAF's contribution was nugatory.

In GHQ, confusion reigned supreme. The Assyria 4 order, issued at 08:30 on October 7, showed that despite the chief of staff's explanation about the change in plans, the GSO thought that after Tagar was completed, Dugman would be executed and that maximum assistance would be given to Northern Command.

Who Gets Air Assistance: North or South?

The decision to cancel Tagar did nothing to improve the defensive battle in Southern Command or relieve the misery of 252nd Division on the morning of October 7, notwithstanding the chief of staff's avowal that the IAF's attack that morning—the preliminary flight on the Egyptian airfields—removed some of the pressure in the south. Unfortunately, this was not true.

At 07:20 Gonen requested air support, and Elazar replied that none would be forthcoming until 15:00. Gonen said he would try to hang on until then. When Dayan returned from the north at 08:20, he said to Peled, "You saved us, now we can provide some air assistance in Sinai."[33]

Southern Command's 09:30 order to break off contact with the strongholds was unquestionably one of the most trying moments for 252nd Division. Elazar, who was aware of the difficulties the defense was undergoing, went to the CCP to see if any air activity could be diverted to the south. By 09:37, Gonen's requests for air assistance multiplied, given that the 252nd was leapfrogging to the rear. Under pressure from the chief of staff—and regardless of his instructions to provide massive support to Northern Command—Peled sent some of his planes to attack in the south.[34]

At 09:51, because of Southern Command's concern that armored divisions were crossing the canal and continuing the momentum of the attack, Gonen demanded air strikes on the bridges that were now straddling the canal, but his request was turned down due to preparations for Dugman and assistance for Northern Command. As soon as the situation improved in the north, Elazar ordered Peled to divert the entire air effort south—though not at Dugman's expense—to bomb the bridges and attack the three Egyptian columns engaged in the breakthrough in a supreme effort to halt them. Referring to the order to transfer all air assistance back to the south,

Brigadier General Rafi Harlev, head of the IAF's Intelligence Group declared: "Enough is enough! We'll continue providing assistance to the north and at the same time prepare for 'Dugman.'"[35]

At the government meeting held between 10:00 and 11:00, the chief of staff acknowledged that the IAF had begun to shift its activity from Tagar to the Golan Heights. In the wake of Gonen's communiqués, Elazar had been reporting on the situation in Southern Command since 09:30. "They [the Egyptians] have [put up] many bridges and their tanks are crossing on them. Opposite them our forces are thinly spread out and exhausted. This is why half an hour ago the air force was ordered to attack three points [Ismailia, Dwersuar, and Shalufa] and by my reckoning our tank attack with air support will delay the Egyptian breakthrough or block it to some degree."[36]

By noon, Dugman 5 had failed. Elazar returned from the CCP and stated that "success [in the north?] had not been exploited because the effort was concentrated, ironically, in the south!" It is difficult to interpret exactly what he meant. At any rate, Gonen repeated his request for urgent air support, and at 11:55 Elazar's aide-de-camp noted that a concentrated effort was being made in the south (the chief of staff ordered the IAF to divert operations from north to south). At 12:00 Elazar informed Dayan, who was at Dvela, of the Dugman 5 fiasco: "Benny [Peled] attacked and the results were not good. It cost us nine [Phantoms]. . . . Now we're making a concentrated effort. Shmulik [Gonen] will get constant air support." Seven minutes later the chief of staff's aide-de-camp jotted in the log: "Immediate assistance to the south." At the same time, Gonen's deputy, Brigadier General Ben Ari, asked the chief of staff for immediate assistance in the south since Dugman was over. Elazar, convinced that the situation there was precarious, told the general of Northern Command that he would have to manage without the air force. At 13:07, following frenzied demands from the north, the chief of staff ordered the IAF to divide its effort between the two commands and provide assistance to both fronts, throwing the air force off balance.[37]

Attacking the Bridges on the Canal

Priority for air assistance changed when the air commander, in consultation with the chief of staff, announced that beginning at 13:30 the rate of sorties in the south would be doubled. The main effort would involve the bridges, although neither the air command nor the squadrons were ready for this increasingly urgent mission. While visiting Dvela at 13:45, Dayan said that air support would be diverted to attacking the bridges, but there was no guarantee they would be destroyed. At 16:00 Peled phoned Forman and ordered him to eliminate the bridges, no matter the price. Within minutes, Peled was at the CCP and updated those present that Dayan had returned from the south claiming that Israel might be facing the destruction of the Third Temple. Shortly after 16:00, in a government meeting with the chief of staff, Peled reported that the IAF "was attacking the bridges regardless of the cost. Two bridges have already been knocked out. . . . The attack on the bridges is taking place at this very moment. Southern Command feels [our] assistance."[38] (The assistance was not felt.) Dayan noted that the report encouraged him to support the next day's counterattack; he suggested that the chief of staff come to the southern front, and "if he decides to attack, then I'm in favor."[39]

The report produced great excitement in the CCP and the Pit, but it was a far cry from the actual situation on the ground. Peled returned to the CCP at 16:43 and informed the chief of staff (over the intercom) of the air force's success in putting the bridges out of commission. "Out of fourteen bridges, I destroyed seven in the first flight and all of the bridges between Bitter Lake and Crocodile Lake. I'm working on the remaining seven and will eliminate them all before and after dark" (see map 10). Elazar and his assistant, Major General "Gandhi" Zeevi, could barely contain their joy. "Come over here and you'll get a kiss," Elazar gushed. Gandhi added, "Anything's possible now." These misleadingly optimistic reports certainly influenced the chief of staff's positive attitude about the next day's counterattack. To encourage the "greens," Peled added, "If I tell them that there's no bridges left that should cheer them up a bit. [Maybe] they'll be ready to counterattack."[40]

Dayan, as his wont, remained skeptical and restrained even after his visit to the CCP at 18:35, where he received reports that eleven of fourteen bridges had been rendered inoperable and the Egyptians had been stopped. In the government meeting that night, he announced that "the IAF has destroyed a fair number of bridges . . . [there were reports of twenty destroyed] but in reality the picture is less than rosy because during the night the bridges were repaired and even if not all of them were completely repaired, it wasn't a total cutoff [of Egyptian crossing forces]. They weren't all destroyed. Some are second and third class bridges. Three of the bridges for tank crossing were missed, and others [the Egyptians] are repairing."[41]

During the night, the IAF attacked only critical targets with loft bombing "until the middle of the night," said Peled, to the extent the air force felt it was necessary. (How exactly was the air force supposed to feel this?) In planning the morning's action, he ordered another attack on the bridges to confirm that they had been knocked out; then he would provide the ground forces with assistance.

Although Elazar had already formulated the basic concept of the counterattack while at Dvela, the IAF and CCP received no update on this important operation in Southern Command until 21:00, despite Dayan's indication that if the IDF launched a large-scale attack on the canal, the air force would have to contribute all the strength it could muster. Dayan added that if the IAF's order of battle remained free and dispatched to the Golan Heights, he would not oppose it.

In the 00:30 operational discussion group, Elazar presented an update on the morning's counterattack. Peled said the air force could allot sixty planes to Southern Command for the whole day.[42]

The IAF's Role in the Counterattack

In the operational discussion group on the night before the counterattack, the chief of staff decided that 162nd and 143rd Divisions would attack with artillery concentrations and a concerted air effort (including cluster bombs) to clean out the enemy infantry armed with antitank missiles. The IAF plan, as it crystallized in the CCP at 03:04, a few hours before the attack, assigned thirty-three pairs of fighters to the Egyptian front. Seven planes would take part in the first flight—bombing seven bridges. This would be followed by a quartet of four-aircraft formations every half hour.

Independent of the counterattack, the air force continued its attempts to destroy the bridges, employing both loft and pop-up tactics. Its efforts, however, were in vain. Peled described the IAF's achievements that day and their impact on the ground forces' ability to hang on: "We had to stop the enemy armor from crossing to the eastern bank on the night of October 8 so that our forces could retain Artillery Road. Without precise information on the bridges' whereabouts . . . the air force set out to destroy them between 13:30 and nightfall. . . . The report on the bridges' elimination prevented the chief of staff from ordering a withdrawal to Lateral Road."[43] All Peled's statements regarding the IAF's destruction of the bridges and its contribution to the ground forces' effort to hold the line at Artillery Road were patently false.

After the gut-wrenching failure of the counterattack and the realization that this was more than the "seventh day" of the Six-Day War, GHQ planners began to recalibrate how best to employ the air force. Elazar finally realized that the main air effort had to be redirected to support the ground forces. Tal agreed that the airfields' destruction was superfluous and that the IAF's order of battle should be allocated to ground assistance. Based on these understandings, the chief of staff set the following day's priorities: the air effort would relieve pressure on the ground forces and give them breathing space and time to reorganize. He ordered Peled to focus on economic targets and to keep his warplanes out of harm's way. "If there's enough strength, we'll attack just two airfields." In a discussion with the chief of staff on Monday evening, the prevailing understanding was that the air force's scattered sorties on October 8 had been a failure. Elazar updated those present on his agreement with Peled: between 05:00 and 10:00–10:30 the air force would send three or four squadrons to relentlessly and massively pound the Egyptian force between the artillery line and the canal; it would avoid attacks against lone tanks. The attack would take place in three sectors according to the crossing areas: Kantara, Firdan, and Hamezach. He also presented Peled's conclusion that IAF planes had disrupted tank crossings overnight and forced the enemy to transfer its ammunition by boat. Elazar informed those present of the air commander's insistence on allotting sixty Phantoms to attack Egyptian airfields the next morning.[44]

Beginning on Monday evening, the air force adopted a new tactic: specialized squadrons in specific sectors. This was a definite improvement in the use of its air potential. At 21:35 a sector attack was ordered for the next day. Each squadron had responsibility for a particular focal point, and each formation consisted of a single plane that would execute a loft bombing and a pair of planes that would carry out a pop-up bombing two minutes after the loft bombing aircraft released its ordnance.

Elazar Halts the Attack on the Bridges

On Tuesday the air force conducted 350 sorties in the southern sector against infantry, armored concentrations, bridges, and enemy forces south of Mitla Road, south of Karat Moora, in the Wadi Mabrook sector, on Yoreh and Pgisha Roads, north of Ras Sudar, and in Ein Musa—the area's missile-packed perimeter. (During the war, the air force adapted its attack method in missile-packed areas to include high-altitude pop-up bombing.) But on Tuesday evening, in view of the IAF's losses on the canal that day, the chief of staff called off the attack, despite Peled's opposition. The IAF commander reported that the air force was damaging bridges and that the loss of four or five aircraft in the course of hundreds of sorties was not so terrible. He claimed that the Phantoms were incapacitating the bridges and destroying everything between Artillery Road and the canal. Harlev, the head of air intelligence, had a more sober view: "We aren't eliminating the bridges. At least three of them are still active. Supplies are being moved to the eastern bank in boats while the bridges serve mainly as a conduit for tanks."[45]

In a private talk with Elazar that evening (but in the presence of assistants), Dayan voiced his dissatisfaction with some of the current commanders and said that he preferred the old guard: Bar-Lev and the IAF's Hod and Tolkovsky. The next day Bar-Lev was given command of the southern front. There were plans afoot to replace Peled, too, but they were ditched.

The IAF Approaches the "Red Line"

At 21:00 on October 9, Peled presented his aircraft inventory: the IAF had entered the war with 320 warplanes; 55 had been lost, and 45 had been damaged but would be operable within two weeks. The following morning the IAF would have 220 fighters, including 55 Phantoms. The IAF commander recommended cutting back on air activity because of the rapid rate of attrition in both material and manpower. Elazar agreed. In reality, the IAF's active order of battle on the morning of October 10 was 258 planes.

On October 11 Peled estimated that on the following day, the IAF would be able to muster 240 top-of-the-line aircraft. But during the chief of staff's situational assessment on October 12, Peled claimed that the IAF would have 233 aircraft that morning: 50 Phantoms, 110 Skyhawks, and 63 planes for interception and protection (simple arithmetic reveals that the total was 223, not 233). He made it clear that at the current rate of attrition, the order of battle would reach a critical point of 220 planes the next day, which was too few to enable an offensive and just enough to provide defense in the heart of the country. His figures had a major impact on Israel's acceptance of a cease-fire.[46]

Senior IAF officers are at a loss to explain Peled's figures. According to Major General Avihu Ben-Nun (Ret.), IAF commander from 1987 to 1992, Peled may have omitted the French combat planes in his count. Major General David Ivry (Ret.) claimed that Peled tried to incentivize the ground forces by omitting the planes undergoing repair from the number of operable aircraft. According to Brigadier General Yiftach Spector (Ret.), Peled told him after the war: "That's right, I [Peled] gave that number, but what I meant was that the IDF should stop jerking off and get on with the crossing. If you wait around a few more days, that's all the planes I'll have left."[47]

After the war, Peled admitted that he had been trying to alert the prime minister to the fact that time was running out and an immediate decision to cross the canal had to be made, without waiting for more tanks to reach the front. According to Peled, the IAF had 330 planes, and at the loss rate of 6 to 8 a day, the situation was becoming perilous. "I said I could wait until we had 220 planes left, but after that I wouldn't be able to provide the crossing effort with serious assistance. . . . We didn't reach the 'red line' until the end of the war."[48]

The commanders' meeting on the afternoon of October 14 convened at a critical moment in Southern Command and at a turning point in the war in the south: the IDF had just smashed the Egyptian offensive that morning. Not a word was said about the Egyptian attack and its significance for the next day's crossing. What was discussed was the lack of war aims.

Flaws in the IAF's Performance

The Egyptian air defense system, which had been established on the canal at the end of the War of Attrition, posed a daunting challenge to the IAF. It represented a tangible threat to its freedom of action and to Southern Command's defensive and offensive plans, at least with regard to support for the ground forces. The air force focused on training, developing a warfare doctrine, producing weapons to eliminate surface-to-air missiles, attacking airfields, and engaging in dogfights. However, many scholars claim that even after the War of Attrition, the IAF overlooked the true significance of Egypt's and Syria's air defense reinforcement and the optimal methods of dealing with it, and it failed to adapt to changes in the region. Pilots were confronted with a multitude of missiles that covered the range of effective flight altitudes: SA2s, SA3s, SA6s, SA7s, and ZSU 23X4 or ZSU 57X2 antiaircraft cannon. With the number of planes being hit, the IAF commander was compelled to drastically limit the type of attacks (loft and pop-up bombings) and the approaches to the canal (only up to fifteen miles)—limitations that seriously impaired the attacks' effectiveness and rattled the pilots' concentration. In other words, the effort to survive the air defense systems detracted from the IAF's performance and rendered its achievements inferior to what had been accomplished in training.[49]

Failure to Adapt to the Enemy's New Air Defenses

The question lingers: was the IAF fully aware of the changes in the enemy's air defenses and the need to find practical solutions? Some of the answers lie behind an intentional haze of casuistry and verbal dissimulation, depending on the identity of the inquirer and the answerer. At any rate, if there were doubts about the IAF's absolute ability—and there were—they dissipated over time with self-assured declarations such as "the regulars [and the IAF] will hold!" and other vague assertions. In his analysis of the IDF's internalization of the missile threat in 1967, Peled listed the flaws in the operational use of the IAF that had taken root between the Six-Day War and Yom Kippur War, and he found that plans had been built on flimsy, unsubstantiated assumptions.

According to Zeira, the head of intelligence during the war, neither the chief of staff nor the defense minister discerned the catastrophic clash between an inflexible defense concept and the changes in the strategic situation produced by the missile array. No one imagined that the IAF would be incapable of carrying out its mission in the holding stage and that, until the missiles were destroyed, the ground forces would be bereft of air support. Only when an Egyptian or Syrian land army advanced beyond the missile umbrella would the air force be able to take full advantage of its power to assist the ground forces. This limitation, Zeira claimed, was neither emphasized nor understood.[50]

In a booklet entitled *Close Air Support to the Ground and Naval Forces* (prepared before the war by the Instruction Department and printed in 1974), there was no mention of surface-to-air missiles as an "influencing" factor in providing assistance to the ground forces. A few lines were devoted to antiaircraft fire capable of neutralizing the value of close air support because of the risk of aircraft loss, but the issue received scant attention in light of the lessons of the War of Attrition. The IAF, however, was definitely limited in its ability to deal with the missiles and lacked an answer for every situation. First the Egyptians and then the Syrians constructed a vast antiaircraft missile system, but the IDF war-fighting doctrine continued to be based on IAF firepower.

Tal expressed the situation best: "We should have realized that because of the anti-aircraft missiles, we couldn't rely on the air force as a source of firepower in a ground battle. We didn't see this coming . . . and we bet all our stakes on the air force. As for the application of ground fire, during the war the air force destroyed no more than a hundred tanks." Even before the war, Tal had harbored doubts about the air force's ability to operate in the air defense environment of Egypt and Syria. He was the first in the GHQ forum to bring attention to the strategic significance of the Syrians' beefed-up antiaircraft missiles in September 1973 and suggested eliminating them in a preemptive strike. (This ran contrary to the chief of staff's statement that the Syrian missiles did not affect the IAF's ability to "finish off" the Syrians in half a day.) According to Tal, ideas were raised in the "Ofek" discussions regarding the status of aircraft in wartime, and they were also broached in GHQ discussions on September 24 and October 1, 1973. Doubts were cast on the air force's ability to fulfill expectations in view of the enemy's enormous antiaircraft capabilities. Some were concerned that the warplane would lose its exalted status and become a mere tactical weapon. Tal went so far as to bring up the failure of the Shrike missile attack in September 1971. (Twelve Shrikes were launched against Egyptian missile batteries after the downing of an IDF Stratocruiser east of the canal, but only one hit its target. All the rest overshot their targets because the Egyptians, who were expecting the attack, had shut off the batteries' radar, which the missiles were homed in on.) "These were red lights," Tal stated. "But they didn't 'goad' anyone and they continued to fight tooth and nail over the air force's budget [claiming that] it was justified that the lion's share of the budget should go to them."[51] Anyone who dared to suggest that the IAF might not be able to carry out its mission was all but lynched. Peled had this to say: "When the Egyptians try to cross the canal—that's when the IAF will repay all the dividends, to the last cent that you're crying over today for investing in us. This will be payback time."[52]

According to Tal, the IDF found itself impotent in the air because it ignored the limitations of airpower under the new conditions. The warning signals were already flashing during the War of Attrition, but the IAF failed to perceive that something essential had changed and that it was losing some of its ability to provide close tactical fire support to the ground battle. The IDF continued to believe that in the future it could count on the air force's overwhelming firepower, which was greater than that of all the Arab armies combined. The painful awakening came in the Yom Kippur War. Ironically, at the IDF's most trying hour on the battlefield, when it desperately needed the IAF's decisive air superiority and overwhelming firepower, the air force no longer had the strength to serve as "flying artillery" for the ground forces. Tal stated that in this war, the IDF lost its superior firepower in the tactical land battle, and the balance of power shifted from the Israeli warplane to Egyptian and Syrian artillery. As early as the May 19, 1973, operational discussion group, Tal had said he "didn't think that the situation in the air would be in our favor if the enemy's on the offensive. But if we gain air superiority and destroy the missiles, then there probably wouldn't be an offensive."[53]

The Syrians and Egyptians, unlike the Israelis, were well aware of the ramifications of their new missile systems, and they planned their military moves accordingly. The Egyptian and Syrian territorial goals did not extend beyond the reach of their missiles. The IAF's decimation of Egypt's Mechanized Brigade No. 1 the moment it headed south to Ras Sudar and stepped outside the range of the Egyptian missiles was the clearest example of the effectiveness of that defensive air umbrella (a negative one, from the Egyptians' viewpoint).

Had the IDF and the government realized from the first hour of the war that the IAF was unable to assist the ground forces and that a new strategic situation existed on the Egyptian and Syrian fronts, they probably would have reassessed their methods of defending the canal and abandoned the defensive positions on the waterline in favor of a mobile defense. As it turned out, the failure to absorb the changes in the combat theater meant that no one had prepared an operational scenario that addressed reality, and the upshot was that the IAF failed to destroy the missiles.

Before the war, the IAF commander had argued that the Egyptian air defense system called for a basic rethinking of plans, as the IAF would not be free to foil an Egyptian offensive until the missiles were completely eliminated. None of this penetrated the consciousness of the ground commanders. The chief of staff shared Peled's view but remained cryptic, whereas Dayan still believed the IAF could stop an Egyptian offensive.

According to Major General Ben-Nun (Ret.), it was obvious that the situation had changed. On July 18, 1970, at the height of the War of Attrition, the Israelis had launched an attack against the missiles on the canal. The plan called for the IAF's entire order of battle to destroy the enemy's ground forces and artillery immediately after the first air attack. But the air commander canceled the plan after the planes of the two squadron leaders spearheading the attack were hit: Lieutenant Colonel Shmuel Hetz's aircraft was downed (Hetz was killed), and Ben-Nun's plane was damaged. Drills for missile evasion, Ben-Nun noted, had been planned and adapted for the SA2 but not for the SA3, which was a smaller missile and was initially mistaken for an SA2. After the failed attack in July, the IAF waged a daily battle against the missiles and scored some successes. The squadrons, however, were furious over the lack of response to the Egyptians' brazen advance of the missile system after the cease-fire. Ben-Nun explained that the experience gained and the lessons learned in the War of Attrition were applied in drills and in devising a combat doctrine, but effective countermeasures were not ready when the Yom Kippur War broke out (they were ready by the time of the 1982 Lebanon War, where they attained superb results).

According to Ivry, at the end of the War of Attrition in August 1970, the IAF lacked a solution for the combined SA2-SA3-SA6 missile array. Although the Egyptians brought the missile batteries forward after the cease-fire, no one pressed for an attack. Everyone, including the air force, was exhausted, and the missile challenge went unanswered. Throughout the cease-fire, the IAF searched for a standoff weapon that could open "corridors" and provide access from the rear, but budgetary constraints precluded the development of an electro-optical device that could relay a picture from the missile to the cockpit. Ivry recalled that the IAF tried the pods employed by the U.S. Air Force in Vietnam, but they were not well suited to the IAF, and the air force felt insecure about challenging the missiles.[54] According to Forman, during the three years of the cease-fire, the IAF developed a makeshift concept that failed to provide serious answers when the war erupted in October 1973.

When war broke out, it was obvious that the air force had failed to come up with something different; it was still fixated on the "big show" scenario in which the entire order of battle attacked the enemy missiles in a deliberate, large-scale, meticulously planned action based on the Six-Day War model. It failed to adapt to the initial conditions of the Yom Kippur War and was psychologically incapable of diverting the order of battle to quality ground targets, even when it was free to do so on October 6, after Meir vetoed even a limited preemptive attack on the airfields in the heart of Syria.

Against the background of these plans—and their limitations—incisive comments from a number of senior IAF officers stressed the link between ground support and destruction of the missiles. Spector noted:

> [There was an] absence of standoff weapons in 1973 to offset the missiles, though there was sufficient force to annihilate the missile layout, albeit at a heavy cost to the IAF. Statistically, the price tag was one aircraft lost for every battery destroyed; in other words thirty Phantoms down for thirty batteries eliminated. In Egypt, with "Tagar" 4 we would have had a free air zone, though that still wouldn't have guaranteed victory over the Egyptians. The 1967 model didn't repeat itself in 1973. In Syria, with "Dugman" 5 the problem was finding the mobile S6 batteries. In any case the IAF wouldn't have destroyed the Syrians' mobile missiles. The air force's warfighting doctrine for attacking missiles—a huge, massive, sophisticated, complex operation against static missile batteries—ignored the SA6s whose mobility required altering the entire warfighting concept.

Spector claimed that Tagar and Dugman interfered with the lead pilots' ability to maneuver and make lightning-quick decisions. The correct method should have been more like a dogfight, in which the pilots are unencumbered by a tight formation. The whereabouts of the missile batteries in Dugman made a shambles of all the plans, forcing the pilots to scuttle around the danger zone hunting for the batteries. According to Spector, the combat exercises developed by Squadron 107 (which he commanded during the war) in July 1973 to deal with the SA6s did away with the need for a large-scale operation, such as utilizing the entire IAF for Tagar and Dugman.[55]

Forman claimed that Dugman 5 contained an inherent flaw: it was based on air reconnaissance photographs taken a few hours prior to the attack, whereas SA6s could be moved around (as they most certainly were). Yet this possibility never entered the operational concept. The overriding faith was that the destruction of the heavy SA2 and SA3 batteries would somehow facilitate the attack on the SA6s. The flaw embedded in Tagar 4 was the concept that the thirty-six to thirty-eight SA6 batteries on the canal did not have to be destroyed—that it would be enough to damage them so the warplanes could enter the fighting zone with minimal exposure. Forman believed that Ben-Nun's offensive concept—an attack with 100 aircraft without exploiting the Israeli pilots' skill at improvisation and target change—was too rigid. "We held fast to the concept of the massive assault."[56]

Major General Amos Yadlin (Ret.) noted the unrealistic timetable the IAF commander presented to the defense minister at 06:00 on October 6. It allowed only one hour to destroy the Syrian air force and a few more hours to eradicate the missile batteries.

According to Brigadier General Amos Amir (Ret.), who would eventually replace Forman, Tagar was superfluous for the same reason that Dugman was a mistake. The IDF's major problem was the Syrian tanks on the Golan Heights, not the missiles that were being shunted from place to place (making air reconnaissance photographs useless). In Amir's opinion, the focus should have been on destroying the bridgeheads on October 7 or attacking the bridging equipment and troop crossings.[57]

Focus on the Missile Threat

Fear of the antiaircraft missile had a negative impact on the IAF's fighting spirit. At the end of the War of Attrition, a concept crystallized that influenced the amount of risk the IAF's senior command was willing to take in offensive air-to-ground operations and in attacking the missiles. This concept had dire consequences, as evidenced by the performance of IAF planners and pilots in actual combat in 1973. Peled noted that the War of Attrition ended before the air force had a chance to recover and formulate a solution to the missile problem. From that moment on, antiaircraft missiles dominated the IAF's doctrine and planning departments.

The air force asked for and received generous funding to find a solution to the missile threat. The result was the sophisticated operational plans—Tagar and Dugman—for the total destruction of the missile array. These plans, which took precedence over air superiority, participation in ground combat, and strategic combat, could have succeeded if they had been carried out in a coordinated manner under optimal conditions:

- A six-hour planning period before H hour (with the joint participation of helicopters, EW, deception, chaff dispersion, and so forth).
- One or two days to complete the destruction of one missile layout on one of the fronts, without massive participation in the ground fighting.
- A ratio of one aircraft lost for each battery destroyed. The attacking force would consist solely of Phantoms.

The Agranat Commission, which took great pains to limit its questioning of the IAF's wartime activities, concluded that even if the tactical flaws in close air support were not completely known to the chief of staff until the outbreak of the war, he should have been aware of the strategic shortcomings stemming from the appearance of Russian missiles in 1970. Close air support, considered second in importance after the protection of Israel's airspace, was relegated to third place in 1970, when destruction of the enemy's air defense system assumed the second spot on the list of priorities.[58]

The missiles, Spector stressed, were merely a nuisance that hampered Israeli planes from reaching their primary targets—the enemy's army and weapons—easily and safely. The missile batteries forced the IAF to engage in irksome fighting and squander its limited supply of invaluable warplanes. Since the Yom Kippur War, Spector noted, planes no longer seemed effective against the enemy's vast number of targets, even when air superiority was acquired or massive destruction on the battlefield was attained. He also questioned the impact of the missiles' elimination on the Syrians' and Egyptians' will to fight. Egypt's airfields did not have to be targeted, he noted; attacking them was superfluous to the battle itself. In the Six-Day War, the destruction of the airfields had been of no strategic value; its effect had been psychological. The sight of the burning airfields had penetrated Nasser's and Egypt's consciousness, and every soldier had understood the significance. The Yom Kippur War was a different story. Attacking the airfields would not undermine the Egyptians, whereas hitting the symbols of government would. In 1973 the missiles were less of a determining factor than in the past; they were not an insurmountable obstacle for the IAF. When targets were clearly marked—even those in high-risk areas saturated with missiles—they were bombed around the clock.

Peled claimed that Dugman 5 failed because most of the aircraft fired on the wrong sites (based on intelligence collected three to four hours earlier), and the IAF was unaware that Syrian armor was sitting on the Phantoms' approach lanes. In this case, the pilots' dedication to mission was flawed.

Yadlin stressed that the air force never gained air superiority. By the end of the war, forty out of sixty or seventy batteries had been destroyed—that is, one-third of them by the ground forces, and one-third by the IAF. The air force's strategic impact was a case of too little, too late. It also failed to create a strategic effect by wiping out the enemy air forces on the ground.[59]

Failure to Execute Bendigo

Bendigo, the joint artillery–air force operation to destroy missile batteries, was not carried out. Gonen justifiably attributed great importance to this operation, and in the war summary, he regretted this omission and noted that it had been a condition for employing the IAF in Dovecote. Southern Command invested a great effort in the preliminary planning stages of Bendigo, and it agreed to allocate one artillery battery for each missile battery. (Another reason that Bendigo required joint planning with the air force was that the Skyhawks could not correct artillery fire.) The operation seemingly fell by the wayside in the rush of events during the first two days of fighting. Furthermore, the artillery group that was supposed to play a pivotal role in Bendigo was not mobilized in the early call-up. The chief of staff apparently did not consider Bendigo a critical element in the elimination of the missiles. After the war, he referred to it as an operation that may or may not have been executed.

When the air force executed Tagar 4 on Sunday morning—before the operation was halted and most of the air support was diverted north—252nd Division's artillery group was not a participant. Even if it had been ordered to take part, it would have been unable to comply because there was no joint planning between the IAF and Southern Command, and most of the artillery units had leapfrogged out of range of the missile batteries. Later, Peled noted that the artillery had been very successful in hitting the missile batteries in Northern Command, unlike in Southern Command (his reasoning, based on Gandhi's interpretation, was wrong).

After crossing the canal, the artillery scored considerable successes, although it was used too late and too haphazardly against the missile bases. Between October 20 and 22 it crippled eight missile batteries north of the city of Suez. Taking part in this late execution of Bendigo were 155mm and 175mm cannon of 209th Artillery Group/252nd Division.[60] The ground forces (421st Brigade/143rd Division, units of 162nd Division, and 252nd Division's artillery) knocked out more batteries on the western bank in six days of fighting than the air force did in the entire war in Egypt. Thus, the ground forces opened a corridor of action for the warplanes—a corridor that continued to expand until the IAF attained almost total control over the western bank.[61]

Amir repeated to the author what he had heard in the CCP when it was discovered that the ground forces were destroying the missile sites on the western bank: "Those blockheads from armor are screwing us out of our missiles." Even Peled saw the ground forces' destruction of the missile batteries as a personal and professional affront: "He [Major General Herzog] says [in commentary on television] . . . that armor had to buy air superiority for the air force so that I'd have something to work with. First of all I find this is very insulting and utterly incorrect."

The ground offensive damaged the missile sites and forced the enemy to scurry off to other positions. Between October 18 and 24 the IDF's accomplishments on the western bank were the result of combined-arms tactics. The ground forces attacked the missile batteries, which in turn enabled the air force to support the ground forces.

Wrong Priorities

According to the IAF's priorities, the destruction of the missiles (followed by the elimination of the Arab air forces) would take about forty-eight hours, and only then would the ground forces receive air assistance. However, in the absence of a genuine dialogue, this concept was not fully internalized, and the ground commanders got wind of it only fragmentarily. Given the adverse conditions at the outset of hostilities, the veto on a preemptive strike, the thinning out of the regulars' order of battle on the contact lines, and the delayed call-up of the reservists—conditions the chief of staff should have been aware of—Elazar should have issued a change of orders at dawn on October 6 or at least ordered the execution of Scratch. Yet Elazar continued to believe that the priorities he had approved on the morning of October 6—ground support in third place—were correct.

In April 1976, two and a half years after the war, Elazar still perceived air support of the ground forces in an area bristling with missiles as unreasonable. "The idea that the air force can ward off an offensive singlehandedly just with the regulars is only in the event of a surprise or catastrophe. This was never the intention." But from the ground forces' point of view, this was precisely the situation on the morning of October 6, and Elazar should have known it. In any case, preference was given to attacking the airfields and missiles rather than employing Scratch or assaulting strategic targets such as bridging and crossing equipment on the western bank.

On Saturday evening, October 6, in light of the situation on the canal, the defense minister expressed one of the major dilemmas of the war in the south and set forth a different set of priorities for the air force:

> I'm skeptical about the IAF's chances of destroying the missiles. On the other hand, we're facing two nights and one critical day of Egyptian armor forces crossing the canal. As I see it, the IAF has to forget the attack on the missile batteries and do everything it can to stop the transfer of Egyptian tanks into Sinai and even if it costs us aircraft. If the IAF focuses on the missile batteries and fails—then we lose either way. In the meantime tanks will be crossing the canal

and conditions will be such that the IAF is without freedom of action.[62]

But the defense minister was a political authority, and the issue was a technical-operational one. The decision remained in the hands of the chief of staff and IAF commander. Dayan, of course, was correct. But on October 6, after the surprise resumption of hostilities, this was not the same feisty, self-assured Moshe Dayan of the past. The blow to his self-confidence and "having his feathers plucked" impaired his ability to force his opinion on others.

The IAF commander in the Six-Day War, Major General Motti Hod (Ret.), also affirmed that destroying the enemy's missiles and airfields should not have been the priority. Many of the losses the air force suffered resulted from the decision that the proper response to the Syrian and Egyptian attack was to attack their airfields. But according to Hod, "in October 1973 there was no need for this because the Arab air forces were not the problem and it was unfortunate to waste the effort on bombing the airfields. On the Golan Heights there were only twelve casualties from air attacks in all of that terrible war in which hundreds of men were killed in tank battles. . . . The misguided use of the air force inhibited it from realizing its potential on the two fronts in their most critical hours."[63]

Was ground support in the event of a surprise attack taken into consideration? Gonen did not think so. The ground forces and the IAF were not prepared for that scenario. "We never analyzed the possibility or thought about what we'd do if the [Egyptians] suddenly leapt up and crossed the canal, and whether the air force could help."[64] Regarding the IAF's limitations in the event of a surprise attack, Peled said that everyone expected the requisite conditions for fighting to be realized, but they were not. The conclusion: The state's defense must not be built on conditions that cannot be guaranteed by those who promise them.[65] A scenario involving a warning of only a few hours was never taken into account; nor was the Scratch option discussed or analyzed.

The complacency among military and security forces, combined with the blind faith that the regulars would hold, created an existential danger on October 6. The IAF has a long history of basing its operational priorities on a sectoral perspective or even an attitude of "we know what's best for the IDF and ground forces." The problem is that the IDF, including the chief of staff, and government officials are generally unversed in the nuances of air matters; therefore, they generally acquiesce in whatever the air force proposes.

The Decision to Scrap Scratch

Colonel Shmuel Gordon (Ret.), a Phantom pilot in the war, claimed that Scratch was fully ready to go, but it was not. Targets and routes could have been prepared in the squadron and relayed to the pilots in flight, based on the latest air photos from October 5 and 6. However, Scratch was not mentioned in the air force's support order on October 6, even though the squadrons had already received operational orders, communications orders, ordnance orders, and so forth. If Motti Hod had been the IAF commander, Gordon observed, he would have given the order: "Execute Scratch!" But no one brought up Scratch in the chief of staff's operational discussion group at 18:30 on October 6.[66]

In contrast, Colonel Shefer (Ret.), the air adviser in Southern Command, asserted that Scratch was only a skeleton order for defense and had to be worked out in detail and coordinated with the greens for concrete ground action. He claimed that Scratch's communications and support systems did not meet the operational needs for issuing commands or relaying targets. According to Shefer, "We couldn't provide any services for Southern Command."[67] These are excuses, from an observer's point of view. What type of concrete ground action did Shefer expect in the maelstrom of October 6? Unfortunately, complaints about the lack of coordination and deficient communications systems have regularly served as excuses for the IAF's failure to carry out Scratch in the emergency situation that existed on October 6. It is not clear to what extent Shefer went the extra mile to ensure that Southern Command would get air assistance, despite all the hurdles.

According to Spector, Scratch was a legitimate plan that had been drilled, but it was not focused and was based on the dispersal of air activity along lines. Ivry, Peled's deputy in the war, explained that the concept was based on Tagar and Dugman. "They tried to go back to 'Tagar' and 'Dugman' but it was impossible because all the time were cries for SOS. We took some elements from 'Scratch'—nighttime attacks on the bridges—for example. Some were used, but not as a complete operational concept. The air force kept the skies clean above Sinai, bagging a couple of helicopters ferrying commandos in the process. This *was* the IAF's success in blocking the Egyptians." In Ivry's opinion, the IAF never received the credit it deserved for its contribution in the war.[68]

In a commanders' briefing on Friday, October 5, Peled said this about Scratch: "If we err and war catches us by surprise tonight and the enemy invades Sinai, which is nearly void of forces, we won't be able to wait until we've eliminated the missiles to carry out air-ground operations. We have to be prepared to enter the fire zone before attacking the missiles. It was for this likelihood that the 'Scratch' plan was devised." Tal confirmed this: "A thousand times the chief of staff and Benny [Peled] said . . . that if the ground forces are in trouble we'll provide them with air support before dealing with the missiles. Everyone's on the highest state of alert . . . and the air force, from the minute the preemptive strike is cancelled . . . will prepare for defense on the ground and in the air."[69]

In reality, the IAF made little effort to carry out Scratch, as demanded by the disastrous turn of events on Saturday. The air force decided not to jeopardize its planes on third-rate missions whose execution was liable to upset the next day's Tagar and Dugman plans. In this way, it catered to narrow sectoral interests rather than addressing the IDF's all-encompassing needs in an extreme situation. Because of the pressure of events, Southern and Northern Commands were probably unaware of their "right" to receive air assistance and did not bang on tables to obtain it.

The defense minister and chief of staff were not willing to order the IAF to carry out this crucial mission, which now topped the IDF's list of priorities. The fact that the IAF could be "bent" had been proved when the chief of staff canceled Tagar on Sunday morning— a legitimate but erroneous decision—and shifted to Dugman. Elazar, like Dayan, was convinced that this was the correct move, given his overview of the two-front war. The excuses raised by Shefer mirror the IAF's wish to stay out of the holding battle—the most urgent problem on October 6 and 7—and use its resources for its own priorities: destroying the enemy's air forces and missiles.

Peled's decision on Saturday afternoon to change the Phantoms' ordnance configuration was not intended to preclude the execution of Scratch. The Skyhawks could have been used on this mission (instead, they conducted sporadic sorties that accomplished nothing and incurred heavy losses). In this emergency, the Phantoms that had not yet changed their ordnance to air defense could have been employed to attack ground targets, but this was not done. In these chaotic conditions, the air force was mainly involved in preparing for the implementation of Tagar and Dugman (in addition to providing air defense and interception) on Sunday morning. The scant air-to-ground support it did provide on October 6–7 was inappreciable and resulted in a heavy loss of aircraft. Therefore, Peled may have judged Scratch (or part of it) to have no operational value.

In 1976 Ben-Nun bluntly and accurately expressed what the IAF really thought about Scratch on Saturday, notwithstanding Peled's remarks about its importance. When asked why Scratch had not been presented to the chief of staff, Ben-Nun answered: "When the air force presents plans, it doesn't present a plan that's bad for the air force. . . . Its job isn't to present every plan as though there's no alternative. Its job isn't to give the chief of staff an opportunity not to call up reservists so that I can wear out the IAF." He continued: "The chief of staff may have figured that the probability of fire breaking out in May was small and told the prime minister that in such an event he would take the risk that if war did erupt, he would hold the enemy back with the air force, knowing that it ran counter to the accepted application of the IAF, but it was preferable to mobilizing the reserves." Ben-Nun explained that the reason for the nonexecution of Scratch on October 6–7 was that it entailed a division of labor. It was a concept rather than a contingency plan, and it was not based on a missile-packed environment. In his opinion, Scratch could have been integrated as a deliberate plan after air superiority had been attained (Tagar), which would have taken a few hours. But if it had been attempted without destroying the missiles, it would have been suicide. If the missile targets had been assigned, then Scratch could have been carried out, even in an area crammed with missiles. Many senior airmen used this excuse to explain the IAF's failure to provide air assistance to the ground forces.[70]

The bitterest criticism of the failure to execute Scratch came from Motti Hod, who called it a terrible mistake by the IAF commander. Hod claimed that the IDF had no illusions about what might happen if it were caught by surprise. The air force prepared exactly for such a situation by devising the Scratch plan, which had been updated two or three months before the war. Yet, despite the surprise attack, it decided to take out the missiles first. Hod explained:

When the war began, the air force forgot about the "Scratch" plan and decided to attack the airfields. There's no logical explanation why it was forgotten and why the air force thought that hitting the airfields would have an effect on the Syrian-Egyptian surprise. The faulty thinking on the eve of the Yom Kippur War was that when the air force was denied permission [for a preemptive strike] it should have . . . informed all its forces to prepare for "Scratch" beginning at a certain hour. "Scratch" meant attacking the Syrian and Egyptian combat structure before the start of the war. They were not in defensive deployment, they were in massive concentrations, and the air force had a plan to attack these concentrations . . . without taking into account the defense layouts. "Scratch" was built on the technique that the attack could be conducted beneath the missile cover so it would avoid getting hit by missiles and only suffer minimum losses. . . . Its ordnance included a large number of small-sized bombs for [maximum] area coverage. This was the first flaw in the rationale, and as a result the entire IDF was caught by surprise and "Scratch" could not be executed. . . . Three hours were needed for its preparation, and the minute this didn't happen . . . [the IAF] was caught with munitions that were unsuited for anything. . . . All the rest that happened in the war was the consequence of this blunder—an error in planning and then performance that went awry.

After the war I took the "Scratch" plan and simulated it for "H" hour, 14:00, when the shells began falling, as though "Scratch" had been ordered in this stage, and checked what would have happened if all of the planes had been armed for "Scratch" and received the order only when the first shell landed. The result was entirely different. It was much more suited to our situation and would have caused us much less heartache and loss than what we incurred in the war. The IAF could have dealt with all of the Syrian and Egyptian brigades like it knows how, when it has air superiority—and it had air superiority throughout the war, even without attacking the airfields. This could have been done much better, much quicker, and at a much lower price. . . . There was flawed thinking in the situation that Israel stumbled into on the eve of the Yom Kippur War and there was defective, mistaken application of the air force.[71]

Failure to Meet the Ground Forces' Unrealistic Expectations

Southern Command's ground forces had unrealistic expectations of the IAF. As a result, they believed that despite the Egyptians' surprise attack, the air force would immediately enter the defensive battle as the main element until the reservists arrived and assist in achieving a stunning operational decision. Southern Command failed to internalize the chief of staff's caveat when he outlined the IAF's operational plans in April 1973: close air support would be provided only after the main objective—Tagar—had been attained. Given the IAF's strength and versatility, leaders in Southern Command thought the reservists might not even be needed for defense, and some of the regulars could be employed in limited offensive actions until the reservists arrived to assist in the development of a major offensive on the western bank. These unrealistic expectations stemmed from a number of factors:

- Unsubstantiated faith in the IAF's tremendous firepower, without taking into consideration its drawbacks and limitations on October 6.
- The absence of a meaningful dialogue and a harmonious working relationship between the air force and the ground forces. Joint planning and approval of plans for support were nonexistent at both the GSO and command levels. The IAF submitted its plans only to the chief of staff; they were hidden from almost every outside element, including the forces designated to receive its assistance. Because of the IAF's obsession with compartmentalization, even Gonen was asked to step out of the room when it presented Bendigo to Southern Command. (Compartmentalization is a phenomenon that still exists to some degree in the IDF, and it is expressed by a supercilious attitude among certain IAF personnel toward the greens because of the latter's so-called nonunderstanding of issues involved in the use of airpower. Recent years have witnessed an improvement in this attitude.)
- Without a defense plan for Western Sinai, no one compiled a list of forces and missions, professional appendixes, and so forth. The air force did not prepare such a plan and was not asked to carry one out. The IAF never clarified how and according to what schedules it would achieve an operational

decision in a defensive battle. The answer to this question remained vague and undetermined among the IAF, the commands, and GHQ.

- Before the war, ambiguity and redundancy characterized the chief of staff's various statements about the IAF's role in the holding stage and how much time would elapse before it could turn its attention to assisting the ground forces. This lack of clarity continued in his postwar summaries. "The IAF was always considered the prime factor in blocking [the enemy advance]. In other words, it would have to contribute to the holding stage. . . . We always assumed that the air force had to be given time to attack the missiles in Egypt and Syria."[72] Note the contradiction: the air force had to contribute to blocking the enemy, but it also needed time to secure air superiority and receive sufficient warning for its preliminary actions.

Gonen admitted he was unaware of the air force's operational limitations, and as far as he knew, he thought he could count on its assistance. No one ever told him, "The IAF can't operate, stop calling on it! They told me that the IAF was needed in the north and couldn't reach the south. . . . Let me say that the rest of the ground people were told the same thing." The chief of staff's imprecise language may have caused the newly appointed general of Southern Command to believe, blindly but not without justification, that the IAF would thwart an attack before neutralizing all the missiles. The chief of staff rejected this version of events. He saw the possibility of some form of air assistance for the ground forces if the situation became critical, but not at the expense of the primary mission. Gonen was asked whether the entire plan was based on automatic approval of an IAF preemptive strike. His answer: "Definitely, if there was a warning in time. . . . This was the foundation of the 'Dovecote' plan—that the air force needed 48 hours to attain air superiority."[73] Stating that the air force would assist in breaking an Egyptian offensive had no logical connection to the chief of staff's definition of its missions. The ground forces' expectation that the air force would act as "flying artillery" immediately created a short-circuit between the IAF's perception of its own capabilities and tasks and the ground forces' perception of them. The air force's meager contribution on October 6–7 removed an important stratum from the assumption that the regulars would hold.

On the gap in expectations between Southern Command and the IAF, Colonel Shefer avowed that brigade commanders were insufficiently aware of the air force's priorities: missiles, airfields, and then support of the ground forces. Tal conceded that no one ever checked whether 300 tanks in Sinai could block the Egyptian invasion force by themselves, without air intervention, until the reservists arrived.[74] Gonen said, "If the war begins without the reservists, and only with the regulars, then it's obvious that the air force's first priority must be to assist in blocking the Egyptian armor. I also understood that the IAF was the main element in 'Dovecote.' The air force was not just an important element, it was the key element."[75]

No operational document has been found to corroborate Gonen's presumption. However, Southern Command had no knowledge that the air force would be occupied for forty-eight hours while dealing with the missiles. In the war summaries, Gonen railed, justifiably, from the bottom of his heart: "I'm arguing and no one's listening. The air force was supposed to play the main role in the holding stage. If the chief of staff tells the ground forces 'you'll have to hang on alone . . . don't expect help from the air force' then he's speaking about our fighting morale. But, if 52% of the annual budget goes to the air force, it means that the main effort in stopping the enemy is the IAF's responsibility. This appears in many documents."[76] Tal backed Gonen's argument:

> We thought that airpower would be the defense against the crossing. Ezer Weizman, the IAF commander in the 1960s, boasted that the air force would take care of the Egyptians, block the crossing, stop them in their tracks, and make sure that they ended up "floating like shit in the canal." The IAF commanders, Weizman, Hod, and Peled said, "It's true there are areas crammed with missiles, but the air force has the answer and will neutralize the Egyptian defense layout within 48 hours [Tagar]." The IDF banked on the IAF, regarded it as all-powerful, and expected it to thwart the enemy in the north and south, obstruct the canal crossing, and find a way to attain air superiority.[77]

It should be noted that Dayan, who was capable of a 180-degree change in opinion, was not exactly thrilled by the IAF's view that missile destruction was its primary mission; he perceived, rightly so, that this was a mistake. Nevertheless, he approved the concept and, as was his custom, refrained from forcing his will. In Saturday's 12:00 government meeting, he explained that IDF's plans were not based on a preventive strike on the Egyptian front during the first night of the holding phase. In the first stage, armor—not the IAF—would deal with the crossing, although the air force might play some part in the action. The following day's plan was to hit the Syrian airfields and missiles, weather permitting.

With or without documentation, it is clear that the air force was expected to do the job. In every forum Gonen attended after the war, he contended that holding the enemy was mainly the air force's responsibility: "The air force comes over and swoops down on the Egyptians while the reservists are mobilizing. The IAF led me to believe that there'd be no crossing if Israeli planes were in the air. . . . My air advisor told me on Saturday that if the air force drops cluster bombs, the Egyptians won't be crossing. But the air force didn't come because they were busy rearming. They came at 16:30, and fell at 17:00." Gonen insisted that the air force never said to him, "We won't be able to help out in the ground battles until the missiles are destroyed."[78]

Tal called attention to the fact that "planes can't hit tanks, but airpower can paralyze an armor force by attacking its logistics bases: concentrations, deployment, and access roads. This was what was meant when they say the air force has to block the enemy, not attack every tank that's crossing the canal. . . . The Egyptian army was concentrated in a large killing zone. . . . It stood row by row on the western side of the canal. If the IAF attacked the Egyptian concentrations on the western bank . . . it meant stopping the enemy . . . and destroying the bridges too."[79]

The chief of staff saw things differently. IAF support of the ground forces was of secondary importance; interdiction was more imperative than close support. "Therefore we weren't too worried that the air force had to divert its attention to the missiles first so it could attain freedom of action." Gonen disagreed with the chief of staff and insisted that Elazar had said the air force would be the main element in blocking the enemy, especially in the event of a surprise attack. "Do you know why artillery wasn't purchased?" he asked rhetorically. "Because the air force was made up of regulars and the dividends had to be paid back."[80]

Thus Southern Command nurtured exaggerated expectations

that the IAF would hold the enemy. At the same time, the fear of dispatching the air force to attack strategic targets contributed to a situation in which the opportunity to obtain an operational decision and the ability to attain air superiority in the ground battle were unexploited.

Unrealistic Timetables

The question of how much time the air force needed until it would be free to assist the ground forces was never brought up for discussion, so the timing remained indefinite. The chief of staff expressed his concept in his summary of the Iron Ram war game in the summer of 1972: "When the crossing begins, the ground forces will have to operate with little artillery support and no air assistance for a few hours [!]. We'll hang on until the complete annihilation of the missile layout is accomplished and then we'll have freedom of action."[81] GHQ knew that destroying the missiles would require forty-eight hours, but it also knew—because the IAF had made it perfectly clear—that only one of the following missions could be carried out simultaneously: destruction of the Egyptian air force, destruction of the Syrian air force, destruction of the Egyptian missiles, or destruction of the Syrian missiles. Gonen believed the IAF would hold the line until the ground forces arrived, especially if there was no prior warning of an attack, and he claimed that Hofi and Tal also believed this.

In retrospect, this critical issue was the essence of the misunderstandings between the senior officers in Southern Command, especially Gonen, and the IAF and chief of staff. The air force assumed it would have as much time as necessary to take out the missiles before being called on to carry out interceptions or support missions. Elazar made note of the order of battle figures, but it is doubtful that he fully comprehended their implications for the regulars, who, despite their depleted state, were required to hold the line without IAF support until the reservists arrived. Locked in this illusion, he continued to convey optimism: the regulars will hold.

In reality, there was no coordinated timetable for the first stages of the war. Although Elazar was aware of the ramifications of the missile threat, his plans did not entail the immediate and massive application of airpower to repulse the invasion.[82] On the contrary, at every opportunity, he stressed that the regulars would have to manage alone for an indeterminate period. He mentioned "a few hours," which was absurd, and like the air force's involvement in the entire defensive battle, this haziness and opacity led to egregious confusion.

Before the war, the ground forces had no timetable for air support. On May 9, 1973, Dayan informed the prime minister, "In the case of a crossing attempt in the evening, it won't be the air force that deals with them. It'll be armor in the first stage. The air force will take care of the missiles the next day and this could go on for a day or two."[83] (He uttered similar statements in the government meeting at noon on Saturday, October 6, two hours before the war broke out.)

After the war, Elazar acknowledged that preparations should have been made for a ninety-six-hour wait until air support reached the ground forces. Had the IAF been given a forty-eight-hour warning before hostilities erupted, it still would have needed an additional forty-eight hours to attain air superiority; in the meantime, the ground forces would have to hold the line on their own until effective air support arrived. In other words, in the event of a surprise attack, the ground forces would have to wait four days before they received air support.

After the war, Peled was asked how much time was needed until the ground forces could be given assistance. His answer: "Our modus operandi naturally depended on the ground forces' situation and amount of time the IAF received [for preparations]. The air war against Egyptian airfields and missiles required 48 hours. If Syria joined in the fighting the air force would need 96 hours from the moment it received a warning until the air war was completed and ground assistance could be provided." The arithmetic is simple: without a warning, the IAF would need 48 hours to prepare for war (especially its EW equipment) and another 96 hours to neutralize the airfields and missiles on both fronts. Therefore, it would take 144 hours for the ground forces to receive air support. The IAF stated that, with sufficient warning time and approval of a preemptive strike, the air offensive could be launched before the enemy's H hour, and its missiles and airfields could be annihilated, at which point the IAF could provide ground support earlier than anticipated. In the spring of 1973 the air force affirmed that an aerial attack on Egypt could begin 48 hours after the order was given; in Syria, it could begin within 24 hours. However, if a 48-hour warning was received and the Rock order of battle (the reservist divisions) was mobilized, the need for air-to-ground assistance would not be as critical (compared with a situation in which the regulars had to hold the enemy alone). Again, basic arithmetic shows that in the event of a catastrophe, after 48 hours and in the dark, the air force would be able to operate only at daybreak on D day + 2, regardless of whether a preemptive strike was authorized, since it would not be able to implement one.[84]

When the IAF commander was asked how long the air force would need in a two-front war before directing its efforts to assisting the ground forces, he was sure that one day would be enough to destroy the missile array on the canal and another day to smash the Egyptian air force; the same timetable would be applicable for Syria. That is, a total of ninety-six hours would pass until the IAF could concentrate on the ground battle. Therefore, if the enemy's H hour was 18:00, as intelligence sources claimed, obliteration of the missiles could not begin earlier than Sunday morning, and air superiority would not be achieved until that evening, if not later.

If this were true, how could the chief of staff assume that the IAF would be able to thwart the crossing?[85] This question should have been brought up on the morning of October 6, and therein lies a fatal mistake in the conduct of the war. When it became clear that the preemptive strike had been called off, the reservists were still mobilizing, and the thinned-out regulars were struggling to stick it out alone, the chief of staff should have ordered the air force to provide immediate and massive assistance to the ground forces. "Execute Scratch now!" should have been the order issued. Furthermore, he should have revised the method of ground defense by evacuating the strongholds and shifting to a mobile defense between the canal line and Artillery Road. Neither of these vital orders was conveyed.

How much time did the IAF really need? There is no clear-cut answer. A careful look at the timetables for achieving air superiority shows that the IAF—which cited various lengths of time on different occasions—gave itself a very generous reserve when it declared that forty-eight hours would be required to neutralize the air forces and missiles on the two fronts (which is inconsistent with the ninety-six hours Peled told the Agranat Commission), and it does not take into account the forty-eight hours needed to prepare for the offensive. The timetables the IAF demanded and received when outlining its plans were dramatically shortened on October 6. At a 07:15

meeting, before the cancellation of the preemptive strike but after Dayan had expressed his opposition to it, Elazar and Peled did their best to retain the option of a preemptive strike against the Syrians. The chief of staff said that despite the opposition to the plan, the IAF would continue its preparations, and if the preemptive strike was conclusively canceled at noon, the IAF would be on immediate stand-by to attack the airfields and go after the missiles three or four hours later. If the Egyptians embarked on a nighttime crossing, the air force would attack the Syrians the following day.[86] The chief of staff's cutback in the IAF's timetable was nothing short of staggering. If the revised timetable was doable, then why did the earlier calculations require the ground forces to wait forty-eight hours before receiving assistance if the air force operated in only one sector —one day for the missiles and one day for the airfields?

In the 11:00 operational discussion group with the defense minister, the IAF commander again presented an astoundingly abridged timetable: one hour (!) to destroy the Syrian air force, and the rest of the day devoted to eliminating the missiles. Afterward (the same day?) it would turn to Egypt. This also deviated fundamentally from the chief of staff's conclusion at 10:00, when he spoke about destroying the Egyptian and Syrian airfields first and then dealing with their missiles, but no one brought this discrepancy to his attention. If these timetables were realistic, then the earlier schedule was both wasteful and irresponsible. If these timetables were unrealistic, then how could they have been suggested as an operational plan in a forum attended by the IAF commander, the chief of staff, and the defense minister just a few hours before the war?

In the chief of staff's operational discussion group at 16:00, the timetables were once again truncated. Instead of the official schedule —forty-eight hours for one sector—it was decided that four missions would be carried out in one day (Sunday): destruction of the two air forces and the two missile arrays. Why, even at this hour, did Elazar remain fixated on this list of priorities? Did he still believe that, despite the vetoed preemptive strike, the IAF could overcome all the glaring shortages and pursue the regular order of priorities?[87]

Was the figure the IAF presented—forty-eight hours—a realistic estimate of the time needed to attain air superiority? Senior IAF officers had different opinions. According to Avihu Ben-Nun, the required time did not depend on the call-up of IAF reservists. There were no helicopter gunships that could have narrowed the interval until the air force could assist in the ground battle, and this message should have been conveyed to the chief of staff and to the ground forces. But the IAF made no effort to do so. Ben-Nun further stated that the timetables should have been drastically reduced and preparations for the attack and the attack itself limited to twenty-four hours in each front.

David Ivry, too, offered a much shorter and more practical timetable. He claimed that the previous IAF commander, Motti Hod, had set the forty-eight-hour figure based on the assumption that the missiles would be destroyed in a preemptive strike. When Benny Peled was appointed commander of the IAF, his plans were based on already existing ones: forty-eight hours for Tagar and Dugman. "Today," declared Ivry, "I would have trimmed the timetable to attacking the missiles not on the entire front but modularly, in select areas." Ivry would have forgone the attack on the airfields, stating, "This was unnecessary given the time constraints. But the missiles could have been targeted in order to provide ground support within 24 hours."[88]

Once the failures of Tagar and Dugman were historical facts, Peled admitted that thirty-six hours would have been sufficient for preparations, and he made it clear that the plans could have succeeded under such conditions: "Fresh intelligence, clear weather, the sun at the right altitude, one operation on one front at a time. Thirty-six hours for preparations if we wanted to include all the elements of the show. Either one or two days for the destruction of one layout, on one front without massive participation in the ground fighting, or, a massive effort for attaining air superiority by attacking the airfields."[89]

The question, then, is why no one challenged the air force's magic number of forty-eight hours. After all the parameters were examined, could the time have been reduced, as claimed by two former IAF commanders many years after the event? Another unasked question: why did the airfields have to be attacked? Did the IAF actually fear that the Egyptians or Syrians would try to exact revenge for their humiliation in the Six-Day War? This overriding concern probably led to Peled's fatal decision to send up so many (superfluous) aircraft for air defense when hostilities erupted. By doing so, other missions that were considered less important had to be passed up, even though these missions could have been carried out while preserving—as planned—the original order of battle for the protection of Israel's skies.

The answers to these simple but nettlesome questions lie in the exalted status of the IAF. Whatever the IAF commanders said was accepted as the "word of God," and neither the chief of staff nor the defense minister seriously questioned their validity or considered that other options might have existed. Elazar blindly accepted the IAF's insistence that it needed forty-eight hours to deal with the missiles, while the ground commanders expected air support immediately upon the outbreak of war. The chief of staff found the self-deception satisfying. The IAF was like a black box, and no one outside of it was privy to its contents.

The Agranat Commission studied the IAF's timetable for providing air support to the ground forces. Of all the air force's operations in the defensive battle, this was virtually the only subject the committee examined in depth. Its members concluded, based on simple calculations, that if an aerial attack on Egyptian airfields and antiaircraft missiles had been made after the Syrian airfields and missiles were destroyed, the ground forces on the canal (given a surprise attack) would have received massive offensive assistance from the IAF only after ninety-six hours had passed, as the following illustrates:

- Two days of light were needed to attack the Syrian airfields and missiles before the effort could be turned to eliminating the Egyptian airfields and missiles, after which effective offensive support could be provided to ground forces in the Syrian sector.
- In the case of an attack on the Egyptian airfields and antiaircraft missiles after the Syrians' had been neutralized, the ground forces could expect full offensive air assistance only after ninety-six hours.[90]

It defies understanding that neither the IAF nor GHQ ever did the basic arithmetic; or if they did, the results were never conveyed to those who needed to know their implications. The ground forces had no idea that assistance on the canal would not be available for ninety-six hours if the "Syria first" plan was implemented.

The Agranat Commission concluded that because the timetables submitted by the IAF to the chief of staff were erroneous, the message received by the ground commanders was inaccurate and muddled, causing confusion about the IAF's participation in the defensive battle. The Agranat Commission asked penetrating questions about the chief of staff's depth of reasoning. His concluding statements about the Iron Ram exercise in 1972 implied that with less than a forty-eight-hour warning, the ground forces would be unable to hold the line by themselves, and the IAF would have to attack the enemy (Scratch) before destroying the missiles. But on October 6, when this harrowing scenario became a reality, the IAF did not proceed according to plan. Thus, the concept that "the regulars and IAF would hold, failed to take into account that the IAF, too, needed a 48-hour warning. We found no expression of these considerations in the IDF's operational orders."[91]

There is no getting away from the fact that the IAF's forty-eight-hour timetable for providing ground assistance was unrealistic. Furthermore, according to operational plans, it should have been perfectly clear that the IAF would not be able to launch a completely effective surprise attack on the airfields and antiaircraft missiles (partially because of the timetable for mobilizing the artillery for Bendigo), and it should have been clear that neutralization of the missiles and airfields would take more time than stated. "On October 6 the conditions that the IAF wanted, as a stipulation for carrying out its missions, did not exist, therefore it was unable to neutralize the missile systems and simultaneously provide assistance to the ground forces. Under these circumstances it found itself in a situation that left no alternative but to focus its primary effort on protecting the state's skies and its secondary effort on attacking the line under any condition." According to Elazar, in this situation, the IAF did not operate according to its designated priorities, thus undermining the assumption that the regulars would hold.[92]

Failure to Carry out Tagar

Even with the IAF's priorities on October 6—that is, ground support in third place—if Operation Tagar had been executed, it would have greatly helped the troops on the canal carry out their defensive assignment. The assumption was that after the attack on the missiles, the warplanes would target the Egyptian forces on the western bank and relieve the pressure on 252nd Division.

The forecast of inclement weather in Syria on the morning of October 6 could have been taken into account on the evening of October 5, and the IAF commander (who was not surprised by the cancellation of the preemptive strike) could have (and should have) prepared an alternative version of Tagar as a preliminary or parallel strike. Tagar could have been carried out on October 6 with high-altitude loft bombing, instead of pop-up bombing, against most of the SA2 and SA3 batteries on the canal. Changing the ordnance setup at such a critical juncture from an attack mission to air defense was one of the IAF's major blunders in the war in general and on October 6 in particular, and it had an adverse impact on the air force's ability to provide immediate assistance to the ground forces.

At 12:50, after the preemptive strike was definitely canceled, Peled ordered the ordnance setup on all the Phantoms switched from ground bombing to air-to-air munitions. This was an egregious error, since Hawk surface-to-air missiles, 57 Mirages of various models, and 12 Phantoms already in a state of air-to-air alert in the squadrons were sufficient—according to IAF plans—to defend Israel's skies. No more than 30 Phantoms should have had their munitions changed. Colonel Giora Forman, head of the IAF's Operations Department, warned Peled that he was making a grave mistake and should leave 80 Phantoms and 160 Skyhawks to attack the enemy's crossing and bridging equipment in a preemptive or parallel strike the moment the Egyptians opened fire. Peled, however, was fixated on air-to-air defense to protect Israel's airspace; he was also under psychological pressure from the government. According to Forman, "with Motti Hod this never would have happened because of his intimate familiarity with how things look from the cockpit."[93]

Peled ordered the ordnance changed at 12:50, and even though he assumed the war would begin at 15:00, there was no way the switch-over could be completed in time. When the sirens sounded at 14:00, no orders were issued to activate the attack plan or execute Scratch, which the squadrons were prepared for. The IAF's decision-making structure began to show signs of cracking.

At 14:05 the Skyhawks were scrambled to assist in the holding action. They conducted pop-up bombing with no targets in sight, without planning, and without orders, and they suffered heavy losses. The Phantoms whose ordnance had already been switched flew off to provide air defense. Phantoms that had not yet changed their munitions released their bombs in the sea and left to assist in air defense. Those in the process of unloading their ordnance could not leave the ground immediately and took off half an hour later, which delayed assistance to the ground forces. Almost none of the Phantoms took part in the attack on October 6. The possibility of improvising a parallel strike was lost once the Phantoms and Mirages flew off, and the possibility of a first flight to assist the ground forces was also frittered away.[94]

IAF Participation: Too Late and Too Sporadic

The question of exactly how many warplanes converted their ordnance (from ground attack to air defense) is critical. The order to do so catapulted the squadrons into frenzied activity, and the IAF entered the fighting late and in fits and starts.

Peled perceived the enemy's air forces as the primary threat, which is why he decided to attack the airfields first and ordered a change in ordnance the moment the preemptive strike was called off. This shift was the result of an error in the IAF commander's priorities, and his misstep rendered the warplanes useless for either attack or defense!

With regard to the ordnance swap, the chief of staff said that he and the IAF commander tried to maximize the time "the air force could stay in an offensive formation until the planes' ordnance configuration had to be changed because they were going to take off. We just didn't know what was happening. At any rate, the IAF's primary mission was to safeguard the skies. Therefore we were in a situation where the air force had to be prepared for their opening move."[95]

The IAF entered the war slowly—twenty minutes passed before the first planes responded in uncoordinated attacks, and they incurred heavy losses. Many quality targets on both fronts were left untouched. The ordnance switch-over and the expectation that H hour would be at 18:00 partially explain the ineffectiveness and lackadaisical response, along with the pilots' surprise when they were scrambled to the fighting zone and encountered a situation similar to that of the tanks. Despite the pilots' awareness of the surface-to-air missiles, the missiles' lethal effectiveness caught them off guard, and many planes were hit by antiaircraft cannon and missiles that day. In the first seventy-two hours of fighting, the IAF made special efforts to cope with the new situation, but most of the sorties for ground assistance were flown at high altitudes and more cautiously than in the past. Thus, although the air force's losses decreased, its effectiveness dropped to less than that in 1967.

The IAF's contribution to the ground battle in the Canal Zone was inconsequential. On October 6, 121 attack sorties were carried out (a trifling number), and their only contribution, though important, was the downing of twenty of the forty-eight Egyptian helicopters ferrying commandos. Dayan, too, affirmed that the IAF's contribution in impeding the canal crossing on Saturday was minimal, even though it executed many sorties (not true). Because of the lack of updated intelligence and the presence of enemy missiles, the pilots released their bombs from a distance, with negligible results. Dayan stated that on October 6 the IAF had only two and a half hours of daylight in the south and could not have operated against the missile batteries; furthermore, it had no updated photographs of the antiaircraft layout (not true). Dayan also raised doubts about there being any targets on the canal that the IAF could have attacked effectively (there were many).[96]

If Tagar had been executed in full on Sunday morning, it probably would have achieved most of its objectives. However, the Egyptians would have promptly rebuilt their missile batteries—maybe even the same night—with missiles supplied by the Soviets to cover their losses. Be that as it may, had Tagar been successful, it would have enabled the exploitation, according to IAF assessments, of the air force's tremendous firepower in this theater. October 7 would have been sufficiently early to disrupt the establishment of Egyptian bridgeheads on the eastern bank, especially in Third Army's sector, and massive air intervention, perhaps beginning on the evening of October 7 or the morning of October 8, could have demolished the Egyptians' ground gains. In practical terms, because of the IAF's involvement in Tagar in the morning and the redirection of operations to the Golan Heights, it did not assist the ground forces on the canal during the worst day of the land battle. As Gonen described the events: "They came in at a quarter to seven, carried out a preparatory fly over, and left the area without so much as informing Southern Command as to what they did."[97]

The inability to obliterate the Egyptian missiles lasted until the IDF crossed the canal and the ground forces on the western bank began to hit the missile batteries with tank and artillery fire, thus enabling the air force to ramp up its activity. Another important point: despite the cancellation of Tagar and the transfer of 100 Phantoms to Dugman in the north, the ground forces could have been helped by approximately 90 EW-supported Skyhawks, but this was not part of the plan. Many senior IAF officers attested that the Skyhawks were not used to their fullest advantage in the war, and even though the Skyhawk was slower than the Phantom, its carrying ability and smaller dimensions would have been beneficial in a missile-saturated area.

The Shift to Dugman

Dayan's anxiety over the campaign in the north was genuine, but there was another reason for the shift from Tagar to Dugman. In discussions on the night of October 6–7, he thought the air effort should focus on attacking the tank concentrations and bridges on the canal instead of neutralizing the missiles. But he did not fight tooth and nail to get his view accepted, and it is doubtful that he suffered any pangs of conscience over the cancellation of Tagar—an operation he never believed in (in fact, he may have experienced a degree of "I told you so" schadenfreude). Ben-Nun backed this view. When Ivry was asked for his opinion on the matter, he said he could not give an answer.

Many IAF personnel had no qualms about criticizing the decision to cancel Tagar and carry out Dugman instead. The squadrons and control units, which had prepared for a day of fighting on the canal, were forced to hastily reorganize for an operation in the north. Dugman 5 was launched with slipshod preparation, and six Phantoms were shot down in very low-altitude flight by regular antiaircraft fire in an area that, according to MI, was supposedly free of missiles. The Syrian air defense layout on the Golan Heights had moved west with the army's advance, and the intelligence had not been updated. Only two of thirty-one batteries were hit by the IAF, which was shocked by the loss of the six Phantoms. The Dugman fiasco led to the decision to cease the attack on the Syrian missiles.

Yiftach Spector, the commander of Squadron 107, described the attack in the north as "running amok." There was no time for briefings, and the pilots received their orders while in flight north. The IAF's main fighting method collapsed immediately. Peled was accused of meekly accepting instructions from Dayan and Elazar without protest. Because of this, a deliberate operation (Tagar) was nipped in the bud, and another (Dugman) was executed frenetically. Harsher criticism was also raised: "The flinty Peled was in fact all wishy-washy inside," and he "called off 'Tagar' because he had always been manic, succumbing to ups and downs."[98]

Canceling Tagar and shifting to Dugman was not the IAF commander's decision. The chief of staff made that call alone, without consulting any GHQ forum (except for Peled). Exhausted and under pressure, Elazar should not have made such a fateful decision on his own. In the air force, Peled was excoriated for not "bang[ing] his fist on the table" and stopping the change in operations. A more seasoned IAF commander with a more rebellious nature certainly would have responded differently to the order to call off Tagar, and here, Peled obviously erred.[99]

The shift to Dugman generated a sense of distrust in the squadrons, and the IAF was unable to return to its deliberate operational plan. Ivry claimed this was because of the calamitous ground situation: "GHQ believed that the regulars would hold for 48 hours until the air force came to their rescue." According to Ben-Nun, the head of the IAF's Operations Department should have participated in discussions with the chief of staff. Peled may have forgotten or been unaware that Squadrons 109 and 110 at the Ramat David Air Base were designated to assist in the fighting on the Golan Heights during Tagar at daybreak. Both Ivry and Ben-Nun made a point of mentioning that in the narrow airspace above Gamla Road, only a four-aircraft formation or a pair of aircraft could have operated and maintained the attack momentum, but because Elazar thought it was impossible to execute Dugman in parallel with Tagar, he canceled the latter. The IAF commander's remark that Mirages could have been diverted from the south to the Golan Heights (excluding Squadrons 109 and 110) indicated that the order of battle was sufficient in the north, and Tagar did not have to be called off. Dayan himself did not demand the cancellation of Tagar, but he did insist on massive assistance for the north. Paradoxically, forces on the Golan Heights had been receiving air-to-ground assistance, but this ceased during preparations for Dugman. When Forman was asked about continuing Tagar with Skyhawks, he answered that, theoretically, it was possible.[100]

In Ivry's opinion, since neither Tagar nor Dugman stood the test, they cannot be judged. Half the IAF could have been allocated to the Golan Heights while the other half continued with Tagar. Tagar could have been carried out without a preliminary flight, as in the War of Attrition, and it could have directly attacked the missiles in the flanks—Port Said and Suez—where there were air defense "openings."

The fact is that the Syrian tanks halted their westerly advance in the southern part of the Golan Heights on Sunday afternoon. The reason for this is still unclear: doctrine; logistical problems; the approach of Musa Peled's 146th Division, which was ascending the southern part of the Heights; fear of leaving the air defense umbrella; IAF activity; or perhaps all of the above.[101]

The IAF Was Thrown Off-Kilter

The zigzag from south to north revealed the IAF's vulnerability despite its highly trained personnel, sophisticated and versatile command and control systems, rapid response in all combat zones, and ability to adapt to sudden changes in activity and mission. Its deliberate plans, rife with stipulations, proved to be extremely complex and intolerant of changes, glitches, or outside intervention. On the Day of Atonement, the IAF had no chance to attain air superiority and freedom of action; thus, it did not operate according to its plans. Had it done so, it would have encountered some irksome problems, but it could have impacted the enemy, disrupted his war objectives, broken his fighting spirit, shortened the time required to achieve the ground forces' objectives, and reduced the number of IDF casualties. Lieutenant General Dan Shomron (Ret.) aptly described the situation: "The side that's caught by surprise always appears to be losing its equilibrium and reacting to events too late, and this is what happened to the IAF." In the consultation group with the chief of staff at 12:45 on October 7, the IAF commander said, "We did everything half way. We carried out half of 'Tagar' on the canal. The chief of staff's calming words—'what we did has already helped us, and is helping [us] now and later'—were irrelevant."[102]

The IAF's October 7 mission merry-go-round after Tagar's cancellation was as follows:

11:30—Attack the missile layout in Syria. Provide massive assistance on the Golan Heights.
12:45—Chief of staff's order to divert the IAF to the canal front (the bridges).
13:45—Provide massive air support on the Golan Heights and

the canal, regardless of the missiles. Continue protecting the
IDF forces and attack the airfields.

Thus, the IAF was being shuffled from mission to mission and from
front to front before it could exert its full force. This was the result of
explicit instructions at the political and military levels that ran counter to the air force's training and tactical principles, and it reflected
a lack of understanding of the IAF's advantages and shortcomings.
Given the zigzagging that day, sanctioned without staff work and
on the basis of personal decisions by the chief of staff and the IAF
commander, the air force was thrown off-kilter, and the pilots no
longer understood what was expected of them. The IAF's Operations Department was not used to responding to recurrent operational fluctuations and indecisive, convoluted orders; its long-held
tradition of issuing reliable, painstakingly examined orders was
upended, and the IAF was thrown into disorder.[103] For example,
Southern Command's IAF adviser, Colonel Shefer, advised the IAF
commander "not to attack the eastern bank [Gonen had demanded
an attack]. Our forces are there. Attack the western bank instead."[104]
  Spector described the madness of that day:

> After the failure of the first round of "Dugman" I was sure
> we were going to refuel, rearm and return north to finish up
> the job, but then came the order:
>   Double time it to Egypt!
>   Egypt? What about the Golan Heights?
>   Forget the Golan Heights.
>   Aren't we going to continue with "Tagar" that we began
> this morning and left off in the middle?
>   No! Attack the bridges that the Egyptians erected on the
> canal for bringing over their armored forces into Sinai.
>   Bridges? What bridges?[105]

Clearly, GHQ did not use the air force effectively on October 7.
It was supposed to fight for air superiority, according to the operational priorities the IAF had approved, but the main air effort was
directed north. The result of the IAF's overwrought activity was that
the Egyptian missiles were not attacked and destroyed. In turn, the
air force had to operate in a missile-saturated environment, which
meant that the ground forces did not receive the assistance they

expected.[106] The most authentic expression of the mood in the IAF that day was uttered by someone in the IAF's CCP post at 10:00: "I've had it up to here with this merry-go-round."

IAF Targets: The Bridges

The bridges the Egyptians assembled on the night of October 6–7, throughout October 7, and on part of October 8 were their chief means of preserving the offensive's momentum and conveying their tanks, antitank weapons, APCs, and artillery to the eastern bank to establish bridgeheads and logistical support for the five infantry divisions that had already crossed the canal. Rafts were also used, but their contribution was nugatory. Thus, knocking out the bridges received top priority in the attempt to provide ground support to 252nd Division, which was single-handedly fighting a savage defensive battle.

The IAF made an enormous effort to attack the bridges. Encouraging reports of good hits (which later proved inaccurate) reached the government meeting in the afternoon. Before Elazar flew to Um Hashiba on Sunday afternoon, he ordered "the air force to destroy the bridges at any price." The IAF commander said that same evening, "We'll have to keep the bridges incapacitated so there won't be any more crossings . . . and provide support to our forces." But IAF headquarters and the squadrons were not prepared for such a mission. Spector stated that he knew nothing about the bridges: "The bridges were across the canal, surrounded by missiles, and no one knew where they were. The attack was conducted when the sun was in our eyes and the bridges looked like thin strands of thread." Spector recalled that, after Dugman 5, Forman instructed him by telephone to go to the canal alone and look for bridges, despite all the missiles there. "I don't know why the IAF didn't ask for aerial photos so it could plan the attack. We knew that the bridges were there" (see figures 1 and 2).[107]

According to Forman, "the attack on the bridges was poorly executed because the pilots feared a low level flight due to the missiles." Ivry has his own explanation for the IAF's failure: "There was a report of sixteen bridges but the air force failed to obtain precise information on their whereabouts. Although the air force conducted routine photo sorties on the canal the whole day, and it turned out there were indeed pictures of the bridges and 'funnels' [traffic snarls of Egyptian forces on both banks], MI kept the photos and the air force received them only at night." Ivry's words, unfortunately, are patently inaccurate and produce an uncomfortable feeling that he was evading responsibility and placing the blame (as usual) on the greens and MI. They also give rise to a number of questions: Who should have provided the IAF with coordinates after the chief of staff ordered it to attack the bridges at any price? The bridges were permanent structures, and the pilots had spotted them and reported them. What prevented IAF decipherers from identifying the bridges, converting their locations to coordinates, and conveying them as targets to the squadrons? Why did the IAF have to wait until MI handed it the data? And even if these were green targets that the air force generally did not deal with, why wasn't an all-out effort made to obtain the information from MI? What did Ivry mean when he said the photographs were received "only at night"? Which night? If they reached the IAF on the night of October 7, the attack could have been carried out at daybreak on October 8. Ivry claimed the planes had to attack the bridges in low-altitude flight and with minimal exposure, with target spotting done in the midst of the attack and after the missiles had been knocked out. Under these circumstances, there was a very good chance of hitting the bridges.[108] But "it was rare to find bridges on the canal most of this day because the [Egyptians] used mainly rafts in transporting their forces and the bulk of the heavy vehicles crossed at night."[109]

Postwar performance analysis shows that although the IAF invested enormous resources in attacking the bridges at the outset of the war, it did little to disrupt the crossing, and the effort had an exhausting effect on the air force because the bridges were heavily defended. Most of them were assembled after dark and then disassembled at daylight and placed next to the canal banks. Of the 240 attack sorties against the bridges in the first four days, the IAF scored only twenty-four hits at best—in fact, probably much fewer. Ten planes were shot down, and six others damaged because of the lethal combination of high- and low-altitude air defenses, which the IAF had no solution for. Due to the rate of aircraft losses, the chief of staff decided to call off the attack on the fourth day. Its failure can be attributed to a number of reasons:

- The bombing method was ineffective. Loft bombing was notoriously inaccurate, and approximately half the attacks employed pop-up bombing in missile-packed areas.

- The ordnance used—cluster bombs and napalm—was designed to eliminate the forces on the bridges, not the bridges themselves.
- Intelligence was not updated. Some of the bridges were transferred or disassembled before the planes arrived.
- Many attacks were conducted at night.
- Many attacks were interdicted.

In addition, the Egyptian defense system on the bridges was simple, effective, and hard to hit, for the following reasons:

- The crossing areas were protected by powerful antiaircraft missiles.
- Bridges were dismantled into rafts during the day and reassembled into bridges at night.
- Every few hours the bridges were shifted to different crossing areas.
- Smoke screens were laid down in the bridges' vicinity.
- Designated forces repaired the bridges close to the crossing areas.
- Antisubmarine nets were strewn from south to north of each bridge.

On October 7 the IAF hit two bridges of Egyptian Third Army's 7th Division at Kilometers 137 and 141, rendering them inoperable until the following evening. During this time, Third Army's sector was without a single working bridge. The same day, 252nd Division's artillery zeroed in on a number of bridges, and the strongholds relayed fire corrections (Mefatseyach was outstanding in this regard), but once contact with the enemy was broken off, the bridges were outside the range of 155mm artillery. Toward the end of the war, the IAF gained freedom of action in Third Army's sector, and all the bridges were destroyed by October 23.

Also on October 7, out of a total of 787 sorties, the air force conducted 317 support sorties for the ground forces in Sinai, 100 attack sorties against missiles, 45 against airfields, and 325 patrolling and interception sorties. Peled claimed that IAF activity stopped the Egyptians from cutting off the Nachal Yam–Baluza Road on October 7, on which 162nd Division was moving, although there is no proof of this. On October 8 the IAF was unable to destroy any bridges on the canal.

Summing up the mission, except for solitary hits, the IAF's prodigious effort to neutralize the bridges on the canal was in vain. Obviously, the mission should have been planned before the war as a basic operation, just as Tagar and Dugman were (although the exact location of the bridges could not be known prior to hostilities, the crossing areas were known). The task of bridge destruction was assigned to the squadrons without updated intelligence (which could have been quickly rectified), a war-fighting doctrine, prior training, or suitable weapons. All these elements should have been checked beforehand in a scrupulous performance analysis. In many ways, this failure to destroy the bridges paralleled the air force's lack of preparation for destroying bridging and crossing equipment on the western bank.

The IAF's Ignorance of the Counterattack

It should be noted that the IAF's plan for assisting in the counterattack was prepared by Colonel Amos Amir—number five in the air force hierarchy—only five hours before H hour, which may be an indication of the amount of attention it was given. Lieutenant Colonel Asher Snir, who sat in the ASC on October 8, had stepped into his role only a few hours earlier and had received no instructions or allocation of forces from the head of the IAF Operations Department. Snir said, "I knew nothing about a counterattack. I'd been briefed only cursorily on what the ASC was. I didn't know how it worked or what my precise authorities were." Snir admitted that his only experience in air support was being "in the forward command post with Arik Sharon in a Southern Command exercise." Snir was not alone in his ignorance. Other senior IAF officers were also in the dark about the planned attack, even though the IAF commander had promised the chief of staff that sixty planes would be available throughout the day, and Amir had prepared a plan to provide assistance. According to Ivry, the air force had no knowledge that a counterattack was intended for October 8. As was his custom, Ivry blamed the greens for not integrating the IAF into Southern Command's counterattack plans.[110] But this was a curious accusation, given that a senior IAF officer—Colonel Shefer—was present in Southern Command's FCG. He should have been aware of what the greens were doing, and he should have known about the chief of staff's visit on the evening of October 7 and his involvement in the matter. If Shefer had cross-checked his information, he might have realized that a counterattack was in the offing, and he could have received plans from the CCP on air assistance and its integration into Southern Command's plan. This was not done. Gonen's criticism reflected his growing despair over the IAF's guarantees of support: "The whole plan for Monday's counterattack was based on air support that never arrived. The same thing happened on Tuesday . . . the day Kalman [Magen] was supposed to capture the 'sandbank' after the air force had 'worked it over' for a whole day—but the warplanes never showed up."[111]

In the absence of organized air assistance in their hour of need, the only thing the ground forces could do was request emergency support to extricate 19th Battalion/460th Brigade, which was pinned down opposite Firdan. In general, even these requests were only superficially answered, and when assistance did arrive after an interminable delay, it was an ineffective response that produced only paltry results.

Some of the IAF's answers to the ground forces' cries for assistance were unacceptable. Thus, at 10:45 on Monday, when the 162nd's flank appeared to be threatened by a brigade of T62s, Gandhi (as acting chief of staff) called the IAF commander and requested that he attack the Egyptian armored brigade. Peled replied that he had lost two warplanes just two minutes earlier, so until the missiles had been neutralized or unless the enemy was actually crossing the canal, he could order only loft bombing. The truth is that a concentrated tank brigade was very suitable for loft bombing, but Gandhi did not press the issue and merely said, "In that case don't do anything." The highest authority—the chief of staff—was needed in this case. After Gonen conveyed his apprehension over Egyptian 15th Brigade in Kantara to the chief of staff and again requested air support, Elazar contacted Peled and ordered him to assist the ground forces, regardless of the missiles.

Three hours later, at 13:20, fearing that the Egyptians were about to attack the entire central sector, Gonen asked the deputy chief of staff, General Tal, to order the entire air force to go after the bridges and assist 162nd Division opposite Firdan and 143rd Division at the Chinese Farm. Peled got in touch with his deputy and ordered him to prepare loft bombing for three possible areas, postpone the attack on the missile batteries until the following day, and commence operations in the Port Said sector (according to the defense minister's orders). As for assisting the 143rd, the IAF commander replied, "Loft bombing in one hour." At 14:45 Southern Command repeated its request for air assistance because of the Egyptian counterattack in the entire sector and received the answer: "Approved!"[112] In both cases, the planes never arrived.

Gonen insisted that the absence of ground support was one of the main factors in the counterattack's failure. He backed this up with a document in which Shefer stated his view of the IAF's participation in the October 8 ground fighting and use of airpower that day. Shefer claimed he could not recall the exact details, but he knew the use of airpower was not massive because the terrain was bristling with antiaircraft missiles. According to the IAF information branch: "The 162nd Division's offensive [was launched] without artillery and [with only] minimal air support [twenty-four sorties]. The decrease in the rate of assistance was due to the loss of a pair of aircraft in the area [!] and the IAF being spread out on the front because the ASC had no prior knowledge of the offensive."[113] After two planes were shot down, Forman asked Shefer to slacken the pace.

The IAF's failure in the counterattack can be summarized as follows:

- The air force slowed the pace of attacks because of the loss of two aircraft.
- Lieutenant Colonel Snir in the ASC was unaware that a counterattack was under way, and he had not prepared planes for an attack.
- The air force attacked sectors on the canal where the ground forces were not engaged. No concentrated effort was made, and the degree of IAF involvement in the northern sector and Port Said was unnecessary.
- The ASC apparently never received the fighting forces' call for massive air assistance.
- On October 8 the air force cut back its activity, partially because of an unfounded report of ground successes.[114]

Since no one at the GHQ level weighed the possibility of prioritizing the air force's efforts on the two fronts, the counterattacks in Sinai and the Golan Heights were conducted simultaneously. The IAF's offensive should have been concentrated on Sinai, for a number of reasons: 252nd Division's desperate situation, Southern

Command's rigid time constraints, and the arrival of the reservists, who needed to be integrated into the battle as quickly as possible. But in general, air assistance for the counterattack in Sinai was inconsequential.[115]

According to Gordon, when the IAF's red line was presented in the first critical week of the war, Peled did not exaggerate its severity. Dozens of planes in the air force's maintenance units and aircraft industry began to be mustered into service on the night of October 5–6 instead of ten days earlier (on the Jewish New Year), when the IAF entered a heightened state of alert. None of the planes were flown before the start of the American airlift. Had the IAF brought them into service earlier, the red line could have been pushed back much further, the chief of staff would not have lowered the pace of air activity, and the prime minister would not have called for a cease-fire.

Disappointment from and in the IAF

The ground forces' disappointment in the air force later found bitter expression in the war summaries. The letdown was mainly due to the ineffectiveness of close air support, the IAF's inattention to the greens' plight, communications breakdowns, broken promises, and inappreciable and token assistance. The ground forces resented the air force's immense budget, given its measly contribution to the overall war effort and its missions in nonessential places (such as Port Said).

Sharon said, perhaps cynically, "I don't understand the disappointment in the air force. The expectations were unfounded and whoever thought that the aircraft is 'flying artillery' doesn't know what he's talking about." Gonen summed up the ground commanders' criticism: "Throughout the war it [the air force] attacked non-risk areas rather than where it should have. At no point did it take part in the battles. . . . The IAF knocked out no more than six batteries in Port Said."[116]

The commanders of the artillery groups responsible for communicating with the aircraft described obstacles, disappointment, and frustration. Colonel Granit, the commander of 215th Artillery Group/162nd Division, recalled, "They'd say 'Receive [support]!' and afterwards 'Sorry—it didn't come.' Then they'd tell us that the north had priority, so we toned down our demands, and even when they told us that we had priority, all they'd send over was a four-aircraft formation or pair of fighters."[117]

Other commanders were more vociferous in their criticism, calling the IAF's support cheap and ineffective and citing feeble attacks in the wrong places, bombing lines that lacked any coordination with the ground situation, communication foul-ups, and aloofness to the greens' predicament. According to the commander of 275th Brigade, "They [the airmen] listen only to the 'blues.' It was incredible! When Colonel Kislev, the 162nd Division's air coordinator arrived, he picked up the phone and suddenly there was a miracle! Everything we wanted for the northern sector suddenly arrived. In other words, it was a question of vested interests."[118]

Tal related an incident that illustrates the different attitude toward risks and losses in the air (airplanes and pilots) versus risks and losses on the ground (tanks and tank crews). At 15:00 on October 6, he checked with the air force about providing support to forces in the Kantara area, where the situation was acute. He spoke with Peled, who "explained that missiles mean losses. . . . This [air support] was possible but several planes would be hit, so I [Tal] decided not to give them support." This was an especially hard decision for Tal, as his son was fighting in the Kantara sector with 9th Battalion. But Scratch was designed exactly for such a scenario—assistance to the ground forces in critical situations, even in missile-packed areas—and Tal was supposed to order the IAF commander to execute Scratch. According to Tal, "Saturday and Sunday proved a tremendous learning experience, and only later did we realize that the air force was incapable of taking out the missiles and bombing the bridges, but on Saturday afternoon and Sunday we still thought it could. . . . When you look back at the total number of sorties, it turns out that the IAF refrained from employing its full strength or even half its strength, and not because of fear of being hit but because of the IAF commander's mismanagement of airpower."[119] Tal also criticized Peled for being too aggressive. The squadron commanders no longer trusted him and would check with the Pit to confirm their orders.

Tal was asked by the IDF History Department why this point had not been brought up in the Pit. His reply:

The field commanders' emergency situation was conveyed to Peled whose answer was "these guys can't understand.

They don't see or know anything." He'd tell us "I'm sending out help now." Gorodish [Gonen] and others in the field
knew they weren't getting air assistance. Benny [Peled]
would counter, "but I'm giving it to them now." Only after
the war did I find out why.

   A. The planes couldn't reach the places where assistance
      was   needed so instead they released their ordnance
      haphazardly at a distance.
   B. Peled sent out very few planes with very few bombs.
      But you [can't] know this in wartime, only after the war.
      . . . When the Iraqis moved into [the Golan Heights]
      the IAF commander was urged to interdict, but Peled
      claimed it was nighttime and [his planes] couldn't find
      [let alone] attack [the enemy].

The IAF commander's responses, Tal lamented, were a disgraceful
symptom of a widespread phenomenon that still exists in the IDF:
the IAF's disparagement of the greens and their demands. From the
airmen's point of view: "They [the greens] don't understand what
they want. . . . We [the air force] understand the situation better
than they do and know what to do. . . . Someone comes and says
he's destroyed all the bridges. . . . Do you realize what this means?
Even on the night [of October 6–7] he says that he's eliminated all
the bridges. . . . I wasn't comfortable with the air force's part in the
holding operation on the canal." Tal added, "The IAF really has to
carry out a thorough examination and internalize the lessons on the
way it was used. The Agranat Commission avoided [investigating]
the air force and everybody was happy."[120]

A lot has been written about the ground forces' disappointment
with the air force, especially in the first three days of the war. The
ground forces have pointed out that not one of the 1,500 Arab tanks
destroyed was a confirmed hit by air ordnance. The IAF's contribution to the land battle was of less consequence than it was in 1967.
Israeli and foreign observers mistakenly assumed that the Arabs'
achievements in 1973 were attributable to the qualitative improvement in their ground forces rather than the effective neutralization
of the IAF by their missiles.[121]

Peled did not shirk the air force's obligation to take part in the
holding battle, and he noted in various forums that between 14:00

and nightfall on October 6, 196 sorties were carried out (121 in the southern front); however, on "Saturday [October 6] it was impossible to bring in anymore because there were no more."[122] He did not explain what "there were no more" meant, but it was obvious that a very large order of battle could have been brought in on Saturday to execute hundreds of sorties in line with Scratch, especially against the funnel targets on the western bank. The standard explanation was that the air force was in the midst of changing munitions after the preemptive strike was canceled, which made it impossible for the planes to go into action. But this fails to justify the meager assistance the IAF extended to the ground forces, and even IAF base commanders said the same.

The author could find no statement or document in which the chief of staff spoke professionally and unequivocally about the IAF's performance in the defensive battle. This is a far cry from the straightforward language of his deputy. Elazar's only relevant remarks on the subject consisted of a diplomatically worded statement made at the senior staff conference: "On Saturday morning, when I realized we were definitely headed for war with this deployment, I knew it was going to be a severe test, and I remembered everything that we discussed about the air force's part in the holding stage. I thought if we looked carefully at everything discussed before the war we'd find that in the final analysis we had planned the right moves but failed in their execution."[123] The chief of staff's statements in the IDF summary of IAF activity are incommensurate with a major combat arm with a lavish budget and on which such high operational hopes had been pinned.

Like the ground forces, the IAF was bedeviled by a sense of lost opportunity and disappointment in its contribution to the war, its priorities, its mission performance in attaining air superiority, and, above all, its inability to destroy the missiles on either front. There was also deep disappointment in the level of assistance it extended to the ground forces and its misinterpretation of their needs and problems.

In addition, there was disappointment over the IAF's "internal affairs." Even Peled admitted that he harbored reservations about the plans to attack the Syrian and Egyptian missiles and the lack of time to implement basic changes in the plans. He was far from satisfied with the ground forces' intelligence collection and IAF control systems, but he could only do his best with what he had. Forman was convinced that the operational concept, which had been tested at the beginning of the war against the missile layouts, was fundamentally flawed and apparently inapplicable. Hundreds of warplanes attacking at intervals measured in seconds (in effect, all at once) precluded flexibility, thwarted the squadron leaders' initiative, and aggravated the effects of stale intelligence.[124]

The battle against surface-to-air missiles on the canal was characterized by overinvolvement in the northern sector and Port Said, despite their secondary importance. This occurred mainly because of Dayan's dream of capturing the city and using it as a bargaining chip in future cease-fire negotiations. The missiles there were attacked on October 8, 12, and 16, despite the absence of any operational need or urgency. Peled's explanations, presented at an October 12 commanders' discussion, were unconvincing. He claimed, "It's good for the IAF not to have missiles in Port Said," and noted that, based on intelligence reports, the enemy was "about to deploy Scud missiles that could reach the refineries in Haifa."[125]

The IAF attacked additional targets, scattering its forces and deviating from the chief of staff's instructions to go after targets where a decision had to be reached. An outstanding example occurred on the morning of October 18. In the midst of the battle on the bridgehead in the central sector, the air force attacked a missile battery in the Kantara area that was much farther north than the chief of staff's intended area. Three planes were hit during the attack. When Elazar learned of this, he called for Peled and gave him a stiff dressing down in private. During the rebuke he hissed, "I couldn't care less about Kantara."[126] By this, he meant that he disapproved of the IAF's independent actions that ignored his instructions and focused on targets that were ancillary to the war effort. Gonen noted that the IAF cleaned out the batteries in the Port Said vicinity three or four times: "I'll be damned why he [Peled] did it. He did it because it was easy there."[127]

Already on October 8, in a discussion among air base commanders, recriminations were leveled against the air force's priorities and its superfluous attack on the airfields. This was the first time the attack on the airfields in Egypt had been characterized as a misuse of resources. The commanders complained that the air force was not substantially assisting the ground forces, and its priorities were off the mark. One of the participants charged that, unlike in the Six-Day War, where a decision had been achieved by eliminating the

Egyptian air force, this was impossible in the current situation, and a decision would have to be made on the line; destruction of Egypt's air capability would be a minor contribution.

Colonel Yakov Agasi, commander of the Ramat David Air Base, thought the IAF warplanes were not being used to their full potential. There were still targets to be attacked, yet the planes were standing idle on the tarmac. "We're asking for ordnance, for something," he said. Peled informed the base commanders that the chief of staff had instructed him not to go after the bridges if it would deplete the air force, and one of the commanders asked Peled sarcastically: "Sir, am I to understand that the IDF has changed its view . . . that our job is only to clean up the skies, that we're not needed anywhere else?" Peled did not alter his position and insisted that the airfields remained the top priority, even if that ran counter to the chief of staff's opinion. In addition, he reasoned that attacking two or three airfields would not influence the amount of support the IAF could give to the line. The base commanders were not convinced. Colonel Ran Pecker, commander of the Tel Nof Air Base, said: "Today we're working at a 60–65% output but we feel our potential is greater."[128]

According to Major General Yadlin, before the Yom Kippur War the IAF had failed to envisage the likelihood of fighting on two fronts. Why were the Phantoms, the spearhead of the IAF, diverted to attacking airfields and not concentrated on the Egyptian divisions crossing the canal? Why didn't the IAF wear down Third Army after the missiles had been neutralized? The IAF's anticipated annihilation of the enemy's air forces and surface-to-air missiles did not materialize, and by the end of the second day, thirty Israeli planes had been lost. Was this fiasco the result of failing to deliver a preemptive blow? With a forty-eight-hour warning, would the IAF have scored better results? Is it wise to rely on a doctrine based solely on intelligence and favorable weather? None of these questions has been investigated.[129]

During the war, the IAF sobered up and came to the realization that whereas it had been the decisive element in previous wars and was the main beneficiary of the defense budget, scenarios could occur in which its contributions fell short. Its priorities—first and foremost, gaining air superiority—had been applied and sanctified before the Six-Day War, but this time, they did not work.

In the first four days of the fighting, the IAF's shortcomings in an intensive, protracted war were revealed, and the IAF commander repeatedly warned that the number of downed warplanes might pass the red line if the fighting continued at the present rate. The arrival of aircraft and weapons from the United States or another source could not be guaranteed, and the air force's strength would have to be conserved for the possibility of prolonged attrition.

According to Spector, it was not the surprise attack or the missiles that were most frightening and distressing; rather, it was the chaos that infected the IAF beginning on the night of October 6–7 due to fluctuating orders and the mad dash from the Golan Heights to the Suez Canal without any substantive gains. He described the loss of confidence, the befuddlement, and the hysteria among the senior leadership. In his opinion, the commanders were unbalanced and had no idea what was happening. Their voices were distraught, their orders incoherent; they were deaf to the feedback coming in from the field, and they repeated their mistakes. Spector felt like the ground he stood on was caving in. He quoted Peled, who said after the war: "We entered the Yom Kippur War like a 'Mickey Mouse' air force, an absurd imitation of the combat arm that we should have been. No need to waste time learning the lessons of this war, it would be better to rebuild the IAF for the next war." Spector continued: "Squadron 107's debriefing affirms that the IAF suffered from a shortfall of targets, and that any attempt to convey lessons to the air command encountered a harsh response. Our blind faith in MI proved to be our weak point. The staff lagged behind the units in knowledge of the enemy. The pervading feeling in the field was that the units are more capable of efficient planning and that in this war the real enemy was the IAF staff itself."[130]

In late 1973 Spector openly accused the senior command of failing in its role. He quoted from a letter by a member of the Pit, who wrote that Spector's criticism of the headquarters under pressure "pales next to what really happened there. The IAF didn't do what it should have done. . . . The decisions whether to continue an operation or halt it in the middle were based on losses, not on reality—because the losses were immediately known and the results only later." Spector, who alleged that certain senior IAF officers believed Peled should be removed from command, accused Peled of failing to comprehend the situation and interfering with everybody's work.[131]

According to Colonel Eliezer Cohen (Ret.), commander of Refidim Air Base in the war, "The IAF had not been a key element before the war and didn't come out [of] it with the feeling of being a victorious air force. . . . The IAF planned to assign the first two days to eliminating the anti-aircraft missile layouts and paralyzing the airfields, but instead it found itself involved in a hasty, fragmented holding operation before it achieved air superiority. The IAF was disappointed that it wasn't able to realize its plans, and the ground forces were no less disappointed that they didn't receive its full support as promised."[132]

Furthermore, the IAF avoided attacking strategic targets in Egypt's depths. Although the Egyptians launched an all-out war with moves that had serious ramifications—such as closing the Bab el Mandeb Strait—the air force refrained from the in-depth bombings it had conducted in the War of Attrition. Fear of Egyptian surface-to-surface missiles being fired into Israel's depths may have deterred the IAF, but this consideration played no role on the Syrian front. Peled regretted that the air force's tremendous firepower had not been exploited to inflict major damage on Egypt's rear-based infrastructure.

The IAF admitted it failed to assist the ground forces in the critical stages of the war. Its official literature drily noted the absence of results on October 7, especially in Second Army's sector during the bungled attempts to provide close assistance: "Between 13:00 and 15:00 the IAF operated in the northern sector to relieve the pressure on Budapest and Orkal—results were nil. In Firdan at 14:35, in Ismailia at 15:20, and in the night of October 7–8, nine loft bombing runs in the Port Said area and Kantara were without significant results."[133]

Cohen was very critical of the IAF:

I'll represent the ground forces. I don't know if you're aware of it but you're not helping us enough. . . . How many [of our] forward command posts needed your assistance and the air force snubbed them? This is how I see it, not as you see it. . . . Right now, this afternoon, I don't know why there aren't two or three four-aircraft formations patrolling Air Control Unit 511 [Refidim] ready to hop over [to help the ground forces] the minute they're needed?

Peled: They were there. . . . Did you expect me to continue the attack with fifty-six Egyptian planes inside?

Cohen: Yes! I expect professional answers. I'm certain that the guys down there needed [our support].[134]

The IAF commander was aware of the rancor and frustration in the squadrons and the CCP, and he shared these feelings. After the war he wrote that the source of this disappointment lay "in the great discrepancy between our expectations of ourselves, not to mention the ground forces' expectations of us, in the conditions that we knew would prevail. The IAF's sense of frustration in realizing this was a hundred fold more painful than the ground forces' complaints." Peled claimed that, in essence, the criticism was justified, but the details were off the mark.[135]

In a commanders' discussion at 19:00 on October 10, the ground forces in Sinai were accused of not deploying for an attack. This spurious charge ignored the chief of staff's order to stabilize the line on Artillery Road. Peled and Major General Ezer Weizman (Ret.), a former IAF commander, correctly sized up the situation. Peled described the "IDF's outstanding feat—from its [inferior] situation on Saturday morning to engaging in combat in the evening." He explained to the IAF commanders that "armor was not fighting a winnable armor-versus-armor battle, but was up against enemy infantry armed with thousands of personal antitank missiles, and most of our casualties were not from tanks but from the infantry that surprised us." Peled observed that "the ground forces are strong enough to hold the enemy, but not strong enough to attack." Weizman added: "You don't know what's happening on the ground. . . . Those guys with their sparse forces . . . the regulars, have suffered a horrific blow. I'm not sure you're aware of how heavy their losses are. . . . We'll have to work in unorthodox concentrations in Sinai. . . . Forget for a minute whether or not the ground forces are moving [to attack]. . . . They won't move until their situation is like that on the Golan Heights." The IAF commanders' responses to the ground commanders reflect more than a modicum of apologetics and a desire to prove that they did the best they could to assist them. Peled rebuffed Gonen's accusation that the IAF did almost nothing on the canal on Sunday, saying, "That's true, but it's because the picture in Southern Command on the night of October 6–7 was that things were going in our favor, while the situation in the north was the exact opposite and forced us to divert almost the entire IAF effort [to the Golan Heights] for nearly all of Sunday."[136]

The Main Problem: Close Air Support

Although the problems involving close air support originated with the pilots and the air force commanders, neither the IAF nor the ground forces made any attempt to redress the combat doctrine and develop emergency drills that could improve cooperation. Even the chief of staff, who took pains to use discretion in the wording of the war summaries, acknowledged, "We can't allow ourselves the luxury of an IAF that only defends the skies and is not used effectively in land battles because we will always be quantitatively inferior."[137]

The failure of close air support—one of most painful shortcomings of the war—had a negative impact on the defensive battle's length, results, and cost. In a Southern Command senior staff meeting, Peled enumerated the main problems with close air support:

- Close support couldn't be given to all the field units because there were too many requests and air space and radio frequencies were limited. It's wasteful and will always be an exception to the rule.
- Air support wouldn't be provided while the missile layout was still operating [up to 6,000 feet]. We were told in joint planning sessions and until the "Oz exercise [a crossing exercise by 162nd Division in March 1972 with full-scale forces] . . . [that if] you need 24 hours [to deal with the missiles] you'll get it, and if you need 48 hours you'll get them too. The main point was to get the job over and done with. The last thing we wanted was the enemy's air force swooping down on ground forces.
- In order to give effective support to the ground battle [not to strategic operations seventy to eighty kilometers in depth] we had to revamp the intelligence collection system on the battlefield. . . . We were strong enough to allocate resources and we tried it in the war because it was impossible to get a clear picture of the battle in the ASC.[138]

Peled highlighted two points: the need to upgrade the level of intelligence and the need to dispense with central control and planning in specific cases. In his opinion, the knottiest problem was gaining a picture of the battle while still in the planning stage of operations.

In 1973 there were two main reasons for the IAF's ineffectiveness: on the tactical level, there was no basis for air-ground readiness and cooperation; on the operational level, no one took into account the enemy's size and the density of the antiaircraft weapons. The following problems explain the failure of ground support:

- According to IAF priorities, air support for the ground forces was a lower priority than destruction of the antiaircraft missiles and the airfields. Although this subject has already been discussed, it cannot be overstated that in certain situations, the combat arms' priorities have to reflect overall war aims rather than a sectoral perspective.
- An "unfinished" and uncoordinated combat doctrine for air-to-ground support had been an issue in previous wars, and at the beginning of the Yom Kippur War, a new support system had not yet been completed.
- Flaws in the air-ground organizational and control structure included the absence of an operational center for air-to-ground attacks (the ASC, in 1973 terms). This center was established on an ad hoc basis on October 6 and was barely mentioned in the IAF's summaries of its linkage with the ground forces. The air force blamed the chief artillery officer for close air support's failure and the failure to relay targets to the air force. That officer, Major General Natan Sharoni (Ret.), claimed he received no calls for support, and from his location in the Pit, he dealt only with artillery matters. In any case, the muddled, opaque delegation of responsibility between the blues (the air force) and the greens (the ground forces) that sufficed in peacetime exploded into chaos when war broke out. The air force tried to shift responsibility to the greens, but the real reason may have been a deep-rooted misunderstanding among GSO, the blues, and the greens.
- The lack of communication between the blues and greens, which was mainly a mental problem and not a technical one, led to a "dialogue of the deaf."
- The pilots demonstrated a lack of devotion to mission accomplishment when it came to supporting the ground forces. In 20 percent of the sorties intended to assist the ground forces, the pilots failed to deliver their ordnance. Peled stated, "The number of warplanes that abandoned their air-to-ground

missions was quite large and should be investigated by a historian."[139]

- The IAF had difficulty obtaining updated intelligence on targets (see below).
- The missile threat affected the air force's ability to assist the ground forces. It also influenced the IAF's planning and performance (the lengthy timetable tied to missile elimination, inaccurate support techniques, fear of entering a missile-saturated environment, no Phantoms allocated for assistance, and so forth). Because of the chief of staff's decision to destroy the missiles first, leading to the cancellation of Tagar and the shift to Dugman, the ground forces were denied effective air assistance on October 7, the most strenuous day of war on the canal. The missile threat also impeded the IAF's efforts to knock out the bridges, which had become the conduit for strengthening and replenishing Egyptian forces on the eastern bank.

Unavailability of Real-Time Intelligence

Peled and many senior IAF officers regarded the lack of near real-time intelligence on targets as the primary reason for the air force's failure to provide ground assistance. The issue was brought up during the war, and Peled said, "An air intelligence layout had to be established that supplies us not only with data on airfields and missiles but also enables us to participate in the ground fighting. We can't leave this in the hands of MI and the commands."[140] Even after his retirement, Peled spent a great deal of time lamenting the air force's lack of intelligence during the war. As an example of a lost opportunity—albeit not a particularly good one—he would wave aerial photographs of massive Egyptian army concentrations and bottlenecks on both banks of the canal that remained static for days and claim, "If only we had known, we could have done a spectacular job." (He claimed he saw some of the photos only two weeks after the war.) What he meant was that if the IAF—which conducted aerial reconnaissance twice a day and relayed the photos to GSO and the commands—had been able to produce independent intelligence on its targets, the war would have gone differently.

Certain senior IAF officers—Ivry and Shefer, for example—blamed the ground forces and the GHQ intelligence branch for not providing the IAF with data on ground targets. Other IAF commanders viewed the problem more evenhandedly and pointed to flaws within the IAF as well. Motti Hod put his finger on the problem: "There was no opportunity or plan to provide close directional support. . . . The problem was to convey the information [the enemy's whereabouts and location of our forces] so that a briefing could be held. . . . There was absolutely no possibility that they [the ground forces and the GHQ intelligence branch] would produce this in real time."[141]

Peled went even further, asserting that Dugman 5 failed because the IAF did not collect intelligence on the Syrian armor's location and the adjacent antiaircraft weapons, which led to the loss of six Phantoms. Peled's accusation raised eyebrows. The IAF had taken photographs on the morning of October 7, so the question was whether air force interpreters analyzed only surface-to-air missile batteries and waited for the GHQ intelligence branch to interpret tank formations and their adjacent antiaircraft protection. Peled claimed that the IAF's dependence on the latest information—which it was not authorized to collect and act on immediately—was a recurring reason for the air force's failure to take part in the ground battle. His main arguments were as follows:

- The IAF had no intelligence tools of its own to gather reports from the battlefield, except for visual or "aggressive" reconnaissance in enemy territory. The IAF did not interpret or analyze the photographs it took to obtain a picture of the ground forces' situation. It was not free to roam Sinai's skies as it had in 1956 and 1967, nor could it safely and comfortably attack targets that had been discovered only a minute earlier by visual reconnaissance.
- All the information the IAF collected, at a rate of almost three times a day, was relayed to the ground forces, which then checked, interpreted, and assessed the information before deciding whether to request the air force to attack.
- Information was supposed to flow from the combat echelons in the field, through a complex network to the ASC, and from there to the attack squadrons, but this did not happen. Due to the fog of battle, the information arrived stale and in bits and pieces, making it unreliable. Aircraft sent out on attack missions had to stay in range of the enemy's antiaircraft weapons

too long, and some were shot down. In contrast, whenever the IAF attacked targets based on exact spotting and immediate identification, the missions were carried out superbly, even in areas protected by surface-to-air missiles.

- The key to success in attacking ground targets, even on the contact line, was the immediate exploitation of rapidly conveyed information.
- The IAF had to obtain intelligence tailored to its own needs. Had it developed its own system for measuring, interpreting, conveying, and assessing the enemy in a given area in near real time, no missiles or antiaircraft weapons would have prevented the use of airpower.

Peled made no distinction between blunders resulting from the ground forces' inaccurate intelligence and foul-ups caused by the IAF, such as its inefficient ASC. He lumped all the shortcomings together and blamed them on the ground forces: the commands and the forces in the field that were supposed to be working with the air liaison system.

Peled presented his doctrine in a symposium in Jerusalem in 1975. There, he stated that information collection must be the IAF's responsibility since, at the end of the day, it would be tasked with attacking the targets. This required real-time intelligence, and he believed the time between the target's identification and its elimination could be cut to thirty minutes.

Peled's idea about an independent IAF target acquisition system may have been valid in principle, but it had nothing to do with the air force's failure to support the ground forces in the war. When hostilities erupted on the Egyptian front, there were giant key targets ("eggs") ripe for attack. These included static funnels on October 6–9 (and even later) that were crammed with military vehicles, tanks, APCs, and other equipment; bridges that, once assembled, became static (though they were often dismantled); and the enormous concentration of Egyptian forces on the eastern bank that remained static from October 7 to 14 (with minor movements). None of these plump targets would have been difficult to attack. Thus, Peled's argument for developing a thirty-minute attack capability was irrelevant as far as the defensive battle in Sinai was concerned; it would have been better suited to daily security operations in Gaza or Lebanon.

The IAF commander stated specifically (and justifiably) that future crossing areas could have been identified before the war by the SA6 batteries deployed next to them. Obviously, they contained huge concentrations of armored fighting vehicles, tanks, APCs, artillery, and logistics appurtenances—in short, they were funnels, first on the western bank and then on the eastern bank. The batteries identified in aerial photographs obtained on October 5 and 6 could have provided the IAF with a reasonably accurate picture of future crossing areas and the location of primary, "juicy" targets. Every pilot operating on the canal must have observed the funnels and reported them, and they could have easily identified and attacked them—if not on October 6, then certainly the next morning. A similar omission occurred with the bridges (see figure 3).

Claiming that the IAF's interpreters were unable to identify these concentrations is preposterous. The funnels were enormous, and recognizing them would have required minimal knowledge in aerial photographic interpretation. Colonel Shmuel Gordon (Ret.) verified that there were interpreters in the air force—graduates of the same course taken by their counterparts in the GHQ intelligence branch and the ground forces—who could have easily deciphered the air photos. Furthermore, according to Gordon, there was not one iota of truth to Peled's claim that the IAF did not have any targets. The air force was aware of the Egyptian concentrations on the western bank and could have attacked them at 14:00 on October 6, according to Scratch or any other plan. They were clearly visible, even with the naked eye, on the aerial photographs.

As to why the IAF made no effort to identify targets, Spector explained that it was fixated on surface-to-air missiles, which it believed would be the tipping point for the Egyptians' collapse. All other targets were secondary. The IAF paid no attention to ground targets and the greens were a "pain in the ass."

If the IAF realized early in the war that the system of conveying intelligence was ineffective, why didn't the CCP or the IAF representative in Southern Command take the initiative and attack the made-to-order targets on the western bank? In fact, there was no need for coordination with Southern Command; an ad hoc short-loop configuration (GHQ intelligence branch–IAF–GSO) could have been set up whereby the air force collected the information and independently attacked the western bank and the eastern one up to Canal Road, similar to its attack against surface-to-air missiles. Southern Command could have continued to collect intelligence for ground targets and request air attacks on the eastern bank east of Lexicon Road, based on the existing doctrine. In the mobile battles on the western bank, after the IDF crossed the canal, the air force actually operated better than in the defensive phase, without any change in the intelligence-collection system—the one Peled criticized so contemptuously. The main differences were joint (blue-green) drills with the old liaison system and the IAF's freedom of action after flight corridors were opened and expanded by the ground forces' advance.

The GHQ intelligence branch, which was responsible for supplying the IAF with green targets, failed in its task. The IAF identified the problem but failed to make emergency changes in the combat doctrine. Instead, it continued to wait for targets from GHQ and the commands while missing the golden opportunity to decimate the Egyptian concentrations on both banks of the canal.

The Unacceptable Price of Ground Support

Why did the IAF avoid taking the initiative and pass up the opportunity to attack the Egyptian targets? Was it deterred by the missile threat? Ivry claimed there was no one to talk to in Southern Command, but he ignored the IAF's ability to bypass Southern Command in a short-loop configuration; nor did the air force initiate any change in the combat doctrine or develop a new drill for ad hoc cooperation. The IAF was not truly involved in the ground war on the canal. When faced with a dense air defense system and the potential for heavy aircraft losses, the cost of ground support became unacceptable. Instead of massive operations or sorties against ground targets (Scratch), all that remained were solo, inaccurate attacks carried out with haphazard coordination with the ground forces.

The operational concept that "the regulars will hold" was based on support from the air force, yet no deliberately organized battle procedure existed for ground-air cooperation in defense and offense; nor were timetables, forces, IAF missions, or professional appendixes—everything needed for a deliberate operational order—prepared in detail. Just as there were no air assistance plans in the ground commands, there were no orders in the IAF for ground support, excluding Scratch.

In one of the commanders' meetings that Peled held during the war, Colonel Oded Marom, commander of the ASC, remarked, "The C.B.U. [cluster bomb unit] was 800 meters off target but it landed and made noise and the ground forces got all that they wanted." This comment expresses in a nutshell the IAF's attitude toward the ground forces; it reflects the blues' total lack of understanding of the greens' needs; it disparages the greens' cries for assistance; and it exudes the supercilious attitude adopted by certain air force commanders during the long and grueling war. In effect, this loathsome, malevolent wisecrack reflects the mental alienation between the two arms—an estrangement that was more counterproductive than any technical deficiency in weapons or doctrine. The IAF relegated ground support to third place on its list of priorities, and to a certain degree, it resented the fact that ground support took pilots away from their primary missions.

Even successful ground assistance conducted outside the range of the missiles (such as the attack on Egyptian 1st Brigade on its way to Ras Sudar or the damage inflicted on 3rd Brigade/4th Division in Wadi Mabrook on October 14) had little effect, either tactically or strategically, on the outcome of the war. The air strikes did not topple the Syrian and Egyptian ground forces, and they proved once again that close assistance was risky and should be carried out only in extreme cases. The realization on October 7 (after the failure of Tagar and Dugman) that neutralization of the missiles would be a long and hard campaign was not translated into an understanding that the IAF's participation in the land battle would have to be different from its role in the past. A doctrinal volte-face, because of the limited time warplanes could hover above a missile-saturated area and the pilots' need to identify targets to be attacked, did not occur.[142] This anachronistic combat doctrine unquestionably contributed to the failure of air support.

Spector reckoned that even if the opening situation had been more auspicious, there would have been no drastic change in the nature of air support; in the state of "avalanche," as he described it, the importance of planning, joint control, and the intelligence bodies was sky-high. The missile threat between the War of Attrition and the Yom Kippur War, as well as the Syrians' motivation to strengthen their air defenses after they were attacked in the First Lebanon War in 1982, has limited the IAF's ability to take part in land battles, and this situation is unlikely to improve. Furthermore, problems of coordination, nighttime operations, weather conditions, target acquisition, and IAF priorities exist, and there is no guarantee that close air support can be provided when the ground forces request it. The IAF's contribution to a future ground war, according to Spector, will be interdiction and the neutralization of strategic targets.[143] The author is in total agreement with this view.

Did the ground forces have any reasonable basis for expecting immediate air support at the start of the war? According to Lieutenant General Rafael Eitan (Ret.), the IAF should never have been involved in supporting the ground forces until it had destroyed the missiles and gained a fair amount of freedom of action. In other words, the ground forces should have been prepared to bear the brunt of the tempest in the initial stages of the war, without dependence on air assistance.[144] However, at the start of the Yom Kippur War, air support was crucial for implementing the "not one step" mission, and the chief of staff had to reverse priorities and order the execution of Scratch—despite the missile menace.

The loose balance of the command structure (GHQ, the commands, and the IAF) between October 6 and 8 added substantially to the failure of ground support, and the system needed a few days to readjust. Even after it got back on its feet on October 9, ground support remained ineffective and desultory, mainly because of the debilitating effect of missed opportunities in target acquisition. The IAF's erosion at the outset, similar to that of the ground forces, was undoubtedly a major reason for its reluctance to put aircraft in harm's way to support the greens (as in the October 8 counterattack).

The chief of staff stuck to his general concept in the war summaries: limited assistance to the ground forces until the missiles were destroyed. As for the price of close air support, he declared, "The October War strengthened my belief that air support meant heavy losses [to our aircraft] and the scope of the losses was out of proportion to the limited results."[145]

The IAF commander stated in no uncertain terms that the air support system (dating back to the 1950s) had been an absolute failure. The entire system had malfunctioned, revealing a total lack of cooperation between the ground forces and the air force to destroy the enemy on the battlefield. Neither arm had taken the trouble to devise war plans in the event of an enemy-initiated surprise attack. In Peled's opinion, the unfavorable physical conditions of the war were not the result of the intelligence concept or inattention to the warning or even the IDF's failure to mobilize. The situation surely could have been better, but then the lessons of the Yom Kippur War would not have surfaced in such sharp relief with regard to a two-front war, air-to-ground cooperation, and combined-arms warfare. Peled pointed out the difficulty of adapting to a situation in which there was no "wham-bam and it's over," especially after paying the high "entrance fee."[146]

The IAF's Impact on the War

Some senior IAF commanders have cited an absence of dedication to mission as one of the main reasons for the air force's limited success in the war. Destruction of the bridges on October 7–8 could have been a decisive factor in the defensive battle, but the IAF failed in this, largely because it had not prepared for such a mission. This setback notwithstanding, Peled presented a disingenuous theory that the illusion of damaging the bridges on October 7–8 averted the order to withdraw to Lateral Road on October 8.

Other commanders disagree with Peled's view that the IAF's activity had a decisive impact on the war's results. Against this backdrop, there appears to be a singular logic to Gonen's claims that more could have been expected from the air force, which received 52 percent of the annual defense budget. Some senior airmen, first and foremost Ivry, claimed that the ground forces' calls for help disrupted the IAF's mission of attaining air superiority. But its inaction against enemy ground forces, in the absence of real-time intelligence on targets and suitable weapons, was the true reason for its poor showing.

The IDF's overall needs (including support for the ground forces) must always take precedence over the needs of a particular arm, and in the general shambles of October 7, decisions had to be made that suited not only the IAF's interests. The air doctrine, important as it is, is not designed solely for the air force; it is an integral part of Israel's general security concept. The IAF's allegations of incompatibility between the IDF's expectations (immediately holding the enemy invasion in check) and the air force's ability to meet them for forty-eight hours ignore the fact that Elazar and Dayan always intended to give the IAF freedom of action, as it requested, but those plans went awry.[147]

Egyptian Assessment of the IAF's Performance

The Egyptians estimated that Israel would launch a preemptive strike against the bridging and crossing equipment in response to their attack. In the event of a surprise, the IAF would have to limit its night attack to small groups of warplanes operating in the crossing area. The Egyptians reckoned that the attack would begin at first light on D day + 1, when Israeli jets would hit the airfields, front-line air defenses, bridges, forces on the eastern bank, and second-echelon operational forces. They assumed the IAF would carry out 400 to 500 sorties on the first day of fighting against targets in Second Army's sector and about 250 sorties in Third Army's sector (greatly overestimating the actual number of sorties). In addition, they thought the IAF would make a concerted effort to provide assistance to the ground forces beginning on D day + 1 by attacking the first operational echelon that had gained a toehold on the eastern bank and the air defenses protecting it.

In the war summaries, the Egyptians noted that the IAF failed to achieve its objectives. Israel's faith in the air force—and its pronouncements that the IAF was capable of responding immediately to Arab aggression in the case of renewed hostilities—proved illusory.[148]

The Agranat Commission's Assessment

The Agranat Commission, which avoided passing judgment on the IAF's performance in the defensive battle, noted in a serpentine sentence in the conclusion of its report: "Since the IAF's freedom of action depended not only on enemy planes, but—from the point of view of direct and indirect offensive assistance [interdiction] also on the resistance of the enemy's anti-aircraft layout—so that the ground forces could act quickly until [the IAF] attained freedom of action, they [the ground forces] had to rely on their own help. In addition, in offensive action against the enemy's rear and supply lines, the air force is the most effective weapon."[149] With all due respect to the committee, this is a convoluted linguistic mélange of the truth: that is, the most effective assistance for the maneuvering formation on the ground came from its own branches—especially the artillery, which must be continuously strengthened and upgraded.

The Agranat Commission's comments on air-to-ground support reflect its unfamiliarity with the subject matter and its inability to serve as an "even-handed mediator" in judging both sides. Disappointment with the air force was the outstanding feature of the ground commanders' testimonies, whereas IAF reports claimed that a great number of sorties had been carried out in perilous conditions. "Obviously these commanders had been expecting another form of air support and their understanding did not take into account the change that the theater had undergone and the effect of the enemy's antiaircraft layouts on the possibility of receiving close support from the air force, the weapons that would be used against it, the information available to the aircraft, and the procedure of requesting air assistance and directing it."[150] The committee's language, in addition to being incorrect, detracted from the ground force commanders' credibility and belittled their professional integrity.

The Agranat Commission devoted all of five and a half pages to the IAF. Other than the issue of the time frame for the IAF's assistance to the ground forces and a few ancillary questions, the committee ignored the IAF's performance in the offensive battle, a subject it was unequivocally mandated to examine. The fact that the lion's share of the defense budget went to the IAF and the fact that the highest echelons in the IDF and the defense ministry regarded it as Israel's ultimate answer to a worst-case scenario—a surprise attack, when only the regulars were on the line—should have compelled the committee to scrutinize the IAF's performance and its role in the defensive battle's failure. This was not done, and there is no explanation why. Moreover, even the IDF's History Department refrained from questioning any of the IAF commanders, from Peled down, even though it carried out an in-depth investigation of the chief of staff and his deputy; the generals of the commands; GHQ intelligence branch staff; division, brigade, and battalion commanders; and other ground force personnel. This too has no official explanation.

To the extent the Agranat Commission touched on the air force, its inquiry was limited mainly to whether the assumption that the regulars would hold included the air force. For some inexplicable reason, the committee decided that it did not. The committee drew no conclusions about IAF intelligence personnel and their significant contribution to the notion that the Egyptians would not launch a war until they were armed with long-range bombers and surface-to-surface missiles. It accepted without question Peled's arguments that the air force was not the solution in every situation, that the possibility of bad weather had interfered with the attack on the missiles, and that the preliminary conditions for a preemptive strike, which the air force made sure to present in exercises and plan approvals, had not been met.

Another reason for the failure to investigate the IAF's role was the absence of an airpower expert on the committee. In addition, there was almost no objective research literature on the IAF's performance in the first days of the war. In debriefings held by Lieutenant Colonel Aboudi, head of the IAF's history branch, the squadron commanders adhered to a defensive position and expressed a lack of confidence in the doctrine before the war, whereas Peled preferred to look to the future. The 1973 war debriefings were relegated to a file labeled "top secret" and ensconced in a safe.[151]

Ivry gave an "elegant" answer when asked by the author why the Agranat Commission did not investigate IAF personnel: "They didn't think the air force did anything wrong."[152] Another IAF commander, Avihu Ben-Nun, replied more modestly, admitting that he did not know. Spector, too, confessed that he could not say why IAF personnel did not appear before the Agranat Commission, but he agreed that the primary reason was probably that the IAF "did all its laundry indoors" and was "something of a foreign army" in the IDF. The Agranat Commission perceived the air force as being above investigation and feared meddling in its business.[153]

According to Lieutenant Colonel Zeev Lachish, formerly of the IAF history branch, it was convenient for the senior military echelon not to examine the IAF separately. It served the IDF's and the IAF's respective interests for the inner workings of the air force to be a mystery to outsiders, and both bodies engaged in mutual deception that everying was okay (the same was true in the two Lebanon wars). Lachish noted that the IAF's orders for the Day of Atonement were ponderous and had been planned by the Six-Day War team for individual scenarios against missiles, not for an Arab-initiated all-out war scenario. For the first two days, the air force thought it was fighting the seventh day of the Six-Day War, and it tried to reenact the Six-Day War miracle until it woke up to reality on Monday evening. Thus, the IAF obsession with air defense on October 6 enabled the Syrian and Egyptian armies to cross the contact lines without interference and without the implementation of Scratch. Lachish stated that the air force focused on Tagar and Dugman rather than "wasting" its strength on a trifling matter like ground support, which was reminiscent of it actions on the first day of the Six-Day War. The air force "sold" slogans and the ground commanders "bought" them. Lachish added that Ezer Weizman told Peled, "The Agranat Commission may have forgiven you but I haven't! You should pack up and go home like the others." But Peled, as we know, remained in his position.[154]

According to Gordon, criticism of the IAF's part in the war was relatively limited compared with the bitter denunciation of the ground army, MI, the defense minister, and the prime minister. Also, IAF personnel in both the standing army and reserves kept their mouths shut when asked about this criticism. It could be that by "closing ranks," the air force preserved its unity and facilitated its recuperation as it faced the next challenge.[155] Closing ranks, however, can hinder constructive criticism and prevent an in-depth correction of deficiencies.

IAF personnel did not appear before the Agranat Commission because of the desire to avoid a war of the generals in the media and because of the IAF's superb skill at hiding its dirty laundry—and that laundry was definitely stacked in large piles. Indeed, the IDF related to the IAF as though it were beyond the comprehension of outsiders and not to be tampered with. Yet the feeling persists that all involved considered themselves experts on all aspects of ground fighting. The Agranat Commission's refusal to investigate the air force defies understanding, given that one of its members, Lieutenant General Laskov (Ret.), once served as IAF commander (however, he was not a pilot and could not be considered an expert in airpower).

5

The Preemptive Strike that Wasn't

Until 1955, Israel's warfare doctrine had no offensive concept, since it assumed that the Arabs would initiate the next war. Only after the 1956 Sinai Campaign, during which the IDF delivered the first strike and transferred the war to enemy territory, did the security concept include a preemptive strike principle in the event Israel was threatened. Between 1956 and 1967 the security concept was predicated on the principle that offense is the preferred shape of battle: leapfrog over the defensive stage, seize the initiative, and transfer the fighting to enemy territory—in other words, launch a preemptive war. The force needed for this goal was built up and organized. The Egyptians were fully aware of Israel's deterrence strategy, and they knew that when Israel wanted to avoid war, as in Operation Rotem in February 1960, it refrained from attacking and immediately backed off.

The IDF and the IAF (as an operational arm) envisioned three ways of responding to a military threat:

1. A preventive strike—a deliberate attack initiated prior to active enemy provocation. Its aim was to destroy the opposing military force.
2. A preemptive strike—intended to anticipate and disrupt the enemy's planned offensive.
3. A parallel strike—intended to pulverize the enemy's forces the moment hostilities commenced and frustrate his offensive plans.

The Preemptive Strike Concept

Israel's unwritten security concept accepted without reservation the need to initiate military actions such as preventive war and the preemptive strike, as defined by Yigal Allon in his pre-1967 book. In Allon's view, a defensive strategy for a state like Israel—that is, with a small population and surrounded by enemies—is impossible; such a state has to rely on deterrence based primarily on the perpetual threat of a preemptive strike as the optimal, and perhaps only, method of maintaining the status quo. If the enemy is not determined to go to war, he must avoid steps that could be interpreted as justifying a preemptive strike. If his objective is war, he cannot claim that Israel thwarted his intentions. Awareness of the possibility of a preemptive strike strengthens deterrence and reduces the likelihood of hostile activity.[1]

Allon leaves no room for doubt about the need to preserve the preemptive strike option. "It is doubtful whether any normal state would be willing to allow the enemy, certainly one with Israel's cramped geographical constrictions, to take the initiative even if the greater percentage of world public opinion condemns it. . . . What it boils down to is that security is the goal of the nation or state, whereas foreign policy is only a means to facilitate its realization, not the opposite. Better that Israel survives and is rebuked defending itself than eulogized on its tomb." Allon emphasizes Israel's moral right to carry out a preemptive strike if it believes its existence is in peril. Nevertheless, he warns of taking such an extreme measure too hastily and advises delaying the attack for as long as possible. The IDF's strength, along with Israel's power and willingness to deliver a preemptive strike, will reduce the need to embark on such a venture. This and Israel's right to self-defense, which includes making the first strike, are the best means of deterrence. A preemptive strike allows a quick and successful end to hostilities with minimal casualties and destruction on both sides. "It is imperative that in certain situations Israel preempts an invasion even by only a few hours; the main thing is to preempt it."[2]

The Folly of Waiting for the Arabs to Start a War

Former chief of staff Yigael Yadin believed that, given the balance of forces between the Israelis and the Arabs, if signs pointed to war, it would be foolish to sit around and wait for the Arabs to start it. A reactive defensive concept would exact a much heavier price in terms of lives and the economy; therefore, Israel had to build an offensive capability and adopt a comprehensive offensive strategy based on the preemptive strike as the key force multiplier. In Yadin's view, Israel had to avoid fighting a war in which the Arabs struck the initial blow, and to prevent this from happening, it would have to act first.

After the 1956 Sinai Campaign, it was obvious that Israel's best approach was an offensive one: Israel could not wait until it was attacked; it would have to initiate a preventive war or a preemptive strike once the enemy's intention to commence hostile operations was ascertained.[3] A change for the worse in the balance of forces increased the value of a preventive war or a preemptive strike.

Lieutenant General Yitzhak Rabin (Ret.) noted that on the eve of the Six-Day War, he felt that Israel's fate depended on whether it took the initiative. The side that began the war would determine the development of the fighting, its results, and the number of casualties Israel would suffer. Given Israel's quantitative inferiority, it had to adopt the first-strike principle and conduct an offensive war rather than a defensive one. Major General Aharon Yariv said, "At the basis of the military thinking for a preemptive strike stood the time factor, superpower involvement, an enforced ceasefire, keeping the Arab countries on the periphery from participating in the war, and the risk, even after 1967, of dependency on the reservist army. A preemptive strike against an enemy that was on the verge of opening hostilities would give Israel a military advantage that offset its inferiority in other areas and would enable it to make gains in its brief timetable."[4]

The preemptive strike doctrine also involved risks. First, the government had to be convinced, with a high degree of certainty, that the enemy intended to go to war in a defined and limited time frame, and such certainty was attainable only proximate to the enemy's attack. Unless the preemptive strike was prepared ahead of time, a short-term warning would limit its planning and execution. Second, although the preemptive strike has an element of deterrence, it is also capable of inducing the opposite result—that is, war may become unavoidable if the enemy senses that a preemptive strike is imminent, in which case he may act first and start a war he did not want.[5]

The Preemptive Strike Falls out of Favor

According to General Tal, when Israel acquired strategic depth in 1967, it jettisoned both the offensive approach as the main security imperative and the propensity to be the initiator of hostilities.

Conventional wisdom held that the depth afforded by Sinai, the West Bank, and the Golan Heights provided the political sphere with greater flexibility and total freedom of action. Political considerations were no longer subordinate to military constraints, and when military threats appeared on one of the borders, Israel could afford to wait for developments and wage a defensive campaign if attacked. Security thinking was no longer riveted to the imperative that the IDF had to deliver the first strike.

The majority of political leaders and some military leaders accepted the change in the security concept. On January 1, 1968, on his first day as chief of staff, Lieutenant General Haim Bar-Lev stated that in a future war, Israel would have to consider not being the first side to launch an air strike. Be that as it may, it would always strive to take quick action and urge the powers that be to allow it to do so, but realistically, there was no certainty that such permission would be granted.

As Israel's strategic depth encouraged the feeling that a preemptive strike was not a military necessity, its political price rose. Dayan instructed the army to base its planning on a "no preemptive strike" strategy and to rely on a warning and sufficient time to mobilize the reservists. In the meantime, the regulars—including the IAF—would hold the line. Israel's second-strike strategy was that, if attacked, it would respond in full force.[6]

It was believed that Israel's territories were its best guarantee of security and lowered the threat of war, so it was understandable that it abandoned the preemptive strike and relegated the responsibility for making peace or war to the other side. In a situation in which the world recognized Israel as a regional superpower, it could not demand the "privileges" of a small, vulnerable state. The logical assumption was that, in the next war, Israel would hold its fire until the Arabs attacked. The IDF would have to block an Arab invasion while the reservists mobilized, and only then would it return to its tried-and-true system of a decisive offensive war.[7]

Golda Meir's government did not debate whether and under what conditions Israel might launch a war. This remained an open question. If emergency conditions prevailed that demanded a decision, Israel would act accordingly. When war broke out on October 6, none of the three basic assumptions at the military level—a sufficient intelligence warning, government approval of a preemptive strike, and mobilization of the reservists—were met. The government, in its desire to preserve the political and military status quo, had to reassess the situation: should Israel execute a preemptive strike or weather the enemy's opening blow? The choice of the defense doctrine was taken for granted. The political-strategic conditions and the limitations of a preemptive strike, backed by the belief that the new lines were best suited for defense, contributed to the decision for static defense on the Bar-Lev Line.[8]

Was Sinai really a buffer zone? The answer is crystal clear. With the Egyptian army deployed en masse in small-arms fire ranges, Sinai ceased to serve as a buffer zone, and the enemy could launch a surprise attack. If this situation had been accorded the attention it deserved, the Israelis would have concluded that, in the absence of a warning, a preemptive strike would be needed to gain time. The strategic depth eroded the preemptive strike principle and the understanding that the reservists had to be called up in proportion to the menace. The comfort zone provided by the strategic depth and the assumption that the regulars and the IAF could hold an offensive by all the Arab armies gave rise to the skewed concept that the reservists could be mobilized after war broke out.

From the Blue White Alert to the Outbreak of War

In the aftermath of the Egyptian force concentration on the western bank that sparked the Blue White alert in April–May 1973, the preemptive strike had to be reassessed, and the chief of staff and defense minister devoted considerable time to the problem. Elazar did not believe the government would approve a preemptive strike, and this may be one reason it was never seriously planned for. Also, some thought that a distinction had to be made between a preventive war that was unrealistic and a preemptive strike that was advisable under certain circumstances.

When the idea of a preemptive strike was first broached on April 27, 1973, Tal, the deputy chief of staff, remarked, "It seems that Yitzhak Rabin [Israel's ambassador to Washington] said that Americans had precisely warned against this." But the defense minister replied that a situation might develop in which the United States would actually be in favor of it. This did not mean that the IDF would be allowed to launch a preventive war or initiate a war with a preemptive air strike, as it had in the Six-Day War, but it implied the possibility of a situation in which a preemptive strike could not be ruled out. The gist of the IDF's assumptions, which the chief of staff presented to the prime minister on May 9, 1973, was that Israel might be prohibited from launching a preventive war, but the IDF was still preparing for the possibility of a limited strike, either before the start of hostilities or parallel to them. Elazar stressed that this was of crucial operational importance: "It can save losses and lighten the burden of war management. Although the plans that we're preparing are based on the assumption that we won't be the ones initiating [the war], . . . we'll want to be ready to face the enemy."[9]

At the May 14 GHQ meeting, Dayan stated, "It's certain we won't be able to initiate a preventive war, and I agree with Talik [General Tal] that it's not necessary. After all, given today's situation there's no interest in a preventive war, but this doesn't mean that a preemptive strike is ruled out of the question. . . . Maybe we won't be able to carry it out for political reasons but that doesn't mean that if there's no preventive war we won't deliver a preemptive strike. If it's possible, we'll do it." On May 18 the chief of staff spoke in the same vein to the foreign affairs and security committee: "We won't be able to initiate a preventive war. The first stage will be the holding stage. We might find ourselves in a situation at the start of the war that we receive information that we can deliver a parallel strike, but not an initiated or preventive war."[10]

On June 13, 1973, the new IAF commander, Benny Peled, showed the defense minister and the chief of staff the air force's operational plans. He made it clear that the attacks on the missiles and airfields in Syria and Egypt would not be carried out unless the IAF was allowed to conduct a preemptive strike and choose the optimal conditions such as time of day, absence of low-level clouds, good visibility, and precise intelligence on the location of the enemy's batteries. After the war, Peled said that Dayan and Elazar told him there was no question that Israel would attack first if there was one iota of suspicion that the enemy was about to do so. According to Peled, he nearly got a dressing down from Dayan when he expressed the slightest doubt about the promise that the IAF would receive permission for a preemptive attack. Ivry noted that during the discussion, it was explained that a surprise attack did not correspond to the political-strategic situation because Sinai's depth enabled holding the line. Nevertheless, the IAF was prepared to deliver a preemptive strike before the Egyptians or Syrians launched a war, and it was ready to carry out Operation Ramming. Peled stated that it was agreed that Israel would attack only if it was clear beyond a shadow of doubt that one of its neighbors was about to initiate a major military action into Israel's territory within days or hours. The hope (which would be replaced by disappointment) that the government would give the IAF the green light to launch a surprise first strike against the missiles in Syria or Egypt went far in stifling criticism of the Tagar and Dugman plans.[11]

In the spring of 1973 Dayan approved the doctrine that Israel was prepared to absorb the first blow, even if circumstances allowed a preemptive aerial strike. On a number of occasions he explicitly instructed the IAF to take this into account and prepare a preemptive strike in case the Arabs renewed hostilities. He spoke to the media in a similar fashion: "If war breaks out, will it be because Israel launched a preventive war? The answer is no! We have no interest in a preventive war. . . . We have no intention to declare the expansion of war and it won't be us who are responsible for a deterioration in the present situation. We will do our best [to] deter the enemy . . . from initiating a new war. We have no intention to implement a preventive war policy."[12]

In the May 21 GHQ discussion after the Blue White alert, Dayan detailed his view of a future war set off by an Egyptian and Syrian initiative: "We have to plan a preemptive strike or preemptive attack. . . . The IDF must prepare a response that will smash the Arabs to smithereens. Preparations have to be made for crossing the Egyptian and Syrian lines. I don't count out preparations for reaching the Nile."[13] During the discussion he issued his much-publicized order: "We, the government, say to the GHQ: Gentlemen, kindly plan for war. . . . Be ready by this summer, and summer begins next month."[14]

The captains of state were aware that war was unavoidable, especially after King Hussein's warning. But, led by Dayan, they hoped to derive maximum benefit from the inevitable confrontation. Therefore, as they saw it, Israel must not appear to be the side that attacked first and initiated the war. This line of thinking influenced Israel's decisions until the outbreak of hostilities.

The chief of staff and the defense minister still tried to come up with ways to execute a preemptive strike. At the April 27 GHQ meeting, Dayan told Elazar: "Look at the Golan Heights with the [Israeli] settlements and you see the [Syrians] concentrating massive artillery there. . . . Nixon won't commit suicide if we deliver [a preemptive strike]. If a provocation is needed, let's say, they opened fire first, we'll get you [a provocation]." Dayan said practically the same thing at the May 14 GHQ meeting: "If it turns out that Tel Aviv is going to be bombed tomorrow, we're not going to sit around waiting." At the following week's GHQ meeting, he added, "How do we explain to the world that we didn't start the war? When we reach that point, we'll deal with it."[15]

The Saga of the October 6 Preemptive Strike

Israel's dilemma on the morning of October 6 was whether to opt for the military advantage that was bound to result from a preemptive air strike, versus the political advantages of not doing so. As soon as the chief of staff realized that war was certain, he requested permission for a preemptive air strike on Syria. He estimated that the IAF would need two or three hours to destroy Syria's airpower, after which it could turn its attention to Syria's missiles.

In practical terms and for various reasons, such a strike would not have been operationally effective, but the government was unaware of this when it denied permission. Even at this late hour, Dayan still thought that war could be averted when he vetoed the chief of staff's request for a general mobilization and absolutely refused to allow an air strike.[16] Tal described the apprehension about initiating a final push toward war: "We shouldn't discredit this line of thinking from a psychological point of view. . . . Elazar, Dayan, Golda, no one stood up and said, 'Hold on a second! Should we give a little push to this huge corpus that's about to roll? Maybe it won't start rolling.' . . . This was the question that we faced until the last second."[17]

What could have been attacked on Saturday? Given the constraints inherent in the Golan Heights—the time factor, the Israeli settlements, and the proximity to the Jordan valley and the Galilee panhandle—compared with the Sinai front, located hundreds of kilometers from Israel's border, Syria was a better alternative. An attack was also proposed on Syria's missiles and airfields. According to Giora Forman, head of the IAF's Operations Department, the proposed attack on the canal front fell through because of the threat of cloud cover in the Nile delta and along the canal on October 5 and 6; therefore, by default, Syria remained the target area. The IAF assumed it would be allowed to implement Dugman 5 on the morning of October 6, but with overcast skies on the Golan Heights, the only alternative was to attack the airfields in Syria's depth, but this too was denied.

Several military commentators have pointed out that in addition to missiles and airfields—the IAF's favored targets—other objectives could have been attacked: C2 (command and control) systems, radar installations, and ground forces, including artillery and strategic targets in both sectors. Bombing the bridging and crossing equipment and communications systems would have been more effective than attacking the missiles and would have disrupted the Egyptian offensive. Certainly the emotional and psychological shock to the enemy would have changed his thinking and impacted his forces' performance.

It is illuminating to track October 6's time line and the fluctuations in the preemptive strike order from early morning through its cancellation at noon and beyond.

04:30. The chief of staff's aide-de-camp phones Elazar and informs him that an Arab offensive will commence at 18:00.

04:40. Elazar orders the IAF commander to prepare a preemptive strike in Syria (missiles and airfields). H hour is expected to be between 10:00 and 12:00. According to Peled, the chief of staff did not mention the possibility of the government rejecting the order.[18]

05:10. Elazar arrives in his office and speaks with his deputy on a number of issues, including the preemptive strike. Elazar says that if the order is given, the strike can be delivered between 14:00 and 15:00.

05:30. The chief of staff convenes the heads of the branches in GHQ, orders an alert for war management, and informs them that the IAF is preparing to attack Syria that day—missiles, the Syrian air force, and the line—between noon and 15:00.

05:50. Dayan asks whether, based on current data, an attack is possible before the Arabs open fire. This is the first time the possibility of a preemptive strike is broached. Elazar recommends a preemptive strike and suggests two possibilities: attacking air bases in Egypt and Syria or attacking only Syria's air bases, missiles, and ground forces on the line. Dayan states that, in his opinion, "the prime minister would say no and I too don't recommend it."[19] He emphasizes that they must avoid a situation in which the Americans suspect that war could have been prevented, even if the Israelis did not initiate it. Dayan brings up another possibility: attacking Syria, even if Egypt alone resumes hostilities. Dayan reasons that Israel has the political right to do so because the settlements close to the Golan front will be in danger. Elazar opines that if a political situation develops that enables an attack, he prefers to target only Syria, but for this, the IAF has to receive an order by 06:00. (Indeed, it receives the order and is ready at 14:00–15:00 for a preemptive strike against Syria or any other action.) Dayan remains steadfast in his view that a preemptive strike cannot be made under the present circumstances: the Americans are sure that the Arabs will not launch a war, and even if they are convinced that the Arabs are about to attack, they will recommend letting the Arabs precipitate it. Although Dayan is opposed to a preemptive strike, he approves a parallel attack—or, as he defines it, "five minutes before"—in the event hair-raising reports are received (for instance, that Tel Aviv is about to be bombed).[20]

06:15. Elazar, participating in a GSO discussion, says that the mobilization method, public or secret, depends on whether Israel opens with a preemptive strike.

06:45. The IAF commander is informed that the weather precludes an attack on the missiles on the Golan Heights. Peled updates Elazar, suggests attacking airfields in Syria's depth, and says he can be ready between 11:00 and 12:00. Elazar decides on 12:00. Thus, the preemptive strike is reduced to "two shin bones and an ear lobe."

07:15. Elazar meets with the heads of the branches, the commanders, and the generals of the commands and again instructs the air force to prepare for a preemptive strike. If it is not approved, the air force will be on standby for immediate action by noon. Elazar states that he is aware of the political ramifications of a preemptive strike but is convinced that if war is imminent, the most important issue will be how to win it as quickly as possible.

08:05. The defense minister outlines his position to the prime minister. Operationally speaking, a preemptive strike is preferred, but Israel cannot carry one out at this time. He adds that a preemptive strike should be ordered on Syria even if Egypt alone starts the war or if worrisome reports come in. Based on current reports, however, Israel cannot hit the enemy with a preemptive strike even five minutes before he attacks. The chief of staff points out that beginning at 10:00 the air force can wipe out the entire Syrian air force and three hours later destroy its missile layout, so if an offensive begins at 17:00, the IAF will be free to deal with Syrian ground forces. A decision has to be made immediately, because a preemptive strike at 12:00 is only four hours away. If this is not possible, the air force will be ready to execute a parallel strike at the start of the enemy's attack. Elazar admits that this is going to be a difficult war but states: "We're preparing for the possibility of conducting partial strikes if they can be implemented before the beginning of or immediately adjacent to the opening of the war, and the IDF's plans are based on the assumption that we won't initiate the war but will have to confront the enemy." Dayan adds that Israel cannot explain a preemptive strike to the world, "but this will be seen as events progress. If the Egyptians launch a war and the Syrians don't join in, we'll hit the Syrians nevertheless."[21]

09:05. Golda Meir sums up the discussion: "A preemptive strike looks attractive but this isn't 1967. This time the world will show its true colors. They won't believe us. If war begins only in the south then it won't be much of a problem, but that we'll find out as the day progresses." Later she asks Dayan, "If the Egyptians open the war, do you think we can attack Syria?" Dayan's response: "We won't wait even two minutes." At the end of the meeting, it is decided to transmit a message to the United States making it clear that Israel knows that Egypt and Syria are about to attack but will not launch a preemptive strike.[22]

09:25. Meir meets with the American ambassador, Kenneth Keating, and informs him that Israel will not initiate a preemptive strike. "To the best of our knowledge, the Egyptians and Syrians are going to attack Israel late this afternoon. . . . We will not start the war. . . . I want to announce to Egypt and the Soviets via the Americans that we are not planning an offensive." When Keating asks whether Israel will strike before the Arabs attack, the prime minister replies categorically, "No! . . . Although this would make things very much easier for us." (Later, in a meeting with Abba Eban, Henry Kissinger makes clever use of Meir's use of the term *announce*.)[23]

Those who have studied this conversation emphasize that the American ambassador did not demand that Israel avoid a preemptive strike. In his memoirs, Kissinger notes that Keating reminded Meir that less than twelve hours earlier, Israeli security officials had assured him that the situation was not dangerous. Meir responded by insisting that Israel would not initiate hostile activity in any way, shape, or manner. The psychological element cannot be overlooked in the prime minister's decision to reject a preemptive strike to avoid the embarrassment of having Israel look like an "undependable" player to the Americans. After all, she had sent Kissinger a telegram a few hours earlier stating that there was a low likelihood of war, but now the situation was reversed and Israel wanted Washington's approval for a preemptive strike!

09:25. The defense minister–chief of staff summary states that the IAF will be ready to attack Syria immediately with the first Egyptian shell, and an alert will be given for a preemptive strike if the Arabs make the wrong move. For some reason, this odd summary assumes that the Syrians will not attack, and with regard to the preemptive strike, it ignores the Egyptian threat. This summary was one of the components of Peled's faulty decision to postpone the switch in the aircraft's ordnance configuration until 12:50, the worst possible time with respect to the enemy's H hour.

09:45. At the chief of staff–IAF commander meeting, Peled explains that the latest hour for a preemptive strike is 16:00; therefore, the order has to be given no later than 15:00. If the strike is canceled, the IAF will have to change the planes' ordnance configuration to defense (as the expected H hour for war is 18:00), and it has to be informed no later than 13:00 if the preemptive strike has been approved.[24]

10:00. In the chief of staff's operational discussion group, Elazar orders the mobilization of all armor brigades and announces that the preemptive strike has been called off.

12:00. At the government meeting, Dayan updates the ministers on his recommendation not to open the war with a preemptive strike, and they adopt his position. The IAF commander is informed that the preemptive strike has been canceled.

12:50. Peled orders the ordnance configuration changed to air defense. This means that the aircraft assigned to attack the airfields are now shifted to patrolling and interdiction missions. Other planes prepare for air support missions on the front.[25] With this decision, any chance of carrying out a preemptive or parallel strike is lost. This decision also has grave consequences on the air force's ability to assist in the ground battle.

13:55. After Elazar is told that the enemy warplanes have taken off, he hurries to the IAF Pit to inquire whether an initiated attack can be carried out in Syria. Peled's answer: "No! The air force isn't organized for this now, but it could be." Elazar: "Then step on it!"[26]

14:30. Elazar reexamines the possibility of attacking the airfields in Syria, but Peled rejects this idea because the main force (the Phantoms) is tied to air defense (armed with air-to-air missiles).
This was one of the greatest omissions of the war. Even in the absence of permission for a preemptive strike, there had been no political veto of a parallel strike. In fact, Dayan mentioned this possibility in the morning and noon discussions. Tal noted that although a preemptive strike had not been approved, a parallel strike was automatically permitted once enemy air activity commenced. Why, then, didn't the air force use the parallel strike option? The answer is complex:

- A parallel strike would have required scrupulous organization, and the IAF was preoccupied with the preemptive strike.
- Changing the ordnance configuration committed the entire order of battle that could have been used for a parallel attack (and air support) to air defense. Had there been a plan for a parallel strike, the whole ordnance fiasco might have been avoided.
- There was no mention of a possible preemptive or parallel strike on the canal, even though Tagar 4 was still in effect.

In postwar conferences, Elazar elaborated on the circumstances surrounding the rejection of a preemptive strike. He stated that it was obvious that the war would be difficult because Israel was poorly prepared for a holding operation, and it was too late to execute Rock. He further noted that he hoped the Americans realized that Israel was on the threshold of war but was not the side that started it.

Israel's Dependence on the United States

The need for superpower (i.e., U.S.) coordination and agreement soared after the Sinai Campaign (during which Israel finally managed to acquire the support of France and Britain). The apprehension over Russian involvement was background to the lengthy political process that triggered Prime Minister Levi Eshkol's and Moshe Dayan's concern, on the eve of the Six-Day War, about capturing the Golan Heights.

The need for coordination with the United States and the anxiety over the Russian response also contributed to the decision in April 1970 to halt the bombings in Egypt's depths during the War of Attrition. The need to obtain Washington's consent was one of the major reasons for not attacking the missiles the Egyptians advanced to the canal immediately after the cease-fire went into effect on August 8, 1970.

The United States had been doing everything in its power since the 1960s to maintain Israel's conventional strength at a level that would preclude its use of a nuclear strategy and possibly even a conventional strategy of a preventive war or preemptive strike. Israel's assessment before the war, based on its daily contact with American officials, was that if it initiated a preemptive strike, the United States would not back it up. Israel had no illusions about the need to avoid a preventive war if it wanted to receive vital American political and military assistance, and it knew that any attempt to initiate a war against one or more confrontational states would be met with American opposition. There was always a chance the IDF might execute a preemptive strike in some extreme situation, but neither the U.S. government nor Israel ever imagined a scenario in which Israel would be caught by surprise, as it was in the Yom Kippur War.[27]

In the few remaining hours before the outbreak of war, no practical attempt was made to reassess these understandings, and the Americans had no time to pressure Israel to abandon plans for a preemptive attack. Israel voluntarily announced that it would not attack first, and although the U.S. government seemed satisfied, it also implied that it would not make any special commitments just because Israel was putting itself at risk. The admonishment not to attack was not accompanied by an official promise that the United States would come to Israel's assistance if the Arabs initiated a war. The Americans assured Israel that they would stand by its side, but the essence and content of U.S. aid remained vague and would be clarified only during the crisis.[28]

Israel realized that if it attacked first, the United States would respond sternly ("Israel won't see a single nut or bolt," warned the Nixon administration after the fighting erupted), whereas if it did not attack, it would be compensated. Indeed, in addition to the political furor over taking an action that ran counter to Washington's wishes, there was deep concern that the United States would withhold material aid that Israel would undoubtedly need when it ran short of aircraft, tanks, and ammunition. Most of this aid, vital as it was, arrived after the war and had to go through a mound of bureaucratic red tape.

Golda Meir assumed that American support depended on absolute proof that Israel did not start the war, and she expected Washington to understand the risk Israel was taking in forgoing a preemptive strike.[29] Meir was aware of "all the reasons 'for' a first strike, but she is against it, because there's always the possibility that we'll need assistance, and if we launch a first strike we won't receive anything from anyone. In her opinion, Elazar, too, did not consider the preemptive strike vital to Israel's security. If Israel attacked we would be at pains to explain to a skeptical world that the Arabs had planned to attack."[30]

To safeguard American support, Dayan was adamantly opposed to a preemptive strike. He claimed that Washington would not give the green light even it was absolutely certain the Arabs were about to attack, and he pointed out that the Americans had warned against making any provocative moves. In a senior command staff meeting after the war, he clarified in detail his opposition to a preemptive strike. "We're sitting on Arab soil, at least as they perceive it and the way the whole world sees us, so the Arabs are justified in going to war. We want to attack them before they attack us, and, from an operational point of view, this is the correct thing to do. . . . It's the chief of staff's duty to recommend it and the political level's duty or prerogative to agree to it or not. Politically, as things stand today, we're attentive to and dependent on one country—the United States. If we lose the very very important support from this one state, we could lose the battle with the Arabs via the Americans." Later Dayan wrote: "We were told that if we started the war with a preemptive strike, even a war that we didn't initiate, the United States wouldn't have supplied us with a single nail." He also wanted to avoid a situation in which the United States suspected the war could have been prevented and Israel did little to avert it. "The need for such an excuse in our relations with the United States may come as a surprise to a foreign observer, but anyone familiar with American-Israeli relations knows that this is not an overstatement."[31]

Dayan's concern over what the Americans might say dominated his deliberations when he received a report that Soviet advisers' families had left Egypt on Thursday night—the clearest signal that the Arabs were headed for war. Dayan wanted to guarantee that no party, especially the United States, could accuse Israel of causing the war. An experienced politician with keen insight, Dayan could have ordered a mobilization, deployment of forces on the line, and so forth on Friday, but he did not—"unless [the Arab attack] actually begins." He remained satisfied with the chief of staff's low-profile proposals within the C-level alert announced on Friday.[32]

Thus, Meir wrote in her autobiography: "Thank God I was right in rejecting the idea of a preemptive strike. It might have saved lives at first but I'm certain that [had it been carried out] we would not have received the airlift that is saving so many lives now."[33]

The American Position on a Preemptive Strike

A distinction has to be made between the American position as reported by journalists and scholars in the postwar period and the Nixon administration's official position at the time. In the unclassified literature written after the war, Kissinger's warning to Israel a few months prior to hostilities is often mentioned: "Do not start a war. Do not launch a preemptive strike. If you fire the first shot, not one 'dogcatcher' in this country will support you. You won't receive the president's support. You'll be alone, completely alone. We won't be able to help you. Do not launch a preemptive strike!"[34]

The author met with Kissinger in his New York office on June 28, 2006, and asked him to comment. He said: "I cannot remember what everyone said after so many years. . . . We didn't think there would be a war." This important admission may explain the absence of documentation; there is no official position paper on the hypothetical question of what the United States would do if Israel "let loose" and launched a preemptive strike. The Americans may not have conceived of such a scenario for many reasons, such as their faith in Israel's military superiority and their certainty that the Arabs would never embark on an offensive that would surely culminate in their defeat.

Kissinger consistently expressed his opposition to a preemptive strike and made this known to Israeli embassy staff in Washington soon after he was appointed secretary of state (a few days before the Yom Kippur War). He said he wanted to break the stalemate before war erupted between Egypt and Israel and prevent the latter from launching a preemptive strike. Kissinger's own words are a reliable historical source (no less than the investigative reports of journalists and researchers) and provide insight into Washington's position on the preemptive strike. Naturally, as a professional diplomat, he would not reveal everything, and we cannot know for certain that what he said was the absolute truth. At any rate, it is important to present his account, since he was in charge of U.S. foreign policy during that period. In his speeches on Israeli television, he avowed, "We never expressed an opinion on Israel's mobilization [of the reservists]. We wanted to avert a preemptive strike by Israel. On the day the war broke out, when the Israelis told us that war would erupt in a matter of hours, we urged them not to launch a preemptive strike. Indeed, it was a matter of three or four hours. A preemptive strike would not have changed much because Israel was unprepared for a first strike."[35]

In a briefing to his senior staff on October 23, Kissinger vigorously denied that the United States had vetoed an Israeli preemptive strike: "This is absolute nonsense! We did not urge them to avoid a preemptive counterattack because we didn't believe that war was about to erupt. There was no reason for us to tell them this. Actually, you could say that we would have been more worried about a war than the Israelis." Kissinger did not see the message sent by Brent Scowcroft from the National Security Council close to midnight on October 5, reporting Egyptian and Syrian military deployment and Israel's uncertainty about whether it was designed for defensive or offensive purposes.[36]

The author asked Kissinger about the preemptive strike and other issues related to the war. His answers follow. Note in particular point 6, about whether the United States would have helped Israel if it had ordered a preemptive strike.

1. "Golda Meir never spoke with me about preempting. If the Israelis had come on Friday and said the Egyptians are going to attack—this would have been another story. On Friday they told us that they do not intend to attack at all, and on Saturday there was war."
2. "Golda acted like this for her own reasons."
3. "Without early consultations with the U.S. government, we would not have liked it [a preemptive strike]."
4. "Abba Eban's quote is exactly right from our conversation on the morning of October 6 [Israel's decision not to deliver a preemptive strike as conveyed to the U.S. ambassador]."
5. "From our experience, when Israel wanted something, it asked us. If only we had been given time to consider the request [for approval of a preemptive strike], but we were not. We could not do much. If they would have come and asked me—this was something serious. During 1973 Israel never consulted with us about a preemptive strike."
6. "We would have supported Israel even if it had conducted a strike, but they didn't consult us and didn't tell us there was going to be a war. If we are told there is no danger of war, how can we say something different?"

The Lack of Coordination with Washington—A Political and Intelligence Fiasco

On the eve of the Yom Kippur War, Israel misread Arab intentions. As a result, as late as the morning of October 6, messages to the United States indicated there was no threat of war. By the time war became a certainty, there was too little time for a political effort to explain to the Americans what had changed and perhaps obtain approval for a preemptive strike. Even if the United States had refused and Israel had insisted on executing it, perhaps the fallout could have been minimized. Obsessed by the low likelihood of war touted by the head of MI, Israel lost the chance to establish political coordination with the United States. Had Israel taken the necessary steps for political and intelligence coordination even a few days earlier, it and the United States might have reached an understanding about a preemptive strike.

Even in the few hours remaining before war erupted, political matters were conducted in a slovenly fashion, and the attempt to coordinate with the United States was marked by dithering and blunders. For example, on October 5 Abba Eban failed to personally deliver an important telegram to Kissinger (although he had been instructed to) because he went to the synagogue to pray on Yom Kippur Eve.[37] The telegram arrived at 17:30 (New York time) and contained the first indication that war was conceivable. It posited two scenarios: (1) Syria, Egypt, or both were afraid that Israel was planning an attack against one or both of them; or (2) Egypt and Syria were in a state of alert in anticipation of initiating hostilities. The telegram requested that Kissinger intercede with the Soviets and the Arabs. The Israeli telegram reached Washington and was conveyed to Scowcroft, who relayed a message to Kissinger. Scowcroft was not overly alarmed because "this is what the CIA knew: [these were] only Egyptian-Syrian defensive measures." Kissinger, who had not seen the telegram, did not consider the matter urgent and did not act on the evening of October 5. At 22:00 Ray Klein, head of the State Department's espionage and research office, vetted the telegram and immediately realized that war would break out the next day or earlier. Despite his trepidation, neither Klein nor anyone else wanted to disturb the secretary of state's rest after a hard day's work. A report on the situation was dispatched to Kissinger's hotel in New York the next morning. Although the report listed all the evidence pointing to war, the bottom line was that war was not expected.[38]

Valuable time that could have been used to reach an understanding with Washington was lost for various reasons. At 22:00 on Friday night, the head of Mossad (Israel's equivalent of the CIA) received information from an Egyptian agent in London that war would break out the following day. However, the prime minister did not speak with the American ambassador in Israel until 09:25 the next day.[39] The five first hours were wasted because of communications malfunctions; Mossad's information did not arrive in Tel Aviv until 02:40 on October 6. Even so, there was no justification for postponing the meeting with Ambassador Keating until 09:25. The prime minister certainly could have spoken with him earlier by telephone and explained the seriousness of the situation. There is no explanation for this time gap.

Thus, because of faulty communications, the Nixon administration learned only in the wee hours of the morning (New York time) on October 6 that Syria and Egypt were about to launch a coordinated attack. Until then, the American intelligence community had estimated the likelihood of war in the Middle East as extremely low. Keating immediately telegrammed the United States after his meeting with Meir; Kissinger claimed he learned of the substance of the meeting only at 06:00 (New York time), when he received the prime minister's telegram and Israel's request to assure Cairo and Damascus that Israel had no intention of attacking them. Many years after the event, Kissinger recalled that the prime minister "sent the telegram without us asking her to. We did not initiate the request. We're talking about a period of one hour from the arrival of the message until the outbreak of war."

In an October 12 press conference, Kissinger emphasized the short time available to deal with the crisis. "A report that hostilities were about to explode at any minute was received at 06:00 and an update on the outbreak of hostile actions around 09:00." He described the whirlwind of telephone calls in and out of his hotel room on Saturday morning and admitted that diplomacy would be useless if the Arab attack was preplanned. Nevertheless, he embarked on a frenetic round of diplomatic moves to prevent a clash, believing the Egyptian and Syrian actions stemmed from a misunderstanding of Israel's intentions. Kissinger's talk marathon came to a halt at 11:25 (New York time), when he told the Russian ambassador in Washington, Anatoly Dobrynin, "Your Arab friends have tricked us in grand fashion."[40]

Since his appointment as secretary of state two weeks earlier, Kissinger had been troubled by Egyptian and Syrian preparations and had tried to alert Israeli intelligence. However, neither the Israeli nor the American intelligence agencies believed the Arabs' activity was anything more than a military exercise. Mobilization of the reservists was never brought up to the Americans. As for the Golda Meir–King Hussein conversation (when the latter conveyed a warning to Israel), Kissinger noted that Hussein might have warned the prime minister of war, but he did not inform the United States. Kissinger also recalled what Abba Eban had told him: nothing dramatic will happen in October. So the war caught

Washington completely off guard. Kissinger said: "We were quite taken by surprise. . . . Israel was truly caught by surprise when the war broke out. The first intelligence assessment held that Israel had started it, not the Arabs, because most of our officials thought it impossible that the Arabs would initiate a war they were bound to lose. This is why it is absurd to say that America gave a silent agreement for war in order to soften up Israel. It's disgraceful to say this."[41]

A week before the war, Simcha Dinitz, Israel's ambassador to Washington, had assured Kissinger that an Arab attack was out of the question. Unconvinced, Kissinger had asked for special intelligence assessments, which deemed the likelihood of an Arab attack very remote. These estimates were verified during the week and again on the morning of the attack. In the privacy of a meeting with his senior assistants, Kissinger vilified Abba Eban, claiming that, "in their conversation in New York, . . . Eban had explained most politely that there was no real need for the peace initiative that I had been urging on him because the military situation was absolutely stable." According to Kissinger, the real surprise was the faulty political analysis by both Israel and the United States. Prior to October 1973, both agreed that Egypt and Syria were militarily incapable of recapturing their territory by force. No one conceived that Sadat was seeking not a military victory but a change in the balance of power; the shock of the war would weaken Israel's sense of military superiority and soothe Egypt's sense of national humiliation.[42]

And what was the Soviet Union's position in these fateful hours? The Soviets probably did not encourage the Arabs to go to war, fearing that the United States would reap the benefits of another Arab defeat. Although the Soviets did not forbid a war, they feared that if they continued to restrain the Egyptians, the latter might switch horses. The Soviets basically told the Arabs, "This is your business." Brezhnev had admonished Nixon at the San Clemente summit in June 1973 that the Arabs were planning a war and were resolved to go through with it this time. The task of evaluating American options in the event of war was given to a low-level State Department official. The attitude was that this was a waste of time, and the work was left unfinished.[43] The CIA interpreted the evacuation of the Soviet advisers on October 4, 1973—as in 1972—as a sign of a crisis in Arab-Soviet relations.

Washington's Likely Response to a Preemptive Strike

As in any examination of an event that did not take place, it is difficult to draw clear and unequivocal conclusions. Based on the statements of politicians and scholars in the United States and Israel after the war, we can assume that, excluding the gnashing of teeth, the United States' position would have been the same with or without a preemptive strike: it would have withheld aid, sought a ceasefire at the end of the first week and on October 22 and 24, and lifted the siege on Egyptian Third Army—regardless of Israel's conduct.

The author believes that a significant preemptive strike against the proper targets in Syria and especially in Egypt could have led— at least in the south—to a shorter war, lower costs, fewer Egyptian gains, and greater IDF achievements. If Israel had hit "hard and fast," Washington's assistance would have been unnecessary, and Israel would have been in a better bargaining position in subsequent negotiations. If a preemptive strike had taken place and caused a vehement American diplomatic reaction, it would have been only lip service. The United States acted as it did in 1973 because it believed it was the wrong time for a confrontation with the Arabs, who were attacking Israeli forces on captured Arab lands; this was different from an attack across a recognized border. On the one hand, the United States regarded the Arab attack as an act of lunacy but not of immorality; on the other hand, given the geopolitics in October 1973, the United States did not want an open confrontation with its ally Israel. After the war Kissinger reiterated: "We never made Israel's refraining from initiating the war a condition for its reception of American aid."[44]

What effect, if any, would an Israeli preemptive strike against the Arab forces have had on U.S.-Israel relations? Over the years, there has been much talk about the political price Israel paid for its relationship with the United States, as well as speculation that Washington would have forced a decision on Israel, as it did after the 1956 Sinai Campaign. These views do not correlate with Kissinger's assertion that "we would have supported you even if you attacked first." Kissinger, an astute and prudent statesman, may have spoken half-truths in some of his interviews, and he may have evaded certain issues, but it is likely that this statement was true.

The conclusion that the United States would not have responded harshly to an Israeli preemptive strike is reinforced by other statements Kissinger made. For example, he expressed the need for a hard and fast Israeli strike to Dinitz on October 7 and to Abba Eban on October 13. He observed that Israel had to be realistic, and if it wanted to enter negotiations in an advantageous position, it would have to strike hard and fast and not skimp on ammunition, since the United States would replenish any shortages later. The American secretary of state wanted Israel to improve its military position because this would help Washington's efforts to save Egypt and block the Soviets, and he cited the United States' desire that Israel come to the cease-fire from a strong position.[45]

The author asked three Israeli statesmen about Washington's possible response to a preemptive strike. Lieutenant General Ehud Barak (Ret.), the former prime minister, replied, "The Americans would probably not have done much in light of the war's results." Former defense minister Moshe Arens stated, "If Israel had carried out a preemptive strike without consulting the Americans they would have let it pass. As for military equipment and diplomatic support, I doubt they would have told us 'deal with it on your own.' Ever since the Six-Day War they've treated us like an ally and would not have let Israel fall. While Nixon could not be characterized as a Jew lover, he regarded Israel as an ally." Arens also noted that when Israel attacked the Osirak nuclear reactor in Iraq in June 1981, "We didn't ask [Washington's] permission . . . and they accepted this as a fact." Shimon Peres claimed, "The Americans would have said 'tsch, tsch, tsch!' or, to put it differently, a rhetorical response could have been expected that would have had no influence on the military and political assistance during the war. . . . In general, there was no need to request permission from the Americans. It doesn't work that way. You only ask permission when you want to warn the other side. Kissinger, the bastard, would not have uttered a word about a preventive war, but neither would he have said 'don't attack.'"

Abba Eban described Kissinger's response during their meeting at the Waldorf Astoria Hotel after Ambassador Keating's telegram reached him: "He [Kissinger] had been studying a report of our prime minister's talk with Ambassador Keating. He [Kissinger] noted the Israeli decision to abstain from preemptive action. He wanted to put on record with me that this was an Israeli decision that was conveyed to the United States after it had been taken. He personally believed it to be the right decision but the United States had no need to express its position on an issue that Israel had already determined for herself."[46] Both Kissinger and Keating refused to discuss Washington's position if Israel had decided to launch a preemptive strike.

What Did Israel Get for Its "Good Behavior"?

An analysis of American activity shows that Israel received nothing of value for the restraint it displayed (other than a few expressions of sympathy). On each of the three main issues—military assistance, forced cease-fires, and the rescue of Egyptian Third Army from the encirclement—Washington acted, as expected, to advance American interests. Therefore, in the event of an Israeli preemptive strike, Washington likely would have judged it pragmatically, based on how well it served the United States. Such a strike might have resulted in considerable American advantages in terms of managing the crisis and its final results.

Military Assistance

After the failed counterattack on October 8, policy makers in Washington realized there would be no quick, decisive two-front Israeli victory this time. The war would stretch out, Israel's dependence on the United States would increase, and an opening would be created to advance American interests in the Middle East.[47] Kissinger's position was that whatever happened later was of no importance; Israel had already suffered a strategic defeat and would be unable to withstand the rate of losses. Therefore, the administration formulated a position that best served U.S. interests: it would find the least conspicuous method of supplying military equipment to Israel in dribs and drabs, while maintaining a low profile and searching for a formula for a cease-fire. Kissinger realized that the United States had an advantage, as it was the only party with ties to all sides in the conflict. The potential benefit, however, depended on Israel not incurring any further setbacks, as this would weaken Washington's bargaining position.

At this stage, Kissinger perceived the Soviet policy to be moderate and restrained, and he affirmed that the United States was avoiding moves that would require military involvement. As opposed to what Israel had been told, the Nixon administration, hoping to safeguard the détente, decided that as long as the Soviet position was conciliatory and a cease-fire was possible, Washington would furnish Israel with only a limited supply of weapons. As long as the Soviets' "clients"—Egypt and Syria—remained in a tolerable position, Moscow acted with restraint; however, the moment the situation changed, and after the Syrians were routed from the Golan Heights, the Soviets began a massive airlift on October 10. The Americans, who feared being criticized for a lackadaisical response to an international crisis, also ratcheted up their aid to Israel. Sadat's rejection of a cease-fire that would preserve the status quo contributed to the United States' decision.

Israel's decision not to attack first was of no consequence in the American equation. Washington's global interests were the determining factor, and the United States made it clear that Israel was of no strategic value.[48] Had Israel hearkened to Kissinger's conversations with Foreign Minister Eban on October 6 and on other occasions and to Ambassador Keating's message, it would have realized that the United States felt no special responsibility for the results of Israel's decision not to execute a first strike, and it was under no obligation to come to Israel's assistance. Presumably, the United States would have acted the same way if Israel had opted for a preemptive strike.

In practical terms, not a single U.S. tank arrived in time to take part in the fighting. Excluding a handful of tanks transported by air, all the rest came by ship after the cease-fire. Air-to-air missiles; a few Phantoms that, according to the IAF, were superfluous; and a few tube-launched, optically tracked, wire-guided (TOW) antitank missiles arrived on October 14. The rest of the arms came on October 24 and 25—after the cease-fire.[49] American assistance included 76 aircraft, 175 tanks, and 50 artillery pieces; in comparison, the Soviets sent 175 warplanes (50 to Syria), about 500 tanks (300 to Egypt), 50 cannon, and 200 APCs. In the final tally, Moscow supplied three times as many tanks and twice as many planes as Washington did. The Americans also shipped tank and artillery ammunition, and despite Israel's unjustified "hysterics" over the lack of ammunition, Washington guaranteed a regular supply of ammunition, which placated the IDF commanders' logistical concerns. Beyond the numbers, the weapons supply was important because it sent an undisguised message: Washington would not sit with its arms folded while massive amounts of Soviet arms and ammunition were reaching the Arabs.

Much has been written in Israel and the United States about the procrastination in assisting Israel. The reasons for the delay can be summarized as follows:

- The secretary of state approved the aid package, but Secretary of Defense James Schlesinger was opposed because of oil supply considerations. He was also against the particular consignment of ordnance. Kissinger explained to Eban that the delay did not stem from technical difficulties but, to a certain degree, from the Defense Department's stance. However, many observers are convinced that Kissinger and Schlesinger were in cahoots: the secretary of state played the "good guy" and the secretary of defense the "bad guy."
- When the civilian airlines refused to handle the airlift, Kissinger vetoed the use of the Military Airlift Command for flights from the United States to the Azores (from there, the cargo was reloaded onto El Al planes for the flight to Israel). In addition, the United States had to coordinate with the Portuguese government for landing rights in the Azores.
- Washington wanted to preserve the détente and keep a low profile to lessen the damage to U.S. policy in the Middle East.
- Kissinger shut off the "faucet" to weaken Israel.[50]

Only when the Nixon administration came to the conclusion on October 14 that the diplomatic process had run its course did it began to act with vigor and determination. This was characteristic of Nixon: whenever he faced a Soviet challenge, he worked to advance the United States' global and regional interests and strengthen its position. In this light, Israel was only the springboard.[51]

A chagrined Dayan wrote, "In the end we received less than half the number of Phantoms we asked for. We asked for tanks—and got one-fifth. We requested APCs and didn't receive any. We asked for various types of aircraft, and received a trickle. We asked for dozens of artillery pieces and they approved only one-third. We asked for TOW missile launchers and were given a quarter of the amount. I'm afraid that someone in Washington isn't overly enthusiastic about our victory." According to Eban, Kissinger acknowledged that the tardiness in conveying military equipment to Israel was aggravating. The Americans wanted Israel to win the war, but not with overwhelming superiority. Israel's success on the battlefield was the key factor in convincing the Arabs and the Soviets to end the fighting.

The arms airlift was the United States' answer to the Soviets, not an anti-Arab move designed to prevent the Arabs from retrieving their lost honor.[52]

In his interview with the author, Kissinger said:

It is not a simple matter to pull off so large an airlift, yet we were accused of delay. Until October 8 you were telling us that you were winning. Only on October 9 did General Gur [Israel's military attaché in Washington] come to me and ask for assistance. We began on October 10 and needed two days to overcome the bureaucracy and organize the airlift. President Nixon was occupied with the Watergate scandal and his vice president had just resigned [Spiro Agnew left office on October 10, after admitting to payoffs and tax evasion]. I couldn't reach Nixon until Tuesday afternoon. Had another constellation been in the White House and not Nixon as president, [the airlift] would have taken longer. The first plane arrived in Israel on October 14 and that was very fast.

In his book *Crisis*, Kissinger (perhaps in self-vindication) notes that Washington may have been unaware of the seriousness of Israel's need until the fourth day of the war. In an unconcealed accusation of Schlesinger, Kissinger states: "The secretary of defense didn't see any problem with a consignment of military aid as long as it didn't involve American technicians, but he was worried that a favorable response to the Israeli requests would reverse the direction of the campaign that the Arabs were winning and would blacken our relations with them for a long time to come. Schlesinger stressed the difference between defending Israel's existence on the pre-1967 borders and assisting Israel in occupying territory captured in the 1967 War."[53]

The cynicism of Washington's foreign policy czar was blatant. At the time, Kissinger wielded unprecedented power in Washington. To Ambassador Dinitz, he seemed to be willing to bend over backwards to help Israel in its hour of need, but this was only to prevent Dinitz from exerting pressure on Congress, the Jewish lobby, and the media. In reality, Kissinger had no intention of assisting Israel, and his explanation for the delay—laying the blame on the Defense Department—was hogwash. Kissinger ran the whole show, and everything was coordinated through him. When the president decided, in the early hours of October 13, to authorize a massive airlift, all the problems suddenly vanished, and everyone involved, including Schlesinger, acted with superb efficiency in carrying out the presidential order as issued by Kissinger.

Forced Cease-Fires

On October 8 Nixon bluntly described the need to impose a cease-fire and jump-start negotiations between Israel and Egypt: "After the Israelis finish pummeling Egypt and Syria, which they definitely will do, they'll be beyond our ability to deal with them—even more than before. We must reach a diplomatic arrangement at this point." Nixon was worried that in the wake of a certain Israeli victory, the Israelis would toughen their position; he hoped to present the sides with a rational proposal that would break the status quo. On the one hand, Nixon's policy required Kissinger to keep the military aid "faucet" shut, so as to avert an overwhelming Israeli victory. On other hand, he did not want Israel to accept a cease-fire too soon, because if the Egyptians were not on the brink of defeat, they would have no incentive to agree to some future solution. Nixon hinted that he would work to postpone the UN Security Council session on October 10–11 to give Israel time to dislodge the Egyptians from the eastern bank.[54]

Israel's agreement to an immediate cease-fire, which it announced on October 12, surprised Kissinger, but it did not move Washington to turn on the "faucet." Israel's military advantage was important to Washington, which was the reason for Kissinger's statement that Israel should strike hard and fast and not conserve ammunition. Only after Sadat rejected the cease-fire and the Soviets accelerated their arms supply did Nixon order a massive airlift to Israel on October 13.

On the same day, after the attempt to broker the cease-fire failed, Kissinger announced that American policy would continue on two tracks: the airlift, and a diplomatic effort in the UN to arrange for a cease-fire. The next morning he crystallized the U.S. position, which stressed the administration's interest in Israel achieving a battlefield decision, especially on the Egyptian front, and thus convincing the Arabs and the Soviets that a cease-fire was imperative.[55] And indeed, Egypt's failed counterattack on October 14 and the IDF's success in crossing and progressing on the western bank proved to Kissinger that a suitable cease-fire that met Washington's conditions could be attained. He exploited the military situation created by Israel to commence negotiations with the Soviet Union from a position of strength and to chalk up points in the global struggle between the superpowers. Kissinger understood that if the dimensions of Egypt's debacle increased, so would its dependence on Washington's goodwill and its need for American aid.

When the Soviets saw that Egypt was headed toward a catastrophic defeat, a diplomatic cyclone ensued. It culminated with Kissinger being called to Moscow and the two superpowers agreeing to an October 22 cease-fire, which Israel was forced to abide by (the Soviet threat of intervention came only after the cease-fire). What Washington actually did was impose the cease-fire on Israel in accordance with American global interests. The first cease-fire fell apart the same night, and the fighting resumed with heightened ferocity. Kissinger, the cease-fire's architect, later wrote: "It seemed that Israel was resolved to end the war with an Egyptian humiliation. We had no interest in seeing Sadat's downfall because of the Israeli provocation during a ceasefire that we had brokered and had extended our joint protection to."[56] Even more than three decades after the war, one senses in Kissinger a residuum of insult and resentment at Israel's violation of the October 22 cease-fire. The United States took practical measures to enforce the date of the second cease-fire too, but by this time, Third Army's encirclement was complete.

The Rescue of Third Army

By forcing Israel to lift the siege on Third Army, the United States and the Soviet Union took away Israel's most valuable bargaining chip in the south. Kissinger was convinced that Third Army's submission would have dashed all hopes for a diplomatic solution and culminated in a perpetual struggle. Had Sadat fallen in the wake of a failed military venture, his place would have been filled, Kissinger assumed, by a radical, pro-Soviet leader; Soviet weapons would have quickly restored a force equal to the encircled army; and, sooner or later, another war would have flared up. The peace process would have been over before it began, and when it was renewed, the Egyptian participant would have been much worse. Kissinger exacted the price for keeping Sadat in power from Israel.

Kissinger privately tried to persuade the Israelis to slacken their chokehold on Third Army so the United States would not have to openly oppose Israel, but his efforts were to no avail. Kissinger described Sadat's increasingly desperate requests as time went by and admitted, "We didn't want Egypt to return to the Soviet camp, and we didn't think it right to drag Moscow into a second round [of negotiations]." The Americans began to ramp up the pressure on the morning of October 26, and Israel resisted until it was presented with an ultimatum. The Americans urged the immediate deployment of UN observers to verify that the cease-fire was being upheld and that food, water, and medical supplies were reaching the trapped army. Israel was forced to acquiesce. Kissinger attributed Israel's desire to annihilate Third Army to its anger at the surprise attack and the exorbitant number of casualties it suffered, but he remained steadfast in his belief that Sadat was the key to peace.[57]

In the author's interview with Kissinger, he affirmed that "the refusal to lift the siege on the Third Army put Israel in a very precarious situation." But, he said, "We would have supported you in any situation, if Russian troops were sent in." It is unclear whether the three-way negotiations—Israel–Kissinger–Egypt—exploited every opportunity to reach a better solution for Israel. Kissinger even intimated this to the author. At any rate, the Israeli government's decision to lift the siege was reasonable under the circumstances.

Due to the political acumen and manipulations of the American secretary of state, the United States racked up impressive gains from the crisis, most of which resulted from limitations slapped on Israeli military activity (or that Israel imposed on itself). So, what did Israel get from all this? The answer: disappointment.

A bitter Golda Meir wrote: "The opinions regarding an Israeli preemptive strike—military gain versus political disaster—are divided. But there is one lesson here for Israel's decision-makers that must not be forgotten. In October 1973 Israel was prevented from achieving a decisive victory because of a superpower's involvement and this impacted on the future political results. The unrivalled victory of 1967, which included a preemptive strike, and the avoidance of a first strike [in 1973], will accompany the Israeli government's future decisions."[58] This statement can be seen as Meir's admission of her error.

Second Thoughts on Forgoing a Preemptive Strike: Then and Now

Doubts surrounding the decision not to deliver a preemptive strike began to be voiced immediately after the war. One of the issues was the nature of the preemptive strike proposed by the chief of staff: attacking only the airfields in Syria's depths, and not before 12:00. The execution of such a preemptive strike would have had only a slight impact on the war, excluding the psychological effects and the postponement of the Arabs' master plan because of their armies' limited ability to improvise.

American political commentators Edward Luttwak and Walter Laqueur claim that Israel could have put 200 warplanes aloft for an attack and still protected the nation's skies (this estimate is excessive and glosses over the political limitations, the weather conditions, and the missile threat). If each plane had carried out five or six sorties before the Arab armies entered full force into the battle, 3,000 tons of bombs and rockets could have been dropped on armored columns and supply facilities on the Golan Heights and western bank of the Suez Canal. Despite the planes' vulnerability to antiaircraft missiles, a devastating blow could have been delivered to the rearward forces, which would have shattered the enemy's morale and saved hundreds of Israeli lives.[59]

Although the chief of staff proposed bombing only the airfields in Syria on October 6, the government ministers, lacking solid information, believed that this was intended to be a massive knock-out strike that would cripple Syria's operational capabilities. They believed this because Elazar presented them with a sumptuous operational prognosis: the Syrian air force would be destroyed within three hours, followed by destruction of the missile layout, which would give the IAF complete freedom of action and enable it to take part in the land battle.[60] Dayan claimed (via his secretary, Aryeh Baron, a few years after the war) that he was against a preemptive strike on the Syrian airfields because of its ineffectiveness unless the missiles were attacked first; however, this does not appear in the notes of the discussions held on the morning of October 6.

Lieutenant General Ehud Barak (Ret.) thought that if a meticulous modular plan for a preemptive strike had been prepared *before-hand*, it might have been possible to consider various scenarios, given the existing level of antiaircraft defense. Had this been the case, a preemptive strike probably would have targeted the missile bases and crossing equipment—at an even higher price in terms of men and material—so as not to put the weakened ground forces to the test. In a *conditioned* plan, said Barak, the military and political advantages and limitations could have been weighed and their benefits assessed. However, in the absence of such a plan, there was only "illusion in the high command posts." Such an operation, according to Barak, became a "monster," and such a complex attack could not be carried out with only a few hours' preparation. Thus, the chief of staff's proposal for a preemptive strike was largely for show—for the sake of saying, we proposed a first strike and they forbade us. In this light, the government's rejection of the plan can be understood. According to Barak, the government was aware that the forces were not ready, but the political leaders believed that the IAF *could* hold the line—based on war games and a concept that had never been thoroughly examined—and that the reservists could be brought to the fronts. The government assumed that there would be a certain advantage in carrying out a preemptive strike—it was not clear how much—but there would undoubtedly be political repercussions as well. It is hard to say to what degree the prime minister comprehended, especially on the bewildering morning of October 6, the operational value (very low) of the chief of staff's proposed preemptive strike. Dayan probably understood it, but Meir anguished over the decision between the political option and the military option, which, as she admitted, could have saved so many lives and changed Israel's fate.[61]

During the war and in the days after it, the government ministers naturally questioned the wisdom of canceling the preemptive strike. At a government meeting held late on the evening of October 7, minister Yigal Allon supported the decision—in stark contrast to what he had written before 1967—despite the military justification for a first strike. This, of course, was because of the opposition from Israel's only friend—the United States. On October 8 Dayan spoke with the chief of staff in the CCP in a rueful tone about his decision to reject the proposal for the preemptive strike. After the war, Meir wrote that she was convinced she had made the right decision in not approving it.[62]

Elazar, too, acknowledged that his main reason for recommending a preemptive strike on Saturday morning was the need to destroy the missiles. He was aware of the political consequences, but he also understood the operational advantage of the preemptive strike. When asked what would have happened if there had been a preemptive strike in Syria, he replied, "We can't analyze a situation that didn't happen. . . . I can idealize the results of a preemptive strike in which we eliminated all of Syria's missiles, acquired freedom of action, and blocked the Syrians by Sunday noon. But I'm not sure if this is how it would have turned out."[63]

Knesset member Menachem Begin's speech on November 13 was the first public political criticism of the prime minister's decision to veto the preemptive strike. Begin, the opposition leader (Gahal party), could not have known that the chief of staff's proposed preemptive strike had no tangible operational value, but his assessment of Meir was incisive and on the mark:

> The chief of staff asked you to understand the difference between a situation in which our enemies start [a war] and conditions in which we initiate what is called a preventive war, and from what he said one can understand that this was his suggestion. . . . You decided not to accept his advice and since you flatter yourselves on your wisdom: go and take a good look, we didn't start the war . . . on noon, the Day of Atonement. Did we have ground forces, armor forces, and infantry available on the two fronts, in the south and north that could have launched a preemptive war against our enemies? You knew that we didn't have any such forces? Any attempt to send them on a preemptive attack was tantamount to suicide. There was only the air force that could have delivered a blow that's called preemptive.[64]

Bar-Lev said that this should serve as a lesson for the future: "In similar cases, plans for a preemptive strike are considered a safety valve against a surprise attack. In other words, surprise has to be met with surprise. A precondition for this is the availability of a mobilized force that can carry out the plan at any given moment. Be that as it may, we cannot over-rely on a preemptive strike as an answer because it isn't applicable in every military or political situation."[65]

Military scholar Ariel Levite quotes Lieutenant General Rafael

Eitan (Ret.) as one of those at the highest level of the security pyramid who believed it was a mistake to abandon the preemptive strike for political reasons:

> We should have carried out a preemptive strike on the Syrians when it was definite they were about to launch a war. An airstrike could have disrupted their opening moves. Afterwards, the prime minister, with other statesmen following suit, claimed that Israel wasn't allowed to carry out a preemptive strike for political reasons otherwise it would be accused of starting the war. I never heard of anything more ridiculous. When a nation's existence is hanging in the balance, its army isn't mobilized, and the media is shut down because of Yom Kippur so that a rapid mobilization of the reservists by a publicly broadcast call-up is impossible— the political consideration is at the bottom rung of priorities. The question what they'll say about Israel isn't worth a wooden nickel. In such a critical hour whoever attributes supreme importance to "what they'll say about Israel" isn't fit to lead this country.[66]

Dayan, the natural-born pragmatist, said in his loose-cannon style on October 8: "The price that the Arabs will pay for this war is that it's the last time in their lives they'll get away without a preemptive strike."[67]

The decision to forgo a preemptive strike and the criticism it engendered crystallized into a realization that the security concept had to be reexamined. Clearly, ceding the advantage to the side that strikes first creates an unstable atmosphere in times of crisis, and mutual fear of a preemptive strike calls for maximum alertness for any change in the enemy's intention and deployment. The cumulative effects of the preemptive strike's advantages—strategic, psychological, and military—will naturally be considered in any discussion of whether to undertake such a move. Based on the logical assumption that a preemptive strike would achieve objectives faster and shorten a war, that would translate into reduced costs in terms of casualties, equipment, and economic damage—including minimizing the time the reservists were mobilized and the concomitant damage to the economy. A shorter war would reduce Israel's dependence on the United States and lessen the window of time for the Arab states in the periphery to enter the fray (the twenty-day-long Yom Kippur War was sufficient for Iraqi, Jordanian, and Moroccan forces to join in the fighting). Israel, with its hypersensitive political culture and growing dependence on the United States, will have to weigh the military value of a future preemptive strike versus its political price, but failure to deliver a preemptive strike also has political, military, and economic repercussions. The pressure to act first has increased in light of the bitter lessons learned from the Yom Kippur War.[68]

Steven Rosen and Martin Indyk's 1976 analysis of the U.S. position on a future preemptive strike is still valid, mutatis mutandis, for the early twenty-first century, including the threat from Syria and particularly Iran's nuclear armament:

- The United States will demand restraint from Israel because various interpretations of the enemy's preparations and intentions are possible.
- Israel's economic and military dependence on the United States has grown, and Israel will probably act only in agreement or coordination with Washington.
- In the event of a future threat, voices will be raised in Israel demanding a preemptive strike.
- The United States is concerned about the global and regional ramifications of a unilateral Israeli move: a rise in oil prices, radicalization in Arab countries the United States is trying to bring into its sphere, escalation of the arms race, and so forth.[69]

If some situation poses an irrefutable threat to Israel's existence, the United States will be asked to coordinate or at least consent to an Israeli action. And in such a case, the United States must understand that ratcheting up pressure on Israel to eschew such a venture will be futile, and sanctions will not be the answer.

In the opinion of Major General Aharon Yariv (Ret.), head of MI before the Yom Kippur War, prevention is better than a cure, just as hitting the enemy before he hits you is the best policy. Yariv is not advocating a preventive war; rather, he is referring to a preemptive attack when all reports and all the signs in the field point to the enemy's intention to attack immediately. The decision to launch a preemptive strike requires full cooperation and awareness on the part of the political leadership, and all political constraints must be fully considered. The preemptive strike is a complementary means of defense that compensates for Israel's lack of strategic depth; it is not designed for territorial conquest, not even for appearance's sake.

In the future, national leaders will certainly examine the political circumstances and weigh the pros and cons of a preemptive strike in the event an inadequate warning precludes defensive deployment. The government's approval is not guaranteed or promised; it will appraise the political implications (vis-à-vis the United States) before making a decision. For this reason, the military must not base its force buildup, deployment, or alert status on a preemptive strike whose implementation remains in doubt. The proper military response must be backed by the defensive element while planning a preemptive strike and coordinating Israel's moves with the United States; however, Israel must be prepared for a situation in which it will not be able to carry out a first strike.[70] Furthermore, the postwar public discourse and the loss of confidence in political and military decisions have compelled the government to consider public opinion on both sides of the political fence, and it must face the fact that public support for a preemptive strike will not be automatic.

Since 1983 (after Operation Peace for Galilee), the defense budget has been steadily cut back, the order of battle reduced, force buildup slowed, and the IDF's area of action narrowed. At the same time, the surface-to-surface missile threat has grown with Egyptian and Syrian rearmament and the Iranian threat. All this is liable to lower the IDF's response threshold and raise the number of voices supporting a preemptive strike or at least an aerial response as long as the threat of war seems palpable. Under these conditions, the government will probably evaluate the IDF's request for a preemptive strike in a different light than it did on October 6, 1973. Because of the taboo on the use of nuclear arms, the strategy of a preventive war or at least a preemptive strike remains an absolute necessity.

Israel must preserve the option of a preemptive air strike against offensive concentrations; it must immediately take the initiative to destroy an attacker's strategy before he can implement it. To stymie the enemy's initiative when it is in the last stages of deployment, the red line for a preemptive strike must be defined; when that line is crossed, the government must choose between making a first strike, with all its inherent dangers, and preparing for the enemy's attack, followed by a counterattack. One lesson of the Yom Kippur War is that the IDF cannot accept ambiguity on this issue.[71]

Regarding advance approval from Washington, it should be noted that in the decades following the Yom Kippur War, Israel has initiated a number of military and political actions that were not coordinated with the United States:

- Preparations for Sadat's visit to Jerusalem in November 1977 and Israel's initial contacts with Egypt were undertaken without the Carter administration's involvement or knowledge.
- Operation Litani was initiated in Lebanon in March 1978 without American agreement, and it ended with a sharp divergence of opinion between Israel and the United States. However, this dispute was forgotten half a year later when Israel and Egypt were invited to Camp David.
- On January 14, 1981, the Knesset ratified the Golan Heights Law without any prior coordination with the United States. In response, Washington withheld the memorandum of understanding. Later, the Americans returned to business as usual.
- Israel's bombing of a nuclear reactor in Iraq in June 1981 was carried out, as far as we know, without updating or coordinating the move with the United States.
- Israel launched Operation Peace for Galilee in June 1982 without the Americans' "blessings," although prior to the war, several attempts were made to reach an understanding with Washington.

To summarize: Israel, in its short history before and after the Yom Kippur War, has embarked on war and entered into peace negotiations without American coordination. Thus, a preemptive strike on October 6, 1973, whether sanctioned by the United States or not, would not have been an earthshaking surprise. Golda Meir's and Moshe Dayan's hypersensitivity to Israel's need for future U.S. military and political assistance was the main reason for their veto of the preemptive strike. There is no evidence of any serious discussions in Israel before the war, and no documents have been found relating to the Americans' prewar position on a preemptive strike.

To complete the picture, take the example of the First Gulf War, when Israel refrained from launching a preventive war or engaging in active hostilities. The Bush administration had asked Israel to stay on the sidelines, and Prime Minister Yitzhak Shamir, who was very circumspect in his responses, stated that Israel had no intention of initiating a preventive war (neutralizing Iraq's ability to launch Scud missiles against Israel). Shamir withstood pressure from Defense Minister Arens and the chief of staff, Lieutenant General Dan Shomron, and was not dragged into military action against Iraq in the air or on ground, even when the Scuds landed in Israel.

How a Preemptive Strike Could Have Changed the War

Could a preemptive or parallel strike against the Egyptian bridging and crossing equipment on the western bank have made a difference in the Yom Kippur War? The answer is yes. It could have changed the direction of the war from the first day and the overall results of the fighting. It could have destroyed a large portion of the enemy's equipment and soldiers concentrated in dugouts on the western bank, and it could have wreaked havoc on the Egyptian armored crossing. And even if a the preemptive strike was canceled because of political considerations, a parallel strike (had it been prepared) could have been executed from the time hostilities erupted (14:00) to last light, making full use of the remaining three and a half hours of daylight. The IDF possessed detailed intelligence on the bridging and crossing equipment, but it was squandered. Based on intelligence reports and the range of effective ground fire, if the artillery had been mobilized and prepared, it could have zeroed in on the enemy's equipment concentrations.

Unfortunately, the IAF and IDF did not recognize the operational value of attacking the bridging and crossing equipment. According to the IAF's operational concept, destruction of the airfields and missiles was of primary importance: Tagar 4 in Egypt, Dugman 5 in Syria, and the Ramming plan to incapacitate the airfields appropriated the lion's share of IAF resources. Yet no one in the IDF or the defense establishment checked for alternatives. Caught up in the prevailing atmosphere, the chief of staff and the defense minister accepted the IAF's focus on achieving air superiority by attacking the missiles and the airfields.

The only specific mention of such an attack came up in the Iron Ram war game (in that scenario, the air force attacked the bridging and crossing equipment on the western bank as soon as the Egyptians opened fire), but the idea never underwent detailed operational planning. At 07:00 on the Day of Atonement, the IAF commander mentioned such a possibility, but nothing came of it:

Today there are four identified crossing points where the
bridging and crossing equipment is located . . . on the other
side of the canal . . . 350 trucks with bridging sections and an
undetermined number of APCs. . . . MI and Southern Command have to provide us with these four defined areas. . . .
I can attack them with loft bombing during the night. Not
a 100-plane flight, but a plane by plane attack . . . [with] a
certain number of bombs, then more bombs, onto the crossing areas. This is possible. Now all I need to know is if I
have to mess up the ordnance configuration that's supposed
to attack the airfields in Syria so we can attack the crossing
areas on the canal. . . . I think you [Forman] have enough
[planes].[72]

Except for the air force commander, who brought up the idea
only once and too late, no one in the IDF was aware of the implications of the equipment concentrations or agreed with the assessment of the attack's importance to the general war effort. No element
ordered or recommended planning an air strike before the air force
began to change its ordnance configuration at 12:50, and especially
not after the prime minister vetoed the preemptive strike. Thus,
another opportunity was missed.

Why the IDF Failed to Act on Intelligence

According to the enemy research team in the IDF Doctrine and
Instruction Department, the Egyptians were expecting the IAF to
try to thwart preparations for the offensive by conducting continuous daytime and nighttime sorties against the air defense layouts
in the Canal Zone, the airfields, the forces in the assembly areas,
and the concentrations of crossing and bridging equipment, with
the aim of inhibiting and disrupting the Egyptians' attempt to reorganize their forces. The Egyptians also saw the possibility of an
artillery attack (Bendigo) on the western bank and the bridging and
crossing equipment.[73]

The IDF did nothing of the sort. It received information on the
Egyptian force concentrations from the 526-T photo sortie on the
canal, carried out at 13:40 on October 4. Lieutenant Colonel Oded
Kam, commander of the interpretation team in Southern Command,
said, "The final findings in the early hours of the morning of Octo-

ber 5 showed a tiger about to pounce. The whole show was obvious."[74] In another photo sortie, 529-T at 09:00 on Saturday, October 6, bridging and crossing equipment was identified north and south of Ismailia, in addition to tank and APC concentrations. The information received no attention whatsoever because, by the time it was distributed, it had no operational significance on the planning or execution of a preemptive attack on the equipment.

Regarding the interpretation of the information gleaned from the two sorties, General Ivry, Peled's deputy, said the ground forces were responsible for ground target intelligence. The IAF interpreters were not knowledgeable enough to interpret ground targets; they could interpret only surface-to-air missiles, radar, and antiaircraft weapons. The ground forces did not convey the bridging and crossing targets to the IAF, and Ivry was aware of no request from the ground forces to attack the equipment. In his opinion, three hours of daylight would have been enough time to do so. The IAF was free for such an action as far as its order of battle was concerned, and it was armed with the suitable ordnance. "If we had been ordered at 12:00, October 6, to attack the bridging and crossing equipment instead of the airfields in Syria, and if they had marked the targets, we could have gotten the job done."[75] Another IAF commander, Avihu Ben-Nun, avowed that since Southern Command was supposed to convey these targets but did not, no one in the IAF thought of attacking them.

"The IAF wasn't interested in targets that were important to the land army. The procedure was that someone [in the commands] gave us targets," explained Giora Forman, head of the IAF Operations Department.[76] He admitted that no one in the IAF was thinking in that direction. Attacking bridging and crossing equipment on eleven sites would have required eight to twelve planes per site, or a total of 100 Phantoms, without Skyhawks. In his opinion, a preemptive strike, before the Egyptians and Syrians opened fire, could have delayed the start of the war. Had there been a decision for a parallel strike, an attack would have been possible at 13:00 on Saturday.

Performance Analysis: Results of a Preemptive or Parallel Strike

According to an analysis of the possible results of an IAF attack on the Egyptian bridging and crossing equipment on the western bank on Saturday, October 6, such an attack would have disrupted the Egyptians' crossing plans and changed the results of the war. Lieutenant Colonel Arik Peer (Ret.) conducted the performance analysis using the IAF's war-fighting doctrine, weapons, and order of battle when the war broke out, along with operational background and data on the Egyptian equipment provided by the author. The research was also based on Egyptian air defenses and weapons as they were thought to be deployed on October 6, and on the deployment of bridging and crossing equipment on the western bank as reinterpreted by Master Sergeant Shvadov of the IDF Deciphering Unit from the two above-mentioned aerial photographs 526-T at 13:40 on October 4 and 529-T or 1887-H at 09:00 on October 6 (see map 11 and figure 4).

Most of the Egyptian armored forces crossed the canal on heavy bridges that were assembled after dark on October 6 and on subsequent days. Some armored forces were transported on rafts. Prior to October 6, the crossing equipment was deployed in a number of advance areas, five to ten kilometers west of the canal. The performance analysis was based on the assumption that the IAF had already prepared an attack against the equipment in these advance deployment areas and was in the possession of updated intelligence on the equipment's location during the attack.

The attack would have required the allocation of either 70 warplanes if it was based on the flight order of battle prepared for Tagar 4 or 120 warplanes if it was based on Dugman 5 (of which 113 would be designated for the attack). Since Tagar 4 was planned for the morning of October 7, attacking the bridging and crossing equipment on October 6 obviously would not have disrupted that operation. Thus, an aerial order of battle of 70 aircraft, or as many as needed, could have been assigned to attack the bridging and crossing equipment on October 6. The optimal ordnance for destroying the crossing equipment would have been cluster bombs.

The ideal time for the attack would have been noon—the hour the IAF was prepared to attack the airfields in Syria. This would have been prior to the Egyptian-Syrian H hour at 14:00 on October 6 or a parallel attack between 15:00 and 17:45 (last light).

The Egyptian crossing equipment, as it appeared in the photos, had been deployed in forming-up areas in the Canal Zone before October 6. Since the armored forces planned to cross the canal on this equipment on the night of October 6–7 (as happened), the equipment would have been moving in the direction of the canal on the evening of October 6 at the latest (in the 529-T photograph, one of Second Army's crossing battalions was identified moving in a convoy toward the canal). In reality, the heavy crossing equipment was deployed on the canal on the night of October 6 and was used to establish the bridgeheads the Egyptian armor crossed on.

The crossing equipment concentrations were also identified in the earlier October 4 photo, and they seemed to be part of the divisional crossing battalions. Each concentration contained several dozen vehicles apparently loaded with crossing equipment in protected dugouts, some of which were covered with camouflage netting. Altogether, five concentrations of crossing equipment were identified in the canal area: Tel el Sabita (Second Army), with approximately fifty-three vehicles, ten kilometers from the canal; Shalufa (Third Army), with approximately twenty-eight vehicles, five and a half kilometers from the canal; Agrud (Third Army), with approximately forty-two vehicles, eleven kilometers from the canal; al Qirsh (Second Army), with approximately thirty-eight vehicles, four kilometers from the canal; and Sarafeum (Second Army), with thirty-two vehicles, three kilometers from the canal.

The main equipment in the divisional crossings included 144 aluminum boats; heavy pontoon bridges (called TPPs) that were assembled with floating posts (steel containers filled with polyurethane foam); a foldable floating bridge (called a PMP) made up of thirty units, each consisting of four parts; and four amphibious mobile bridges. Other equipment may have been placed along the canal embankment before October 6. The equipment was carried on various types of trucks. The number of trucks in each crossing battalion was based on the following standard: the TPP battalion had 145 trucks (136 ZIL 157s, 3 KrAZ 53s, and 6 half-ton trucks), and the PMP battalion had 56 trucks (16 ZIL 157s, 36 KrAZ 255s, and 4 half-ton trucks).

If the spotted concentrations were part of the PMP battalion, then each concentration included 50 to 100 percent of the crossing battalion. If the identified concentrations were part of the TPP battalion, then each concentration included only 25 to 30 percent of the crossing battalion.

There were 55 surface-to-air missile batteries, antiaircraft cannon, and shoulder-fired SA7s in the Canal Zone. The antiaircraft layout consisted of both static cannon and Gandish mobile cannon. Each of the crossing concentrations was located in a missile-saturated area protected by a surface-to-air missile brigade. Three of the concentrations near the canal were protected by a large number of antiaircraft weapons, including Gandish cannon.

There were two possible methods of attack:

1. Loft bombing: The chances of hitting the target were much lower with loft bombing than with pop-up bombing. In loft bombing, the planes would have to approach close to the missile batteries. Since the flight in the direction of the target was over flat terrain, the aircraft were at great risk of being discovered at an early stage and encountering missile fire. Equipment concentrations close to the canal could be attacked, but the assembly areas were too far away for loft bombing without entering Gandish-saturated areas.

2. Pop-up bombing: The acute antiaircraft missile threat in the Canal Zone undoubtedly called for a pop-up attack in roundabout paths and the use of EW and antiradiation missiles to neutralize the Egyptian missiles during the attack. Areas with heavy concentrations of antiaircraft and shoulder-fired missiles could be avoided in a pop-up attack, and only the surface-to-air missile threat would have to be dealt with. Therefore, the chances of hitting the target were better.

The performance analysis was based on the following data:

- There were two attack plans: one with 70 warplanes and the other with 110 warplanes.
- Since five crossing battalions had been spotted on the western bank, one-fifth of the attacking force was allocated to each battalion—in other words, fourteen aircraft per concentration in the first attack plan, and twenty-two planes per concentration in the second attack plan.
- The planes were armed with cluster bombs (each aircraft carried four bombs—the usual number was three) and attacked the assembly areas in pop-up runs. In each pair of planes, one was armed with CBU-52s and the other with CBU-58s; both aircraft attacked in the same direction.
- Ten percent of the planes failed to attack because of breakdowns or missile threats on the way to the targets.

According to the performance analysis, 20 to 30 percent of the vehicles in the targeted sites would have been destroyed. In the Agrud site, where the vehicles were deployed over a very large area (almost one square kilometer), the attacking planes would have covered a smaller percentage of the area.[77] The identified forces sometimes included only part of the crossing battalion; therefore, an attack on the sites where the crossing equipment was protected in dugouts probably would have destroyed only 15 to 25 percent of the equipment (perhaps even less in the TPP battalion).[78]

The lethality criterion in the results relates only to vehicular, not human, vulnerability. The soldiers in the crossing battalions likely would have remained at the sites, close to or inside the vehicles, so some of them would have been killed and wounded. This was especially true in Tel el Sabita, Shalufa, and Sarafeum, where 85 to 100 percent of the vehicles in the area would have been hit with CBU-58 cluster bombs, and a very high percentage of the Egyptian troops would have been killed or wounded. Incapacitating a large percentage of Egyptian soldiers in a crossing battalion probably would have neutralized it for several days.

If the convoy spotted in the al Qirsh area had been attacked, every vehicle would have been covered by the ordnance of several warplanes, and close to 100 percent of the vehicles would have been destroyed. In addition, all the Egyptian troops would have been near or inside the vehicles in the convoy and would have been killed or wounded. Since the convoy consisted of thirty-eight vehicles, if it was part of the PMP battalion, the attack would have neutralized greater than 70 percent of the battalion—in practical terms, paralyzing it for the entire war. If the convoy was part of the TPP battalion, the attack would have neutralized approximately 25 percent of the battalion, which would have delayed its mission by at least a few days.

From the time the convoy was photographed at 09:00 on October 6 until the attack, several hours would have passed, during which time the photograph would have been interpreted, that interpretation relayed to the planners, plans devised according to the latest intelligence and passed on to the pilots, and the mission prepared in the squadrons. Meanwhile, the convoy would probably have been on the move, in which case the attacking aircraft might not have been able to identify and attack it.

In conclusion, if a designated plan had been prepared for attacking the crossing equipment spotted near the canal, it would have been executed in the form of either a preemptive strike on October 6 before the renewal of hostilities or a parallel strike sometime between 15:00 and 17:45. If such an attack plan had been carried out, it would have annihilated a large percentage of the Egyptian troops where the crossing equipment was concentrated, as well as 15 to 25 percent of the battalions' crossing equipment (trucks and the bridging and crossing equipment loaded on them). The murderous effect on the troops would have neutralized the PMP battalion for several days and retarded the implementation of the TPP battalion's mission.

Attacking the convoy would have destroyed most of the vehicles and killed or wounded a major portion of the Egyptian soldiers in it. But such an attack would have taken place several hours after the convoy was photographed, and it is doubtful that it would have been in the same place during the attack.

Thus, had such an attack been executed, it probably would have delayed the heavy bridging across the canal in at least four sectors of the five crossing divisions. Egyptian headquarters would have had to decide whether to allow heavy bridging to proceed only in 2nd Division's sector, where the bridging battalion was in transit and might not have been hit. The rest of the bridging battalions would have been incapacitated to varying degrees.

The combination of a devastating blow to the troops operating the equipment and damage to the equipment itself would have delayed the heavy bridging operations for tank crossing by several days and knocked the whole plan off kilter. Under these circumstances, it is not at all certain that the Egyptian General Staff would have let the infantry remain on the eastern bank—presumably for two to four days—without the chance of a linkup with the tanks, even if motorized ferries could have transferred a small number of tanks to the eastern bank.

The decision not to conduct a preemptive or parallel strike on the bridging and crossing equipment was unquestionably one of the IDF's most grievous blunders. It highlighted flaws in the operational concept with regard to the use of the air force—that is, it should be used for missions of general importance to the IDF, not just missions preferred by the IAF, such as destroying surface-to-air missiles and achieving air supremacy.

According to standard military criteria for performance analysis, an air attack of this type would have completely disrupted the Egyptian armored crossing plan. Without tanks on the eastern bank, the bridgeheads could not have been expanded, and the Egyptian General Staff probably would have recalled the infantry forces to the western bank, with heavy losses. The artillery in the Rock order of battle, which had completed its deployment on October 9, could have neutralized the infantry on the eastern bank between the canal and Lexicon Road within forty-eight hours. In this scenario, the severe disruption of the armored crossing would have enabled the IDF to hold the Egyptian attack on Saturday night, neutralize the forces on the eastern bank by October 11, and reach a quick decision within four or five days.

Afterword

Forty-one years have passed since the Yom Kippur War, and the sights and sounds are still present. As the years go by, the list of studies and books grows, revealing newly discovered details.

This book abounds with descriptions of the oversights and miscalculations of the political leaders and senior military commanders in the application of forces and the conduct of operations. Both levels were responsible for the regulars' inability to hold and their failure to succeed in their mission of not yielding one step, given the absurd balance of forces. The concept fostered by the IDF—the regulars will hold!—failed in its three main components: deterrence, warning, and reliance on the air force.

Like many combat veterans of Sinai, the author is still sickened by the missed opportunity. Despite the IDF's flagrant shortcomings and mistakes in 1973 and the impossible conditions in which the war began, if a defensive battle had been fought, a battlefield decision could have been reached on the eastern bank of the Suez Canal within a few days, the IDF's losses would have been significantly reduced, and the Egyptian army would have been severely incapacitated. This could have been the result if certain actions had been taken and blunders avoided.

These painful revelations notwithstanding, and leaving aside the omissions, mistakes, and impossible circumstances when war erupted on Saturday, October 6, 1973, it is important to remember that at the end of the Yom Kippur War, the IDF was 101 kilometers from the Egyptian capital. The courage, moral strength, and perseverance of the rank-and-file soldiers and junior officers were the number-one factor in the IDF's endurance and recovery. And—lest we forget—this book is a memorial to those who fell in that war.

The outcome of the Yom Kippur War led to peace with Egypt, the largest and strongest country in the Arab world, but formidable challenges still lie ahead. The question lingers: until when? As an answer, here are Moshe Belinson's words from Elhanan Oren's *History of the Yom Kippur War*: "Until the might of the Jewish people in their country dooms any and every enemy attack to defeat. Until the most zealous and audacious in the enemy camp, in all enemy camps wherever they are, knows: no means exist that can break Israel's strength because its survival is a necessity, and no other way is acceptable. This is the meaning of the campaign."

Acknowledgments

I am deeply grateful to many people for their help in completing this book. Unfortunately, because of space limitations, I cannot mention all of them.

Special thanks are due to the late Major General Israel Tal (Ret.), deputy chief of staff during the Yom Kippur War, for his lucid explanations of the General Staff's concept of the defense strategy in Sinai. I am also indebted to him for writing the foreword to this book.

I am indebted to Lieutenant Colonel Roger Cirillo, U.S. Army (Ret.), for going above and beyond the call of duty to get the English version of this book published.

I wish to thank Major General Gadi Eisencott, who, as head of operations in the IDF, permitted me access to historical material from 1973 and provided generous assistance in processing operations research and war games.

Colonel Shaul Shay (Ret.) and Lieutenant Colonel Shimon Golan (Ret.), both from the IDF Historical Division, and Professor Stuart Cohen from Bar-Ilan University gave me invaluable advice and guidance at the outset of this work.

Thanks are due to Lieutenant Colonel Avi Gur (Ret.), deputy commander of B Company/52nd Battalion (the battalion I commanded in the Yom Kippur War) for allowing me to use the photographs he took during the war.

The late Major General Avraham Adan (Ret.) and Major General Yeshayahu Gavish (Ret.) and Colonel Omer Bar-Lev (Ret.) provided inestimable assistance in the chapter on the formulation of the defense concept in Sinai. I sincerely thank them.

While writing the main chapter of this book—chapter 3 on the defensive battle—my conversations with the following were invaluable: the late Lieutenant General Dan Shomron (Ret.), Lieutenant General Ehud Barak (Ret.), Major General Haim Erez (Ret.), Major General Amnon Reshef (Ret.), Brigadier General Baruch Harel (Ret.), and Brigadier General Avraham Baram (Ret.).

I extend my sincerest thanks to Brigadier General Gideon Avidor (Ret.) for his helpful liaison with AUSA and for providing incisive details about 252nd Division's defensive battle. I am also grateful to Brigadier General Shai Tamari (Ret.), who clarified the intricacies of Southern Command's thinking on the defensive battle in Sinai in the prewar period under the command of Ariel Sharon and during the war under Major General Shmuel Gonen.

I thank my colleagues Brigadier General Yom Tov Tamir (Ret.), Brigadier General Beni Taran (Ret.), Brigadier General Uzi Levtzur (Ret.), Brigadier General David Shoval (Ret.), and Colonel Haim Adini (Ret.) for their helpful insights.

A special debt of gratitude is owed to Lieutenant Colonel Gil Sirkin, head of the systems analysis branch in the Administration for the Development of Weapons and Technological Infrastructure, for his help in explaining the historical data related to the chance of damage to both IDF and Egyptian tanks. Thanks also to Major Yaron Dantes, who analyzed the results of virtual tank battles on October 7, 1973.

I am grateful to Brigadier General Dani Asher (Ret.) for his generous assistance in clarifying the Egyptian war plan and to Colonel Ilan Sahar (Ret.) and Lieutenant Colonel Jacky Locker (Ret.) for providing me with important historical tools.

I extend my heartfelt thanks to all those who helped me understand the dilemmas and malfunctions in air assistance during the ground battle: Major Generals David Ivry (Ret.) and Avihu Ben-Nun (Ret.); Brigadier Generals Giora Forman (Ret.), Yiftach Spector (Ret.), and Amos Amir (Ret.); and Lieutenant Colonels Moti Habakuk and Zeev Lachish (Ret.).

Colonel Shmuel Gordon (Ret.) enlightened me on this subject during the course of our many conversations and made me aware of the parameters that must be taken into consideration to obtain a comprehensive picture.

I received generous assistance on chapter 5 from Master Sergeant Vadim Shvadov, who interpreted air reconnaissance photographs from October 4 and 6, 1973, related to the deployment of Egyptian bridging and crossing equipment. I also thank Lieutenant Colonel Zion Suliman (Ret.) for his help in this effort.

In addition, Master Sergeant Shvadov's interpretation of the October 8 reconnaissance photographs gave me a broad picture of the Egyptian army's deployment on the eastern bank. This was necessary for the operations research on IDF artillery fire carried out by Lieutenant Colonel Shachar Cohen and Lieutenant Colonel Hershkovitz (Ret.), both from the chief artillery officer's headquarters.

I am indebted to Lieutenant Colonel Arik Peer (Ret.) for carrying out operations research on the results of a theoretical air strike against Egyptian bridging and crossing equipment on October 6, 1973.

I am grateful to Amir Oren for his help in gaining access to the Kissinger Papers and for his insight on the American position regarding a preemptive Israeli strike.

My conversations with former prime ministers Shimon Peres and Ehud Barak and former defense minister Moshe Arens were of inestimable benefit, and I thank them dearly for their time.

I also wish to thank Dr. Henry Kissinger, U.S. secretary of state during the Yom Kippur War, for personally clarifying the American position during an interview on June 28, 2006.

I would like to extend my appreciation to Brigadier General Ron Kitri (Ret.) and Lieutenant Colonel Shoshana Tene (Ret.), who helped in the initial editing of this book, and to editor Dani Dor, who struggled through the military jargon to make it readable (in Hebrew).

I thank Professor Efraim Inbar and Dr. Gadi Kreuzer from Bar-Ilan University; they instructed me in the processing of historical material so that it would measure up to the highest academic standards. In addition, I am grateful to Professor Aharon Meir, also from Bar-Ilan University, who encouraged me to write this book.

My sincerest thanks go to the translator, Master Sergeant Moshe Tlamim (Ret.), for his skill and patience in rendering this book into English for a global audience.

It has been my privilege to convey, through this book, the deepest respect and admiration for my comrades, veterans of the Yom Kippur War in Sinai, and especially to my subordinates, the troops of 52nd Battalion, so many of whom fell in that bitter war.

Last but not least, I owe the greatest debt of gratitude to my loving family, who shouldered the burden of my long years of service in the IDF: my wife, Edna, and my children Vered and Avner, as well as my eldest son, Yoav, who, as a soldier in the Golani Reconnaissance Unit, fell in battle in Lebanon on September 5, 1986.

Appendix 1

The 252nd Division's Order of Battle, 14:00, October 6, 1973

Tanks

- 14th Brigade: 54 tanks on the line—52nd Battalion, 32 tanks in the southern sector; 184th Brigade, 22 tanks in the central sector (two tank companies)
- 275th Territorial Brigade: 34 tanks (9th Battalion/14th Brigade)
- 401st Brigade: 85 tanks in the rear, at Bir Tmadeh–Gidi–Refidim
- 46th Battalion: 28 tanks at Bir Tmadeh
- 79th Battalion: 25 tanks at Refidim (under the command of 460th Brigade on October 6 and later under the command of 14th Brigade)
- 195th Battalion: 32 tanks at Gidi
- 460th Brigade (Armor School): 110 tanks in the Bir Tmadeh–Refidim area
- 198th Battalion (tank commanders' course): 44 tanks at Bir Tmadeh and Refidim
- 196th Battalion (armor officers' course): 66 tanks at Refidim

Artillery

The 209th Artillery Group: 3 medium 155mm battalions consisting of 10 batteries, with 7 on the line (28 cannon)

Southern Sector

- One medium artillery battalion under 52nd Battalion's command
- One reduced battery in the Navarone stronghold (Mevaded)—fixed-position cannon
- Karat Moora battery near the Notsa fortification

- Gidi battery south of the Mitzva fortification
- Reinforcements according to the Dovecote order: two 160mm mortars from Refidim to Mevaded; one entered the line

Central Sector

- One battery from 55th Heavy Artillery Battalion (175mm) at the Kishuf fortification, under 184th Battalion's command
- Reinforcements according to the Dovecote order: one battery from 403rd Medium Artillery Battalion (155mm) was carried on transporters to the central sector at 10:00; the rest of the battalion arrived in Tasa on its tracks and was on the move at the beginning of hostilities
- Two batteries (10 tubes) from Artillery Training Base No. 9 reached Refidim on the morning of October 6, traveled on their tracks from Refidim to the central sector during the night of October 6–7, and entered action on October 7 and 8

Northern Sector

- 404th Medium Artillery Battalion
- Two fixed-position cannon in the Budapest stronghold
- One 155mm M50 battery in the Yoram fortification
- One battery near the Maror fortification
- On standby at Refidim: 403rd Medium Artillery Battalion

Total artillery deployment: one battery for every 23 kilometers on the canal front. In a number of places, two or three batteries were able to concentrate their fire, but in some areas, only a section operated, not a battery.

Mechanized Infantry/Reconnaissance

- On the line in the southern sector: a reconnaissance company from 14th Brigade (under 52nd Battalion's command) at Telepatia (a former Egyptian missile base); on October 13 a mechanized infantry company of reservists linked up with 52nd Battalion
- On the line in the central sector: a reduced mechanized infan-

try company, J Company/184th Battalion. in the Televizia fortification

- On the line in the northern sector: a reduced company from 424th Battalion (under command of 275th Territorial Brigade) for patrols on the sandbar, and a platoon of mechanized infantry from J Company/184th Battalion in the Martef fortification
- In the Ras Sudar sector: under the division's command—424th Battalion less one company
- In the rear: under 401st Brigade's command—one mechanized infantry company from 46th Battalion tasked with security assignments at Um Hashiba, Southern Command's command post (returned to the battalion on October 15)
- A mechanized infantry company from 79th Battalion linked up with 9th Battalion on the night of October 6–7

Engineers

- 601st Engineers Battalion (a half-track–borne company and two companies without mobile means)

Appendix 2

The Strongholds: Location and Manning

Northern Sector: Manned by 16th Brigade

On the Mediterranean coast:

- Traklin observation stronghold, manned by 6 soldiers from Budapest
- Budapest: on the coastal sandbank, 63 soldiers and 2 tanks (8 crew members) from 9th Battalion that were attached to the stronghold according to the Dovecote order

North of Kantara:

- Orkal A—the northernmost stronghold 5 kilometers south of Port Fuad: 20 soldiers and 2 tanks (8 crew members) from 9th Battalion in permanent deployment
- Orkal B: 17 soldiers
- Orkal C: 19 soldiers
- Lahtsanit: 17 soldiers
- Derora: 19 soldiers
- Ketuba: 21 soldiers

Kantara: Milano—a stronghold manned by 28 soldiers—and three unmanned strongholds next to it

South of Kantara: Mifreket, opposite El-Balah Island—28 soldiers

Central Sector: Manned by 16th Brigade

- Hizayon stronghold (opposite Firdan): 20 soldiers (21 according to 14th Brigade)
- Lakekan stronghold (on the lakeshore): 10 soldiers from 16th Brigade

Southern Sector: Manned by 16th Brigade and 904th Nahal Unit

- Botser (on the tongue of land between the lakes): 26 soldiers from 16th Brigade (27 according to 14th Brigade) and 3 tanks (12 crew members) from 52nd Battalion, attached to the stronghold according to the Dovecote order; due to a lack of coordination, another 3 tanks (12 crew members) from 46th Battalion were sent to the stronghold on the night of October 6–7
- Lituf A (at the western opening of Gidi Road on the shore of the Little Bitter Lake): 29 soldiers from 16th Brigade (27 according to 14th Brigade)
- Lituf B (a daytime observation stronghold): 3 soldiers from Lituf A
- Mefatseyach A (at the western opening of Mitla Road): 28 Nahal soldiers (31 according to 14th Brigade)
- Mefatseyach B (a daytime observation stronghold): 3 soldiers from Mefatseyach A
- Mefatseyach C: thinly manned
- Nisan (Hakfar; next to A Shat Village): 20 Nahal soldiers (19 according to 14th Brigade)
- Masrek (Hamezach; opposite Port Tawfik): 30 Nahal soldiers (42 according to 14th Brigade) and 4 tanks (16 crew members) from 52nd Battalion; 2 tanks were brought in according to the Dovecote order, and 2 tanks were deployed there at the outset of the war to treat soldiers wounded outside the stronghold
- Egrofit (at Ras Masala on the shore of the Gulf of Suez): 5 Nahal soldiers; the stronghold was reopened four days before the war

The total number of soldiers in the strongholds was approximately 450, including administrative personnel.

Appendix 3

The Egyptian Ground Forces' Order of Battle

Overall Order of Battle

Approximately 2,200 medium tanks (plus 180 Stalin tanks, SU100s, and PT 76s), of which 1,650 were medium tanks and 140 were various types for the formations
Approximately 2,950 APCs
Approximately 2,400 artillery tubes
Approximately 800 antitank launching systems
12 Frog 7 launchers
9 Scud launchers
Various types of amphibious and bridging equipment

Order of Battle Employed in the War

1,700 tanks
2,500 armored vehicles
2,000 artillery tubes (field artillery, medium and heavy artillery, mortars of infantry and armor formations)
1,500 antitank cannon
700 antitank missile launchers
Several thousand RPGs
Thousands of the RPG 43 antitank grenades

Overall Organization

2 army headquarters
2 armored divisions
3 mechanized divisions
5 infantry divisions

3 to 5 independent tank brigades (2 under construction)
2 independent mechanized brigades (one of them, 130th Marine
   Brigade, operated within the framework of Third Army)
4 independent infantry brigades
3 airborne brigades
24 commando battalions

Organization for the Attack

2 army headquarters
5 reinforced infantry divisions
2 armored divisions
12 (approximately) commando battalions

GHQ Reserves

3rd Mechanized Division (less 130th Marine Division, which
   was allocated to Third Army)
1 tank brigade—Presidential Guard
1 mechanized brigade—Presidential Guard
2 to 3 airborne brigades
2 to 3 commando groups

Appendix 4

Report on the 526-T Photo Sortie, October 4, 1973

Southern Command/Intelligence sent the following classified report to 252nd Division/Intelligence, Unit 399, and the intelligence officers of 162nd and 143rd Divisions, interpreting the artillery and armor changes revealed by sortie H/1866, 526-T.

1. Date of sortie: October 4, 1973
2. Date of interpretation: October 5, 1973
3. Area of coverage: Kantara–Suez
4. Sortie level: intermediate
5. Summary of findings:

   A. Artillery
   1) 62 additional batteries were identified in the entire canal sector (total number in sector—206 batteries).
   2) In the Kantara sector—4 additional field artillery battalions were identified.
   3) In the Ismailia sector—an additional 3 field artillery guns and 1 battalion of antitank/field battery were identified.
   4) In the Dwer-Suar sector—an additional medium artillery battery and 4 field artillery battalions were identified, and a battery of Katyusha rocket launchers disappeared.
   5) In the Shalufa sector—an additional medium artillery battalion and 4 field artillery battalions were identified.
   6) In the Suez sector—an addition of 2 field artillery battalions was identified.
   7) 6 artillery batteries disappeared in Abu Suweir.

   B. Armor
   1) Tanks

a) An additional 87 tanks were identified in the entire sector (total number of tanks in the sector—351 tanks and 22 SU-100 tank destroyers).

b) A tank brigade was identified in the Salahiya area (not included in the total number of armored vehicles in the canal sector).

Appendix 5

Order for the Alert in 14th Brigade/ 252nd Division, October 3, 1973

The 14th Brigade headquarters sent the following urgent order regarding the alert status and its effect on leaves to 52nd/184th Battalion's commander and operations officer, the reconnaissance company commander, and the brigade headquarters camp commander, with the commander of 9th Battalion to be informed and the order distributed to unit commanders.

1. The following order is in force until further notice.
2. The level of alert in the brigade will be:

   A. All forces on the line will be on 5 minutes alert.
      1) Whoever is not on duty in the strongholds from 2400 until 0430 is allowed to sleep undressed.
      2) The mechanized infantry and tank companies, except for the platoon on immediate standby and people on duty, are allowed to sleep undressed from 2200 until 0430.
   B. There will be night patrols on the embankment on all sectors according to the daily activity plan.
   C. Commanders in all strongholds will be on watch until midnight, commanders' lookouts remain in force (one half hour before first light until two hours after first light, two hours before last light and one half hour after last light).
   D. In all of the strongholds/fortifications, installations, and camps, a commander will be awake the entire night.
   E. Morning patrols will go out under sector control and only after manning at least 80 percent of the regular lookout positions of the enemy. TOCs will be manned by an operations officer/S3.
   F. Unit headquarters will remain close to their permanent place.

3. Leaves:
    A. Leaves for reservists will continue as before.
    B. Restrictions on leave will be as follows:
        1) All officers and career soldiers are forbidden to go on leave, except:
            a) Battalion commander/deputy battalion commander.
            b) Staff officers/assistants.
        2) Headquarters company + brigade headquarters up to 10 percent for special needs.
    C. Sections 1 (a) (b) and 2 require further telephone confirmation.
4. Execute as necessary.

Appendix 6

The Strongholds: Manpower, Casualties, and Fate

Stronghold	Manpower on Oct. 6	Number of Tankers Added	Rescue Attempt?	Under Attack?	Killed and Missing	POWs	Rescued	Time of Evacuation	Time of Surrender
Traklin	6	—	—	—	—	—	—	—	—
Budapest	63	8	—	Yes	3	—	—	Not evacuated	Did not surrender
Orkal A	20	8	Yes	Yes	39	19	5	07:17:00	—
Orkal B	17	With Orkal A	—	—	—	—	—	07:17:00?	—
Orkal C	19	With Orkal A	—	—	—	—	—		07:17:00
Lahtsanit	17	—	—	Yes	9	8	—	—	—
Derora	19	—	Yes	Under fire	3	1	15	07:14:30	—
Ketuba	21	—	Yes	Under fire	2	—	19	17:14:00	—
Milano	28	15	Yes	Yes	13	6	24	07:23:30–08:06:00	—
Mifreket	16	—	Yes	Yes	5 (4?)	6 (7?)	5	07:17:00	—
Hizayon	20	—	—	Yes	12	8	—	—	09:09:00

Stronghold	Manpower on Oct. 6	Number of Tankers Added	Rescue Attempt?	Under Attack?	Killed and Missing	POWs	Rescued	Time of Evacuation	Time of Surrender
Purkan	33	—	Yes	Yes	—	—	33	09:02:30	—
Matsmed	34	—	Yes	Yes	2	32	—	—	09:08:00
Lakekan	10	—	Yes	—	—	—	10	07:17:00	—
Botser	26	12 + 12	Yes	Under fire	—	—	40	09:02:00	—
Lituf	29	—	Yes	Yes	18	11	—	07:13:30 (attempt)	07:13:30
Mefatseyach	28	—	—	Yes	5	23	—	—	08:14:00
Nisan (Hakfar)	20	—	—	Yes	10	10	—	—	09:15:00
Masrek	30	16	Yes	Yes	5	37	—	—	13:11:00
Egrofit	5	—	Yes	—	—	—	5	06:19:00	—

Source: Zeev Eitan, "'Dovecote'—Planning and Execution in the Test of Fire," *Maarachot* 276–77 (October–November 1980): 48. The data on the number of soldiers are slightly different from those in the book *The Yom Kippur War, October 1973* (14th Brigade Internal Document, October 1975).

Appendix 7

The 252nd Division's Tank Order of Battle, October 7, 1973

Before dividing the canal sector with the Rock divisions, 252nd Division had 114 operable tanks on October 7, deployed as follows.

Northern Sector

At 07:09:15 (162nd Division received responsibility at 07:30), there was a total of 32 tanks:

9th Battalion: 8 tanks
198th Battalion: 17 tanks
Force Lapidot: 7 tanks

Central Sector

At 07:14:20 (143rd Division received responsibility at 16:00), there was a total of 41 tanks:

184th Battalion: 16 tanks
79th Battalion: 11 tanks
196th Battalion: 14 tanks

Southern Sector

At 07:21:52 there was a total of 41 tanks (for which 252nd Division retained responsibility):

52nd Battalion: 15 tanks (3 at Botser, 3 at Ras Sudar, 4 at Hamezach, and the tanks of C Company, under the command of 46th Battalion; in effect, the battalion had 3 tanks until the morning of October 8)

195th Battalion: 10 tanks
46th Battalion: 16 tanks

During October 7, 14th and 460th Brigades were removed from 252nd Division's order of battle. During October 8, the 252nd was reinforced with 875th (mechanized) Brigade and 164th (tank) Brigade. The number of tanks in the division stood at 130 to 140 between October 8 and 18.

Notes

Introduction

1. Barry R. Posen, *The Sources of Military Doctrine* (Ithaca, NY: Cornell University Press, 1984), 105–37.

2. Elizabeth Kier, *Imagining War* (Princeton, NJ: Princeton University Press, 1997), 89–92; Elizabeth Kier, "Culture and Military Doctrine: France between the Wars," *International Security* 19, no. 4 (Spring 1995): 65–93.

3. Israel's military "concept" refers to two conditions that precluded an Arab-initiated war: (1) Syria would not undertake a war with Israel without Egypt's assistance, and (2) until Egypt obtained long-range bombers and surface-to-surface missiles, it would not go to war to avenge Israel's devastating air strike on June 5, 1967.

4. Max Hastings, *Armageddon: The Battle for Germany 1944–45* (Or Yehuda: Dvir Publishers, Defense Ministry Publications, 2007), 19.

5. Colonel Yehoshua Nevo, *The Defense of the Golan Heights: Doctrines and Concepts* (Tel Aviv: IDF Department of History, 1990), 3.

1. Development of the Defense Concept in Western Sinai

1. David Arbel and Uri Neeman, *Madness without Atonement: The Surprise that Wasn't and the Strategy that Failed* (Tel Aviv: Yediot Achronot, Sifrei Hemed, 2005), 16.

2. Major General Meir Amit (Ret.), "The Sinai Campaign, the IDF's First Test as a Standing Army," *Maarachot* 306–7 (December 1987): 206–7.

3. Lieutenant General Yitzhak Rabin, interview, *Ma'ariv*, September 29, 1967.

4. Ariel Levite, *Israel's Military Doctrine: Defense and Offense* (Tel Aviv: Hakibutz Hameukhad, 1988), 122. Elazar quoted in Louis Williams, ed., *Military Aspects of the Israeli-Arab Conflict* (Jerusalem: Minister of Defense, 1975), 250.

5. Avraham Adan, *On Both Banks of the Suez* (Tel Aviv: Idanim, 1979), 148.

6. Author's interview with Major General Yeshayahu Gavish (Ret.), May 7, 2007.

7. Quoted in Levite, *Israel's Military Doctrine*, 122.

8. *Agranat Commission Report*, Third and Last Report (1975), vol. 1, 1350, 4011–12; hereafter cited as *AGCR*.

9. Stuart Cohen, "Limitations on the Use of the Reserves: Lessons from the Yom Kippur War," *Maarachot* 366–67 (1999): 56–79.

10. Israel Tal, *National Security: Few against Many* (Tel Aviv: Dvir, 1996), 203–4; author's interview with Israel Tal, December 21, 2005; Yaacov Bar-Siman-Tov, *The Yom Kippur War: 25-Year Retrospective* (Jerusalem: Ministry of Education and Leonard Davis Institute for International Relations, 1999), 46.

11. Carmit Guy, *Bar-Lev: A Biography* (Tel Aviv: Am Oved, Sifriyat Poalim, 1998), 150–51.

12. Ibid.

13. Moshe Dayan, GHQ Operational Discussion: "Our Border with Egypt," November 21, 1968, 3–33.

14. Ibid.

15. Guy, *Bar-Lev*, 171–79.

16. The IDF circulated maps with code names for areas, roads, strongholds, and so forth. The maps themselves were also given code names—in this case, "Sirius." Every few years, or in the event they fell into enemy hands, the maps' names and code names were changed.

17. Israel Tal, GHQ Discussion, "Maoz" Plan, December 19, 1968, 3–26.

18. Ibid.

19. Ibid.

20. The posts of chief of GHQ and deputy chief of staff were sometimes filled by one individual (e.g., General Tal in 1973) and sometimes by two different generals (e.g., Haim Bar-Lev as deputy chief of staff and Ezer Weizman as chief of GHQ in 1967), in which case the deputy chief of staff had seniority. GHQ organized the general staff's work.

21. Israel Tal, GHQ Discussion, "Maoz" Plan, December 26, 1968, 3–27.

22. Guy, *Bar-Lev*, 180–81.

23. Adan, *On Both Banks*, 47–48.

24. Guy, *Bar-Lev*, 179.

25. Emanuel Wald, *The Curse of the Broken Vessels* (Tel Aviv: Schocken, 1984), 101–3.

26. Eli Zeira, *Myth versus Reality: Failures and Lessons of the Yom Kippur War* (Tel Aviv: Yediot Achronot, Sifrei Hemed, 2004), 82–83.

27. Yosef Hochbaum, "The Yom Kippur War with the Chisel of Staff Work," *Maarachot* 276–77 (October 1980): 79–80.

28. Guy, *Bar-Lev*, 182–83.

29. Dani Asher, *Breaking the Concept* (Tel Aviv: Maarachot Publications, Defense Ministry, 2003), 40–41.

30. Avraham Zohar, *The Struggle for Israel's Security* (Tel Aviv: Israeli Fund for Military History, Tel Aviv University, 2003), 160.

31. Tal, *National Security*, 154–56.

32. Guy, *Bar-Lev*, 190–91, 196–97.

33. Ezer Weizman, *You Got the Sky You Got the Land* (Tel Aviv: Maariv, 1975), 194.

34. Ibid., 196–97; Edward Luttwak and Walter Laqueur, "Kissinger and the Yom Kippur War," *Commentary* (September 1974): 38.

35. Tal, *National Security*, 154–56.

36. Asher, *Breaking the Concept*, 54–55.

37. Elhanan Oren, *The History of the Yom Kippur War* (Tel Aviv: IDF Doctrine and Instruction, History Department, 2004), 44–45.

38. Moshe Dayan, *Milestones* (Jerusalem: Idanim, 1976), 523.

39. Israel Tal, "The Defense of Sinai," October 13, 1970, Document AR587-310.

40. Guy, *Bar-Lev*, 191.

41. Ibid., 231.

42. Author's interview with Gideon Avidor, June 21, 2006.

43. Avner Yaniv, *Politics and Strategy in Israel* (Tel Aviv: Sifriat Poalim, 1994), 222–23.

44. Author's interviews with Brigadier General Shai Tamari (Ret.), January 3 and 24, 2007.

45. Ibid.

46. Author's interview with Brigadier General Dov Tamari (Ret.), February 23, 2009.

47. *AGCR*, Testimony, Head of the Intelligence Corps, vol. 1, 28.

48. *AGCR*, Third and Last Report, vol. 1, 131.

49. Arbel and Neeman, *Madness without Atonement*, 239; Asher, *Breaking the Concept*, 75.

50. Dov Tamari interview, February 23, 2009.

51. *AGCR*, vol. 2, "The Development of the IDF Order of Battle on the Fronts," 206.

52. GHQ, General Collection 1–3, Warfare Doctrine, vol. 2, Defense (Tel Aviv: Department of Doctrine, November 1964), 1–52.

53. Aviezer Golan, *Albert* (Tel Aviv: Yediot Achronot, 1977), 185–86; Asher, *Breaking the Concept*, 76–77.

54. Adan, *On Both Banks*, 54.

55. *AGCR*, vol. 2, "The Development of the IDF Order of Battle on the Fronts," 194–96.

56. Asher, *Breaking the Concept*, 66–68.

57. See Shimon Golan, *The Yom Kippur War: Research of the GHQ* (Tel Aviv: IDF History Department, 1996, 2006), pt. 1, vol. 1, 89. This unpublished work consists of two editions: the 2006 edition covers part 1, "Background to the War" (2 vols.); the 1996 edition covers part 2, "The War and Its Management" (4 vols.); hereafter cited as *Research of the GHQ*.

58. Ibid., pt. 1, vol. 1, 135.

59. Major General Shmuel Gonen (Ret.), testimony before the IDF Department of History, February 8, 1977, 11–12.

60. Lieutenant General David Elazar, Senior IDF Staff Meeting, February 12, 1974.

61. Oren, *History of the Yom Kippur War*, 414.

62. Ibid., 22.

63. Shmuel Gonen, testimony before the IDF History Branch, July 20, 1976, 10–11.

64. Avidor interview, March 21, 2006.

65. *AGCR*, book 4, vol. 3, 1339, 1464.

66. Yaniv, *Politics and Strategy*, 43.

67. Golan, *Research of the GHQ*.

68. Cohen, "Limitations on the Use of the Reserves," 64.

69. *AGCR*, book 1, vol. 2, 228–30.

70. Ibid., 231.

71. Golan, *Research of the GHQ*, pt. 1, vol. 2, 404–5.

72. *AGCR*, vol. 1, 14, 19.

73. *AGCR*, vol. 2, pt. 2, 283–84; Cohen, "Limitations on the Use of the Reserves," 65–66.

74. Haim Herzog, *The Thirtieth Anniversary of the Yom Kippur War, Day of Judgment War*, special ed. (Tel Aviv: Zmora-Beitan, Yediot Achronot, 2003), 59.

75. *AGCR*, vol. 1, addenda, 14–16, 45.

76. Tal, *National Security*, 9, 85–88.

77. *AGCR*, Additional Partial Report, Arguments and Addenda, April 1, 1974, vol. 1, 149–50.

78. *AGCR*, vol. 1, 150.

79. *AGCR*, vol. 2, chap. 2, 230.

80. Dov Tamari, "The Reserves: A Unique Israeli Phenomenon" (PhD diss., Haifa University, 2007), 349–50.

81. *AGCR*, vol. 2, pt. 2, 228–30.

82. Golan, *Research of the GHQ*; see Elazar's notes on the draft of the chapter "Viewing the War and Its Goals, April 1976."

83. Oren, *History of the Yom Kippur War*, 8–9; Jehuda Wallach, *Not on a Silver Platter* (Jerusalem: Defense Ministry Publishers, 2000), 110–11; Tal, *National Security*, 173–74.

84. Wallach, *Not on a Silver Platter*; Saad El Din Shazly, *Crossing the Canal* (Tel Aviv: Maarachot Publications, 1988), 197; Hasan El Badri, Teh El Magdoub, and Zahari Aldin, *The Ramadan War: The Fourth Arab-Israeli Round, October 1973* (Tel Aviv: Hatzav, IDF Translation Publications, 1974), 65.

85. Zeira, *Myth versus Reality*, 188–89.

2. Initial Blunders

1. *AGCR*, Third and Last Report, vol. 3, 1347.

2. This defect still prevailed in the command style of some IDF commanders in the Second Lebanon War (July–August 2006).

3. *AGCR*, Third Report, vol. 3, Supplements, 1315.

4. *AGCR*, chap. 2, sec. 28, 23, 270–71, 277, 282.

5. *AGCR*, vol. 1, 23.

6. Operation Rotem was Egypt's clandestine deployment of three divisions to deflect military escalation in the north between Israel and Syria following a number of border incidents. See Tal, *National Security*, 179.

7. Shmuel Gonen, testimony before the IDF History Department, February 8, 1977, 27–28.

8. Cohen, "Limitations on the Use of the Reserves," 71.

9. Golan, *Research of the GHQ*, 15, 67.

10. Gonen testimony, July 15, 1976, 21–23.

11. Lieutenant Colonel A., "The Yom Kippur War, Strategic Decisions," *Maarachot* 276–77 (October–November 1980): 27–28.

12. Author's interview with Brigadier General Dov Tamari (Ret.), February 23, 2009.

13. Lecture by Major General Yehoshua Saguy (Ret.), in *A Series of Symposiums Summing Up Intelligence's Role in the Yom Kippur War* (Tel Aviv: Intelligence Training Base 15, 1994), 75.

14. Ehud Barak, IDF lecture, November 8, 1993.

15. *AGCR*, vol. 1, 60.

16. Barak lecture, November 8, 1993.

17. Arbel and Neeman, *Madness without Atonement*, 63–65.

18. Southern Command Intelligence (classified report), Artillery and Armor Changes Following the 526-T Sortie, October 4, 1973.

19. Colonel Oded Kam (Kaminitz) (Ret.), in *Series of Symposiums*, 46.

20. Aryeh Baron, *Moshe Dayan in the Yom Kippur War* (Jerusalem: Idanim/Yediot Achronot, 1992), 57; Uri Bar-Yosef, *The Watchman Who Fell Asleep: The Yom Kippur War Surprise and Its Sources* (Lod: Zmora-Bitan Publishers, 2001), 297–98.

21. *AGCR*, vol. 1, 372–74.

22. *AGCR*, vol. 2, pt. 6, "Explanations on the Personal Level," chap. 1 (partial report, sec. 28).

23. *AGCR*, 263–69, 5770 in the Protocol.

24. Lieutenant General Elazar, General Staff Conference, February 12, 1974.

25. Avidor interview, April 4, 2006.

26. *AGCR*, vol. 1, 108–9; *AGCR*, Partial Report, vol. 2, 320–21.

27. *AGCR*, 1252–53; author's interview with Brigadier General Baruch Harel (Ret.), April 4, 2006.

28. Tal, *National Security*, 85.

29. Colonel Dan Shomron, testimony before the IDF History Department, Major Ziskind, December 13, 1973.

30. *AGCR*, vol. 2, sec. 28, 23, 269.

31. Barak lecture, November 8, 1993.

32. Harel interview, April 4, 2006.

33. Colonel Shomron's testimony before Major General Menachem Meron, December 1973.

34. Author's interview with the late Lieutenant General Dan Shomron, January 4, 2006.

35. Golan, *Albert*.

36. *AGCR*, vol. 2, chap. 1, 241–44, 3964–67.

37. Documents from the archive of Albert's widow, Shula Mandler.

38. Author's interview with Brigadier General Benny Taran (Ret.), December 31, 2006.

39. Amiram Ezov, *Holding: Southern Command's Defensive Battle in the Yom Kippur War, October 6–7, 1973* (Tel Aviv: IDF History Department, 2001), 173; Harel interview, April 4, 2006.

40. *AGCR*, Third and Last Report, vol. 3, 1469, 1495; General Tal's recommendation for the establishment of a ground force headquarters, GHQ discussion, August 18, 1969.

41. Golan, *Research of the GHQ*, pt. 1, vol. 1, 17.

42. Colonel Roland Aloni (Ret.), "The Logistics of IDF Forces in the Yom Kippur War," *Maarachot* 361 (1998): 31.

43. *AGCR*, vol. 1, 163, 166.

44. Tal, *National Security*, 145–46.

45. *AGCR*, 1354–55, 1437–40.

46. A. H. Cordesman and A. R. Wagner, *The Lessons of Modern War*, vol. 1 (New York: Westview Press/Mansell Publishing, USA, 1990), chap. 2.

47. Golan, *Research of the GHQ*, pt. 1, vol. 2, 434–35.

48. *AGCR*, 4005–6.

49. *Shlav bet* were new immigrants in their mid-twenties to mid-thirties who, after basic training, served a few months on active duty and then became part of the reservist framework.

50. Herzog, *Thirtieth Anniversary of the Yom Kippur War*, 142; Golan, *Albert*, 75; Arbel and Neeman, *Madness without Atonement*, 139–40.

51. Major General Ariel Sharon, Southern Command Lessons Learned Conference, July 25, 1975.

52. Lecture by Major General Yehoshua Saguy (Ret.), in *Series of Symposiums*, 74–76; *AGCR*, vol. 6, pt. 1, 275; Asher, *Breaking the Concept*, 78.

53. Dani Asher, "The Antitank Weapon as the Answer—Egyptian Plans for Using Antitank Weapons in the Yom Kippur War," *Maarachot* 346 (February 1996): 6–10.

54. *AGCR*, Conclusions, 1346.

55. Adan, *On Both Banks*, 38.

56. *The Yom Kippur War, October 1973*, 14th Brigade Internal Document, October 1975, 12–28; *AGCR*, Additional Partial Report, vol. 2, 210–11.

57. Avidor interview, May 15, 2006.

58. *Yom Kippur War, October 1973*, 12–13; *AGCR*, Additional Partial Report, April 1, 1974, vol. 2, 209.

3. Ground Forces in the Defensive Battle

1. Guy, *Bar-Lev*, 288.

2. Brigadier General Yiftach Spector (Ret.), *Loud and Clear* (Tel Aviv: Yediot Achronot, Sifrei Hemed, 2008), 257.

3. The IAF commander expected to be granted permission for a preemptive strike; therefore, he stalled for as long as possible. At 12:50 he ordered the squadrons to switch from general-use ordnance for Dugman 5 (the preemptive strike in Syria) to munitions adapted for air defense. The siren sounded while all the F-4 Phantoms were in the midst of rearming, so they could not be sent aloft immediately.

4. Harel interview, April 4, 2006.

5. Golan, *Research of the GHQ*, pt. 1, vol. 2, 456–57.

6. *AGCR*, vol. 1, 46; author's interview with Victor Shem Tov (minister of health in 1973), January 8, 2006.

7. *AGCR*, vol. 1, 33.

8. Ibid.

9. Ibid., 34.

10. Ibid., 40; Exhibit 57, ibid., 42–43.

11. Ibid., 40–41.

12. Author's interview with Shimon Peres, March 21, 2006.

13. *AGCR*, vol. 2, 193.

14. Tal interview, June 5, 2006.

15. *AGCR*, vol. 2, 285–86.

16. Golan, *Research of the GHQ*, pt. 1, vol. 2, 454–56, 481; Oren, *History of the Yom Kippur War*, 64.

17. Gonen, testimony before the IDF History Department, December 17, 1975.

18. Shalev, testimony before the IDF History Department, December 1, 1977.

19. *AGCR*, vol. 2, sec. 28, 287–90.

20. Statements made at a senior staff meeting, February 12, 1974.

21. *AGCR*, vol. 2, 289; Protocol 4081; Oren, *History of the Yom Kippur War*, 62–63.

22. *AGCR*, vol. 2, 289; Protocol 4089; Oren, *History of the Yom Kippur War*, 62–63.

23. Shalev, testimony before the IDF History Department, December 1, 1977.

24. Ibid.

25. Golan, *Research of the GHQ*, pt. 1, vol. 2, 480–83; Gonen, testimony before the IDF History Department, January 14, 1976, 35.

26. Golan, *Research of the GHQ*, pt. 1, vol. 2, 471; reinterpretation dated November 22, 1978, and signed by the head of the History Department, Colonel Ayalon, Notebook F; *AGCR*, vol. 2, 289–91.

27. *AGCR*, vol. 2, 292.

28. Ibid.

29. Ibid.

30. Ibid.

31. Ibid., 294.

32. Golan, *Research of the GHQ*, pt. 2, vol. 1, 18.

33. Statements made at a senior staff meeting, February 12, 1974.

34. Elazar, testimony before the IDF History Department, February 27, 1976.

35. Golan, *Research of the GHQ*, pt. 1, vol. 2, 471.

36. Elazar, testimony before the IDF History Department, April 13, 1976.

37. *AGCR*, vol. 2, 335–37; Oren, *History of the Yom Kippur War*, 64.

38. Gonen, War Summary Conference in Southern Command, February 5, 1974, 5–6.

39. Gonen, testimony before the IDF History Department, July 20, 1976, 2.

40. *AGCR*, vol. 1, 148.

41. *AGCR*, vol. 2, 134.

42. Oren, *History of the Yom Kippur War*, 62–66.

43. Ezov, *Holding*, 138.

44. War Summary Conference in Southern Command, February 5, 1974, 5–6.

45. Elazar, testimony before the IDF History Department, February 17, 1976.

46. *AGCR*, vol. 2, 337.

47. Ibid., 337–39.

48. Ibid., 341.

49. Ibid., 342.

50. Ibid.

51. Ibid., 340.

52. Gonen, testimony before the IDF History Department, January 15, 1976, 35.

53. *AGCR*, vol. 2, 340, 342.

54. Gonen, testimony before the IDF History Department, January 15, 1976, 35.

55. *AGCR*, vol. 2, 341.

56. Colonel Pinchas Noy (Ret.), commander of 275th Territorial Brigade, War Summary Conference in Southern Command, February 5, 1974, 36; Harel interview, April 4, 2006.

57. *AGCR*, vol. 2, 295–96.

58. Ibid.

59. Tal, testimony before the IDF History Department, January 29, 1979, 52, 83–84.

60. Ibid., December 13, 1978, 5–7, 13–14; memo from Mrs. Shula Mandler to Agranat Commission.

61. Tal, testimony before the IDF History Department, March 7, 1977.

62. Ibid., January 29, 1974, 16–23.

63. Ibid., 27.

64. Ibid.

65. Major General Ariel Sharon (Ret.), Southern Command Lessons Learned Conference, July 25, 1974.

66. Ronen Bergman and Gil Meltzer, *The Yom Kippur War: Real Time* (Tel Aviv: Yediot Achronot, Sifrei Hemed, 2003), 74.

67. Ezov, *Holding*, 372 (Eitan Haber's interview of Gonen).

68. Herzog, *Thirtieth Anniversary of the Yom Kippur War*, 168.

69. Colonel Zeev Eitan, "'Dovecote'—Planning and Execution in the Test of Fire," *Maarachot* 276–77 (October–November 1980): 44–46.

70. Adan, *On Both Banks*, 70.

71. *AGCR*, vol. 2, 213.

72. Major General Shmuel Gonen, Senior IDF Commanders Meeting, February 2, 1974.

73. Colonel Amnon Reshef (commander of 14th Brigade), Summary of Moves in the Yom Kippur War, Southern Command, July 24, 1974.

74. Brigadier General Gabi Amir, IDF Command and Staff College, June 15, 1980, in Ezov, *Holding*, 286.

75. Colonel Dan Shomron, Southern Command Conference, March 5, 1974.

76. Colonel Dan Shomron, Summary of the Moves in the Yom Kippur War, Southern Command, July 24, 1974.

77. Statement by Lieutenant General Dan Shomron (Ret.), in *Series of Symposiums*, 67–68.

78. Brigadier General Baruch Harel, Southern Command Lessons Learned Conference, July 25, 1974.

79. *AGCR*, vol. 2, 212; testimony of G-3 of 14th Brigade, Major Sokol to Colonel Hisdai, 7, 10; *Yom Kippur War, October 1973*, 10–11, 36, 55; *AGCR*, vol. 2, 210–11.

80. *AGCR*, vol. 1, 220.

81. *AGCR*, 1350–51.

82. Ibid.

83. Baruch Harel, Southern Command Conference, March 5, 1974.

84. Colonel Dan Shomron, testimony to the chief of the Instruction Department, November 28, 1973.

85. Avidor debriefing, IDF History Department, Doctrine and Instruction Department, November 10, 1974, 3; Ezov, *Holding*, 263.

86. Hanoch Bartov, *Dado, 48 Years 20 Days* (Tel Aviv: Sifriat Maariv, 1978), 40.

87. Eitan, "Dovecote," 39–46.

88. *AGCR*, vol. 1, log of the chief of staff's aide, October 6, 1973, Exhibit 285, 227.

89. Author's interview with Lieutenant General Dan Shomron (Ret.), January 4, 2006.

90. Guy, *Bar-Lev*, 285.

91. Ezov, *Holding*, 273; Harel's testimony before the head of the Doctrine and Instruction Department, November 1973.

92. Golan, *Research of the GHQ*, pt. 2, vol. 1, 234, 254n143.

93. Tal, *National Security*, 175.

94. Lieutenant General Ehud Barak, lecture at Senior Staff Officers' Conference, November 8, 1993.

95. Colonel Dan Shomron, Summary of the Moves in the Yom Kippur War, Southern Command, July 24, 1974.

96. Major General Shmuel Gonen, Southern Command Lessons Learned Conference, July 25, 1974.

97. *AGCR*, Shula Mandler's memorandum, Exhibit 238.

98. Ezov, *Holding*, 208.

99. *AGCR*, Third and Last Report, vol. 1, diary of the chief of staff's aide-de-camp, October 6, 1973, Exhibit 285.

100. Ibid., chief of staff at the 06:18:35 operational meeting; Bartov, *Dado*, 40–42.

101. *AGCR*, Third and Last Report, vol. 1, 227B–C.

102. Lieutenant General David Elazar, Senior Staff Conference, February 12, 1974.

103. Colonel Dan Shomron, testimony before the IDF History Branch, December 13, 1973; Herzog, *Thirtieth Anniversary of the Yom Kippur War*, 183.

104. Avidor debriefing, October 11, 1974, 31–33.

105. Brigadier General Baruch Harel, Southern Command Conference, March 5, 1974; Summary of the Yom Kippur War, 252nd Division (internal paper), 100.

106. Gonen, Southern Command Lessons Learned Conference, July 25, 1974.

107. Ibid.

108. Major General Shmuel Gonen (Ret.), Summary of the Moves of the Yom Kippur War, Southern Command, July 24, 1974; Herzog, *Thirtieth Anniversary of the Yom Kippur War*, 149.

109. Ariel Sharon, conversation with Brigadier General Baruch Harel, Southern Command Conference, March 5, 1974.

110. Avidor interview, May 15, 2006.

111. Author's interview with Brigadier General David Shoval (Ret.) (commander of 46th Battalion/401st Brigade), March 28, 2006.

112. *AGCR*, Third and Last Report, vol. 1, 220.

113. Dayan, *Milestones*, 590.

114. Avidor interview, May 15, 2006.

115. *AGCR*, Third and Last Report, vol. 1, 227D.

116. Ibid., 227.

117. Dayan, *Milestones*, 597.

118. Golan, *Research of the GHQ*, pt. 2, vol. 1, 171.

119. Ibid., 153.

120. Ibid., 278–79.

121. Eitan, "Dovecote," 45; Summary of the Yom Kippur War, 252nd Division, 44.

122. Lieutenant General David Elazar, Senior Staff Conference, February 14, 1974, High Command Document.

123. Dayan, *Milestones*, 580, 583.

124. Adan, *On Both Banks*, 36.

125. *AGCR*, Third and Last Report, vol. 1, 226.

126. Brigadier General Baruch Harel, testimony before the head of the Doctrine and Instruction Department, November 1973.

127. Conversation between the commanders of 401st Brigade and 52nd Battalion, morning of October 7, 1973, History, Radio Tapes, Operational Frequency "Dahlia"—Southern Sector, Doctrine and Instruction Department, IDF Archives.

128. Ibid.

129. Colonel Dan Shomron, testimony before the IDF History Branch, December 13, 1973.

130. Avidor interview, May 15, 2006.

131. Testimony of Captain Yaron Ram, commander, C Company/46th Battalion, in War Summary, 401st Brigade (internal document).

132. Shoval interview, March 28, 2006.

133. *AGCR*, Third Report, vol. 3, 1221.

134. *Yom Kippur War, October 1973*, 51–52, 55; testimony of Lieutenant Gideon Eldar, operations officer, 184th Battalion, ibid., 50.

135. *AGCR*, Third Report, vol. 2, 218.

136. Ibid., 325, 621.

137. Yona Bendman, "The Third Army Crosses the Canal, October 6–8, 1973," *Maarachot* 296 (December 1984): 26–30.

138. *AGCR*, Third Report, vol. 1, 232.

139. Tal's testimony, ibid., 237.

140. Oren, *History of the Yom Kippur War*, 92, 96.

141. *AGCR*, Third Report, vol. 1, 233; Radio Tape Exhibit 349, Film No. 1.

142. *AGCR*, Third Report, vol. 1, 229.

143. Golan, *Research of the GHQ*, pt. 2, vol. 1, 128, 139.

144. *AGCR*, Third Report, vol. 2, 159–60, 321.

145. Ibid., vol. 3, 1220–21, 1240–43.

146. Golan, *Research of the GHQ*, pt. 2, vol. 1, 121.

147. *AGCR*, Third Report, vol. 2, 621.

148. Shmuel Gonen, Summary of the Moves in the Yom Kippur War, Southern Command, July 24, 1974.

149. *AGCR*, Third Report, vol. 1, 241–42.

150. Golan, *Research of the GHQ*, pt. 2, vol. 1, chaps. 1–2, 94.

151. Dayan, *Milestones*, 506, 597.

152. *AGCR*, Third Report, vol. 1, 184–85.

153. Baron, *Dayan*, 196; *AGCR*, Third Report, vol. 1, 184–85; Golan, *Research of the GHQ*, pt. 2, vol. 1, chaps. 1–2, 130, Defense Minister's Third Diary, October 7, 1973, 19–20.

154. Bergman and Meltzer, *Real Time*, 73.

155. *AGCR*, Third Report, vol. 1, 184–85, 233; Gonen, Summary of the Moves in the Yom Kippur War, Southern Command, July 24, 1974.

156. Adan, *On Both Banks*, 75; Oren, *History of the Yom Kippur War*, 93; Bergman and Meltzer, *Real Time*, 73.

157. Golan, *Research of the GHQ*, pt. 2, vol. 1, chaps. 1–2, 138.

158. *AGCR*, Third Report, vol. 1, 235–36.

159. Ibid., 237–38.

160. Bergman and Meltzer, *Real Time*, 78.

161. Ibid., 228; Dayan, *Milestones*, 600.

162. *AGCR*, Third Report, vol. 1, 187–88.

163. Ibid., 192.

164. Ibid., 187–88, 192.

165. Ibid., 238, 243–44; tape from the chief of staff's office.

166. Ibid.

167. Ibid.

168. *AGCR*, Third Report, vol. 1, Protocol Eli Mizrahi, Exhibit 57A, Document 14, 249–54.

169. *AGCR*, Third Report, vol. 1, 259–60.

170. Golan, *Research of the GHQ*, pt. 2, vol. 1, 166–67.

171. Ibid.

172. Ibid., 173.

173. *AGCR*, Third and Last Report, vol. 1, 136.

174. Roger Ashley, *On War: A Short Guide to Clausewitz* (Tel Aviv: Maarachot Publications, 1977), 161–63.

175. Lieutenant General Ehud Barak, lecture at General Staff Personnel Conference, November 8, 1993.

176. *AGCR*, Third and Last Report, vol. 1, 285.

177. Brigadier General Dov Tamari (Ret.) interview, February 23, 2009.

178. *AGCR*, Third and Last Report, vol. 1, 135; Eil Barzel War Game Summary, 6–7.

179. Eil Barzel War Game Summary, 7.

180. Ibid., 17.

181. *AGCR*, Third and Last Report, vol. 1, chief of staff's summary of Eil Barzel War Game, 135; *AGCR*, vol. 2, chief of staff's statements, May 2, 1973, 96.

182. Golan, *Research of the GHQ*, pt. 2, vol. 2, chaps. 1–2, 31.

183. Amiram Ezov's interview with Brigadier General Avner Shalev (Ret.), February 13, 2007, in Ezov, *Holding*.

184. *AGCR*, Third and Last Report, vol. 1, 272–74.

185. Ibid., 184, 230.

186. Ibid., 228.

187. Ibid., 238; tape recording from the chief of staff's room, 13:10, October 7, 1973.

188. David Elazar, Yom Kippur War Summary, Southern Command, July 24, 1974.

189. Golan, *Research of the GHQ*, pt. 2, vol. 1, , 158; tape recording from the chief of staff's room, Tape No. 2, 18–19.

190. Golan, *Research of the GHQ*, pt. 2, vol. 1, 155; log of the chief of staff's aide-de-camp, October 7, 1973, 13.

191. Golan, *Research of the GHQ*, pt. 2, vol. 1, 166.

192. Ibid., 211n35.

193. Statement by Lieutenant Colonel Shimon Golan (Ret.), in *Series of Symposiums*, 30, 59; Dayan, *Milestones*, 600.

194. Adan, *On Both Banks*, 79–80.

195. *AGCR*, Third and Last Report, vol. 1, 279.

196. Ibid., 121–22.

197. Ibid.

198. Ibid., vol. 2, 520.

199. Ibid., 488.

200. Golan, *Research of the GHQ*, pt. 2, vol. 1, 160–61.

201. Avidor interview, May 15, 2006; Bendman, "Third Army Crosses the Canal," 26–30.

202. *AGCR*, Third and Last Report, vol. 1, 271; Golan, *Research of the GHQ*, pt. 2, vol. 1, 207n8.

203. *AGCR*, Third and Last Report, vol. 1, 272.

204. Ibid.

205. Ibid., 282.

206. Ibid., 274–82.

207. Ibid.

208. Ibid., 321–22.

209. Ibid., 276–77.

210. Tal interview, June 7, 2006.

211. *AGCR*, Third and Last Report, vol. 1, 281–83.

212. *AGCR*, Third Report, vol. 3, 1405–8.

213. Ibid., 1399.

214. Ibid., vol. 1, 311.

215. Ibid., 289–91 (based on the log of Southern Command's aide-de-camp).

216. *AGCR*, Third and Last Report, vol. 1, 291–93.

217. Ibid., 310.

218. Ibid., 310–13.

219. Ibid., 1311–12.

220. *AGCR*, Third Report, vol. 1, 320–21.

221. Ibid., 293–94.

222. Ibid., 297–98.

223. Ibid., vol. 2, 623.

224. Ibid., vol. 1, 317.

225. Ibid., 303.

226. *AGCR*, Third and Last Report, vol. 1, 285.

227. *AGCR*, Third Report, vol. 1, 316–18.

228. Ibid., vol. 2, 532.

229. Dayan, *Milestones*, 604.

230. *AGCR*, Third Report, vol. 2, 1282.

231. Ibid., vol. 1, 308.

232. Ibid., 309–11.

233. Ibid., vol. 2, 348–45.

234. See the notes of Major General Rehavam "Gandhi" Zeevi, "Change of Direction: The 162nd Division to Cross at Hizayon."

235. *AGCR*, Third Report, vol. 2, 388.

236. Ibid., 593, 611.

237. Ibid., vol. 3, 798.

238. Bergman and Meltzer, *Real Time*, 123.

239. Ibid., vol. 2, 586; author's interview with Colonel Haim Adini (Ret.), April 15, 2007.

240. "Loft bombing" or "toss bombing" is a bombing method in which the attacking pilot pulls the aircraft skyward while releasing the bomb load, thus enabling the bomb to begin its ballistic path with an upward vector, giving it additional flight time.

241. *AGCR*, Third Report, vol. 2, 604.

242. Ibid., 642–54.

243. Ibid., 659–60.

244. Author's interview with Brigadier General Uri Ben Ari (Ret.), January 10, 2007.

245. *AGCR*, Third Report, vol. 1, 322.

246. Ibid., vol. 2, 556, 679; ibid., vol. 1, 520.

247. Ibid., vol. 3, 775.

248. Ibid., vol. 2, 537.

249. Ibid., 562.

250. Dayan, *Milestones*, 660.

251. Colonel Pinhas Noy, commander of 275th Brigade, Southern Command Conferences, February 24 and March 2, 1974.

252. *AGCR*, Third Report, vol. 1, 161; Golan, *Albert*, 191–93, 202; Golan, *Research of the GHQ*, pt. 2, vol. 1, 185.

253. *AGCR*, Third Report, vol. 1, 257.

254. Golan, *Research of the GHQ*, pt. 2, vol. 1, 166.

255. *AGCR*, Third Report, vol. 2, 347–48.

256. Ibid., 327–31, 341, 347–48.

257. Ibid., 355.

258. Ibid., 732; author's interview with Brigadier General Shai Tamari (Ret.), January 3, 2007.

259. *AGCR*, Third and Last Report, vol. 1, 318.

260. Ibid., 733.

261. *AGCR*, Third Report, vol. 3, 510, 733.

262. Ibid., vol. 2, 718, 749.

263. Ibid., 1314–16, 1390–93, 1397–99.

264. Ibid., 338.

265. Ibid., 357.

266. Ibid., 364.

267. See Gandhi's notes, "Requesting Permission for the 162nd Division to Cross at Hizayon."

268. See Gandhi's notes, "Bring the 143rd Down to the Gidi."

269. *AGCR*, Third Report, vol. 3, 764–65; Bergman and Meltzer, *Real Time*, 117.

270. *AGCR*, Third Report, vol. 2, 390–91, 395, 380–81.

271. Ibid., 390, 397.

272. Ibid., 397.

273. Golan, *Research of the GHQ*, pt. 2, vol. 1, 285; *AGCR*, Third Report, vol. 2, 401.

274. See Gandhi's notes, "Sending the 143rd Division to a Crossing at Hakfar and Capturing Suez."

275. *AGCR*, Third Report, vol. 3, 733; *AGCR*, vol. 2, 388.

276. Ibid.

277. *AGCR*, vol. 2, 499–503.

278. Ibid.

279. Ibid., 430.

280. Ibid., 377–79, 512; *AGCR*, vol. 3, 512.

281. *AGCR*, Third Report, vol. 3, 785–87, 778–94, 512; *Yom Kippur War, October 1973*, 59; Wald, *Curse*, 106–7.

282. *AGCR*, Third Report, vol. 3, 767.

283. Wald, *Curse*, 836–37.

284. *AGCR*, Third Report, vol. 3, 794–95; *AGCR*, vol. 2, 410.

285. *AGCR*, Third Report, vol. 3, 798; Golan, *Research of the GHQ*, pt. 2, vol. 1, 299; *AGCR*, Third Report, vol. 2, 425–27.

286. Ibid.

287. Golan, *Research of the GHQ*, pt. 2, vol. 1, 300.

288. *AGCR*, Third Report, vol. 2, 815.

289. Ibid., 711, 714–18.

290. Ibid., vol. 3, 816.

291. Ibid., vol. 2, 442, 723–36, 707, 709.

292. Avidor interview, May 15, 2006.

293. Colonel Dan Shomron, commander of 401st Brigade, Southern Command Conference at Refidim, March 12, 1974.

294. Gideon Avidor debriefing, November 14, 1974, 9–10, IDF History Department.

295. Ibid., 12–17; Oren, *History of the Yom Kippur War*, 127.

296. Avidor debriefing, 9–10.

297. Ibid., 15–17.

298. *AGCR*, Third Report, vol. 1, 409.

299. Ibid., vol. 3, 845, 821, 865–66.

300. Bergman and Meltzer, *Real Time*, 123–24.

301. *AGCR*, Third Report, vol. 2, 509; Avraham Rotem, "Rules and Principles in Desert War in View of the IDF's Campaigns in Sinai," *Maarachot* 254 (1977): 865–66.

302. *AGCR*, Third Report, vol. 1, 513.

303. Golan, *Research of the GHQ*, pt. 1, vol. 1, 288n264.

304. *AGCR*, Third Report, vol. 3, 1270–72, 748; ibid., vol. 1, 580–81; ibid., vol. 2, 682–83.

305. Ibid., vol. 2, 371.

306. Ibid.

307. Ibid.

308. Ibid., 469.

309. Bergman and Meltzer, *Real Time*, 128.

310. Ibid., 128, 467–68.

311. *AGCR*, Third Report, vol. 2, 428–29.

312. Ibid., 431.

313. Lieutenant General Ehud Barak, lecture at Senior Staff Conference, November 8, 1993.

314. Rotem, "Rules and Principles," 10, 12.

315. *AGCR*, Third Report, vol. 2, 507.

316. Ibid., 514.

317. Ibid., 503–10, 514–16.

318. Ibid., 440–49; Golan, *Research of the GHQ*, pt. 2, vol. 1, 304.

319. Golan, *Research of the GHQ*, pt. 2, vol. 1, 304.

320. Ibid.

321. *AGCR*, Third Report, vol. 2, 469.

322. Golan, *Research of the GHQ*, pt. 2, vol. 1, 326–27; *AGCR*, Third Report, vol. 2, 461–63; statement by Lieutenant Colonel Shimon Golan (Ret.), September 22, 1993, in *Series of Symposiums*, 61–62.

323. Golan, *Research of the GHQ*, pt. 2, vol. 1, 349.

324. Ibid., 343.

325. Bergman and Meltzer, *Real Time*, 133 (tape recording of the chief of staff's aide-de-camp).

326. Golan, *Research of the GHQ*, pt. 2, vol. 2, 4.

327. Ibid.

328. Ibid., 6.

329. Ibid., 12.

330. Ibid., 13–14.

331. *AGCR*, Third Report, vol. 2, 471–77.

332. Ibid.

333. Ibid., vol. 1, 8, 12, 137–38; Golan, *Research of the GHQ*, pt. 2, vol. 2, 17–22.

334. Golan, *Research of the GHQ*, pt. 2, vol. 2, 49, 52.

335. Ibid., 55.

336. Armor Corps Headquarters, Armored Divisions in the Yom Kippur War, Southern Front, 252nd Division, October 1974, 23.

337. Colonel Dan Shomron debriefing, IDF History Department, December 13, 1973.

338. Lieutenant Colonel Emanuel Sakal, commander of 52nd Battalion, testimony before the IDF History Department.

339. Golan, *Research of the GHQ*, pt. 2, vol. 3, 43–52.

340. Tal interview, December 21, 2005.

341. Golan, *Research of the GHQ*, pt. 2, vol. 1, 105–6.

342. Ibid.

343. Field Marshal Mohamed Abdel Ghani El-Gamasy, *The 1973 October War: Memoirs of Field Marshal El-Gamasy* (Tel Aviv: IDF Intelligence Training Base 15, 1994), 131 (comments by Colonel Zusia Kaniajer [Ret.]).

344. Asher, *Breaking the Concept*, 235–36.

345. Oren, *History of the Yom Kippur War*, 184.

346. Lieutenant General Ehud Barak, lecture at Senior Staff Conference, November 8, 1993; Golan, *Research of the GHQ*, pt. 2, vol. 1, 123.

347. *AGCR*, Third Report, vol. 3, 1270.

348. Ibid., 7209.

349. Ibid., vol. 4, pt. C, 1362–63, 8783–90.

350. Ibid., 1365.

351. Major General Ariel Sharon (Ret.), Southern Command Lessons Learned Conference, July 25, 1974.

352. *AGCR*, Third Report, vol. 1, 75, 322, testimony of Colonel Keren, commander of 500th Brigade; Colonel Gonen, commander of 274th Brigade; and Brigadier General Tamari, deputy commander of 162nd Division.

353. *AGCR*, Third Report, vol. 3, 1339.

354. Ibid.

355. Ibid., 1342–43.

356. Ibid., 1443–49.

357. In Northern Command, 24 percent of the hits were from hollow charges, of which 13 percent were Sagger missiles.

358. Herzog, *Thirtieth Anniversary of the Yom Kippur War*, 591.

359. Major General Shmuel Gonen, Southern Command Lessons Learned Conference, July 25, 1974.

360. *AGCR*, Third Report, vol. 2, 526, 530.

361. Golan, *Research of the GHQ*, pt. 1, vol. 2, 468.

362. *AGCR*, Third Report, vol. 1, 135–36.

363. Ibid., vol. 3, 1206–7.

364. Ibid., 1368–71.

365. Ibid., 228–29.

366. Statement by Lieutenant General Dan Shomron (Ret.), in *Series of Symposiums*, 67–68.

367. *AGCR*, Third Report, vol. 3, 1369.

368. Ibid., 1372.

369. The first supradivisional headquarters was established in 1974 under the command of Major General Sharon.

370. Shomron debriefing, IDF History Department, December 13, 1973.

371. Major General Amos Yadlin (Ret.), "The Air Force's Role in the Yom Kippur War, 30 Years in Retrospect," in *The Yom Kippur War and Its Lessons* (Tel Aviv: Ha'universita Hameshuderet, 2003), 70.

372. Oren, *History of the Yom Kippur War*, 287.

4. Air Support for the Ground Forces

1. GHQ discussion, "Situation Assessment Summary," June 26, 1972, 7.

2. Iron Ram War Game Summary, August 24, 1972, IDF History Department Archive.

3. Golan, *Research of the GHQ*, pt. 1, vol. 1, 110.

4. Dov Tamari interview, February 23, 2009.

5. *AGCR*, Second Report, vol. 2, 278.

6. Golan, *Research of the GHQ*, pt. 1, vol. 1, 109.

7. Ibid., 101; Baron, *Dayan*, 32.

8. Tal, *National Security*, 65.

9. Cohen, "Limitations on the Use of the Reserves," 65–66.

10. Lecture by Brigadier General Giora Forman (Ret.), "The Seven Year War in the Air Theater," no date; Golan, *Research of the GHQ*, pt. 1, vol. 1, 277–78.

11. Golan, *Research of the GHQ*, pt. 1, vol. 1, 80–85, 107–8, 264.

12. Ibid., 105.

13. Ibid., 109.

14. Bartov, *Dado*, 12; Golan, *Research of the GHQ*, pt. 1, vol. 2, 470.

15. Brigadier General Dani Asher (Ret.) and Lieutenant Itai Asher (Ret.), "Israeli Artillery on the Southern Front in the Yom Kippur War," *Maarachot* 354 (1999): 17.

16. Golan, *Research of the GHQ*, pt. 1, vol. 1, 277.

17. *AGCR*, vol. 2, chap. 2, 236.

18. Golan, *Research of the GHQ*, pt. 1, vol. 1, 112–14.

19. Lecture by Lieutenant Colonel Motti Habakuk, no date.

20. IAF History Branch, Commanders' Discussions in the Yom Kippur War, 22–23.

21. Ibid., 9.

22. *AGCR*, vol. 2, 217.

23. Ibid., 218.

24. IAF History Branch, Commanders' Discussions in the Yom Kippur War, 22–23.

25. AGCR, vol. 2, 219; Bartov, *Dado*, 67.

26. Oren, *History of the Yom Kippur War*, 99.

27. *AGCR*, vol. 2, 317.

28. Bartov, *Dado*, 49; Golan, *Research of the GHQ*, pt. 2, vol. 1, 62–63.

29. Golan, *Research of the GHQ*, pt. 2, vol. 1, 77; author's interview with Colonel Shmuel Gordon (Ret.), March 1, 2006.

30. Golan, *Research of the GHQ*, pt. 2, vol. 1, 77.

31. Colonel Shmuel Gordon (Ret.), "The Paradox of October 7," *Maarachot* 361 (1998): 47; Gordon interview, March 1, 2006; Dayan, *Milestones*, 595–97; Herzog, *Thirtieth Anniversary of the Yom Kippur War*, 236.

32. Golan, *Research of the GHQ*, pt. 2, vol. 1, 96, 104.

33. Gordon interview, June 13, 2006.

34. Golan, *Research of the GHQ*, pt. 2, vol. 1, 120–21; Habakuk lecture.

35. Gordon interview, March 1, 2006.

36. *AGCR*, Third Report, vol. 1, 230.

37. Ibid., 231; Golan, *Research of the GHQ*, pt. 2, vol. 1, 128–29; Gordon interview, March 1, 2006.

38. Golan, *Research of the GHQ*, pt. 2, vol. 1, 168.

39. *AGCR*, Third Report, vol. 1, 259–61.

40. Bartov, *Dado*, 70; *AGCR*, Third Report, vol. 1, 262–63.

41. *AGCR*, Third Report, vol. 1, 215.

42. Ibid., 227.

43. Benny Peled, *Days of Reckoning* (Ben Shemen: Modan, 2004), 335.

44. *AGCR*, Third Report, vol. 1, 316–19.

45. IAF History Branch, Commanders' Discussions in the Yom Kippur War, Base Commanders' Discussion, 09:07:17.

46. Shmuel Gordon, *30 Hours in October, Fateful Decisions: The IAF at the Start of the Yom Kippur War* (Tel Aviv: Sifriyat Maariv, 2008), 411–12.

47. Author's interview with Brigadier General Yiftach Spector (Ret.), June 6, 2007.

48. Wald, *Curse*, 109.

49. Cordesman and Wagner, *Lessons of Modern War*, vol. 1, chap. 2 (translated into Hebrew by Colonel Ron Kitri), in *Series of Symposiums*, 34–36.

50. Zeira, *Myth versus Reality*, 52.

51. Israel Tal, testimony before the IDF History Department, December 8, 1978, 22–30.

52. Ibid.

53. Tal, *National Security*, 205.

54. Author's interview with Major General David Ivry (Ret.), May 31, 2007.

55. Spector interview, June 6, 2007; Spector, *Loud and Clear*, 235–36.

56. Author's interview with Brigadier General Giora Forman (Ret.), March 11, 2006.

57. Author's interview with Brigadier General Amos Amir (Ret.), January 12, 2006.

58. *AGCR*, vol. 2, 214.

59. Yadlin, "IAF's Performance in the Yom Kippur War," 80–81.

60. Asher and Asher, "Israeli Artillery on the Southern Front," 17.

61. Jehuda Wallach, *Not on a Silver Platter* (Jerusalem: Carta, in cooperation with Defense Ministry Publishers, 2000), 120.

62. Golan, *Research of the GHQ*, pt. 2, vol. 2, 62–63; Dayan, *Milestones*, 588, 594; Baron, *Dayan*, 91–92.

63. Lecture by Major General Motti Hod (Ret.), "The Air Theater in the Yom Kippur War," Professional Day No. 7 at Efal, May 4, 2000.

64. Major General Shmuel Gonen (Ret.), testimony before the IDF History Department, February 8, 1977, 20–24.

65. Peled, *Days of Reckoning*, 332.

66. Gordon interviews, March 1, 2006, and September 11, 2007; Golan, *Research of the GHQ*, pt. 2, vol. 1, 28–32.

67. Statement by Colonel Shefer (Ret.), Southern Command, June 15, 1980, in Ezov, *Holding*, 233.

68. Ivry interview, May 31, 2007.

69. Peled, *Days of Reckoning*, 421; Gordon, *30 Hours in October*, 208.

70. Golan, *Research of the GHQ*, pt. 1, vol. 1, 110n170.

71. Hod lecture, "Air Theater in the Yom Kippur War," May 4, 2000.

72. Golan, *Research of the GHQ*, pt. 1, vol. 1, 106–7.

73. *AGCR*, Protocol 4786; *AGCR*, Additional Partial Report, vol. 2, 335.

74. *AGCR*, vol. 2, chap. 2, Protocol 2450.

75. *AGCR*, vol. 2, chap. 2, 236.

76. Gonen, Southern Command Summary of the Yom Kippur War, July 24, 1974.

77. Author's interview with Major General Israel Tal (Ret.), June 7, 2006.

78. Shmuel Gonen, testimony before the IDF History Department, July 20, 1976, 9.

79. Israel Tal, testimony before the IDF History Department, August 11, 1976, 18.

80. Wald, *Curse*, 120; lecture by Major General Benny Peled (Ret.), "Not Attacking Strategic Targets in the Yom Kippur War," May 6, 1979.

81. Oren, *History of the Yom Kippur War*, 13.

82. Arbel and Neeman, *Madness without Atonement*, 127; Bartov, *Dado*, 257.

83. Golan, *Research of the GHQ*, pt. 1, vol. 1, 108.

84. *AGCR*, vol. 2, 227, 275–76; *AGCR*, vol. 1, pt. 1, 270.

85. Zeira, *Myth versus Reality*, 86.

86. *AGCR*, vol. 2, 217.

87. Bartov, *Dado*, 67.

88. Ivry interview, May 31, 2007.

89. Peled, *Days of Reckoning*, 346–47.

90. *AGCR*, vol. 2, 227, 275–76.

91. Ibid., 232.

92. Ibid., 219, 227.

93. Forman interview, March 11, 2006.

94. Gordon interviews, March, 1, 2006, and September 11, 2007.

95. Lieutenant General David Elazar, Senior Staff Conference, February 12, 1974.

96. Dayan, *Milestones*, 592.

97. Gonen, testimony before the IDF History Department, July 15, 1976, 9.

98. Spector interview, June 6, 2007.

99. Yadlin, "IAF's Performance in the Yom Kippur War," 78; author's interview with Zeev Lachish, May 8, 2007.

100. Forman interview, March 11, 2006.

101. Yadlin, "IAF's Performance in the Yom Kippur War," 70.

102. Golan, *Research of the GHQ*, pt. 2, vol. 1, 139.

103. Gordon, "Paradox of October 7," 47–48; Bergman and Meltzer, *Real Time*, 69–70; lecture by Colonel Shefer (Ret.), IDF Command and Staff College; Gordon interview, March 1, 2006; Ido Ambar, "The IAF's Participation in the Ground Battle," in *The Crossing that Wasn't*, ed. Uri Milstein (Tel Aviv: Yaron Golan Publisher, 1992), 279.

104. Gordon interview, March 1, 2006.

105. Spector, *Loud and Clear*, 246; Spector interview, June 6, 2007.

106. Oren, *History of the Yom Kippur War*, 99.

107. Spector, *Loud and Clear*, 247–49; Spector interview, June 6, 2007.

108. Ivry interview, May 31, 2007.

109. Statement by Lieutenant Colonel Oded Kam (Ret.), in *Series of Symposiums*, 247.

110. Interview with Asher Snir, July 16, 1977, in Peled, *Days of Reckoning*, 232; Spector interview, June 6, 2007; Ivry interview, May 31, 2007.

111. Shmuel Gonen, War Lessons Summary, March 12, 1974.

112. *AGCR*, Third Report, vol. 2, 407–8.

113. Habakuk lecture.

114. IAF History Branch, *The Yom Kippur War,* vol. 2, *The Air Force's Participation in the Ground Fighting* (Tel Aviv, 1979), 150.

115. Wallach, *Not on a Silver Platter,* 120.

116. Gonen, testimony before the IDF History Department, July 15, 1976, 3, 20.

117. Statements by the commander of 215th/162nd Artillery Group, March 12, 1974, in Ezov, *Holding,* 332–33.

118. Colonel Pinkhas Noy, commander of 275th Territorial Brigade, Senior IDF Commanders' Meeting, February 14, 1974.

119. Tal interview, December 21, 2005.

120. Tal, testimony before the IDF History Department, December 17, 1975, 1–2.

121. Trevor N. Dupuy, *Elusive Victory: The Arab-Israeli Wars, 1947–1974* (London: Harper and Row, 1978), 555–56.

122. Benny Peled, Senior IDF Commanders' Meeting, February 12, 1974.

123. Lieutenant General David Elazar, Senior Staff Conference, February 12, 1974.

124. Forman lecture, "Seven-Year War in the Air Theater."

125. IAF History Branch, IAF Commanders' Discussion, October 12, 1973.

126. Lieutenant Colonel Shimon Golan (Ret.), "I Couldn't Care Less about Kantara," *Zrakor* (October 2002): 9–11, 79.

127. Gonen, testimony before the IDF History Department, July 15, 1976, 3, 20.

128. IAF History Branch, IAF Commanders' Discussion, October 8, 1973, 29.

129. Yadlin, "IAF's Performance in the Yom Kippur War," 70, 72–73.

130. Spector, *Loud and Clear,* 276.

131. Ibid.

132. Colonel Eliezer Cohen (Ret.), *The Sky Is Not the Limit: The Story of the Israeli Air Force* (Tel Aviv: Maariv, 1990), 524–25.

133. IAF History Branch, Participation of the IAF in the Land Battle in the Yom Kippur War in Southern Command, 1984, 103–4.

134. IAF History Branch, IAF Commanders' Discussion, October 8, 1973, 29.

135. Peled, *Days of Reckoning,* 32.

136. Major General Benny Peled, Southern Command Conference at Refidim, May 12, 1974.

137. Elazar, Senior Staff Conference, February 12, 1974.

138. Benny Peled, Senior IDF Commanders' Meeting, February 12, 1974.

139. Peled, *Days of Reckoning,* 380.

140. Ibid., 356.

141. Major General Motti Hod (Ret.), Southern Command Conference at Refidim, March 12, 1974.

142. Ambar, "IAF's Participation in the Ground Battle," 268.

143. Spector interview, June 6, 2007.

144. Lieutenant General Rafael Eitan (Ret.), interview with Dov Goldstein, in *Story of a Soldier* (Tel Aviv: Maariv, 1985), 146–47.

145. Quoted in Colonel Trevor N. Dupuy (Ret.), "Military Aspects of the Israeli-Arab Conflict," in *International Symposium, October 12–17, 1975, Hebrew University of Jerusalem* (Tel Aviv: University Publishing Projects, 1975), 242–43.

146. Peled, *Days of Reckoning,* 378, 428.

147. Gordon, "Paradox of October 7," 46, 52–53.

148. Almajdub Albadri Aladin, "The Ramadan War, the Fourth Arab-Israeli Round," statements by Thomas Chatham, United Press journalist in Tel Aviv, October 16, 1973 (IDF internal publication, 1974), 68.

149. *AGCR*, Third Report, vol. 3, 1511.

150. Ibid., Summary Volume, 1442.

151. Yadlin, "IAF's Performance in the Yom Kippur War," 68–69, 76–77.

152. Ivry interview, May 21, 2007.

153. Spector interview, June 6, 2007.

154. Interview with Lieutenant Colonel Zeev Lachish (Ret.), January 9, 2006.

155. Gordon, "Paradox of October 7," 44.

5. The Preemptive Strike that Wasn't

1. Yaniv, *Politics and Strategy*, 31.

2. Yigal Allon, *Screen of Sand* (Tel Aviv: Hakibutz Hameukhad, 1960), 69–70, 74, 76–79; Levite, *Israel's Military Doctrine*, 12.

3. Yaniv, *Politics and Strategy*, 79.

4. Major General Aharon Yariv (Ret.) quoted in Levite, *Israel's Military Doctrine*, 20–21.

5. Ibid.

6. Steven J. Rosen and Martin Indyk, "The Temptation to Preempt in a Fifth Arab-Israeli War," *Orbis* (Summer 1976): 276.

7. Yaniv, *Politics and Strategy*, 242–46, 467.

8. Herzog, *Thirtieth Anniversary of the Yom Kippur War*, 12–13; Bar-Siman-Tov, *25-Year Retrospective*, 42.

9. *AGCR*, Third Report, vol. 1, 131; Golan, *Research of the GHQ*, pt. 1, vol. 1, 85.

10. *AGCR*, Third Report, vol. 1, 1499–1500.

11. Peled, *Days of Reckoning*, 341, 347, 371–72, 401, 407.

12. Bar-Siman-Tov, *25-Year Retrospective*, 43.

13. Arbel and Neeman, *Madness without Atonement*, 174.

14. Golan, *Research of the GHQ*, pt. 1, vol. 1, 125–26.

15. GHQ Discussion, May 21, 1973, IDF History Department Archive; Baron, *Dayan*, 28.

16. Cohen, "Limitations on the Use of the Reserves," 64.

17. Major General Israel Tal (Ret.), testimony before the IDF History Department, December 7, 1978 , 79–81.

18. Peled, *Days of Reckoning*, 361.

19. *AGCR*, vol. 1, 32.

20. *AGCR*, vol. 2, 216.

21. Ibid., 229.

22. Baron, *Dayan*, 75.

23. Lieutenant Colonel Shimon Golan (Ret.), "The Preemptive Strike at the Onset of the Yom Kippur War," *Maarachot* 373 (November 2000): 56; Golan, *Research of the GHQ*, pt. 1, vol. 1, 466.

24. Ibid.; *AGCR*, vol. 2, 217.

25. Author's interview with Colonel Shmuel Gordon (Ret.), September 11, 2007; Golan, "Preemptive Strike," 57; Ambar, "IAF's Participation in the Ground Battle," 274.

26. Golan, "Preemptive Strike," 52–53.

27. Yishai Cordova, *United States Policy in the Yom Kippur War* (Tel Aviv: Maarachot Publications, 1987), 32.

28. Yaniv, *Politics and Strategy*, 319–20.

29. Arbel and Neeman, *Madness without Atonement*, 68.

30. Golda Meir, *My Life* (Tel Aviv: Steimatzky, 1975), 358–59.

31. Dayan, *Milestones*, 575, 663.

32. Arbel and Neeman, *Madness without Atonement*, 241.

33. Meir, *My Life*, 358–59.

34. Marvin Kalb and Bernard Kalb, *Kissinger* (Jerusalem: Idanim, 1975), 221.

35. Henry Kissinger, transcript of the Channel 1 television series *Idan Hageneralim* (Age of the Generals), 203.

36. Amir Oren, "Kissinger Documents," *Haaretz* (Israeli Hebrew-language daily), October 9, 2003.

37. *AGCR*, vol. 1, 57–58; Kalb and Kalb, *Kissinger*, 219–20.

38. Kalb and Kalb, *Kissinger*, 220.

39. Abba Eban, *Autobiography* (Tel Aviv: Steimatzky, 1977), 500.

40. Henry Kissinger, *Crisis* (Jerusalem: Shalem, n.d.), 36.

41. Kissinger, "Age of the Generals," pt. 5.

42. Kissinger, *Crisis*, 7.

43. Brigadier General Yoel Ben-Porat, "The Yom Kippur War: A Mistake in May and Surprise in October," *Maarachot* 299 (July–August 1985): 5–7; William Quandt, *Decade of Decisions: American Policy towards the Arab-Israeli Conflict, 1967–1976* (Berkeley: University of California Press, 1977), 166–67.

44. Kissinger, "Age of the Generals," pt. 10.

45. Cordova, *United States Policy in the Yom Kippur War*, 82; Eban, *Autobiography*, 517.

46. Eban, *Autobiography*, 502.

47. Kalb and Kalb, *Kissinger*, 224; Luttwak and Laqueur, "Kissinger and the Yom Kippur War," 33.

48. Rose and Indyk, "Temptation to Preempt," 274; Yishai Cordova, "The Political Background to the American Airlift in the Yom Kippur War," *Maarachot* 256 (June 1977): 50.

49. Author's interview with Brigadier General Giora Forman (Ret.), March 11, 2006.

50. Luttwak and Laqueur, "Kissinger and the Yom Kippur War," 33, 39.

51. Cordova, *United States Policy in the Yom Kippur War*, 77.

52. Quandt, *Decade of Decisions*, 184.

53. Kissinger, *Crisis*, 122.

54. Shlomo Nakdimon, *Low Probability: The Dramatic Story that Preceded the Yom Kippur War and What Happened as a Result* (Tel Aviv: Revivim, Yediot Achronot, 1982), 200.

55. Cordova, *United States Policy in the Yom Kippur War*, 90–91.

56. Kissinger, *Crisis*, 266.

57. Ibid., 314–15.

58. Meir, *My Life*, 363.

59. Luttwak and Laqueur, "Kissinger and the Yom Kippur War," 38.

60. Tal, *National Security*, 171.

61. Shmuel Segev, *Maariv* (Israeli Hebrew-language daily), March 29, 1976.

62. Meir, *My Life*, 363.

63. Lieutenant General David Elazar, Senior Staff Meeting, February 12, 1974.

64. Menachem Begin, Knesset debate on the government's announcement on the political situation, November 13, 1973.

65. Quoted in Williams, *Military Aspects of the Israeli-Arab Conflict*, 259.

66. Levite, *Israel's Military Doctrine*, 146.

67. IAF Information Branch, recordings, head of CCP, October 8, 1973.

68. Rosen and Indyk, "Temptation to Preempt," 265.

69. Ibid., 283.

70. Levite, *Israel's Military Doctrine*, 95–97.

71. Yaniv, *Politics and Strategy*, 392.

72. IAF Information Branch, Commanders' Discussion on the Yom Kippur War, 06:05:00, 8.

73. Lieutenant Colonel Shai Avi, "The Approaching Yom Kippur War: War Aims and Egyptian Offensive Plan," *Maarachot* 250 (1976): 18.

74. Quoted in *Series of Symposiums*, 46.

75. Author's interview with Major General David Ivry (Ret.), May 31, 2007.

76. Forman interview, March 11, 2006.

77. The calculations are based on an attack in the entire Agrud area. However, an actual attack almost certainly would have focused on the dugout concentrations at the site, so in practical terms, a greater number of vehicles would have been hit.

78. These calculations were based on the assumption that the vehicles at the site were part of a PMP battalion. The calculation also includes a case in which the sites were part of a TPP crossing battalion. Although the ZIL trucks in the TPP battalions were more vulnerable to cluster bombs than the KrAZ trucks, which made up 70 percent of the vehicles in the PMP battalions, the percentage of trucks destroyed would have been smaller if the site was part of a TPP battalion rather than a PMP battalion.

Selected Bibliography

Books and Articles in Hebrew

Adan, Avraham. *On Both Banks of the Suez.* Tel Aviv: Idanim, 1979.

Allon, Yigal. *Screen of Sand.* Tel Aviv: Hakibutz Hameukhad, 1960.

Aloni, Colonel Roland (Ret.). "The Logistics of IDF Forces in the Yom Kippur War." *Maarachot* 361 (1998).

Amit, Major General Meir (Ret.). "The Sinai Campaign, the IDF's First Test as a Standing Army." *Maarachot* 306–7 (December 1987).

Arbel, David, and Uri Neeman. *Madness without Atonement: The Surprise that Wasn't and the Strategy that Failed.* Tel Aviv: Yediot Achronot, Sifrei Hemed, 2005.

The Armor Corps Doctrine—Armor Formations in the Yom Kippur War. Tel Aviv: Southern Front—252nd Division, 1974.

Asher, Dani. "The Antitank Weapon as the Answer—Egyptian Plans for Using Antitank Weapons in the Yom Kippur War." *Maarachot* 346 (February 1996).

———. *Breaking the Concept.* Tel Aviv: Maarachot Publications, Defense Ministry, 2003.

Asher, Brigadier General Dani (Ret.), and Lieutenant Itai Asher (Ret.). "Israeli Artillery on the Southern Front in the Yom Kippur War." *Maarachot* 354 (1999).

Ashley, Roger. *On War: A Short Guide to Clausewitz.* Tel Aviv: Maarachot Publications, 1977.

Avi, Lieutenant Colonel Shai. "The Approaching Yom Kippur War: War Aims and the Egyptian Offensive Plan." *Maarachot* 250 (1976).

Barkai, Aviram. *On the Edge of the Abyss: The Story of the 188th Brigade in the Yom Kippur War.* Tel Aviv: Sifriat Maariv, 2009.

Barkai, Mordechai. *"The Path of Fire": The 52nd Battalion in the Yom Kippur War.* Tel Aviv: Bereaved Families Publications, 1975.

———. *The "Steel Tracks" Armored Brigade in the Yom Kippur War.* Tel Aviv: Chief Education Officer—Defense Ministry, 1977.

Baron, Aryeh. *Moshe Dayan in the Yom Kippur War.* Jerusalem: Idanim/Yediot Achronot, 1992.

Bartov, Hanoch. *Dado, 48 Years 20 Days.* 2 vols. Tel Aviv: Sifriat Maariv, 1978.

Bar-Yosef, Uri. *The Watchman Who Fell Asleep: The Yom Kippur War Surprise and Its Sources.* Lod: Zmora-Bitan Publishers, 2001.

Bendman, Yona. "The Third Army Crosses the Canal, October 6–8, 1973." *Maarachot* 296 (December 1984).

Ben-Porat, Brigadier General Yoel. "The Yom Kippur War: A Mistake in May and Surprise in October." *Maarachot* 299 (July–August 1985).

Bergman, Ronen, and Gil Meltzer. *The Yom Kippur War: Real Time.* Tel Aviv: Yediot Achronot, Sifrei Hemed, 2003.

Brody, Bernard. *War and Politics.* Tel Aviv: Maarachot Publications, 1980.

Cohen, Eliezer. *The Sky Is Not the Limit: The Story of the Israeli Air Force.* Tel Aviv: Maariv, 1990.

Cohen, Stuart. "Limitations on the Use of the Reserves: Lessons from the Yom Kippur War." *Maarachot* 366–67 (1999).

Cordova, Major Yishai. "The Political Background to the American Airlift in the Yom Kippur War." *Maarachot* 256 (June 1977).

———. *United States Policy in the Yom Kippur War.* Tel Aviv: Maarachot Publications, 1987.

Cordova, Major Yishai, and Lieutenant Colonel Yona Bendman (Ret.). "The American Effort for a Ceasefire in the First Week of the Yom Kippur War." *Maarachot* 289–90 (1983).

Dayan, Lieutenant General Moshe (Ret.). *Diary of the Sinai Campaign.* Tel Aviv: Am-Hasefer Publications, 1965.

———. *Milestones.* Jerusalem: Idanim, 1976.

Eitan, Colonel Zeev (Ret.). "'Dovecote'—Planning and Execution in the Test of Fire." *Maarachot* 276–77 (October–November 1980).

El Badri, Major General Hasan, Major General Teh El Magdoub, and Brigadier General Zahari Aldin. *The Ramadan War: The Fourth Israeli-Arab Round, October 1973.* Tel Aviv: Hatzav, IDF Translation Publications, 1974.

El-Gamasy, Field Marshal Mohamed Abdel Ghani. *The 1973 October War: Memoirs of Field Marshal El-Gamasy.* Tel Aviv: IDF Intelligence Training Base 15, 1994.

Ezov, Amiram. *Holding: Southern Command's Defensive Battle in the Yom Kippur War, October 6–7, 1973.* Tel Aviv: IDF History Department, 2001.

Gaon, Major Benny. "The Standing Division and the Defensive Failure in the Yom Kippur War." *Maarachot* 361 (1998).

Gelber, Yoav. *History, Memory and Propaganda: The Historical Discipline in the World and Israel.* Tel Aviv: Am Oved, Sifriat Ofakim, 2007.

Golan, Aviezer. *Albert.* Tel Aviv: Yediot Achronot, 1977.

Golan, Lieutenant Colonel Shimon (Ret.). "I Couldn't Care Less about Kantara." *Zrakor* (October 2002).

———. "The Preemptive Strike at the Onset of the Yom Kippur War." *Maarachot* 373 (November 2000).

———. "The Scud that Deterred Israel." *Zrakor* (October 2002).

Golan, Matti. *The Secret Conversations of Henry Kissinger.* Tel Aviv: Schocken Books, 1976.

Gordon, Colonel Shmuel (Ret.). "The Paradox of October 7." *Maarachot* 361 (1998).

———. *30 Hours in October, Fateful Decisions: The IAF at the Start of the Yom Kippur War.* Tel Aviv: Sifriat Maariv, 2008.

Guy, Carmit. *Bar-Lev: A Biography.* Tel Aviv: Am Oved, Sifriat Poalim, 1998.

Hashavia, Aryeh. *The Yom Kippur War.* Tel Aviv: Zmora-Bitan, Modan, 1974.

Hastings, Max. *Armageddon: The Battle for Germany 1944–45.* Or Yehuda: Dvir Publishers, Defense Ministry Publications, 2007.

Head Education Officer. *Battles on Both Sides of the Canal: The Yom Kippur War.* Tel Aviv: Head Education Officer, Doctrine and Instruction Branch, 1974.

Hisdai, Colonel Yaakov (Ret.). "The Yom Kippur War: Surprise? Victory?" *Maarachot* 275 (1980).

Hochbaum, Major Yosef. "The Yom Kippur War with the Chisel of Staff Work." *Maarachot* 276–77 (October 1980).

IDF General Staff. *Battle Doctrine*, vol. 2, *Defense*. Tel Aviv: IDF Instruction Department, November 1964.

———. *Lexicon of Warfighting Terms*. Tel Aviv: IDF Doctrine and Instruction, General Staff, 1996.

Inbar, Efraim. *Rabin and Israel's National Security*. Tel Aviv: Defense Ministry Publications, 2004.

Kalb, Marvin, and Bernard Kalb. *Kissinger*. Jerusalem: Idanim, 1975.

Kfir, Ilan. *My Brothers, Heroes of the Canal: Stories of the Fighters Who Won the War*. Tel Aviv: Maariv, 1990.

Kissinger, Henry. *Crisis*. Jerusalem: Shalem, n.d.

Levite, Ariel. *Israel's Military Doctrine: Defense and Offense*. Tel Aviv: Hakibutz Hameukhad, 1988.

Manchester, William. *American Caesar*. Tel Aviv: Maarachot Publications, 1982.

Meir, Golda. *My Life*. Tel Aviv: Steimatzky, 1975.

Nakdimon, Shlomo. *Low Probability: The Dramatic Story that Preceded the Yom Kippur War and What Happened as a Result*. Tel Aviv: Revivim, Yediot Achronot, 1982.

Oren, Lieutenant Colonel Elhanan (Ret.). *The History of the Yom Kippur War*. Tel Aviv: IDF Doctrine and Instruction, History Department, 2004.

Peled, Benny. *Days of Reckoning*. Ben Shemen: Modan, 2004.

Peled, Major General Matti (Ret.). "How Israel Did Not Prepare for War." *Maarachot* 289–90 (October 1983).

Rotem, Major General Avraham. "Rules and Principles in Desert War in View of the IDF's Campaigns in Sinai." *Maarachot* 254 (1977).

Sakal, Major General Emanuel (Ret.). *The Shortcomings in Preparing the Ground Forces for War in the Summer of 2006*. Ramat Gan: Begin-Sadat Center for Strategic Studies (BESA), 2007.

Schiff, Ze'ev. *Earthquake in October*. Tel Aviv: Zmora-Bitan, 1974.

A Series of Symposiums Summing Up Intelligence's Role in the Yom Kippur War. Tel Aviv: Intelligence Training Base 15, 1994.

Shazly, Saad El Din. *Crossing the Canal*. 2nd ed. Tel Aviv: Maarachot Publications, 1988.

Shem-Tov, Victor. "Golda's Omissions, 30 Years after the Yom Kippur War—The View from the Government's Table." *Kivunim Hadashim* 10 (2004).

Spector, Yiftach. *Loud and Clear*. Tel Aviv: Yediot Achronot, Sifrei Hemed, 2008.

Sprinzak, Ehud. *Everybody Does What's Right in His Eyes: Illegality in Israeli Society*. Tel Aviv: Sifriat Poalim, 1986.

Tal, Israel. "National Security: Background and Dynamics." *Maarachot* 253 (1979).

———. *National Security: Few against Many*. Tel Aviv: Dvir, 1996.

Wald, Emanuel. *The Curse of the Broken Vessels*. Tel Aviv: Schocken, 1984.

Wallach, Jehuda. *Military Doctrines and Their Development in the 19th and 20th Centuries*. Tel Aviv: Maarachot Publications, 1977.

———. *Not on a Silver Platter*. Jerusalem: Carta, in cooperation with Defense Ministry Publishers, 2000.

――――. "The Omnipotent Tank." *Maarachot* 276–77 (October–November 1980).

Weizman, Ezer. *On Eagles' Wings: The Personal Story of the Leading Commander of the Israeli Air Force.* Tel Aviv: Maariv, 1975.

Wexler, Yishai, and Yehuda Tal. *The 198th Tank Battalion in the Yom Kippur War: A War Story.* Tel Aviv: Defense Ministry Publications, 2001.

Yadlin, Major General Amos. "The Air Force's Role in the Yom Kippur War, 30 Years in Retrospect." In *The Yom Kippur War and Its Lessons.* Broadcast University Series. Tel Aviv: Ha'universita Hamishuderet, 2003.

Yaniv, Avner. *Politics and Strategy in Israel.* Tel Aviv: Sifriat Poalim, 1994.

Yishai, Major Cordova. "The United States Position on the Preemptive Strike Issue." *Maarachot* 276 (October–November 1980).

The Yom Kippur War, October 1973. 14th Brigade Internal Document, October 1975.

Zeira, Eli. *Myth versus Reality: Failures and Lessons of the Yom Kippur War.* Tel Aviv: Yediot Achronot, Sifrei Hemed, 2004.

Zohar, Lieutenant Colonel Avraham (Ret.). *The Struggle for Israel's Security.* Tel Aviv: Israeli Fund for Military History, Tel Aviv University, 2003.

Books and Articles in English

Asher, Dani. *The Egyptian Strategy for the Yom Kippur War.* Translated by Moshe Tlamim. Jefferson, NC, and London: McFarland, 2009.

Bar-Siman-Tov, Yaacov. *The Israeli-Egyptian War of Attrition, 1969–1970: A Case Study.* Tel Aviv: Westview Press for the Jaffee Center for Strategic Studies, 1985.

――――. *The Yom Kippur War: 25-Year Retrospective.* Jerusalem: Ministry of Education and Leonard Davis Institute for International Relations, 1999.

Bar-Yosef, Uri. "Trends in the Historiography of the Yom Kippur War: A Thirty-Year Perspective." *Journal of Israeli History* 2 (September 2005).

Cohen, Eliot, and John Gooch. *Military Misfortunes.* New York: Collier Macmillan, 1990.

Cordesman, A. H., and A. R. Wagner. *The Lessons of Modern War,* vol. 1. New York: Westview Press/Mansell Publishing, USA, 1990.

Dupuy, Colonel Trevor N., USA (Ret.). *Elusive Victory: The Arab-Israeli Wars, 1947–1974.* London: Harper and Row, 1978.

――――. "Military Aspects of the Israeli-Arab Conflict." In *International Symposium, October 12–17, 1975, Hebrew University of Jerusalem.* Tel Aviv: University Publishing Projects, 1975.

――――. *Numbers, Predictions, and War.* New York: Bobbs-Merrill, 1979.

――――. *The Practical Numerical, Deterministic Model.* Annandale, VA: Dupuy Institute, 2006.

――――. *Understanding War: History and Theory of Combat.* New York: Paragon House, 1987.

Eban, Abba. *Autobiography.* Tel Aviv: Steimatzky, 1977.

Horowitz, Dan. *Israel's Concept of Defensible Borders.* Jerusalem: Hebrew University of Jerusalem, Leonard Davis Institute for International Relations, 1975.

————. *The Israeli Concept of National Security and the Prospects of Peace in the Middle East: Dynamics of a Conflict.* Princeton, NJ: Humanities Press, 1975.

Inbar, Efraim. *Israel's National Security: Issues and Challenges since the Yom Kippur War (Israeli Strategic Thinking after 1973).* New York: Routledge, 2008.

Inbar, Efraim, and Shmuel Sandler. "Israel's Deterrence Strategy Revisited." *Security Studies* 3, no. 2 (Winter 1993–1994): 330–58.

Kier, Elizabeth. *Imagining War.* Princeton, NJ: Princeton University Press, 1997.

Luttwak, Edward, and Walter Laqueur. "Kissinger and the Yom Kippur War." *Commentary* (September 1974).

Menzis, Perter. *Stanford Encyclopedia of Philosophy, Metaphysics Research Lab.* Palo Alto, CA: Stanford University, 2001.

Posen, Barry. *The Sources of Military Doctrine.* Ithaca, NY: Cornell University Press, 1984.

Quandt, William B. *Decade of Decisions: American Policy towards the Arab-Israeli Conflict, 1967–1976.* Berkeley: University of California Press, 1977.

Rosen, Steven J., and Martin Indyk. "The Temptation to Preempt in a Fifth Arab-Israeli War." *Orbis* (Summer 1976): 265–85.

Index

CPSIA information can be obtained
at www.ICGtesting.com
Printed in the USA
LVOW10*2311200218
567370LV00001B/5/P